Foreign Policy

of the

American People

Foreign Policy

OF THE
AMERICAN PEOPLE

Charles O. Lerche, Jr.

Associate Professor of Political Science
Emory University

Englewood Cliffs, N. J.
PRENTICE-HALL, INC.

First printing .... January, 1958
Second printing .... January, 1959

Library of Congress Catalog Card No.: 58—7828

Printed in the United States of America
32671

Preface

Everyone agrees that Americans should be interested in their foreign policy; more of them are actually concerned with it today than at any time in their nation's history. Foreign affairs is truly everybody's business. Many citizens are realizing that fulfilling the duties of citizenship demands both more attention to and more competence in dealing with the subject matter of the foreign relations of the United States. It is as a contribution to this augmented "attentive public" that this book seeks its justification.

This is an analytical-topical study of American foreign policy. Its objective is not to transform its readers into top-level experts on all phases of American foreign policy, both procedural and substantive; a more modest purpose has governed the selection and presentation of its content. If it suggests some clues to a sounder and more inclusive understanding of a rapidly moving and often bewildering sequence of events, and if it points out a few avenues and techniques for more effective popular decision and choice, its author's goal will have been thoroughly achieved. Throughout the discussion that follows, therefore, more emphasis has been placed on "principles" and long-term problems than on details; a self-conscious attempt has been made to concentrate on the "big picture." Historical, organizational, and administrative data, as well as elaborate region-by-region surveys, have been avoided.

The material has been selected and organized with reference to a set of three assumptions, and perhaps evaluation of the value judgments found throughout the book will be facilitated if they are stated explicitly: (1) American foreign policy can be usefully analyzed in terms of a generalized conceptual pattern of foreign policy. (2) Contemporary American foreign policy has accumulated enough historical antecedents to be analytically conceived of as a whole and discussed in such terms, rather than being described as a series of more or less independent and unrelated enterprises. (3) The crucial point of reference in discussing the foreign policy of the United States is "the American people"; mass attitudes, responses, values, and demands are of central importance to any analysis. With each of these three propositions there is admittedly room to disagree, and selection of some other assumptions would have resulted in a different book. The author, however, can enter two justifications for his adherence to them: first, they represent his own position; second, they have proved to be useful postulates upon which to ground his exposition.

One final point should be made. If it were possible to develop a scale for the measurement of relative optimism and pessimism, this book would be placed well over toward the optimistic pole. The point of view expressed here is hopeful—even confident—that the problems facing the United States are soluble by the means presently available and that neither catastrophe nor Armageddon are necessary outcomes of American foreign policy. No guarantee is made that the solutions will actually be found; indeed, the book concludes by leaving open a question on that very point. But the author is convinced that the answers can be found; considering the apocalyptic character of so much contemporary comment on America's role in international politics, such a profession as this one automatically moves its maker into the camp of the cheerful.

ACKNOWLEDGMENTS

Leading the list of those to whom gratitude is due for assistance in the preparation of this book are the hundreds of students who have passed through the author's graduate and undergraduate courses in American foreign policy at several institutions. Out of classroom interplay and the necessity of organizing and sharpening teachable concepts grew the skeleton of this study. From among this large group, Hoke L. Smith should be singled out; as undergraduate and graduate student he has helped many of the ideas take shape by subjecting them to his own brand of incisive, searching, and fruitful criticism.

The author is also particularly grateful to Professors Arno Mayer of Brandeis University, J. David Singer of Vassar College, and Robert L. Smith of Southern Methodist University, whose insights and suggestions helped immeasurably in giving form to an almost amorphous project. The author's colleagues in the department of political science at Emory University, particularly Professors Lynwood M. Holland, Charles D. Hounshell, and Ronald F. Howell, all read parts of the manuscript and gave generously of suggestions and encouragement,

Professors H. Field Haviland of Haverford College, Charles P. Schleicher of the University of Oregon, and Harold Sprout of Princeton University read all or part of the manuscript. Their severest criticisms were uniformly just; many an egregious error has been spared the reader due to their patience and wisdom.

Mrs. Judith Watkins Smith performed the unenviable task of translating a heavily edited manuscript into coherent form and served as a constant watchdog on idiosyncratic grammar and whimsical spelling.

The foregoing share credit for what is creditable in what follows. For all sins of omission and commission, however, the author bears full responsibility.

C.O.L., Jr.

Emory University, Georgia

to **Margaret**

and **Herky**

Table of contents

ix

Contents

VIII. LOOKING AHEAD

part I:

A CONCEPTUAL FRAMEWORK

1 : What is
a foreign policy?

This volume is an essay on the foreign policy of the United States. It is one of the truisms of political science that every state has a foreign policy, just as every state also has a constitution, a locus of sovereignty, and several other distinguishing characteristics. Each sovereign political unit, existing as it does in a world that contains approximately 90 other states, cannot escape having some kind of relations with them; common sense would seem to dictate that these relations should, if possible, be ordered and governed by some kind of more or less rational plan. Foreign affairs, always one of the major fields of government action, has grown in importance under the conditions of modern technology so that today it is the principal concern of many states and is of primary significance to all.

Our major interest in this study will be the foreign policy conducted by the government of the United States in the name of the American people. We shall devote the bulk of our attention to a consideration of the ways in which both government and people meet and attempt to solve the peculiar problems of international relations that fall to them. We shall be making our examination in terms of an analytical device that we may call our "conceptual scheme." We shall develop a number of general concepts and will then suggest some relationships among them; this device, it is hoped, will permit us to view our subject as more of a whole than it sometimes appears to be, and will also provide a number of insights into both the strengths and the weaknesses of American foreign policy. In this opening chapter, therefore, we shall attempt to lay most of these preliminary foundations.

THE CONCEPT OF "FOREIGN POLICY"

What is it that we are talking about in this book? What do we mean when we say that "every state has a foreign policy"? No more fundamental starting point for our inquiry could be found than a clarification of this, our basic concept.

In this book, by "foreign policy" we mean the courses of action and the decisions relating to them that a state undertakes in its relations with other states, in order to attain national objectives and to advance the national interest.[1] Such a definition contains several terms that themselves require definitions, and it obviously stands in need of further analysis and refinement. We shall devote ourselves to this task in this chapter. This definition, as expanded, will incorporate the system by which we shall analyze American policy.

The nature of foreign policy

Foreign policy, as an area of government action, shares many of the characteristics of any public policy; many of the generalizations about the conduct of public affairs developed by political scientists and other students of government are applicable to the study of the foreign relations of any state.[2] We shall not attempt to enumerate these here, nor to isolate the features that make the formulation and execution of foreign policy different from other forms of state action. Instead, in this chapter we shall discuss some of the considerations fundamental to an understanding of our subject without direct concern for their relevance to other problems of government.

The Components of "Policy." Foreign policy, as we analyze it here, has three major components, from the interaction of which various discrete steps develop. In the order of their appearance in the foreign policy process, they are: (1) the state's criteria of measurement, which we usually call national interest; (2) the situational factors impinging on the state; (3) the action taken by the state. Although the possible action pat-

---

[1] Compare the following definition advanced by Charles B. Marshall, then a member of the Policy Planning Staff of the Department of State: "...the foreign policy of the United States [is]...the courses of action undertaken by authority of the United States in pursuit of national objectives beyond the span of jurisdiction of the United States." *Department of State Bulletin* (March 17, 1952), p. 415.

[2] On the governmental process in general. see for example David Truman, *The Governmental Process* (New York: Alfred A. Knopf, Inc.. 1951).

terns states may follow are so numerous that their classification and description fall outside our purpose in this book, an analysis of the first two notions is necessary to our analytical method. In a moment we shall attempt to clarify both the notion of national interest and the typology of situational factors; later in the chapter we shall examine both of them in some greater detail.

Foreign Policy as Process. Before proceeding, however, we should emphasize that foreign policy is here conceived as a social and political process. It is an on-going affair, not one that may be seized and studied in all its ramifications at a particular moment in time. Dynamism is the keynote of all international relationships, and our analysis should be so oriented as to take account of unceasing evolution and change. Only by devising techniques that encompass the notion of process can we develop a picture of foreign policy that is at all relevant to reality.

Of what does the foreign policy process consist? If we define "process" as action consisting of a series of steps each leading to the next and all aimed at a predetermined end, we may put the matter this way: the foreign policy process consists of the repeated application of a set of relatively constant criteria to an infinitely variable pattern of situational factors, and the subsequent adjustment of state action in response to the conclusions reached from such application. We can list the steps of the process as follows: (1) the establishment of the criteria; (2) the determination of the relevant variables in the situation; (3) the measurement of the variables by the criteria; (4) the selection of a goal; (5) the elaboration of a strategy to reach the goal; (6) the decision to act; (7) the action itself; (8) the evaluation of the results of the action in terms of the original criteria.[3]

We should further postulate that this process, since it goes on within every state and since all states function within a dynamic system, is for analytical purposes deemed to be unending. The criteria, as we shall see in a moment, tend to be less constant in practice than in theory; the ends of state action themselves are notoriously prone to revision in response to stimuli both rational and irrational; the system itself usually operates so as to frustrate the ultimate purposes of states. Though we can possibly conceive of an international order in which what we are calling "foreign policy" would no longer be present, the actual world in which we live is one in which the process not only goes on constantly but also shows no sign of diminishing either in importance or in complexity.

---

[3] Contrast the process here suggested with the simpler formulation found in the Brookings Institution's study, *The Administration of Foreign Affairs and Overseas Operations* (Washington, D. C.: U. S. Government Printing Office, 1951), p. 13.

What Is a Foreign Policy?

The Notion of National Interest. National interest is considered as the prime criterion (or criteria) in terms of which a state judges situational factors, determines the relative priorities to be given to different goals, and establishes and evaluates courses of action. It is the closest approximation to a fixed factor the policy process affords, but the nature of its components, its lack of absolute specificity, and the variety in the techniques by which it is formulated debar it from postulation as a true constant. Its rate of evolution and change, however, is much slower than is the case of the other raw materials of policy, and its role as the significant criterion gives such consistency as may be present in any foreign policy.

In most states, and certainly in the United States, national interest as a generalized concern arises from two sources. The first (and less specific) is what we call the "myth" of national purpose in international affairs: those mass-shared values in foreign policy whose maximization by government is demanded by a broad consensus. The ego-image a national group has of itself as it views the world cannot help but be basic to the specific foreign-policy steps it takes. The second source of national interest is the group of practitioners of foreign policy (the "decision-makers") themselves. Though forming part of the mass we call the nation and, as such, themselves partakers in the national myth, their insights, experience, and collective responsibility for action—as well as their peculiar bureaucratic point of view—often lead them to conceive the national interest differently than does the mass, and to apply somewhat different criteria to its formulation. Occasionally such varying views of long-range public purpose are the cause of serious internal conflict.[4]

Categories of Situational Factors. Situational factors that influence policy are infinite in both number and variety, but here we may subsume them under three general heads: (1) the international milieu in which the state is operating; (2) the specific actions taken by other states to which responses of one sort or another are appropriate; (3) the state's own capabilities for action. Elements from each of these categories inter-

---

[4] There is a steadily growing literature on the subject of national interest, revealing the extent to which scholars are grappling with the problem of its clarification and also the lack of agreement which generally prevails. Among the leading works we may mention Hans J. Morgenthau, *In Defense of the National Interest* (New York: Alfred A. Knopf, Inc., 1951), Robert Osgood, *Ideals and Self-interest in America's Foreign Relations* (Chicago: University of Chicago Press, 1953), and Frank Tannenbaum, *The American Tradition in Foreign Policy* (Norman: University of Oklahoma Press, 1955). Several leading articles have also appeared in such journals as the *American Political Science Review, World Politics,* and the *Political Science Quarterly.*

act to create the situation to which the criterion of national interest is applied.

Objectives and Courses of Action. When national interest is applied to a situation that calls for decision and action, the outcome is the selection of an objective: a reasonably clearly defined state of affairs the accomplishment of which the decision-makers feel would be advantageous, at least under the controlling conditions. An objective is a target of state action: a goal the state wishes to reach. Its justification is the net gain to the state that its achievement would either bring about or make possible. The selection of an objective is followed by the development of a strategy to reach the goal and the subsequent execution of that plan; this last step is the purer (or at least narrower) referent to the term "policy."

The "Chain" of Policy. We have now reached the point in this highly generalized survey of the concept of foreign policy at which we may suggest some sort of causal relationship among the various steps. We can conveniently put this in the form of what we might almost call a "chain reaction."

Step 1. Popular traditions and official points of view, applied to (relatively long-range and fixed) conditions, interact to produce a formula of national interest.

Step 2. A formulation of national interest, applied to (middle-range and evolving) conditions, results in the selection of precise objectives.

Step 3. An objective, analyzed in terms of (short-range and immediate) conditions, leads to the selection of a course of action (a policy).

The energizing factor that moves the reaction from step to step is, of course, the varying impact of the situational factors impinging on the state. Foreign policy does not just happen; the state's decision to act is always the result of some change in the situation—internal or external—with which it is faced. Since we have agreed that the situational elements of international politics are in constant flux, it would be logical for us to conclude, as we suggested above, that the foreign-policy process is constantly operative, each step leading to the next and each new situational change touching off a new chain reaction of adjustment.

Foreign policy and the state system

Although in our study we shall be interested primarily in the purposes and actions of one state—the United States—we shall be reminded at every turn that its foreign policy must be planned and executed within the confines of the state system. In many ways and at all times the requirements of the system affect the behavior of any of its members, and success most frequently comes to those states that best fit their policy into the peculiar demands of the society of which they are a part.

Although no purpose would be served by reviewing here a detailed theory of international politics, a summary of some fundamentals might throw a little light on our subsequent discussions. We shall briefly examine three notions: (1) the state's freedom of choice; (2) the channels of state action; and (3) the limiting controls on such action.

The State's Freedom of Choice. The mystique of sovereignty confers one important area of freedom on the members of the state system: the freedom to choose. No external force can rightfully dictate to a state what its national interest should be; each state, in terms of its internal processes and dynamic, reaches and ratifies its own version of what is best for it. Each state is similarly free to make such situational analyses as suit its concerns and to select such objectives as it wishes. And finally, each state may adopt such policies as it sees fit, using such combination of techniques as to it seems expedient and wise. Interest, objectives, and policy are all—from the state's point of view—egocentric; each member of the state system may choose any policy at all and owe responsibility for its decision to no one outside itself. The basic motivations of foreign policy are therefore to be found within the state.[5]

The Channels of State Action. State action in pursuit of an objective may assume any of a great variety of forms. Modern technology has added greatly to the supply of foreign-policy techniques available to the statesman. Despite their increased number, however, they all fall into one of the four traditional categories of tools and techniques, the four channels of state action. These four are: political action, through the mechanisms of diplomatic representation; economic action, through the productive and distributive system of the state; psychological action, through the techniques of mass persuasion; military action, through armed force. From among these four types, a statesman chooses in such combination as seems to him to be best suited to the particular purpose he has in mind. Many forms and degrees of action are available to him within each category, but the number of categories cannot be expanded. There are no other areas in which the state can act in pursuit of its objectives.[6]

---

[5] One of the early developments of this point among American scholars was by Nicholas J. Spykman, in *America's Strategy in World Politics* (New York: Harcourt, Brace and Co., 1942), Chapter I: "Power Politics and War."

[6] See E. H. Carr, *The Twenty Years Crisis, 1919-1939,* Sec. Ed. (London: The Macmillan Co., 1946), Chapter 8, and Harold and Margaret Sprout, eds., *Foundations of National Power,* Sec. Ed. (New York: Van Nostrand, 1951), pp. 40-43.

The Limits on State Action. There are both formal and informal limits on the possible action any state might take in pursuit of an objective. Their combined effect is largely to inhibit the state's real freedom.

We may sum up the formal limits as international law and international organization. International law incorporates a body of rules prescribing acceptable state conduct in a broad variety of situations. Although the system is incomplete and of uncertain enforcement, all states recognize its existence and admit it to be—to a substantial if imprecise extent—a limiting factor. International organization—most clearly epitomized in its major contemporary manifestation, the United Nations—limits state action both by its statutory competence to sit in judgment on state behavior and by its unique ability to form and express a mass international consensus. Although the formal limits on state action are yet rudimentary, and despite the fact that states occasionally succeed in evading their restraints, their over-all limiting effect is perceptible and sometimes controlling.[7]

The informal limits on state action grow out of the dynamic of the state system itself. Each state, in pursuing its own policies, is confronted by all its fellows doing the same thing. Each therefore is faced with the ominous likelihood that any interstate relationship in which it becomes involved will be a competitive one and may well develop into open conflict. No state can afford to be engaged in disputes simultaneously with all other states; it must therefore seek to adjust its pattern of relations so as to maintain a satisfactory balance of support, sympathy, noninvolvement, and nonopposition from those states with which actual or potential conflicts are minimal or nonexistent. In this way it conserves its energy and power for use against those states with which it is involved over more important matters.[8]

In any such direct confrontation, another type of limit is operative. The principle of expediency that governs state action in a relativistic world demands that a state not press its cause against another beyond the point of its own capacity. No matter how insistently a state's national interest may demand victory over an opponent, no possible action will produce such a triumph if the state simply lacks the competence to achieve it. The absence of effective institutional controls over state action

---

[7] See, for a thorough demonstration of this point, Charles de Visscher, *Theory and Reality in Public International Law*, trans. P. E. Corbett (Princeton, N. J.: Princeton University Press, 1957).

[8] See this point as developed by George F. Kennan, in *Realities of American Foreign Policy* (Princeton, N. J.: Princeton University Press, 1955), Chapter II: "The Non-Soviet World."

9

tends to make each international dispute a clash of power, with victory going to the state better able to enforce its will. The point here is that prudent statesmanship allows for this condition and accepts as a limit on state action the general rule that a state should not become involved in a controversy in which its position would be, on balance, weaker than that of its opponent.

NATIONAL INTEREST

We have identified "national interest" as denoting the relatively constant criteria by which a state judges the evolving situation it faces and in terms of which operating decisions are made and policies undertaken. We have also pointed out that it arises, in somewhat different forms, from two sources: the controlling myth and value system of the nation as it contemplates the international scene, and the somewhat more sophisticated and operationally more precise notions that emanate from specialized official personnel. Each of these aspects merits some further examination.

The myth of national mission

Within any nation of more than rudimentary political experience there exists a more or less well-formulated image of its national mission: this, indeed, is one of the characteristics of the modern nation-state. There may be some sovereignties in the world in which the population is so politically inert that such a myth does not exist, but such states would be few in number and of relatively minor importance in world affairs. Politically significant states all incorporate some such notion, and its role in articulating national interest and in determining the direction and frequently the methods of foreign policy is always large and sometimes dominant.

The Importance of Mass Attitudes. It is axiomatic today that foreign affairs is no longer the exclusive plaything of a small group of political insiders, but that the mass of citizens—at least in democratic states—is deeply involved in the process. State objectives have become so broad and the effort demanded to attain them involves so many facets of national power that no statesman dare run the risk of alienating the support of any large portion of his people. This makes nationalism, the mass

10

political emotion, a factor always to be taken into account in policy decisions.[9]

What this means for most policy-makers is that the actions they contemplate must be attuned to mass attitudes. If their projected plan falls within the area permitted or demanded by the national myth, they can proceed confidently; if it does not comport with what the dominant attitude feels is satisfactory, a preliminary problem in political leadership must first be solved. The mass must either be persuaded to expand or reorient its values by means of educational or propaganda techniques, or the policy must itself be altered or reinterpreted so as to bring it into conformity with the commands of the popular tradition.

Statesmen frequently chafe under the restraints imposed by such a myth, but contemporary political life affords few clues about how they may escape it. The mass may be manipulated, tricked, cajoled, temporarily evaded, or even tyrannized, but it cannot permanently be ignored. To the extent to which the mass tradition of international mission is clearly formulated and based on genuine value consensus, it is an absolutely controlling determinant of national interest. Statesmen must develop their own formulations within such freedom of action as it permits them.[10]

Popular Preferences and Foreign Policy. In conceptualizing the myth of national mission, we must be wary not to draw over-rigid inferences from our notion. Even in a tightly-knit authoritarian society organized under a system of rigid social controls, voluntary unanimity on ultimate national purposes is usually impossible to achieve in any notable detail; in a fluid social structure, consensus seldom develops spontaneously except on extremely narrow issues and then only for limited periods. Such myth as exists in a democratic society usually finds expression either in broad value generalizations permitting great flexibility in official interpretation and application to specific situations, or else in emotional slogans equally subject to manipulation by skilled leadership.

Popular preferences, therefore, as a source of national interest only rarely tie official hands completely. In a free society there is competition among individuals and groups who seek to express the controlling version of the myth; a variety of voices purport to speak the basic ("true")

---

[9] See Karl Deutsch, *Nationalism and Social Communication* (New York: John Wiley & Sons, Inc., 1953); for specific examples from Britain and France, see Arnold Wolfers, *Britain and France Between Two Wars* (New York: Harcourt, Brace and Co., 1940), Chapters III, XIII.

[10] Gabriel A. Almond, in *The American People and Foreign Policy* (New York: Harcourt, Brace and Co., 1950), deals extensively with this problem.

national interest. This situation often gives officialdom an opportunity to move shrewdly to cultivate the positions of which it approves and to play a constructive part in shaping the myth to dimensions appropriate to the action demanded at the moment.

Even in this looser version of the concept of the national myth, however, we must nonetheless recognize its basic irrationality. Popular attitudes may seize upon an objective, a technique, or a condition, and sanctify it as an integral part of basic national interest. Against such a move the statesman is helpless; as long as the myth is speaking, official discourse is powerless to be heard. Governments must cope with such commands as best they can.[11]

We may repeat, however, that ordinarily the "national interest," to the extent that it is imbedded in the culture as a prevailing myth and value system, finds expression only in the most general terms and is subject to most elastic interpretation. As a rule, officials responsible for government action find it a hurdle not impossible of clearance, although only rarely are they able to ignore it completely. An orderly analysis of the national interest of any particular state must recognize the peculiar role of mass value preferences and make its first task an estimate of their dimensions and effect.

National interest as a policy determinant

When we turn from national interest as myth and consider it in its more material role as perhaps the prime determinant of government policy, we find ourselves capable of somewhat more precision, even though the literature of political science is replete with controversy over the exact meaning of the term. Although defining it in a way satisfactory to everyone has so far proved impossible, we can discover sufficient consensus to permit clarification of the concept to a degree sufficient for our purposes. Certain notions reappear regularly in the discussions of scholars and the pronouncements of statesmen; the concrete formulations of interest made by states resemble one another relatively closely with reference to a handful of broad concerns. From these sources we may draw a few tentative conclusions.

The Idea of National Interest. As we analyze the role of interest in

---

[11] See, for a thoroughly critical comment on this situation, Walter Lippmann, *The Public Philosophy* (Boston: Little, Brown and Co., 1955), especially Chapter II: "The Malady of Democratic States."

the foreign policy of actual states, we find that all of them seem to be perennially concerned to some important degree with the same three considerations. We may phrase these common desires of states as (1) self-preservation, (2) security, and (3) well-being. It is probable that for most states these three are listed here in their normal order of priority.

But these three areas of interest, as stated, are too generalized and abstract to be of much use, either for analysis or for policy-making. They must be given a more specific content. Each government makes such an elaboration with regard to the generalized situational context in which it is operating and to its long-range aspirations within that situation (the latter consideration is the peculiar province of the myth we discussed in the preceding section). This translation of interest into relatively precise and long-lived wants and needs results in the working criterion by which the government measures the changing milieu. We need scarcely point out that, since no two states face the same situation, no two formulations of national interest are the same. For our purposes, therefore, the "national interest" as a determinant of policy consists of formulations of those (at least) semi-permanent ends, phrased at a high level of generalization, the accomplishment of which the state feels is necessary to its self-preservation, its security, and its well-being.

"Interest" vs. "Interests." We have come a little way in making the notion of national interest more intelligible and useful, but our term is yet too abstract to be used as an analytical tool. We will recall that our "chain of policy" made situational factors the motivating element in policy; circumstances also play their part in translating the national interest into useable and concrete terms. One attempt to formulate the process put the matter this way:

> The *national interest* may be defined as the general and continuing end for which a state acts.... This is, of course, a highly generalized definition. But any lower level of generalization tends to lose substantive meaning, and the term becomes increasingly ambiguous. The reason for this is that the requirements of security and well-being not only change with circumstances but are, in addition, matters of judgment and calculation and hence open to varying interpretations....[12]

To replace the general notion of "the national interest," the authors of this selection suggest the plural term "interests," because such usage not

---

[12] William A. Reitzel, Morton A. Kaplan, and Constance G. Coblentz, *United States Foreign Policy 1945-1955* (Washington, D. C.: Brookings Institution, 1956), Appendix A, "Definition of Terms," pp. 471-2. Italics in original. Reprinted by permission.

13

only reveals that interests "may conflict in any given set of circumstances," but also that a choice must be made among them "in terms of priorities and values" before specific objectives and policies can be selected. "Interests" are defined as "what the decision-making group in a government determines is important to the maintenance of the state." [13]

Such a substitution of "interests" for "the national interest" as an analytical tool has a good deal to recommend it on grounds of clarity and utility; it makes a great deal more sense to say about a particular situation that "the United States has an interest in . . ." than "the national interest of the United States is . . ." The use of "interests" makes it possible for the statesman or analyst to proceed directly to concrete situations and speeds the process of reaching a policy decision. But there seems to be some danger in relegating the more general term to the discard and in concentrating entirely on what "the decision-making group" in a state thinks is important. Conflicts between competing interests within a state are frequent, and the quotation above admitted that they are to be resolved by a choice made "in terms of priorities and values." It does not seem illogical to suggest that such a choice might well be made in terms of a generalized version of interest rooted in mass tradition.[14] But the use of the plural term is most helpful in analyzing and explaining detailed problems; our conceptual system will frequently make use of this device.

"Ends" and "Means" in National Interest. If we accept the plural notion of "interests" and admit that there is a likelihood that interests will conflict with each other, further examination of the package of interests pursued by most states leads to a rudimentary system of classification. The interests of a state may be catalogued as end-interests (goals valuable in themselves) or means-interests (with a value relevant to an already-posited end). End-interests, closely related to the myth of national purpose, are postulated *a priori;* means-interests, on the other

---

[13]Reitzel, Kaplan, and Coblentz, *op. cit.,* p. 472. Reprinted by permission.

[14] Reitzel, Kaplan, and Coblentz use the term "principles" to refer to such a criterion: "*Principles* is used to mean the enduring modes of behavior or the relatively established guides to action that characterize nations. . . . The decision-making group, concretely concerned with *interests,* tends to think of *principles* as more-or-less subjective and to find them in occasional conflict with *interests.* Nevertheless, *principles* are deeply imbedded in the general culture and political philosophy of a society and are powerful, if intangible and subjective, guides to action. . . . they represent the underlying patterns of value that guide national action and to which determinations of *interests, objectives,* and *policies* over the long run tend to conform." *United States Foreign Policy,* pp. 472-3; italics in original. Reprinted by permission. Such a definition seems to fit quite closely what we are calling the "myth" of national mission and may well be used as a definition for it.

hand, are usually derived by a process more or less rational. End-interests, accordingly, do not permit of analysis and evaluation by rational techniques; means-interests can usually be criticized in terms of their efficiency in reaching the desired end.[15]

Since ends and means are primarily analytical devices and any such classification as we have attempted runs the risk of drastically over-simplifying reality, we cannot expect to find a state's concerns neatly labelled "ends" and "means" as it pursues its policy. The distinction is most useful as a possible guide to priority judgments made by statesmen; generally speaking, we would not expect a rational policy-maker to endanger an end-interest in order to advance a means-interest.[16]

National Interest: the Final Criterion. One final point needs to be made in this connection about national interest. It is more than the standard by which situational factors are given relevance and action inspired; it is also the ultimate criterion by which the state's "success" or "failure" is measured. A "good" foreign policy is one that advances the notion of interest that inspired the action in the first place; a "bad" one fails. Other possible outcomes are largely ignored. Thus we might aphoristically say that the concept of interest is both the starting point and the end of the foreign-policy process, and the entire sequence of action acquires a peculiarly circular character.

The permanence of national interest is, of course, only relative. Nothing stands still in international relations, and interest is no exception to this rule. But we must emphasize that a state's devotion to its self-preservation, its security, and its well-being (in other words, to its end-interests) remains constant, however different may be the forms in which problems present themselves. New political, economic, demo-

---

[15] "[I think] of foreign policy as relating to means and ends and to the gap between them. . . . Ends are concepts. Means are facts. Making foreign policy consists of meshing concepts and facts in the field of action." Charles B. Marshall, *Department of State Bulletin* (March 17, 1952), p. 416. See also the brief but powerful development of the same point in Walter Lippmann, *United States Foreign Policy* (Boston: Little, Brown and Co., 1943), Chapter II: "A Fundamental Principle of Foreign Policy."

[16] See Karl Von Vorys, "The Concept of National Interest," in Vernon Van Dyke, ed., *Some Approaches and Concepts Used in the Teaching of International Politics* (Iowa City: State University of Iowa, 1957), pp. 49-54. Professor Von Vorys establishes the following classifications of interests: (1) ultimate end-interests postulated with a high degree of regularity (utopian images of the international order); (2) proximate end-interests postulated with a high degree of regularity (self-preservation, territorial integrity, military security, subsistence); (3) means-interests regularly pursued (security techniques, economic measures, anti-subversive techniques, etc.); (4) means-interests irregularly pursued (all atypical state goals, such as the renunciation of war). Reprinted by permission.

graphic, psychic, or technological facts may work great changes in the means-interests pursued by the state or even in the pattern of postulated end-interests. In this sense, interest unquestionably evolves in its detailed expression. But this mutability that we can see in the concept does not vitiate its key role in the policy process; some formulation of national interest provides the foundation for all subsequent steps in making and executing foreign policy.

SITUATIONAL FACTORS

We indicated earlier that the situational factors in response to which policies are initiated fall into three categories: (1) the international milieu in which the state is operating; (2) the specific actions of other states; (3) the state's own capabilities for action. Later in this book we shall devote a chapter to each of these as they apply to the United States; here we need only clarify their content briefly to see how they fit into our conceptual system.

The international milieu

The milieu of state action—including both the fixed factors confronting the state and the general "climate" of international affairs—is the source of a large share what some call the "givens" of foreign policy. The setting in which policy is made and conducted itself influences the decisions states make and the actions they take.[17]

Fixed Factors in the Milieu. Each state is faced with a number of relatively fixed factors as it charts its course in international affairs. Some of these relate uniquely to itself, such as its size and location; these are generally considered as part of the tangible component of state capability. Others appertain more directly to the state system and its effect on the state concerned, and must be fed into the policy calculations the state makes. Examples of these might include the global distribution of power, the existing international institutions and their effectiveness, the stability or disorganization of international society, and so on.

The Climate of International Politics. But we have made the point

---

[17] A systematic survey and critique of the various interpretations of the milieu has been made by Harold and Margaret Sprout, in *Man-Milieu Relationship Hypothesis in the Context of International Politics* (Princeton, N. J.: Center of International Studies, 1956).

several times already that no fixed scheme of relationships can convey an accurate impression of the international scene. Dynamic forces also form part of the milieu, and tend to influence the interpretation and modify the impact of the fixed factors. The cumulative effect of the dynamic forces at work at any one time is to create the "climate" of international politics: the general atmosphere of state relationships. Measures appropriate to an era of caution would be totally out of place in an age of adventure, and vice versa. Some of the dynamisms that might contribute to the climate are the broad trend toward revolution or toward reaction, mass attitudes on war and peace (the "expectation of war"), the state of ideological disputation, and the level of nationalist identification among large groups of people.

The actions of other states

What we really mean when we say that other states affect the course of policy-making by any government is that the state system itself forms a situational factor. What is there about this system that obliges a state to take into account the known and predictable reactions of its associates when it is planning a policy move?

The Dual Impact of Other States. Each state impinges on any other in two ways. In the first place, as policy is executed, resistance by other states is encountered. Such opposition may be overt and extensive, it may be covert and nominal, it may even be passive. Each form of resistance must be anticipated as accurately as possible and measures devised for dealing with it. Second, each state must devote a large portion of its capability to coping with policy moves made by other states, resisting, cooperating, or accommodating as its own interest dictates. A surprisingly large share of each state's effort is spent in dealing with situations arising from action originating outside its own boundaries.[18]

Competition in the State System. The fictions of sovereignty—the independence and equality of all states—produce a system that in logic is absolutely competitive. States are free to—and often do—select policies the accomplishment of which would require the attainment of absolute objectives. When all states seek the same absolute goals, their attainment in a world of dispersed power is impossible to any of them.

---

[18] This and the succeeding points are discussed at greater length in the present author's *Principles of International Politics* (New York: Oxford University Press, 1956), Chapter V.

The state system is thus inherently frustrating; every member of it is doomed to permanent dissatisfaction as it doggedly plods on in search of illusory objectives. This frustration lends a certain peevish quality to interstate relations; it often seems as if states feel that as long as they cannot really accomplish their goals, they are determined to do the next best thing: to deny their accomplishment to others.

The international order is an intensively competitive one. Each state realizes that at bottom every other state is its actual or potential rival; each views the international scene with the assumption that its fellows would be perfectly willing to deny it the fruits of any of its efforts.

This is a strong statement, and one often belied in practice. We must recall, however, that absolute competition is often modified by the working of the principle of national interest. For particular states and in appropriate circumstances, cooperation in the pursuit of a shared objective may be more mutually advantageous, and competition is laid aside. But if (or when) their interests—determined by each state for itself—again diverge, intense competition would immediately replace the earlier harmony.

The Pursuit of Compensation. The actual working of the competitive principle usually takes the form of the pursuit of "compensation." Especially among states who are admitted rivals (in other words, between which competition has come out into the open), an advantage gained by one state—usually some move that attains an objective or at least brings it nearer realization—touches off a search for compensation by the others. They may attempt to offset the gain by resistance or by retaliatory action; they may readjust their relations with each other so as to reestablish the former relationship; they may seek gains of their own to restore the balance.

International politics may be viewed as a complex series of such initial moves followed by compensatory reactions. Statesmen contemplating policy moves must assume that any but the most minor steps will precipitate such an attempt at compensation by some states.

The Effect of Other States. When a statesman makes his judgment about the reactions his move will provoke, he knows that a broad range of action is open to the affected states. Some will agree with him, and perhaps will actively cooperate; others will be affected only slightly, and their moves in either direction will be minimal; still others will be in opposition and will initiate compensatory policies. The task of the policy-maker is to move through these permutations and combinations as deftly as he can and to extract from the situation such freedom of action—usually brought about by balancing favorable reactions off against opposing ones—as will permit him to make some contribution to the notion of interest he is serving.

State capability

By "capability" we mean the ability of a state to achieve its objectives.[19] This definition, being almost perfectly circular, does not define; perhaps it is more accurate to say that capability is the measure of the capacity of a state to have other states agree with it on matters in which it is interested. Among sovereignties the only way differences can be eventually terminated is by agreement, and it is immaterial whether such agreement is forced or free.

Force and Consent. There are, as we have suggested, two different ways by which a state may secure agreement from other states. It may either compel agreement by force—the application of coercive or semi-coercive techniques—or it may win agreement from them by free consent. Both force and consent, as devices for obtaining agreement, form parts of capability.[20]

Generally speaking, the more free consent a state can command in support of its policy, the less need it has of force to reach its objective. Conversely, the less consent available, the greater the amount of force needed. Since under most circumstances agreement by consent is preferable to agreement by force (for reasons both of permanence and of economy of effort), states as a rule endeavor to maximize their area of consent.

There is, however, an inherent limit on this effort. No state would dare to depend entirely on the voluntary consent of other states in estimating its ability to fulfill its mission. Neither, for that matter, can a state trust itself entirely to force for any but the briefest of periods or the narrowest of objectives. "Capability" must, for each state, be a measure of the effective action open to it in the particular context, such effectiveness being composed variously of its coercive power and its command of the free consent of its associates.

---

[19] For systematic attempts to give content to the concept of capability (or "power"), see Harold and Margaret Sprout, *Foundations of National Power*, Chapter IV, and Stephen B. Jones, "The Power Inventory and National Strategy," *World Politics* (September, 1954).

[20] This notion is extensively developed by Louis J. Halle, in his *Civilization and Foreign Policy* (New York: Harper & Bros., 1955), and earlier in his "Force and Consent in International Affairs," *Department of State Bulletin* (September 21, 1953).

The Content of Capability. A state's ability to achieve its objectives is so much a function of time, place, and situation that we cannot ever attain anything like mathematical precision in its analysis.[21] We can, however, suggest here the broad areas of state life that bear directly on the concept; in Chapter 11 we shall fill in some of the details as they apply to the capability of the United States.

Capability involves both tangible and intangible factors. The former are to a great extent susceptible to measurement by objective criteria; the intangibles defy exact measurement—and often exact formulation as well —by statistical techniques. Students of international affairs as well as statesmen realize, however, that both sorts of concerns contribute to the total ability of the state to act constructively.

The tangible factors are usually listed under five heads: (1) geography; (2) population and manpower; (3) natural resources; (4) industrial and agricultural production; (5) military organization and power-in-being. Each of these has been studied in detail; a wealth of information about their status in the majority of states is now available, and a host of revealing comparisons has been and is being made. Insofar as capability analyses can be made by the yardsticks represented by these five categories, we can do the job quite presentably.[22]

Intangibles are nonquantifiable (as are indeed many of the aspects of the tangibles in the list above), but estimates must nevertheless be made of their effect if capability judgments are to have any utility at all. Among the many ways of listing the nonmaterial components of capability, the one that follows is an attempt at synthesis; other lists might have more or fewer entries, but the general points included would be generally the same. We stipulate four categories: (1) the political, economic, and social structure of the state under consideration; (2) the educational and technological level; (3) the state of national morale; and (4) the international strategic situation of the state—its need for allies, its opponents, its general leader-follower status in international society, and the amount and kind of consent it can command.

The Relativity of Capability. Capability is a slippery concept, for it acquires meaning only in a relative sense. A state is not "capable" or

---

[21] "Capability analysis proceeds from the tangible and easily measured factors to those which though still very tangible—indeed crucial—involve so many imponderables as to defy measurement." John S. Reshetar, Jr., *Problems of Analyzing and Predicting Soviet Behavior* (Garden City: Doubleday, 1954), p. 33. Reprinted by permission.

[22] For example, the United States Air Force, in its AFROTC program, devotes a large part of the program of the fourth year to a course entitled "Military Aspects of World Political Geography."

"incapable" in any absolute way; instead, it is "capable" or "incapable" of doing some particular thing. A capability judgment about a state is comprehensible only when a decision is being reached about whether or not it can attain an objective it has in mind. A state may be able to reach a particular goal when opposed by one state, but may be impotent when confronted by another; one objective may be within its capacity while another is completely out of reach.[23]

Thus each time a policy decision is under consideration, a capability judgment about the attainability of the various alternatives helps influence the choice of one of them. Capability is not a status to which states attain, but rather a device of measurement by means of which policy-makers can judge the relative feasibility of different courses of action.[24]

The Dynamism of Capability. Another controlling characteristic of the concept of capability is its dynamism. The several factors interact so subtly and in such a variety of ways that capability judgments must be made, so to speak, on the run.

We can almost say that it is impossible to reach any conclusion about the relative capabilities of states that is not at least partially obsolete at the time it is made. Many of the factors influencing such a judgment are moving so rapidly that even the latest information is out of date. This makes the detailed measurement and comparison of capabilities really a matter of isolating the significant trends of development within each relevant component, and then projecting each of these into the future. In this way calculations of relative competences of states become the best possible guesses about conditions yet to arise.

The Time Factor. The relativism and dynamism of capability combine to suggest another qualitative element: the pervasive influence of time. Questions of "now" and "then" enter into every judgment. A state's capability to reach an objective may be inadequate at one moment, but ample a short while later after conditions have changed. In like manner, time may work against a state. The components of capability change at an uneven rate, and the determination of the moment of maximum capacity

---

[23] This warning is even more apposite when the notion of "power" is under discussion in the same sense that "capability" is being used here. It is easier to visualize a "powerful" state than a "capable" one, and even more deceptive to do so. "Power" does not convey as clear an implication of the ability to perform a specific act as does "capability"; this is perhaps one of the more compelling reasons why the latter term has come generally to be regarded as both more accurate and more useful than the older one.

[24] See Feliks Gross, *Foreign Policy Analysis* (New York: Philosophical Library, 1954), p. 124, for an elucidation of this point.

for a particular course of action requires that the statesman carefully coordinate a number of factors moving at different speeds. The effect of time appears at every turn in international politics, and success in foreign policy rests to a great extent upon the ability of the policy-maker to calculate the optimum moment for action.

OBJECTIVES AND POLICY

We turn now to two more concepts that play an important role in the foreign policy process: objectives as goals of state action, and policy considered as a course of action designed to reach an objective.

Objectives

The Nature of Objectives. Foreign policy involves action in the national interest, but such action must be purposive. Each state organizes its purposes into a set of objectives that represent the goals it seeks to reach by deliberate action. We have defined an objective generally as a state of affairs that a state attempts to bring about. It may be positive in nature and demand affirmative action; it may be negative and demand only that a particular position be held against external pressure. Objectives are preferably verbalized in concrete terms that afford some criteria for determining when and if the objective is attained and for devising strategies for their attainment.

From Interest to Objectives. In the policy process, the development of a situation to the point where it either requires or suggests action by the state calls for the application of the yardstick of national interest. Every government asks itself a question more or less as follows: "Considering the situation as of this moment, what possible state of affairs would be most advantageous in terms of the national interest?" The answers it discovers to the question furnish the objectives it accepts and will seek to attain. Objectives, as we have seen, arise out of the situation as interpreted by a notion of interest.

The Mutability of Objectives. Realizing that any formulation of interest is subject to modification and that many situational factors themselves are inherently unstable, we are led to conclude that objectives (derived from these two elements) are themselves absolutely liable to change along some minimum-maximum continuum. It is no wonder that states are constantly overhauling their patterns of objectives. Some goals

22

are discarded as either no longer valuable or as beyond attainment; some are modified in the light of situational change; some entirely new ones are adopted. No state can safely assume that the application of its version of interest to a general situation will produce the same result twice in succession; indeed, the contrary assumption is usually safer. Objectives provide targets at which to shoot and combine to indicate a direction in which policy moves, but only rarely does a state reach the exact goal after which it originally set out.

The Pattern of Objectives. Every state, of course, has a number of objectives. Each of the components of national interest normally gives rise to a more or less numerous family of specific concerns ("interests"), in response to each of which some concrete objective is selected from the situational context. It is only seldom that these objectives fall neatly into a homogenous or harmonious relationship with each other; usually there is some degree of inner contradiction within the larger outline of interest and policy.

When this contradiction involves fundamentals, a real dilemma confronts the policy-maker; sometimes he may advance his state's interest in one area only by doing it serious or irreparable damage in another. Normally at this point major readjustments become necessary. More frequently, however, conflict among objectives is resolved in terms of time priority (Objective A, being urgent, must be achieved as soon as possible; Objective B, contradictory but less immediately critical, may be attacked at a later time) or some other rationalizing device.

If the controlling notion of interest is sufficiently clear, we would expect that all the specific objectives of a state could be comprehended within its terms, even if only at a very high level of generalization. Conversely, some approximation of what a state considers its interest may be reached by induction from an analysis of the motivations underlying its choice of objectives. In any case, a rationally conceived foreign policy, maintaining a working relationship with an understood and accepted notion of interest, would normally have more of harmony than of contradiction.

Policy

Early in this chapter we defined foreign policy and warned that this definition would require further analysis. Between that point and this one we have examined the foreign policy process and various of its components. We now return to the subject of "policy" itself, initially in a much narrower frame of reference than in our original definition, and later in its original broader sense. "Policy," as we are discussing it here, is not necessarily the same thing as "foreign policy."

The Meaning of Policy. Our concern at this point is with "policy" considered in a strategic and tactical sense. Policy in these terms assumes an objective to have been already selected, and refers to a method for its attainment. The term therefore has two connotations: it means either the actions actually taken to accomplish a purpose, or the principles that govern such action. It may refer either to a series of overt moves made by a state in order to reach an objective, or to the prepared plan under which such steps are taken. Both meanings are useful, and analytically the distinction between them is important; as we use the word in this discussion, however, the particular reference will usually be indicated by the context.

Reaching a Policy Decision. Making a policy decision to act in accomplishment of an objective is a power monopolized by the official decision-making personnel of a government. Action in international affairs occurs only by government mechanisms, and only those officials authorized in the name of the state to commit the government to act can make meaningful decisions. Considerable study has been made of the process by which decision-makers, particularly in the United States, perform this task.[25]

Without going into the minutiae, however, we may sketch in a skeleton outline of the method most frequently used. Governments are scrupulous to follow the general pattern of reaching a decision that we have suggested. Particular emphasis, especially after the objective has been selected, is placed on canvassing all the possible alternatives of action. Each course that has any feasibility at all is spelled out, and each is evaluated rigorously in terms of the prevailing idea of national interest, the impact of the developing situation, and its possible success in attaining the objective. The final selection (at least in theory) is made of the one that seems to promise the greatest success (or, sometimes, the minimum loss) in the fulfillment of the demands of national interest.

Various states formalize this process of developing alternatives to different degrees, and within any state it may vary from one situation to

---

[25] Three useful, although very different, analyses of the foreign-policy process are Richard C. Snyder, H. W. Bruck, and Burton M. Sapin, *Decision-making as an Approach to the Study of International Politics,* Foreign Policy Analysis Series No. 3 (Princeton, N. J.: Princeton University, 1954); Kurt London, *How Foreign Policy Is Made* (New York: Van Nostrand, 1949); and Philip W. Buck and Martin Travis, eds., *Control of Foreign Relations in Modern Nations* (New York: W. W. Norton & Co., Inc., 1957).

another. But some approximation of the technique is used in every government that takes foreign affairs seriously. No less detailed method would take enough of the variables into account.[26]

The Flexibility of Policy Decisions. Policy decisions, being concerned more with "how" than with "what," are as often as possible taken with an eye to their possible revision as conditions evolve. This is one major reason for the elaborateness with which the open alternatives are frequently analyzed; if the strategy selected should prove unworkable, the state presumably can fall back on the policy line originally judged next best. States normally attempt to preserve the maximum room for maneuver; sometimes an objective will prove beyond reach by any possible policy technique, and then a new objective must be fixed and a new program accepted to reach it. Flexibility is sought in time, in quantity, in kind, and indeed in every dimension by which policy is measured.

The dynamism of the state system swiftly penalizes the state that neglects to allow for change. A rigid policy—based on the (explicit or implicit) assumption that conditions will continue unchanged indefinitely —stands in constant danger of becoming irrelevant to new situational elements. If a policy supported by commitments of power faces the loss of effective rapport with its milieu, the state may well be forced into the expensive and hazardous effort of extemporizing to buy time while it adjusts to the new dimension of its problem.

"Policy" and "Foreign Policy." In this discussion we have been emphasizing that "policy" refers to the course of action a state follows in pursuing a single objective. A state thus has many policies—as many as it has objectives—and it follows each of them simultaneously. It is in this connection that we speak of a "policy decision": a decision to commit the government to act in a certain way in order to achieve an objective.

But, despite the built-in ambiguity that results, "policy" has another meaning. As used in the phrase "foreign policy," "policy" refers to the general pattern and direction revealed by the aggregate of a state's specific undertakings and the broad principles that undergird them. Thus we may say that Soviet foreign policy is expansionist, and we may also say that the Soviet pursues the policy of cultivating the friendship of the uncommitted states. There is no easy escape from this confusion of language; we may, however, suggest one possible clue. "Policy" as a generic concept is usually verbalized in general or abstract terms, while

---

[26] Examples of this process are provided by the specimen "problem papers" included in each volume of the series prepared by the International Studies Group of the Brookings Institution, *Major Problems of United States Foreign Policy* (Washington, D. C.: Brookings, 1947-54).

a particular policy of a state is (or, at any rate, should be) precise and concrete in its referents. Further than this we must fall back on the context to clarify the sense in which the term is being used.

AMERICAN FOREIGN POLICY: CONTENT AND METHOD OF ANALYSIS

Up to this point, we have been outlining and commenting upon a conceptual scheme for a reasonably rational analysis of foreign policy. With some modifications it could be used to reach some conclusions and evaluations about the foreign policy of any state in the world; generally speaking, the key notions of interest, situational factors, and state action apply to all states with approximately the same force. But our aim in this book is to consider American foreign policy, and the purpose of this chapter is to lay out the method of inquiry we shall be using in our consideration of the foreign relations of the United States. Here in the concluding section of the chapter, we should spell out as precisely as possible just what phenomena we shall be examining and just how we shall attack them.

The content of "American foreign policy"

In approaching American foreign policy by way of the leads furnished by our over-all system, we can find over a dozen different categories of data into which we should inquire. Each of them has some relevance to the foreign policy the United States is conducting at the present time, and each has a place in our model of the foreign-policy process. Each therefore forms part of the "American foreign policy" with which we are concerned. The list that follows includes 13 separate components of our study:

1. The national interest of the United States as tradition and concept.
2. Specific formulations of the national interest.
3. The historical background of American policy.
4. The mechanisms and procedures for making and executing American policy.
5. The international milieu in which the United States is acting.
6. The policies of other states to which the United States must react.
7. The capabilities of the United States, general and specific.
8. The general international action pattern of the United States.
9. The specific objectives sought by the United States.

10. The courses of action taken by the United States to attain its objectives.

11. The evaluation of the policies of the United States.

12. The unresolved issues remaining in American policy.

13. The probable future course of American policy.

An Analytical Scheme. The chapters that follow this one are an attempt to fit these separate areas of inquiry into a reasonably coherent analysis of American foreign policy. The remainder of this book divides the material into sections, each one constituting a segment of our generalized concept of foreign policy or logically deriving from it. An effort has been made to present the material in logical sequence, both within each part and from part to part.

Part I includes this opening chapter. Parts II and III deal respectively with the structures and processes for making and executing American policy and with the historical antecedents of contemporary American action. They are considered at the outset because of their relatively fixed and continuing impact on policy: as part of the "givens" of American foreign affairs they constitute bases on which we build other factors.

Part IV deals with the national interest, including both the national value system that we have called the myth of national mission and the operating formulations that American decision-makers have derived from this broad-gauge image of the national good. Part V devotes a chapter to each of the three major categories of situational factors affecting the United States: the international milieu, the actions of other states (in this case largely the USSR), and American capabilities.

Part VI considers American action in the contemporary era. One chapter discusses the general pattern of American policy; another gives a chronological overview of the first decade of cold war organized around the concept of bipolarity.

Part VII examines certain continuing issues of American policy that have continued to be important through all the situational changes that have taken place. Part VIII concludes the study with an attempt at some limited-range forecasting of the future of American policy.

Such an organization not only encompasses the 13 areas we listed as being of interest, but also puts to the test the general conceptual scheme this chapter has outlined. If we have made an accurate list of the important considerations and if our analytical techniques are reliable, we should emerge from our study with a better rounded and more consistent understanding of at least the fundamentals of American foreign policy.

part 2:

MAKING AND EXECUTING
AMERICAN FOREIGN POLICY

part 2:

MAKING AND EXECUTING
AMERICAN FOREIGN POLICY

2 : Policy formulation: the decision-makers

Foreign policy, as we suggested in Chapter 1, does not just happen. It is the result of a long, difficult, and never-ending process. Although in a democracy such as the United States every effort is made—for reasons both of ideology and of practicality—to take popular opinion into account and to make government action square as much as possible with the wishes of the people, by its very nature the actual making and executing of foreign policy is a government monopoly. In considering who makes policy, how it is made, and how it is carried out, we must initially concentrate on the sprawling structure of the government of the United States.

But, despite the truism that the manipulation of the raw materials of policy is the exclusive province of those who hold official position, our inquiry cannot stop there. American ideology is democratic; American foreign policy must therefore be, in some way, a democratic policy. It is not enough for the official elite itself to verbalize its belief in the values of democracy; in a popular government, mechanisms must be developed for the registration of public opinion and its translation into specific action by the government. Our analysis of policy formulation must therefore be extended to include the ways in which public opinion is brought to bear on officials. In broader terms, we might phrase a "democratic dilemma," stemming from the impasse brought about by the conflicting claims of an expert bureaucracy, informed and competent, on the one hand and the demands of a democratic public on the other.[1]

---

[1] Among the many discussions of this point in the literature, one of the most thoughtful and recent ones is Max Beloff, *Foreign Policy and the Democratic Process* (Baltimore: John Hopkins Press, 1955).

One further complication might be mentioned at the outset. So important and complex has foreign policy become that the machinery for making decisions has become very elaborate. Many people in government "speak for the United States" and have the power to commit it to action. Responsibility is highly concentrated, as we shall see below; authority to act, however, is dispersed throughout most of the official hierarchy. This will oblige us to confine ourselves in this chapter largely to generalization and summary; any detailed study of policy-making would carry us far beyond our allotted scope.[2]

We shall divide our discussion of the process of policy formulation into two chapters. In this one, we shall consider the formal governmental mechanisms for reaching decisions; in the next, we shall examine the socio-political domestic factors that influence these decisions.

THE EXECUTIVE BRANCH

Executive leadership

The executive branch of the federal government has a greater responsibility in making foreign policy than have its two fellows. Logic, history, law, and necessity unite to confer on the President and his subordinates a peculiarly advantageous position in making the decisions that govern American action. From among the several reasons for such executive pre-eminence, we may select three that are especially pertinent.

In the first place, the executive branch has access to, and possesses a great fund of, information without which action becomes impossible, useless, or dangerous. Second, the executive branch is the medium of official international contact; it deals directly with the other states of the world. This creates the intimate relationship between decision and execution that places the executive in the position of being prepared to act quickly. Third, the executive branch has the expertise, the competent

---

[2] Such detailed studies include: William Yandell Elliott, *et al., United States Foreign Policy, Its Organization and Control* (New York: Columbia University Press, 1952); Brookings Institution, *The Administration of Foreign Affairs and Overseas Operations* (Washington, D. C.: U. S. Government Printing Office, 1951); H. H. Bundy and J. G. Rogers, *The Organization of the Government for the Conduct of Foreign Affairs*, Task Force Report on Foreign Affairs, Hoover Commission (Washington, D. C.: U. S. Government Printing Office, 1949); Arthur Macmahon, *Administration in Foreign Affairs* (University, Alabama: University of Alabama Press, 1953).

agents, who know the "how" and the "where" of policy and are thus able more effectively to suggest the "what" and the "why."

We must not assume, however, that executive leadership in foreign policy means executive monopoly. There are many important functions of policy-making that are shared with Congress; competition and frequent conflict between legislature and executive are as normal as is cooperation. Whether or not this is desirable cannot be answered in any absolute way, for opinions may legitimately differ; a good case can be made that it is, in any event, inevitable.

The presidency

If we agree that the executive branch is central to policy formulation, it follows that the President is the heart of the whole policy-making process. It is often said that the presidency is the most powerful political office in the world. Not the least of the factors contributing to this judgment is its great span of control over foreign affairs.

The Nature of the President's Role. Executive power in the United States has long been a subject of interest to both American and foreign students. The study has been all the more fascinating because of its vagueness; the exact nature of the role of the President in any context is often difficult to define in detail. His actual conduct is often the result of the interaction of a variety of formal and informal factors, and what generalizations we offer must therefore be very broad.[3]

In the first place, in international affairs the President's position is that of ultimate responsibility for all executive decision and action. Both international law and the United States Constitution make him the official voice of the United States in foreign relations. Only he can make final policy decisions. He may and usually does delegate a good deal, most, or sometimes all his operative authority to subordinates, but these latter individuals make binding commitments only because of their acquisition of fiduciary presidential power and subject to his final (perhaps only implicit) ratification. The President cannot escape his final responsibility for any policy decision emanating from the executive branch; even in

---

[3] See Edward S. Corwin, *The Presidency: Office and Powers*, 3d ed. (New York: New York University Press, 1948); a more introspective study is Clinton Rossiter, *The American Presidency* (New York: Harcourt, Brace and Co., 1956).

the case of decisions virtually forced upon him by Congress, his responsibility for execution and implementation cannot be shifted.

A second policy-making function of the President is his power to set a general line. In a fashion open to no one else, he can formulate ultimate objectives, develop verbalizations of the national interest, and delineate future emphases. Once made, these general decisions usually provide the framework for more detailed action undertaken by subordinates; his control over his aides is sufficient to enforce compliance with his wishes. This power of initiation is the President's alone, even though frequently he exercises it only by adopting proposals brought before him by his assistants.

It is a further characteristic of the President's position in foreign affairs that he may make decisions personally at any level of detail. Ordinarily, administrative requirements confine him to the broadest considerations and to the vital and complex task of coordination. But he may, at any time he wishes, assume the authority that is his alone and decide any part, or the whole, of any issue. Various Presidents have exercised this function to different degrees, but it is a power open to any of them at any time.

In summary, therefore, we may characterize the President's role in making foreign policy roughly as follows: (1) he bears ultimate responsibility for all decisions; (2) he usually outlines the general policy line to be followed on important questions; (3) he makes personally such decisions as he chooses. He is, in short, the apex of a policy-making pyramid, and may make his own role in it just about as large as he pleases.

Constitutional and Legal Powers of the President. The Constitution confers on the President a limited number of very important foreign-affairs powers. He alone negotiates treaties; he appoints American ambassadors; he "receives" ambassadors from other states (thus giving rise to the important power of recognition); he is commander-in-chief of the armed forces; he may negotiate executive agreements and often implement them without congressional approval. Each of these, when interpreted broadly, carries a tremendous grant of competence in foreign policy.

In addition to these, Congress has made literally dozens of special grants of power to the President. Some of these, to become effective, require the proclamation of a national emergency; others are simple delegations, effective without further action. Included among the latter are some of the most significant policy moves taken by the United States in recent years, among them the series of bills (1947-56) making up the foreign-aid program. In each of these the President was given broad grants of discretionary power by simple act of Congress.[4]

And yet, formidable as the list of the legal powers of the President may be, they are not enough. The requirements of international life load on the President such a variety of responsibilities that it is obviously impossible to encompass them all in a legal framework. In the leading case on the subject, the United States Supreme Court admitted that the President has "a degree of discretion and freedom from statutory restriction which would not be admissible were domestic affairs alone involved."[5]

We may put this another way. The United States, if it is to function effectively in international society, must be presumed to have all the powers that appertain to a sovereign state. Some of these powers the Constitution distributes; others are covered in congressional statutes; the remainder are not specifically dealt with in American law. International practice therefore vests these in the only official international voice of the United States, the legal chief of all foreign affairs personnel, the President. As the Court indicated in the *Curtiss-Wright* case, we cannot assume that the President has any fewer powers than are necessary for him to perform his task as the chief architect of American foreign policy.

The President as Leader. The legal powers of the President, of course, tell only part of the story. The modern development of government in the United States has made the presidency the seat of real political leadership. He speaks not only for the legal abstraction called "the United States," but increasingly also for the vast bulk of the American people— and especially when he deals with international issues. Despite the impossibility of distinguishing completely between the President as party chieftain and as foreign-policy spokesman, it is an obvious fact that the concept of the chief executive as the national leader has a firm grip on the imagination of the American people.

As the public's expectations of presidential action have increased, his power to act in this way has steadily grown. If he maintains effective rapport with public attitudes, he has an almost ready-made consensus to support whatever decisions he may reach. His peculiar status also helps him create support for his own decisions (or those with which he chooses to identify himself). It is difficult for opposition to crystallize against a decision that a reasonably popular President has made and is actively

---

[4] See, for example, Title I of the Foreign Assistance Act of 1948, Public Law 472, 80th Congress.

[5] *United States v. Curtiss-Wright Export Company,* 299 U. S. 304 (1936).

defending before the public. No other executive official enjoys this advantage. We may recall the constant opposition Secretary of State Dulles faced between 1953 and 1957 and contrast it with the almost complete support received by President Eisenhower, even when they were advocating substantially the same policies.[6]

The executive staff

Because of the President's status as legal head of all executive foreign-affairs activity and his unique policy-making function, there has been gathered about the chief executive an elaborate staff organization. Its purpose is to assist the President in performing his mission of initiating, coordinating, and bearing responsibility for action. The staff agencies are of various sizes and degrees of intimacy with the President.[7] The ones discussed here (except for the Joint Chiefs of Staff) are subsumed under the administrative grouping known as the Executive Office of the President.

The White House Office. The White House Office contains the President's personal staff. It consists of a relatively small number of administrative and personal assistants, aides, and secretaries. It performs such duties as are set for each of the members by the President himself and, especially under President Eisenhower, has taken over a significant number of more or less routine executive functions. Included in this group, but of special importance, is the Special Assistant to the President, whose mission is entirely in foreign affairs and who, under Presidents Truman and Eisenhower, gained a relatively large degree of freedom in making policy decisions on his own.

The Joint Chiefs of Staff. The Joint Chiefs of Staff include the uniformed chiefs of the three armed services plus a chairman selected from one of the three services (who does not vote). Legally the JCS is

---

[6] An instructive example of the impact of presidential leadership was furnished by the controversy between Congress and the President during February, 1957, over the prospect of United Nations sanctions against Israel. Although congressional leadership was virtually unanimous against sanctions, the President's position, strengthened by a radio-television speech on 21 February, remained substantially unchanged. The final resolution of the issue—Israel's agreement to withdraw from Egyptian territory—was on the terms stipulated by the executive rather than those suggested by Congress. The day-by-day story of the issue is covered in the *New York Times* for February and the first few days of March, 1957.

[7] E. H. Hobbs, *Behind the President* (Washington, D. C.: Public Affairs Press, 1954), discusses the executive staff in detail.

the principal military adviser to the President, responsible for basic strategic recommendations. We shall consider military influence in and on American policy below; for the moment let it suffice to say that the JCS provides the official channel through which the point of view of the armed services reaches the President.

The Office of Defense Mobilization. As something to a counterpart to the JCS the Office of Defense Mobilization, under a Director, heads up the nonuniformed component of the governmental organization for defense. The Director is the principal adviser to the President on all questions of domestic mobilization other than the military, including such matters as production, manpower, economic controls, and so on. He is also concerned with the relationship of overseas aid programs to mobilization at home, with stockpiling, with economic stabilization, and a host of related affairs. It should be emphasized, however, that the ODM is more than just a staff agency; in addition to its advisory function, it has extensive operational duties given it both by law and by executive delegation.

The Council of Economic Advisers. The inclusion of the Council of Economic Advisers in this list illustrates the pervasive influence of foreign affairs in American life today. The CEA, established in 1946, has no direct connection with foreign policy, but it is axiomatic today that economic strength is a major international weapon of the United States. The task of CEA is to make recommendations to the President on measures to be taken to maintain the maximum productivity and prosperity of the American economy; its recommendations must mesh with those of ODM or serious conflict and possible maladjustment will result.

The National Security Council. The National Security Council, although part of the Executive Office of the President, is a unique body, both in its composition and its function. Created by law in 1947, it is the high strategy board for American security policy—called by one author "the American Politburo."[8] It consists of the President as chairman, the Vice-President, the Secretary of State, the Secretary of Defense, the Director of ODM, and—in practice—such other high officials as the President may invite. Under President Eisenhower, the Secretary of the Treasury, the Chairman of the JCS, the Director of CIA, and certain others regularly attended.

The NSC has a permanent staff headed by an executive secretary, who —despite his anonymity and his lack of command authority—is often thought of as one of the half-dozen most influential men in the govern-

---

[8] John Fischer, *Master Plan USA* (New York: Harper & Bros., 1951), Chapter I.

ment in the field of foreign policy. He has direct access to the President and assists him in planning the agenda of the weekly meetings of the Council.

The Council's function, in practice, is double. In the first place, it makes recommendations to the President on all matters that bear on the security of the United States and that require Presidential decision. Second, it brings together—at the highest level—the most important officials concerned with foreign policy and provides a setting for full and frank discussion among them. In these matters the NSC is of critical importance; evidence is accumulating that its already major significance will become even greater in the future as successive Presidents learn more about its usefulness and its limitations.[9]

The Central Intelligence Agency. The Central Intelligence Agency, established by the National Security Act of 1947, can be most usefully conceived of as an intelligence clearing house, directly subordinate to the National Security Council. The United States has a number of other agencies engaged in gathering information upon which to base policy decisions; the CIA seeks to coordinate all of them, and to serve as a central agency for the distribution of intelligence data, as a correlator of intelligence emanating from other sources, and as a synthesizer of "intelligence estimates." It performs a number of intelligence activities of its own, but (according to law) only those that are most efficiently performed centrally. Its detailed operations are one of the most security-cloaked activities of the government.[10]

The Bureau of the Budget. The final executive staff agency to merit mention is the Bureau of the Budget. Students of American government know something of the Bureau's key role in all budgetary matters and of its authority to review all requests for legislation made by the various departments. With foreign affairs—broadly conceived—now representing roughly three-fourths of the expenditures of the government, the role of the Bureau in passing on, approving or disapproving, and raising or lowering requests for appropriations is obviously of great total impact

---

[9] Sidney W. Souers, "Policy for National Security," *American Political Science Review* (June, 1949), p. 530; Helen P. Kirkpatrick, "The National Security Council: Adviser or Policy Maker?" *American Perspective* (February, 1949), p. 447; Robert Cutler, "The Development of the National Security Council," *Foreign Affairs* (April, 1956).

[10] For a general discussion of the importance of strategic intelligence in the formulation of foreign policy, see Sherman Kent, *Strategic Intelligence for American World Policy* (Princeton, N. J.: Princeton University Press, 1949); see also, Roger Hilsman, *Strategic Intelligence and National Decisions*, (Glencoe, Ill.: The Free Press, 1956).

on the substance of policy. Added to this is the Director of the Bureau's role as one of the major fiscal advisers to the President.

The state department

The Department of State, headed by the Secretary of State, constitutes the major single source of foreign policy decisions in the entire governmental structure. Under the pressures of international problems that have forced American policy mechanisms to proliferate, the Department has been obliged to renounce its once-exclusive control over foreign policy, but yet retains a central position. Even when interdepartmental consultation and coordination is necessary, it is most often the Department of State that serves as the principal medium of cooperative action.

The Role of the Secretary of State. The Secretary himself is perhaps the most important decision-maker. As the President's major adviser on foreign policy, his exact role is largely dependent on his personality and that of his chief, on the problems that arise during his tenure, and on the specific issues that fall to him to decide.

The Secretary's relationship to the President is an elastic one. The law of 1789 that created the office did not give the Secretary any detailed responsibilities in foreign affairs, but directed him instead to assist the President in any way that the latter directed. This legal directive empowers the President to establish almost any kind of relationship he wishes.

He may give the Secretary his head and pointedly refrain from having any policy of his own; although fairly frequent during the nineteenth century, such a relationship would be suicidal today. He may go to the other extreme and become "his own Secretary of State." This practice also may be effective for a short time (President Roosevelt, for example, often simply ignored Secretary Hull during much of World War II),[11] but in the long run the State Department is too important to be left out entirely. In practice, some form of teamwork based on an agreed division of labor seems to be the most effective form of rapport; the blueprint of presidential functions we outlined above would leave the Secretary's role both well-defined and critical. Within the broad limits thus laid down by the chief executive the Secretary of State could move with some freedom in making decisions of his own.

---

[11] Robert Sherwood, *Roosevelt and Hopkins* (New York: Bantam Books, 1950). II, 374.

Today perhaps the most important policy-making role carried on by the Secretary is that of coordination. While the Department's functions and staff have increased, its relative share in foreign policy has diminished. The military establishment, special agencies of all sorts, and Congress itself all play much larger parts than before 1941. As the key individual advising the President, however, and as the "senior" member of all varieties of coordinating bodies (such as the National Security Council), the Secretary is in a strategic position to exert major influence in determining decisions, whether or not he makes them himself.

The Department as Policy-maker. As the observer looks at the Department, he is forcibly struck by the extent to which the power to make policy decisions is decentralized within the structure. The administrative theory behind this practice is clear: each administrator at each level makes policy over the area of his responsibility; these decisions serve as directives to his subordinates who make decisions of their own within these limits, and so on down the line. However rational this may be in theory (and it is perfectly justifiable on those grounds), the result is that binding policy decisions are made at all operational levels except the very lowest.

Recent reorganizations of the Department have set up control mechanisms to improve communication from top to bottom (and vice versa), as well as to enforce upon subordinates the decisions made by higher-level officials. But within as large a structure as the Department, one of the major problems will always be that of coordination. Making certain that decisions made in one part of the Department harmonize with other decisions made by other officials is a task whose difficulty has not yet been matched by the success of its accomplishment.

Equally perplexing, and perhaps even more important, is the problem of coordinating State Department decisions with those of other departments. We shall see below something of the extensive network of coordinating agencies that have been created to bring all "interested" points of view into harmony before a final decision is reached. But what is to be done about the conflicts and disharmonies that develop after two or more agencies have committed themselves and it is discovered that they do not agree? The solution most frequently advanced for this awkward outcome—to bring it to the White House for resolution—is at best imperfect, for it adds another burden to an already overloaded set of officials.

The Department as a Staff Agency. Another problem lies in the relationship of the Department to the remainder of the governmental struc-ture: is it a staff agency pure and simple, or does it have responsibilities for executing programs? During the Topsy-like era during and after the war, when new duties were loaded on the Department nearly every day, this issue was academic. Once the cold war began in earnest, however, and the American government settled down to the long-term operation of framing and executing a permanently-expanded foreign policy, it became necessary to clarify the Department's real function.

There are persuasive arguments in support of the contention that the State Department should have a broad area of operational responsibility, and these have been advanced many times in many guises during the long controversy over the place of the Department in the over-all foreign-policy design of the United States. The trend between 1950 and 1955, however, was toward the gradual elimination of responsibility for programs from the Department and its final designation as a staff (policy-making) and negotiating body. Under the reorganization plans of President Eisenhower in 1953, the Department's role was spelled out most clearly: it was to be an advisory agency with only the slenderest kind of operating authority. The later (1955) centralization of all foreign aid in the International Cooperation Administration and the latter's inclusion in the Department seemed to be a step backward from this ideal. For practical purposes, however, the ICA is operationally autonomous, and only the Office of the Secretary concerns itself with it.

At the same time, if the Department is to be primarily a policy-formulating body, it must have some kind of ground rules to specify its function in this area. The same plans that stripped the Department of many operating functions also stressed its key role in policy-making by authorizing the Secretary of State to give policy guidance to such operating bodies as the Foreign Operations Administration and the United States Information Agency, and by directing the heads of such agencies to seek guidance from the Secretary. A recent indication of the continuing importance of policy to the Department was the elevation of the post of Chief of the Policy Planning Staff to that of an Assistant Secretary, thus giving him equal status with the major operating subordinates of the Secretary.

What all this means is that the major job of the Secretary is to deal with policy—both in terms of advising the President and of making decisions himself—rather than with administration. Concentrating directly on the details of a particular program might create the danger of over-looking broader concerns of total policy, and this is a trap into which the Secretary should not be allowed to fall. Yet we must admit that the dichotomy between "policy" and "administration" is much more real in theory than in practice; the Department—being composed of human

41

beings—often simply cannot develop a program and then turn it over to some other agencies for administration. It tends rather to keep a finger in the administrative pie, if only through the magic of that elastic word, "coordination."

The Departmental Point of View. As the result of its own history, traditions, and place in the governmental hierarchy, the Department of State has developed a distinct point of view toward the problems with which it is called upon to deal. Although this attitude has elements of real strength, such as its emphasis on professionalism, its concern with the concrete and the practical, and its insistence on the service of its notion of the national interest, it also has a number of shortcomings that affect its role in modern American society and government.

Some of the deficiencies in the departmental point of view are not peculiar to it, but grow instead out of its status as a major government department. Many of the familiar bureaucratic vices are present in the State Department, some of them in excessive amounts. The Department often seems obsessed with procedure and routine; many of its members are hypersensitive to considerations of career, prestige, and power; effective coordination is difficult to achieve.

More peculiar to the State Department itself is the sharp sense of cleavage between departmental personnel (domestic or foreign) and the American public at large.[12] This may be explained to some extent by the unique relationship the Department has with the American people; after all, the argument sometimes runs, the Department's clientele is not the American public at all. "State" deals with foreign governments rather than with American citizens. In whatever way one may defend or explain it, however, the fact remains that a sense of nonidentification with the American mass public has led to two clear consequences of great importance. On the part of the Department, it has helped foster the growth of elitism: a self-generated impression that only the Department knows fully the real problems confronting the United States and what should be done about them. Large segments of the public have reciprocated by developing disdain, contempt, and distrust for departmental personnel. On both sides this is a disquieting outcome.

Operationally, the Department's point of view stresses caution, a faith in precedents (substantive and procedural) proved by time, and a preference for "making policy on the cables." Despite the lessons learned during the period since 1945 and many reorganizations of structure, and

---

[12] *Toward a Stronger Foreign Service* (Washington, D. C.; U. S. Government Printing Office, 1954).

also despite uncounted high-level directives stressing the need for pre-vision and an adequate operational plan, the Department retains much of its pre-1941 disinclination to plan in advance. Agencies exist within the Department whose function it is to plan, acting under the general direc-tion of the Assistant Secretary for Policy Planning; much effort is expended in devising blueprints for the future. The objective observer, however, is still impressed by the extent to which the usual desk officer refuses to "deal with hypothetical questions" and seems to get consider-able satisfaction out of making the "brush fire" approach a normal operating procedure.[13]

The military

One of the significant changes in American foreign-policy making since 1945 has been the systematic inclusion of the military point of view. This, as we shall see later, is not part of the traditional image of how American foreign policy is made; military and foreign affairs were usually thought to be two separate worlds, to be kept apart at all costs. Today, however, the picture is completely reversed; most of the contro-versy over the point deals with whether or not the views of the armed forces receive too much consideration rather than too little.[14]

Military Calculations in American Policy. What sort of military con-siderations are appropriate to American policy decisions, and why has it become so important since World War II that they be included? The answer lies in certain basic relationships between ends and means in any state's foreign policy.

The ends of policy—the objectives of the state—must be served by such means as are available and appropriate. Military power is one of these possible means open—at least to some limited extent—to every state. Any policy-maker, therefore, should take account of his state's abil-ity to apply military pressure and, conversely, of its ability to withstand any probable similar pressure applied by other states. As long as inter-

---

[13] Hugh Gibson, *The Road to Foreign Policy* (Garden City: Doubleday, Doran, 1944), discusses the difficulties before and during World War II. His comments, despite their dated referents, have a good deal of relevance today.

[14] The general subject of military influence on foreign policy is discussed critically in Burton M. Sapin and Richard C. Snyder, *The Role of the Military in American Foreign Policy* (Garden City, N. Y.: Doubleday, 1954); see also Samuel P. Hunting-ton, *The Soldier and the State* (Cambridge, Mass.: Belknap Press of Harvard Uni-versity Press, 1957).

national politics goes on within the state system as we know it today, such judgments will continue to be necessary.

American policy, therefore, must in part be based on two kinds of military judgments. In the first place, American decision-makers must have an understanding of American military capability in the context under consideration, for no objective needing military support should be chosen that lies beyond the military capacity of the United States to achieve. Second, the United States should confine itself to positions that it can defend against the military pressure of other states. Thus the military point of view in American planning requires both the calculation of the affirmative employment of military measures and the provision of defensive measures against hostile (or potentially hostile) measures taken by others.

One final statement seems in point. Means-ends analysis is a very tricky subject. In practice means often look disconcertingly like ends, and vice versa. Particularly so is this true in American military policy. Weapons supremacy, such as in strategic bombardment aircraft or in thermonuclear bombs, in theory is significant primarily as a means to some other policy objective, such as superiority over a potential enemy; as actually carried out, however, weapons leadership over all comers (or, as sometimes among air-power enthusiasts, over any combination of comers) becomes a policy end of the first priority. This point has led to more controversy over the military contribution to American foreign policy than perhaps any other.[15]

The Pentagon and Foreign Affairs. The Department of Defense and the three service departments under its direction share directly in the foreign policy process at all levels. The Secretary of Defense is, of course, a member of the Cabinet where—especially during the Eisenhowever administration—his views have been solicited by the President. He is also a permanent member of the National Security Council where his special concerns are even more directly in point.

The Secretary of Defense and the three service secretaries each have special foreign-policy assistance in the form of an assistant secretary or other high-ranking civilian official who is charged with direct responsibility for making the department's contribution to all interagency or joint decisions. Since so many operational decisions are taken on a multi-departmental basis via the National Security Council or lower-level joint

---

[15] From the many statements made by Alexander P. De Seversky, one of the most outspoken advocates of supreme air power for the United States, one of the most carefully worked-out is *Air Power: Key to Survival* (New York: Simon and Schuster, 1950).

bodies, it can be seen that great care is taken to have the "military point of view" represented in almost every sort of decision-making body of more than routine importance.

The Joint Chiefs of Staff. The preceding paragraphs considered the Secretary of Defense as the spokesman for the military, even though most of the top leadership of the Defense Department is civilian. It is via the Joint Chiefs of Staff that the viewpoint of the uniformed services is expressed.

The Joint Chiefs are the principal military advisers to the President, the National Security Council, and the Secretary of Defense. Their approach is professional and technical; they personify the "means" role of the military. Their advice in theory does not concern itself with any aspect of policy other than its military feasibility and/or its military consequences. Much of the dispute over the role of the Joint Chiefs (such as the heated battle that developed as the aftermath of the Indochina crisis of 1954) stems from the widely-shared suspicion that they often slip out of their purely instrumental role into an advocacy of substantive policy.[16] To the extent that this charge can be substantiated, there is some basis for arguing that civilian supremacy is being undermined and that the always unclear distinction between substantive policy ends and purely military means is also being eroded.

Other executive agencies

Foreign-policy making power is widely shared in the executive branch.[17] To make a catalogue of the exact part played by each of the hundred-odd agencies that participate in one way or another would exhaust both compiler and reader. All we can do is to sketch some of the broader outlines and to indicate one or two bodies of special importance.

---

[16] Admiral Arthur B. Radford, the then Chairman of the Joint Chiefs, presented his notion of the role of the group in an interview in *United States News and World Report* (February 25, 1955), entitled "We Give Military Advice Only."

[17] A famous chart appearing in the Hoover Commission's Task Force Report on Foreign Affairs indicated the "Organization Units of the Executive Branch Participating in the Conduct of U. S. Foreign Affairs." What was striking was the small number—less than twenty—of executive agencies that did not in some way share in foreign policy; even some of these were open to debate. Among the few that the Task Force felt did not qualify were the National Archives, the Office of the Housing Expediter, the Indian Claims Commission, the National Labor Relations Board, the National Capitol Park and Planning Commission, the Railroad Retirement Board, and the Commission on Fine Arts. Also in this group was the Selective Service System; many a recent draftee might argue that this agency plays a great—if indirect—part in American foreign policy!

The Treasury Department. The Treasury Department constitutes the third in the foreign-policy "big three" Cabinet departments. In part, this stems from the central proposition that foreign affairs consumes the great bulk of the annual budget of the United States; with so much money involved, the Cabinet's fiscal expert naturally becomes a key figure. Under President Eisenhower, Secretary of the Treasury George Humphrey's recommendations on taxation and expenditure frequently served as a limiting factor on policy, particularly military and foreign-aid programs.[18] The requirements of a budget in balance, or at least in near-balance, in time of peace often could have great controlling and directing effect on American policy.

But the Treasury Department has operating responsibilities as well; a good share of American policy deals with financial and monetary matters and the Treasury makes basic decisions in this area. There is in the department an Office of International Finance concerned entirely with this general problem; perhaps its major concern is with American membership in the International Monetary Fund and the International Bank for Reconstruction and Development. Tariff administration, direct international loans, and other aspects of economic foreign policy are other areas in which Treasury recommendations carry great weight. Its importance is underscored by President Eisenhower's decision to include the Secretary as a regular member of the National Security Council.

Other Cabinet Departments. All the other Cabinet departments share in policy-making, although in unequal amounts. All of their administrative heads participate in Cabinet meetings and thus have access to the President when international issues are being discussed. All of them, in addition, enter the foreign policy field to some extent in performing their statutory duties.

Perhaps the most significant of this group are the Departments of Commerce and Agriculture, for reasons that are largely self-evident. Commerce is responsible for the whole matter of foreign trade; Agriculture enters such fields as the international movement of food products and the procurement of agricultural experts for American technical assistance programs. The rest of the Cabinet departments—Labor, Post Office, Justice, Interior, and Health-Education-Welfare—have roles that, while equally as direct as those of Agriculture and Commerce, are not as extensive. Labor, for example, functions through the International Labor Organization; the Post Office represents the United States in the Universal

---

[18] Secretary Humphrey's reaction to the 1957 budget message was one of near-horror. Unless the government reduced its spending, Mr. Humphrey told a press conference shortly after the budget was released, he foresaw "a depression that would curl your hair." *New York Times* (January 17, 1957).

Postal Union; the Justice Department controls immigration and resident aliens; Interior administers American overseas possessions.

Non-Cabinet Agencies. One of the administrative problems of American government—a perennial concern of all attempts at reorganization—is the large number of administrative bodies that lie outside the Cabinet-department structure and are responsible only to the President. This condition applies in foreign affairs as well as in any other area; some of the most significant policy decisions are made and implemented by non-Cabinet bodies.

Perhaps the most important of these, now that foreign aid has once again been taken directly into the Department of State, is the Atomic Energy Commission. It is responsible for dealing with all aspects, domestic and international, of the development of atomic energy—a subject most Americans would admit is of considerable importance today.

Other independent agencies with foreign-affairs functions include the Maritime Commission, the Civil Aeronautics Board, the Federal Communications Commission, the Export-Import Bank, and the United States Tariff Commission. Each of these to some extent makes policy in its own area and influences decisions—often by representation on interdepartmental bodies—on questions in which it is interested.

Coordination in the executive branch

The Decentralization of Policy. It has become clear in the foregoing discussion that policy-making is highly decentralized in the executive branch. The power to commit the United States to action has been widely diffused. Foreign policy today is so multiformed, with so many aspects of human action having relevance to the objectives of the United States, that it is difficult to conceive how such decentralization could have been avoided. It is true that total responsibility for all executive action lies on the President, but it would not be humanly possible, or even desirable, to force him to actually make all the decisions for which he is responsible. He must, in some way, delegate authority so as to reduce his own task to manageable proportions.

But administrative theory and the needs of foreign policy agree that delegating decision-making power is not in itself a sufficient answer. Guidance and control must be exercised by the delegating authority; a general policy line must be stipulated and mechanisms developed to guarantee that the action taken by subordinates agrees with the over-all orientation. We might suggest that one index of the efficiency and effectiveness of American foreign policy is the extent to which detailed

47

decisions made by operating personnel are consistent with the broader policy directives issued by higher-ranking officials.

The Need for Coordination. Since policy-making is so extensively decentralized, some apparatus for coordination becomes necessary. This task has dimensions both horizontal and vertical. Horizontally, there must be agreement at any level among the various agencies making policy so that their cumulative effort is exerted to a common end; this basic harmony must be both intra-departmental and interdepartmental. Vertically, units lower in the hierarchy must coordinate with those higher up (even though in a different department). Only if this be done successfully can excessive confusion, contradiction, and frustration be avoided and something like a single American foreign policy be forged.

The Forms of Coordination. In the attempt to devise a sufficiently high working level of coordination, four sorts of devices have been developed and are used individually or in conjunction.

(1) The first, dealing mainly with vertical coordination, involves the President himself and the White House Office. The prestige and position of the chief executive make it possible for him to demand—and usually to receive a considerable amount of—effective harmony in making and executing policy. Much of the apparatus surrounding the Executive Office is for the purpose of helping the President reach sound high-policy decisions and to ensure their effective implementation. The National Security Council is the archtype of this kind of coordinating body; the Bureau of the Budget, in a different way, performs the same task.[19]

(2) A second coordinating device consists of assigning coordinating authority over a particular policy area to a single department. Such agency is directed to provide general guidance to all other interested agencies and to see to it that their various efforts mesh into a coherent whole. This method has the virtues of simplicity and centralization of responsibility, but such is the bureaucratic ethic that it has been productive of a good deal of interagency dispute. The Department of State has been most frequently given this sort of directive; we have seen that part of the Eisenhower reorganization plan involved giving State a policy coordinating authority over a number of new operating agencies. The Treasury has something of a similar role with regard to a number of multi-agency financial programs.

(3) Most commonly, coordination is attempted by means of the interdepartmental (or interagency) committee. On these bodies—of which there are dozens—all "interested" units are represented and are suppose to achieve a happy harmony, both in reaching decisions and in

---

19 Hobbs, *Behind the President*, *op. cit.*, Chapter 2, "Bureau of the Budget."

seeing to their execution. Although hallowed by much use, and despite the very considerable success that some of them have enjoyed, the interagency committee remains a technique of only limited utility. Their numbers have multiplied to the point where membership on any of them is apt to be conferred on such low-ranking members of the department that none may authoritatively speak for their own agencies; so widespread has representation become that it has become quite difficult to come to any consensus on most of the committees. If the appropriate committee cannot do its job of providing coordination, this leaves the department that has the inside track on the policy area in question to enjoy virtually a clear field.

(4) Finally, a "super-coordinator" was created in 1955 when the Operations Coordinating Board came into existence by executive order. This body consists of the Undersecretary of State as chairman, the Deputy Secretary of Defense, the Director of CIA, the Director of the United States Information Agency, a representative of the President, and a representative of any other agency the President selects. The Special Assistant to the President for National Security Affairs and the Director of the International Cooperation Administration also attend.

This high-level body is supposed, as one wag put it, to "coordinate the coordinators." Its coordinating function is obviously top-level, and is designed to oversee the implementation of the National Security Council's operational plans, primarily those involving interagency planning and action. Its history is too short to furnish the basis for any general estimate of its effectiveness.

It appears from this analysis that coordination in foreign policy, despite the obvious need, has not yet been achieved. This judgment may be confirmed by any reasonably sophisticated newspaper reader; the evidence is unmistakable that there are dozens of foreign policies in the executive branch rather than a single American policy. Yet the problem is being attacked; this same sophisticated reader cannot fail also to be impressed by the extent to which a unity of purpose and effort actually permeates much of what the United States does. That it is not done better is no reason to discount how well it is being done.

CONGRESS AND FOREIGN POLICY

Although it has become commonplace to point out that the part played by Congress in foreign policy has increased, both relatively and absolutely, during the decade since the end of World War II, we must nevertheless admit that even this augmented role remains secondary to that of the executive. From the very beginning of the Republic, Congress has chafed at the logic that has made the presidency the chief inspiration for foreign policy; the history of legislative-executive relations over international issues is one of recurrent dispute. In recent years the legislative branch has made some progress in defining its own place in the foreign-policy process; today Congress has a role that is of major importance.[20]

But this is not to say that the national legislature has achieved equality in policy-making, or that it is desirable that it should. As we suggested in our discussion of the executive's function in foreign affairs, law and logic agree that the initiative and the lion's share of the decisions naturally reside "at the other end of the [Pennsylvania] avenue." This would lead us to suppose that Congress's role in the process is essentially a reacting one; we would expect its function to be that of modifying, amplifying, and expediting decisions already taken by the President or his assistants. Recognizing the operation of checks and balances in the American system, we would further assume that Congress would be peculiarly prone to exercise some form of negative control on executive decisions, either by refusing to accept them or by changing their substance, direction, or timing. These indeed seem to represent the nature and extent of Congressional power over foreign policy.[21]

We should make one further qualification before briefly examining the ways in which Congress affects the course of policy-making. Although Congressional *power* itself has definite and measurable limits, the same cannot be said for Congressional *influence*. Being generally more sensitive to the tides of electoral politics than is the President (this is especially true of the House, whose members must face the voters every two years), Congress is prone to reflect shifts of public opinion that its members detect (or think they detect). This gives Congressional opinion great weight in the executive branch whenever the responsible bureaucrats believe that the legislators are convinced that they are expressing a popular consensus. This matter of Congressional influence, so difficult to measure, often goes farther to explain the legislative impact on foreign policy than does any detailed consideration of the legal powers of Congress.

Congressional functions

How does Congress enter overtly into the policy-making process? While admitting at the outset that there is very little that Congress does

---

[20] The leading study is Robert Dahl, *Congress and Foreign Policy* (New York: Harcourt, Brace and Co., 1950).

[21] See especially Daniel Cheever and H. Field Haviland, *American Foreign Policy and the Separation of Powers* (Cambridge, Mass.: Harvard University Press, 1952).

50

that is completely without relevance to American foreign policy, we may nevertheless distinguish a short list of definite functions.

The Senate: Treaties and Appointments. Of the two houses, the Senate enjoys superior power and prestige in foreign affairs. Part of this primacy arises from the popular notion of the Senate as the "upper house"; part from the greater age, average length of service, and freedom of discussion that characterize Senators. But the bulk of Senatorial leadership comes from two specific constitutional provisions: the power to approve treaties and the power to confirm executive appointments.

The Constitution gives the President the power to make treaties with the "advice and consent" of two-thirds of the Senate. As students well know, the "advice" part of this provision is a dead letter except as the President chooses to consult with individual Senators during the negotiation phase of a treaty. "Consent" involves a two-thirds vote of the Senate in favor of a treaty, the effect of which is to open the document to ratification of the President.

The Senate thus enjoys, as one author puts it, a "treaty veto";[22] it may simply refuse to approve the treaty. Such action voids the entire enterprise. The Senate, however, may not change the treaty in any way. It may suggest amendments which, if made, would make the document acceptable; what happens to these proposed amendments, however, depends on the President. He may choose to renegotiate the treaty and seek to have the amendments written into the agreement; on the other hand, he may find them unacceptable and simply drop the whole affair. The treaty veto has been a favorite subject for discussion by critics of the American constitutional system ever since the defeat of the Treaty of Versailles in 1919;[23] the historical record indicates, however, that only a small minority of all treaties have been defeated. Nor should we overlook the fact that executive agreements are free from any necessary Congressional control, although much Congressional opinion feels that a legislative veto should be placed on these agreements as well.

Appointments of ambassadors, ministers, and consuls—the entire foreign service—must receive Senatorial approval. Occasionally, as in the struggle over the confirmation of Mr. Charles Bohlen as Ambassador to the Soviet Union in 1953, this power has great significance for foreign

---

[22] D. F. Fleming, *The Treaty Veto of the American Senate* (New York: Putnam, 1930).

[23] For a textbook summary of the arguments against Senate approval of treaties, see Robert K. Carr, Donald H. Morrison, Marver H. Bernstein, and Richard C. Snyder, *American Democracy in Theory and Practice* (New York: Rinehart, 1951), pp. 997-999.

policy. It has been generally felt in the Senate, however, that the President should have a free hand in selecting his foreign-policy personnel and it is seldom that Senatorial confirmation of a diplomatic appointment becomes a really important issue.

Legislation. It is in the general function of legislation that the whole Congress comes squarely to grips with foreign policy. There are only a few areas of foreign policy in which the President can move freely without the necessity of any legislation; usually some implementing law must be passed before policies can be effectively carried out. This means that most major programs must be submitted to Congress in the form of bills. Here is where the legislature may exercise its amending or negating authority, and it is rare for an executive suggestion to pass through the Congressional mill without being reshaped in some way.

So important is the potential impact of Congress on any project that the executive tends to consult with Congressional leaders in advance so as to tailor his requests to what Congress will accept; sometimes—as in the case of the Marshall plan—Congress will run away and develop its own program anyway.[24] To the extent that policy declarations come to be formalized into specific programs of action—and this is a great extent indeed today—Congress has great power to alter the executive designs; at the very least, such a constant possibility requires that the President and his advisers always take Congressional opinion into account.

The legislative history of the so-called "Eisenhower doctrine"—the administration's Middle East proposals of early 1957—illustrates this relationship. Before submitting the proposals in his special message of January 5, the President consulted with leaders of both houses; the Congressmen, on their part, were irritated that details had been leaked to the press before they had been informed. Once in the legislative mill, amendments were offered in profusion, and the administration was hard put to keep the proposals in anything like their original form. Their final passage revealed that, although the general framework had remained intact, a number of changes had been made, the effect of which was to place Congressional controls over executive action. A typical example of the way Congress functions in this regard was the requirement that the President should inform Congress of his intention to obligate any of the funds involved in the act at least 15 days before such expenditures were to become effective.[25]

---

[24] John C. Campbell, *The United States in World Affairs, 1947-48* (New York: Harper & Bros., 1948), p. 503.

[25] *New York Times* (March 6, 1957).

Appropriations. What is true of legislation applies even more sharply to one special manifestation of legislative power: the appropriation of funds. American foreign policy demands money in great amounts, and no funds at all are forthcoming from the United States Treasury except as a result of Congressional appropriation. Congress tends to be more generous in authorizing appropriations than in actually making them; the appropriations committees of Congress (particularly in the House) are more wary of granting funds than are the substantive committees. This means that often the executive must fight the same battle four times, once before each foreign-affairs committee and again before each appropriations committee; sometimes, indeed, he must return and fight it before each house, for a total of six. This gives Congress several chances at the executive program, each usually resulting in a slight scaling down or other modification.

Investigations. We must also recognize the importance of investigations by Congressional committees to foreign policy. This is a case of influence rather than power; the net effect of such committee investigations as those of the late Senator McCarthy or of Senator Symington (on the state of American air power in 1956) is to create powerful currents of public opinion for or against particular policy emphases. On occasion these have had great impact on the executive branch by affecting mass opinion and forcing department heads to conform to the wishes of the particular committee. Obviously the extent to which an investigation succeeds in this regard depends on public reaction; such popular concern—although sometimes unfortunate—occasionally results in an improved policy. What direction is taken usually depends on the orientation of the committee's efforts.

Resolutions. Also in the category of functions of influence is the device of the Congressional resolution, either by one house or—more effectively—by both. A resolution, expressing the "sense of the house(s)" but without legal effect, serves notice to all concerned that the Congressional mind has been made up on the particular point. Such resolutions are most effective (1) when they represent accurately the state of public opinion on the questions and (2) when they are passed prior to the making of a firm commitment by the executive. Examples of important resolutions include the so-called "Vandenburg" resolution in 1949 that was in effect an advance acceptance of the North Atlantic Treaty and the several resolutions of the House between 1953 and 1956 opposing Communist China's admission to the United Nations. Such resolutions, of course, do not have the force of law.

53

Congressional characteristics on foreign policy

Recognizing that generalizations about 531 legislators are hazardous we may nevertheless suggest a few common characteristics revealed by Congress as it copes with the issues of foreign policy. Perhaps the safest and broadest statement we can make is that the legislative branch is quite well equipped to perform its checking and amending function and does so with reasonable success; when it turns from this, however, and attempts to make positive policy on its own, the outcomes are usually ineffectual or —in some cases—unfortunate.

Negativism. One reason for this limitation on the effectiveness of Congress is that body's fundamentally negative orientation to foreign policy. Because of the nature of the problem and its place in the scheme of government, Congress is best fitted for saying "no." It usually cannot efficiently take the initiative; its function is commonly confined to reacting to proposals emanating from the executive offices. It exercises its authority by denying power to the executive or by placing conditions on such power as it grants. Only in special and infrequent cases is it possible for Congress to play a positive role. There is a great deal of evidence that many Congressmen and Senators find this a stultifying and frustrating position, but there does not seem to be a great deal that they can do to modify it. The frequent pleas for Congress "to seize the initiative" in foreign policy have uniformly failed to mark out any clear procedure whereby the legislature could make its will effective in opposition to the President.

Conflict with the Executive. A second characteristic grows out of the first. Under the checks and balances system of American government, competition and conflict between legislature and executive is to be expected; this is the reason why Congress is made to share in so many executive powers. On purely domestic policy, Congress may and often does take the initiative, and the resulting relationship with the executive is more nearly an equal one. But on foreign policy, certain advantages inhere in the President, and Congress's exercise of its checking role gives rise to much controversy. Many Congressional moves in foreign policy defy rational explanation on any other ground than its simple determination to differ with the executive and to make disagreement effective. An interesting example occurred in 1956, when Congress insisted upon appropriating a billion dollars more for the Air Force than President Eisenhower and Secretary of Defense Wilson contended was necessary.

Political Orientation. We have already alluded to the all-too-obvious

54

fact that Congress in general, and the House of Representatives in particular, tends to be more responsive than the President to short-range voter (or interest-group) pressure. What this means in foreign policy is clear to any newspaper reader. Repeatedly the executive has recommended programs that, although open to question on their merits, at least were devised in all seriousness as an attempt to advance the prevailing idea of national interest. When the Congress seized upon them and attacked the problem of their implementation, far too often for comfort the dominant concern of many members was not whether the programs would be advantageous to the nation. Rather their preoccupation was with the effect of such policy implementation on their individual political fortunes. Foreign-aid and military appropriations have been especially obvious footballs in this respect; an articulate and powerful bloc in Congress has consistently felt that voters in the grip of a cold war would never object to large military expenditures but that they would resent "giveaways" of which foreigners were the beneficiaries.

But although a major indictment can be made of Congress on the grounds of a short-sighted truckling to vociferous and self-serving elements of public opinion, it would not do for us blithely to dismiss the political approach of Congress as being entirely without justification. We must not forget that there is always an "ivory-tower" tendency in any government bureaucracy, and particularly in a foreign-affairs bureaucracy; it is all too easy to dismiss mass opinion as beneath serious consideration. To the extent that the top echelon of decision-makers becomes divorced from the tides of popular attitudes, it is thoroughly salutary for Congress continually to remind them that there is an American public and that its wishes must be taken into account. Of course, the value of this function depends on whether Congress is accurately reading the mass temper and is not mistaking well-organized minority pressures or the political preoccupations of its members for the broad-gauge voice of the people.

Deliberateness and Lack of Information. Two final characteristics of Congressional activity in foreign policy remain to be noted. Congress tends to operate slowly, and it almost always acts upon incomplete and inaccurate information. The first stems from its function as a deliberative body; it would be violative of the Congressional responsibility in American democracy for it to be expected to reach its decisions with great speed and in total silence. Yet, even after granting this, we may still contend that much of Congress's slowness is unnecessary; it seems evident that it could work more rapidly without sacrificing anything essential to the legislative process.

The poverty of Congressional information is a much more serious problem. In the past ten or fifteen years, Congress has made great efforts, and with some success, to improve the amount and the reliability of the information on which it must base its decisions. Yet the question is still unsolved, and may even prove insoluble. How can Congress play its part in shaping American policy if it simply does not have available enough data to make the right kind of decisions? The information that is necessary is often by definition a secret; to open the executive files to Congressional investigation would make extremely delicate matters subject to heated, partisan, and very public debate. Alongside this we must place the lack of mutual trust and confidence between Congress and the executive department.

If Congress must depend on the executive for all its information, there is a real danger that the data fed it will be—in the delicate bureaucratic word—"selective": that is, deliberately chosen and slanted so as to influence Congress in the direction the bureaucracy desires. The most the legislative branch has been able to do up to this point is to staff its specialized committees on foreign affairs and related subjects with experts of its own, and to try to develop such liaison with the executive as is possible and effective.

Legislative-executive cooperation

There is little purpose in our reiterating the need for legislative-executive cooperation in foreign affairs. Everyone realizes that the United States cannot afford to have its President and its Congress always at swords points over foreign policy. There is likewise no advantage in wishing more or less plaintively (as many scholars have done)[26] that the United States had a parliamentary system such as that of Great Britain, in which the problem would simply never come up. The United States has separation of powers and checks and balances, and there is no possibility of their abandonment in the foreseeable future. Within their context Americans must devise a workable mechanism of foreign policy.[27]

Consultation. The most frequently relied-upon device for achieving some such sustainable level of agreement is that of formal or informal consultation. The President frequently calls meetings of Congressional

---

[26] See, for example, the argument advanced in James MacGregor Burns, *Congress on trial* (New York: Harper & Bros., 1949).

[27] This problem, and some recommended solutions, are dealt with in Cheever and Haviland, *American Foreign Policy and the Separation of Powers.*

leaders (not necessarily limited to foreign-policy experts) and briefs them, sometimes submitting to questioning. Less often, similar sessions are held by department heads. Informally, legislative-executive contacts are extensive and frequently quite productive; an outstanding recent example was the daily meeting between Senator George of Georgia, then chairman of the Foreign Relations Committee of the Senate, and Secretary Dulles during the summer and autumn of 1955. There is no doubt that consultation has been at least a qualified success in reducing the chasm between Congress and the executive; how effective it is in any particular case depends on both the political climate and the personalities involved.

Liaison. Recently executive departments have begun to add to their staffs specialists on Congressional liaison. The State Department has an Assistant Secretary for Congressional Relations whose mission is, as one department official put it privately, "to keep Congress happy." President Eisenhower added a liaison specialist (General Wilton B. Persons) to his personal staff; other agencies have done the same. In this way the executive, needing the support of Congress, has sought to establish a favorable relationship. We may perhaps regret that no reciprocal effort may be remarked on the part of Congress.

Commissions. Less widespread than the first two, and by nature perhaps destined to remain so, are the mixed legislative-executive investigating commissions. Part of their membership is appointed by the President, the remainder consists of members of Congress; the Congressional representation is usually drawn from both parties in both houses. Such a body, once it deals with an issue and makes a recommendation, represents a fusion of opinion that cannot help but be reflected in some way in subsequent policy. Outstanding examples of recent years are the two Hoover Commissions on administrative reorganization and the Randall Commission on foreign economic policy.[28]

The Permanence of the Need. But none of these devices has solved the problem; legislative-executive relationships on foreign affairs are always uncertain and, as we know, often hostile. It is probable that the issue can never be thoroughly resolved as long as the United States retains its peculiar political system. No one would deny, however, that the importance of maintaining enough cooperation to ensure the adoption and implementation of adequate policies is great enough to justify continuing effort, however much we may despair of final perfection.

---

[28] The Randall Commission's report: Commission on Foreign Economic Policy, *Report to the President and Congress, January 23, 1954* (Washington, D. C.: U. S. Government Printing Office, 1954).

3 : Policy formulation:
forces that shape decisions

As we suggested in the opening paragraphs of the preceding chapter, although the general arrangements for policy in the American government are roughly similar to those of most modern states, there is one significant difference between the United States and many other states. The United States is a democracy. Whatever that much-abused word might mean in differing value systems, it seems pretty well agreed that an essential element in any democratic government is the establishment and use of mechanisms for the formal registration and implementation of popular attitudes. Government in a democracy is a device by means of which public opinion is translated into public policy. This proposition holds as true in foreign affairs as in any other area of government action.

And so we come to the central concern of this chapter. A democratic government like that of the United States is ideologically committed to follow, as nearly as it can, the dictates of its constituents. This means that the policy-makers cannot confine their attention to the national interest as they perceive it themselves, but must always heed whatever they feel the voice of the people is saying. Popular influence on the decision-makers, present to some extent even in the most dictatorial of governments, is different in a democracy primarily in that it is thought to be normal, is constantly taken into account, and is accepted as controlling most of the time.

If we admit that responsible policy-makers have the duty and the necessity of shaping policy in response to mass wishes, a dilemma inherent in the democratic idea immediately arises. Does the public have an equivalent obligation? Can (or should) the people exercise their right of ultimate policy determination in happy irresponsibility, or should they confine their function to those areas in which they can operate effectively? Who speaks for the public? Does "the people," considered as a single factor, verbalize something called "the national interest" as well as, better than, or not as well as the official experts who are both better trained and closer to the scene of action?

This list of questions could be prolonged indefinitely, although to little purpose. All we are saying here is that the troublesome theoretical and practical issues of democracy are no more easily resolved when the significant problems are those of foreign policy. The interlocking roles of officialdom and the mass public remain difficult either to disentangle or to rationalize. We shall look at this dilemma again at the end of the chapter.

THE DECISION-INFLUENCERS

Those government officials, executive and legislative, that actually make the decisions in foreign policy have the influence of the public brought to bear on themselves from a variety of sources. These "decision-influencers" speak variously for the entire people or for significant sub-sections of the body politic, and each exerts its effect in a different way.

Public opinion

We should begin with a brief and general consideration of that amorphous and slippery shibboleth, public opinion. Students of democracy have long realized that although the concept of "public opinion" is in some way relevant to democratic thought, attempts either to define it precisely or to locate it empirically have largely come to grief. This is not to say that the idea, because it is not susceptible to free quantitative manipulation, is useless; our principal concern is to make as clear as possible just what we mean by the term.

What Is Public Opinion? There follows one attempt to give content to this mystic and elusive phrase. We ought initially to clear the ground somewhat by stipulating what public opinion is *not*: it is in no sense a single, mass entity always the same and always operating in the same way. Whatever public opinion is, it is not a commodity that can be packaged, divided up, computed in an equation, or seen. It is both more and less than that.

59

In the first place, "public opinion" is merely a shorthand way of expressing something basic in democratic ideology, at least in the United States: total opinion is the sum of individual opinions. There are, as we shall see in a moment, several "publics," and each has its own peculiar type of "opinion." But the fundamental ingredient in all of them is the individual member of the social group who—under whatever influences—makes up his own mind.

"Opinion" in this sense has two components. In the first place, it sums up all the *attitudes* that individuals have toward such questions as make an impression on their consciousness. On each such issue the individual has an attitude that may be the result of a sophisticated rational process or the crudest type of emotional response, that may be the outcome of a lonely private struggle or merely a pumped-in predigested stand originating in an organized group. In any case, the individual reaches his conclusion by his own devices, subject only to the overriding influence of the second component, the prevailing mood.[1] Out of these individual attitudes certain common patterns emerge, to be ascertained impressionistically by observers, journalists, or Congressmen, or to be measured statistically by survey and poll techniques.

The Several Publics. Students of public opinion agree that there are several "publics" that share in what is called public opinion. Gabriel Almond distinguishes three such within the American society:

> One may speak of a "general public" if one keeps in mind that while it is characterized by a sense of identification and reacts to general stimuli, it also contains a variety of interests and groupings which are affected differentially by both general and specific stimuli. Second, there is an "attentive public" which is informed and interested in foreign policy problems, and which constitutes the audience for foreign policy discussions among the elites. Third, one may speak of the policy and opinion elites, the articulate policy-bearing stratum of the population which gives structure to the public, and which provides the effective means of access to the various groupings.[2]

Professor Almond feels that the "elite public" is the only portion of the whole that has policy relevance, since the competition among its various sub-sections (political, administrative, interest, and communications elites) is what really determines "public" opinion. "The 'masses,' " he contends,

---

[1] Gabriel Almond, in *The American People and Foreign Policy* (New York: Harcourt, Brace and Co., 1950), analyzes the American mood in terms of movement along several axes: withdrawal-intervention, optimism-pessimism, tolerance-intolerance, idealism-cynicism, and superiority-inferiority (pp. 53 ff.)

[2] Almond, *American People and Foreign Policy*, p. 138. Reprinted by permission.

"participate in policy-making in indirect and primarily passive ways."[3] The attentive public listens to the discussions among the elites and, presumably, plays the most important role in making up the mass mind by telling it what to think.

Whether or not one accepts the whole of Professor Almond's rigorous analysis, it is difficult to question either its thoroughness or its fruitfulness. His catalogue of the various elites is roughly adapted for use in this chapter; succeeding sections will deal with the impact of interest groups, political parties, mass media, and nonpolitical ("prestige") leadership on American foreign policy. His major proposition remains beyond doubt; there are indeed several different publics, each with its peculiar characteristics, of which policy-makers must take account.

The Problem of Measurement. After one isolates the various components of the public, the next problem is the determination of just what each of them has by way of attitudes toward actual policy questions. The various elites, being fairly homogeneous and unified, usually take clear positions; the crucial group, however, is the mass. If policy-makers are bound by mass opinion (even at the restricted level admitted by Professor Almond), it is important to know what that opinion is. By the application of various sampling and statistical techniques, cross-sections of mass attitudes on many questions may be roughly synthesized. Here is the province of the public-opinion poll and the survey. However imperfect these may be—and attacks on them are legion—they draw the clearest picture policy-makers have yet been able to discover.[4] Other indices—letters to Congress and to bureaucrats, electoral results, and so on—are even more unreliable for measuring opinion on a particular issue.

Who Speaks for the Public? All of this discussion returns to one major point. "The public" has no voice of its own; someone must speak for it. The policy-maker who, either because of ideological conviction or from sheer prudence, wishes to guide his conduct generally by the commands of the public must decide for himself whose voice is authentically that of the mass.

There are many who wish to speak for the public and who claim to do so; we shall see in a moment how at least some of them function. But there is almost always some confusion of voices; the mass rarely speaks unanimously through one spokesman. The policy-maker therefore knows in advance that whatever decision he makes will please some of those who

---

[3] Almond, *American People and Foreign Policy*, p. 139. Reprinted by permission.
[4] Assistant Secretary Francis H. Russell, "The Function of Public-opinion Analysis in the Formulation of Foreign Policy," *Department of State Bulletin* (March 6, 1949).

clamor for his ear, and that it will displease others. The best he can hope for is that his decisions will not violate the implicit consensus that under-lies all the Tower of Babel we call public opinion. On details the suc-cessful (or lucky) official may fly in the face of mass opinion; on funda-mentals, however, and over any significant period of time, he must stay within the bounds the mass public lays down.

The Functions of the Public. We may, at this early stage of our general discussion, suggest three functions of the "public" with respect to foreign policy: (1) the determination of the outermost limits of permissible gov-ernment action (Professor Almond's point); (2) the delineation of a general direction in which policy should move and the isolation of certain landmark objectives and techniques; (3) the debate and decision of crucial issues so important in themselves that the governmental elite dare not proceed until public sentiment has come to rest. We shall be return-ing to these points in the latter portion of this chapter.

Interest groups

Many sophisticated students of American government claim that the dominant political characteristic of the American people is their divi-sion into interest groups.[5] According to this line of analysis, the indi-vidual today lacks political significance. He gains importance only to the extent to which he allies himself with an organized group that represents his particular interests. The group, large enough to be important and led by skilled manipulators of pressure, can fight actively for the public policy desired by its members and obtain a much greater degree of success than all its members, acting individually, could accomplish by themselves. In this way the role of government is primarily that of referee among the competing groups; out of the warring factions of private and group interest will come some working approximation of the national interest.

This doctrine, as we can easily see, does violence to the democratic myth of individualism. Yet one need not be a confirmed "interest-grouper" to admit that these particular organizations have tremendous significance in the determination of public policy (including—perhaps especially—foreign policy) and that they form one of the major influence elements in policy decisions.

---

[5] A leading exposition of this point of view is David Truman, *The Governmental Process* (New York: Alfred A. Knopf, 1951).

The Organization of Interest. An interest group scarcely needs elaborate definition. It is a group of individuals organized on the basis of a single common interest or set of interests; for our purposes, we might add that this interest is something that all the members want the government to do (or refrain from doing). The purpose of the group is to use any combination of a long list of techniques—all subsumed under the rubric of "pressure"—to persuade the appropriate government officials, legislative or bureaucratic, to decide in its favor. Almost every conceivable interest in American life has been organized today; on major policy issues, both domestic and foreign, there are groups that represent almost every possible opinion.

Individuals join these groups in response to their own interests. Since very few well-adjusted persons have only one interest in their lives, it is normal for any individual to belong to, or at least to accept the program of, several different groups. In this way unperceived contradictions often develop. A college professor, for example, may maintain membership simultaneously in the American Association of University Professors and in the American Legion. The AAUP opposes loyalty oaths for college faculties; the Legion favors them. On which side does the professor stand?

The leaders of each group (who collectively form the "interest elite" Professor Almond discusses) each claim to speak for their total membership—including our hypothetical professor. Obviously at least one of the spokesmen is mistaken. And yet the policy-making official is unable to know definitely to what extent the interest elite is taking unwarranted liberties with its constituency. Frequently he must accept their claims at face value for want of reliable evidence to the contrary.

The Mechanics of Pressure. Interest groups apply pressure of two kinds on government officials, usually termed "direct" and "indirect." Direct pressure is applied by the group leadership upon the officials personally. Techniques are varied: persuasion, threats of political reprisal (more effective on elected office-holders), technical information (even on foreign policy private groups may be better informed on special issues than are the responsible officials), promises of voting support for the official's party, and so on. The object of direct pressure is to impress the group's wishes forcibly on the decision-making official(s).

Direct pressure has certain limitations. In the first place, it is largely dependent on the ability of the group's leadership to gain access to the decision-makers. It does no good to exhaust one's armory of persuasive techniques on officials who do not have the power to grant the group's wishes. More importantly, even if a group can penetrate directly to the key officials, this advantage is largely vitiated unless it can command a near-monopoly of the bureaucratic ear. This happy situation seldom arises. Even when applying pressure to the appropriate official, the group must realize that other groups, arguing the opposite point of view, can probably do the same thing.

Indirect pressure concentrates on the creation of an active mass opinion that will in turn exert pressure on officials to take the desired steps. This usually involves disseminating propaganda aimed at the least common denominator of the public and stressing a simple action formula. The interest group's victory comes nearest to completion when it is able to stir up the public to the point where policy-makers face an opinion *fait accompli* to which they have no choice but to bow. Quantitatively, it is probable that the significant majority of interest group effort is expended in this kind of indirect pressure.

But again we must note the competition among the groups for the public ear. When major policy questions are at issue, the "average citizen" is bombarded with appeals from every point of the compass. The battle of the propagandists is never-ceasing. From among the various "messages" the individual chooses and takes his place on one side or the other of the question. One unexpected outcome of this group conflict is anathema to propagandists but increasingly evident to observers: there seems to be a growing tendency among members of the mass, when confronted with such a barrage of appeals for action, to express their confusion by a simple withdrawal and a refusal to take any stand at all. To a thoughtful person this appears to be a perfect parody of democratic procedure.

Categories of Interest Groups. To call the roll of the interest groups that bear on foreign policy would require a list many pages long. Gabriel Almond provides a convenient scheme of categories.[6] We should remember only that within each classification are many separate subgroups, each considerably different from all the others in its pattern of desires. Almond identifies seven groups: (1) labor groups (AFL-CIO); (2) business organizations (United States Chamber of Commerce, National Association of Manufacturers); (3) agricultural groups (American Farm Bureau Federation, National Grange); (4) veterans' groups (American Legion, Veterans of Foreign Wars, AMVETS); (5) women's groups (League of Women Voters, National Federation of Business and Professional Women's Clubs); (6) religious organizations (Federal Council of Churches of Christ); (7) ethnic groups (Jews, Germans, Italians, Poles).

---

[6] Almond, *American People and Foreign Policy*, Chapter VIII. Reprinted by permission.

Political parties

Another source of influence on American decision-makers is the institution of the political party. American parties operate in a fashion almost diametrically opposed to pressure groups. Where the interest group is tightly identified with a specific program, the party by definition is decentralized and pluralistic. Where the interest group is largely concerned with policy, the party's focus is on government personnel. Where the interest group seeks to sharpen issues, the party attempts to blur them.

The Parties and Foreign Policy. In the American two-party system, each party approaches foreign policy somewhat ambivalently. Foreign policy is a perfectly valid election issue and party politicians see no fundamental difference between foreign issues and domestic ones; each type is important to them only to the extent to which it wins or loses votes. Consequently, we find professional politicians manipulating foreign-policy questions as expertly as those of domestic policy; party divisions on international issues run as deep as they do on any others.

Yet, in the past decade or more, the increasing significance of foreign policy to the United States has penetrated even into the high councils of the specialists in winning elections. There seems to be a feeling that decisions about NATO may, in the last analysis, be more important than those concerning agricultural support prices or public power in Tennessee or Idaho. There has, in other words, begun to evolve something like an interparty consensus on foreign policy that has tempered the party battle to some extent. Disagreement between the parties now tends rather to center on the preferred methods of implementing policies rather than on basic approaches to them. So far has this progressed that many serious-minded and independent citizens are concerned because there is often no "respectable" way to dissent from current American policy since the parties have reached such a high level of agreement.[7]

The President and His Party. This raises an interesting issue. The President is responsible for his administration's foreign policy; he is also his party's leader. His party must stand on the President's record. If the opposition is to defend its own position, it must attack the President; such is the logic of American politics. But, if the interparty consensus has been operative during the previous two or four years, for the opposition to challenge the President's foreign policy would require it to

---

[7] H. Bradford Westerfield, *Foreign Policy and Party Politics* (New Haven: Yale University Press, 1955), analyzes this trend in terms of Congressional votes on foreign policy issues between 1943 and 1950.

question a program with which it largely agrees. Here the dual role of the President—as national leader and as party chief—serves to confuse the operation of the American political system.[8]

President Truman's foreign policy was supported by the votes of all but an extreme wing of Republicans between 1947 and 1952; in the 1952 campaign the Republicans solved their dilemma by adopting—as ostensible party policy—the arguments of the "radical right" wing, but by selecting General Eisenhower as their candidate. Eisenhower not only approved of the Truman foreign policy; he was personally identified with it. In this way a broad voter appeal was created without committing the party to abandon a foreign policy it wished to retain. In the 1956 campaign the Democrats were caught in something of the same vise; their approach consisted mainly in supporting the general line but quarreling over details, except for a last-minute disagreement over Middle East policy.

More difficult is the problem of maintaining presidential leadership in foreign policy over all elements of a party. This is particularly applicable to Congress, and especially to Senators. The decentralized structure of American parties makes it impossible for a President to keep his fellow party members completely under control; belligerent independence of executive leadership is often good politics for a Senator. Senator Knowland of California, the Republican Senate leader under President Eisenhower, persistently broke with his chief and never suffered politically. Often the President must act like the leader of an interest group and use indirect pressure on his party, stirring up public opinion to demand action from the recalcitrant legislators.

Party Splits on Foreign Policy. Since 1945 it has become apparent that both major parties are split into two or more groups on major questions of foreign policy. American parties are not "responsible"; they owe no official allegiance to any central leadership, although the national con-

---

[8] This problem concerned the Democratic leadership in the Senate during the debate on the "Eisenhower doctrine" for the Middle East during early 1957. Although Democratic attacks on the President were the most direct and outspoken of any during the entire Eisenhower period up to that time, the party found itself in a dilemma when faced with the necessity of supporting or opposing a specific measure; to disagree with the details of the President's proposal was politically sound, but to vote against the resolution was dangerous. Senator John Kennedy of Massachusetts, speaking for a group of "moderates," rationalized his position in a statement stressing his disagreement with the policy but calling for support of the proposal as "better than nothing." Democratic votes in opposition came from the extreme wings of the Southern conservatives and the ultra-liberals. On the other hand, the Republicans had no problem; only three Senate Republicans voted "no," all from the extreme right wing. For the Kennedy statement, see the *New York Times* (March 2, 1957); for the roll call vote in the Senate, see *Congressional Record* (March 5, 1957), p. 2776.

ventions purport to exercise such authority through their party platforms. Much more revealing of party attitudes toward foreign affairs than any platform is the behavior of the party delegations in both houses of Congress, and here is where the sharp cleavages reveal themselves.

Both parties suffer from what may be called—somewhat inaccurately—an isolationist-internationalist division. There are not really two clear camps in each party, but rather a continuum covering the entire spectrum of foreign policy. But on crucial foreign-affairs votes in Congress, something like definite points of concentration appear on either side of the boundary between these two popular terms.[9]

The Republican split is best known, taking roughly the form of a separation between the Middle West on the one hand and both coasts on the other. Under the leadership of President Eisenhower, the importance of the Midwest group declined both relatively and absolutely, but was never completely eliminated. The Democratic cleavage was less obvious for a time, but came into the open during the first years of the Eisenhower administration. Fundamentally it represents a split along North-South lines, with the South developing something that observers tended to identify with prewar Middle West isolationism.[10]

The upshot of the parallel divisions in both parties—at least in Congress—has been the development of informal foreign-policy coalitions that transcend party lines. Southern Democrats ally themselves with Republicans from the Middle West; northern and western Democrats make common cause on foreign policy with Republicans from the same regions. Like most generalizations about party politics, this conclusion cannot be elevated to the status of a hard and fast rule (the same is true of the "conservative coalition" on domestic policy, whose membership is often roughly the same as that of the isolationist bloc). It is sufficiently applicable, however, to qualify sharply any serious attempt to delineate party positions or party programs on foreign-policy matters. The illusory specificity of party platforms should not be permitted to obscure the fact of the actual lack of "party" foreign policies.

Bipartisanship. Were the parties to develop clear lines of distinction on foreign policy, it might be possible to conduct America's international relations on a "partisan" basis: that is, one party would be responsible for

---

[9] Westerfield, *Foreign Policy and Party Politics*, pp. 51-52.

[10] An editorial, "Ike Doctrine Vote Slaps Isolationists," in the *Atlanta Constitution* (March 7, 1957) said: "Approval by the Senate of the Eisenhower Doctrine ... is a convincing slap at what looked like a budding isolationist revolt in that body." Although the editorial mentioned no names, its target was obviously those Southerners who followed Georgia's Senator Russell in his attempt a few days previously to strip all aid provisions from the measure. Reprinted by permission.

all policy and the other would constantly criticize it, always ready to take charge if public support were withdrawn from the incumbents. This is more or less the way British government functions. To do this, however, would require a degree of party unity on foreign policy that does not seem possible under the American federal system, where national parties are loose confederations of "sovereign" state organizations. If pure partisanship is out of the question as a guiding principle, some form of "bipartisanship" becomes necessary.

In a strict sense, bipartisanship is as difficult as pure partisanship, for it really means that the parties in effect remove foreign policy from the area of controversy and that their positions on specific questions are substantially identical. To be effective, this would require that party leadership control the rank and file and that there be distinct party positions that could be harmonized. As we have seen above, this is most unlikely; there is no workable way at present for both parties to share equally in the responsibility for foreign policy.

H. Bradford Westerfield has coined the word "extrapartisanship" to describe what actually happens in the American government and what is probably the best compromise attainable under the present conditions of party politics. The President remains as the most important policy maker and clearly identifies the bulk of his party with his own policy. The support of the opposition is brought about by deliberately including some of its leadership in the policy process by invitation of the President, and then trusting these opposition leaders to swing enough of their party membership behind the joint policy to guarantee a workable consensus. Ordinarily it is most profitable to include the opposition's foreign-policy spokesmen in Congress in the group of consultants, provided only that they be of sufficient prestige to carry real weight. Of the many examples of extrapartisanship, Mr. Truman's close association with Republican Senator Vandenburg of Michigan during 1948-9 and Mr. Eisenhower's working arrangement with Democratic Senator George of Georgia during 1955 are outstanding.

But ever since at least 1940, there has been some kind of two-party support in Congress for the policy of whatever administration has been in power.[11] Straight party-line votes are always rare in Congress, but they are especially so on foreign policy. If a President keeps his policy in reasonably good tune with the prevailing currents of popular opinion, he can frequently count on constituent pressure (among other techniques) to

---

[11] Westerfield, *Foreign Policy and Party Politics*, Part 3, "The Record of the Parties in Foreign Affairs, 1939-1950."

bring the bulk of both houses of Congress over to his side. The development of extrapartisanship only makes this principle more workable.

Mass media

The media of mass communication—newspapers, radio, television, motion pictures, magazines, advertising, and—to a lesser extent—books, have become of tremendous importance in American culture as it has become more complex and dehumanized. Face-to-face contacts are of less significance in the transmission of ideas today than at any earlier time in the history of American culture. If mass media are indispensable and if foreign-policy ideas are the most important political concerns of our time, we would expect the media to play a large part in shaping foreign policy.

The Mass Media and Public Attitudes. A mass medium is a technique of communicating simultaneously (or nearly so) with a large number of people. In every case the audience is one that, by definition, transcends the limits of face-to-face contact. Mass media became possible by the advance of technology—printing, electronics, high-speed transportation, and so on; mass communication has become almost a necessity because of the increasing impersonalization of modern civilization.

Being aimed at people in the mass, the messages brought by mass media are usually phrased in terms that will have a broad appeal: simple, brief, and striking. They must place no insuperable burden on the absorptive capacity or the tolerance of their consumers. Their content must be tailored to the sensed needs and desires of the audience; such changes as they bring about in audience attitudes are gradual, usually enlarging rather than breaching the existing bounds of acceptance.

In some intellectual circles it is currently fashionable to argue that mass media are positively dangerous to American democracy because of their grip on the imaginations and the value systems of the mass public. Horrifying pictures are painted of the ease with which the "architects of consensus" can create public demands for particular programs, and dark prophesies are made of the fate of freedom if the tycoons of mass communication were ever to make full use of the power that is theirs. This picture is somewhat overdrawn, although to the casual observer it might seem as if Americans take all their standards from Hollywood, the television studios, and the picture magazines.

69

Mass media can, to a considerable extent, play successfully on the pre-existing prejudices of people; they have proved to be able to sell soap, sex, and sensationalism. But there is little persuasive evidence that they are able to change significantly the patterns of mass wants and needs; audiences simply leave them when they seek to work substantive alteration in fundamental systems of preferences. As long as the mass media are kept within these limits, we may regret that they do not elevate the public instead of pandering to it[12] but there seems little reason to fear overmuch that they will destroy freedom.

Mass Media and Foreign Policy. What generalizations can we make about the impact of mass media and their manipulators on the foreign-policy process? We must first repeat our general conclusion that such effect as they have takes place generally within the pre-existing preference pattern of the mass public. If any attitudinal change takes place among the mass, the media may well be in a position to capitalize on it[13] but they have been so far unable to bring about any such change themselves.

Within these limits, however, we may identify at least three different effects of mass media on foreign-policy decision-making. (1) The media help focus issues during a period of readjustment and reassessment by means of constant and extensive discussion of various alternatives. (2) They do a non-discreditable job of mass education, informing the public of data and points of view that otherwise would not receive wide circulation. That this is done often for reasons other than public service should not detract from its value. (3) On the debit side, it must be admitted that the mass media approach to foreign policy stresses its controversial and sensational aspects and minimizes its continuing, affirmative, and harmonizing functions. We are familiar with the cynical attitude of many newspaper employees that "nobody buys a newspaper to read good news"; this assumption underlies much of what all the mass media do in the foreign-policy area.

Nonpolitical leadership elites

The final entry in this brief listing of the decision-influencers is the most difficult to specify, and yet it may well be as important in shaping public

---

[12] David Riesman, Nathan Glazer, and Reuel Denney, in *The Lonely Crowd* (Garden City: Doubleday [Anchor Books ed.], 1953), point out, however, that the mass media have done considerable service in the elevation of mass taste in such fields as furniture and architectural design (p. 339).

[13] The manner in which some more sensational American newspapers and magazines seized on the issue of Communist China after public attitudes crystallized after 1949 is an apt example of this adaptation to a new mood.

attitudes as the more formal groupings we have been considering. This is the existence, at all social levels, of unofficial but powerful "opinion leaders" whose attitudes—however derived—are influential in shaping the opinions of large numbers of their associates. Their role is central to any study of public opinion in the United States.[14]

An Elite of Influence? Students of American society all agree on the existence and importance of the opinion leaders, although they disagree widely as to the nature of their role and its impact for good or bad. Whether it is argued that this leadership constitutes a "power elite" that really rules America[15] or that the leadership merely operates on the periphery of important decisions, that there are nonpolitical leaders whose effect is perceptible although difficult to measure seems beyond doubt. It would seem likely that in the aggregate they are more powerful in changing mass attitudes (through mass response to their own shifts) than are the mass media. There is some empirical evidence to support this thesis.[16]

The Characteristics of Opinion Leaders. Generally speaking, the non-political elite consists either of those individuals in any segment of society who occupy some prestige position, either personal (wealth, beauty, notoriety, social-economic group leadership), or status (the clergy, teachers, attorneys). Americans are famous for their willingness to lend weight to the opinions of prestigeful individuals on any subject, even one on which the particular leader is unqualified to speak. This propensity gives any such leader a ready-made followership prepared to accept many of his opinions as their own.

If this be true, the characteristics of this opinion leadership—if any such can be adduced—are of great importance to the substance of mass opinion on foreign policy. Even though such disparate figures as Norman Vincent Peale and Marilyn Monroe may be included in the group of prestige leaders, we may nevertheless hazard a few generalizations about them.

By and large, opinion leadership tends to come from the upper economic brackets, to be better educated, more widely traveled, and somewhat more catholic in taste and outlook. Their opinions, however, cover the entire possible spectrum, and their influence is exerted in many

---

[14] Floyd Hunter, *Community Power Structure*, (Chapel Hill: University of North Carolina Press, 1953), makes an exhaustive analysis of the structure and pattern of community leadership in "Regional City" (reputedly Atlanta, Georgia).

[15] See, for example, C. Wright Mills, *The Power Elite* (New York: Oxford University Press, 1956).

[16] Paul Lazarsfeld, B. Berelson, and H. Gaudet, *The People's Choice* (New York: Duell, Sloan, and Pierce, 1944), Chapter XVI, "The Nature of Personal Influence."

different ways; there is no necessary implication in what we have been saying that their influence is always—or usually—exerted on the side of enlightenment, of reason, or of tolerance. If it turns out to be, however, it goes far to contribute to a more effective mass opinion within the area of its effect. There are some scholars who attribute much of the growing popular sophistication about international affairs to the work of this kind of leadership.

The Elites and Pressure Groups. The key role of opinion leadership has long been recognized by the directors of interest groups. These organizers and manipulators of pressure always seek to enlist the services of leadership elites at every possible level, from the small community to the entire nation. We are all familiar with the imposing letterheads of such groups that feature a long list of "sponsors" with well-known names who—for one reason or another—have lent their prestige to the particular cause involved. If the member of the elite contents himself with the use of his name, his effect will be limited, although real; if he actively busies himself with the promotion of the cause, he will gain converts and play a significant part.

The Elites and Foreign Policy. It is difficult to generalize further about the special impact of the prestige elites on foreign-policy decisions. Gabriel Almond calls them "the articulate policy-bearing stratum" of the public and feels that they have the truly critical role; they "give structure to the public."[17] This is true at the national level, and in concentrated metropolitan communities; there is some difficulty, however, in conceiving of a smalltown clergyman or high school teacher as a member of Professor Almond's elite public. It might be safer to allocate a minority of them to the elite public, the bulk to the attentive public, and another relative handful to the mass public, at least as far as their reaction to international issues is concerned.

If this group—the prestige leadership—comes together on one side of any foreign-policy issue, a solid public opinion on that issue is as good as made. The cumulative impact of all local, regional, and national opinion leaders all urging the same thing on their followers would be tremendous; there would indeed be few left to dissent. On most issues, however, such unanimity does not develop; the opinion leaders divide among themselves and compete for mass support. The side of the question that gains the consensus of the prestige elite generally carries mass opinion with it; this is the "public opinion" of which government officials usually take account. This fact explains why local opinion leaders are such important targets

---

[17] Almond, *American People and Foreign Policy*, p. 138. Reprinted by permission.

of organized interest groups. As Almond suggests, "who mobilizes elites, mobilizes the public."

A DEMOCRATIC FOREIGN POLICY?

We now turn to the somewhat more detailed consideration of a question that has been implicit through the entire discusssion in these two chapters. Can American foreign policy be truly democratic? American ideology demands that it be; American government is alleged to be responsive to the demands of the people. And yet, as we shall see, there are both strong arguments and objective facts that may lead us, and have led many people, to conclude more or less regretfully that the nature of the foreign-policy problem is such that the democratic ethic provides no guides, but only pitfalls. No issue can be imagined that is more fundamental to the outcome of the American experiment in democracy.[18]

The democratic dilemma

The conduct of foreign policy in the state system is carried on under a set of formal and informal principles as old as the system itself. These operative concepts became institutionalized during the period following the Peace of Westphalia in 1648, and diplomatic procedures were therefore stabilized on the basis of a society of absolute monarchies. The relations of states were actually the relations of sovereign princes, and the concerns of national interest were actually the wants and needs of the crowned heads. In international politics, the apochryphal remark attributed to Louis XIV made a good deal of sense: "I am the state"—in foreign policy.

The French Revolution democratized foreign policy; modern nationalism culminated in conferring on the mass of the people of a state the right and the power to "make" foreign policy, at least in its broad outlines. In return, the populace acquired a reciprocal duty, that of executing the policy of which they were at least the partial architects. Com-

---

18 For a somewhat different attack on this problem, see the symposium, "Can Foreign Policy Be Democratic?" *American Perspective* (September, 1948); also Max Beloff, *Foreign Policy and the Democratic Process* (Baltimore; John Hopkins University Press, 1955).

pulsory military service was the first new civil responsibility; additional burdens of taxpaying, economic activity, intellectual pursuits, and other fields were added until today it is possible to speak of a "total" foreign policy in almost the same sense as we use the term "total war." Corresponding to the increase of mass responsibility for service in behalf of the national foreign policy came an increase in the degree of control popular attitudes exercised over foreign policy.

The more "democratic" foreign policy became, however, the more difficult became the foreign-policy process itself. The demands mass opinion made on government tended steadily to become less and less concrete, and more and more absolute, and ultimately often verging on the unattainable. Caught between the pressures of emotionally involved and articulate public opinion on one side and the inexorabilities of the state system on the other, statesmen in many countries found themselves involved in an unhappy dilemma. They were either obliged to follow the whims of popular demand and undertake policies they thought unwise, or else to flout their people and run the risk of repudiation.

So acute has this issue become in the United States in the middle of the twentieth century that there is a body of informed opinion that contends that foreign policy cannot be democratic or, alternatively, even if it were possible, it would be highly undesirable. On the other hand, to remove openly that area of government action which is currently the most important from popular control would be to do violence to the entire tradition of American government. The issue is a subject of frequent debate.

The Undemocratic Nature of Foreign Policy. It is often said that foreign policy, by its history and by its nature, is inherently undemocratic. Of the many reasons advanced to support this generalization, we shall consider four of the most frequently encountered.

(1) Foreign affairs is a government monopoly. The relations of states are carried on among governments, and in the exercise of the function officials must be free from close checking by irresponsible laymen.

(2) Foreign policy requires, if it is to have any success, both speed and flexibility. Governments must be able to move quickly to meet unexpected contingencies; they must also be able to adapt their actions to meet whatever conditions prevail. Obviously speed and flexibility are closely connected; neither is fully significant without the other. Both these qualities collide with the practice of democratic states generally and the United States particularly. American democracy, except in the most extreme emergency, does not operate with any notable speed. Once

committed, the United States finds it difficult to change its policy (domestic or foreign) in response to new conditions.

(3) Foreign affairs necessitates a constant concern with secrecy. Negotiations usually take considerable time to consummate and during that time the premature release of information often would endanger the whole enterprise. Nothing more fundamentally opposed to American ideology can be imagined. The idea that the government is keeping secrets from the people immediately gives rise to powerful currents of resistance, resentment, and opposition.

(4) A foreign policy must concern itself with what are often called "multiple constituencies." The American government is serving not only the American people, but also the populations of its forty-odd allies; furthermore, the clientele of American foreign-policy personnel also includes all the opponents and enemies of the United States. This means that the requirements of policy often demand that the State Department (for example) accede to the wishes of a foreign state rather than to those of the American people. This is also ideologically repugnant; a democratic government is popularly supposed to serve its people first and always.

We might add a fifth undemocratic requirement of foreign policy: the definition of the national interest. In later chapters we shall consider both the myth of American foreign policy and the working notion of interest that governs contemporary government action. In practice, however, the operating definition and formulation of interest is undertaken by the official elite.[19] This again suggests some conflict with democratic principles.

The Claims of Democratic Ideology. The democratic myth,[20] on the other hand, has certain strong implications for foreign policy. They may be formulated as a series of propositions.

(1) There is something called a "public interest" that is composed of the arithmetic total of individual interests. This is the national interest that the government should serve in foreign policy.

(2) The "average citizen" knows and understands his own interests

---

19 "Hence the national interest becomes defined in practice as what those in power declare it to be." Thomas I. Cook and Malcolm Moos, "The American Idea of International Interest," *American Political Science Review* (March, 1953), pp. 28-44, at 30. Reprinted by permission.

20 This term is used in the sense that it is employed by Gabriel Almond, "The democratic myth is that the people are inherently wise and just, and that they are the real rulers of the republic," *American People and Foreign Policy*, p. 4. Reprinted by permission.

and those of his fellows; in other words, he knows where his private concerns fit into the total public interest.

(3) The average citizen possesses the intellectual and moral resources satisfactorily to comprehend the issues of foreign policy.

(4) The average citizen can—and will—make meaningful decisions on those issues, and the total of individual decisions will constitute a clear directive to his servants in the government hierarchy.

(5) The average citizen is a better (because disinterested) judge of basic alternatives than are special interest groups or even highly specialized experts.

These propositions arise from the application of the individualist faith of traditional democracy to the questions of foreign policy. They incorporate a deep suspicion of special interests, government experts, institutional mechanisms, and indeed of any social structure that stands between "the citizen and his government." In their total impact they collide directly with the essentially undemocratic aspects of foreign policy we noted above. These two alternatives—expertise or popular will—constitute the two horns of what we call the "democratic dilemma."

Leadership: the elite of the competent

We shall first consider the effect of elite leadership on the ideal of a democratic foreign policy. During the years that foreign affairs have been a major concern—since 1945—much attention has been lavished on the determination and evaluation of the role of leadership. Certain general characteristics both of the leadership itself and of its apologists and defenders have become apparent.

Government: The Monopoly of Decision. Foreign-policy leadership is of course concentrated in the government hierarchy. It is axiomatic that foreign-policy decisions in the technical sense can be made only by responsible officials,[21] and that only they can conduct relations with other states. Furthermore, only they have access to the steady flow of information upon which to base intelligent decisions. All of these elements contribute to making the "political" leadership the central element in all foreign-policy discussion.

Whenever official personnel feel called on to justify their stewardship,

---

[21] Richard C. Snyder, H. W. Bruck, and Burton Sapin, *Decision-Making As An Approach to the Study of International Politics* (Princeton University, N. J.: Foreign Policy Analysis Series No. 3, 1954), is devoted to an elaboration of this thesis and an inquiry into how decision-making may be most profitably analyzed.

their attitude finds expression in several general lines, whose net effect is a plea for public tolerance and a continued free hand.

First, they stress the difficulty of the task: "... foreign policy is a tapestry of infinite complexity, and even the expert can only hope to achieve familiarity with a part of its intricate designs."[22] Second, they emphasize the inherent limits on their real freedom of action.[23] Third, they imply that the problems are really beyond the understanding of ordinary citizens.[24] Fourth, they elaborate on the importance—indeed, the critical character—of their own function.

There is no intention here to challenge the importance or the ability of the official leadership group; American national interest is best served by having the most efficient and dedicated official personnel obtainable. What does give rise to some concern, however, is the implication that a final dichotomy exists between the general public and the government bureaucracy and that, when all is said and done, the ultimate safety of the United States rests on the skill and insight of its officials rather than on the morale, intelligence, and patience of the people.[25] There would seem to be some grounds for argument that no leadership can be more than a magnified reflection of the people it leads, and that improving the quality of American leadership without also bettering the political performance of its people smacks a little of building a house by starting at the roof and working down.

The "Democratic Elites": The Monopoly of Knowledge. Implicit in the newer studies in the political process in the United States is the more or less specific assumption that only a part of the public is of any policy significance: the "democratic elites," to use Almond's phrase.[26] Our earlier overview of the various publics indicated that there is indeed a division of labor between the so-called attentive public and the mass. The former is distinctive because of its near-monopoly of knowledge over the data of foreign policy, the viable alternatives, and the preferable courses of action. In the sense in which we are using the general term

---

[22] Almond, *American People and Foreign Policy,* p. 143. Reprinted by permission.

[23] Charles B. Marshall, *The Limits of Foreign Policy* (New York: Henry Holt and Co., 1954). See also his "The Nature of Foreign Policy," *Department of State Bulletin* (March 17, 1952), pp. 415 ff.

[24] A former member of the Policy Planning Staff of the Department of State, Dorothy Fosdick, disagrees with this position, however. See her *Common Sense and World Affairs* (New York: Harcourt, Brace and Co., 1955).

[25] Thus Almond says: "The problem of contemporary American foreign policy is not so much one of mass traditions and resistances as it is one of resolution, courage, and intelligence of the leadership," *American People and Foreign Policy,* p. 88. Reprinted by permission.

[26] See especially Truman, *The Governmental Process,* Part II: "Group Organization and Problems of Leadership."

"leadership" in this discussion, we are therefore including these elites in the leadership group in the United States.

The knowledge possessed by this minority is more than sheer information. If they actually possess more data, it is not necessarily because they have access to more sources than does the uninformed mass; rather, their advantage arises from their concern that motivated them to take the time and trouble to become better informed. But by the constant exercise of their perceptive and critical faculties the elite groups have acquired a facility in at least the elementary analysis and synthesis of foreign policy issues; they have made a beginning at competence.

The division of "the public" into two unequal groups, the smaller consisting of those who have knowledge, the larger encompassing the unsophisticated, raises a question basic to democratic thought. Is it in any sense "right" to allow the raw, emotional and uninformed opinion of a member of the mass to cancel out the thoughtful and serious judgment of a member of the informed elite? To argue the negative is to condemn democratic policy always to be tied to the level of the lowest stratum of the mass public. But to agree that not all opinions are equally valuable is to open the door to a host of elitist and nonegalitarian doctrines of social and political action. Officials, for example, may well be tempted to deal frankly only with the informed minority and to content themselves with manipulating the masses by the crudest stimuli.[27]

The Professional Attitude. It is natural—and probably wholesome—for foreign-policy officials to acquire a professional attitude toward their own calling, and to regret the circumstances that force them to bow to the wishes of the uninformed. George F. Kennan put this very forcefully:

> ... I cannot refrain from saying that I firmly believe that we could make much more effective use of the principle of professionalism in the conduct of foreign policy; that we could, if we wished, develop a corps of professional officers superior to anything that exists or ever has existed in this field; and that, by treating these men with respect and drawing on their insight and experience, we could help ourselves considerably. However, I am quite prepared to recognize that this runs counter to strong prejudices and preconceptions in sections of our public mind, particularly in Congress and the press, and that for this reason we are probably condemned to continue relying almost exclusively on what we might call "diplomacy by dilettantism."[28]

---

[27] Almond, *American People and Foreign Policy*, p. 233: "An effective approach to public information on foreign policy questions will therefore be selective and qualitative. It will be directed toward enlarging the attentive public and training the elite cadres." In another connection Almond speaks of the "containment of mass moods." Reprinted by permission.

[28] George F. Kennan, *American Diplomacy, 1900-1950* (Chicago: University of Chicago Press, 1951), pp. 93-4. Reprinted by permission.

By "professionalism" Mr. Kennan clearly means that attitude among foreign-policy specialists that conceives their mission as a service calling, dedicated to a self-devised code of ethics beyond nonprofessional scrutiny. The analogy that springs readily to mind comes from other professions, such as the law, the clergy, medicine, and university teaching. None of these groups admits the right of the public to interfere with its own professional conduct; each of them formulates its own mission within only the broadest of general limits; each feels it should be responsible ultimately only to itself.

The hope for professionalism undoubtedly has its roots in a sincere concern for the welfare of the United States. It is not surprising that these specialists generally feel that knowing *how* to perform a function qualifies them to determine *whether, when,* and *under what circumstances* it shall be performed. It does little good to contend that the "how" function is a question of administration while the others are matters of policy; many shrewd analyses demonstrate that it is impossible completely to separate policy and administration. The next step, of course, is to argue that policy control by right belongs to the administrators.[29] A cynic might be pardoned for wondering whether or not one of the less explicit reasons for the professional urge is a desire on the part of the officials to escape from the annoyance of popular control.

The Denigration of the Mass. The argument that official personnel should be free from popular control is often complemented by a denial of the ability of the mass to function in any effective way. One critic puts it in this way:

> There are inherent limitations in modern society on the capacity of the public to understand the issues and grasp the significance of the most important problems of public policy.... The layman ordinarily cannot formulate alternatives so that he can see how and in what way his interests are engaged.[30]

George Kennan echoes this position:

> ... a good deal of our trouble seems to have stemmed from the extent to which the executive has felt itself beholden to short term trends of public opinion in the country and from what we might call the erratic and subjective nature of public reaction to foreign-policy questions.[31]

---

[29] Dwight Waldo, in *The Administrative State* (New York: The Ronald Press, 1948), has brought together in Chapter VI, entitled "Who Should Rule?", most of the orthodox arguments on the superior right of administrative expertise in the determination of public policy.

[30] Almond, *American People and Foreign Policy*, pp. 5, 8. Reprinted by permission.

[31] *American Diplomacy*, Kennan, p. 93. Reprinted by permission. See also Walter Lippmann, *The Public Philosophy*, for an elaboration of this thesis.

The picture that is presented by this school of thought is of a mass public that is ordinarily inattentive to public affairs except as it is stirred to emotional excesses by misunderstood events or vote-conscious politicians. The general public is thought to be incapable of judging issues on their merits, of understanding their complexities, or of appreciating the delicacies and subtleties of the problems of dealing with them. The mass public is not to be consulted or followed; it is to be appeased, manipulated, and led by forceful leadership backed by the resources of mass communication and modern public relations.[32]

Granted this *a priori* judgment of the inability of the general public to act in any affirmative way, it is natural for the advocates of government and elite control to argue that the bulk of the populace be kept as far away from foreign policy questions as possible. "Let those who can, make policy; let those who can't, pay their taxes and follow the orders of the competent" seems to be the slogan of the more extreme defenders of this position.[33]

Followership: the role of the general public

What of the public in this equation? Is there a scope of action for the mass of American citizens, even if we grant that the more extreme criticisms of the mass mind have some validity? Must we accept some form of government-elite domination?

Earlier in this chapter we suggested a three-part function for the general public in dealing with foreign affairs. We said the public acts as a limiting factor, as a direction-setter, and as a court of last resort on certain issues. If this formulation should prove to have some utility, it would

---

[32] One State Department official once confided his dismay at the American people to the author: "You can't handle these people. If you scare them too much they go crazy; if you don't scare them enough, they go fishing!" See also John D. Millett, *Management in the Public Service* (New York: McGraw-Hill Book Co., Inc., 1954), ch. 6: "Public Relations."

[33] See, for example, Walter Lippmann's attack on contemporary democracy in *The Public Philosophy* (Boston: Little, Brown and Co., 1955), pp. 24-5: "There is no mystery about why there is such a tendency for popular opinion to be wrong in judging war and peace. Strategic and diplomatic decisions call for a kind of knowledge—not to speak of an experience and a seasoned judgment—which cannot be had by glancing at newspapers, listening to snatches of radio comment, watching politicians perform on television, hearing occasional lectures, and reading a few books. It would not be enough to make a man competent to decide whether to amputate a leg, and it is not enough to qualify him to choose war or peace, to arm or not to arm, to intervene or to withdraw, to fight on or to negotiate." Reprinted by permission.

give most Americans something affirmative to do about international affairs, something perhaps more positive than being merely a "crude and passive instrument." We are here advancing the contention that the democratic ideology will not die away, and that for an indefinite period Americans are going to have to live with some form of popular opinion and mass action on foreign policy. If this be so, it seems a worthwhile inquiry to explore the possibility of a more effective way for the bulk of the populace to participate.

How the Public Functions. We have already noted that "the public" does not function as a single anthropomorphic entity, but instead brings its influence to bear in several different ways. It operates initially, and perhaps most frequently, by way of interest groups whose impact is usually quite specific in the advocacy of particular points of view. Secondly, and more broadly, the public functions as the electorate after the political parties have performed their function of polarizing the many possible alternatives into a simple choice (or sometimes, as we have seen, into no real choice at all). Finally, the public affects decisions through the national mood: the more broadly-based mental sets that govern the popular threshold of tolerance of government action.

The Public as a Limiting Factor. Nearly all observers admit, whether regretfully or happily, that popular opinion acts as a limiting factor on government action. Substantively and procedurally, mass opinion fairly clearly indicates how far the government can go in conducting foreign policy. To cite two extreme examples: American opinion would not tolerate a policy aimed at the conquest and annexation of Canada (substantive) nor would it approve immediate American entry into a world federal government (procedural). Policy-makers do their best to have as accurate an idea as possible of the outlines of their area of operating freedom as described by these limits, and accept them more or less as "givens" of the situation in which they have to act. Even the most outspoken critics of American attitudes on foreign affairs grant the effectiveness and the relative permanence of this degree of control.

The Public as Direction-Setter. But this does not, it would seem, exhaust the positive function of the public. In addition, a picture emerges from the various indices of public-opinion measurement, revealing that the general public sets a general direction in which government must aim its policy. Without concern for detailed situational influences or operational timetables, the popular image of national destiny, more or less clearly formulated, perforce imposes the broad outlines of policy on the decision-making officials. To put it in other terms, we may say that the general public, by a process admittedly cumbersome, formulates at

81

least the skeleton of the notion of national interest that government must implement.

This process is probably more intimately connected with the general evolution of American society and the consequent changing pattern of socio-political values that it is with any conscious application of rational effort to international issues. It represents the translation into foreign-policy terms of the prevailing complex of wants and needs within the society at any given time. And yet, vague as this may be and difficult to discover, policy-makers (if they are interested in maintaining effective rapport with the public) must seek valiantly to "tune in" on this social wavelength. Failure to do this may well result in their tacit repudiation.

It seems probable, for example, that formulating American national interest as "peace, order, and stability" as we shall do later is a reflection of the pattern of social expectations of the bulk of the American people. This is, to put it bluntly, the kind of world most Americans (when they specifically think about it) want to live in; they feel that it is up to their government to get it for them. Nor may policy-makers afford the luxury of consistently disregarding these inchoate and inarticulate urges of the mass in favor of the more insistent clamor of the interest groups. No more dangerous mistake could be made than to assume that popular silence on fundamentals always means apathy; let the government unthinkingly violate an element of the unspoken consensus and the resulting storm might well blow the responsible officials into a keener realization of the importance of public sentiment.

The Public as Decision-Maker. The heading of this paragraph is not to be taken literally; we know already that the public cannot really "make" decisions. Its figurative import, however, illustrates another basic function of mass attitudes. Many occasions arise in the conduct of foreign policy when new conditions, either predicted or unforeseen, create the necessity for new categories of government action. If these are of relatively minor importance, if they fall within the area of pre-existing consensus, no difficulty is presented to the responsible officials. But if they involve far-reaching new consequences or if there is real doubt in Washington about what the reaction of the general public might be, something like a public decision must be made before the government can, or will, act.

Arriving at a mass consensus under such circumstances is preceded by a widespread debate within each of the various publics. It usually begins with discussion within the various elites, with the attentive public being drawn in as the concentric rings of controversy widen. Ultimately, whether in accurate or in over-simplified form, the issue comes to the attention of the mass public. Not until the bulk of the people have become aware of the problem and, on some basis, made up their minds can the top layer of officialdom feel confident in committing themselves to a course of action. The consensus must be clear; until then policy must remain in suspension.[34]

Elitists of one school or another tend to regret the fact that the public retains this key role and take pains to point out the shaky foundations of much individual opinion. But there seems no other convenient way to handle the problem of gaining support for new ventures foreign to the immediate experience and attitudes of the mass. On the other hand, there is some reason at least to hope that recent experience indicates that public attitudes provide not only a necessary base for policy, but also a frequently effective one.

A democratic compromise

Can these positions of leadership and followership on foreign policy be rationalized? Is it possible to resolve the democratic dilemma? Can Americans develop a working partnership between their officials and themselves, in which each set of parties will contribute its best features and in which the shortcomings of each are at least partially neutralized?

It is no function of a textbook to prescribe cures for social ills, and we shall not elaborate any formulation of a perfect situation here. A description of the ideal made some years ago by a State Department official, however, illustrates some of the requirements:

> Our national policies should reflect the will of the people, a will that is not distorted by false propaganda or slogans, that is based upon a solid knowledge of all the facts, that has taken into account all factors and considerations, and has resulted from open and active debate so that all points of view have been thoroughly aired and discussed.[35]

Fortified by the support of a rational and temperate opinion such as this, officials could operate efficiently and to good purpose in making the decisions and executing the policies that come before them.

---

[34] From the recent past we may cite a few of the more significant "great debates": on the Truman Doctrine in 1947, on the Marshall Plan in 1948, on the North Atlantic Treaty in 1949, on "troops for Europe" in 1951, on "liberation" in 1952, on entry into the Indochina war in 1954, on "going to the summit" in 1955, and on sanctions against Israel in 1957.

[35] Francis H. Russell, "The Function of Public-Opinion Analysis in the Formulation of Foreign Policy," *Department of State Bulletin* (March 6, 1949). Mr. Russell was at this time Director of the Office of Public Affairs of the Department.

Policy Formulation: Forces That Shape Decisions

If Elysium is represented by a sophisticated and alert public opinion cooperating with a democratically-minded, responsible, and dedicated officialdom, it is perfectly clear from our discussion that the United States has not yet arrived there. What can be done to improve effective relationships between public and bureaucracy?

A Two-way Relationship. One basic consideration seems to have been rather generally overlooked in most of the discussions about the possibility of a democratic foreign policy. Reflection on the leader-follower relationship suggests a conclusion that it is a street that runs two ways. The governmental elite has the responsibility of initiative, but it also has the duty of effective communication with its mass constituency. The executive department must tell the people what, in good conscience, the people ought to know; leaders, however, must also listen to what their followers say. The people have the obligation to use their political power to select the leaders they trust, but then they must trust them; democracy is in no way advanced by a constant ill-tempered squabble between the bureaucracy on the one hand and Congress and the public on the other —for Congress, at least in this particular context, is really a part of the public.

If an effective working relationship is one that calls for the best efforts of both sides, if we are not to accept the somewhat repellent hypothesis (repellent at least to anyone who believes that the democratic idea retains vigor and pertinence in the twentieth century) that only a small minority of co-opted elites can speak for the public, progress toward a more democratic foreign policy will require conscious effort from both the personnel of government and the public, however organized it may be. Some concrete suggestions can be advanced that promise some improvement without smacking of illusory utopianism.

The Duties of Leadership. Each of the points included in this paragraph could be expanded into a detailed discussion, but we shall content ourselves with a brief listing. Some of the steps that government officials —perhaps in cooperation with the elite publics—might take to improve the democratic character of American foreign policy would include: (1) a real effort to trust the good sense of the general public; (2) an attempt to acquaint the people with the peculiar method of analysis used by government; (3) a policy of formulating issues for public discussion in the actual terms used by government; (4) an end to thinking of the "mass" as something to manipulate for short-run purposes and a new emphasis on long-term education of public opinion; (5) a minimization of the tendency to play politics with foreign policy; (6) a greater reliance on candor, explaining the real reasons for government action

84

to the maximum extent commensurate with real national security. This set of suggestions is by no means thought of as a panacea; it would seem logical to expect, however, that their adoption would represent a not inconsiderable contribution to a healthier public opinion.

The Responsibility of the Public. But, as we suggested above, this responsibility works both ways. There are few indeed who would argue that the present conduct of Americans constitutes a model worthy of imitation by all democratic peoples. There are a number of things that individual Americans, be they members of the elite, attentive, or mass publics, could themselves do that would contribute to the over-all improvement of public opinion on foreign-policy matters. None of them aim at creating a nation of experts; expertise is best left to the government officials themselves. The aim of this set of suggestions is rather better to fit the general public and its individual component parts for the foreign-policy mission that is rightfully theirs.[36]

Any list like this will probably err either on the side of brevity or of prolixity; the present one probably fits the first description. We may say that the tone of public opinion on foreign policy would be noticeably improved if any substantial portion of the American people would do any or all of the following things: (1) attempt to formulate a clearer picture of the kind of world that Americans would be satisfied with—thus giving the government a more constant pattern of interest within which to work; (2) gain some awareness of the limits on the capability of foreign-policy instruments—thus allowing government to set more realistic objectives for itself; (3) take such strides as are possible toward acquiring patience—thus freeing the government from the maddening insistence on immediate results that plagues officialdom today; (4) make more efficient use of the sources of information presently available—thus making it possible for the government to operate on the basis of a more informed consensus without any necessity to "educate" public opinion all over again each time new decisions are called for. That these four steps would help make American policy more genuinely democratic seems self-evident. Persuading enough people to take them, however, calls for leadership, political and nonpolitical, of the highest order.

---

[36] "Not expertness but improved understanding is the target which the public should be urged to set for itself." Almond, *American People and Foreign Policy*, pp. 6-7. Reprinted by permission.

4 :   The execution of American policy

In this chapter we shall consider the organization and to some extent the operation of the governmental machinery for the execution of American foreign policy. By "execution" we mean all the implementing action that follows a policy decision, up to the point where the effect of the original decision is felt on its objects. We should admit, of course, that such a concept is valuable primarily as an analytical tool; it is impossible actually to isolate a single policy decision and then to trace out to its end a single chain of execution. In practice, each action taken by a government usually requires that additional policy decisions be made in implementation, and the process rarely reaches full completion; furthermore, so many policies are being executed simultaneously that each of them impinges on and modifies many of the others. By defining the term the way we do, however, we are able to obtain a focus of concentration that will differentiate our present discussion from our earlier one.

We shall first consider the Department of State as an operating agency. Next we shall analyze other operating bodies in terms of their policy functions: military, economic, and psychological. Some comment follows on the overseas representation of the United States. The concluding section will note certain special procedures in negotiation, especially the roles of the President, of special emissaries, and of American delegations to the United Nations.

86

THE DEPARTMENT OF STATE

General organization

We discussed the policy-making function of the Department of State in the preceding chapter; here we shall consider only its role in the execution of policy. The basis of our discussion will be the accompanying chart.

The organizational chart of the Department reveals certain natural groupings. The first is the Office of the Secretary, containing the department head, the Undersecretary, and Executive Secretariat. The next group is at the "Deputy Undersecretary" level, containing deputy undersecretaries for economic affairs, political affairs, and administration, as well as the Director of the International Cooperation Administration. The third group, as well as the fourth and fifth, are at the "Assistant Secretary" level. The third includes a number of special-purpose advisers to the Secretary; the fourth, the "functional bureaus"; the fifth, the "geographic bureaus." These are not equally important for our purposes in this discussion; our subsequent analysis will omit the administrative segment entirely and will touch only lightly on the formal organization for policy-making.[1]

Office of the Secretary. The Office of the Secretary is the nerve center of the Department. The Secretary is the administrative chief of the entire establishment and thus falls heir to a normal complement of supervisory duties. He issues directives, resolves disputes, sets tasks, and acts generally in his area as do his fellow department heads in the Cabinet. He is assisted by the Undersecretary, who shares the burden of responsibility and who stands in for his chief during the latter's absences. The Office is served by the Executive Secretariat with a broad variety of functions.[2]

The Deputy Undersecretaries. The three Deputy Undersecretaries have functional roles differentiated by their titles; they shall receive only

[1] Many studies dealing with the Department have been published in recent years, although of course they cannot keep up to date on the rapid—one is tempted to say constant—reorganizations. Among the most significant are Graham Stuart, *The Department of State* (New York: The Macmillan Co., 1949), Brookings Institution, *The Administration of Foreign Affairs and Overseas Operations* (Washington, D. C.: Brookings, 1951), and James McCamy, *The Administration of American Foreign Affairs* (New York: Alfred A. Knopf, Inc., 1951).

[2] Former Secretaries of State Cordell Hull and James F. Byrnes have spelled out their functions in their memoirs. Cordell Hull, *Memoirs* (New York: The Macmillan Co., 1948), and James F. Byrnes, *Speaking Frankly* (New York: Harper & Bros., 1947).

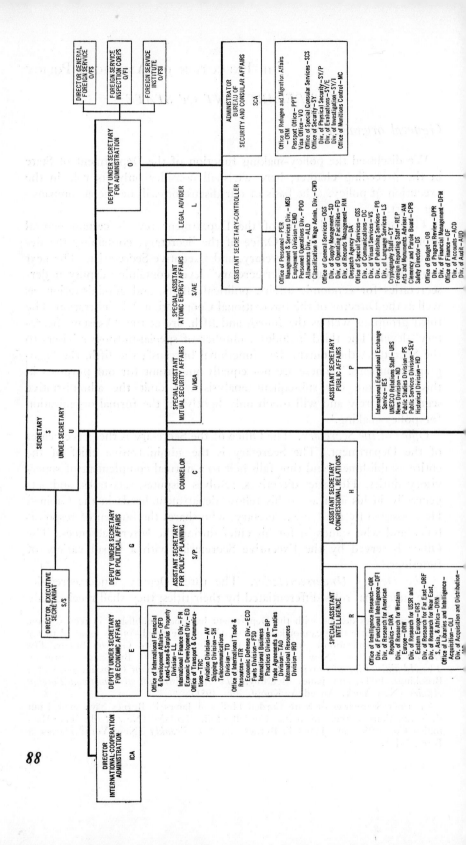

SECRETARY
S

UNDER SECRETARY
U

DIRECTOR, EXECUTIVE SECRETARIAT
S/S

DIRECTOR GENERAL FOREIGN SERVICE
O/FS

FOREIGN SERVICE INSPECTION CORPS
O/FI

FOREIGN SERVICE INSTITUTE
O/FSI

DEPUTY UNDER SECRETARY FOR ADMINISTRATION
O

ADMINISTRATOR BUREAU OF SECURITY AND CONSULAR AFFAIRS
SCA

Office of Refugee and Migratior Affairs — ORM
Passport Office — PPT
Visa Office — VO
Office of Special Consular Services — SCS
Office of Security — SY
Div. of Physical Security — SY/P
Div. of Evaluations — SY/E
Div. of Investigation — SY/I
Office of Munitions Control — MC

ASSISTANT SECRETARY-CONTROLLER
A

Office of Personnel — PER
Management & Services Div. — MSD
Employment Division — EMD
Personnel Operations Div. — POD
Allowances Div. — ALD
Classification & Wage Admin. Div. — CWD
Office of General Services — OGS
Div. of Supply Management — SD
Div. of Operating Facilities — FD
Div. of Records Management — RM
Despatch Agency — DA
Office of Special Services — OSS
Div. of Communications — DC
Div. of Visual Services — VS
Div. of Publishing Services — PB
Div. of Language Services — LS
Cryptography Staff — CY
Foreign Reporting Staff — REP
Arts and Monuments Adviser — AM
Clemency and Parole Board — CPB
Safety Director — DS
Office of Budget — OB
Div. of Program Review — DPR
Div. of Financial Management — DFM
Office of Finance — OF
Div. of Accounts — ACD
Div. of Audit — AUD

LEGAL ADVISER
L

SPECIAL ASSISTANT ATOMIC ENERGY AFFAIRS
S/AE

SPECIAL ASSISTANT MUTUAL SECURITY AFFAIRS
U/MSA

DEPUTY UNDER SECRETARY FOR POLITICAL AFFAIRS
G

ASSISTANT SECRETARY FOR POLICY PLANNING
S/P

COUNSELOR
C

ASSISTANT SECRETARY CONGRESSIONAL RELATIONS
H

ASSISTANT SECRETARY PUBLIC AFFAIRS
P

International Educational Exchange Service — IES
UNESCO Relations Staff — URS
News Division — ND
Public Studies Division — PS
Public Services Division — SEV
Historical Division — HD

SPECIAL ASSISTANT INTELLIGENCE
R

Office of Intelligence Research — OIR
Div. of Functional Intelligence — DFI
Div. of Research for American Republics — DRA
Div. of Research for Western Europe — DRW
Div. of Research for USSR and Eastern Europe — DRS
Div. of Research for Far East — DRF
Div. of Research for Near East, Ot. Asia, & Africa — DRN
Office of Libraries and Intelligence Acquisition — OLI
Div. of Acquisition and Distribution —

DEPUTY UNDER SECRETARY FOR ECONOMIC AFFAIRS
E

Office of International Financial & Development Affairs — OFD
Lend-Lease & Surplus Property Division — LL
International Finance Div. — FN
Economic Development Div. — ED
Office of Transport & Communications — TRC
Aviation Division — AV
Shipping Division — SH
Telecommunications Division — TD
Office of International Trade & Resources — ITR
Economic Defense Div. — ECD
Fuels Division — FSD
International Business Practices Division — BP
Trade Agreements & Treaties Division — TAD
International Resources Division — IRD

DIRECTOR INTERNATIONAL COOPERATION ADMINISTRATION
ICA

88

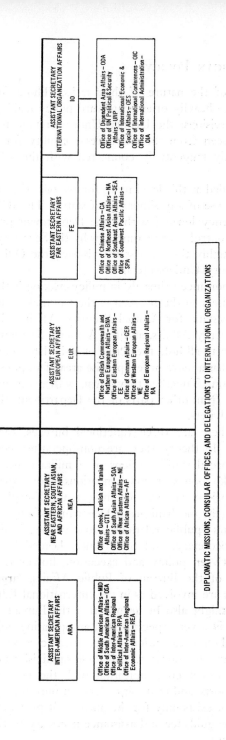

ORGANIZATION OF THE DEPARTMENT OF STATE

JUNE 1, 1956

DIPLOMATIC MISSIONS, CONSULAR OFFICES, AND DELEGATIONS TO INTERNATIONAL ORGANIZATIONS

ASSISTANT SECRETARY INTER-AMERICAN AFFAIRS — ARA
- Office of Middle American Affairs — MID
- Office of South American Affairs — OSA
- Office of Inter-American Regional Political Affairs — RPA
- Office of Inter-American Regional Economic Affairs — REA

ASSISTANT SECRETARY NEAR EASTERN, SOUTH ASIAN, AND AFRICAN AFFAIRS — NEA
- Office of Greek, Turkish and Iranian Affairs — GTI
- Office of South Asian Affairs — SOA
- Office of Near Eastern Affairs — NE
- Office of African Affairs — AF

ASSISTANT SECRETARY EUROPEAN AFFAIRS — EUR
- Office of British Commonwealth and Northern European Affairs — BNA
- Office of Eastern European Affairs — EE
- Office of German Affairs — GER
- Office of Western European Affairs — WE
- Office of European Regional Affairs — RA

ASSISTANT SECRETARY FAR EASTERN AFFAIRS — FE
- Office of Chinese Affairs — CA
- Office of Northeast Asian Affairs — NA
- Office of Southeast Asian Affairs — SEA
- Office of Southwest Pacific Affairs — SPA

ASSISTANT SECRETARY INTERNATIONAL ORGANIZATION AFFAIRS — IO
- Office of Dependent Area Affairs — ODA
- Office of UN Political & Security Affairs — UNP
- Office of International Economic & Social Affairs — OES
- Office of International Conferences — OIC
- Office of International Administration — OIA

passing mention here because of the nature of their tasks. Those for economic and political affairs are heavily oriented toward policy-making rather than the execution of decisions; the Deputy Undersecretary for Administration has, as can be seen from the chart, responsibility for a group of operating services only tangentially connected with the substance of policy.

The Director of ICA is included at this level more for reasons of convenience of discussion than because of any similarity of status. The ICA is an autonomous operating agency located within the Department primarily as a means of exercising control over its functions by the Secretary. In this way its Director has roughly the same status vis-a-vis the Office of the Secretary as do the Deputy Undersecretaries.

The Special Advisers. Of importance primarily in policy-making is the group of "special-purpose" advisers to the Secretary: the Counselor, the Legal Adviser, the Special Assistant for Mutual Security Affairs, the Special Assistant for Atomic Energy Affairs, and the Assistant Secretary for Policy Planning. These officials all hold the actual or assimilated rank of Assistant Secretary and each has a more or less precise area of responsibility for policy recommendation. Together they form, with a varying number of Assistant Secretaries from other parts of the Department, the Secretary's "senior staff" of advisers.

The Functional Bureaus. There are three functional bureaus, each dealing with one specific area. In theory they are non-operating, corresponding roughly to the "special staff" sections of a military headquarters; their task is to make policy recommendations about their particular areas of concern. Their names are to some extent self-explanatory: Congressional Relations (the mechanisms of Department-Congress coordination) and Public Affairs (public relations, broadly conceived), each headed by an Assistant Secretary, and Intelligence, headed by a Special Assistant. The line between policy and execution, however, is unclear; certainly in the case of the Bureau of Public Affairs, large-scale operational responsibilities are involved as in the International Educational Exchange Service. It might also be argued that the Bureau of Congressional Relations is also, in a very special sense, an operating unit.

The Geographic Divisions. Policy execution, in the specific sense, is the primary mission of the geographic bureaus. It is these subdivisions of the Department that maintain direct communication with the Department's foreign posts, receive reports, and transmit orders. In pure theory, the remainder of the Department exists only for the purpose of providing the geographic bureaus with the guidance and assistance necessary to the efficient performance of their duties.

90

"Geographic bureau" is something of a misnomer. Of the five operating bureaus, only four are organized geographically; the fifth, that of International Organization Affairs, is geographic only in the far-fetched sense that the United Nations headquarters area in New York City is a particular policy area of the world. An explanation for including international organization affairs in a separate operating agency is that the problems of American membership in the United Nations and other such bodies are independent of, or at least largely transcend, a purely regional framework. The Bureau of International Organization Affairs thus has a separate mission, but its effectiveness obviously depends upon how well it cooperates with the geographically-oriented units.

The geographic bureaus in action

The Division of the World. All foreign offices divide the world into regions for the execution of policy; the basis on which such division is made usually reflects the pattern of interests of the state. The State Department has, in addition to the Bureau of International Organization Affairs, four regional subdivisions. They are the Bureau of European Affairs, the Bureau of Far Eastern Affairs, the Bureau of Inter-American Affairs, and the Bureau of Near Eastern, South Asian, and African Affairs.

This division is quite informative. Since all four are headed by Assistant Secretaries of equal rank, it means that all four are thought of as roughly equal in importance; that is, the vast and populous area of Africa, the Middle East, and India is no more significant—organizationally—to the Department than is Latin America. During 1957, however, steps were taken toward the creation of a separate African bureau. Furthermore, the geographic breakdown cannot be perfect; as far as the Department is concerned, the entire Commonwealth of Nations is dealt with in the Bureau of European Affairs, although most of the Commonwealth members fall into some other geographic area.

These geographic breakdowns are not irrevocable; changing circumstances—both international and intra-departmental—bring about modifications in the bureau structure. Some years ago inter-American affairs were the direct responsibility of an Undersecretary and were outside the ordinary hierarchy entirely; German affairs were formerly dealt with by an office distinct from the geographic bureaus whose chief reported directly to the Secretary. Prior to World War II there was very little effective coordination on any regional basis; the country "desk officers" recognized no operative superior except (occasionally) the Secretary of State himself. The future will see more changes in the particular responsibility of each geographic bureau.

The Mission of the Assistant Secretary. Each of the geographic bureaus is headed by an Assistant Secretary of State. His duties may be grouped under four headings, although of course in practice he is responsible for whatever matters are appropriate to his bureau and that find their way to him for disposition. Normally, however, he must: (1) communicate in all directions—upwards to the Undersecretary and the Secretary on all matters needing their attention, downward to the subsections of his bureau and the "desk officers" within them, and laterally to his fellow Assistant Secretaries and others who may be interested parties; (2) make decisions on questions that fall within his scope, on which he is empowered to decide, and on which he has appropriate general directives for guidance; (3) coordinate the offices within his bureau so that in his particular geographic area United States policy is both consistent within itself and also coordinated with American efforts in other parts of the world; (4) make recommendations on policy to the higher levels of the Department. This is indeed a formidable task; situated roughly in the middle of the organizational pyramid as he is, the Assistant Secretary in charge of a geographic bureau is obviously one of the key figures in the execution of American policy.

The Desk Officers. Within each bureau there is a further subdivision, still on a regional basis. The Bureau of Near Eastern, South Asian, and African Affairs, for example, contains four "offices": Greek. Turkish, and Iranian Affairs; South Asian Affairs; Near East Affairs; African Affairs. Each of these function within their restricted scope with an office chief in charge; each is further divided into "country desks."

In theory, there is one desk, occupied by one man, for each state with which the United States has relations; in practice, however, two or more small or relatively unimportant states are often lumped into one desk. Thus, in the Office of Greek, Turkish, and Iranian Affairs, there is one "officer in charge" of Greek Affairs, one of Turkish Affairs, and one of Iranian Affairs.

The desk officers are the real operating personnel of the Department. It is they who deal directly with the American missions abroad; it is they who conduct routine business; it is they who, in the course of their day-by-day activities, make what is in the aggregate probably a majority of all the policy decisions made in the Department. The desk officers are of long standing in the Department; most of the administrative superstructure above them was added fairly recently. As a result, the desk officer traditionally regards himself as the true specialist on his particular country, and is more or less reluctant to fit himself into a regional or global pattern of policy made by (what are to him) nonspecialists.

Coordination among the desk officers has thus been often difficult to achieve; the need for some workable principle of harmony has been one of the major motivations for the many reorganizations of the Department. The idealized model of the State Department is one that concentrates on two administrative entities: the Secretary and the desk officer. Let the Secretary make the correct decisions; let him transmit the policies to the desk officer for execution; let the latter carry out both the spirit and the letter of the policy; this is administrative perfection. Every administrative apparatus between the Secretary and the desk officer is for the single purpose of helping one or the other to perform his mission more efficiently.

Geographic-functional Relations. The Task Force on Foreign Affairs of the first Hoover Commission dealt with a very ticklish issue in the internal functioning of the Department: what should be the relationship between the functional and the geographic bureaus? From the time that functional units began to be added to the Department, there was confusion about their relative roles. Geographic units often included functional personnel of their own, such as economic specialists; the functional divisions were engaged, often by specific directive of the Secretary, in the active execution of programs. Overlapping, competition, and open conflict resulted as the duties of the Department multiplied. Obviously some final decision was necessary.

The present structure and operating theory of the Department is largely a result of the Commission's recommendation: the geographic bureaus are the only action units, while the functional bureaus are supposed to confine themselves to staff (advisory and informational) tasks.[3] The responsible geographic office is not required to secure the approval of the appropriate functional branch before taking action, although it is supposed to "consult" with it. This directive, however, has been only imperfectly implemented; action units do not always consult, and a residue of operating responsibility yet remains in the functional bureaus.

In theory, of course, the functional unit is deemed to consist of experts whose lot it is to be "on tap, not on top." The action officer in the geographic bureau is supposed to call on expert advice from all appropriate areas in the functional stratum, and then to make his own decision for which he will stand responsible. Let us put ourselves in the place of the Assistant Secretary of State for Near Eastern, South Asian, and

---

[3] Hoover Commission, Task Force on Foreign Affairs, *A Report to the Congress* (Washington, D. C.: U. S. Government Printing Office, 1949), p. 46.

African Affairs as he confronts a situation requiring a decision involving American aid to Pakistan and Indian objections thereto. We will consult the appropriate experts in the Bureau of Economic Affairs; we will call for information from the South Asian specialists in the Office of Intelligence Research; we may consult with the Special Assistant for Mutual Security Affairs, the Legal Adviser, and the Assistant Secretary for Congressional Relations (to sound Congressional opinion). When we have gathered all the information and recommendations these sources can provide, and have done such canvassing of our own subordinates as we care to, we make our decision—communicating it upward, downward, and laterally. The decision and the responsibility are both ours alone—provided we remain within the bounds laid down by higher echelons of policy-makers.

The Problem of Overlap. One other problem of policy execution should be mentioned. In an era of global policy, it is often very difficult to attack problems within a purely regional framework; questions have a tendency to spill over into other regions than the one in which they originated. How should these be handled?

Here again, it is easier to lay down a principle than it is to put it into practice. A problem that cannot be handled within one desk should be shared by the smallest possible number of people, supervised by the lowest ranking superior that has jurisdiction over all the units involved. The aim, of course, is to confine the responsibility to the lowest possible administrative level. This rule, perhaps more easily applicable to other administrative agencies, causes serious problems in the Department of State.

When the overlapping takes place within a subregional office, the office chief can take charge of coordination; when it takes place within a geographic bureau, the Assistant Secretary is responsible. But if the overlap occurs between two desks, one in—for example—the Bureau of Far Eastern Affairs and the other in the Bureau of European Affairs (such as the Indochina crisis of 1954), there is no one below the Deputy Undersecretary level who can assume the responsibility for coordination. Since this sort of overlap is as much the rule as the exception, a crushing burden is placed on officials who already have the outsize task of ensuring affirmative harmony. Settling jurisdictional disputes (to which such overlaps frequently lead) occupies an inordinate amount of time and effort. Complicating this factor is the further fact that the bureau chiefs, being Assistant Secretaries, have access to the Secretary and many such issues are dealt with at the very top. Time spent by the Secretary in arbitrating power disputes must be taken away from other duties.

OTHER OPERATING AGENCIES

The execution of military foreign policy

Nearly every branch of the executive establishment has some sort of operating responsibility in foreign affairs. In this section we shall be dealing with three selected functional areas of policy: military policy, foreign economic assistance, and informational activities.

One index of the growing maturity of American foreign policy has been the gradual although yet incomplete meshing of military policy with foreign affairs. There is little disagreement today that foreign policy has a military dimension and that armed might is both an end in itself and a means to the accomplishment of other American objectives. A good deal of what the United States does in international affairs today is oriented to military calculations. The execution of what we call military foreign policy therefore becomes a separate problem.[4]

Generally speaking, operational responsibility for the military aspects of foreign policy—with the principal exception being the negotiation of treaties of alliance, agreements on bases, and so on—rests with the Department of Defense, acting usually through the Secretary or his principal assistant for these matters, the Assistant Secretary for International Security Affairs. The three service departments have roughly similar arrangements in their respective hierarchies for the accomplishment of the same general purposes. We must remember, however, that administrative mechanisms in this area tend to be extemporized to meet changing needs.

War. Perhaps the most obvious, but also the most basic, military operation with a foreign-policy implication is the conduct of war. We shall remark in a later chapter on the time-honored American tendency to regard war as an interruption in the orderly course of international affairs, and to conceive the spheres of diplomacy and warfare as occupying different universes. This idea has virtually disappeared among policy-making officials; there is also some reason to believe that its acceptance is declining among the general public.

There is no more important foreign-policy mission than the prosecution of a war. This is the supreme test of a nation's ability to achieve its objectives; to exert the enormous effort required for modern warfare without having a concrete political objective in mind is today a waste

---

[4] See Burton M. Sapin and Richard C. Snyder, *The Role of the Military in American Foreign Policy* (Garden City, N. Y.: Doubleday, 1954).

that not even the United States can afford. The Korean conflict—despite General MacArthur's valedictory to the effect that "in war there is no substitute for victory"—is an example of a military struggle that was kept always at the service of a reasonably clear set of political objectives. No more effort was expended than was necessary to reach those goals; once they were attained, it was immaterial to American interest whether or not the military test was settled conclusively.

Today, with hydrogen bombs, intercontinental ballistic missiles, biological warfare, and the other horrors of modern total war, there is considerable doubt about the long-range utility of large-scale warfare as an effective instrument of national policy. The time may come when a military establishment will lose all utility in executing policy and become instead merely an example of national conspicuous consumption; mankind, however, is not yet at that point. As long as total war remains a possibility in the international order, the United States must be prepared if necessary to implement at least the bare minimum of its objectives —continued survival—by military means.

Occupation of Defeated States. Following World War II another example of the execution of foreign policy by military means was provided by the American occupation of the defeated enemy nations.[5] Occupation had a political purpose; to occupy Germany and Japan merely for the sake of revenge would have been childish. The military outcome of the war required physical occupation of the terrain as the only way the Allies could make any beginning on their ambitious plans for postwar reconstruction. The Allied plan called for the reasonably early replacement of military by civilian control over the Axis; the cold war, however, intervened and the whole project was drastically remodeled. It is generally agreed, however, that the military branches performed their share of the mission creditably.

Military Aid. In the contemporary period, one of the major preoccupations of the military establishment of the United States is the administration of the American military aid program. Since the cold war became acute the military buildup of America's allies has been a major order of business. Starting with the Mutual Defense Assistance Program of 1949 and including the various Mutual Security Acts, furnishing military assistance to growing numbers of foreign states has been

---

[5] For Germany, see E. H. Litchfield *et al.*, *Governing Postwar Germany* (Ithaca: Cornell University Press, 1953); for Japan see Russell Brines, *MacArthur's Japan* (Philadelphia: J. B. Lippincott Co., 1948), and Robert B. Textor, *Failure in Japan* (New York: John Day, 1951).

96

a major element of American policy. The execution of these programs has been entrusted to the Department of Defense.

Control over military aid, under the terms of the various statutes, is vested in the Secretary of Defense and exercised by the Assistant Secretary for International Security Affairs. To supervise the general assistance program by coordinating requests from the various states, there was created the Joint American Military Advisory Group (JAMAG) that works in close harmony with the Assistant Secretary. In each foreign state receiving American military aid there is a Military Assistance Advisory Group (MAAG) that cooperates with its host government in developing recommendations for aid. Both JAMAG and MAAG are composed of representatives of the three uniformed services.

Another form of international military assistance, often coupled with the supply of materiel, is a training mission. The Department of Defense and the service departments have sent a sizeable number of training missions to states in Europe, the Middle East, the Far East, and Latin America. Obviously the military establishment of a nonindustrialized nation that receives large shipments of American equipment—Turkey, for example—needs considerable instruction in its employment. Even if formal assistance in "military end-items" is not involved, it is in the interest of the United States to see to it that its allies have as efficient a military force as possible.[6]

Alliances. One final form of policy executed by the military is the fulfillment of continuing American responsibilities in the various mutual-security pacts to which the United States is a party: NATO, SEATO, ANZUS, OAS, and a number of bilateral agreements. If, as some current military thinking insists, the chief contribution the military makes to American security is its deterrent effect, it would seem that this elaborate alliance structure plays a major part in discouraging communist attack.

Of all the alliances, NATO is both the most elaborate and the neatest example; military planning and military action in the others are not nearly so advanced. NATO is, of course, under civilian control at the highest level, the North Atlantic Council. From there on, however, it is a military matter, organized into a Supreme Headquarters, various subordinate commands, and elaborate logistical arrangements. Throughout all of these American military personnel may be found; the post of SACEUR—Supreme Allied Commander, Europe—has never been filled

---

[6] See Arthur Macmahon, *Administration in Foreign Affairs* (University, Alabama: University of Alabama Press, 1953), pp. 132-137.

except by an American.[7] In 1956, however, efforts at discovering a political dimension to NATO were intensified, and the appointment of Paul-Henri Spaak of Belgium as Secretary-General of the organization seemed to presage a new era for the alliance.

We shall consider NATO in more detail in later chapters. It is mentioned here as perhaps the most detailed contemporary example of the implementation of American foreign policy by the military.

Foreign aid

One of the most dramatic departures in American policy after World War II was the popular acceptance of responsibility to extend large-scale assistance of all sorts—economic, military, and technical—to friendly foreign states. With the details of that program we shall be concerned later; at the moment we are interested only in the organizational pattern for administering this aid as it has developed since 1947.

The State Department and Foreign Aid. From the very beginning of the aid program there was serious disagreement about the most efficient and expeditious method of its administration and now, after more than a decade, the issue is in no way settled. The central problem has always been the relationship of the Department of State to the over-all aid program. Obviously, if the Department is the principal agency for policy recommendation, and if foreign assistance is to be at or near the center of American policy, there are good reasons for the State Department to exercise some manner of control over the whole operation. On the other hand, the serious diminution of the Department's prestige with Congress and the public, and the formidable arguments against loading the Department down with extensive operating responsibilities, raised doubts about the value of giving it direct responsibility for the program. Various solutions have been attempted, involving virtually every possible form of relationship between the Department and the aid program, but no clear verdict has yet been rendered.[8]

The ECA: Vague Equality. The first organization to administer foreign aid was the Economic Cooperation Administration (ECA), set up in 1948. The ECA was a separate agency headed by an Administrator (Mr. Paul Hoffman) of Cabinet status. Congress deliberately made the ECA independent of control by the State Department and, although it is

---

[7] Between 1951 and 1956, the several commanders were Generals Eisenhower, Ridgeway, Gruenther, and Norstad.

[8] The various alternatives are discussed in the 1951 Brookings report, *The Administration of Foreign Affairs*, pp. 90-101.

generally agreed that the ECA was well operated and that it accomplished its mission with an enviable degree of success, its exact status vis-a-vis the Secretary of State was never defined. President Truman attempted to maintain the integrity of the State Department by insisting that it was primarily responsible for policy and that the ECA was to take direction from it; the Foreign Assistance Act, however, gave the ECA such autonomy that the actual implementation of the Department's primacy was difficult to achieve.

The MSA: Complete Independence. By 1951, when ECA was dissolved, the foreign-aid program had acquired a new dimension. ECA had been concerned only with economic assistance to Europe; the Korean conflict had launched large-scale military assistance programs in Europe, Latin America, and the Far East. Some new administrative device seemed appropriate.

The result was the creation of the Mutual Security Administration (MSA) in 1951. The general tenor of expert opinion during 1950 and 1951 favored the consolidation of all foreign assistance in one agency that would be responsible for all action in the field—that is, it would be entirely independent of the Department of State. This provision Congress wrote into the new law; the MSA was in no sense to be subordinate to the Secretary of State, and had jurisdiction over all phases of assistance except technical cooperation, which retained a semi-autonomous status in the Department of State as the Technical Cooperation Administration (TCA).

Although Mr. Averell Harriman, the Mutual Security Administrator, actually did create mechanisms for coordination with the State Department, the Department of Defense, the Treasury, and other interested agencies, the significant fact is that he did this by preference, not by law. The clear intent of Congress at this time was to debar the Department of State from any direct part in foreign aid administration; the law even deprived the Department of any control over the military aid program, which was divided between MSA and the Department of Defense.

The FOA: Policy Direction. President Eisenhower, by executive reorganization directive, abolished MSA in 1953 and created in its place the Foreign Operations Administration (FOA). This new body's sphere of authority was extended to include not only all the duties of MSA but also those of the Technical Cooperation Administration. FOA brought all aid operations except the supply of military end-items (vested in the Secretary of Defense) under a single operating control; the Administrator (Mr. Harold Stassen) was charged with coordinating the military aid program with the others.

Although FOA had complete action responsibility, it was not in as independent a position as had been MSA. The Secretary of State, according to the reorganization plan, had direct policy control over the FOA Administrator; even "subordinate levels of the Department of State" were given authority to furnish direction to FOA. FOA's organizational structure paralleled the geographic bureaus of the Department, and it was clearly expected that at all levels coordination between FOA and State would take the form of policy direction to the former by the latter. The net effect of the shift from MSA to FOA was a gain in policy authority by the State Department that more than balanced its loss of operating responsibilities.

The ICA: Back to the Department. The most recent organizational shift took place in 1955 when FOA was abolished and replaced by the International Cooperation Administration (ICA), which—so much for a "non-program" State Department—was brought within the administrative structure of the Department.[9] ICA performs all the functions of FOA; the difference is purely hierarchical. ICA is a division of the Department; the Administrator (Mr. John Hollister was the first) is a subordinate of the Secretary of State and is as completely under his authority as any Assistant Secretary. The new arrangement had one great advantage, in that it finally gave the Secretary the power directly to coordinate non-military foreign aid activities with other aspects of foreign policy, something the need for which had been felt from the very inception of the program. On the other hand, it immediately revived the old arguments about whether or not the Department should have program responsibility.

International information

Another policy area of great significance is "international information," a delicate euphemism for the somewhat more blunt words "propaganda" and "public relations." Like military foreign policy and foreign aid, the development of large-scale information programs was an event of the postwar period. Propaganda for political purposes is a pursuit in which Americans do not yet thoroughly feel at home (although why this should be so is somewhat difficult to understand; in the United States advertising is a fine art), and the record compiled by the various information programs is not breath-taking.[10]

---

[9] See the statement by Secretary of State Dulles, (January 23, 1956), *Department of State Bulletin* (February 6, 1956).

[10] For an interesting and recent statement of the problems of informational activi-

The Propaganda Program. The pressures of the cold war forced the United States to develop an elaborate, if somewhat helter-skelter, propaganda program. The State Department was central to the process from the beginning, with its own activities being conducted by the International Information Administration. The two major areas of the Department's work in this field prior to 1953 were the Voice of America, a global network of radio stations beaming propaganda at hostile and neutral nations, and the United States Information Service, under whose auspices hundreds of American "information centers" were set up throughout the world. These last provided outlets for American publications of all sorts, and gave thousands of foreigners their first insights into what the United States was really like.

But the Department of State was not alone in the field. It is a characteristic of American government today that every operating agency in the executive branch is acutely sensitive to the need for good public relations, and nearly every one of the many agencies with responsibilities in foreign policy began to handle the propaganda aspects of its own mission. The State Department's principal competitor in this field was the series of foreign-aid agencies, notably ECA and MSA. Rapid turnover in personnel, persistent attacks from all directions by a variety of opponents, discontinuity in policy, and a failure in its own public relations made the International Information Administration a somewhat less than popular agency. Its critics pointed it out as a glaring example of the inadvisability of conferring program responsibility on the Department of State.

Psychological Warfare. Further complicating American information policy was the concept, born apparently some time in the early stages of the Korean war, of "psychological warfare." This phrase implied something new in foreign policy, aimed at undercutting the strength of opposing regimes by destroying the bonds of loyalty between the people and their governments. It was argued that, if the United States were to use the resources of modern techniques of persuasion in a coordinated attack on the stability of opposition governments, it might be possible to solve all the problems of the cold war at one blow, with great economy in manpower, resources, and money.

---

ties and their administration, see the report by Howland H. Sargeant, "Information and Cultural Representation Overseas," in Vincent Barnett, ed., *The Representation of the United States Abroad* (New York: The American Assembly, Columbia University, 1956), pp. 67-119. This volume is the report of the findings of the Ninth American Assembly, on the subject of American representation overseas, held May 3-6, 1956.

Interagency committees of various sorts were created to develop an over-all strategy of psychological warfare and to coordinate its execution by the appropriate departments. Between 1951 and 1953 a great deal of effort was expended with little perceptible change in the pattern of propaganda being put forth by the United States overseas.[11] President Eisenhower, shortly after taking office, instituted an entirely new survey of the entire field of psychological warfare by the so-called Jackson Committee. The committee's report, made in mid-1953, exploded the entire concept of psychological warfare as a specialized technique, susceptible of manipulation by specialists in persuasion, and capable of ending the cold war speedily and economically. The committee contended that all policy had its psychological aspects, that they could not be separated from other facets, and that everyone engaged in policy implementation was in effect carrying on psychological warfare.

The United States Information Agency. The United States Information Agency (USIA) was created in 1953 by executive reorganization directive. This body was the counterpart in its field of the Foreign Operations Administration; it took over all information programs from whatever agencies had been carrying them on. In particular, it absorbed the International Information Administration and the Voice of America. Again like the FOA, its operational monopoly was not matched by equal freedom in policy. Instead it was ordered to follow the policy direction of the Secretary of State; the material it distributed (whether by broadcast or by printing) was subject to censorship by the Department.

Even more illustrative of the status of the Agency was the relation of its overseas representatives, known as Public Affairs Officers (following the delicate nomenclature of the Division of Public Affairs [relations] in the Department of State). These propaganda chiefs were to be part of the American diplomatic mission in the country to which they were assigned and, although under the general administrative direction of the Director of USIA, were also under the operational control of the resident American chief of mission. Both in Washington and in the field, the propaganda arm of American policy is now under the day-by-day control of the State Department.[12] This development is part of the broader plan of clarifying the status of the Department as chief policy-maker for the entire government.

---

[11] An interesting view of the early stages of the American "sykewar" effort is presented by Edward W. Barrett, former Assistant Secretary of State for Public Affairs, in his valedictory, *Truth Is Our Weapon* (New York: Funk and Wagnalls Co., 1953).

[12] Sargeant, in Barnett, *Representation,* thoroughly approves of this status for public affairs officers (p. 79).

OVERSEAS REPRESENTATION OF THE UNITED STATES

The United States, like all sovereign states, executes a large part of its foreign policy by means of its representatives stationed in foreign countries. The new international status of the United States has resulted both in a vast increase in the size of the American representation abroad and in the growth of a number of new problems stemming from it.

Historically, the bulk of the task of representation was carried on by the State Department through the United States Foreign Service. The multiplication of programs and the discovery of new channels of power has created new categories of representation. This has led to problems of duplication, overlapping, and competition. This section will deal with both the traditional representatives of the State Department and the broader question of multiagency participation.

The foreign service

Prior to World War I, the overseas representation of the United States —diplomatic and consular—was generally considered to be the legitimate prey of the spoils system. As long as foreign policy was a minor adjunct to the important business of the United States, no need was felt for a professional approach, and overseas posts were thought of as particularly juicy rewards for faithful political service. This principle applied at all levels of appointment, from ambassadorships to clerkships.

It was not until the 1920's that some realization of the folly of permitting foreign policy to be implemented by unskilled amateurs or political opportunists penetrated the congressional consciousness. With the creation of the career foreign service by the Rogers Act (1924), the United States accepted the idea of professionalism in overseas representation, and the modern history of the foreign service began.[13]

The Career Foreign Service. The theory of the Rogers Act was that there should be recruited, by an extremely selective process, a highly skilled, very intelligent, and supremely dedicated elite corps of foreign service offices. These men were to spend their careers in representing the United States abroad in both the consular and diplomatic services

---

[13] A valuable sketch of the history and the problems of the American foreign service is contained in J. Rives Childs, *American Foreign Service* (New York: Henry Holt & Co., 1948); an eloquent defense of the career service is made by former Ambassador Hugh Gibson, in *The Road to Foreign Policy* (Garden City, N. Y.: Doubleday, Doran, 1944), Chapters III, IV.

(which were administratively combined by the Act). They were to be available for short-term assignments in the Department itself, but it was expected that the bulk of their duty time would be spent in overseas assignments.

The career idea, of course, never was extended to the very top of the system. Chiefs of mission were specifically excluded from the foreign service; the practical maximum of career opportunity was that of Counselor of Embassy (the second ranking post at an embassy) or that of consul general. Politically significant posts were still to be filled by presidential appointment and subject to confirmation by the Senate.

Over the years the selection system produced a career service that corresponded closely to the original idea. Success on the entrance examinations required both a highly specialized education—usually involving graduate study—and a particular personality type (measured by an oral examination before a panel of Foreign Service Officers). Advancement in the Service in practice required acceptance of the unwritten (and to some extent written) traditions of the Department; failure to fit the pattern usually resulted in a blighted career. As the Service matured during the 1930's, a definite "Foreign Service type" began to emerge, characterized by technical facility, a faith in order and tradition, a code of gentlemanliness, a profound distrust of novelty in substance or procedure, and great personal charm. We should also note that salary schedules were maintained at a level where a foreign service career virtually demanded an outside source of income.

And yet, despite the shortcomings of the foreign service, we must admit that it performed very creditably—within its self-imposed limitations—up to 1941. It was not charged with making policy in broad terms; this was the responsibility of the civil service personnel at home in the Department. Its mission was that of execution, and under the narrowly conceived policy of the 1930's, it fulfilled this responsibility with great skill.

Civil Service Vs. Foreign Service. The difficulties of the foreign service began during World War II. As the State Department added new functions every day, most of which involved some form of overseas representation, it was soon discovered that there were not enough Foreign Service Officers to go around. "Non-career" representatives—civil-service employees of the Department or even civilians—were sent overseas and worked side by side with the FSO's themselves. After the war, when the Department absorbed entire agencies such as the Office of Strategic Services, even more such agents appeared abroad. The career foreign service found itself in danger of being engulfed by a tidal wave of what some of its members felt to be lesser beings.

As the postwar period progressed and as the responsibilities of the Department showed no signs of diminishing, a serious split developed in the overseas establishments. The FSO's, aware of their prestige advantage and led by long-time members of the group who had risen to high rank, deliberately set out to "take care of their own"—or so the story went as told by non-career employees. Charges of favoritism, of social and professional discrimination, of policy "freezeouts," and so on began to be leveled at the FSO's; on their part, the career personnel alleged their privileged right to leadership in overseas missions, even at the expense of higher-ranking "non-career" specialists.

At the same time, the stay-at-home civil service staff of the Department, charged with policy-making and the direction of the overseas personnel, was undertaking a small-scale cold war of its own. FSO's on home assignment found it difficult to function effectively with the permanent staff. The Department was in danger of losing much of its efficiency in a squabble over personnel status.

The Wriston Report and "Integration." The obvious solution had long been known. In a permanent large-scale operation such as that in which the Department was engaged, there was no rational reason to continue a bifurcated personnel system. It made no sense to deny the United States the policy-making wisdom accumulated by long overseas service by the career personnel; it was equally nonsensical to require that policy be made by men who usually had no personal experience in the areas for which they were responsible. Amalgamation of the two services would solve both these operating difficulties at once.

Between 1948 and 1953 several attempts had been made to put some such plan into operation, but without success. The Foreign Service wished to keep its exclusive status; many of the civil-service group had no interest in overseas service. It was not until 1954, under the direction of Secretary Dulles, that amalgamation was accomplished. It came about as the result of recommendations by the Secretary's Public Committee on Personnel, known as the "Wriston Committee" after its chairman, Dr. Henry Merritt Wriston, the former president of Brown University.[14]

"Integration"—a word that became common currency in the Department for several years—involved the classification of virtually all the nonclerical posts of the Department, both overseas and home, as "dual": that is, capable of being filled either by career FSO's or civil service

---

[14] The Committee's report, *Toward a Stronger Foreign Service* (Washington, D. C.: U. S. Government Printing Office, 1954), was submitted to the Secretary on 18 May 1954. See also Dr. Wriston's *Diplomacy in a Democracy* (New York: Harper & Bros., 1956).

personnel. A directive from the Secretary then ordered the gradual integration of the two services, not to be accomplished by the creation of an entirely new hierarchy, but by the absorption of the great bulk of the civil service policy personnel into the Foreign Service by "lateral entry." Civil service employees not wishing to become liable for overseas service were to be separated without prejudice. The upshot was to be the creation of a vastly augmented Foreign Service capable of manning the policy desks in the Department or any post overseas.

Integration proceeded steadily throughout 1954, 1955, and 1956. There were many administrative difficulties involved in lateral entry, and not a small amount of hard feelings; by and large, however, there was general satisfaction that the Foreign Service under the new scheme was destined to retain a sizeable amount of its old esprit and at the same time to benefit from the large infusion of new blood.

The New Foreign Service. The Wriston Report also dealt with another difficulty of the old Foreign Service. A combination of a peculiar philosophy of selection and restricted personnel budgets had made the FSO's an over-homogenous group. The Committee argued that recruitment policies should be amended to attract candidates from a broader social, economic, educational, and geographical base. Its assumption, though never made explicit, was that the Service should be "democratized." [15]

Beginning in 1955 the recruitment recommendations were put into effect. An entirely new examination procedure was instituted, stressing general education and innate intelligence rather than specialized knowledge. Emphasis was placed on obtaining young men and women whose training encompassed such diverse fields as agriculture, accounting, and law. The first round of appointments under the new system revealed greater diversity than any under the old, and there was some ground for hoping that the Committee's ideal of a "more representative" Foreign Service would be, to some extent, realized.

The Organization of an Overseas Mission. The organization of American diplomatic missions overseas vary of course according to the importance of the host state to the United States and to the volume of business transacted, but certain organizational patterns are common, at least among the larger ones. The mission is headed by the "chief of mission," of whom three-fourths are ambassadors and the remainder ministers. His immediate aide is usually the counselor of embassy, who succeeds (as charge d'affaires) when the ambassador is absent. Below the counselor the mission splits into operating sections according to the

---

[15] *Toward A Stronger Foreign Service*, pp. 39-44.

nature of the work load; political and economic sections are universal, while cultural sections are increasingly common. Outside the normal hierarchy of the mission, but full parts of it, are the various special attaches. In addition to the familiar military, naval, and air attaches, commercial, agricultural, legal, labor, and several other types of attaches exist. The attaches have a peculiar status. Although they are full-fledged members of the ambassador's staff, they remain employees of other agencies than the State Department. They are nominated by the Departments of Commerce, Agriculture, Army, Navy, Air Force, Justice, and so on; they remain administratively under their home department's control.

Multiagency representation

We have earlier remarked on the growth of other agencies than the State Department in the execution of American foreign policy. In 1951 the Brookings Institution discovered that 43 different Federal agencies were maintaining overseas staffs and executing programs.[16] Their relationships with the regular diplomatic missions varied widely, with no single principle governing. Many members of the regular diplomatic staffs complained that their function was being degraded and their efforts bypassed. All recent studies of the execution of American foreign policy have dealt with this question.

Categories of Representation. The non-State Department representatives abroad can be grouped in the same three categories discussed in the previous section: military, foreign-aid, and informational. Between 1947 and 1954 each of the three types of representation grew to the point where in many states it rivalled the American diplomatic mission in prestige and in importance.

Military representation occurred through the various service attaches in the embassies, through the military-aid missions, and through the training groups. Foreign aid representation was at its height under ECA where the various "country chiefs" of ECA had more money to dole out and consequently were in a position to maneuver the resident American ambassador off the stage and into the wings. A few of them, it might be noted, did exactly that. The MSA, since it simplified the administration of American aid, somewhat improved this situation. Informational

---

[16] *The Administration of Foreign Affairs*, p. 244; see also Macmahon, *Administration in Foreign Affairs*, Chapter 3: "Field Structure for Foreign Programs."

activities were never the threat to regular diplomats that the first two types were, largely because State carried on so many itself.

The Attack on the Problem. We have already suggested the outlines of the solution recommended by the Brookings study and the Hoover Commission. In line with the general doctrine now governing the execution of American policy that State is the single agency *primarily* responsible for foreign *policy*, and that coordination is to be brought about under State Department *leadership*, the moves taken in the past five or six years have all been aimed at strengthening the position of the senior foreign-affairs agency. We have seen how USIA is clearly under the policy direction of the Department, both at home and abroad. Foreign and technical aid are now joined in ICA, which is an integral part of the Department. The MAAG in each foreign state is now ordered to work under the general direction of the American diplomatic mission there, although the administration of military aid is in the hands of the Department of Defense.

The theory behind the attack on multiagency representation abroad can be summed up in President Eisenhower's language when he sent the foreign affairs reorganization plans to Congress in 1953: "[It shall be the duty of] each Chief of Diplomatic Mission in each foreign country [to] provide effective coordination of, and foreign policy direction with respect to, all United States Government activities in the country."[17] Unassailable as this administrative principle is in the abstract, our knowledge of the tenacity of the bureaucratic urge to survive will make it a reasonably safe assumption that the full implementation of the directive will require a formidable amount of time.

A NOTE ON NEGOTIATION

The day-by-day conduct of relations between the United States and foreign states that we call "diplomatic negotiation" is a highly complex subject and a fascinating one. We cannot, however, discuss it in the detail it deserves in this study. The "negotiation" with which we are concerned here is negotiation of a special type—or, rather, three special types—that takes place outside the normal diplomatic ambassador-foreign minister relationship. We shall consider the President as negotiator, the use of special negotiating emissaries, and American delegations to the United Nations and international conferences. In each of them we shall find problems that will throw some light on the accomplishment of American policy objectives.

---

[17] *Congressional Record* (June 1, 1953), p. 5849.

The president as negotiator

We know that every President, in one sense or another, does a great deal of negotiation. Usually this is at one remove, by advising or directing the American personnel involved in the bargaining; occasionally the President has face-to-face contact with ambassadors of foreign states. But the development of the Presidency into an instrument of close-quarter and detailed negotiation is a fairly recent development.

A significant precedent was set by Woodrow Wilson, who left the United States to go to Paris to help work out the Peace of Paris in 1919. During the 1920's President Hoover received visits from many foreign chiefs of government, notably Premier Laval of France and Prime Minister MacDonald of Great Britain. These were not mere state visits, but hard-working bargaining sessions. It was during World War II that Franklin D. Roosevelt, executing his mission as chief of grand strategy for the United States, met with Winston Churchill, Marshal Stalin, Chiang Kai-shek, and several other chiefs of state in an important series of conferences. Here basic decisions were made and hard bargains struck.

Presidents Truman and Eisenhower kept the tradition alive after 1945 by frequent meetings with the heads of allied states. The most dramatic recent reinforcement of the practice occurred in July, 1955, with the famous "summit" conference at Geneva that marked what came to be thought of as the end of the parliamentary phase of the cold war.

When the President Should Negotiate. Presidential negotiation is appropriate under certain circumstances. Perhaps the most compelling reason is the desire to deal with a question that, for whatever reason, must be handled only at the highest level. There is very little real advantage in the President dealing personally with ambassadors, foreign ministers, or other lower-ranking foreign officials; he is most effective when he is facing his opposite numbers. This means ordinarily that the President copes best with broad and important questions that defy solution lower in the hierarchy because of their complexity, their sensitivity, or their public significance. It would also seem that the President's role is most aptly that of either opening or closing a negotiation; there would seem to be little value in taking an on-going discussion out of the hands of professional diplomats and giving it to the President. When he is able to initiate an entirely new area, however, such as Mr. Eisenhower's "open sky" disarmament proposal at Geneva, or terminate a long controversy (as Mr. Roosevelt did at Yalta on the issue of voting procedure in the United Nations Security Council), Presidential negotiation may be of major usefulness.

109

Strengths of Presidential Negotiation. Presidential negotiations have certain inherent strengths. In the first place, a top-level conference is always newsworthy and everything done there is invested with a quality of drama and portentousness. Agreement reached under such circumstances is almost certain to receive popular support. This leads to another strength: Presidential action is admirably suited to breaking impasses, either by widening the agenda (proposing new formulas in a highly charged atmosphere) or by making drastic shifts in policy on his own initiative. Granted good will on the other side of the table, top-level negotiations can cover more ground more quickly than can discussions at any other level. This is largely because of the time advantage gained by having the President directly involved (a third strength). Channels are bypassed, agreements can be rapidly pinned down, and rapid transformation of a large area of dispute is possible.

Weaknesses of Presidential Negotiation. Some of the advantages, however, are offset by corresponding weaknesses. The President is always to some extent the prisoner of his staff; he can seldom bring to a discussion any more information and alternatives than have been given him by his subordinates. If the executive staff work is faulty, mistakes can be made that will be all the graver because the President himself committed them.[18] We might note that the very flexibility that the President possesses might be the cause of serious disruption in the more orderly patterns of policy being developed by the State Department; this is a serious danger if the President's information is incomplete or inaccurate. Another objection, not to be dismissed lightly, is that Presidential negotiation serves further to degrade the operation and significance of the regular diplomatic corps by denying it the right to deal with matters of major significance.

For better or worse, however, modern transportation and communication facilities make it convenient for the President to step into a negotiation whenever he or his advisers think it appropriate. The advantages of the device, added to its relative ease, promise to make it long-lived, if of relatively infrequent appearance.

The use of special emissaries

Another atypical negotiating technique is the employment of special emissaries of one type or another to take charge of a particular problem.

---

[18] There is some feeling that President Roosevelt was the victim of some bad staff work at Yalta.

Several of the considerations involved in Presidential negotiating apply in these cases also.

The Secretary of State as Negotiator. To an even greater extent than the President, the Secretary of State has become a top-level negotiator. He acts more and more frequently in face-to-face relationships with his opposite numbers everywhere in the world. His activities in this area have many of the strengths of Presidential intervention, plus some advantages uniquely his own. The disadvantages of the Secretary's practice of negotiation likewise to some extent are shared with the President.

Affirmatively, the Secretary of State is free to travel more widely than is the President; a visit from the American Secretary of State is much less of a great event in the affairs of a foreign capital. It is also much less difficult for the Secretary to break away from Washington. His discussions with other foreign ministers, whether in Washington or not, are less likely to be front-page news everywhere in the world, and the prospects for significant compromise are thereby increased.

The major disadvantage of negotiating by the Secretary of State arises from the dilution of his primary role of chief foreign-policy adviser to the President. When he is abroad he cannot be in as close touch with affairs in the Department; to some perhaps minor extent the effectiveness of the Department is reduced as a result. His frequent involvement in negotiation places a heavier burden on his own chief assistants, and the caliber of the Department often thus depends on the ability of the second-level administrators.

Both the advantages and the disadvantages of Secretarial negotiation were demonstrated by the two recent Secretaries of State who indulged in the practice most freely, James F. Byrnes and John Foster Dulles. Mr. Byrnes spent most of his year in office in one long round of foreign-ministers' meetings dealing with the postwar settlement; Mr. Dulles set what must have been a record, if not a pattern, for Secretaries of State by an almost incessant shuttling about the world between 1953 and 1958. Mr. Dulles apparently viewed his role as that of a trouble-shooter; whenever American relations with any important non-communist nation became troubled or complicated, Mr. Dulles made a hurried trip to the scene to smooth things over. It seems clear that Mr. Dulles' skill and experience as a negotiator led him to place a high premium on this aspect of his task.

Perhaps because we are so close to it in time, the attempt to judge the effect of direct negotiation by the Secretary leads one to consider the question in the light of Mr. Dulles' record. There is some evidence that his many journeys did succeed in straightening out many thorny impasses in American policy; outstanding examples are the rationalization of American and British positions on the negotiation of SEATO in 1954 and the improvement of United States-Indonesian relations in 1956. But there is little doubt that he impaired morale in the Foreign Service by his almost brusque disregard of the full-time American representatives in the countries he visited; there is some reason also to believe that his frequent absences served to freeze American policy into almost a fixed mold. This was particularly unfortunate since the rapid change in Soviet policy late in 1955 coincided with President Eisenhower's first serious illness, and there was great need for someone to impart flexibility to the American response to the new challenge.

The Use of Personal Representatives. Less common today than during the wartime period is the employment of personal representatives of the President for special, "one-shot" negotiations. Ever since President Truman startled the world during the 1948 presidential campaign by proposing to send then Chief Justice Fred Vinson to Moscow to negotiate directly with Stalin, officials have been reluctant to use this technique. During the war, Harry Hopkins—the private and unofficial representative of Mr. Roosevelt—served an extremely useful purpose, performing missions that could not have been handled in any other way. The long-run course of American policy today, however, minimizes the possibility of extensive recourse to the "presidential agent" as an instrument of negotiation. Barring war or other extreme emergency, the President himself or the Secretary of State will be able to take over the delicate and high-level conversations that Hopkins (and, during World War I, Colonel Edward M. House) undertook.

American representation to the United Nations

The United Nations is, like the League of Nations before it, the scene of what some called "permanent negotiation." It is diplomacy with a difference, however, and negotiation there offers problems and opportunities that are unique.

The Nature of American Representation. American representation at the United Nations is headed by a permanent representative with the rank of Ambassador. He acts usually as the American representative on the Security Council and also acts as chief of the United States delegation to the General Assembly. He is assisted by a permanent American delegation that sits on the various commissions and councils in which the United States has membership.

The delegation to the General Assembly is deliberately chosen to incorporate variety. The Secretary of State himself usually appears for part of the session, most commonly during the opening general debate. The remainder of the delegation is composed, more or less equally, of professional diplomats, governmental personnel, both executive and legislative, and what we might call "public" representatives. Among the more noteworthy of the recent laymen chosen for the General Assembly delegation was Mr. Henry Ford II.

The Nature of United Nations Negotiation. United Nations negotiation differs from ordinary diplomacy in several important ways. In the first place, it is continuous; communication and contact are constant, thus eliminating many of the delays to which diplomacy is often subject. Second, it is multilateral. Almost all of the member states maintain permanent delegations that are available immediately to enter into any negotiation in which they are interested. Conference diplomacy has great strengths and equally great weaknesses, and the United Nations is conference diplomacy at its zenith. Finally, a great deal of United Nations negotiation is either carried on in public or else becomes public property almost immediately. Public opinion is therefore a factor of which every United Nations discussion must take due account, and the requirement of public debate and voting makes for a much more careful calculation of the propaganda effects of policy than is the case otherwise.

part 3:

THE HERITAGE OF THE PAST

5 : Nineteenth century trends

For many Americans, "foreign policy" as something about which the citizen should concern himself dates from some point in the period between 1940 and 1946. Prior to the crisis that brought about World War II, American disinterest in international affairs was endemic; popular ignorance and unconcern about international relations was a dominant cultural trait in the United States between 1920 and 1939. Foreigners have often remarked about the non-historical outlook of American culture and its alleged effect of eliminating a sense of continuity between the present and the past. In no area is it more true that Americans are unaware of the record of their own past than it is in foreign affairs.

But American foreign policy has a history, and a long and complicated one at that. Ever since the Treaty of Paris in 1783 that established American independence, the United States has been dealing with other nations in the complex process that we call international relations. There has been, as we have conceived the term, an American "foreign policy" during the entire century and three-quarters that the United States has been a sovereign state; during these decades commitments were made, lines of action laid down, and concepts of interest formulated. Americans now alive are in large measure the heirs of the record, good and bad, made by their ancestors. That the statesmen of another day are today often without honor or even any particular recognition by their descendants in no way minimizes the importance of their work to an understanding of the foreign policy problem the United States faces today.

This chapter and the next one will attempt to characterize the course of

American foreign policy up to the end of World War II. We shall be concerned in this chapter with the broad trends of emphasis and development during the nineteenth century; Chapter 6 will deal with the first forty-five years of the twentieth century, a much shorter but much more crowded period. We shall not attempt to detail, or even to summarize, the continuous story in a strict chronological sense; excellent studies of superb scholarship and considerable literary value have already performed this task for us.[1] Our task will rather be to extract from the whole of the history of American foreign policy those particular elements, whether broad trends or uniquely important events, that have special pertinence to contemporary American foreign relations.

THE FORMATIVE CENTURY

The nineteenth century—by which we mean the period of somewhat more than a hundred years between the Treaty of Paris (1783) and the Open Door notes of 1899 and 1900—may be called the "formative era" in American foreign policy. During this time two sorts of things happened that have had consequences far beyond their historical setting. First, a number of relatively fixed policy lines aimed at particular objectives were developed by the American government and came to acquire the semi-sacrosanct character of fixed commitments. With the more unfortunate consequences of some of these undertakings the United States is still struggling. Second, and related to the first by the normal processes of democratic government, a rather clear popular tradition of American participation in foreign affairs became an article of faith with the bulk of the politically articulate and active population. Much of the substance of American policy and much mass opinion about it derives, directly or indirectly, from the nineteenth century experience. We shall consider the major elements of this tradition in Chapter 7.

Continental expansion: "Manifest Destiny"

Certainly the most obvious foreign-policy trend of the nineteenth

---

[1] The leading diplomatic histories are those by Samuel Flagg Bemis, *A Diplomatic History of the United States,* third ed. (New York: Henry Holt, Inc., 1950); Thomas A. Bailey, *Diplomatic History of the American People,* third ed. (New York: Crowell, Inc., 1949;) Julius A. Pratt, *A History of United States Foreign Policy,* (Englewood Cliffs, N. J.: Prentice-Hall, Inc., 1955); and Dexter Perkins, *The Evolution of American Foreign Policy* (New York: Oxford University Press, 1948). Among the many shorter collections of documents, one of the most useful is Ruhl J. Bartlett, *The Record of American Diplomacy,* third ed. (New York: Alfred A. Knopf, Inc., 1953).

century was the process of continental expansion that began almost as soon as the new United States set itself up in business as an independent sovereignty. We should recapitulate briefly the series of moves that brought the United States to its present continental boundaries within a short fifty-year period of active expansion.

The Louisiana Purchase. The first great acquisition—and the largest single one—was the purchase of the Louisiana Territory from France in 1803. This transaction, one of the greatest bargains in history, was consummated by President Jefferson as the result of a complex maneuver in the game of European power politics.

In 1800 Napoleon of France had persuaded Spain to cede him the Louisiana Territory. This disconcerted the British, who were already preparing Bonaparte's ultimate destruction. The United States also became uneasy at the thought of having powerful France as its neighbor to the west instead of weak Spain, as well as at the possibility of being forever barred from access to the port of New Orleans. Napoleon, on his part, soon lost his interest in Louisiana in the light of his pressing need for funds to continue his European conquests. Jefferson, supported by Britain, offered to purchase Louisiana for $15,000,000. Napoleon agreed, and in one stroke of a pen the United States had more than doubled its area.

The Floridas. The next step took the United States southward. "The Floridas," comprising today all of the state of Florida and the Gulf coast of Alabama and Mississippi, were under Spanish sovereignty at the time of the Louisiana purchase. For fifteen years after 1803, American expansionism clashed with weak Spanish rule; border incidents involving violence and protracted (and sometimes questionable) negotiations succeeded only in perpetuating an impasse. Finally, in 1818 Secretary of State John Quincy Adams presented Spain with a virtual ultimatum. The Bourbons surrendered; in 1819 Spain ceded the United States all her lands east of the Mississippi (as well as her claimed right to Oregon) in return for some token concessions from the United States, chiefly an American waiver of an admittedly shaky claim to Texas.

Texas. In 1845 the independent republic of Texas was annexed to the United States by joint resolution of Congress. Texas had seceded from Mexico in 1836 after a successful war of independence and had thereupon sought admission to the Union. Political pressures, generated largely by the slavery issue, made it impossible to secure the necessary two-thirds majority in the Senate in favor of a treaty of annexation. A bare majority could be scraped up in both houses for a joint resolution, and this somewhat questionable device was used to approve the annexation of the only independent sovereignty ever to become one of the United States.[2]

Oregon. The Oregon territory, including most of the northwestern corner of the United States and part of present-day British Columbia, had long been claimed by both Great Britain and the United States. After the election of President James K. Polk in 1844, the United States determined to settle the question once and for all. Supported by an expansionist fervor in the United States that was to result also in the annexation of Texas and the war with Mexico, Polk took a strong diplomatic line with the British in 1845. By mid-1846 a relatively favorable compromise was reached. The boundary, running along the 49th parallel, added a rich and large territory to the existing United States.

The Mexican Cession. By the terms of the Treaty of Guadalupe Hidalgo that terminated the war with Mexico, in 1848 the United States gained another enormous bloc of territory. The area ceded included present-day California, Nevada, Utah, and parts of Arizona, Colorado, New Mexico, and Wyoming. Vast as this new acquisition was, it almost failed to satisfy the expansionist elements in the United States. The "all-Mexico" movement gained such momentum that total annexation was seriously discussed in high government circles.[3]

The Gadsden Purchase. The territory won in the Mexican War filled in the outlines of the continental United States of today with a single exception: the Gila River valley in southern Arizona and New Mexico. In 1853 (a half-century after the Louisiana purchase) the American minister to Mexico, James Gadsden, successfully negotiated the purchase of this area from Mexico for $10,000,000. Subject to some minor frontier rectification, the limits of the United States on the North American continent had been reached.

Hemisphere hegemony: The Monroe Doctrine

To many Americans, the phrase "Monroe Doctrine" has a familiar ring. Depending on their historical knowledge, their political sophistication, and their educational background, they know a variety of things about it. Most people suspect that it has something important to do with Latin America; a smaller number understands that it also has implications

---

[2] Pratt, *A History of United States Foreign Policy*, pp. 231-233, discusses the political maneuvering. It is worth noting that Hawaii was also an independent republic at the time of its annexation by the United States.

[3] Bailey, *Diplomatic History of the American People*, p. 278.

for the "Old World" in general and Europe in particular. Its more subtle ramifications tend to be overlooked in its contemporary relevance as a symbol of the "good old days" in American foreign policy.

Apart from its political significance, the Monroe Doctrine as developed during the nineteenth century became perhaps the most important, and certainly the most fixed, principle of United States foreign policy. A large part of its earlier significance has evaporated under twentieth century conditions, but enough remains that it merits continued study. American preoccupation with the western hemisphere is as great today as it ever was, despite that area's relative decline in popular awareness under the pressures arising from other parts of the world.

The Original Declaration (1823). The "Monroe Doctrine" proper refers to certain paragraphs in President James Monroe's annual message to Congress on December 2, 1823. In these sections he dealt with the problem of the newly-independent republics of Latin America and the growing possibility that the European powers might intervene to return them to the European colonial powers. On the basis of this specific issue a doctrine was formulated that went far beyond the crisis at hand.

Monroe's message first declared that the "American continents" were "henceforth not to be considered as subjects for future colonization by any European power." Any attempt on the part of the European states "to extend their system to any portion of this Hemisphere" would be considered as "dangerous to our peace and safety." The New World was thereby declared to be evermore out of bounds to new European imperialism, although the United States specifically refused to make any statement about such colonies as then existed. In return for forbidding European penetration in the Americas, Monroe then restated the intention of the United States to refrain from interfering in exclusively European matters.[4] This latter point, often thought of as one of the doctrinal roots of isolationism, we shall discuss later in this chapter.

The Polk Restatement (1845). The doctrine, so bravely enunciated, lapsed without application until the Oregon crisis in 1845. As a part of the vigorous diplomacy he was conducting with Great Britain, President Polk's message to Congress in December, 1845, averred flatly that "no future European colony or dominion shall with our consent be planted or established on any part of the North American continent."[5] This carried Monroe's original doctrine a step farther. The original

---

[4] The relevant portions of Monroe's message are quoted in Bartlett, *Record of American Diplomacy*, pp. 181-3.

[5] Dexter Perkins, *Hands Off: A History of the Monroe Doctrine* (Boston: Little, Brown and Co., 1941), p. 62.

doctrine had been intended to inhibit European colonization or armed intervention; Polk's reformulation was expanded to include even diplomatic action as falling within the forbidden area.[6] Polk's exhumation of the Monroe Doctrine created a binding precedent; thenceforth it exerted a measurable influence on American attitudes toward the hemisphere.

The Mexican Crisis. The first real test of the Monroe Doctrine came during the American Civil War when Napoleon III of France established his puppet, Maximilian of Austria, as Emperor of Mexico. This was an open defiance of the doctrine, and despite sometimes frenzied diplomacy during the Civil War, the French-supported regime in Mexico survived until after Appomattox. Once the American decks were cleared by the end of internal conflict, however, the situation changed. American pressure on the increasingly uncomfortable Napoleon induced him to withdraw his troops, and the native Mexican forces destroyed Maximilian's *papier-maché* empire. The Monroe Doctrine had been vindicated; an open European attempt to penetrate an American preserve had been turned back.

We should pause here a moment to consider another point that we shall later be dealing with in more detail. The Monroe Doctrine, from its birth through the Mexican affair, represented an undertaking whose implementation was beyond the unassisted power of the United States. The American government alone was physically unable to exclude European power from the western hemisphere. What made the doctrine successful was the unadmitted but real harmony of interest between the United States and Britain. The British, for political, strategic, and economic reasons of their own, were as interested as were Americans in keeping continental states out of Latin America. For the successful establishment of American hemisphere hegemony that came after 1865 the United States can in large measure thank British policy between 1820 and 1870.[7]

The Establishment of American Dominance. After the Civil War, the United States turned to Central and South America as a matter of right. With American power demonstrated both in internal warfare and in its relations with France, the United States came to interpret the Monroe Doctrine as meaning something more than merely the defense of the hemisphere against European penetration. As evidence multiplied that the little republics to the South were caught in an apparently chronic instability and periodic revolution and crisis, it became respectable in the United States to argue that somebody should take care of them, so as to

---

[6] Perkins, *Hands Off*, p. 90.

[7] George Lipsky, *John Quincy Adams* (New York: Crowell, 1950), pp. 305-6.

protect their people from the worst consequences of their failure to govern themselves properly. What could be more natural and just than for the United States to assume this civilizing duty? The Monroe Doctrine had long before made clear the peculiar American interest in Latin America, and now the time had come for the United States to fulfill its claims of benevolence.

How much of this argument was sincere and how much merely a cover for jingoist expansionism or simple greed is difficult to determine, but from our point of view it is largely irrelevant. Little by little, beginning in the Caribbean and working gradually southward, an increasing measure of American control over Latin America became apparent under the cloak of the Monroe Doctrine. So far had this gone by 1885 that Secretary of State Olney could claim that "the United States is practically sovereign on this continent, and its fiat is law upon the subjects to which it confines its interposition." [8] The development of this trend into what was known as "dollar diplomacy" did not occur until after 1900, but the principle was well established long before the turn of the century.

Anglo-American cooperation: the unadmitted alliance

We have already referred briefly to the fact that British cooperation with the United States contributed largely to the success of the Monroe Doctrine in its early period. This condition had even larger implications throughout the nineteenth century.

What is remarkable about the long record of Anglo-American relations during this period was that neither party would openly admit the fact of cooperation. The burden of responsibility for this condition rests mainly on Americans; the popular image of Britain as the enemy of American independence made open and admitted coordination of effort a political near-impossibility. "The redcoats are coming" had too strong a hold on American ideology for any formalization of what was for many years a real—if tacit—working agreement.

The Harmony of Interest. The design of Britain's nineteenth-century foreign policy found a secure place for the expanding and maturing United States. London built its approach on the foundation of the European balance of power. It was definitely in British interest for the

---

[8] *Foreign Relations of the United States, 1895*, I, 558 (Washington, D. C.: U. S. Government Printing Office, 1896).

United States to remain out of the circle of European states. American noninvolvement in Europe and its fixation on the western hemisphere, both springing from indigenous roots in the United States, suited British desires perfectly. London and Washington, each pursuing its own interest, found much in common on which to concert their action.

Britain and the Monroe Doctrine. The actual end of the post-Revolutionary era of dispute between Britain and the United States came with the Treaty of Ghent (1814) that ended the War of 1812, but it was not until the crisis of the Spanish-American colonies that cooperation became real. Although the United States rejected Prime Minister Canning's proposal for joint action because of Secretary of State Adams' disinclination "to come in as a cock-boat in the wake of the British man-of-war" [9] the American government's decision for a unilateral declaration was clearly founded on an assumption of Britain's approval.[10] Canning himself gloated that he had "called in the New World to redress the balance of the Old."

The Shield of Sea Power. It was British sea power that made the Monroe Doctrine effective; it was British sea power that made American continental expansion possible. Britain, for reasons that we have suggested above, had no interest in weakening the United States during the nineteenth century; on the contrary, the more power Americans controlled (in their own chosen areas), the greater the gain to British policy.

Under the technological conditions of the nineteenth century, the United States profited from its geographical isolation. Continental Europe could not break through the wall of ships thrown up by Britain to strike at the United States; neither, for that matter, could the United States easily exert much influence on European affairs. This whole situation pleased London immensely. At least until the United States entered into the Pacific and came into direct contact with the states of Europe there, most American dealings with continental states were conducted, either directly or at one remove, via the British Foreign Office. Though Americans would have bitterly resented being told so, the facts are that the United States was, during most of the nineteenth century, the protege of British sea power.

The Civil War and Mexico. This generalization can be supported by reference to British policy toward the American Civil War and the

---

[9] John Quincy Adams, *Memoirs*, ed. C. F. Adams (Philadelphia: J. B. Lippincott Co., 1875), Vol. VI, p. 179.

[10] Walter Lippmann, *United States Foreign Policy: Shield of the Republic* (New York: Pocket Books, Inc., 1943), p. 14.

Mexican crisis. Economic self-interest impelled Britain toward the recognition of the Confederacy, but London held back because of its larger concern with its identity of interest with the Union. There was a long period of debate within the British government as well as many acrimonious exchanges with American diplomats, but ultimately the cement of common interest proved strong enough to withstand the divisive pull of Southern cotton.

The same point can be made with regard to Napoleon III's Mexican adventure. Britain refused to follow the French lead into Mexico at least partly because of its unwillingness to offend the United States. London brought what pressure it could upon France to withdraw from Mexico and was—for its own reasons—delighted to see Maximilian finally collapse.

The Latter Half of the Century. After the Civil War the nature of the Anglo-American relationship changed, at first subtly and then radically.[11] In the western hemisphere itself, the burgeoning American feeling of competence encouraged the United States to act vigorously on its own, even—as in the Venezuelan boundary dispute of 1895—to the point of defying Britain itself. Britain found that the young American republic was no longer a protege in Latin America, but a rival.

Meanwhile, both the United States and Britain were expanding into the Pacific. Here the old relationship was untenable; American sea power was, at least in the central and eastern Pacific, superior to the British. By the time of the rise of Japan, Britain found itself obliged to accept the United States as an equal power in many Pacific ventures and in some cases to defer to American leadership.

Even Britain's European position deteriorated so sharply in the face of German dynamism that Canning's idea of the "new world redressing the balance of the old" came to take on a new meaning. Instead of wanting to keep the United States out of Europe, Britain began to think wistfully of the advantages of having it as a full participant in the system.[12] Active American entry into European affairs was to wait until after 1900 and the presidency of Theodore Roosevelt, but long before that time Britain was planning to extend Anglo-American cooperation into the area of European great-power relationships.

---

[11] For this general point, see Crane Brinton, *The United States and Britain* (Cambridge: Harvard University Press, 1945), pp. 122-132; for a graphic elucidation of the necessity of Anglo-American cooperation in sea power, see Eugene Staley, "The Myth of the Continents," in H. F. Armstrong, ed., *The Foreign Affairs Reader* (New York: Harper & Bros., 1947), pp. 317-333.

[12] See L. M. Gelber, *The Rise of Anglo-American Friendship* (New York: Oxford University Press, 1938).

Noninvolvement in Europe: "isolationism"

We come now to one of the most misunderstood elements in nineteenth-century American foreign policy, as well as being perhaps the most abused term in the entire language of discourse about the external relations of the United States: isolation. No other single idea has had such an influence on the shaping of American attitudes toward the outside world, nor can we name any that has had a more complicating effect on the American task of coming to terms with the international issues the United States faces in the twentieth century.

What tends to obfuscate any discussion of isolation is the complex of emotional reactions that are called up today when nearly any American hears the word. No matter what his intellectual equipment and training, it is a rare citizen who is not "for" or "against" something called "isolationism"—even though he may be hard put to it to give any concrete content to the term. In some circles in the United States, "isolationist" ranks with "fascist," "communist," or "plutocrat" as an epithet of deep contempt; in other regions, it is still (or again) fashionable to stake out an isolationist position whether or not one actively identifies himself with the word.

A brief look at history, however, will clear away at least the most troublesome underbrush that impairs the landscape of comprehension. In this section we shall give the term a fairly narrow (and, it is hoped, precise) meaning. By "isolation" we mean the policy and the tradition followed by the United States during most of the nineteenth century that may be summed up as one of political "noninvolvement" in the affairs of Europe.

If we here sketch out briefly the rationale and the major steps in the development of the principle, we shall be better equipped to deal with its twentieth-century ramifications and its contemporary manifestations. In Chapter 7 we shall look at isolation as part of an American tradition of foreign policy.

Europe and the Young United States. Americans sometimes forget that the accomplishment of American independence was only partially due to the valor and the patriotism of the Revolutionary generation in the United States. The war of American independence was only one part— and a relatively minor part at that—of the long series of great-power struggles that persisted in Europe for nearly two centuries. The Treaty of Paris that ended the American war marked a phase in this Europewide conflict; the next era opened with the wars against revolutionary

France only a few years later. The birth of the United States was a direct outcome of a convulsion in the society of European states and several of its members naturally looked on the new state as a creature of their system.

The Post-Revolutionary Involvement. This suspicion was born out by events. During the thirty-one years between the Treaties of Paris and Ghent, the young United States was buffeted by the tides of great-power politics. American policy was tossed back and forth by the three great powers of the period: Britain, France, and Spain. With Britain the United States fought the War of 1812 and relations with France included an undeclared war and twenty-five years of bickering over navigation, commercial regulation, and so on. With Spain was opened the tedious and ill-tempered maneuvering that continued until the cession of the Floridas in 1819.

The early experience of the United States with the states of Europe was an unhappy one. Young, weak, inexperienced, and sensitive, the American government found its abrupt introduction to the ways of great-power politics an event not to be celebrated and if possible to be avoided in the future.

The Monroe Doctrine. The Congress of Vienna, in 1815, ended the long period of general European war and ushered in the peaceful century of what is sometimes called the *pax Brittanica.* As soon as the European states adjourned their game of maneuver and crisis, the pressure on the United States rapidly relaxed. Affairs with the British adjusted themselves; the problem of France disappeared, not to reappear until the Civil War; Spain ceased to be a concern until American imperialism spilled outside the boundaries of the United States much later in the century. By 1820, more or less, Europe had released the United States to its own devices.

This left the way open for the brave pronouncement of the Monroe Doctrine. We will remember that President Monroe's statement not only denied the western hemisphere to future European colonization, but also foreswore any American interest, present or future, in "the wars of the European powers, in matters relating to themselves...." "The political system of the allied powers [in Europe] is essentially different in this respect from that of America," he went on. This was the genesis of formal American isolation.

There is little doubt, however one may question the wisdom or the feasibility of the doctrine as it pertained to the Americas, that the generalizations about the American attitude toward Europe made good sense. By 1823 the United States had turned westward to the great task of filling up the continental hinterland, and it was quite true that Americans had little inclination to "interfere in the internal concerns" of any of the powers of Europe. American national interest lay in the western hemisphere. It was also good practical politics. Europe was settling down, and the great powers were delighted to learn that the United States was going to remain on its side of the Atlantic, however little effect they may have thought American intervention might have had if it had actually taken place.

Up to 1900. The principle of noninvolvement, thus promulgated at a moment when the times were most propitious to its success, endured throughout the rest of the nineteenth century as the basis of American attitudes toward Europe.[13] It was because of its operational feasibility, given the political and technological conditions, that isolationism became so firmly imbedded in the American consciousness. We shall consider the reasons for its success in a moment. Before this, however, we should examine two of its implications as it was worked out during the latter half of the century.

In the first place, it was never intended that isolation should be complete to the point of nonintercourse. Monroe had pointed out that it was only the problems peculiar to Europe in which the United States was to avoid involvement; in other areas, where presumably the United States had a direct interest, American relations with European states were to be frequent and intimate. The later history of the Far East was to demonstrate the validity of this deduction. As the century wore on, moreover, the original self-denying ordinance was watered down. The United States little by little began to play a part in the European political process; its noninvolvement engagement was then modified into something less rigid than full nonparticipation. In practice, it meant generally a continuing attempt to avoid fixed commitments on the European continent.

Indeed, the very word "isolation" did more to confuse than to illuminate. Perhaps the more accurate term to characterize American policy toward Europe would be "independency." [14] This word carried

---

[13] One of the most famous later expressions of the principle was that of Secretary of State Seward in 1862: "The American people must be content to recommend the cause of human progress by the wisdom with which they should exercise the powers of self-government, forbearing alliances, intervention, and interference." Quoted in John Bassett Moore, *Digest of International Law* (Washington, D. C.: U. S. Government Printing Office, 1906), Vol. VI, p. 23.

[14] The word was popularized by the late Charles A. Beard, who developed his ideas in detail in several works including *The Idea of National Interest* (New York: The Macmillan Co., Inc., 1934), *The Open Door at Home* (New York: The Macmillan Co., Inc., 1935), and *The Devil Theory of War* (New York: Vanguard Press, 1936).

a double connotation. In the first place, it suggested that the United States would intervene in European affairs only when, under the circumstances, and to the extent that American national interest demanded. It also implied clearly that such intervention would never create a precedent but would always be a matter of circumstance. American engagements would end the moment American interest was satisfied, regardless of what effects American withdrawal might have on other states. This formulation fairly accurately represents the actual approach of the United States, at least during the last quarter of the nineteenth century.

The second major point about the practice of noninvolvement is that is was never intended to be, and seldom was during the nineteenth century, a policy of mere passive watchful waiting. It left the United States ample room for affirmative action in non-European areas, and gave it justification to act in Europe as it saw fit.

The Ideology of Noninvolvement. We shall examine the ideological justification for isolation in the course of our later analysis of the American popular tradition of foreign policy. At this point, however, we may anticipate somewhat and suggest some of its doctrinal roots.

In the first place, isolationism flowed naturally from American history. Europe had oppressed the United States until Americans had made good their escape after 1820; to drift back within the European political orbit, the ideology claimed, would place American freedom in jeopardy. The democratic dogma also played its part in this connection. Implicit in the Monroe Doctrine and in dozens of later pronouncements by American statesmen was the idea that American democracy brought to its citizens individual freedom, political rights, and economic opportunity. All of these ideas were absent, Americans felt, in the Europe from which most of them had fled. The best way to keep the peace and to preserve American advantages was to have nothing to do with the enemy of all that America stood for: Europe.

A number of other forces also played a part in shaping the American attitude toward isolation. There was, as we shall see, a basic insecurity in Americans as they faced the old courts of Europe; they nursed a well-concealed fear that the United States would be unable to hold its own. Cultural particularism and provincialism, intensified by the dominant intra-continental preoccupation of American society, found a great satisfaction in scorning the effete and polyglot states of Europe. There was a final moral revulsion against power politics and the feeling that the United States, by not joining in the European struggle, was avoiding the moral smirch inherent in politics of the traditional type.

Operational Bases of Noninvolvement. Why did noninvolvement work so well for so long? What were its working bases? What happened to make it irrelevant after 1900? There are three sorts of reasons for the effectiveness of the policy and its eventual obsolescence.

The first reason is geographic. The United States was separated from Europe by an ocean, and this fact (the importance of which was often overlooked in the nineteenth century) does more to explain isolationism than do many more complex exegeses. The three thousand miles separating Europe from the Atlantic coast of the United States might as well have been three million; they made America as remote from European concerns as if it had been on the moon.

The second explanation has a political root. We have already remarked on the role played by British sea power in the development of American dominance in the hemisphere. The great aim of Britain was to keep the European states pinned down on the Continent, confronting each other in an uneasy balance engineered in London, while Britain itself ranged the world in its imperialistic and economic policy. British success in this effort during all but the last quarter of the century left the United States with only one possible enemy: Britain itself. We have seen that the harmony of interest between Britain and the United States prevented any fundamental clash from developing out of this relationship. Thus the United States again had Britain to thank, this time for making the reality of isolationism some approximation of the ideal.

Finally, we must mention technology; here we find a situational explanation both for the success and the failure of noninvolvement. In 1823 all the great powers were European and played their major roles on that continent. As long as the technology of warfare and statecraft enable Europe to maintain its global dominance, the principle of American noninvolvement squared with the facts of international life. When the great British effort collapsed in the face of the new technology, the bases of American policy were washed away. The extension of the European state system to non-European areas, the breakout of Germany into rivalry with Britain, and the rise of Japan all spelled the end of *pax Brittanica* and of American isolation.

Beginnings of a Pacific policy

American interests in the Pacific grew bit by bit during the nineteenth century. As we have noted above, the original base of American entry into the affairs of Asia and the Pacific rested on non-political foundations. It was a combination of economic and missionary activities, plus the urge to abolish the humiliating status ceremonies that all Westerners endured before Oriental courts, that brought the United States into the Pacific in the first place. American Far Eastern policy was already a reality before the outcome of the war with Spain made the United States a full-fledged Pacific power.

China: the Cushing Treaty. In 1844, Caleb Cushing succeeded in concluding with China the famous Treaty of Wanghia. This instrument provided a base for an already-established American trade with China and was followed by a vast increase in Chinese-American commerce. The principle of extraterritoriality that was to plague later relations between China and the western powers was also included.

Although the United States was one of the leaders in the commercial penetration of China, it refused to follow Britain and France into the practice of extracting economic concessions by strong diplomacy and, occasionally, by force. Candor compels us to admit, however, that American insistence on the most-favored-nation clause in dealings with China usually resulted in any new concessions won by Britain and France being extended to the United States in turn. This technique was later formalized as the "Open Door."

Japan: the Perry Expedition. In 1854 the famous expedition of Commodore Matthew C. Perry succeeded in forcing Japan to open its gates to the outside world. It was this American action that brought the Japanese to the point of deciding to adopt Western organization and technology. Throughout most of the rest of the century a succession of able American diplomats played a large part in Japan's transformation. So important was their work that one scholar has said that "Japan at the turn of the century was in considerable measure the child of American diplomacy." [15]

The Purchase of Alaska. In 1867 the United States acquired Alaska by purchase from Russia.[16] Although this enormous territory is a part of the North American mainland, its strategic significance is more Asiatic than American. Its acquisition gave the United States a base overlooking the entire North Pacific; the outermost Aleutian Islands commanded Japan from the North and brought the American flag to within a few miles of Asia. The importance of Alaska was for a long time considered

---

[15] Bailey, *Diplomatic History*, p. 336.

[16] A brief survey of the negotiations leading to the purchase of Alaska is found in W. A. Williams, *American-Russian Relations, 1781-1947* (New York: Rinehart Co., 1952), pp. 21-2; see also Pratt, *History*, pp. 324-8.

to be entirely economic; it was not until after 1941 that its key role in strategy and statecraft was fully realized.

Samoa. Much less vivid in American recollection is the United States entry into the South Pacific. In 1878, after a protracted and frustrating series of negotiations, the United States concluded a treaty with the native government of Samoa that provided for the establishment of an American naval station at Pago Pago, and threw American protection over the native rulers vis-a-vis any foreign government. This was a significant move that made a shambles of any hope to extend noninvolvement to the Pacific.

There then ensued a three-cornered international squabble over Samoa, involving the United States, Britain, and Germany. For a decade there was constant tension and rising tempers. In 1889 at Berlin, a three-power condominium was established as the least embarrassing way out of the dilemma; by its terms the three states assumed a joint protectorate. Finally, after Britain withdrew in 1899, Germany and the United States obliterated the native government and divided the islands between them.

Hawaii. A much longer and complicated story surrounds the annexation of the Hawaiian archipelago. The Sandwich Islands had become involved in American commerce with China as a convenient stopping place and considerable American settlement—traders and missionaries—took place during the nineteenth century. In the 1840's the United States had unilaterally guaranteed the continued sovereignty of the native kingdom of Hawaii—thus extending the American security frontier far out into the Pacific. By 1875 a commercial treaty of reciprocity was concluded that tied the islands closely to the United States by means of the flourishing sugar industry. A subsequent renewal of the treaty in 1887 conferred Pearl Harbor on the United States for use as a naval base.

By the 1890's the critical position of the sugar industry led the leading planters—most of them Americans—to join forces with the expansionists on the mainland in pressing for annexation. By a somewhat comic-opera series of events the native government fell in 1893 and the "republic" of Hawaii (dominated by annexationists) drew up a hasty treaty of annexation with the United States. President Cleveland, suspicious of the motives of the disciples of annexation and personally unconvinced of the need for American imperialism, repudiated the treaty. He failed, however, in his attempt to restore the native government. The independent republic of Hawaii endured until the end of the Cleveland administration.

Under President McKinley a new treaty was negotiated in 1897. Difficulties at home among recalcitrant Democrats and abroad in the form of Japanese objections delayed ratification until the beginning of the war with Spain. Admiral Dewey's victory at Manila provided the spark; Hawaii was thereupon annexed. It is worth noting, however, that the device of the joint resolution authorizing an executive agreement was called upon in this case; even in an atmosphere of war hysteria there was doubt that the two-thirds majority could be garnered in the Senate for the approval of the treaty.

Summary on American Pacific Policy. This brief recital of American penetration into the Pacific and the Far East suggests one or two conclusions. First, isolation, or noninvolvement, was never a reality in the Orient. American expansion in that region had a long history, and the United States was perfectly willing to come to grips with the great powers of Europe in an Asiatic setting. Second, there is little evidence that most Americans—or their government, either, for that matter— were self-consciously pursuing a crystallized idea of national interest in the Orient. Each step in United States policy in the Far East was either accidental, prompted by a special interest group, or brought on by a vague nationalist expansionist urge. By the time the war with Spain made the United States a major power, Americans already had large Pacific commitments without being overly sure of what they were supposed to do with them.

THE BIRTH OF GREAT-POWER STATUS

Historians often divide their time periods into centuries, with each hundred years characterized in a different way. This device is sometimes artificial; very seldom does human history move from one era to another just as a century ends. In the case of United States foreign policy, however, this method fits the actual facts with more than a casual approximation. During the last two years of the nineteenth century the United States passed through a major change in status; it entered the twentieth century with a new set of problems and a new orientation to them.

At the risk of oversimplifying, we may call this brief two-year period that during which the great-power status of the United States was being born. Prior to the war with Spain and its outcome, Americans were citizens of a nation of great potential importance but of limited actual impact on the course of world affairs; after 1900 the United States had acquired full title to all the rights and privileges that appertain to membership in the handful of great powers.

133

The war with Spain

It was the American victory over the decaying monarchy of Spain that signalled the arrival of the United States at full international maturity. Out of this brief and in many ways sordid conflict came the new posture that has so radically altered the foreign policy of the United States.

The Coming of the War. It is no part of our mission to analyze the complex and unedifying train of events that led up to the American decision to go to war.[17] Perhaps most important was the Cuban insurrection that was so bloody on both sides and so close to the territory of the United States. This struggle was one on which American opinion was ready-made; to most citizens who were at all aware of it, it was the familiar story of a suppressed subject people striving for independence against decadent European oppression. On this count immediate popular sympathy for the insurgents was natural and proved to be extensive.

But there were other factors at work. The expansionist urge, fortified by the Samoa and Hawaii incidents and especially stimulated by American truculence in the Venezuelan dispute with Great Britain, had long focused on Cuba as a possible addition to the United States. Many Americans were frankly searching for someone upon whom to test their newly-realized national strength. It is hard to escape the suspicion today that the United States was looking for a fight in 1898, and was not particularly concerned with whom the argument was picked.

We must also recognize that it was during this era that "yellow" journalism, whose stock in trade was sensationalism aimed at circulation-building, began to have a major influence on mass attitudes on foreign policy. Each episode in the Spanish-American crisis (such as the sinking of the U.S.S. *Maine* in Havana harbor) was given extreme and provocative treatment in such newspapers as the New York *Journal* and the New York *World.* Just as it seemed as if diplomacy had succeeded in adjusting all legitimate (and even quasi-legitimate) American claims against Spain, public opinion—whipped up by the yellow press— shook off all restraint. Popular clamor for war, supported by a belligerent Congress, forced a reluctant President McKinley to accept battle.

Military Victory. Although marred by stupidity and ineptitude, the Spanish-American war resulted in an American victory in an *opera bouffe* atmosphere. The Spanish fleet was destroyed at Santiago, Cuba, and

---

[17] See Walter Millis, *The Martial Spirit* (Boston: Houghton-Mifflin Co., 1931), for a highly critical study of the preliminaries of the war.

Admiral Dewey sank the Spanish naval force in Manila harbor in the Philippines—a long way, we may note, from the Cuba the United States was allegedly fighting to liberate. On land, the fighting in Cuba was fitful and inconclusive, although admittedly sanguinary. The Americans won a few small victories in Cuba, occupied Puerto Rico, and looked around for more worlds to conquer. But Spain had had enough.

Legal war with Spain had begun on April 21, 1898; on August 12, hostilities were ended by a protocol signed (on behalf of Spain) by the French ambassador to the United States. The peace conference convened in October at Paris. Negotiations continued until the peace treaty was signed in December; the treaty was approved by the United States Senate in February, 1899. By the terms of this agreement the United States served notice on the world that a new great power had been born.[18]

Territorial acquisition

What had the United States accomplished by the war that resulted in such a change in status? Why is the war with Spain, a small-scale affair even in nineteenth-century terms, today looked on as a watershed in American foreign policy?

Not the least of the reasons for the great importance given to the outcome of the Spanish-American war to the destiny of the United States is the fact that by the terms of the treaty the United States succeeded to what was left of Spain's world position: a colonial empire in the western hemisphere and a position as a major power in the Pacific. The new American empire brought the United States prestige, power, duties, and unpleasant responsibilities. Before analyzing the meaning of the new possessions, we ought to look quickly at the territories that were won.

Cuba. Cuba, the ostensible pretext for the war with Spain, achieved independence by the terms of the treaty of peace. There was considerable sentiment in the United States for outright annexation of the island, despite the wartime aim that Cuba be "liberated." Obstructing this natural consequence of expansionist attitudes of many Americans in the 1890's was the fact that Cuba had become involved in party politics and the Democratic party had become adamant against annexation. There was also the matter of the so-called Teller Amendment affixed to the Con-

---

[18] For an interesting analysis of the peace negotiations, see A. L. P. Dennis, *Adventures in American Diplomacy, 1896-1906* (New York: E. P. Dutton & Co., Inc., 1928).

gressional joint resolution that had precipitated the war. By the terms of this self-denying pledge, Congress had disclaimed any intention on the part of the United States to annex Cuba.

Unwilling to go so far as annexation, and yet concerned lest a weak although free Cuba might prove a temptation to some European imperial power (possibly Germany), the United States settled on a compromise. The "Platt Amendment" to the army appropriation bill of 1901 made Cuba, for all practical purposes, a protectorate of the United States and more or less settled the Cuban issue until the wholesale revision of American policies toward Latin America that took place during the 1930's.

The Philippines. The annexation of the Philippines, which put the United States within a few hundred miles of the Asiatic mainland, came almost as a surprise to Americans. The United States steadily revised its demands upwards while negotiations progressed on the Philippine issue. As Americans contemplated the rich archipelago, they discovered that the promptings of imperial pride demanded more and more satisfaction. At first interested only in a naval base at Manila, the United States moved to an insistence on the entire island of Luzon, and ultimately to demanding the entire group of islands.

What to do with them? There was a good deal more doubt about the wisdom of annexing an island group thousands of miles across the Pacific than there was about the acquisition of Cuba or Puerto Rico. The current of opinion in the United States seemed to be running in the direction suggested by Mr. William Jennings Bryan, who argued for American acceptance of the Philippines only for the purpose of granting them early independence. This generous, if somewhat impractical, impulse was thwarted by the Filipino insurrection that broke out in February, 1899. Two years of nasty jungle fighting ensued before the rebels were worn down, and after that episode Americans were in no mood to confer independence. Strategic and imperial reasons interfered with broad-gauge justice, and World War II was to intervene before the promise of 1898 was to be fulfilled.

Puerto Rico, Guam, Wake. Of the rest of the new empire, Puerto Rico was the most important segment. Annexed outright—apparently because there had been less of an independence movement there before 1898— Puerto Rico was to serve as a base for American military operations in the Caribbean for many years. Guam, also won from Spain, was transformed into a naval base, completely under Navy rule until after World War II. Wake Island was occupied by an American naval vessel during the war and must also be included in the booty.

The expanded frontier

The most visible result of the vast (or, at least, far-flung) acquisitions of the United States was that the American security frontier had been tremendously expanded. In the two areas where American naval power could be expected to exploit the new bases most effectively, the Caribbean and the Pacific, the outcome of the war presented the United States with entirely new situations.

The Caribbean. We have noted that American hegemony over the Caribbean and northern Latin America had been claimed before the Spanish-American war, most explicitly by Secretary Olney during the Venezuelan boundary dispute. After 1898, with the acquisition and occupation of advanced offshore bases in Cuba and Puerto Rico, American influence in the Caribbean became paramount beyond any doubt. Operating from Cuba and Puerto Rico, President Roosevelt was to find it relatively simple to maneuver the winning of the Panama Canal Zone; the maintenance of a force-in-being made the later intervention policy much more feasible.

A natural outgrowth of the new bases was the southward extension of the area of Latin America in which the United States was able to exercise primacy. Before the war, Mexico, the West Indies, and Central America had marked the effective limits of American power; after the war American control extended to substantially all of South America north of the "bulge" of Brazil.

The Pacific. The principal effect of the war, however, resulted from the changed American status in the Pacific. The annexation of the Philippines opened unsuspected vistas to the United States. It is doubtful that Americans realized fully just how deeply they had put themselves into Asia; even after the Japanese attack on Pearl Harbor in 1941 it came as a shock to many Americans to realize that to go from Tokyo to Manila required a compass setting to the southwest. By taking the Philippines the United States leaped almost 5,000 miles west of Hawaii and into Asia's front yard. Only about 700 miles separated Manila from the coast of China; the northern tip of the Philippines was only 350 miles from Formosa, while the southern end of the archipelago blended into the then Netherlands East Indies. The other Pacific acquisitions of this era—Guam, Wake, Samoa, and Hawaii—formed a series of stepping stones that made it possible for the United States to sustain its advanced base in the Philippines. The most obvious lack was an understanding of just what being in the Far East actually involved.

The United States arrived in the far Pacific just as the late phase of European imperialism in Asia was reaching its height. The European powers were busy at work trying to carve up and divide the last rich imperial prize, the apparently prostrate China. Japan had just come on the scene as an imperial power to be reckoned with; the Sino-Japanese War had just ended, and the Russo-Japanese War was just a few years away. The "Open Door" policy of the United States, enunciated almost at the very moment that Washington was settling uneasily into its new seat among the mighty, marked the new departure in American policy. The expanded security frontier of the United States had brought Americans into the thick of what was probably the most important theater of great-power controversy at the turn of the century, the ticklish question of Asiatic imperialism.

The new imperialism

At various points in the preceding pages we have had occasion to note the growing expansionist spirit that seized Americans during the last 15 or 20 years of the nineteenth century. We have suggested that in some ways the war with Spain and its consequences were the logical aftereffects of this new spirit. If being tagged with the opprobrious term "imperialist" was an outcome of achieving the new version of American manifest destiny, most Americans were willing to bear that burden.

Most, but not all. The ratification of the peace treaty with Spain provoked a bitter fight in the Senate and the two-thirds vote that finally passed it was a bare minimum. The Senate battle was only a pale reflection of a deep division among the public, one that was never to heal fully.[19]

Anti-imperialist Attitudes. Anti-imperialism drew its justification from ideological, historical, and logical bases. Ideologically the opponents of empire claimed a fundamental disharmony between the professions of democracy and the possession of an overseas empire of subject peoples. Historically, they raised the issue of isolationism, the negative aspects of the Monroe Doctrine, and the wisdom of the American record of staying out of great-power embroilments. Logically, they pointed to the folly of undertaking a war to free Cuba and then becoming a Pacific power on the opposite side of the globe from the Caribbean.

Underlying anti-imperialist sentiment we can detect a combination of

---

[19] For the American debate over imperialism, see Julius Pratt, *Expansionists of 1898* (Baltimore: Johns Hopkins University Press, 1936), generally.

what our era would call guilt feelings and insecurity. Imperialism as a too familiar manifestation of power politics seemed to many people to be something that the American political genius was constitutionally incapable of carrying off successfully. The guilt arose from a sense that America, in succeeding a corrupt monarchy as ruler over alien peoples, was betraying its faith in individual dignity and freedom. The prospects of imperial rule were admittedly intoxicating, but many well-meaning people wondered if, in gaining the renown of the world, Americans were not running the danger of losing their own souls.

Imperialist Attitudes. The imperialists, if they felt such scruples, kept them well under cover. We need not recite the catalogue of imperialist arguments in detail; they are all familiar to students of modern history. Economic advantage, strategic gain, the siren call of prestige, the iron law of history, the beckoning finger of destiny, and the requirements of Christianity were all pressed into service in the fight—as indeed they had been used in every state that felt the call to imperial greatness. Perhaps the rationalization that played the largest part in carrying the day for the imperialists—in addition to popular resentment at the Filipino insurrection —was the seductive idea of the "white man's burden."[20] Today a term of derision, in 1898 and 1899 it provided the ideological escape hatch through which many worried citizens could make their way to the acceptance of imperialism.

The Practice of Imperialism. We need not concern ourselves in detail with the practice of the new imperialism; we shall have occasion to consider it in the next chapter. Once committed to imperialism (albeit of a somewhat different sort) Americans busily set out to make the most of it. Both in the Caribbean and in the Pacific, government and private action accelerated its pace so as to capitalize on the new American empire.

Cuba, Puerto Rico, Hawaii, and the Philippines all became the scenes of frenzied private investment and of extensive programming by the American government. All tropical and all insular, these possessions

---

[20] Rudyard Kipling's poem, "The White Man's Burden" (1899), helped persuade Americans where their duty lay. The most impressive of the poem's seven stanzas is the fifth:

> "Take up the White Man's Burden —
> And reap his old reward:
> The blame of those ye better,
> The hate of those ye guard —
> The cry of hosts ye humour
> (Ah, slowly!) toward the light: —
> 'Why brought ye us from bondage,
> 'Our loved Egyptian night?'"

Quoted from *McClure's Magazine* (February, 1899).

offered lucrative opportunities for capital investment in the production of such commodities as sugar, hemp, and other tropical agricultural products. Naval bases and other installations, provision for which had been made in the various instruments of annexation, were rushed to completion. The United States began to present to the outside world what had come to be thought of as the normal appearance of an imperial power.

The United States among the great powers

The New American Attitude. The more informed and sophisticated among the Americans of 1900 had a fairly clear understanding that the United States had come to the end of an era. The new overseas territories of the United States meant a good deal more than just a vast augmentation in prestige, however satisfying to nationalist appetites that might be in itself. They required the United States to walk a new path in foreign affairs, to concern itself with new problems and to solve them in new ways.

The administration of President Theodore Roosevelt understood this, at least to some significant extent. Under Roosevelt some systematic attempts were made to grasp the requirements of world-power status and to design a policy appropriate for it. But even here Mr. Roosevelt's approach was largely the product of the American past. It does not seem overcritical to characterize it as an attempt to apply an old tradition to a new set of problems. What success he enjoyed was due largely to a keen appreciation of the dimensions of the issues; his failures stemmed from certain basic inadequacies in his techniques.

But even though informed opinion grasped the implications of the new role of the United States only imperfectly, not even that much can be said about the general content of public opinion. If we may generalize about a dangerous subject from the vantage point of over half a century, it seems probable that the mass of the American people in 1900 did not realize what had happened to them. There was great pride in the victory over Spain; there was a good deal of self-congratulation at being an imperial people; there was considerable misssionary zeal for spreading the message of the American way to backward peoples. But except for a few belligerent and quasi-chauvinist voices, there seems to have been little inclination to recognize the fact that, for good or ill, the United States had left the past behind. The oceans still existed and the British navy still sailed upon them; Europe and the great powers still seemed as far away as they had a hundred years before.

This failure to awake to the responsibilities of great-power status has sometimes been called one of the greatest errors that Americans have ever committed. This judgment seems, if not overly harsh, at least somewhat beside the point. There was no error involved at all, if by "error" we mean a deliberate choice of what turned out to be a wrong alternative. Instead, most Americans never understood that there was any choice to be made at all; they simply assumed that now that the war with Spain was over and the predictable result had taken place, things would somehow readjust themselves and the United States could again rock along in its pleasant insularity. So deep-seated was this idea that it was to take two wars and a depression to disabuse Americans of it.

The Attitude of the Other Powers. If the United States was ignorant of what had happened to it, this happy state was not shared by the other great powers. As much earlier as the time of the American Civil War, the European states, contemplating the awful military might that the United States mobilized on both sides, realized that America was ready then to join the circle of the internationally elect. By 1900, as the European state system analyzed the American victory over Spain, each of its major members thought through what the entry of the United States into their councils might mean.

Great Britain, almost alone among the major powers, welcomed the birth of American power; we have already examined some of its reasons. British influence was unable any longer to sustain Britian's commitments; with real harmony of interest and with a long history of unspoken co-operation with the United States, London contemplated the arrival of a potential ally.

Germany, on the other hand, was unhappy. Anti-German sentiment had been growing in the United States; long before 1900 American opposition to German moves was obvious. During the Samoa episode bad feeling had almost boiled over; it flared again in Manila Bay after Dewey's victory. With Germany obviously aiming at undermining British control of the seas, the addition of the American potential to British strength was admitted to be a bad omen for the Kaiser's dreams of empire.

France and Russia, the other important European members of the system, were less directly involved. France had had little direct conflict with the United States during the century except for the Maximilian affair, and that had been forgotten with the disappearance of the Second Empire. The French were relatively neutral toward the United States. Russia had carefully nurtured its policy of friendship toward the United

States and officially was moderately pleased at the new American posture. This attitude was to bear fruit a few years later as President Roosevelt helped extricate the Czar from the embarrassment of the Russo-Japanese War.

There remains only Japan. Like the United States, Japan was just coming into acceptance as a major state at the turn of the century, and (we can see today) Nippon had its eye on some form of Asian hegemony. The abrupt arrival of the United States in the Pacific and the Far East, just as Japan was beginning its own program of expansion there, meant that the Japanese had suddenly come upon a new and formidable obstacle to their own ambitions. Though it was not to become palpable for over two decades, Japanese reaction to American great-power status was one of hostility.

6 : The first half of the twentieth century

During the period between 1900 and 1945, the years covered by this chapter, American foreign policy may be interpreted as a struggle between the forces of history and the reluctance of the American people to recognize what was demanded of them. Each of the several phases into which we can divide the less than 50 years between the Spanish-American war and V-J Day made more clear the difference between the real world and the world as the mass of Americans saw it. No similar period in history provides such a dramatic demonstration of the truism that one cannot solve a problem until he first recognizes that the problem exists.

The American record in international affairs during the first half of the twentieth century is not an especially edifying one. It is filled with lost opportunities, missed chances, and deep-seated misunderstandings, only partially retrieved by occasional great efforts. Too often for national comfort, American policy-makers were busy doing too much or too little, too early or too late. We can find in retrospect almost an unspoken conspiracy among people and leaders to avoid the tedious but ordinarily necessary task of harmonizing national interest, commitments, objectives, and capabilities. The public took refuge from reality either in outbursts of missionary zeal or in equally irrational withdrawal; statesmen manipulated shibboleths and formulas and sought a quick-and-easy way out of such dilemmas as they recognized.

But it is not our purpose in this chapter to point a moral that, if it has any value at all, is by this time obvious. We shall be tracing the broad lines and critical events of the first half of the twentieth centry for a somewhat more useful purpose. We shall be suggesting the extent to which American policies of the pre-World War II era have carried over into the contemporary world, and we shall attempt also to indicate certain aspects of the national attitudes that have survived the transition from the age of innocence to the age of bipolarity.

THE FIRST PHASE, 1900-1914

The first phase of American policy in the twentieth century began with 1900 and ended with the opening of the war of 1914-18. It was marked, as we suggested at the end of previous chapter, by a real although limited attempt to go forward from the new platform provided by the war with Spain.

The Caribbean

During this period, American action in the Caribbean took a frankly imperialistic turn. The Monroe Doctrine was modified into a justification of American hegemony, and governmental action in this direction was vigorous.

The Canal Zone. The first great achievement of the United States was the acquisition of the Panama Canal Zone.[1] This first required that treaty relations with Great Britain be modified in order to get London's approval of American construction and fortification of the trans-isthmian canal; this step was taken by the second Hay-Pauncefote Treaty (1901). After deciding finally on a route across the Isthmus of Panama, the project ran into difficulty because of the obduracy of the Congress of the Republic of Colombia, whose flag then flew over Panama. In 1903 there occurred a "revolution" in Panama, in which American naval forces figured strangely. As soon as the new Republic of Panama had proclaimed itself, President Roosevelt extended American recognition; two weeks after the revolution the United States had negotiated a satisfactory treaty with Panama (the Hay-Bunau-Varilla treaty), giving it perpetual control over the Canal Zone. The exact responsibility—moral, legal, and political —for the peculiar chain of events is still a matter of dispute;[2] the fact

---

[1] On this episode, see H. C. Hill, *Roosevelt and the Caribbean* (Chicago: University of Chicago Press, 1927), Chapter 3.

[2] Roosevelt asserted in a later speech that "I took Panama." S. E. Morison and H. S. Commager, *The Growth of the American Republic*, revised ed. (New York: Oxford University Press, 1940), II, 404.

144

remains, however, that out of the episode the United States gained the Zone and the Canal, and the new strategic advantage necessary to American policy in Latin America.

The Corollaries to the Monroe Doctrine. The international financial irresponsibility of the Central American republics contributed to certain additions to the Monroes Doctrine. The "Roosevelt Corollary" of 1904 claimed a right of American intervention into the domestic affairs of Latin American states to force them to pay their bills; this was justified as the only sure means of forestalling non-American intervention. This power, once claimed, was actively exercised. In 1912 there came the so-called "Lodge Corollary," a Senate resolution that was tacitly accepted by the executive branch. By its terms the United States expressed disapproval of the transfer of strategic areas in the hemisphere to non-American private companies that might be acting as agents of a foreign power. Both of these declarations, in addition to others less formalized, served notice on the world that the United States considered the Caribbean an American lake.[3]

Dollar Diplomacy. Not peculiar to the Caribbean but especially well known in that area is the policy dubbed "Dollar Diplomacy." Under Roosevelt and particularly under President Taft, the government no longer contented itself with protecting private American investments in sensitive areas, but instead took the lead in actively promoting them. Dollar diplomacy was justified as being something more than simple greed; its rationalizations gave it a high-policy aspect. If American capital were to go into Latin America, it must have guarantees of government stability. Such stability the United States government, by intervention if necessary, would create. Thus order would replace the normal anarchy of the region; this would be to the advantage of the United States, since it would discourage foreign penetration in the neighborhood of the Panama Canal. At the same time, private investment would bring advantages to the Latin American region. Justified or not, dollar diplomacy contributed largely to the lasting unpopularity of the United States in Latin America.[4]

The Far East

In the Caribbean after 1900 the United States began to act the part of an imperialist power; in the Pacific it found itself saddled with the

---

[3] On the corollaries of the Monroe Doctrine, see Perkins, *Hands Off*, Chapter VII: "The Policeman of the West."

[4] See the criticism in Scott Nearing and Joseph Freeman, *Dollar Diplomacy* (New York: The Viking Press, 1925).

responsibilities of one among a group of major states. The first decade of the twentieth century was a period of American involvement on the mainland of China and of bickering with Japan.[5] Both Chinese and Japanese relations were to have consequences that have endured to the present day.

The Open Door in China. The policy of the "Open Door" with regard to China is one of the landmarks of American statecraft. Not because of its effects on events in the Far East, which was actually insignificant; rather because of the great grip it obtained on the emotions of the American people and the consequent commitments Americans have felt ever since to some such notion.

The policy itself was laid down in a set of three notes sent out by the United States to the major European powers with interests in China. The first was dispatched in 1899, the others in 1900 and 1902. The doctrine evolved in this series of communications was both economic and political in nature.

Economically, the United States was attempting to establish the principle of equality of opportunity among the great powers in staking out imperialist spheres in China. Secretary of State John Hay hoped to prevent the creation of exclusive preserves by one or another of the major states. Politically, the United States declared itself in favor of "Chinese territorial and administrative entity." What both points amounted to was a picture of China as viewed by American interest. The United States wished China to remain sovereign, politically independent, and territorially united; if foreign economic penetration was to take place —and there seemed no way to prevent it—the United States insisted on equality for all rather than the erection of semi-sovereign enclaves on Chinese soil.[6]

Put this way, we can see that the Open Door policy was never from the beginning the high-minded philanthropy that popular legend sometimes claimed it to be. American interest demanded a balance of power on the Asian littoral, and this meant the continued existence of China. To prevent its dismemberment, the United States was prepared to oppose Japan, Germany, Russia, or any other state that seemed willing to take over China.

One flaw in this policy appeared after only a few years. However

---

[5] A. Whitney Griswold, *The Far Eastern Policy of the United States* (New York: Harcourt, Brace and Co., 1938), Chapters 2, 3.

[6] George F. Kennan has a wryly humorous—and heavily critical—interpretation of the Open Door episode in *American Diplomacy, 1900-1950,* Chapter II, "Mr. Hippisley and the Open Door."

uncompromising the expressed American attitude toward the possible breakup of China, the United States had no bargaining position in implementing its position. Americans were, to put it briefly, unwilling to use force to save China. As long as world opinion supported the America position, the Open Door had some influence; when agressors appeared who were willing to use violence, the policy rapidly degenerated to an empty catchword.

Japanese Relations. The new American posture as the defender of China did not escape the attention of Japan. Japan planned to expand into the mainland of Asia, and China was its most tempting prize. The United States fanned Japanese resentment by forcing Tokyo to scale down its demands on Russia at the close of the Russo-Japanese War in 1905; confusion was compounded during 1906 in the quarrel over the continued immigration of Japanese to the United States and the education of their children in California. The United States flexed its muscles in 1907-08 by sending the American battleship fleet around the world, and it appeared as if tension between the two nations was mounting to the point of danger.

But Japan was not anxious for any kind of a showdown with the United States at this time. On the initiative of the Japanese government, in 1908 the Root-Takahira agreement was consummated. This arrangement settled the major points at issue in the Pacific (the immigration question had been disposed of earlier by a so-called "Gentlemen's Agreement"). The two states agreed to maintain the status quo in the Pacific, to respect each other's territorial possessions, to uphold the Open Door, and to support the "independence and integrity of China." Although the agreement seemed to remove the grounds for controversy, it was obvious that the era of Japan's sponsorship by the United States had passed. Both states were major powers; both had interests in the Pacific that conflicted with the other. Competition and controversy seemed inevitable in the future.

A note on Morocco

We must note in passing that the United States injected itself into one major issue of purely European concern. The Moroccan crisis of 1905, involving Germany and France directly and the other European powers indirectly, seemed for a time to threaten general war. President Roosevelt offered his good offices to help settle the crisis, and it was largely due to this effort that the Algeciras Conference was called. At this conference the United States had official delegates; there was no pretence of isolation. Americans negotiated, composed differences, and played a large part in the proceedings.

There was some soul searching in the United States over this adventure, for it was in clear violation of the noninvolvement policy of hallowed memory. Nobody was particularly pleased about it, but its apologists justified American intervention on grounds of sheer necessity. One scholar suggests that Roosevelt added a new corollary to the Monroe Doctrine: the United States would be justified in intervening anywhere in the world if it seemed necessary to maintain world peace.[7] Monroe Doctrine or not, the Moroccan intervention foreshadowed the eventual total irrelevance of noninvolvement in Europe to the working interests of the United States.

THE FIRST WORLD WAR

The first major consequence of American great-power status was the historical process that drew the United States into the first world war. We have seen that the United States owed its birth to a general European war, and until it successfully disentangled itself from the European state system in 1820, the United States was part of the general society of states. Between 1820 and 1900, however, the United States stood outside the mainstream of world affairs and escaped all the wars that occurred within it. When Americans rejoined the family of nations, there was no way for them to avoid being caught up in the next major upheaval. What makes the 1914-1918 period important for us is the extent to which this— the war's major lesson to the United States—was missed by Americans.

The effect of Wilsonianism

American policy during the era of the first world war was materially affected, if not actually governed, by the fact that its major architect was President Woodrow Wilson. Mr. Wilson brought a distinct philosophy of foreign affairs to the presidency and self-consciously sought to order the behavior of the United States according to its principles. Both his great successes and its ultimate repudiation grew out of this preoccupation.

Wilson's Philosophy of Foreign Affairs. Wilson adopted a "democratic"

[7] Bailey, *Diplomatic History*, p. 567.

theory of international relations entirely in harmony with what Walter Lippmann called the "great illusion" of the nineteenth century.[8] He submitted the behavior of states to the measurement of moral criteria, derived from the democratic ideology of the United States and a strict Puritanical conscience. He accepted a set of morally desirable values: peace, self-determination, the rights of small states, the superiority of public opinion to the calculations of diplomats, and the abolition of self-seeking national interest. He attempted to circumvent the apparatus of traditional power politics and to substitute therefor a new methodology in world affairs stressing the implementation of the democratic dogma. In so doing he was giving forceful and very literate expression to long-standing and basic popular attitudes in the United States.

Wilson was obliged, however, to cope with some hard realities. Up to the time of American involvement in the war, his foreign policy forced him to deal with a series of problems inherited from his predecessors. To do Wilson justice, he attempted—with some success—to alter American tactics in Latin America and in relations with Great Britain; the record of his prewar policy is not a discreditable one.

Latin American Intervention. President Wilson, despite his good intentions of dismantling Dollar Diplomacy, was unable to halt the trend. Not only did he continue—although on a lesser scale—the promotion of American investment in Latin America, but he was forced into a series of interventions more extensive than even those of Roosevelt or Taft. Best remembered is the long and tedious quarrel with Mexico that at times verged on all-out war. Through it all, however, he clung to his basic idea: American intervention was only a holding operation, designed to keep affairs in order until the spontaneous will of the people could be expressed. His approach, however imperfect it may have been in practice, helped prepare for the day of the liquidation of Dollar Diplomacy after the war and its ultimate replacement by the Good-Neighbor policy.

Anglo-American Relations. Important for its later effect on American attitudes toward the war was Wilson's achievement in solidifying Anglo-American relations by the settlement of the Panama Canal tolls problem. The solution—that American shipping would have no preferential treatment on tolls—not only cleared the road for American cooperation with Britain in the years ahead, but also represented a large step in the direction of Wilson's goal of placing moral principle ahead of immediate material advantage. The improvement in relations with Britain helped produce the pro-Ally bias toward the war that was so strongly to affect future American policy.

---

[8] In *United States Foreign Policy* (Boston: Little, Brown and Co., 1943), p. 30.

Neutrality and its failure

The coming of the European war in August 1914 at first had little impact on Americans. Here, mass attitudes seemed to imply, was another European struggle of the old type, growing out of certain inherent flaws in the political structure of Europe and the states within it. In this kind of conflict the United States had no interest. The proper role for Americans was to remain on the sidelines and to capitalize on their advantage by dealing with problems nearer home. With this popular attitude President Wilson and his advisers, principally Secretary of State William Jennings Bryan, were in general agreement.

Neutrality vs. Unneutralism. At the onset of the war, therefore, the United States issued proclamations of neutrality almost as a matter of routine.[9] As Americans watched the course of the fighting, however, they discovered that noninvolvement could not and did not mean impartiality. The sympathies of the bulk of the people were unquestionably on the side of the Allies. Certain ethnic groups in the United States were either pro-German or anti-British, but the predominant attitude was pro-Ally. Here again the government, although better informed and somewhat more sophisticated than mass opinion, shared its predilections; Mr. Wilson himself was tortured by the conflict between his pro-British leanings and his insistence on a policy of noninvolvement. Only Secretary Bryan, by now almost a confirmed pacifist, was relatively untroubled by any bias in favor of Britain.

The Violation of American Rights. The unneutral attitude of Americans was strained by the studied violation of American "neutral rights" by both sides from almost the very beginning of the war. The war of 1914-18 is sometimes called the first modern war, and one evidence of the new nature of warfare was the utter collapse of the nineteenth-century idea of neutrality. Both sides, fighting a total war for the first time, found themselves unable or unwilling to concede the freedom that neutrals had traditionally claimed, and both systematically interfered with American commerce. All the old legal ideas, including contraband, continuous voyage, visit and search, and so on were given new and (to Americans) unnatural interpretations by the belligerents. Americans discovered that the lot of a neutral, particularly a neutral great power, was an unhappy one in a general war.

During the first part of the war, Britain seemed to be the more per-

---

[9] The standard work is Charles Seymour, *American Neutrality, 1914-1917* (New Haven: Yale University Press, 1935).

sistent violator of American rights. Given the control of the sea enjoyed by the British navy, it was relatively easy for Britain to impose vexing controls over American trade with Europe. The United States grew restive under the constant diet of harrassment, and the considerable agitation for forthright action was barely offset by the persistent Anglophilia of the government and the people.

The British, however, enjoyed another natural advantage in the struggle for American sympathy. Germany, without enough of a surface navy to challenge British supremacy, turned to the submarine as its preferred weapon against seaborne commerce. Submarine warfare, by definition, made mincemeat out of the ordinary rules of neutral shipping, rules that the British had retained in principle however drastically they might have interpreted them in practice. The crowning blow, and the one event that tipped American sympathies irrevocably in favor of the Allies, was the sinking of the *Luisitania* in 1915.

The German Choice Forces War. The United States responded quickly to the German challenge. Secretary Bryan resigned rather than approve a stronger American policy, and President Wilson took over active direction of American strategy. He sought by vigorous diplomacy to persaude Germany to limit its submarine warfare and, for a time, seemed to have won his point as Germany promised to restrain itself.

By early 1917, however, Berlin made a deliberate calculation of what was involved and elected to resume unrestricted submarine warfare. The imperial government realized that this might bring about American belligerency; it reasoned, however, that it could win the war before American participation could tip the scales. The United States immediately broke off diplomatic relations; in April, after the revelation of German plots in Mexico and the revolution in Russia, the United States declared war.[10]

The United States and the war

American participation in the war furnished almost a laboratory example of the traditional American attitude toward war in general. The war, as popular opinion saw it, was forced upon the United States by vicious and depraved men. The American government had been patient; it had reasoned with the aggressors; it had sought to stave off battle as

---

[10] For critical studies of American entry into the war, see Walter Millis, *Road to War* (Boston: Houghton-Mifflin Co., 1935), and Charles C. Tansill, *America Goes to War* (Boston: Little, Brown and Co., 1938).

long as possible. Finally, given no choice, the United States went to war. America had no sordid objectives of material gain or the satisfaction of national interest; its concern was with principle. After the war was won, Americans were prepared to help straighten out the world before they went back to their own concerns.

American Idealism. Put as baldly as we have stated them above, these propositions seem almost fatuous and puerile to a more skeptical generation of Americans. Later scholars (and some contemporary ones) have proved that President Wilson was as sensitive to the requirements of the European balance of power as were his associates in Britain, and American entry into the war was a natural decision to attempt to forestall German hegemony on the continent.[11] And yet—and this is a danger peculiar to our time—we must not overlook an historical fact. Most Americans believed that these abstractions were what they were actually fighting for—and so did most foreigners, enemy and Allied alike. Part of the difficulty into which Wilson later drifted arose from the inability of the other Allied leaders to believe that American objectives were actually as simple and ideal as they seemed. But mass sympathy—at home and abroad—with American idealism was a weapon of unsuspected effectiveness. We must never forget that Germany surrendered on the basis of the Fourteen Points, Wilson's most ambitious effort to translate his own idealism into practical terms.

Wilson's War Aims. President Wilson thought himself fighting the war for a single objective: peace—durable, honorable, and satisfying. To him, the only kind of peace settlement that stood any chance of enduring was one that incorporated his own (and his country's) philosophy of international relations and applied it to the settlement of concrete issues.

As Wilson saw it, peace for the world required the simultaneous application of a handful of general prinicples. These were self-determination (points 6 'hrough 13 of the Fourteen Points dealt with self-determination in one form or another), political democracy (the old American bias against monarchic rule as being inherently warlike), untrammeled intercourse between peoples (freedom of the seas, abolition of economic barriers, freedom of movement), and international organization (Point 14—the crucial one for Americans in dealing with the Treaty of Versailles—dealt with a "general association of nations" to guarantee "political independence and territorial integrity" to all states). He wrapped all

---

[11] See Edward Buehrig, *Woodrow Wilson and the Balance of Power* (Bloomington: University of Indiana Press, 1956). Compare this recent study, however, with another that takes the opposite position: John M. Blum, *Woodrow Wilson and the Politics of Morality* (Boston: Little, Brown and Co., 1956), especially Chapter VIII.

of these up into a single operating hypothesis that was in turn dependent on a basic article of faith: that the spontaneous common opinion of mankind, if given the chance to speak freely, would always declare for peace, justice, and freedom. He dedicated the United States to the cause of creating mechanisms for the expression of that mass will.[12]

Equally revealing was the absence of any of the "normal" war aims ordinarily expected of a sovereign state in a major war. The United States, according to its official statements, was interested neither in territory, indemnities, nor military bases. It disclaimed any hostility toward the German people, reserving its enmity for the military masters of the state. It was unconcerned about the interests of its allies except insofar as they fitted into the postwar scheme envisaged by Wilson. In general, the United States was not interested in the usual kind of peace settlement at all, based on the submission of the vanquished. Wilson genuinely hoped a "peace without victory," or, more exactly, a peace in which all— victors and vanquished alike—would be ultimate winners.

The United States and the Allies. The fundamental distinction that Americans drew between their own war and that being fought by the rest of the Allies is shown by the amorphous relations between them. The United States never became an "Ally," but remained only an "Associated Power" to the end. This legal distinction left America free to set its own course and—if need be—to negotiate a separate peace (an event which, as history worked out, actually took place[13]). During the weeks of negotiation preceding the Armistice, the half-concealed divergence of views between Wilson and the Allied leaders broke out into the open, and it required some none-too-subtle threats of a separate peace to force Clemenceau and Lloyd George to accept the Fourteen Points as the basis for peace. At the Paris Peace Conference itself, Wilson (although the popular idol of the European masses) ran into constant opposition from his opposite numbers around the table, and finally fell between the two stools. He failed to get the kind of peace settlement he wanted

---

[12] Wilson's war message (April 2, 1917) put this proposition at its simplest:

"Our object . . . is to vindicate the principles of peace and justice in the life of the world as against selfish and autocratic power and to set up amongst the really free and self-governed peoples of the world such a concert of purpose and of action as will henceforth insure the observance of those principles. . . .

"We are glad . . . to fight thus for the ultimate peace of the world and for the liberation of its peoples . . . : for the rights of nations great and small and the privilege of men everywhere to choose their way of life and of obedience." *Congressional Record*, LV, 103, 104 (April 2, 1917).

[13] After the failure of the Treaty of Versailles in the Senate, the United States made peace with Germany by joint resolution of Congress, signed by President Harding July 21, 1921.

at Versailles, but what he did get was too much for the United States Senate. Neither Europe nor the American people were ready for a Wilsonian peace in 1919.

THE RENAISSANCE OF ISOLATIONISM

Looking back to the 1920's, we can suggest several explanations for the renaissance of isolationism that flowered after the end of the war. It was perhaps inevitable that a people whose insight was so limited that they could not grasp the meaning of great-power status, who had fought their greatest war with emotional slogans and crusading zeal and without any rational understanding of how to approach their idealistic goal, and who thought of war as a matter of punishing sinners, would lapse into disillusionment when Heaven proved difficult to locate. Party politics, always a factor in American political decision, played its part as well in bringing back isolationist prejudice; President Wilson's unbending insistence on his own particular way alienated many otherwise sympathetic internationally minded people. But it serves no purpose to analyze the motives of 1920. For good or ill, Americans once again turned their backs on the world. Their action had a perceptible effect on the course of events during the next twenty years, called by E. H. Carr "the twenty years crisis."[14]

The rejection of the League

The genesis of neo-isolationism is found in the struggle over the ratification of the Treaty of Versailles and American entry into the League of Nations. Once this battle was over and the concept of "normalcy" had captured American political life, the emotional drive for noncommitment had taken charge of American policy. The issues raised during the 1919-1921 period were not to be settled until after V-J Day.

Wilson's Tactics. To a considerable, although immeasurable, extent, the rejection of the League of Nations was the outcome of the political tactics of President Wilson. Never noted as a compromiser, and prone to insist on his way if he felt a moral issue was involved, he laid a political trap for himself in the manner in which he handled the issue of international cooperation.

His first error was made prior to the congressional election of 1918; he urged the election of a Democratic Congress as the surest way to

---

[14] E. H. Carr, *The Twenty Years Crisis, 1919-1939* (London: The Macmillan Co., 1940).

guarantee a successful peace settlement. Such an identification of either party with superior virtue or patriotism is never especially good politics in the United States and, under the circumstances, practically guaranteed the eventual Republican victory. The election meant that Wilson went to Paris after what amounted to a popular repudiation—an outcome he could possibly have avoided. What was worse, the delegation he chose to accompany him included no Senators and only one Republican—and a lukewarm one at that. It would seem that Wilson had omitted-doing nothing that might antagonize the majority party in the Senate.

After the treaty was submitted, the President made his lot even more difficult. He rejected the Lodge reservations which, had he accepted them, would have permitted American membership in the League on a slightly different basis (Britain and France were both prepared to accept the Lodge reservations). Instead, he insisted on his own version of the League and expressed his determination to stand or fall on it. Even after all of this (and the President's physical collapse that further complicated an already tangled situation), there was enough Republican support for the Treaty that it fell only eight votes short of the required two-thirds.[15]

The Election of 1920. The presidential election of 1920, coming after the long and bitter battle over the League, sealed the fate of the United States. Although the victorious Harding was, as a candidate, vaguely in favor of "an association of nations," the Democratic defeat was correctly interpreted as a mandate. The American people were turning away, not only from the League, but from the broader idea of systematized and institutionalized action to preserve peace. During the Republican era of the 1920's—and even during Franklin D. Roosevelt's first term—it was axiomatic in American politics and in American foreign affairs that the United States was not to become involved in any permanent international arrangements requiring political commitments. The interwar isolationism was much more a state of mind—popular and official— than it was a matter of practical policy. The people had spoken and, this done, turned to other matters.

The United States and International Cooperation, 1920-1932. Although committed to the popular demand for isolationism, the United States found itself unable to escape frequent, extensive, and organized intercourse with the states of Europe. Interwar isolationism meant essentially that American relations with Europe (and the state system generally) were restricted to what Americans thought of as non-political activities, such as disarmament and finance. Even on these relatively innocuous

---

[15] See generally Denna F. Fleming, *The United States and the League of Nations, 1918-1920* (New York: Putnam, 1932).

points, the American approach to the other great powers was wary, tentative, and reluctant. Such a mild enterprise as adherence to the Statute of the Permanent Court of International Justice proved impossible of fulfillment; the Senate was firmly convinced that "the World Court is the back door to the League," and this less-than-half-truth amounted to a death sentence on the project.

Even so, the United States did become involved with the League of Nations in a variety of projects, especially disarmament. So rigid was American public opinion, however, that much of this had to be done almost by stealth, and almost all American efforts were weak and ineffectual. The ubiquitous American "observer" sitting in on League sessions, unauthorized, uneasy, and impotent, eventually became something of a laughingstock at Geneva.

Disarmament

Perhaps the most conspicuous and well-meaning effort of the United States toward the establishment of a peaceful order during the interwar period was the long attempt at "disarmament." The word is put in quotation marks here, although in the minds of Americans of the day it was taken literally to mean the ultimate abolition of all weapons of war.

The United States saw little reason and no need to try to construct peace among the major powers by means of either institutional arrangements (the League) or political understandings (diplomacy leading to treaties). Traditional American theory considered war an abnormal event; peace could be achieved if men and nations divested themselves of the weapons of war and the legal right to wage it. Power politics, rooted in military force, could thus be eliminated and American security preserved without any necessity for either permanent commitments or political effort.

The disarmament movement suited American predilections exactly. By stripping nations of their capacity to fight a war, the desire to fight would be eliminated; by making a commitment for peace, peaceful process would be guaranteed. Foreign policy for the United States would then consist only of trade relations with the outside world and the exploitation of America's natural hegemony, principally in the western hemisphere.

The Washington Conference. In 1922 the United States led the way in moving toward disarmament. The Washington Conference, called on the initiative of the United States, attempted to arrest the postwar naval race among the United States, Britain, and Japan. Although the United States had a construction program under way that would have made it the world's greatest naval power in a few years, America agreed to suspend the building effort and to the stabilization of the three greatest navies on a capital-ship ratio of 5-5-3. France and Italy were added to the ratio at 1.75 each, and it seemed as if a great stride had been taken for peace.

The Conference also dealt with the political problems of the Pacific, where a dangerous rivalry had developed after the war. Out of the negotiations came the Four-Power Treaty that abrogated the Anglo-Japanese alliance and substituted an agreement among the United States, Britain, Japan, and France to respect each other's rights in the Pacific and providing vaguely for consultation and possible joint action in case of a threat by another power. The Open Door was reaffirmed by the Nine-Power Treaty (the four above and Belgium, China, Italy, the Netherlands, and Portugal) that pledged the signatories to respect the "sovereignty, the independence, and the territorial and administrative integrity" of China.[16]

The Geneva Conference. The Washington Conference had provided a ratio by which to control capital ships, but left the door open to a new naval race in smaller vessels. President Coolidge therefore called for a new naval disarmament conference in 1927, to meet at Geneva. Here the United States sought to extend the 5-5-3 ratio to all classes of warships, but it proved impossible to reach any agreement. The conference ended in a total fiasco.

The Kellogg-Briand Pact. In this connection we should mention the ill-starred Pact of Paris, the Kellogg-Briand Pact for outlawing war. This document, once thought of as one of the major diplomatic triumphs of the United States, renounced war "as an instrument of national policy" and promised that the settlement of international disputes would not be attempted "except by pacific means." Almost all the states of the world finally ratified it, but many (including the United States) added significant reservations that permitted "defensive" war. Signed in 1928, the Pact became politically irrelevant in 1931, when Japan's invasion of Manchuria ended the myth of achieving a warless world by proclamation.

The London Conference. The next disarmament effort was made in 1930. After long preliminary negotiations between Britain and the United States, the five major naval powers met at London. Here some concrete results were achieved, although the total reduction in naval strength was

---

16 See Raymond Leslie Buell, *The Washington Conference* (New York: Appleton, 1922). A more recent study is John Chalmers Vinson, *The Parchment Peace* (Athens: University of Georgia Press, 1955).

negligible. The major result of the conference was to stabilize the relative strength of the three largest navies. The United States and Britain agreed to complete parity in all types of vessels; Japan accepted smaller ratios than the other two in every category except submarines; a ceiling was placed on the construction of all types of ships. The naval race seemed halted, except for the famous "escalator clause." This provided that the ratios were to be null and void in case a nonsignatory power entered into a naval race with any of the parties to the treaty.

The World Disarmament Conference. In 1932, after over a decade of preparation, the League of Nations "World Disarmament Conference" finally convened. The great goal of this gathering was the creation of some limits for land armaments analogous to those hammered out for naval vessels. The United States participated and tried its admittedly feeble best to promote something concrete; President Hoover even went so far as to propose an immediate one-third cut in all existing armaments. But the politics of security in Europe and Japan's Manchurian adventure cast a pall over the conference, and it broke up without any progress. The next year Hitler came to power in Germany and the entire discussion became irrelevant.

The United States and Disarmament. It is impossible to find fault with American intentions during the whole long and ultimately tragic history of the attempt at disarmament. The difficulty with the American conception was its general irrelevance to the actual problems with which it was designed to deal. It was no use to dismiss French concern with security as frivolous and stubborn; it was pointless to shrug off Japanese insistence on naval parity as presumptuous. The political problems of the interwar period were real and pressing, regardless of the fact that they may have seemed slightly indecent to Americans. The way to peace was not to be found—at least in the 1920's—by voluntary acts of self-abnegation by sovereign states.

The depression

During the period we have been considering, European relations had changed swiftly from crisis in 1924 (marked by French occupation of the Ruhr) to a remarkable degree of reconciliation after 1925 (the year of the signature of the Pact of Locarno). Between 1925 and 1930, the climate of international relations in Europe raised hopes for permanently improved relations. This was the era of the Pact of Paris and the heyday of the League of Nations. This more or less halcyon phase came to a close with the depression of 1929.

Even before the stock-market collapse that touched off the world-wide economic distress, economic relations between the United States and Europe had been complicated by the question of the so-called "war debts."[17] The coming of the depression elevated what had been an annoyance to the level of a major crisis.

The Debt Question. About two-thirds of the debt owed the United States by its European allies had originally been contracted during the war; the remainder had taken the form of a post-Armistice loan. The end of the war found the Allies at first arguing for cancellation of the entire debt; this the United States rejected as being both a matter of bad faith and of bad business. The next European contention was to assert that there was a connection between the interallied debt and the collection of reparations from Germany. This the United States found equally unacceptable, since there was already (by 1922) a suspicion that the reparations bill would prove uncollectible.

The United States persuaded the major European debtors to accept repayment plans that in themselves involved a huge reduction in the total bill. In attempting throughout the 1920's to keep the payments coming in, Washington was forced unofficially to intervene into the reparations issue; in 1924 the "Dawes plan" provided for a less onerous scale of reparations payments from Germany; in 1929 the "Young plan" drastically lowered the total due. Throughout it all, payments trickled in from the European debtors accompanied by a rising tide of ill will. To millions of Europeans, the United States became "Uncle Shylock," intent on getting his pound of flesh at whatever cost. American attitudes, already sensitive toward European criticism, retaliated by becoming more belligerently nationalistic and isolationist.

The Moratorium and Default. In 1931, President Hoover attempted to reverse the disastrous trend of international economic relations by proposing a one-year moratorium on the payment of Allied debts. During the year, the European powers substantially cancelled the reparations due from Germany (by the terms of the Lausanne Agreement, 1932) and then looked expectantly to the United States for the cancellation of their own debt. President Hoover refused; his example was followed early in 1933 by Franklin D. Roosevelt. American public opinion would not tolerate cancellation in any form for any reason. Despairing of obtaining relief from the United States and offended by the Johnson Act (1934) forbidding private American loans to governments in arrears, almost all the debtors defaulted by June 1934. The single exception was Finland, whose

---

[17] See Harold Moulton and Leo Pasvolsky, *War Debts and World Prosperity* (New York: Century, 1932).

debt was miniscule and who reaped a harvest in favorable publicity over the years worth far more than its negligible payments.

Economic Isolationism. One final word must be said about American economic foreign policy during the depression. By 1933 the European states realized that only an international solution could be found for an international depression. Accordingly, an International Economic Conference convened in London in June to consider some form of joint international action to restore prosperity. After some encouraging progress, the discussion turned to the gold standard and currency stabilization. Here was the rock on which the conference foundered.

The Roosevelt New Deal, it must never be forgotten, was in the grand tradition of American reform movements; as such, it emphasized domestic policy and was profoundly and quaintly isolationist in spirit.[18] Currency manipulation was part of its program for fighting the depression at home; it had no intention of sacrificing any part of its control over the American economy on behalf of any illusory scheme of international cooperation. As a result, President Roosevelt intervened in the Conference, rebuking the membership for considering joint currency stabilization and cutting the ground out from under the American delegates (Secretary of State Cordell Hull and Mr. Raymond Moley), who had earlier indicated some willingness to go along with the program. With the United States clearly unwilling to merge its economic destiny with that of other states, the conference failed. The United States had joined the major states of Europe in a policy of economic nationalism that was to endure until World War II.

One break in the otherwise solid front of economic nationalism was the Reciprocal Trade Agreements Program, originally enacted in 1934. This program authorized the negotiation of bilateral executive agreements covering tariff reductions. By means of the most-favored-nation clause, reductions brought about in American duties under the terms of one of these agreements were given application to many other nations. By 1941 the Reciprocal Trade Agreements Program had brought about an over-all reduction in American tariff barriers that, although encouraging, was never any more than moderate.[19]

The liquidation of dollar diplomacy

One credit mark in the record of American foreign policy prior to

---

[18] Eric F. Goldman, *Rendezvous with Destiny: A History of Modern American Reform* (New York: Alfred A. Knopf, Inc., 1953), pp. 374-9.

[19] For further discussion of the program and its more recent history, see p. 469.

World War II was the liquidation of dollar diplomacy in Latin America and the adoption of the Good Neighbor policy. Credit for this movement in the direction of the abandonment of imperialism must be divided between the administrations of Hoover and Roosevelt.

The Reinterpretation of the Monroe Doctrine. From its beginning, the Hoover administration made clear that it was abandoning the more extreme interpretations of the Monroe Doctrine popular under Theodore Roosevelt, Taft, and Wilson. In 1930 there was published a long and detailed *Memorandum on the Monroe Doctrine*, written in 1928 by Undersecretary of State J. Reuben Clark.[20] This document returned to the original conception of the doctrine as a policy vis-a-vis Europe rather than Latin America. During the Hoover administration the government remained generally faithful to its new principles, recognizing *de facto* governments in the western hemisphere without concerning itself with their legitimacy and withdrawing American forces from Haiti and Nicaragua.

The Good Neighbor. The New Deal followed up the initial advantage. The Montevideo Inter-American Conference (1933) resulted in a pact, supported by the United States, that denied any right of intervention. Later the President specifically underscored the end of intervention and dollar diplomacy by a studied policy toward recurrent Latin American crises a good deal different from former American tactics. The United States entered World War II with the hemisphere more united and less hostile toward the "Colossus of the North" than at any time in sixty years, although provisions for multilateral action in enforcement of the Monroe Doctrine—hemisphere cooperation against outside threats—were not worked out until later.

THE RISE OF THE DICTATORS

The rise of Hitler, Mussolini, and imperial Japan to the point where the United States finally recognized them as menaces marks one of the major turning points in the history of American foreign policy. Before a rational course of action could be decided on, however, the last full measure of noninvolvement was to be tried and found wanting.

The new threat of totalitarianism

The Totalitarian Menace. In the policies of Nazi Germany, Fascist

---

[20] J. Reuben Clark, *Memorandum on the Monroe Doctrine* (Washington, D. C.: U.S. Government Printing Office, 1930).

161

Italy, and a newly intransigent Japan the United States found something for which it was unprepared. The dictators of the 1930's were the outstanding exponents of "the pragmatic revolt in politics"; they ignored accepted codes of behavior, did not act like gentlemen (or even normally civilized persons), rejected the dogmas of individualism, preached war as the noblest exercise of men, and ranted about "master races" and world conquest. The initial American reaction to such irrational behavior was simply one of shocked incredulity; the United States could not take such preposterous talk seriously.

When Americans finally realized that these governments meant exactly what they were saying, something like panic replaced the earlier bemusement. It seemed as if the dictators had discovered the secret of successful foreign policy in direct, forceful action; the democracies appeared to be almost hypnotized by the speed and precision with which the dictators won victory after victory. After a quasi-hysterical attempt at total withdrawal, the United States came at last to realize that there was only one way to deal with the sort of menace it faced: to meet force with greater force.

First Step: Manchuria. Japan opened the dictatorial drive for world power by invading Manchuria in 1931. The United States, both because of its interest in the Open Door and its concern with peace, opposed the move and ultimately gave voice to the "Stimson Doctrine": the United States would not recognize any territorial changes brought about in violation of treaty obligations.[21] This was a weak move at best, and when Britain and France refused to follow the American lead (the relative positions of the democracies were now strangely reversed) the attempt collapsed.

The Japanese invasion of Shanghai, in 1932, produced a stronger reaction in the United States. Public opinion at last grew seriously concerned and urged strong action against Japan. The government of the United States, however, contented itself with strong protests. Japan finally withdrew, but the damage had been done; Tokyo had broken the peace and had been permitted, not only to escape punishment, but to retain most of the fruits of its aggression.

Ethiopia and Spain. There then ensued a pause of some three years while Hitler came to power in Germany and Mussolini poised to strike. In 1935 Italy invaded the African kingdom of Ethiopia and succeeded in making good its conquest in the face of an abortive attempt to impose

---

[21] For the "Doctrine" itself, and for a picture of the crisis from the point of view of a major participant, see Henry L. Stimson and McGeorge Bundy, *On Active Service in Peace and War* (New York: Harper & Bros., 1948), pp. 226-239.

sanctions by the League of Nations. In 1936 civil war broke out in Spain, with the rebels receiving open support from Hitler and Mussolini. Once again the best efforts of the European democracies were weak and futile; the dictators scored another victory.

Isolation by law

How was the United States reacting to the rise of totalitarian power? In the first place, there was the depression to combat at home; this absorbed the bulk of official and popular attention. When foreign affairs finally forced themselves on American attention, the reaction was all too familiar. The United States attempted to legislate isolation.

The Neutrality Acts. In the mid-1930's, Americans were profoundly disillusioned about international affairs in general, and particularly about the institution of war. This was the era during which thousands of college students signed pledges that they would never fight in any war. The only way war could come to the United States, Americans felt, was by deceit. The United States would fight only if tricked into it by the wiles of European diplomats or by the selfish manipulation of war profiteers—the "merchants of death" who became famous through the activities of investigating committees of Congress. So the United States sought to protect itself from these twin dangers by passing laws: the Neutrality Acts of 1935, 1936, and 1937.

The 1935 act made it illegal to sell or ship munitions to belligerents. In 1936 loans to belligerents were prohibited. In 1937 the law was extended to include such civil wars as were proclaimed by the President. One concession was written into the 1937 law: the "cash-and-carry" rule that raw materials could be sold to belligerents if they paid cash and took them away in their own ships. This provision had only a two-year life; this turned out to be important because World War II was to begin within a few weeks after this provision expired.

The Neutrality Acts were misnomers; they represented the complete abandonment of neutrality rather than any protection of it. The United States had abdicated all of the traditional rights of neutrals to use the high seas in time of war, and instead was trying to shut out all sight, sound, or other evidence of fighting. However much we may dispute the historical or legal impact of these laws, their purpose was clear: to keep the United States out of war by any possible means. Their effectiveness, of course, would depend in practice on an intangible: would the United States remain sufficiently impartial in a major war so that both sets of belligerents could be treated alike, particularly if the prospective victor had interests inimical to the United States? This question, to be answered during the 1939-41 period, was not raised while the acts were being passed.

The Naval Race. But American policy during this era was not all a matter of head-in-the-sand. The 1935 London Naval Disarmament Conference failed because of Japan's withdrawal and Italy's nonadherence to the draft treaty. Recognizing finally that disarmament was a futile effort during the 1930's, President Roosevelt moved to build up the United States Navy to treaty strength. By 1938 the United States was active again in the naval race.

"Quarantine" and Munich

By 1937 the Roosevelt administration had at last learned that the dictators were actual dangers rather than mere annoyances, and that the United States could not afford any longer to ignore them without seriously undermining American security. In Europe and in the Far East American policy began to grapple with the threat of totalitarianism, at first hesitantly and then later with more determination (if with but little more effectiveness).[22]

The "Quarantine" Speech. The first clear sign that a new American policy was in the making was the famous "quarantine the aggressors" speech of President Roosevelt in October 1937. Attacking what he called "international lawlessness," he emphasized the American interest in peace, and suggested that aggressors should be "quarantined." The President declared that 90 per cent of the world wanted to live in "peace under law" and according to accepted moral standards, and that the ten per cent who were lawless should be restrained. "There must be," he said, "positive endeavors to preserve peace."

Though forcefully stated, Roosevelt's speech represented only the line of official thinking rather than any clear action program. Public opinion, although probably inclined toward his position, was neverthe-

---

[22] For American policy beginning with the "Quarantine" speech and leading up to American entry into the war, the literature is already enormous. Worthy of special note are the two volumes by William L. Langer and S. Everett Gleason, *The Challenge to Isolation* (New York: Harper & Bros., 1952) and *The Undeclared War* (New York: Harper & Bros., 1953), and Basil Rauch, *Roosevelt from Munich to Pearl Harbor* (New York: Creative Age, 1950). Bitterly critical of United States policy during this period are the two works of Charles A. Beard, *American Foreign Policy in the Making, 1932-1940* (New Haven: Yale University Press, 1946) and *President Roosevelt and the Coming of the War* (New Haven: Yale University Press, 1948), and Charles C. Tansill, *Back Door to War* (Chicago: Regnery, 1952).

less divided; the American people had not gone as far as had their government in awakening to the changed situation. But the speech had one constructive effect: it not only put the dictators on notice that the United States disapproved of what they were doing, but also that the American government was willing to consider action to stop them.

Troubles with Japan. Meanwhile, troubles were multiplying in the Pacific where, earlier in 1937, Japan had initiated the "China incident," a euphemism for a general war of aggression against China. With the conflict spreading throughout that distraught nation, it was inevitable that episodes would occur involving Americans. The most serious event was the sinking of the United States gunboat *Panay* in December, 1937.

In the diplomatic dispute that then ensued, Japan announced a "New Order in East Asia," the end of the Open Door and the establishment of Japanese hegemony. This the United States was obviously unprepared to accept and, in mid-1939, the government abrogated its commercial treaty with Japan preparatory to the establishment of a munitions embargo. This provocative step clearly showed the Japanese that America was in earnest and served for a while to slow Tokyo's timetable.

Munich and the Threat of Hitler. Up to this point Japan and Italy had been the most conspicuous dictatorships; Germany's Hitler was a semi-comic figure with many apologists in the United States. During 1938, however, Hitler moved to the front as the leader of the new Axis of fascist states and became the most ominous threat to American security.

After destroying the Versailles Treaty in 1935 by rearming and by reoccupying the Rhineland, Hitler struck next in 1938. Early in the year he annexed Austria by a superlatively efficient coup; in the autumn came the great crisis over the Sudetenland area of Czechoslovakia. The issue grew so tense that many during that summer thought that the dread day of a general war had arrived. In this critical moment the United States moved quickly and, in contrast to some of its earlier efforts, to some effect. President Roosevelt personally urged Hitler and Mussolini to accept a peaceful solution to the crisis and, when the fateful Munich conference was convened, felt relieved that war had been averted.[23] American policy was by this act deeply involved in the tangled course of European affairs.

But the United States swiftly learned the folly of what was already being called "appeasement." Peace—of a sort—had been sustained at Munich, but only at the price of giving the dictators what they de-

---

[23] Arthur S. Link, *American Epoch* (New York: Alfred A. Knopf, Inc., 1955), p. 473-4.

manded. The contemptuous attitude of the Nazis after their bloodless victory rapidly dissipated what little was left of American goodwill, and diplomatic relations between Germany and the United States hung on the brink of open rupture. When, in the spring of 1939, Hitler tore up the Munich agreement and annexed all of Czechoslovakia, to be followed shortly by Mussolini's rape of Albania, the United States placed itself in support of Britain and France in their attempts to prepare for what now seemed to be an inevitable open clash. During the last six months of peace, American policy sought to mobilize world opinion against the dictators and to give what help it could to the democracies who were struggling to get ready for the war they had hoped they would not have to fight.[24]

The coming of the war

The Polish Crisis. Hitler, who seemed to be timing his moves to coincide with the equinoxes, began his next aggression during the late summer of 1939. His target this time was Poland; his focus Danzig and the Polish Corridor. Poland, backed by the now-spirited allies, Britain and France, resisted Nazi pressure; the western democracies were busy negotiating a pact with the Soviet that, they hoped, would prevent Hitler from going to war. These plans evaporated late in August when the famous Nazi-Soviet nonaggression pact was announced. Hitler had won the diplomatic battle.

War and Neutrality. President Roosevelt made one more attempt to head off the conflict, personally urging Hitler, the President of Poland, and the King of Italy to submit the dispute to peaceful settlement. But the time had long passed when this kind of appeal had any utility; Hitler was ready for the battle and saw no reason to defer either to public opinion or to any adjusting agency. On September 1, the Nazi forces invaded Poland. On September 3, Britain and France declared war on Germany after the Nazis had ignored their ultimatums; on September 5, the United States issued its proclamations of neutrality. The Neutrality Acts (unamended, since an administration effort to change them had failed earlier in the year) were invoked, and President Roosevelt told the American people: "As long as it remains within my power to prevent it, there will be no blackout of peace in the United States."[25]

---

[24] For Roosevelt's policy in this period, see Link, pp. 472-475.

[25] New York Times (September 4, 1939), quoted in Bailey, Diplomatic History, p. 754.

THE WAR YEARS

With the course of battle during World War II, we have little to do; what is important from our point of view is the basic reorientation in American foreign policy that took place during the fighting. During the second great war Americans finally learned a good deal of what they should have known before the first.

Cooperation before Pearl Harbor

The United States, although sympathetic toward the Allies, was determined to remain out of the war. Up to the fall of France in June, 1940, American policy sought more and more ways of making explicit its policy of noninvolvement. This approach was inspired by a widespread belief that Allied military strength was sufficient to dispose of Hitler and that American action could safely be confined to cheering on the victors. Hitler's sensational victories in the West in 1940 overturned this illusion; once the Allied foothold in Europe had been reduced to the British Isles, American statesmen were forced into a frenzied recalculation of the entire situation. Never before had it been so clear that American success in remaining uninvolved in Europe depended on the British navy; if Britain fell, there would be nothing to protect the United States from the full wrath of the dictators.[26]

The End of Neutrality. The American government immediately began giving extensive "aid short of war" to the Allies. Arms shipments were made under strained interpretations of the law—or even in defiance of it; British warships were repaired in American shipyards; the United States provided sites and personnel for the training of British flying crews. The most spectacular of these moves, made in September, 1940, was the famous transfer of 50 overage destroyers to Britain in return for a series of sites for American naval bases in a number of British possessions in the western hemisphere. There was no doubt that the United States had scrapped any notion of neutrality; America was becoming a nonbelligerent ally.

Lend-Lease and Convoying. But more was to come. Early in 1941 the United States adopted the Lend-Lease Act that converted America into the "arsenal of democracy." Under this law, the United States pledged itself to "lend" or "lease" defense commodities of every sort to any

---

[26] On this period, see especially Langer and Gleason, *The Undeclared War.*

government that the President saw fit to support in this way.[27] Since everyone knew that all such aid was to be given to those states fighting the Axis, the distinction between lend-lease and outright war was a very slender one; this, however, was about as far as American opinion cared to go at the time. The United States was cooperating with those states with which it had a common interest, but it would not go to the point either of formalizing such an arrangement into an alliance or of going all the way to war.

During the spring and summer of 1941, German submarine sinkings of Allied convoys reached the point of real danger, capped by open Nazi attacks on American shipping. By July the United States Navy was convoying merchant vessels and defending them against submarine attacks; in September Roosevelt ordered American ships to "shoot on sight" at submarines; in October the Neutrality Acts were repealed and American merchant ships began to be armed. Most Americans by this time regarded the United States as virtually at war.

The Atlantic Charter. All of this was in at least the quasi-military realm. In the purely political area the most sensational single event of the pre-Pearl Harbor era took place: the "Atlantic Charter" issued by Roosevelt and Churchill in August 1941. This eight-point program was a joint declaration of peace terms (they could not be called "war aims," since the United States was not officially a belligerent) and were widely discussed at the time, during the war, and afterwards. The particulars were not novel; one author calls them a "mixture of the New Deal and the old Fourteen Points." [28] However innocuous the Atlantic Charter was in substance, and however little influence it had on the shape of the ultimate terms of peace, it is undeniable that it served as a rallying point for a good deal of pro-Ally public opinion during the war. From our point of view, however, its chief significance is that it tied the United States to Britain in working for a common peace—an enterprise that could be accomplished only by fighting a common war.

The Japanese Explosion. As all Americans know, World War II came to the United States via the Pacific. Japan had capitalized on the Nazi victory in Europe to launch a strong diplomatic offensive aimed at establishing its "New Order" in Asia, with the wealth of Indochina and the East Indies as the tempting lure that drew it on. American opposition grew in turn more rigid, and throughout the latter half of 1941 the respective positions hardened. Japan insisted on American recognition of

[27] E. R. Stettinius, *Lend-Lease: Weapon of Victory* (New York: The Macmillan Co., 1944).

[28] Bailey, *Diplomatic History*, p. 784.

Japanese economic and political pre-eminence in Asia; the United States demanded nothing less than the abandonment of Japan's foreign policy line after 1931 and Tokyo's retreat to its pre-Manchuria position. It seems obvious today (and, as a matter of fact, it was obvious at the time) that there was no way to reconcile these two positions.

The Tojo cabinet that took office in Japan in October 1941 was pledged to no retreat, and during the last phases of Japanese-American negotiation, Tokyo was making secret military preparations. President Roosevelt made one last try on December 6, personally appealing to Emperor Hirohito to keep the peace. It was too late; the Japanese task force was already at sea. Early in the morning of December 7, Japan attacked Pearl Harbor and war had come to the United States.[29]

The immediate policy decision was really no decision at all; Congress did not even declare war, but merely responded to the President's invitation to recognize that "a state of war"" already existed by virtue of Japan's action. On December 11, Germany and Italy announced that they considered themselves at war with the United States, and again Congress had merely to ratify an action taken by the enemies of the United States.

The United Nations

Unlike American experience in 1917-18, almost from the very beginning the United States was part of a massive international body for fighting the war. The United Nations Organization—the wartime fighting alliance—was not only the closest and most intimate arrangement ever created among so many states for such a large object, but it also provided within itself the basis for the establishment of permanent cooperation and organization for postwar unity. The United States received its baptism of fire in the troubled arena of joint action during the war; the lessons learned were to be applied later.

The United Nations Declaration. On January 1, 1942, the formal structure of cooperation was set up by the signature of the Declaration by the United Nations, adhered to originally by twenty-six anti-Axis states and finally by over forty. This document bound all the signatories to the principles of the Atlantic Charter and pledged no separate peace. Thus the specific provisions of the Roosevelt-Churchill agreement ac-

---

[29] The most dramatic of the many accounts of the events leading to the attack is that by Walter Millis, *This Is Pearl!* (New York: William Morrow & Co., 1947); more sober and factual is Herbert Feis, *The Road to Pearl Harbor* (Princeton, N. J.: Princeton University Press, 1950).

quired a policy significance as official war aims that they had not previously had, and involved the United States—at the very beginning of its part in the conflict—in the accomplishment of a set of specific objectives.

Russian Relations. One consequence of the war was to throw the United States into intimate contact with the Soviet Union, an experience for which Americans were not emotionally or politically prepared. After American recognition in 1933, the Soviet's relations with the United States were limited, formal, and incomplete. Once the two nations became allies, each was forced to learn how to deal with the other, a task complicated by the fact that it had to go on in the midst of a frustrating, expensive, and total war. With so little of a historical background to their relations and with such a narrow area of agreement, what is remarkable today is that Soviet-American contacts were as amicable as they were during the war.

Moscow had is share of objections to American policy. Many were petty, but some had a good deal of substance. The Russians never felt that they were receiving an adequate share of lend-lease equipment throughout the period during which they were holding off the entire weight of the Nazi armies. They objected to some of the more questionable features of American wartime diplomacy—among them the highly equivocal deal with the pro-fascist French Admiral Darlan in North Africa in 1942. They found fault with the Allied policy toward the governments-in-exile in London, particularly the openly anti-Russian Polish regime. Most specific was their constant cry for a second front in Europe so as to relieve the pressure on the Red Army and to speed the defeat of the Axis.

American criticism of the Soviet proceeded generally from an ideological root of anti-communism. Policy-wise, the United States never understood Russia's refusal to go to war against Japan until victory was already assured; there was also considerable official resentment at Moscow's reserved and suspicious attitude toward its western allies.[30]

Even so, after 1943 American-Russian (or—more accurately—Allied-Russian) cooperation proceeded adequately. By means of top-level conferences and an elaborate hierarchy of coordinating committees, liaison officers, and so on, the governments kept each other passably well informed. There was a considerable degree of consultation on major strategy and a lesser amount of tactical coordination.

---

[30] See John A. Deane, *The Strange Alliance* (New York: The Viking Press, 1947), and W. A. Williams, *American-Russian Relations, 1781-1947* (New York: The Rinehart Co., 1952), pp. 258-82.

The Conferences. The new dimensions of American foreign policy were demonstrated for all to see by something that, although not entirely new, was completely novel in its scope. This was the policy-making device of the top-level conference permitting the heads of the allied governments to meet face-to-face and informally to make basic decisions. The "Big Three" of World War II was a familiar group to newspaper readers during the war.

The list of the wartime conferences is impressive: Washington, D. C., December-January 1941-2 (Roosevelt, Churchill); Washington, D. C., again, June 1942 (Roosevelt-Churchill); Casablanca, January 1943 (Roosevelt, Churchill, De Gaulle); Washington, D. C., May 1943 (Roosevelt, Churchill); Quebec, August 1943 (Roosevelt, Churchill, and a Chinese representative); Cairo, November 1943 (Roosevelt, Churchill, Chiang Kai-shek); Teheran, November-December 1943 (Roosevelt, Churchill, Stalin); Yalta, February 1945 (Roosevelt, Churchill, Stalin).

In all of these President Roosevelt participated personally, yet probably the most important single conference of the war years was the Foreign Ministers' Conference at Moscow in October 1943. Here the log jam in Russo-American relations was broken and it was on this occasion that Britain, the USSR, and the United States (joined by China) pledged themselves to the establishment of a new international organization to preserve the peace.

The conferences were large-scale diplomacy with a vengeance. It seemed shocking to many Americans, even in the midst of a global war, that their President should sit in a room with the Prime Minister of Great Britain and the dictator of communist Russia and jointly remake the map of the world. There seemed something so final, so Olympian about this way of doing business that much public opinion was alienated. When, at the end of the war, the information about the "secret protocols" of the Yalta agreement leaked out, public opinion was strong. The mass revulsion against strong executive action in foreign affairs, originally set in motion by the wartime conferences, continued into the postwar period in the form of such proposals as the so-called Bricker Amendment.

Planning for the postwar world

On one count the United States in World War II clearly improved over its record during the earlier conflict; planning for the peace. In the first place, many Americans recognized that there was going to be a peace and that all American problems were not going to end with the consummation of the magic formula of "unconditional surrender." The existence of the United Nations Organization and the record of the top-level conference also impressed on United States policy-makers, if not particularly on the mass public, the need for some kind of plan of action to follow the defeat of the Axis. Indeed, the postwar difficulties into which the United States drifted were not a result of the want of a plan, but rather of having too many plans. Perhaps the most accurate way to put the point is this: the deficiency was not in the plans themselves, but rather in the fact that the plans were drawn to cope with a situation that never arose, while the actual problems that appeared were foreign to the blueprints under which the United States was trying to operate.

We shall examine the political strategy of the United States at various places in our discussion in later chapters. At this point, we shall consider only one very special type of postwar plan, one that its architects felt was the most crucial of all and the one that would spell success or failure to man's attempt to guarantee the peace he was winning with such effort. This was, of course, the project to establish a new international organization to replace (and improve upon) the defunct League of Nations. In this operation the United States was a leader.

The Moscow Declaration. The Atlantic Charter, in words of studied vagueness, had pledged Britain and the United States to work for the creation of some new kind of world organization. This idea languished, as we have seen, during the early years of the war. It was only with the Moscow Conference of foreign ministers, in October 1943, that the promise was made specific. This, the original germ of the United Nations, merits quotation. In the communique the following statement was made:

> 4. That they [the United States, the United Kingdom, the Soviet Union, and China] recognize the necessity of establishing at the earliest practicable date a general international organization, based on the principle of the sovereign equality of all peace-loving states, and open to membership by all such states, large and small, for the maintenance of international peace and security.[31]

Preliminary Activity. With the Moscow Declaration as proof that the great powers were committed to permanent international organization, the attack on the postwar world went forward during the fighting. In the spring of 1943, there had already been held the United Nations Conference on Food and Agriculture that led to the creation of the Food and Agriculture Organization of the United Nations. The United Nations

---

[31] *Department of State Bulletin* (October 16, 1943, p. 254).

Relief and Rehabilitation Administration (UNRRA) was created in November 1943. In the summer of 1944, the Bretton Woods Conference on monetary and financial questions—with forty-four nations represented—met and hammered out a plan to meet the financial and monetary problems of the postwar world. These proposals ultimately became the International Bank for Reconstruction and Development and the International Monetary Fund.

Dumbarton Oaks and Yalta. The major effort in direct implementation of the Moscow Declaration was the Dumbarton Oaks Conference of August-October, 1944. Here representatives of the four major allied powers worked out a draft of a world organization. Despite general agreement that the new structure was to have "teeth" as contrasted with the powerless League of Nations, the thorny question of the voting formula to be used in controlling the enforcement action of the organization could not be finally decided.

This was solved—after a fashion—at the Yalta Conference. It was at this meeting that the much-discussed "veto" provision, requiring the unanimous vote of all permanent members for the Security Council to take any action on a nonprocedural matter, was decided upon by Roosevelt and Stalin. With this out of the way, the call was issued at Yalta for the United Nations Conference to draw up the Charter of the proposed organization.[32]

The San Francisco Conference. From the dates of its meeting (April 21–June 25, 1945) the San Francisco Conference belongs in a discussion of the war years, but it may also be thought of as the beginning of the postwar era. Before the Conference adjourned, Germany had surrendered and the final blows were being prepared for the destruction of Japan. Another reason for considering it a postwar development was the appearance at San Francisco of what were to become some of the most ominous lines of cleavage in postwar politics: the East-West split and the great power-small state controversy.

The Charter of the United Nations emerged from the Conference much as it had come from Dumbarton Oaks and Yalta. The smaller states made a few significant amendments, mainly in the direction of increased emphasis in structure and function on "non-political" questions—economic, social, and technical. They also succeeded in reducing slightly

---

[32] See E. R. Stettinius, *Roosevelt and the Russians* (Garden City: Doubleday, 1949), Chapters 7, 10; also John N. Snell, Forrest C. Pogue, Charles F. Delzell, and George A. Lensen, *The Meaning of Yalta* (Baton Rouge: Louisiana State University Press, 1956).

the almost complete monopoly over security issues that the Big Five had originally hoped for. But in the main the Charter was close to what its original sponsors had planned.

Unlike the Covenant of the League, the Charter had no difficulty winning ratification. The quick action taken by the United States Senate marked something of the distance the United States had come since 1919. The Foreign Relations Committee held only brief hearings, Senate debate lasted only six days, the final vote was eighty-nine to two, and the United States was the first state to ratify. Americans, having come out of one war into attempted isolation and almost complete frustration, were determined to try a different tack as they emerged from the second.

part 4:

THE NATIONAL INTEREST:
MYTH AND YARDSTICK

part 4.

THE NATIONAL INTEREST:
MYTH AND YARDSTICK

7 : The popular tradition of foreign policy

W hat a people thinks it is often largely determines what it actually is; what it thinks it ought to do has a great effect on what it actually does. Each nation has a more or less formalized ego-image: a psychic picture of itself as it performs its mission in the world. Perhaps no more fundamental starting place can be found for our study of American foreign policy than an inquiry into what Americans think they are and what they think they are doing in their relations with other peoples.

Our analysis in this chapter will be made generally in terms of what we call the "tradition" of American policy: those ideas, impressions, and feelings about the external relations of the United States that have their roots deep in history and are widely shared among, deeply felt by, and virtually self-evident to the mass of the American people today. Being imbedded so firmly in popular political consciousness, this tradition represents a relatively constant and fixed factor that must be taken into account by both American and foreign policymakers. The image of America's international role, like any tradition, changes only slowly and reluctantly; the fast-moving world of today has done violence to many of the most cherished presuppositions and preferences of Americans. Many newer attitudes compete for acceptance among the people. Although modified to some extent by the impact of circumstances, the tradition endures to this day, alternately strengthening and stultifying the government's attacks on international problems.

We shall analyze this popular orientation to international relations from three points of view: (1) a brief consideration of the continuing American tradition of foreign policy, including some traditional formulations of national interest; (2) a survey of American operational preferences; (3) a study of some of the characteristics of American public opinion as applied to international questions.

177

THE TRADITION OF AMERICAN FOREIGN POLICY

The American people have approached foreign policy in general agreement on certain basic assumptions. These have grown out of native American history and culture and have reflected certain basic characteristics of the whole of American life. This was indeed inevitable; a nation's foreign policy may perhaps be less than its over-all *Weltanschauung*, but it can never be more.[1]

The secondary nature of foreign affairs

We may lay down a basic postulate at the outset. Foreign affairs, however exciting they may have become during particular crises, in the long run have been of only secondary importance to Americans. They have felt that their ultimate salvation was to be found within the United States and, while agreeing that they must accept the world, they have argued that they dare not trust themselves entirely to it.

The Importance of Domestic Affairs. Initially, this notion grew out of a very natural preoccupation with domestic affairs. The size of the United States, its great natural and man-made wealth, the complexities of the social, economic, and political problems Americans must solve, America's long period of immunity from the pressures of the outside world, and the grandeur of American civilization all combined to turn American eyes to matters within the borders of the United States. Americans have tended to be most interested in those things that were either close to them in space or that affected them directly, and for most citizens the rest of the world was far away. Today it is less far away than it used to be, perhaps; yet the immediacy of international problems is seldom as great for most Americans as that of local, municipal, state, or national ones.[2]

Nowhere has this been more clearly indicated than in the dominant popular attitude toward domestic politics. Presidential elections are traditionally fought out essentially on national issues, and Americans have

---

[1] For somewhat different approaches to the problem discussed in this section, see, among other works, the following: Dexter Perkins, *The American Approach to Foreign Policy* (Cambridge: Harvard University Press, 1952); Robert Osgood, *Ideals and Self-interest in America's Foreign Relations* (Chicago: University of Chicago Press, 1953); Frank Tannenbaum, *The American Tradition in Foreign Policy* (Norman: University of Oklahoma Press, 1955).

[2] For an explicit example of this attitude, emphasizing the minor importance and essentially amoral character of foreign affairs, see Felix Morley, *The Foreign Policy of the United States* (New York: Alfred A. Knopf, Inc., 1951).

178

had some difficulty in grasping the supranational significance of their political struggles. "Foreign policy" has been an election issue to be dealt with by both parties in such a way as to harvest the greatest number of votes from it; it has been no different—and of no more importance— than agriculture, labor relations, tax policy, or any of a dozen other perennial problems that help decide elections.

Distrust of the Outside World. A second explanation for the relatively low place occupied by foreign policy in the American attitude has been a genuine distrust of the outside world. This is by no means to say that Americans have been totally uninterested in what goes on abroad; indeed, American curiosity about alien cultures is famous everywhere in the world. But the political overtones of this curiosity have been suspicion, reserve, and mistrust.

This apparently innate American characteristic has been noted by many observers, foreign and American, ever since the United States appeared as a nation. It would require far more than our limited space to list all the explanations that have been advanced for this phenomenon, each having some considerable historical and analytical support. The most we can say here is that Americans, as a group, have tended to approach the world armed with a genuine cynicism about the motives and the behavior of other peoples and other states.

Since Americans have had to make their way in a world peopled by men who, if not actually doing evil, were at least capable of it, their tradition tended to place a low estimate on what they could achieve in dealing with them. The rewards of foreign policy were thought to be by their very nature limited in extent, and of only an inferior order of worth. For what good the United States could achieve in the world Americans felt they must count ultimately only on themselves.[3]

Cultural Isolationism. A final explanation of the basic popular skepticism about foreign policy grows out of the first two. Culturally Americans have been in the past— and to a considerable extent still are—isolated from many of the main streams of social development. Most adult Americans—and most of their forbears—grew to maturity in a climate relatively unsullied by alien influences and free from direct concern about the size or the complexities of other societies.

Thus unaware of the cultural diversity of men, or—more accurately— aware of the diversity but insensitive to the difference such cultural varia-

---

[3] This idea was the foundation of the later foreign-policy thinking of the late Professor Charles A. Beard. See especially his *Open Door at Home* and *The Devil Theory of War*, as well as his polemics on American entry into World War II, *American Foreign Policy in the Making* and *President Roosevelt and the Coming of the War.*

tion made, Americans have tended to judge the world by their own standards. Mass attitudes indicated a strong preference for peculiarly American ways and a rejection of possible contributions from the outside world. Americans were peculiarly proud of their country's history as a "melting pot"; they found a society in which widely divergent elements were fused into a single mass culture something of which to be proud. Their self-identification was epitomized in the famous phrase from Washington's Farewell Address: "Why quit our own to stand on foreign ground?" "Why, indeed?" have echoed generations of Americans; foreign policy thus came inevitably to reflect a dominant cultural particularism.

The uniqueness of the United States

Despite the secondary place of foreign policy in the American attitude, Americans nonetheless recognized early in their history that they must deal with the rest of the world. Into their contacts with other states they carried the second element of their evolving tradition: a profound conviction that they were a unique people, unlike any other and therefore subject to different standards of behavior and judgment.

The Sense of "Difference." American history led to the conclusion that Americans are different from any other people. Geographically isolated, culturally separate, politically self-determined, socially fluid, and economically self-contained, the American people early drew a clear distinction between themselves and other societies. Nobody, they felt, was quite like Americans, and it was unfair to expect them to behave quite like anyone else.

The international role of the United States, therefore, came to be conceived as different from that of any other state. Americans claimed to be uninterested in the ordinary goals pursued by ordinary governments; they felt that they were engaged in a (regrettably) necessary but ultimately loftier enterprise than the common run of nations. The United States was in the world—this much Americans would admit—but it was emphatically not of it. The nation contended that it would not make any compromises with its principles in order to gain advantages that, at best, could never be more than temporary. The United States would achieve its own objectives in its own way, regardless of cost.[4]

---

[4] For example, Washington's Farewell Address pointed out: "Our detached and distant position invites us and enables us to pursue a different course [from that of the states of Europe]." James D. Richardson, ed. and compiler, *A Compilation of the Messages and Papers of the Presidents* (New York: Bureau of National Literature, 1897), I, 214.

Moral Superiority. This sense of detachment from the world rapidly led into a manifestation of what anthropologists call "ethnocentrism." The difference between other peoples and Americans came popularly to be regarded as measures of the extent to which outsiders fell short of the high American moral standards. Morality became the index of uniqueness; Americans were simply "better" people.

One of the unspoken but ubiquitous premises of American foreign policy has been that the United States was always dealing with its moral inferiors. Particular states, of course, varied in the degree to which they fell short of the American standard; generally, the more closely they resembled the United States the greater amount of moral conviction they were admitted to have. Generally Great Britain was agreed to rank the highest. But since no one could ever be quite like Americans, no one could quite come up to their moral level.[5]

An International Double Standard. Being different, and this difference being epitomized and most clearly demonstrated by moral preeminence, it was only a short step for Americans to argue that they should be judged by a different set of standards than those applied to lesser states. It would have been unjust, the argument ran, to expect the United States to conform to rules made for ordinary peoples; it was nothing more than equitable to recognize American uniqueness and to apply different criteria in judging American acts. This argument was seldom spelled out in detail; it was generally subordinated to an evocation of the mission in which the United States was engaged. But even in this way it became an accepted part of American dogma.

In this way deeds wrong in themselves when done by other peoples became perfectly permissible; other forms of state action, regarded as normal by the international community, were barred to the United States. It was not "imperialistic," for example, for the United States to annex overseas territories, since American purposes were high-minded and philanthropic; the United States was to rule colonial peoples for their own good. According to the converse of the same principle, "power politics" was "un-American" and immoral; Americans would not indulge in it, no matter how widespread the practice might be among other states.

For a long time Americans overlooked the ethical trap they were laying for themselves by the advocacy of this double standard. The constant evocation of uniqueness and moral superiority prepared the way for the

---

[5] For a sharp critique of American moralism in international affairs, see George F. Kennan, *American Diplomacy, 1900-1950*, pp. 95-103; for an indignant demand that Americans return to the historic moral base of their foreign policy, see Morley, *Foreign Policy*, pp. 154-156.

dangerous doctrine that the ends always justify the means. It has been only recently that this dilemma has finally forced itself on the popular consciousness.[6] Today many Americans are wrestling with the issue, but without reaching any broadly satisfying answer.

American Utopianism

Finally, the American approach to foreign policy has been essentially Utopian. This term has been used variously as an anathema or as an accolade, but its substantive import has been fairly consistent. The Utopian assumption has been one of the more durable and versatile components of the American tradition, and it survives almost intact to the present day.

A Sense of Mission. In the first place, Americans have been called Utopian because they have recognized and have accepted a sense of mission. The popular attitude toward foreign policy, once the United States has actively entered the international arena, has usually been an urge to "set things right." Americans disapproved of purposeless action; they affirmatively have sought a goal of improvement, of rectification, or of organization.

Remembering their unique orientation to the world, we would expect that the missions accepted by the American people would be thought of as being of a higher and more moral nature than would ordinarily be expected of a state. There has been a strong popular preference for objectives expressed as moral absolutes: Americans have attempted to "end war," to "make the world safe for democracy," to settle disputes "by pacific means," to "establish a world of law," or to "stop communist aggression." Only seldom have national missions gained popular expression in either concrete or egocentric terms.[7]

---

[6] For example, we may note the embarrassing situation in which the United States found itself in the aftermath of the crisis created by Egypt's nationalization of the Suez Canal in 1956. The United States government, speaking through Secretary of State Dulles, insisted that Suez be "internationalized" but was sharply taken aback when demands arose that the Panama Canal be given the same treatment. The United States rapidly abandoned its insistence on internationalization of Suez and began considering whether or not Panama might profitably be transferred to international administration. See statements of ex-President Truman, *New York Times* (August 10, 1956) and Senator Flanders of Vermont, *New York Times* (September 10, 1956).

[7] Although hackneyed by much quotation, Woodrow Wilson's speech on the Fourteen Points merits one more repetition because of its admirable evocation of the idea of "the American mission": "We entered this war because violations of right had occurred which touched us to the quick and made the life of our own people impossible unless they were corrected and the world secured once for all against their recurrence.... The program of the world's peace, therefore, is our program...." *Congressional Record*, LVI, 691 (January 8, 1918).

The Goal of Perfection. Utopianism has been also apparent in the deliberate pursuit of the goal of perfection by Americans. Implictly Americans have seemed to assume that all international problems have a "right" answer, discoverable by men if only they put all their resources of reason and good will to work on it. Americans have therefore frequently made a conscious effort to bring about a perfect state of affairs or, if this were beyond reach, to move actively in that direction. This, to Americans, was "progress," a goal which all loyal citizens were thought enthusiastically to accept.

The right answer usually was one that forever settled the problem and removed it to the category of the not-to-be-thought-about-again. Not only were single issues attacked in terms of finding the correct solution for each of them, but the long-range target was frequently formulated as a world organized into a single, self-regulating system. Such perfection, Americans thought, would obliterate forever the irrational scourges of war, crisis, and turmoil. To this end American policy should be directed.

Leadership by Example. But we must not infer that Utopianism led Americans into active commitment to the cause of the perfect order they desired. On the contrary, the dominant popular conception of the role of the United States was that of leadership by example rather than that of direct participation in concrete cooperative projects. The best way to bring about a world of law and justice, Americans felt, was for them to act always as the United States wished everyone else to act, to be prompt to point out the failures of other peoples, and to be willing to give advice as to how they should behave. In this way the sheer force of example would do more to bring about a better day than would self-defeating involvement in the imperfect and frustrating process of day-by-day international politics.

This kind of role gave the United States a double advantage: it preserved the image of American uniqueness and moral leadership, and yet it freed the nation from the necessity of direct follow-through on its policy pronouncements. No greater strain has been placed on Americans since 1945 than the necessity of abandoning a purely didactic view of world affairs and of dealing with concrete problems in an increasingly relativistic context.

Traditional formulations of the national interest

Within the developed tradition of foreign policy, the American people developed a number of concrete formulations of interest that reflected the national sense of mission. Mass attitudes accepted and sanctified a series of particular purposes and hardened them into fixed commitments. Many of these traditional interests have been carried virtually untouched into the contemporary era; others have been abandoned in favor of newer formulas. As we saw in Chapter 1, however, whatever forms the myth of national purpose may take, it remains as a major factor influencing the decisions made on concrete issues made by the responsible officials of the American government. In times of stress or sudden crisis the spontaneous reaction of much of public opinion is to revert to traditional concepts of interest; to accept some new formulation usually demands an effort of mass will spurred by self-conscious leaders.

Chapters 5 and 6 sketched some of the major historical developments that contributed to this traditional package of interests. We shall not restate the conclusions that we reached in those chapters, but we shall rather briefly consider here how particular undertakings became institutionalized into parts of a working tradition.

The Myth of Isolationism. We should first dispose of a pernicious but remarkably tenacious component of the American myth: the notion of isolationism. We have already seen that the word itself was more a tool of political manipulation and a component of the mystique of democratic politics than it was descriptive of the actual content of American foreign policy. There is little concrete evidence that the working notion of American national interest was ever based on any purely isolationist premise.[8] Total nonintercourse with the outside world has never been seriously attempted by the United States, and the term is almost meaningless on any other basis. Even the use of a more restrictive word, such as "independency" or "noninvolvement," still leaves many historical facts unaccounted for. The record indicates that the American tradition of national interest has been too many-sided to be successfully fitted into any slogan as rigid as "isolationism." It has taken a different turn in each major region of the world, and we must consider it in terms of its principal specific manifestations.

Hemisphere Hegemony. No element of American foreign policy received such unanimous acceptance by the public nor a more solid place in tradition than the principle that the United States should be absolutely dominant in the western hemisphere. The Monroe Doctrine is, as we have pointed out, a phrase with which almost all Americans are familiar,

---

[8] See the elaborate synthesis made by Albert K. Weinberg in "The Historical Meaning of the American Doctrine of Isolation," *American Political Science Review* (June, 1940).

and the package of emotional reactions that it evokes has had a powerful impact on the actual policy of the United States.[9]

As worked out by the interaction of doctrine and practice, the American interest in the western hemisphere consisted of three related concerns: (1) The United States insisted on the exclusion of non-American power from the hemisphere except for the minor colonial holdings of Britain, France, and the Netherlands. (2) The United States was to brook no real rivals in the region; America was to regard the hemisphere as a United States preserve in which Washington reigned unchallenged, eliminating rivals and rearranging internal and international affairs to suit its convenience. (3) The Americas were to be organized into a single more or less cohesive entity under United States leadership; the resulting unity was to be primarily of service to the foreign policy of the United States.

European Noninvolvement. We have already pointed out that the principle of "isolationism" was relevant only to Europe, and then only in a rather special sense. Tradition energetically foreswore any entanglement in intra-European politics, a game which Americans felt themselves unequipped to play. Even today this instinctive distrust of Europe's political concerns lies deep in the American subconscious; many Americans are still uncomfortable at the thought that they may be caught in a political web in the capitals of Europe from which they can never escape.[10] Such participation in European affairs as the United States could not avoid was reluctant and broken off as soon as possible.

We should also note again, however, that noninvolvement was more a matter of geography than of an antipathy to the European states as such. The traditional interests of the United States have always permitted extensive relations and even binding commitments with the powers of Europe on questions that were non-European in nature. It was only at European problems, narrowly defined, that the United States drew the line; in Latin America and in the Pacific, American tradition approved of intimate dealings with the world of Europe.

Balance of Power in Asia. "Intervention" is as much a key word to characterize American traditions in Asia—or, more properly, the Far Eastern littoral—as "noninvolvement" is appropriate to the American out-

---

[9] This story is well told in Dexter Perkins, *Hands Off: A History of the Monroe Doctrine;* and Samuel F. Bemis, *The Latin American Policy of the United States* (New York: Harcourt, Brace and Co., 1943).

[10] Typical—although somewhat extreme—examples of this attitude can be found throughout Harry Elmer Barnes, ed., *Perpetual War for Perpetual Peace* (Caldwell, Idaho: Caxton, 1953).

look toward Europe. In the Pacific and on Asia's eastern face, crystallized interests called for the United States to follow an active policy and to enter into the thick of affairs.[11]

America's original interests in Asia were not, in the usual sense, political at all, but rather economic and missionary. Commercial penetration and winning converts to Christianity freed the United States from concern either with the political forms that developed in the Far East or with the extent to which the region became a zone of great power rivalry. Trading and preaching occupied Americans in the Orient until the turn of the twentieth century. A real political interest in Asian politics arose only when the rising tide of international problems there began to threaten the more limited undertakings Americans were pursuing. As soon as the United States adopted a position on pressing political issues, Americans were obliged to adopt a vigorous policy.

Simplifying drastically, traditional American interests in the Far East can be reduced to three interdependent propositions, whose application with varying degrees of skill to changing circumstances can tell the story of American policy in the region since 1900. These three propositions are:

1. The overriding concern of the United States is with the internal and international stability of the Far East.
2. Stability in the region can best be achieved by ensuring a balance of power on the Far Eastern littoral; that is, the area must not be permitted to fall under the domination of any single power.
3. Stability and the balance of power, in turn, depend upon the fate of China; only if China were guaranteed "territorial integrity and political independence" could Asia be structured according to American interests.[12]

Imperialism: American Style. Most Americans would reject the bald statement that imperialism is any part of their traditional version of national interest. The word and the idea both run counter to what has been expressed as the "different" international role of the United States. Yet Americans, although late starters, did get caught up in the international race for overseas colonial possessions, and a rationale for such a policy became incorporated into the American tradition.

The American empire was not particularly large, though it was admittedly widespread. In its acquisition and exploitation Americans revealed the common characteristics of an imperial people, primarily that

---

[11] See Griswold, *The Far Eastern Policy of the United States.*

[12] See the Open Door note of 1899 and the circular telegram of 1900, quoted in Bartlett, *The Record of American Diplomacy,* pp. 409-11, 413.

of rationalizing their colonizing mission into one of philanthropy.[13] The United States purported to be interested primarily in the betterment of the unfortunate peoples for whose destinies the American government made itself responsible.

What made the imperial tradition of the United States unusual, however, was the fact that Americans took their own professions quite seriously. Regardless of American motivation, the record reveals a constant—although unevenly effective—attempt to live up to the repeated claims of good will. The more "civilized" colonies—Puerto Rico, Hawaii, and the Philippines—were prepared for self-government and, in the case of the Philippines, ultimate independence. The backward peoples were the objects of a host of programs of betterment, all carried through with considerable zeal if with occasional questionable judgment. In this effort the United States government was responding to a genuine and deep-seated urge growing naturally from the self-image of the American people.

TRADITIONAL TECHNIQUES OF FOREIGN POLICY

Corresponding to their traditional formulations of the national interest, Americans developed what we might call a traditional methodology of foreign policy. It is compounded, in roughly equal parts, of the American ego-image, of a growing but imperfect understanding of the world and its political system, and of the accumulated experience of the century and three-quarters during which the United States has had a foreign policy.

The mass of the American people—particularly the less informed, relatively unsophisticated groups—have accepted this tradition as the way foreign policy *should* be conducted and as the way it *will* be conducted when the world is finally arranged the way it should be. Part of the problem of managing American foreign affairs in the contemporary world arises from the necessity felt by officials to meet concrete problems effectively without at the same time doing irreparable violence to the nation's procedural tradition.

One final warning is necessary before we briefly list the elements of the American operating tradition. There is a temptation among sophisticated observers to dismiss all of it—particularly its details—as outmoded and irrelevant to present-day concerns. It does contain much that is

---

[13] For a general discussion of this point, see for example J. A. Hobson, *Imperialism: A Study*, 3rd ed. (London: Allen and Unwin, 1938), pp. 196-8.

admittedly anachronistic. Many of its elements, however, are capable of justification on practical grounds; Americans would finally discard them only to their own disservice. We might profitably remind ourselves that the valid test of a tradition is empiric rather than chronological. The past is neither good nor bad in itself.

The distrust of power politics

Traditionally, for reasons both too well known and too complex to develop fully here, Americans have distrusted power politics and the United States has practiced it only under duress, and then with great embarrassment and no great skill. Power politics, the amoral and opportunistic pursuit of national interest by all expedient means, is historically repugnant to Americans. They have preferred instead to prosecute their policy by other—and morally more defensible—methods.

The Immorality of Power Politics. As a nation whose history has been called "the vindication of Puritan morality," it was strictly in character for the American people to reject power politics on grounds of immorality. The world of states in practice pays more homage to Machiavelli than to Moses; the cynicism of many statesmen about human motives and their crass calculations of expedient alternatives have repelled the American conscience and driven them to search for some "finer" principle upon which to base their international conduct.

It has seemed to Americans that power politics as carried on by the courts and chancelleries of the "Old World"—Europe—was a pastime of men whose intellect had overwhelmed their moral sense. The United States, by playing the game by the same rules, would dirty its own hands with the same pitch. To attempt an American version of power politics would be to sully the national ideals and to cheapen the very truths the United States was seeking to universalize.[14]

American Inadequacies. To be honest, however, we must also admit that popular disgust with power politics had another root. Not only were Americans outraged by its immorality; they also entertained shrewd doubts about their ability to hold their own in it.

Americans seem to have had a difficult time escaping some of the aftermaths of their long-ago colonial status. One heritage from this era and the struggle for independence with which it closed was a chronic fear of American political inadequacy. Not so strong as to be called a

---

[14] From among the many criticisms of this position, see Reinhold Niebuhr, "Eisenhower's Theory of Power and Morals," *The New Leader* (March 11, 1957).

national inferiority complex, it has taken the more restrained form of a reluctance to put the United States to the test of active entry into open diplomatic competition with other states. As the late Will Rogers put it, "The United States never lost a war or won a peace."

We find very few clear admissions of this concern with America's fear of its own possible ineptitude, either in the pronouncements of statesmen, the fulminations of editors, or—until recently—the writings of scholars. Americans have preferred to rest their case for eschewing power politics on moral grounds and to seek their goals by other means. It would be useless to deny, however, that this same fear of proving unequal to the task of close-quarter diplomacy and the strategy of force and counter-force is still at work in the American people in the middle of the twentieth century; for proof we need look no further than the popular impatience with diplomacy and the constant discussion of a "showdown" with the USSR.

Armed force in the American tradition

A logical outgrowth of this strong opinion about power politics is the traditional American view of armed force as an element in foreign policy. Not sharing the prevailing assumptions about the nature of interstate life, the American people developed some indigenous ideas about the role of military power in it.

The Nature and Purposes of War. According to the traditional American idea, war can be either of two things. It may be the outcome of the diabolical schemes of cynical and depraved aggressors; it may, on the other hand, be merely the result of the diseased outlook of unsound rulers. Whether rational but unprincipled or the end product of sheer insanity, war is considered always as an abnormal event. It is never deliberately selected as a technique by worthy statesmen; organized hostility is a departure from the rational norm of international affairs.

Since war was viewed as a pathological phenomenon, it followed that Americans saw no need to take it into account in normal international intercourse, nor to plan for it except as one always makes some kind of plan to take care of unexpected illness or other catastrophe. The ideal world was one without war. Americans based much of their approach to international affairs on the assumption that this ideal could some day be achieved by the United States' refusing to accept war as an integral part of the international political process.

Once the United States became involved in a military struggle, the tradition also provided a guide to the conduct of the conflict. Americans have felt a strong compulsion to fight only for some "higher" purpose than mere selfish interest. Usually American war aims were phrased as lofty abstractions that furnished such popular gratification as might come from doing an unworthy act for the noblest of reasons. The national attitude toward an enemy has stemmed from the same root: Americans tended to see their foes as needing chastisement for their anti-social behavior and for their temerity in disturbing the peace. The object of war was to inflict a military defeat; Americans could not see any connection between the war they had won and the political concessions that might be gained from the victory.[15]

The Armed Forces in Peacetime. The American conception of armed force has been of a piece with this theory of warfare. Until recently the United States did not see the necessity of having a peace-time armed force of more than token size. Americans clung to the myth of the invincibility of the "embattled farmer" of the Revolution, and trusted in the native fighting ability of the ordinary American citizen who, armed with the products of American industrial ingenuity and the reinforcement of a just cause, could withstand any any possible combination of enemies.

This distrust of "standing armies" led the United States to place relatively greater trust in sea power as the primary guarantor of its security. The American people have been far more willing to support a large navy than a large army; in recent years air power has moved to the top of the list in public acceptance, even ahead of the navy. Two factors might help explain this traditional preference for sea and air power: both are less greedy of manpower than is a land army, and both tend to exert their influence beyond the limits of the United States and are less obvious in the midst of American society, either as an unpleasant reminder or as a veiled threat.

American Policy and the Military. Seeing no necessary connection between armed might and an orderly foreign policy, and distrustful of a major military establishment in peacetime, it is no wonder that Ameri-

---

[15] George F. Kennan puts the point this way in *American Diplomacy, 1900-1950*, pp. 65-66: "Democracy fights in anger—it fights for the reason that it was forced to go to war. It fights to punish the power that was rash enough and hostile enough to provoke it—to teach that power a lesson it will not forget, to prevent the thing from happening again. Such a war must be carried to the bitter end.

"This is true enough, and, if nations could afford to operate in the moral climate of individual ethics, it would be understandable and acceptable. But I sometimes wonder whether in this respect a democracy is not uncomfortably similar to one of those prehistoric monsters with a body as long as this room and a brain the size of a pin...." Reprinted by permission.

cans traditionally have given little thought to overt military calculations in foreign policy. The United States in the past seldom considered the military implications of any particular policy move nor did it reckon closely the nation's military capability to carry it through. The popular image of foreign policy made it the province of diplomats; only when negotiations failed completely was the matter supposed to be turned over to the military.

This has meant that the advice of military men was not sought when policy moves were being considered. Traditionally, foreign policy was none of their business. The military function was thought to be limited to two tasks: (1) to guard the security of the United States; (2) to fight —and win—a war at the command of the civilian authorities. With the circumstances leading up to that war, they were not to be concerned; neither did they have any interest in its political outcome.

The American method in foreign policy

Since tradition rejected the usual basis of international affairs—power politics—and its necessary motive force—military power—Americans had to develop a foreign-policy method of their own. Its dominant characteristic was its great reliance upon persuasive and nonviolent techniques; starting from its assumptions, it could scarcely have done otherwise. We must note, however, that the American version of persuasion did not take the form that it did in other conceptions of foreign policy, that of diplomacy. Diplomatic haggling and adjustment smacked too strongly of the immorality of power politics; Americans tended instead to prefer persuasive procedures more in harmony with their own predispositions.

The Appeal to Reason and Morality. Perhaps most characteristic of the United States and most consonant with its general position was the technique of appealing to the good sense and the good will of the states with which it was in contact. Democratic ideology taught that men were possessed of reason and morality, and that they would respond to appeals made in those terms. Americans therefore attempted to stake out positions that were justifiable by both rational and ethical criteria, and to apply these norms in relations with other states.

This approach often had two practical advantages. In the first place, when the United States espoused the cause of abstract reason and morality, it frequently put its opponents in an uncomfortable position. To disagree with truth and right as defined by Americans often meant favoring or apologizing for irrational and immoral conduct. Many instances could be cited in which this device left the United States in an unassailable position. Second, anyone who opposed the United States was—according to Americans—*per se* a "bad" (irrational and/or immoral) person, and Americans were thus in a better frame of mind to prosecute the ensuing struggle.[16]

The Invocation of Public Opinion. In complete harmony with democratic ideology was a great faith in the wisdom and the omnipotence of "public opinion." Believing in *vox populi, vox dei,* Americans saw in the voiced wishes of the masses of men a sovereign technique of universal applicability. The policy of the United States has long been to attempt systematically to influence mass attitudes everywhere and to identify American policy with what were taken to be the commands of popular opinion.

Woodrow Wilson's vision was of the harmony of interest of all men and of the certainty of peace if ways could be found to express this consensus clearly. It is one of the most explicit formulations of what has been a basic commitment of the American tradition.[17] Native political ideas assumed a disharmony between the people of any "autocratic" or "dictatorial" state and their government, and Americans felt that it would not be difficult to win the masses of men to the American side in any dispute. Men, the argument ran, are inherently reasonable and just; American policy is reasonable and just; all rational and moral men will automatically support the United States if only they know the truth; the ultimate vindication of the American position is therefore certain.

The operational problem of United States policy therefore resolved itself primarily into one of communication. All the United States had to do was to make its own position clear beyond misunderstanding (being sure to orient it on objective truth and moral right), and then to discover mechanisms to bring its message to the world. Public opinion

---

[16] For a provocative treatment of this point—and the American preference for rational and moral techniques generally—see the article by Hans J. Morgenthau, "The Mainsprings of American Foreign Policy: the National Interest *vs.* Moral Abstractions," *American Political Science Review* (December, 1950), pp. 833-54. See also the "great debate" touched off by this article, especially Frank Tannenbaum, "The Balance of Power *vs.* the Coordinate State," *Political Science Quarterly* (June, 1952), pp. 173-197; and Professor Morgenthau's reply, "Another Great Debate: the National Interest of the United States," *American Political Science Review* (December, 1952), pp. 961-88.

[17] In his "peace without victory" speech in 1917, Mr. Wilson said: "Any peace which does not recognize and accept this principle [of consent of the governed] will inevitably be upset. It will not rest upon the affections or the convictions of mankind." *Congressional Record,* LIV, 1742 (January 22, 1917).

everywhere would recognize the justice of American policy, and all wise and good men would demand that their respective governments immediately accede to the wishes of the United States. No regime, however inimical it might be otherwise, could resist this pressure.

The Development and Use of "Law." Another traditional nonviolent technique much favored by Americans has been a heavy reliance on law, legal reasoning, and legal rules. This also has an indigenous root; no nation in the world is more the slave of its lawyers than are Americans. In international relations the United States has been sensitive to the existence of legal rules and has usually attempted to shape its policy in accordance with them.

Not only has the United States attempted to "have the law on its side," but also it has sought to foster the continual elaboration of international legal rules. To Americans, social relations sanctioned by juristic norms are always preferable to extra-legal ones; a "world of law" would be better on all counts than a "lawless" one. The United States has pioneered in the extension of the international legal frontier so as to encompass more and more of interstate life.

Economics: the Punitive Sanction. But what if reason, justice, law, and public opinion were to prove inadequate; what was the United States to do if the forces of evil did not yield to these rational techniques? The American tradition, although repudiating armed force except in extremes, nevertheless made allowances for a punitive sanction. Such open coercion as was necessary was to be accomplished by economic means.

This again was only to be expected. In a highly materialistic culture in which major emphasis is placed on the rewards of economic activity, the promise of economic reward or the threat of economic deprivation has come to have a distinctly coercive character. What could be more natural for Americans than to conclude that this weapon would prove as efficacious in international relations as it was in their private lives?

And so the United States came to feel that its productive power made it really unnecessary for it to fight wars or to play the more ordinary forms of power politics. All America really needed to do was to use its immense economic strength coercively and any possible opponent would be, if not stopped, at least handicapped to the point where it would be susceptible to the influence of the American techniques of persuasion.

PUBLIC OPINION AND AMERICAN FOREIGN POLICY

The first two sections of this chapter have dealt with the popular image of foreign policy as it was formed during earlier periods of history.

We have considered the mass attitudes and preferences that are still alive today in the subtle and complex phenomenon we call "public opinion." This concluding section will deal with American public opinion as it bears upon specific issues of foreign policy. In this connection we shall confine ourselves to an estimate of its strengths and weaknesses; we have made an analysis of its constructive role in Chapter 3.

The Characteristics of Public Opinion. We shall be enumerating certain common characteristics of mass attitudes in the United States. It seems scarcely necessary to remind ourselves that any such list contains certain inherent shortcomings: (1) no single person demonstrates all the following characteristics, either of strength or of weakness, in his own attitudes; (2) the general public seldom exhibits all the characteristics simultaneously; (3) no single characteristic is present in the public all the time.

If these limitations be kept in mind, it is possible to construct two almost parallel lists, one including the major weaknesses of American mass opinion, the other its significant strengths, as both apply to questions of international affairs.

The Role of Public Opinion. Scholars differ widely as to the proper role of the public in foreign policy, as well as to the actual effect of mass opinions. From among the many different arguments advanced, it seems safest to reject both extremes: the one that is frankly elitist, denying the public any rightful place in the process; and the way of hyperdemocracy that insists that all acts and decisions receive formal or informal popular ratification. The easiest position to defend, and the one that squares most closely with the way decisions are reached in the United States, makes the public a partner with the responsible officials. It assigns mass opinion control over certain important areas of action and gives it a sort of suspensive veto over the remainder. This is the notion we developed in an earlier chapter.

Weaknesses of American public opinion

It has been fashionable for a number of years for scholars to find ample fault with the American mass mind as it comes to grips with international problems.[18] Either because of an admiration for the "superior" efficiency of dictatorial or aristocratic governments or because of a deep and sincere faith in the greater wisdom of professional officialdom, many

---

[18] A recent example is Walter Lippmann, *The Public Philosophy.*

writers have made very detailed and thoughtful criticisms of the way Americans think about foreign affairs. We may find their conclusions unpalatable and their recommendations controversial, but we must admit that they have made a very sizeable indictment of American public opinion.

Lack of Information. Perhaps the most far-reaching, and the most difficult to contradict, of the asserted weaknesses of American opinion is its uninformed character. Americans have access to a greater amount of information than does any other people in the world; newspapers, magazines, radio, television, and every other mass medium pour forth data in a great flood. The stark fact remains, however, that mass audiences do not take advantage of the available data to the extent that one might expect them to. Americans are not at all as well informed as they could be—and as they should be.

No one expects laymen to have complete information about all the problems facing the nation. Even if it were possible to make all the data available, only those to whom the subject is a full-time mission could be justly expected to be fully informed. But the "ordinary citizen" does not seem to have enough information at his command to play even his limited public part with full efficiency. Public-opinion polls reveal a startling lack of knowledge about such important matters as the United Nations, NATO, the nature of communism, and so on. Without basic data, it is a near-impossibility for individuals to make intelligent decisions —or even any decisions at all.

Impatience. Americans are an impatient people. Their culture emphasizes direct social action with speedy results; they tend to prefer immediate solutions to problems, with no excuses accepted for delay. When applied to foreign affairs, in which progress is often tortuous and usually slow, this cultural trait can cause serious conflict.

Impatience makes Americans fretful under the tedious and delicate course of most diplomacy; it frequently leads to the advocacy of "showdown" or "all-out" techniques when less extreme measures might be preferable. It makes continued crisis difficult to endure, eroding national self-control and perspective. It generates tremendous pressures for action that officials find to be very difficult to withstand.

Emotionalism. Emotion bulks large in American international attitudes. Americans go to greater lengths in indulging their international loves and hates than do the people of any other major state. It is difficult to maintain mass enthusiasm for the controlling constant of national interest; the public most commonly follows the course dictated by current likes and dislikes. This gives American opinion toward major issues a

195

peculiar wavelike quality arising from its tendency to great emotional swings from one extreme to the other.[19]

The Preference for Dichotomies. Finally, we must mention the American preference for dichotomies. Americans generally have an all-or-nothing attitude in international affairs; the dominant national assumption is that the only alternative outcomes of a situation are extreme ones. Public attitudes think only of total peace or total war, total love or total hatred, Russian friendship or Russian enmity. This simple black-or-white formulation of problems grows out of the first three points we have made above, and in turn influences each of them.

Since Americans lack adequate information about issues, problems can be easily simplified into a choice between only two alternatives. Since they are impatient, if one alternative proves unworkable it is easy and quick for the public to seize on the opposite extreme and to vigorously urge its prosecution. Finally, a simple one-or-the-other choice makes it possible for Americans to distinguish between the absolutes of good and evil, love and hate, virtue and sin; it is much easier to indulge the national predilection for emotional judgments.

Strengths of American public opinion

Less frequently discussed, at least in any objective fashion, are the positive strengths of American public opinion. It is somewhat surprising that this is so; in a democracy in which public opinion is given a significant role to play we would expect that considerable effort would be expended in analyzing the positive contributions made by mass attitudes. Yet it is relatively rare to find a systematic study of the sources of strength provided by the public.

We may nevertheless prepare a list suggesting some of the favorable or advantageous characteristics of American public opinion on foreign policy. We must keep these in mind in reaching any over-all judgment on the democratic process as it applies to international affairs. Concentrating only on popular shortcomings prepares the way for the possible acceptance of some doctrine of elitism and might ultimately lead to at least a partial rejection of the entire democratic idea. The strengths of American opinion at least help balance the most glaring of its weaknesses.

The Debating of Major Issues. One of the chief strengths of American

---

[19] A recent example is provided by the shift in American attitudes toward Britain and Israel between November, 1956, and March, 1957. At first condemning the two states for their military action against Egypt, four months later public opinion was largely in support of them.

public opinion is a popular insistence on thorough public airing and debate of major international issues. For this we may thank, among other factors, the tendency of Americans to organize into pressure groups. On any important question nearly every possible point of view has at least an organization or two to express its views. As each prosecutes its case, the basic alternatives often receive a thorough airing. Political parties also share in keeping debate and disagreement alive, with the party in control of the White House (and therefore presumably responsible for policy) usually defending its record and the opposition engaged in attacking and criticizing.

Common Sense. The next characteristic we mention might at first seem contradictory when set alongside our earlier indictment of American emotionalism. There is in American public opinion a strong strain of common sense that historically has often come to the rescue just as it seemed as if emotional excesses were to sweep the United States away.

Americans seem to need their periodic emotional indulgences; perhaps they provide an outlet for pent-up frustrations and tensions. But after each of these outbursts of love or hate, there comes a reaction. Often it goes too far in the opposite direction, and the new attitude is actually as emotional as the old. But ultimately the pendulum tends to come to rest, and most Americans—emotionally purged—take a stand on the dead center of common sense.

If this model be accurate, and if we may assume that such common-sense judgments are usually satisfactory, we may regret that the American people seemingly must go through their initial emotional sprees. How much better it would be if they clung to their down-to-earth practicality all the time! But, at least up to this point in history, the American people have not been able to dispense with their preliminary reliance on pure sentiment; perhaps we should comfort ourselves with the realization that up to the present the United States has been able eventually to extricate itself from the worst of its emotionally-rooted errors. And it would be a brave man indeed who would argue that American public opinion would be always of a higher type if all emotional preferences were abandoned and all judgments made on the basis of cold common-sense calculation. A good case can be made in defense of at least some feeling in American mass attitudes.

Altruism. American public opinion, finally, is genuinely altruistic. We commented earlier on American Utopianism, and tried to suggest some of its failings. No one, however, can question its sincerity. Americans do generally wish everyone well, and devote an unusually large share of their efforts to trying to improve the lot of man.

It is dangerously easy to deride the simple good-heartedness of Americans; easy, and with some basis in fact as well. But we must not blind ourselves to another reality: America's genuine concern for other peoples is widely recognized abroad, and this disinterestedness historically has been often taken for granted by other states. What Americans have not realized is that their reputation for altruism is itself a source of great strength in their dealings with other states. In the past it was often the only weapon the United States had available; today, when a vastly more complex foreign policy is carried on, it still serves as a source of additional (and often unexpected) power.

Preliminary verdict on public opinion

Balancing strengths against weaknesses, what can we say at this point about American public opinion on foreign-policy issues, particularly in the light of America's international ego-image as we developed it in the first part of this chapter? In one sense, to answer this question is the purpose of this book, and an attempt to do so is made in the final chapter. But, even at this early stage of our inquiry, certain points can safely be made.

It would be inaccurate to condemn American attitudes as inherently unsound, but equally as erroneous is the assumption that public opinion is an infallible guide to policy. The weaknesses of American opinion are all dangerous to intelligent planning; no policy-maker could safely trust himself and the national interest to the whims of a rapidly-shifting, stereotype-ridden, impatient, and highly-emotional body politic. Coping with this phenomenon raises problems of political leadership of a grave difficulty. On the other hand, the advantages we saw in American attitudes each strengthens the hands of American statesmen and gives them freedom of action (once opinion has come to rest) that makes it possible for the government to act in accordance with the major outlines of a preconceived strategy.

Both the strengths and the weaknesses of American opinion, therefore, have an impact on American policy. The concern of both the statesman and the public would seem to be one of curbing the excesses and capitalizing on the advantages of this situation so as to produce a workable relationship between the demands of mass opinion and the concrete purposes of official leadership.

8 : The contemporary version of the national interest

In Chapter 1 we saw that an operating concept of national interest forms the basis of any foreign policy. In Chapter 7 we pointed out that the popular image of the international role of the United States has played a large part in creating a generalized, mass myth of American purpose; we also indicated that the American ego-image and the popular consensus about what the United States ought to be doing clashed on many points with the contemporary situation in which the United States must operate. In this chapter we approach the problem of American national interest in a different way. Rather than focusing on popular myth and tradition, we shall attempt to stipulate the basic ingredients of the actual (or at least the dominant) concept of national interest accepted by the American government, and, applying this notion to the prevailing conditions facing the United States, to formulate a pattern of generalized goals and objectives.

This is a difficult task for anyone not of the government hierarchy, but by no means an impossible one. The American outlook on the world and the imperatives of international affairs in the mid-twentieth century combine to exert a powerful influence on the substance of the contemporary foreign policy of the United States. Certain lines of action are virtually closed to the American government, others are virtually ineluctably demanded of it; between these extreme compulsions we can find a broad complex of choices. Even in this area, however, we may suggest a set of reasonably well-clarified wants and needs—what we can call interests—that largely govern the rational choices made by American policy-makers. An understanding of these preoccupations will throw a good deal of light on what has been done and will be done in the future by the government of the United States.

The classification of foreign policies

We should first undertake a preliminary exercise in political taxonomy. We shall be fitting American policy and the concept of national interest that undergirds it into a rough system of classification. From such a scheme, we may draw certain inferences from the general category into which United States policy falls. So as to sharpen our tools and to ensure that we shall be talking about the same thing when we use a particular descriptive term, our first task should be to delimit our classifications.

The Dichotomy of State Attitude. Were we quickly to analyze inductively the basic assumptions of the foreign policy of each of the 80-odd states in the world, we would discover at least the rough outlines of a generalized dichotomy in their approach to each other. Despite the obvious fact that no two states have the same foreign policy, and the equally self-evident conclusion that there are many subtle shades of difference among even very similar ones, in the most general sense some type of either-or proposition underlies everything that any state does. There seems to be a single choice that every government makes, consciously or unconsciously; once made, its subsequent action flows naturally and almost inevitably from it. Major change in its foreign policy is difficult and unlikely unless this original decision is reversed.

This crucial determinant, the major criterion of our system of classification, is the state's attitude toward the world situation in which it finds itself. Any state must somehow determine which of two possible alternatives it will choose: it may either accept—at least in general—the combination of advantages and disadvantages that together give it a status relative to all other states, or it may be dissatisfied with its role and determined to improve its place. Which decision it makes, and how and by what means that decision is reached, is determined by forces within the particular state, although external factors must be taken into account. The choice of a fundamental outlook determines the form and the direction of the greater part of all its later action. The two groups of states, divided by this watershed of attitude, provide the two categories of our system of classification.

Status Quo vs. Revisionism. Scholars have given names to the two halves of our dichotomy. The first group of states, satisfied with what they have and interested primarily in preserving it, is most commonly called the "status quo" states. Other suggested names, carrying roughly the same connotation, include "have" states, "satiated" states, or (not always accurately) "passive" states. The other group, interested in overturning the prevailing distribution of rewards and power, is usually called "revisionist," although often also termed "expanding," "have-not," or "active" states. Oppositions other than status-quo revisionist are open to serious question because the descriptive words tend to carry policy implications that are not really necessary to the classification. In our discussion we shall confine ourselves to the simple status-quo-revisionist antinomy.[1] We may draw certain limited but basic conclusions about the general foreign-policy line of these two types.

A status-quo state normally pursues policies aimed at preserving its status: policies of limited objectives that are in the broadest sense defensive in inspiration. Generally such a state is more concerned with devising responses to problems that arise from external sources than with initiating positive long-range programs of its own. It usually has a major interest in peaceful international intercourse, particularly in the process of peaceful change. Switzerland is perhaps the archtype of the status quo.

A revisionist state, on the contrary, is actually or potentially on the offensive. Committed by the terms of its initial decision to constant effort aimed at the improvement of its status, it must be on the alert for profitable opportunities to move towards its goal. Revisionist policy assumes the strategic initiative, actively exploring any situation that promises advantage. We cannot generalize that such an outlook must be one that looks forward to or plans war, but we can safely stipulate that the choice between war and peace made by a revisionist state is governed only by considerations of operational expediency and utility rather than by any basic demand of national interest; it is a "means" rather than an "ends" decision. Nazi Germany in its heyday, dedicated as it was to incessant attack, is a classic example of revisionism in action.

The Limits of Classification. We shall be using the status-quo revisionist dichotomy as an analytical device throughout our discussion of American foreign policy. Its usefulness will perhaps be demonstrated as we progress, but at the outset we must enter a large caveat. The "science of

---

[1] See Hans J. Morgenthau, *Politics Among Nations,* second ed. (New York: Alfred A. Knopf, Inc., 1954), Chapters IV, V, and VI, for an extended discussion of the classification of foreign policies. Professor Morgenthau finds three types of policies: status quo, imperialist, and prestige. We include the latter two under the more general rubric of "revisionism."

international politics," of which taxonomy is such a large part, is still rudimentary and imprecise. Our system of classification can do no more than to suggest certain rough categories divided by a line often difficult to discover and frequently violated in practice. The inferences we draw from the status-quo or revisionist status of any state can never be any more than tentative; any conclusion we reach must be submitted to the test of rigorous empiric verification.

One additional warning seems in point. Any objective analysis of foreign policies must proceed on the assumption that the choices that states make are rationally determined. No one would be foolhardy enough today to insist that all states (or, for that matter, any state) will follow a policy dictated only by the calculations of pure reason. We are constantly confronted by examples of status-quo states undertaking moves that would seem logical only within a revisionist context; less frequently we see the opposite. Here is the province of the inescapable irrational factor,[2] and to the extent that it controls the behavior of states the usefulness of our classification is seriously impaired.

THE UNITED STATES AND THE STATUS QUO

The United States is, by our criteria, assumed to be a status-quo state whose major interest is in the preservation of its present advantageous position. We shall modify this generalization as we examine American interest more closely, but in its essentials it will remain as the fundamental consideration of our analysis of the basic American motivations in foreign policy.

The United States as a "have" power

The Satiation of the United States. What sort of things make a state a "have" power? Why does a state become a defender of the status quo, at least as it perceives it? By answering this question with particular reference to the United States we may examine the broader issue.

Generally speaking, a state accepts a status-quo position for either of two reasons. In the first place, it may lack the capability to achieve any more of its objectives; it therefore settles for the most it can get from the given situation. This might be called the "status quo by default." Sweden's open renunciation of its ambitions after 1721 resulted in such

---

[2] Feliks Gross calls this "factor *x*," to be allowed for in all policy analyses. *Foreign Policy Analysis* (New York: Philosophical Library, 1954), pp. 124-5.

a status-quo position. On the other hand, the status quo may be accepted simply because the state concerned has reached all the objectives it deems important and such as remain unattained would require more trouble than they would be worth. Although capable of getting more, the state elects to content itself with what it has. This might be the "status quo by deliberate choice."

It seems clear that if the United States is a status-quo power, it arrived at this position by the second route. It has only been since 1945 that the status quo as a policy channel became fully rationalized to American policy-makers and has served as a base for calculated strategic and tactical decisions. At the moment that the more or less deliberate choice was made to defend the status quo, the United States possessed ample capability—both of force and of consent—to reach an entirely new set of goals. American statesmen, acting in harmony with popular attitudes as they understood them, instead chose to concentrate on the defense of the post-war situation of the United States.

The objectives that states pursue can be categorized in various ways, subject to the warning we entered above about the limitations on any system of classification. One set of categories that has considerable utility lists the concerns of states under the headings of independence, security, territory, prosperity, power, and prestige. In 1945 there was little disagreement among either officials or citizens that the United States had reached virtual satiation in each of these areas. The United States no longer had any obsessive objectives; there were no major international adventures upon which Americans were determined to embark. Left alone, Americans would bother no one, conquer no new territory, overthrow no governments, start no wars. They wished only to be free to enjoy the advantages of their civilization and—within reason—were willing to permit everyone else the same right to enjoy their own.

The Nineteenth Century. As we saw in Chapter 5, American preoccupation with the status quo is a relatively recent development. During much the nineteenth century the United States had a dynamic, expanding foreign policy that was an accurate reflection of the dominant American revisionism.[3] Until the United States achieved continental expanse, hemisphere hegemony, and economic maturity, it had longstanding purposes to whose accomplishment successive administrations devoted themselves. During the first century and a quarter of American history as a sovereign state, therefore, the United States became involved in a series of major disputes with most of the great powers and fought

---

[3] See, for example, Julius Pratt's two studies, *Expansionists of 1812* (New York: The Macmillan Co., 1925), and *Expansionists of 1898.*

three large-scale international wars: with Great Britain in 1812, with Mexico in 1846, and with Spain in 1898. Having finally achieved the American "manifest destiny" by 1900 (and having added a fillup to it by falling heir to a far-flung colonial empire), the approach of the United States changed. During the twentieth century the United States had been concerned mainly with holding on to its winnings rather than in adding to them, although full realization of this role did not come until after 1945.

Self-preservation, Security, and Well-being. In Chapter 1 we postulated that the basic concerns of every state are self-preservation, security, and well-being. As Americans faced the world in 1945 and attempted to apply these general terms to their own situation, the condition of the United States was revealed as one of high satiation. Although there was room for some improvements, the nation was considered to be so well off on all three counts that most Americans thought that to seek major alterations in an already happy situation might jeopardize the foundations of America's enviable status. No responsible leader sought to construct a version of security or well-being that called for extensive action to bring about further shifts in favor of the United States. Indeed, any extreme policy was felt to be dangerous. The decision that was reached and ratified was that no adventuresome expansion would be undertaken and that henceforth the major American effort would be in defense of already established positions.

The American attitude toward change

One of the dangers inherent in our necessary classification of states into status-quo and revisionist is the likelihood of drawing an over-specific inference from the mere fact of classification. "Status quo" as a policy orientation has a reasonably precise meaning that derives from a state's attitude toward the world situation as it sees it. It is dangerously easy, however, to take the next step and to conceive a status-quo policy as merely involving holding a particular position and of resisting and attempting to prevent any and all change. This conclusion does not necessarily follow from a status-quo assumption; only an outdated and superlatively short-sighted version of the idea would demand immobility. Indeed, one of the distinguishing marks of the American approach to world affairs is the activist implication that is built into the defensive posture the United States assumes on most substantive questions.

The Avoidance of Stand-pattism. It is a dangerous misjudgment to assume (and it has been done often, by Americans and foreigners alike) that because the United States considers itself a status-quo state, it is committed to rigidly opposing either evolutionary or revolutionary change. The kind of world in which Americans want to live is one that cannot be achieved by simply holding fast and letting the rest of the world take care of itself. The United States cannot stand pat. It dares not take on the thankless task of Meternich's Austria and seek to destroy any deviations from the American version of "legitimacy." This would be impossible under the conditions of modern technology and national self-consciousness; what is more, even if it were feasible it would be unwise and possibly disastrous.

Change in the American Interest. We shall be examining the more specific components of long-range American interest in the next section of this chapter. Without anticipating what we shall say there, however, this point can be demonstrated out of our own individual experiences. Let anyone attempt to visualize the kind of international society in which he would feel personally secure, and then let him ask himself if this kind of order can ever be born without first making significant change in the world as it is at present. The answer, at least as given by most rational and well-intentioned people, would in most cases call for action and change on a broad front; the world of today is not one that will permit the United States the luxury of ignoring it.

The basic interests of the United States and the American people demand, not stagnation and immobility, but fundamental change in many parts of the world. Americans want peace and recognize the need to work for it, but anyone will admit that the world abounds with potential wars. It would be fatuous for Americans to prate solemnly of "order" or "stability" in the world while at the same time their government neglected or inhibited efforts to remove the conditions that breed war. The final guarantee of the American concept of the status quo demands action; the United States cannot retain its preeminence by denying improvement to everyone else or by neglecting action to create the conditions conducive to peace. In this sense the United States violates the stereotype of the status-quo state; Americans are instead— on this point—truly revisionist.

The Requirement of Affirmative Action. Nor does the American identification with the status quo confine the United States indefinitely to a passive, negative policy of doing nothing until some kind of threat arises, and then of confining its action to mere countermeasures. Defense —military, political, ideological, and economic—has a real place in Ameri- can strategy, but it is by no means the only or even the most important concern of policy. The kind of peaceful order that Americans seek —to speak metaphorically—is not the peace of the cabbage patch, but rather the peace of the beehive.

The notion of interest that we are developing here demands, therefore, that the heart of the foreign policy of the United States consist of vigorous, positive action to create the kind of world that Americans want. This means an international order in which the United States and its citizens will be free to enjoy their advantages in the maximum possible security. This means—and this is as good a formulation of American national interest as any—a world of peace, order, and stability.

The procedural status quo

Thus far we have argued that the United States is basically a status-quo power with a major concern with the defense of its own situation, but with the additional qualification that to a very real extent the United States is also committed to at least some of the principles of what we have called revisionism. Can we now reconcile these two positions and, in doing so, clarify the content of the American adherence to the status quo?

The Scope of American Revisionism. We may put the matter in this way: as regards the bulk of the substantive questions of international politics, the American attitude is either actually or potentially revisionist. The United States excepts from its general tolerance of change only such substantive issues as bear adversely and immediately upon American self-preservation, security, and well-being—nor is it necessary for us to define these terms in any especially sweeping way. While insisting on the continued maintenance of those factors that contribute to the concrete and apparent advantage of the United States, American policy-makers generally retain an open mind on the prospects of material change elsewhere.

We are not claiming here that the American attitude of substantive revisionism makes the United States always in favor of change. The American government is not committed to a principle of constant dynamism any more than it is to simple stagnation; its attitude instead is highly pragmatic. Some forms of substantive change contribute to the advancement of American interest, and these the United States approves, urges, and seeks to bring about; an apt example is the American concern for the improvement of underdeveloped areas. Others are potentially or actually inimical, and these the United States disapproves and seeks to prevent; for example, American opposition to the nationalization of the Anglo-

Iranian Oil Company in 1951. In between these extremes are many developments and evolutions that do not permit of such ready categorization. American interest demands that each of these be scrutinized, measured against the yardstick of relevance to American concerns, and then favored or opposed in its terms.

The American Concern with Procedure. Where the American identification with the status quo is complete, however, is the general area of international procedure. The United States insists that the mechanisms of international contact, adjustment, and necessary change must be peaceful and orderly. On this point the United States makes no concession. Peaceful process—the mark of an orderly society—is the central ingredient of the status quo Americans seek to preserve.[4]

This was the major operational decision involved in the post-World War II policy choice made by the United States.[5] Americans recognized, as we shall see below, that the situation in 1945 demanded extensive long-range planning and action by their government if the full results of victory were to be achieved. There was little of the traditional status quo in that decision, except for the central commitment to the ideal of an orderly world. Peace and (international) stability—of a sort—existed after the surrender of Germany and Japan and the creation of the United Nations; it was this kind of system—improved, filled in, and institutionalized—that the United States was determined to retain. To this commitment the American government and (to a large extent) the American people have remained generally faithful.

PEACE, ORDER, AND STABILITY

We summarized American national interest above as a continuing concern with permanent peace, order, and stability in the international

---

[4] No more graphic demonstration of this premise could be made than American reaction to the Anglo-French-Israeli invasion of the Suez Canal Zone in 1956. The basic ingredient in American policy was the principle that no provocation, however extreme, justified the adoption of force as a technique. See President Eisenhower's speeches on October 31, 1956, (*Department of State Bulletin*, November 12, 1956, p. 743), and February 20, 1957 (*Department of State Bulletin*, March 11, 1957, p. 387-90). In the latter speech, he said: "If we agree that armed attack can properly achieve the purposes of the assailant, then I fear we shall have turned back the clock of international order. We will, in effect, have countenanced the use of force as a means of settling international differences and through this gaining national advantages. . . . We cannot consider that the armed invasion and occupation of another country are 'peaceful means' or proper means to achieve justice and conformity with international laws."

[5] See the analysis made at the end of the war by Nathaniel Peffer, *America's Place in the World* (New York: The Viking Press, 1945).

society as the best way to guarantee American independence, security, and well-being. We turn now to a more detailed analysis of this generalization.

The United States and International Equilibrium. We may begin by generalizing that the controlling interest of the United States is in some system of international equilibrium. The details of any such arrangement would depend so much on factors of time and place that for us to attempt to spell them out would be useless. We may say, however, that what the United States is seeking is a flexible and adaptable international order without any drastic modifications in the traditional patterns of state behavior; the greatest novelty would be the introduction of a set of fixed outer limits on permissible state action. One of the long-run objectives of American policy, therefore, is the development and application of a set of controls on the freedom of action of all states and the creation of self-activating mechanisms of adjustment in the international order.

What we mean by "controls" and "self-activating mechanisms of adjustment" can be simply stated. We are referring to procedures and institutions that will: (1) prevent states from resorting to war at their own decision, and (2) provide satisfactory solutions to problems so as to make war unnecessary. War, therefore, is the focus of the entire enterprise. If state action could be confined to nonviolent procedures, the worst dangers of the state system would be eliminated. Within the structure of peaceful process as thus conceived, the concerns of states could be dealt with with much less fear of the consequences of failure.

This notion, of course, underlies the idea of collective security, and its applicability to the United Nations explains a large part of American support of that organization. The attempt to place controls on state action by United Nations action squares exactly with American interest, and it is only to be expected that the United States would support most such moves. But the general realization that the United Nations, by itself, is not enough has kept the American government active in other areas, attempting in many ways to make some form of dynamic equilibrium a reality.

The American interest in peace

We have already dealt briefly with two matters bearing directly on the American interest in peace, whether we consider it either as a technique of international politics or as a condition of state life. We have suggested that the status-quo identification of the United States necessarily implies peaceful process as the preferred vehicle of international adjustment, and we have also noted American concern with the development of a condition of international equilibrium that incorporates peace as a way of life. There remain several additional comments to make about peace as being in the American interest.

Are Americans a Peace-loving People? We should first recognize an old issue. In Chapter 7 we saw that the American ego-image is one of uniqueness, particularly in the national attitude toward war. Americans generally think of themselves not only as inherently peace-loving, but as superior to other peoples in this regard. The national self-image is of a people tolerant to a fault, slow to anger, but mighty in its wrath when aroused. The United States has never gone to war, Americans normally argue, except to administer just punishment to vicious and unprincipled aggressors.

It comes as a blow to many Americans to be told that this picture is not shared by most foreign peoples, either in Europe or Asia. The United States is frequently thought of instead as being impatient, trigger-tempered, and liable to explosion at any moment. American history, foreigners point out, is speckled with big and little wars, many of them (including the War of 1812, the Mexican War, the Spanish-American War, and countless campaigns against the Indians) suspiciously similar to acts of aggression. During the nineteenth century American troops were engaged in combat more of the time than were the forces of any state on the European continent. Today many of the allies of the United States are genuinely concerned about American bellicosity and the danger to peace that it represents (although they often express equally strong doubts about American steadfastness).

The Peaceful Imperative. Whether or not Americans are, as a people, actually peace-loving is to a large extent irrelevant to American policy. American interest calls for peace not on any ground of moral superiority, but for reasons of calculated advantage. The nation has virtually everything to gain by a policy of preserving peace and very nearly everything to lose by initiating war.

The Disappearing Utility of War. War, as an instrument of national policy, is neither inevitable nor accidental. Wars do not simply happen; they come about as the result of a deliberate policy decision by some state (though it is true that external conditions play a major part in making such a decision probable). The technology of warfare in the twentieth century has made war less and less useful to the foreign policy of major states. The costs of large-scale conflict today are so prohibitively high that there is only a tiny handful of objectives—most of them intimately connected with self-preservation—whose worth would justify a state coolly electing to initiate a total war.

This is especially true of the United States; indeed, this is the principal explanation of the general American status-quo position. There are additional prizes that the United States could win if popular opinion thought them worth their cost; more territory, greater economic advantage, and so on. But their achievement would exact a tremendous price in money, matériel, and lives, a price that Americans are unwilling to pay.[6] With the possible rewards of war so nearly balanced (or actually outweighed) by its predictable costs, American national interest has embraced wholeheartedly the desirability of permanent peace.

What is applicable to offensive war applies, with some modification, to defensive warfare as well. The United States cannot afford to accept a military challenge thrown out by a potential aggressor unless it first exhausts all alternative methods of coping with the threat. Defensive war is a rational alternative for Americans only if they are convinced that there is literally no other endurable way out of the crisis. Accordingly, since 1945 the United States has ignored numerous provocations and threats that, under other circumstances or at some earlier time, might have resulted in a decision to retaliate with force. The American government will wage defensive war only when forced to do so.[7]

The American Interest in a Peaceful World. But America's interest in peace is more extensive than the mere urge to stay out of war itself. It involves, as we have noted above, the broad ideal of a world in equilibrium and organized without the technique of violence. What this means in practice is a constant American concern with the progressive elimination of war as a practice in the state system and the working objective of a warless world.

War anywhere is a threat, either direct or—occasionally—remote, to the interest of the United States. It is not enough for the American government to meet threats to the peace, from whatever source, as they arise. American interest demands a continuing effort to broaden the area in which peaceful process is the controlling technique of international relations, both from the United States and from such other states as can

---

[6] President Eisenhower, in his speech accepting renomination in 1956, emphasized this point by calling war "not only perilous, but preposterous." *New York Times* (August 24, 1956).

[7] A certain school of militant publicists, journalists, and public figures in the United States reacted strongly to the demonstration of this position by the American government in the autumn of 1956 at the time of the Anglo-French-Israeli invasion of Egypt. There was considerable public discussion that the American attitude was degenerating into pacificism and an abdication of intelligent policy in favor of the decisions of the General Assembly. For examples, see "The Price of Peacemongering," *The Reporter* (November 29, 1956), and many similar editorials in the *National Review* between November, 1956, and March, 1957.

be mobilized in this effort.[8] A peaceful world obviously requires that each state limit its policy objectives to those that can be gained peacefully; part of the American concern with peace is a continuing insistence that other states make this kind of self-denying commitment in response to similar action by the United States.

Order and stability

The remaining two components of broad-gauge American interest are order and stability in international society. As used here, "order" refers to the existence of peaceful and regular *methods* of conducting international affairs, while "stability" is the *condition* that will prevail when these orderly techniques are so widely used that state behavior will be, in great measure, predictable. Together, the two terms fill in the outline of the general concept of "peace" and make it a more comprehensive guide to American policy.

The Role of Law and Legal Rules. In Chapter 7 we noted the traditional American preference for social relationships that are regulated by legal rules. Here is one of the many instances in which a popular, non-rationalized impression is also very good practical policy for the United States. Despite the many chronic overestimations of the potentialities of legalisms as control factors in international relations, it is undeniable that order and stability, as we have defined them, can be permanently realized in international life only when they rest on a sub-structure of legal principles.

Scholars have pointed out that law has an intimate relationship to social stability; the more stable the society, the more complex and inclusive are the legal rules that govern individuals. The causal relationship, however, is unclear; there is disagreement among various schools of jurisprudence as to whether a legal system creates social stability or is only a reflection of it. In any case, the general principle is relatively clear: a world of peace, order, and stability will also be a world in which fundamental relationships will be under legal control.[9]

---

[8] From the many official statements of this position, we may cite the two Presidential speeches, one almost immediately after World War II and the other quite recent: Mr. Truman's Navy Day speech, October 27, 1945 (*New York Times*, October 28, 1945), and Mr. Eisenhower's campaign speech of September 27, 1956 (*New York Times*, September 28, 1956).

[9] Ralph Linton, in *A Study of Man* (New York: Appleton, Century, Crofts, Inc., 1936), points out: "The only cases in which new forms of society have been established successfully have been those in which the plan for the new society has included a large body of concrete rules for behavior" (p. 97). Reprinted by permission of Appleton, Century, Crofts, Inc.

It is therefore quite apparent that American national interest should include some appreciation of and concern with the extension of the scope of international law. This may be implemented in two ways, capable of being undertaken simultaneously. On the one hand, the United States may seek to assist in the development of new legal rules to formalize evolving international relationships that have reached or are reaching stability; one contemporary example is the question of international civil aviation.[10] The other area in which the United States could take the lead is in the formulation of principles of law incorporating the verb "ought," and the attempt to bring the actual conduct of states into conformity with these humanitarian rules. Perhaps the best known recent example of this is the United Nations Convention on Human Rights, a document in whose drafting the United States played a leading part.

The Necessity of Organization. But order and stability require more than just a system of legal rules. The effective operation of the kind of world order the United States is seeking necessitates a more elaborate structure of institutions, a more detailed organization.

Institutions—predictable behavior patterns plus some form of external formal structure—play an important role in the social life of individuals. They channel and limit individual behavior; they provide frameworks for action; they incorporate value systems shared by the members; they are the means of joint and collective action on behalf of these shared values. A hierarchy of institutions is one of the marks of a civilization.

International society is distinguished by a relative scarcity of these agencies of joint action. Although the institutional structure of interstate life is not entirely lacking, we must admit that it is no more than rudimentary. There is a lack both of control mechanisms and of instruments for joint action; in times of crisis, both types must be extemporized.[11] Many scholars have noted that this shortcoming of the state system is responsible for the tendency of international problems to fail to reach complete resolution except by violence.[12] The converse of this proposition is self-evident; if an adequate institutional structure were to be created, much of the strain and crisis of international politics would be

---

[10] See the International Air Services Transport Agreement, drawn up at the Chicago Conference on air transport in 1944. *Proceedings of the International Civil Aviation Conference* (Washington, D. C.: Department of State, 1948-9).

[11] For example, the United Nations Emergency Force recruited to enforce the Middle East cease-fire in 1956 was created in great haste in the midst of an extremely dangerous situation.

[12] Clyde Eagleton, *International Government*, revised ed. (New York: The Ronald Press, 1948), p. 19; J. L. Brierly, *The Law of Nations*, fourth ed. (Oxford: Clarendon, 1949), pp. 42-6.

eliminated. This principle leads the United States to its interest in the progressive elaboration of international institutions.

We must not infer from this general statement that the American government is irrevocably pledged to any particular type or form of organization. Such agencies as the United Nations, NATO, UNESCO, and the Joint Inter-American Coffee Board each has a place in the general concept of organization, and no one is necessarily any more in the American interest than any other.

Nor are we saying that, as of any particular moment, the more organization the better. Although there may be room for real dispute as to whether law creates stability or vice versa, on the question of institutions there is less ground for disagreement. No institution can be created until the social setting is prepared; men must be aware both of the social need and the suitability of the proposed organization for satisfying the need before they will permit its creation and participate in it.[13] The most we can say is that—as of any particular moment—the United States has an interest in seeing to it that the level of international organization—both in terms of extent and of effectiveness—is at its practical maximum. As the acceptance threshold of the society of states lowers, more and more organization can be introduced.

Where will it end? Are we saying that the national interest of the United States demands that ultimately the organization principle should be carried to its logical extreme in the form of a world government? We are not going so far, at least at the present stage of our discussion. We are generalizing only to state that order and stability in international relations demands organization, and that the more that international politics is fitted into an effective organizational scheme, the more orderly and stable it will be. Since 1945 the United States has accepted this idea and has been more or less consistently acting upon it.

Peaceful Change. One final aspect of order and stability, implicit in the preceding discussion of law and organization, merits some consideration in itself. This is the discovery, acceptance, and utilization of the techniques of peaceful change. It would not be overly far-fetched to argue—as many students have done—that this is the central political problem of our time.[14] Man seems to have tacitly agreed that war can no longer be used for the settlement of disagreements among great states; the ques-

---

[13] Marion Levy, *The Structure of Society* (Princeton, N. J.: Princeton University Press, 1952), pp. 102 ff; Ralph Linton, *The Tree of Culture* (New York: Alfred A. Knopf, Inc., 1955), p. 31.

[14] For a recent survey of the rationale of peaceful change and the pacific settlement of international disputes, see Inis L. Claude, *Swords into Plowshares* (New York: Random House, 1956), pp. 219-30.

tion that perplexes everyone is what shall be used as a substitute for violence in international affairs. If men could develop an acceptable method of coping with this issue, most of the other political dilemmas of contemporary life might prove to be less fearsome than they seemed when confronted in the face of the specter of war.

Change, as we have seen, is of the very essence of international relations. Other than violence there is no technique of change of guaranteed efficacy. The abandonment of war will not eliminate the need for allowing for constant evolution. A stable world order must contain procedures that will make change possible, feasible, and acceptable, all the while limiting state action to something short of war.

The national interest of the United States naturally leads to American acceptance of the doctrine and—to a lesser extent—the practice of peaceful change. Despite the degree to which its necessity has been obscured by the exigencies of the cold-war decade, a backward look today will reveal that the United States has made real, if limited, progress in promoting the principle. How this has taken place we shall see in later chapters.

ACTION PRINCIPLES: THE CONSTANT INTERESTS

From the highly generalized concept of American national interest that we have been developing, summarized as a continuing concern with the creation of a world of peace, order, and stability, there flows a small number of what we call "action principles." These are the relatively permanent enterprises that are so fundamental to the accomplishment of any part of the American design that their inclusion in actual American foreign policy is axiomatic. These principles might be thought of as an initial step in translating the idea of interest into the concrete courses of action that we call policy.

As presented here, the action principles of American foreign policy are three. First, the United States must look to its own self-defense. Second, the United States must cooperate actively with those states that share the American interest in a world of peace, order, and stability. Third, the United States must oppose any state that violates (or threatens to violate) the procedural status quo, grounded in peaceful process, that the United States is committed to defend.

Self-defense

It might seem almost redundant to make the detailed point that the United States has a great interest in its own self-defense, but the concept

214

of "defense" and the mythology that surrounds it today requires us to examine the point systematically.

The Status Quo in Practice. We must always remind ourselves that the new world of peace, order, and stability that the United States is seeking to create does not yet exist. The society of states in which the United States fits is one still dominated by the doctrine of sovereignty and the egoistic promptings of national interest. So long as this condition persists—and for safety's sake we must assume its indefinite existence, no matter how the United States attempts to modify it—American national interest must depend for its satisfaction primarily on the acts of the American people and the government of the United States.[15]

Our starting point in this analysis of American interest was the postulate that the United States is a status-quo state: the consensus among Americans is that the present situation of the United States is sufficiently advantageous that the major effort of the American government should be directed at its perpetuation. All subsequent developments of American interest stem from this central proposition; peace, order, and stability are ultimately in the American interest because through them the United States hopes to preserve its uniquely favorable status.

From this review of the logical sequence within the American concept of interest, we can see the fundamental place occupied by the requirement of self-defense. Americans wish to preserve their advantages; in the long run the best way to accomplish this is by helping to develop a world in which all states and all people can feel secure. But, if the long-range plan fails, or at least during the period before it is consummated, the defense of the status quo as it affects Americans must rest on the United States itself.

Multiple Defense. The preceding paragraphs review the basic logic of self-defense. It is less clear, however that "self-defense" has a different connotation in the middle of the twentieth century than it has had in any earlier epoch.

Traditionally, "defense" has meant the development of the capacity to resist armed attack; this is the classic idea of "security" as a state objective. But one of the paradoxes of modern world politics is the increasingly clear

---

[15] This is an elementary example of what is called the "minimax" theory of strategy, drawn from the mathematical theory of games. It is based on the construction of a plan of action that assumes that the worst possible outcome will be the result of the game; by planning in this way the player's losses are held to a minimum and yet he remains in a position to maximize his gains if events are more favorable than he had assumed. See Martin Shubik, *Readings in Game Theory and Political Behavior* (Garden City: Doubleday, 1954), especially the essay by Karl Deutsch, "International Politics and Game Theory."

fact that technology, as applied to warfare, is a sword that cuts two ways.[16] It vastly increases the destructive power of weapons and has made it operationally feasible to destroy an entire civilization. On this count it would seem that defense against military attack is more necessary than ever. But the events of the cold-war decade suggest that just to the extent to which weapons have grown more fearsome and efficient, the likelihood of their use in all-out conflict has decreased. And so military defense—as we shall see in detail in a later chapter—has assumed a new dimension today; deterrence, rather than battlefield mastery, has become the dominant military concern of the United States.

But the decline in the purely military component of self-defense has been matched by a corresponding increase in its other forms. The military danger to the United States may be less today than heretofore, as many experts believe; other sorts of threats, however, pose problems each as acute in its way as a military one would be. "Political warfare," economic conflict, ideological and propaganda war, and the frequently overemphasized but always real danger of subversion are only a few of the areas in which the United States is called upon to defend itself.[17]

There is very little inclination in the United States today to argue that unilateral self-defense is the route to ultimate salvation for Americans. Most Americans realize that, in seeking some approximation of the late Senator Taft's "fortress America"[18] the United States would be voluntarily sacrificing many of the happy domestic circumstances that American foreign policy is pledged to preserve. The "go-it-alone" argument, once popular, today makes sense only as a last resort if all of the more affirmative approaches of the United States should fail. It would be stupid for the United States to seek to build a better world without first paying due attention to its own defense, but it would be catastrophic for it to make self-defense, narrowly defined, its only principle of action.[19]

---

[16] W. F. Ogburn, ed.,*Technology and International Relations* (Chicago: University of Chicago Press, 1949); Bernard Brodie, ed., *The Absolute Weapon* (New York: Harcourt, Brace and Co., 1946); Henry A. Kissinger, *Nuclear Weapons and Foreign Policy* (New York: Harper & Bros., Inc., 1957).

[17] For an excellent early summary of the multidimensional problem of American defense, see Hanson W. Baldwin, *The Price of Power* (New York: Harper & Bros., Inc., 1948); see also W. W. Kaufman, ed., *Military Policy and National Security* (Princeton: Princeton University Press, 1956).

[18] In *A Foreign Policy for Americans* (Garden City: Doubleday, 1951).

[19] See, however, the comment of Senator R. B. Russell of Georgia, on February 27, 1957, with reference to the so-called "Eisenhower Doctrine" for the Middle East in which he doubted the value of non-military measures. *New York Times* (February 28, 1957).

Cooperation for peace

If self-defense alone is not enough, and if positive action toward a world of peace and order is demanded in the American interest, we come next to the major question of how the United States is to proceed in this task. Here we consider a much-debated question: the necessity for, and the most desirable extent of, "international cooperation."

The Limits on Unilateral Action. We may take it as axiomatic that the United States cannot build the new world alone. The detailed framework of a peaceful order will be so many-sided, so complex, and so extensive that even the tremendous potential capability of the United States would be insufficient to construct it without help from outside. The United States cannot enforce peace by its own unaided efforts; it cannot order all the relationships of men, groups, and states; it cannot alone require that all forms of state action everywhere should be confined within the limits declared to be acceptable. The American interest in a new basis for international society is of such dimensions that assistance from other states is a *sine qua non* of success.

This is not to say, of course, that the United States cannot or should not make a major contribution to the common task, nor that it cannot or should not be at least one of the leaders of a peaceful coalition. No other state, no matter how sincere its dedication to international order, can hope to match the potential American contribution to its realization; no other state could build an effective grouping in pursuit of this objective that did not include the United States. America's role in the task must be a major one, but final success lies beyond even the great capability of the United States. It must have partners if its long-range plans are to bear fruit.

Harmony of Interest Within the Status Quo. What makes American national interest, as we are formulating it, a viable basis for policy is the fact that there is a sizeable group of states that share the general idea of the status quo as defined by the United States and that have no major disagreement with its particular American version. There are at least several dozen fundamentally status-quo states; that is, they are not revisionist and are willing indefinitely to sustain the present distribution of rewards as it affects them.[20] Though most of them have some quarrel with the United States on points of detail, none makes its abasement a matter of primary concern. Thus a genuine harmony of interest obtains

[20] See, for example, Barbara Ward, *Policy for the West* (New York: W. W. Norton and Co., Inc., 1951).

within this group on the two points of critical importance to Americans: first, all of them are more or less committed to the principle of a world of order; second, all are generally willing to accept American advantages as part of the world system they are interested in preserving.

The Structure of Cooperation. Granted a harmony of interest in the maintenance of the procedural status quo and the absence of fundamental disagreement on the minimal substantive status quo that Americans demand, the discovery and application of methods of cooperation becomes a matter of operational technique. Cooperation between states is always possible—and usually practical—if it is based on a genuine, unforced, harmony of interest.

States, however, do not cooperate just for the sheer joy of cooperating. Joint action, if it is to serve a useful purpose, is purposive: it is aimed at specific goals and involves the exchange of definite commitments to do particular things. American interest demands, therefore, that any cooperative enterprise have a predetermined objective in mind, that the participants be limited to those states that share the particular purpose, that the mutual obligations be precisely stipulated, and that each such venture be evaluated rigorously in terms of its contribution toward the long-range purposes of the United States. Under these assumptions the United States has associated itself with many states in a broad variety of cooperative schemes, each one pinpointing a specific objective and the membership of each determined by the interest the members have in its purpose. Some, like NATO, have had relatively productive histories; others, like the abortive Suez Canal User's Association of 1956, have failed. Such failures have generally been due to the nonapplicability of one of the criteria above to the project.

Hostility to nonpeaceful states

If we agree that cooperation with like-minded status-quo states is demanded by the national interest of the United States, is the converse of the proposition true? Does American national interest demand hostility toward all revisionist states? If we remember the particular connotation that we have given to the American version of the status quo, if we confine the idea of revisionism to procedural matters, and if we define revisionism sharply enough, this proposition can be defended.

The Defense of Peaceful Process. The logic of American national interest leads the United States to oppose any state that seems willing to

218

violate the structure of peaceful process in international relations. This is the procedural status quo, pure and simple. American opposition to this form of revisionism is independent of the specific objectives that the state is seeking; it is conceivable that the United States might approve or even actively support an identical program if it were to be prosecuted peacefully.[21] If it is an order of permanent peace that is the goal of American policy, simple logic and common sense both would seem to demand that the United States offer immediate and absolute opposition to any state openly defiant of this end. Failure to take this step would vitiate much of the rest of what the United States is trying to do.

The Case of the Cold War. This principle is the basis of the anti-Soviet line that has bulked so large in post-war American policy. We shall be considering the rationale of the cold war in some detail in Chapter 12, but some reference to American assumptions about the Soviet will serve to illustrate the point we are making here.

The United States has no inherent interest in the destruction of the communist government in Moscow, nor in the permanent frustration of its legitimate interests. American anti-Soviet policy has been based instead upon the Kremlin's demonstrated willingness to advance its interests by means of perpetuated disorder, frequent crisis, and threatened war. The Russian line in the post-war decade was directly opposed to American purposes; to have permitted Moscow to have its way without opposition would have been tantamount to abandoning the whole of American foreign policy.

The Indivisibility of Peace. Peace, as the United States defines the term, is indivisible. It is not sufficient for the United States to oppose only those disturbers of the peace that directly threaten purely American interests; any state anywhere that is willing to rupture peaceful international relationships runs equally afoul of American concerns. We can argue that communist China represents a direct and immediate threat to the United States, and that American hostility to Mao Tse-tung can be explained on that basis; no such claim could be made, however, for American resistance to the ambitions of President Nasser of Egypt, to the Communist regime in Guatemala, or even to India's provocative be-

---

[21] This point may be made with regard to the American attitude toward Israel following the 1956 Middle East crisis. The American position, as developed during the long controversy precipitated by Israel's refusal to evacuate the Gaza strip and the Gulf of Aqaba area, was that the United States opposed Israel's use of force while generally supporting the specific objectives Israel claimed to be seeking. See the speech of President Eisenhower, February 20, 1957, *Department of State Bulletin* (March 13, 1957).

219

havior on the issue of the Kashmir, to mention a few cases in addition to the most spectacular demonstration of American adherence to the principle, the opposition to Britain and France in the Middle East in 1956.

It is the principle of peaceful process to which the United States is committed as a matter of national interest. Affirmative action in its behalf is naturally to be expected, but so is the policy of resistance to any state that would go to war. Peace, order, and stability require not only that the United States build a new institutional edifice, but also that it also protect its work against those who would destroy it.

part 5:

SITUATIONAL FACTORS
IN CONTEMPORARY AMERICAN POLICY

9 : The United States in a new world: 1945

The end of the four-year war effort between 1941 and 1945 brought the United States to the threshold of a major departure in its foreign policy. It was a new world in which Americans had to find their way; a world in which many of the calculations and assumptions by which Americans had—for better or worse—guided their policy in the past had become invalidated. There were several factors with which policymakers in Washington and citizens everywhere had to deal for the first time; their cumulative effect was to create an almost entirely novel foreign-policy problem.

In this chapter we shall discuss the broader dimensions of this new world. We shall consider many individual factors, but some order may be brought into our analysis by subsuming them under three broad headings. The first section will consider the major features of the postwar international scene—the "givens" of the foreign policy theorem. We shall next enumerate and characterize briefly the postwar dynamics: the new forces that have lent movement to the course of affairs since 1945. The chapter will conclude with an examination of two new elements in the "internal setting" [1] of American policy: those broadly-based components of prevailing public attitudes in the United States that reflected the reordering of the world. This chapter, therefore, is the first in our series of three that will consider the major situational factors affecting American policy.

---

[1] See Snyder, Sapin, and Bruck, *Decision-making as an Approach to the Study of International Relations,* for an explanation and analysis of this concept.

THE UNITED STATES: 1945

THE POSTWAR INTERNATIONAL SCENE

All wars of any importance rearrange the political relationships of nations. World War II, however, set a new mark in this respect, even surpassing the overturns that resulted from the first general war of the century. No quarter of the globe escaped major effects, and every state in the world was in some significant manner influenced by the struggle. The arena of international politics after 1945 was only in small measure the same as that of before 1939.

The redistribution of power

World War II, as perhaps its most widespread effect, produced a wholesale redistribution of power on the grandest scale in history. The pre-1939 classification of states into "great powers," "middle powers," and "small powers" was completely invalidated; in its place the postwar world offered the strange spectacle of the overwhelming bulk of the available power concentrated in two states, while at the other end of the scale huddled all the rest, differing from one another only in the degree of their weakness relative to the two giants. The world has been struggling with the consequences of this imbalance ever since.

The Abasement of the Old Powers. In 1939 it was generally agreed that there were seven "great powers" in the world.[2] Four of them were primarily European: Great Britain, France, Germany, and Italy. Two, the United States and Japan, were non-European; the seventh, the USSR, straddled Europe and Asia. Five of the seven were summarily removed from the category as a result of the war. Three—Germany, Japan, and Italy—were defeated, humbled, occupied, and in a fair way to be remade by the victors. Britain and France, although technically on the winning side, had both been so drained by the war that neither could rightfully claim membership among the handful of dominant states. Britain, of course, carried considerable additional weight with the support of the Commonwealth and Empire[3] but, as we shall see in a moment, the centrifugal force of nationalism was to make the British role less than its apologists had imagined it to be.

---

[2] Frank L. Simonds and Brooks Emeny, *The Great Powers in World Politics,* new ed. (New York: American Book Co., Inc., 1939), p. 154.

[3] William T. R. Fox, in *The Super-Powers* (New York: Harcourt, Brace, and Co., 1944), conceived of Britain (and the Commonwealth-Empire) as one of the three peacekeeping "super-powers" of the postwar world.

Opinions differed in 1945 as to the permanence of the reduced role of the erstwhile great powers. There was general agreement that Italy, whose prewar position had always been built on a shaky foundation, would never again be a serious contender for top rank. There was much the same opinion about France, although that nation's domestic potential and extensive colonial empire made its case less clear. Germany presented a different problem, since the Allies agreed in principle that the world's future would be safer if Germany were kept permanently weakened; there was a good deal of disagreement, however, about how best to proceed to dismantle Germany's power base. Japan also offered a ticklish issue; no one was certain how to keep permanently in secondary status a nation of over 80 million people, occupying a strategic economic and political position, armed with a vigorous pride and tradition, and equipped with an elaborate industrial plant.

Britain's status as well was uncertain. Although badly battered by the war, both British prestige and the remnants of British power argued for a fairly rapid return to leadership. Safely installed as the key ally of the United States and as co-author of many postwar plans, Britain was determined to exploit its remaining advantages. British determination not to retreat to secondary status kept London afloat during the period when it seemed as if its former grandeur might be gone forever.

The Rise of the New Leaders. Of the old great powers, only two survived the war intact. Not only had the United States and the Soviet Union come through the war without serious debilitation; their power positions had improved both relatively and absolutely. The gap between them and the rest of the world had widened, but not only because the weak had become weaker; the strong had become stronger as well.

The USSR, although injured by having been an active theater of combat, had nevertheless become the second military power of the world; it had held off and beaten back the full weight of the Nazi war machine. The war had also ended what was left of its pariah status; Stalin had been a close collaborator in the planning of high strategy during the war and in the framing of the United Nations. The United States, on its part, had dazzled the world with its incredible productivity and, by the end of the war, with its massive military power as well. Economically and militarily, the United States was the most powerful state in the world and, with the Soviet, controlled all but a small fraction of its total available power.

The Small States. The end of the war left the small states—the nongreat powers of 1939—in a precarious position. All of them to some degree damaged by the war, the familiar pattern of international relationships gone, dependent on outside sources for sheer survival, most of them had little real hope of maintaining significant freedom of action. They were obliged to turn to the leaders for assistance.

The new giants

The Soviet Union: Out of the Shadow. From the point of view of Americans, the most important single fact of the postwar world was that the United States was forced into an intimate relationship with the Soviet Union. The Soviet, out of the shadow, had a problem of adjustment of its own. Revolutionary as had been the impact of the war on the United States, its effect on the USSR was even greater.

In 1939, the Soviet was still something of an international outcast.[4] The states of the "civilized" world had been forced to admit that Bolshevik rule in Moscow was a fact, but very few admitted it as permanent. Most seemed to assume that some day the communist edifice would fall, either from collapse, internal revolution, or external conquest. There was some feeling in the West that Hitler's attack in 1941 would be the *coup de grâce* to Lenin's experiment. When the Red Army refused to submit and finally beat back the Nazis, Soviet Russia's prestige was vastly revised upward.

The USSR emerged from the war one of the avowed masters of the world. It had recaptured its "lost" territory in Europe; it stared the West in the eye in the center of Germany; it had become the leading land power in Asia; it sat in the councils of the victors. Moscow had joined the world; a great many people felt in 1945 that the world would have been just as pleased if this development had never taken place. Furthermore, the Soviet's conduct during and immediately after the war did nothing to reassure the uneasy; Moscow proved itself to be a difficult capital with which to do business.[5]

The United States: Unsuspected Strength. The status of the United States in late 1945 was unique in the history of the world. American performance during the war had verged on the fabulous. The United States had fought two wars, one in Europe and one in the Pacific, supplying its troops with incredible amounts of materiel; it had been a

---

[4] Frederick L. Schuman, *International Politics,* fifth ed. (New York: McGraw Hill Book Co., Inc., 1953), pp. 418-22. See also his *Soviet Politics at Home and Abroad* (New York: Alfred A. Knopf, Inc., 1946).

[5] For an early postwar estimate of the Soviet position, see *Major Problems of United States Foreign Policy, 1948-49* (Washington, D. C.: Brookings, 1948), pp. 16-17, 22-26.

major source of supply for all its many allies; it had—despite this flood of war production—maintained a wartime standard of living superior to that of most states in time of peace; and yet it ended the war rolling in private and public wealth. Its military power was overwhelming everywhere except within the Soviet sphere; its leadership among the victors was questioned by no one except Stalin.

Looking back on that era, we can see that very few Americans realized fully just what had happened to them. There was very little popular inclination to capitalize politically on the preeminence of the United States, and none at all to establish anything like world hegemony. The prevailing attitude was one of relief that the war was ended and of determination to finish the task of reconstruction. Other states, however, were acutely aware of American power and were curious and not a little perturbed about how the United States was going to use it. Considerable suspicion existed abroad (particularly in Europe) that America would either repeat its 1920 performance and withdraw, thus condemning the world to continued instability, or that it would instead proceed with reckless abandon, unaware of the responsibilities attendant on enormous strength.[6]

The eclipse of Europe

The modern state system was born in Europe and reached its most elaborate development there; from 1648 to the end of World War II, the European subcontinent was the center of the world's political activity. In 1939 four of the great powers were European and one was at least half-European; it is no accident that the war that began in that year, originating in a squabble over a tiny bit of territory, ultimately spread to engulf all the continents and the bulk of the world's people.

The End of European Dominance. The end of the war saw the eclipse of Europe; the world was no longer ruled from half a dozen European capitals. What had ended its long period of dominance? Why, after surviving so many wars, did Europe undergo a "political collapse"[7] after this one? What had brought man to "the end of the European era"?

We shall consider these questions in detail in later chapters, but at this point we may hazard two general answers. First, the two wars of the

---

6 See Harry S. Truman, *Year of Decisions* (Garden City, N. Y.: Doubleday, 1955), Chapters 30-34, for the former President's version of America's situation at the end of the war.

7 Hajo Holborn, *The Political Collapse of Europe* (New York: Alfred A. Knopf, Inc., 1951).

twentieth century brought the states of Europe to the point of mutual exhaustion. Economically, demographically, psychologically, and spiritually Europe was virtually spent by 1945. Ruling the world demanded that the states of western Europe maintain high morale and adequate power-in-being; World War II had sapped their interest in world dominion as well as their ability to maintain it. The problem of life for millions of the people of Europe had been reduced to sheer survival, and there was little room left for the contemplation of past glories or the meditation of new ones.

The second reason is one over which the Europeans themselves had little control. By 1945 technology had progressed to the point that Europe could be said to be suffering from political obsolescence. This is true on the twin grounds of size and location. The end of the war ushered in the age of the giants: the United States (170 million people, over three million square miles, continental expanse) and the USSR (210 million people, eight and a half million square miles, continental expanse). The states of Europe, much smaller and much less populous, no longer could compete with them on any basis of even near-equality. Second, the seats of power had moved away from Europe; both the United States and the USSR were peripheral, and there was no effective way in 1945 for the European states to exert direct influence on them. The only significant exception was Britain, whose global Empire and Commonwealth gave London a supra-European status.

Target Europe. The end of the European era was signalled by a complete reversal of that continent's historic role. Europe was transformed from an area in which power was wielded and out from which power flowed all over the globe, into the principal target of power originating outside itself. Europeans, who had traditionally used non-European peoples as pawns in their own games of power politics, found themselves becoming counters in a competition on an even more massive scale.

The major controversy during the first phase of the cold war was for the mastery of Europe. This was most clearly revealed in the struggle for the political heart of the new Europe, Germany. To many neutral observers, there was something ironic in the postwar spectacle of the late allies bitterly disputing over the prostrate figure of their former enemy. In such a situation very few expected Germany to remain long impotent; her remarkable revival was at least partially due to the strategic advantage arising from its position as an object of courtship by both sides.

But the rest of Europe was not afforded the same opportunity to play

East and West off against each other. As the primary target of the policies of the two super-powers, the bulk of the European states found themselves forced to join one side or the other in the cold war; target Europe was divided down the middle by the Churchill-described "Iron Curtain." It was not for a decade, until the cold war apparently changed character in 1955 and 1956, that Europeans again won some little freedom of maneuver.

Asian instability

One of the "war aims" of the United States between 1941 and 1945 was "the restoration of the balance of power in Asia." To the extent that this was verbalized during the period of active combat, it turned out to mean largely that the United States was hoping to restore the Asian status quo of about 1937, with the single exception that Japan was to be deprived of all her gains and forced to retire to her home islands. Otherwise the map of Asia was to remain substantially unchanged.

Insofar as this was a real aim of the United States, the war was a failure. Asia after Japan's surrender refused to return to its prewar configuration. Instead of the (perhaps illusory) stability of Asian politics between 1920 and 1931, the entire enormous land mass seethed with powerful and upsetting new forces after V-J Day. All the way from India to Japan instability was endemic.[8]

The Disappearance of Historic Power. Perhaps the principal reason for the new round of instability in Asia was the disappearance of the historic sources of power in Asia. The Far East, between 1920 and 1939, was collectively dominated by Great Britain, France, Japan, the Netherlands, China, and the United States. The upshot of the war was the obliteration of Dutch, Chinese, and Japanese power and the serious diminution of the British and French. Russia emerged as the dominant land power in Asia and the United States, operating at the end of a 6000-mile supply line and tied to the sea, was unable and unwilling at the time to bring controlling force to bear. In all of Asia there was no indigenous power center; only the USSR and the United States seemed to be in a position to exert significant influence.

The End of Imperialism. Another dynamic force in the new Asia was

---

[8] See Ernest Minor Patterson, ed., "Lessons from Asia," *Annals of the American Academy of Political and Social Science*, vol. 276 (July, 1951). This volume contains articles by specialists that cover the several aspects of Asian instability in the immediate postwar period.

anti-imperialism. The obvious weakening of European authority, Japan's success in puncturing the myth of white supremacy even despite its eventual defeat, and the hard experience in self-government gained in the resistance movements, all combined to awake the masses. Colonial peoples in southeast Asia strongly resisted being returned to European control; the Indian independence movement was so strong that it could no longer be resisted. Asian imperialism, if not yet completely dead, was changing out of all recognition.

There is only one way to dislodge an imperial power from a colonial possession—short of the unlikely possibility of voluntary withdrawal. Such a change can be brought about only by creating a mass movement built on nationalism that welds a people into a single political instrument. At least half a dozen former colonies in Asia contained such movements, and in each an at least partially successful revolution took place. But the situations did not stabilize with victory over European rule. New nationalism is a powerful force, and Asian nationalism persisted, acting as a forceful dynamic making for continued instability.

Economic and Social Discontent. There were more than political pressures shaking Asia. The war brought the twentieth century to Asia, and the masses had awakened to some of the possibilities of self-improvement. A common demand for economic and social betterment, canalized into a dozen or more distinct nationalist movements and often coupled with a program calling for political independence, began to be voiced throughout the continent. The western world has come to call this the "Asian revolution."

We shall be referring to the Asian revolution frequently in subsequent chapters, and shall discuss its outlines in the next section of this one. We need only point out here that several years were necessary before the western world realized its full significance. By the time the United States came to understand the dimensions of the problem, the American position in Asia had deteriorated badly and an originally complex problem had been made unnecessarily acute. Other states in the western community were similarly embarrassed; only the Soviet and its allies recognized the true nature of their problem and were in a position to capitalize swiftly upon it.

The defeated enemies

One of the postwar phenomena that, although admittedly temporary, nevertheless exercised a pervasive influence on the international order was the status of the defeated Axis nations. Omitting their minor satellites, Germany, Italy, and Japan totalled 200 million people and together represented an enormous potential productivity. Although the victorious allies agreed on the necessity for making certain that no repetition of Axis aggression could be possible, no such harmony existed on exactly how this was to be carried out. During the immediate postwar period, the former enemies were at least as important to the victors as they had been during the war.

The Problem. What made the defeated enemies so critical an issue was the question of their ultimate destiny. The short-run program was clear, at least in theory: Germany, Italy, and Japan were to be punished for their actions by territorial reduction, the exaction of reparations, and the reconstruction of their governments. The first step in this procedure was clearly military occupation. But what was to become of these states finally?

One school of thought—known popularly in the United States as the "Morgenthau Plan" after President Roosevelt's Secretary of the Treasury, Henry Morgenthau, Jr.—proposed the permanent reduction of Germany (and, by extension, Japan) to the level of an agricultural state supplying raw materials.[9] This technique, by denying the Germans industrial capacity, would make any military renaissance impossible. Critics insisted that this approach was unrealistic; the population levels of Germany and Japan depended on the maintenance of a high level of industrialization and it would be simply impossible to force the people back to pastoral agriculture. The focus, argued these observers, should be on the rehabilitation of the Axis; let them be democratized and pacified, and the world would no longer need to fear the use to which their industrial genius would be put.[10]

There was also a major difficulty involved in the development of a framework of international cooperation for the joint rehabilitation of the Axis. No issue more clearly demonstrated the breakup of the wartime alliance between the Soviet and the western world than the rapid development of separate national approaches to the problem of dealing with the defeated enemies. Reparations, the form of government, occupation policy, and social and political reconstruction proved to be the specific issues on which interallied cooperation came to grief.

The Occupations. The occupations of Germany and Japan provided

---

9 Henry Morgenthau, Jr., *Germany Is Our Problem* (New York: Harper & Bros., Inc., 1945).

10 For a forthright statement of this position, see Freda Utley, *The High Cost of Vengeance* (Chicago: Regnery, 1949).

instructive contrasts. Germany, conquered by both the Soviet and the western armies, was divided into four zones of occupation with coordination among the occupying powers supposed to take place at the topmost command level by means of the Allied Control Authority (ACA). Each zone was in turn administered separately. Japan, on the other hand, was almost entirely an American occupation. International control was exercised by a multi-state Far Eastern Commission of civilian representatives, transmitting directives for unilateral implementation by the American commander.

The German occupation broke down early; by mid-1946, it was apparent that great-power disagreement over Germany's future was splitting that unhappy state into fragments. Each of the four occupying states governed its own section of Germany to suit itself; cooperation among the three western powers in common opposition to Soviet obduracy was not to come for three years. Japan, on the other hand, escaped the worst consequences of the nascent cold war. East-West disagreement might paralyze the Far Eastern Commission, but General MacArthur's command remained intact. Japan received a unified and relatively uniform occupation despite the disruption of allied unanimity.

The United Nations

The final item in this brief list of the new situational elements in the postwar world is the existence of the United Nations. The new international organization appeared on the scene enjoying certain operational advantages over its ill-starred predecessor, the League of Nations. Most important was the fact that no significant major-power controversy marred its birth. The wartime allies agreed that there should be a permanent organization to keep the peace they were winning; during the closing days of hostilities there was a rash of new declarations of war on the Axis from erstwhile neutrals to enable these states to claim charter membership in the United Nations. There was a general expectation that the organization would be of assistance to everyone as the world settled down after the war.

The Impact of the Charter. The Charter, and particularly its preamble, had a profound symbolic effect. The stirring statement of purposes with which the document opened furnished a vision of the world of the future that was deeply appealing. There was, however, relatively little vacuous Utopianism in this attitude. Practical statesmen were aware that the instrument created at San Francisco did not institutionalize per-

232

fection; they realized that there were mechanical difficulties standing in the way of effective international cooperation; they knew that the past was not to be erased merely by a cessation of hostilities. But, even so, the first sessions of the United Nations were greeted by a remarkably spontaneous outburst of enthusiasm from governments and peoples alike. The Charter represented hope; the operational problem of realizing that hope was not felt to be beyond solution.

The Super-Powers and the Charter. The United States and the USSR, at least at the very opening of the postwar era, conceived of the United Nations as the instrument by means of which they and their major associates could police the world and keep it at peace. The Charter revived the ancient doctrine of the "concert of power": the structure of the Security Council, complete with veto, made clear that the maintenance of peace and security was to be a monopoly of the great powers. The states that had carried the burden of the war were to be prominent in guaranteeing the peace. The "big five" of the United Nations—the permanent members of the Security Council—thought of the organization primarily as a political tool whose significant functions were to be in the area of guaranteeing the security of its members.

The Smaller States and the United Nations. Not so the smaller states who made up the vast majority of the membership. Most of them had been members of the League and recalled the successful effort made there to shackle the major states; so successful had the smaller powers been in this task that the great powers felt themselves in an uncomfortably weak position in that organization. The lesser powers, acutely aware of their increased insecurity vis-a-vis the giants, were not particularly reassured by the sight of the Big Five sitting in total command of all the security mechanism of the United Nations.[11]

But there was little they could do about it, at least in 1945 and 1946, before the cold war became universal. The great powers, as long as they chose to cooperate, were in an impregnable position in the Security Council. The small states, therefore, chose to concentrate on the so-called "non-political" functions of the United Nations, under the jurisdiction of the veto-free General Assembly (in which they formed a majority) and centralized in the Economic and Social Council.

The very creation of the Economic and Social Council at San Francisco was a victory for the smaller states, and from the very beginning they argued that the security function of the United Nations was to have no more than equal rank with the long-range attack on the causes

---

[11] See H. V. Evatt, *The United Nations* (Cambridge, Mass.: Harvard University Press, 1948), for an able exegesis of the small-state thesis.

of war. The reduction of economic, social, psychic, and demographic tensions, argued the small nations, would make a more lasting contribution to the elimination of war than the putative use of military force to punish aggression. The postwar era opened with this serious division of opinion among the United Nation's most devoted supporters.

NEW FORCES IN WORLD POLITICS

We have just catalogued the major modifications in the postwar international scene; we shall turn now to consider some of the new dynamisms that were operative in the post-1945 world.

These forces gave new directions, new structures, and new emphases to the course of international politics. None of them, of course, was entirely novel; the impact of the war, however, had been to accentuate their effect and change their nature so that each had an influence on the affairs of states many times greater than before 1939. In the aggregate they forced governments to adopt a new set of guiding principles as each state pursued its national interest in a world that was in many respects a new one.

Economic prostration

World War I had been an extremely expensive enterprise; World War II far surpassed it in cost; the cumulative effect of two massive struggles within thirty years was to prostrate enormous segments of the world economy. In Europe industrial machines were laid waste; in Asia agricultural production was brought to a standstill and elaborate distribution systems destroyed. Outside the United States, in 1945, there were only a few relatively unimportant areas in the world in which economic activity was either normal or healthy; the bulk of mankind entered the new era engaged in a grim struggle against poverty and, in some cases, actual starvation.[12]

The Loss of Productive Capacity. War is an economic waste; great amounts of national wealth are simply blown up and disappear. For most of the productive areas of the world the war had been a long

[12] For the problem in Europe and the impact of American policies, see Howard Ellis, *The Economics of Freedom* (New York: Harper & Bros., Inc., 1950), and William A. Brown and Redvers Opie, *American Foreign Assistance* (Washington, D. C.: Brookings, 1953). For a brilliant statement by a European, see Barbara Ward, *The West at Bay* (New York: W. W. Norton and Co., Inc., 1948).

interruption in normal economic life marked by tremendous economic loss. Financial resources were exhausted, making rehabilitation impossible. Industrial plants—those that had not been removed or destroyed by the war—were obsolescent, in need of modernization and repair, and revealed evidence of the large-scale cannibalism that had kept them going during the struggle. Agricultural production was upset by the devastation of the land, the dispersal of labor forces, and loss of markets, and the dislocation of distributive mechanisms. Transportation facilities were worn out, destroyed, or inadequate. The general picture revealed an impairment of productive capacity that could be alleviated only by wholesale reconstruction.

The Paralysis of Trade. With production at a normal rate impossible for all but a few states, it followed naturally that international trade as well was paralyzed. Nations do not live in economic vacuums; to some extent each trades with the rest of the world. Industrial states import food and raw materials; agricultural states import manufactured goods. With neither type of state able to produce its specialty in significant amounts, there was simply no way for the exchange of goods to take place. What was produced tended to be consumed at home; trade, that requires some form of surplus production, had nothing on which to feed.

The Politics of Economics. Many states faced a new situation in 1945: the politics of economic survival. As nations set about living in this new world, the content of their foreign policies tended to be based on securing what each felt was necessary for its continued subsistence. To a large extent this was a politics of food, since to many peoples the problem was that basic. For others, procuring raw materials, capital goods, and manpower would make an industrial revival possible; the agricultural states required implements, fertilizers, and markets.

Much of the world has made a significant recovery from the economic low point of 1945, but the "politics of economics" is a concept that has not lost its importance today. For many states, their currently prosperous status is precarious, and any interruption in their delicately balanced economies might be disastrous. American recognition of this fact has resulted in the concept of "foreign aid" becoming at least a semi-permanent feature of American policy.

Political instability

The economic distress of much of the world was matched by a corresponding instability in politics. The war had been fought to establish democratic values once and for all as against totalitarian aggression; in its aftermath, however, the democratic regimes set up by the victors proved dangerously insecure. In no area was the disruptive effect of the war on social institutions more clear than in the matter of orderly government.

Europe: Political Apathy. Most startling was the distressing condition of liberated Europe. Americans expected that Europe, the historic seat of democratic ideology and individual rights, would have few political difficulties once the blight of Nazi rule was removed. The United States assumed that Germany would require considerable reeducation, and Italy a lesser amount (after all, the Italians had turned against Mussolini as early as 1943); the rest of western Europe, it was felt, had had its fill of authoritarian regimes. France, the Low Countries, Scandinavia, and Britain were safe; the prospects were good that dictatorships would fall relatively swiftly in Spain and Portugal. American expectations were less clear about central and eastern Europe as well as the Balkans; wartime agreements with the Soviet, however, had provided for free elections leading to the establishment of democratic governments throughout this region.

The actual course of events in Europe came as a shock. Britain and Scandinavia did prove to be able to make a relatively smooth transition from war to peace, but all the other American hopes faded. France and Italy set up democratic regimes, but on so shaky a basis as to constitute a permanent danger. The Balkans and Slavic Europe fell into the Soviet sphere, exchanging one totalitarianism for another; Greece alone adopted a westward orientation, and it was in its turn torn by a vicious civil war. Spain and Portugal gave no indication of being anxious or willing to rid themselves of their dictators; even Belgium was beset by constitutional crises.

What was even more disheartening to Americans were the clear signs of mass apathy in Europe toward the democratic idea. Postwar Europe seemed to have lost much of its faith in the dignity of man and human capacity for self-government; and democracy had poorer prospects in 1945 than it had had in 1939. It was easy to make a list of reasons for this loss of faith: the ignoble record of democracy before 1939, many failures of leadership, the inroads of communism, the corrupting influence of Nazi rule, economic crisis, and general war-weariness all helped in understanding what had happened. But explanation did not remove the stark fact that, in the region apparently most committed to democracy, self-government was in danger of being uprooted. This left the way open for attacks by the new totalitarianism, communism. The political battle for Europe was to bulk large in the cold war.

Asia: Change and Crisis. Throughout Asia and North Africa, change and crisis marked the new political climate. The war had ended the old Asia for all time and the western world had to come to terms with something new. The historic Asian political structures—imperialism, feudalism, despotism—were challenged everywhere by a variety of new forces. In some parts of the continent, old orders were swept away almost without a trace; in others the outer appearances of prewar society were retained despite enormous inner modifications.

Such a massive development could not be expected to proceed smoothly. At the end of the war, Asia erupted. At one extremity was Japan, whose entire semi-feudal structure was shaken by the deliberate American policy of unleashing new social and economic forces. The liberation of women, the establishment of labor unions, the diversification of corporate ownership, and the erection of a parliamentary system all began to work their effects. In far southwest Asia was the Arab world, being transformed by nationalism, independence, and petroleum. Everywhere in between new elements were added to the political pattern whose combined effect was to transform a once-static situation into a highly dynamic one.

The Significance of Political Flux. It was extremely significant that political forms in the postwar world were widely regarded as being susceptible to rapid and drastic change. It meant that no permanent shape could be given to international relationships, no coherent pattern of interstate alignments could emerge, until domestic political life had first been stabilized. Consistent foreign policy can rest only on consensus, and in dozens of states there was no such broad agreement on fundamentals. The arrangements made in this postwar international society could not escape being tentative and exploratory, subject to sudden revision in the light of the rapid pace of political change in most of the world.

The impact of communism

For many Americans the most important—and the most baleful—of the new forces abroad after 1945 was communism; for some, indeed, it was the only important one. We shall see later how the popular tendency in the United States to blame all America's difficulties on the official Soviet ideology has resulted in serious policy distortion; we can thoroughly understand the impact of communism only in relation to the

1945 setting and to the other dynamisms of the postwar period. At this point, however, we shall consider communism only in terms of its general impact on the pattern of world politics.[13]

The Rise of Communism. Communism, as doctrine, was nothing new to students of ideas. Marx had written the "Communist Manifesto" in 1848, nearly a century before; Marxist and Communist parties had long been part of the European political scene. Since 1917 Russia had been under communist rule, and its agents had been active in every part of the world. The world knew communism, and thought it understood it. Yet, at the end of the war, this dogmatic ideology broke out as one of the controlling forces of world affairs. How did this sudden rise take place?

The major reason is of course the parallel revolution in the status of the Soviet Union. Courted instead of shunned, powerful instead of weak, one of the arbiters of the world, Bolshevik Russia had become a global giant. It was inevitable that its doctrine should be upgraded in proportion to its rise in political stature, since all good Bolsheviks attribute all their success to the universal applicability of their ideology. Nothing succeeds like success, and Moscow had undoubtedly succeeded in its greatest test. Communism received much of the credit.

There were other reasons as well. In the resistance movements against the Axis occupations between 1940 and 1945, communists everywhere had set examples of courage, organization, ingenuity, and devotion. In Europe they earned—and received payment on—a great debt of gratitude for their wartime services. In Asia they sought positions of leadership in native nationalist movements and used their new respectability to consolidate themselves against the day of peace. In both Europe and Asia, peace found communists either in or near the seats of power in many states, and in all they had improved their positions.

Communism and the Discontented. But the success of the Soviet Union and the wartime record of communism only explain part of the new impact of the doctrine. We have seen that political and economic instability were widespread at the end of the war. The prevailing mood throughout much of the world was one of discontent, whether sullen and passive in Europe or active and revolutionary in Asia. This presented the communists with a tempting opportunity.

Communism, as its students can testify, is a very elastic ideology; it can be given almost any turn appropriate to circumstances. This gives its manipulators a tactical advantage, in that they can shape their appeal to attract supporters in a great variety of situations. During the imme-

---

[13] From among the many histories of communism, one of the most useful is Hugh Seton-Watson, *From Lenin to Malenkov* (New York: Praeger, 1953).

diate postwar era communism, modified to meet differing situations, was aimed squarely at the discontented masses.

The communists preached only one message with infinite variations: hope for a better world. Whatever the complaints peculiar to the society, communism was the one nostrum guaranteeing a cure. The Soviet Union, "the place where communism works," was held out as the one state that was interested in the problems of the "working people" of France (or of Greece, or of India, or of Indonesia, or anywhere else). Let the people follow the communists, let them create the socialist Paradise in their homeland, let them accept direction from Moscow, and all their troubles would be over. Discontent would be satisfied and all social, economic, and personal problems would be solved.

The communist appeal to the discontented was all the stronger because of the seemingly reactionary character of much of its opposition. Democracy in Europe seemed to look backward to 1939 for its ideal; imperialism and authoritarianism in Asia likewise sought to turn back the clock. It seemed to many as if only communism held promise for the future, as if only the communists were advancing any new ideas. Democratic foreign policies in the cold-war patterns have had great difficulty in devising effective responses to this claim.

Communism and Soviet Foreign Policy. Another explanation of the new importance of communism was its extensive and effective use as an instrument of foreign policy by the government of the Soviet Union. Stalin had long established completed hegemony over all foreign Communist parties. The strategy and the tactics of each of them was laid down in Moscow, with only one objective: the advancement of the interests of the USSR. This was the test of a loyal communist.

After the war, the high command in Moscow attempted to coordinate the programs of local Communist parties everywhere. In a theme modified only by local conditions, communists strove for power, created mass movements of the discontented, and preached the virtues of the Soviet Union. It made no difference that the export-variety doctrine bore only a superficial resemblance to the working ideology of the Russians themselves. The Russian purpose was not really to bring about a world revolution and a classless society, but rather a continuous augmentation in Soviet power and prestige.

Communism had another advantage during this period: it was backed by Soviet military power. Ideology for export was not the whole of Moscow's foreign policy; it was one of a kit of tools that the Kremlin used interchangeably to accomplish a complex pattern of objectives.

239

But it served a most useful purpose, giving Moscow a leverage in many situations beyond the reach of Russian arms.

Communism and Change. Perhaps one more comment might further clarify what we have been saying. Communists, whose stock in trade (outside the USSR) is the constant advocacy of change, were admirably suited to thrive in the climate of political opinion in much of the postwar world. In 1945 it appeared that only communists were preaching change in economics, in politics, and in society. Many Americans more or less naturally identified communism with all the other revolutionary forces that became significant at this time: nationalism, anti-imperialism, collectivism, and so on. The unfortunate consequences of such a telescoping was that American anti-communism came often to mean opposition to all varieties of change. This, in an era when change was the order of the day, was a guarantee of inevitable frustration.

The Asian revolution

Asia, the seat of the world's civilizations, had become the football of European politics by 1900. The first half of the twentieth century witnessed the first stirrings of Asian self-consciousness in an industrialized world; it was not until the defeat of Japan, however, that the billion and a half Asians asserted themselves firmly. They set in motion the enormous mass movement that we have already called the "Asian revolution," whose consequences are now shaking the world and that may yet prove to be the most significant outcome of World War II.

A Revolution of Multiple Dimensions. There is no such thing as "Asia" as a political entity, but only a number of separate peoples, cultures, and states coexisting within a geographic area known as Asia. In the same way the very term "Asian revolution" is deceptive. There is no single revolution, but rather fifteen or twenty individual revolutions scattered throughout the continent, each following its own course and each seeking its own fulfillment. On this basis it is inaccurate to discuss the "Asian revolution" at all.

But each of these individual mass movements resembles, at least to some degree, all of the others; they are enough alike that it is possible to find certain common features. The social, economic, and political breeding ground of revolt throughout all of Asia was roughly the same; there is a model of *an* Asian revolution, if not of *the* Asian revolution.

In the first place, revolution in contemporary Asia is multi-dimensional. It is neither exclusively political, entirely economic, nor purely psychic, but instead partakes of all three characteristics. Particular groups may emphasize one element or another, but success in no single one would satisfy any revolutionary movement; the goal each of them seeks is nothing less than a new posture toward the outside world. Nor is it feasible for the West (or for the communists either, for that matter) to devise a single formula for satiating all Asian revolts individually or the Asian revolution in general. Despite their general similarity, each movement is rooted in indigenous factors and the technique for coping with them must be conspicuously flexible and capable of infinite adaption.

Roots of the Revolution. To analyze fully the roots of revolution in Asia—if any non-Oriental could do it successfully—would require an extensive and detailed history of the impact of the West on the East. We may at least suggest, however, a very general cause: Asia is now determined to receive its just due in its relations with the rest of the world.[14] Most of the details of political developments in Asia since 1945 can ultimately be traced to this motivating urge.

That western imperialism—political, economic, and cultural—was a technique for the perpetuation of Asia's inferior status was long known to the intellectual and political leaders of the Orient. As long as this insight was confined to a tiny and impotent section of the population, however, effective resistance to the West was impossible. It required the catalyzing action of the war to make the masses throughout Asia aware of this situation and to inspire them to end it. The object lesson of Japan, the resistance propaganda of the allies, the improvement in transportation and communication, and a number of other factors contributed to the awakening of new nationalism. Once political self-consciousness had been born, the leaders in each country were able to capture the mass movements and to provide them with both platforms and programs for action. The Asian revolution represents a reaction against the past and a hope for the future; it has been called "the revolution of rising expectations."

Positive and Negative Aspects. Not the least of the confusing aspects of the new Asia is that its revolution has both a positive and a negative side. Affirmatively, the common demands of the various mass movements stress the necessity of developing an equitable basis of relationships with the rest of the world. The most common components of the positive creed are political self-determination, economic independence, and cultural and social equality; none of these, we will note, are unfamiliar to Americans. Asians are demanding the same deference values as do other

---

14 See Arnold J. Toynbee, *The World and the West* (New York: Oxford University Press, 1953), Chapter V: "The Psychology of Encounters," for an interesting development of this theme.

peoples. Negatively—and frequently overlooked even by western sympathizers with Asian aspirations—there is a significant element of revenge involved. At last free from the more humiliating aspects of tutelage by the West, many Asians are deeply committed to demonstrating their new freedom, often in a most flamboyant way. All the old scores that weigh heavily on the conscience of the West are being settled; Asia is determined to balance its psychic accounts.

No one can yet foretell the direction that revolutionary Asia will eventually take. Communism early moved to take advantage of it, and many of the nationalist movements acquired a distinct pro-Soviet tinge. But as long as communist ideology requires subservience to Moscow, there is little prospect of a permanent communist victory in Asia; the Orient did not liberate itself from western imperialism in order to offer itself to Moscovite hegemony. The problem facing both the West and the communists is not how to control the Asian revolution (it is too massive for "control" in any ordinary sense) but rather how to come to terms with it.

The impact of technology

It has long been a subject of somewhat ironic comment that the greatest technological advances tend to be made during a time of war. Basic scientific principles may be discovered at any time, but in the western world they are generally not exploited unless they have immediate economic significance. Only in wartime, when ordinary cost calculations become irrelevant, are new scientific findings likely to receive their maximum utilization. Then, after the war, peacetime pursuits often receive the benefits of the new developments.

World War II fit this pattern. During the fighting, hundreds of technological applications of already-known scientific truths were made; some of them were of major significance in combat. The impact of at least some of them on the postwar world was so significant as to make technology one of the major new forces in international politics. We shall consider here only three examples of the technological revolution: transportation and communication, medicine, and the implications of nuclear fission.

Transportation and Communication. The major relevant development in transportation during the war was, of course, in aviation.[15] Air trans-

---

[15] See William F. Ogburn, "Aviation and International Relations," in W. F. Ogburn, ed., *Technology and International Relations* (Chicago: University of Chicago Press, 1949), pp. 86-101.

port matured between 1939 and 1945. The end of the war found the entire world tied together by a network of airlines; no corner of the world was so remote as to be completely unapproachable by the airplane. It is banal, but unquestionably true, to point out that the net effect of the rapid growth of air transportation was to make the world a much smaller place. This had, of course, an ambivalent effect; it made nations much more interdependent, but at the same time increased their mutual vulnerability. This was particularly relevant to the United States; obviously American security problems changed if Europe were only twelve hours away instead of seven days. The same may be said, of course, of Europe's security concerns vis-a-vis the United States.

Other transportation developments had perceptible effects. The requirements of warfare had caused highways to be built in many places where no modern roads had existed before; the Ledo Road in Burma is a prime example, although its peacetime use was admittedly negligible. Many societies became oriented to motor transport, with the American jeep becoming commonplace everywhere. At sea, despite the wartime losses, the world's merchant fleet largely survived the fighting and nations set about replacing the lost tonnage. Railroads alone did not share in the extension of transport facilities; wartime devastation outside the United States seriously reduced both trackage and equipment.

In communication, both wire and wireless facilities had been extended. Radio, telephones, radio telephony, and telegraph systems proliferated under the stimulus of a world-wide war, and remained largely intact after the fighting. Instantaneous communication across continents and oceans was a technological factor of great importance to future world politics.[16]

Medicine. It would require a long list compiled by a specialist to include all the wartime medical advances bequeathed to the postwar world. We shall mention only a few: the use of DDT as an insecticide; new drugs such as atabrine (replacing quinine as a treatment for malaria), the sulfas, and penicillin; the near-miracles worked in the transportation, storage, and employment of whole blood and plasma; and the mastery of a whole battery of new surgical techniques.

General gratification over these successes in the war against disease tended to obscure certain potentially troublesome implications. Many of these new techniques had public-health applications. This meant that death rates from disease could be drastically reduced by fairly simple

---

[16] See Hornell Hart, "Technology and the Growth of Political Areas," in Ogburn, ed., *Technology and International Relations.*

and economical methods. What this might mean for the already over-populated areas of Asia was generally neglected.

Demographers, ecologists, and agronomists warned of the likelihood of "population explosions," creating serious social stresses, pressures on food supplies, and the danger of new expansionist foreign policies as governments wrestled with the tensions caused by constantly increasing populations.[17]

Atomic Energy. Best known of the technological feats of the war was the American success in harnessing nuclear energy. The overpowering implication of nuclear fission was of course military; we shall discuss this aspect below. But scientists and technologists realized that atomic energy had a significance that far surpassed its use in bombs; it carried profoundly revolutionary overtones for the whole of international society.

Atomic Energy and Industrialization. Atomic energy, despite its spectacular nature, is merely another kind of energy; atoms produce heat as do other kinds of fuel. As such, it is capable of being put to the uses to which other energy sources are put; this means, most commonly, turning the wheels of industry. The principal industrial energy sources today are coal, petroleum, and, less importantly, hydroelectric power. Atomic fuels produce fantastic amounts of energy in proportion to their weight and volume and thus would seem to be ideal for industrial purposes.

This meant that, if the time were to come when men would be free to use atomic power for industrial purposes, the modernization or extension of a mature industrial structure would be no very complicated matter, and the creation of an entirely new one would be very much simplified. As the long-range aspect of atomic energy was pondered, many discussions began to be heard about a "new industrial revolution." [18]

The Equalization Factor. But if a new industrial revolution were indeed coming, it was destined to be a very different one. The coal-iron technology of the industrial age that began in the eighteenth century tied industry to its energy base; nations without extensive endowments of coal were seriously handicapped in the race for industrial power. This factor, more than any single other one, determined the location of the economic and political giants of the twentieth century.

The introduction of nuclear fuels, however, would change this picture

---

[17] Among the more outspoken of these arguments are William Vogt, *Road to Survival* (New York: Sloane, 1948), Fairfield Osborn, *Our Plundered Planet* (Boston: Little, Brown and Co., 1948), and Harrison Brown, *The Challenge of Man's Future* (New York: The Viking Press, 1954).

[18] See S. H. Schurr and J. Marschak, *Economic Aspects of Atomic Power* (Princeton, N. J.: Princeton University Press, 1950), and Laura Fermi, *Atoms for the World* (Chicago: University of Chicago Press, 1957).

greatly. Relatively inexpensive and needed only in small volume, their procurement and exploitation is beyond the reach of only the smallest and weakest of states. If a new industrial race were to begin, most states would start approximately even; the advantages enjoyed by the handful of presently dominant economies might disappear quickly. This point was understood by both the industrialized and the nonindustrialized states, and the ultimate implications of atomic power were one of the unknowns as the world entered the postwar era.

The new warfare

The technological speedup during the war had created new concepts of warfare. Many of the old assumptions about the place of armed force in international politics were largely outmoded by the new techniques, and almost all had to be sharply revised. The course of world affairs after 1945 revealed the effects of the change.

Total Weapons. World War II had ended with atomic bombs; it was generally agreed that any World War III would begin with them. Weapons of totality, capable of destroying great amounts of property, devastating broad expanses of territory, and killing millions of people at one blow, had been developed. The atomic bomb came to symbolize what was really a whole family of weapons that raised the prospect that man could wipe himself off the planet.[19]

Chemical weapons, such as the odorless, tasteless "nerve gas" that kills in seconds; biological weapons of all degrees of horror; guided missiles with atomic warheads; pilotless aircraft of great range; rockets; recoilless cannon capable of being fired from the shoulder; atomic artillery; long-range submarines: all of these (and many others) were either used during the war or were in an advanced stage of planning. Even the scientific and technological principles of the thermonuclear reaction—the hydrogen bomb—were no secret in 1945. Given normal scientific progress, anyone could predict that weapons would continue to become more and more devastating. Warface was evolving toward the point of mutual saturation, with victory probably going to the nation that could achieve strategic surprise.

Total War. The new weapons required a new theory of war. Classically, the object of warfare was to "destroy the enemy's will to resist" and to have him bend to your will. This concept entailed the prosecu-

[19] See Bernard Brodie, ed., *The Absolute Weapon* (New York: Harcourt, Brace and Co., 1946).

tion of combat by uniformed armed forces, fighting according to a generally understood code. The new weapons, however, had only limited utility under tactical conditions; their most effective targets were the productive centers of the enemy, where they could exert maximum effectiveness on the concentration of facilities and the congregations of people. Total weapons thus led to a theory of total war.

Total war is total in every respect: total in weapons, total in targets, total in strategy, total in mobilization, and finally total in objectives. Total war is war for annihilation. Its alternative objectives are the abject surrender of the enemy or his total obliteration. Negotiated peace becomes a thing of the past; all peace terms are to be either dictated after surrender or else irrelevant because the enemy no longer exists. If total effort be required for total victory, objectives become absolute as well; nothing less than absolute hegemony over the defeated is a sufficient enticement to make the effort and risks worth while.[20]

The Inexpediency of Military Power. However consistent the new theory of war may have been with its premises and its techniques, it broke sharply with the traditional theory of international politics. War is usually conceived as an instrument of national policy, as the only ultimately efficacious technique available to a state for the enforcement of its will on others. Total war, however, is an efficient instrument only for the accomplishment of total objectives; if total war is the only kind of war that a state is in a position to fight, its less extreme policies are seriously handicapped. It lacks the means of applying force in amounts graduated according to the objective sought and the resistance encountered, and thus is brought to face a hard choice. Objectives less than total must either be prosecuted without any real reliance on military techniques—a frustrating and often futile enterprise—or expanded so that they become important enough to justify the new warfare.

In the immediate postwar period, a deliberate recourse to total war by any state capable of waging it was unthinkable; popular war-weariness made any such thought utterly untenable. Although the United States held a monopoly of atomic weapons and a long lead in the other total techniques, very few serious students expected this condition to endure for long. The time was destined to come when the major states would confront each other in full possession of the armory of new weapons, each capable of waging a total war of extermination. What would happen to international relations at that time, when the state system might

---

[20] See B. H. Liddell Hart, *The Revolution in Warfare* (New Haven, Conn.: Yale University Press, 1947), and W. W. Kaufmann, ed., *Military Policy and National Security* (Princeton, N. J.: Princeton University Press, 1956).

well be forced into the poignant choice between total war and no war at all, could be no more than guessed at. Agreement was general, however, that the new warfare would modify many of the traditional assumptions about the nature of international relationships.[21]

THE AMERICAN ATTITUDE

This, then, was the general shape of the new world in which the United States found itself at the end of World War II. It was a world in which the fixed points had been moved and in which powerful new forces, dimly understood and often unsuspected, were at work. The international scene bristled with problems; the future, although hopeful, was certain to be complex. What about the American attitude toward the world; how did the United States face its problem?

We may synthesize two general themes from the welter of voices that spoke for American opinion at that time. In the first place, Americans generally accepted the end of the era of noninvolvement; isolation had been abandoned and most Americans admitted that they had joined the world. Second, there was widespread acceptance of some kind of responsibility. The United States was obviously to be required to act purposively in the future, and American thinking was to be both broader and deeper than at any similar period in history.

The end of disentanglement

The effect of World War II was not to bring the United States into the world; that had happened nearly half a century before. Its effect was rather to persuade mass opinion in the United States to accept the broader implications of America's full membership in the community of states. There was little joy and considerable regret in the American reaction to the new conditions of foreign policy, but there was also little inclination to shrink from the prospect. The postwar world was not one in which a policy of withdrawal stood any chance of success; wartime victory had brought its consequences.

The End of Innocence. The years of war had contributed largely to the development of the political sophistication of the American people.

---

[21] For a vigorous attack on the attempt of professional military men to fit the new concept of war into a traditional operational plan, see B. H. Liddell Hart, "Military Strategy vs. Common Sense," *The Saturday Review* (March 3, 1956), pp. 7 ff. This problem is discussed further in Chapter 15 below.

Many of the easy assumptions about the immorality of power politics, the sovereign virtues of public opinion, and the inevitability of victory for the virtuous had been sloughed off in the hard years of fighting and sacrifice. There was less of a tendency to consider the United States a nation apart, subject to its own set of values and rules. Instead there was more awareness of the common plight of all states and the necessity for Americans to play the game according to the common rules. The end of American innocence came as the immediate result of the increase in popular understanding of three fundamental factors in the foreign policy of the United States.

(1) Americans ended the war more cognizant of the sheer power of their country than they had ever been. The massive battles that had smashed the Nazi machine and humbled Japan had demonstrated the United States to be the most powerful nation in the history of the world. However dimly, many Americans understood the global consequences that would follow from whatever action the United States took, even in the form of refusing to do anything at all; it was a sobering thought that the slightest shift in American policy would be felt in Europe, in Asia, and in the Soviet Union itself.

(2) The same war that revealed American strength also indicated the dimensions of the problem that the United States was facing. The war ended with armed Americans in China, in the South Pacific, in Japan, in Czechoslovakia, in North Africa, and in Iran. Where the war had gone, there also were born problems of postwar settlement; unless Americans were willing to repeat the error of 1919 and permit everyone else to make the peace that the United States had largely contributed to making possible, they were obligated to project American policy to all these out-of-the-way places.

(3) There was also some appreciation of the responsibilities that go with power. We shall consider some of the details of this point in a moment, but at this point we may stress that the war had made clear that with great power comes a duty to use that power wisely. No longer did Americans feel that their great strength was theirs alone to use as they saw fit; the happy irresponsibility of another day had largely disappeared. The only way in which American power could bring real security to the United States was by its application to the affirmative purpose of making good the wartime victory. Merely contemplating American grandeur and reposing in isolated splendor would be suicidal.

Other Attitudes. What we have been describing was the prevailing public mood in 1945. It must not be supposed that these opinions were unanimous. There were other attitudes widely shared within the public that ran directly contrary to these, and that were to become increasingly important during the cold war.

We might first mention the most important dissent to the general abandonment of disentanglement, that of the so-called "isolationists." Geographically concentrated in the Middle West, drawing (at least according to some students) their strength from the pro-German, anti-British prejudices of large segments of the rural population in that region, the isolationists stubbornly resisted what they felt was a dangerous trend.[22] Speaking principally through such newspapers as the Chicago *Tribune* and a bloc of conservative United States Senators, they denied both the necessity and the desirability of any departure from "traditional" American policy.

As their argument matured, they shifted their ground from the naive noninvolvement argument of 1919 and 1937. Recognizing—as did most Americans—that it was futile to order the rest of the world to leave the United States alone, the new isolationism devised a formula for coping with it. Instead of preaching withdrawal, they advocated an aggressive expansionism. The United States was to "go it alone," but it was nevertheless to conduct a vigorous—nearly imperialist—policy. Great areas of the world were to be marked out as American spheres within which the United States would tolerate no competition; the rest of the world was to be watched warily and any real threat to American hegemony was to be scotched immediately. Permanent arrangements with other states, especially through the United Nations, were to be avoided as much as possible; all dealings with foreigners were to be tentative and subject to early termination.

At the other pole were the new Utopians, as much the legitimate heirs of an old American tradition as were the isolationists. This group saw in the post-war era an opportunity for the United States to remake the world in a new and more perfect form. Various schemes, including those of such organizations as the United World Federalists, urged the commitment of American power to far-reaching reconstruction of the political organization of the world. The reformers had little patience with the ordinary routine of diplomacy and many seriously questioned the value of the United Nations. Founded on the doctrine of national sovereignty, the United Nations was, according to some more extreme

---

[22] Samuel J. Lubell, in *The Future of American Politics* (New York: Harper & Bros., Inc., 1951), is an outstanding advocate of the pro-German interpretation of isolationism. See Chapter 7: "The Myth of Isolationism."

Utopians, bound to repeat the errors of the past. The United States, the argument ran, should make a clean break with history and start a fresh page.[23]

The acceptance of responsibility

The dissolution of the mirage of disentanglement brought with it an understanding that the United States had acquired broad and longlasting responsibilities. American foreign policy was in the future to be constantly sensitive to the existence, the needs, and the wishes of other states; the free-wheeling assumption that the United States needed to concern itself with no one but itself was discarded. New responsibilities were immediately shouldered by Americans in four major areas.

Peacemaking. Following on the heels of the wartime agreements, the United States plunged into the thorny question of making the peace. The latter half of 1945 and the entire year of 1946 was spent in a continuous round of peace negotiations with the major allies. Although peace terms with the major states of Germany and Japan—as well as the final disposition of Austria—proved impossible of formulation, arrangements with the minor Axis powers were concluded in 1947.

The United States remained true to its pledge of no separate peace with the Axis long after any real hope for a common settlement had evaporated. East-West negotiations over Germany were not broken off until 1948; the policy of treating West Germany as a separate state was not adopted until 1949; a separate peace treaty was not signed with West Germany until 1952. Japan's peace treaty was negotiated in 1951 only after formally extending an invitation to the Soviet to participate in its formulation and offering Moscow an opportunity to adhere to the final document.[24]

Rehabilitation. Americans, true to their humanitarian tradition, leaped into the problem of rehabilitating the devastated areas of the world almost before the fighting was over. In addition to direct American assistance to distressed populations via the armed forces, the first international

---

[23] An extreme version of this Utopianism is the *Preliminary Draft of a World Constitution* (Chicago: University of Chicago Press, 1947), prepared by the "Committee to Frame a World Constitution," of which Robert Maynard Hutchins was Chairman and G. A. Borgese was Secretary.

[24] On peacemaking, see Redvers Opie and associates, *The Search for Peace Settlements,* (Washington, D. C.: Brookings, 1951); on the Japanese treaty, see Bernard M. Cohen, *The Political Process and Foreign Policy* (Princeton, N. J.: Princeton University Press, 1957).

agency created to cope with the human and material backwash of war was the United Nations Relief and Rehabilitation Administration, to which the United States made the bulk of the contributions. UNRRA eventually evolved into the International Refugee Organization, again the recipient of major American support. The American government made many large grants of money, equipment, and foodstuffs to its former allies during the initial period after the war; to Europe alone these grants of various sorts totalled over eleven billion dollars by the spring of 1947. In all of these enterprises popular feeling completely supported the governmental action.

Atomic Energy. Among the most interesting evidences of the new American sense of responsibility was United States policy toward atomic energy. Aware both of its potential destructiveness and its possibilities for good, the American government early began studying the most efficient and safe method of making its knowledge available. From the beginning American policy contemplated the internationalization of atomic energy on some basis that incorporated safeguards against atomic war. The Acheson-Lilienthal report of 1945 and the Baruch proposals of 1946 represented serious attempts to salvage the good out of atomic energy while neutralizing the bad. That these attempts failed and that the world settled down to an atomic arms race is not the fault of the good will of the American people. In 1945 popular attitude supported the idea that atomic energy, for good or ill, was something that was to be shared with all people, and not to be kept for the exclusive use of Americans. There were elements both of moral conviction and of hard common sense in this position; Americans realized that an atomic monopoly was practically impossible as well as morally indefensible.

The United Nations. Finally, we must again mention American opinion toward the United Nations as a more general indication of the new sense of responsibility. There were, as we have noted, some opposition voices, but American acceptance of the United Nations was widespread. The controlling mood was one of mixed repentance (for having destroyed the League by abstention) and hope (for what the United Nations might achieve). On both grounds the United Nations received such deep approval that some scholars later felt that it had been "oversold" and that Americans expected too much from what was, after all, an admittedly imperfect instrument.

But more fundamental that whether or not the mass of people were over-sanguine about what the United Nations could do is the fact that Americans accepted the organization in full realization that they were accepting a long-run commitment. The arguments that had doomed the Treaty of Versailles and the League—the loss of sovereignty, alien control, and so on—seemed irrelevant to the conditions of 1945; Americans sensed that their own freedom depended on that of other peoples. We may therefore infer that the acceptance of United Nations membership—done with reasonable insight into the nature of the act—symbolizes the final break with the past. Americans were ready to do their part, at least insofar as they understood it.

10 : The Soviet threat
1945-1946

This chapter is the second in the three that deal with the situational factors out of which have grown American policy decisions since 1945. We shall be considering the threat presented by the postwar policy of the USSR. Were it possible (or worthwhile) to classify all American policy moves in the past decade in terms of their situational motivation, there is little doubt that we would discover that the vast majority would owe their original inspiration to Soviet policy. The behavior of the Soviet Colossus has been the most significant fact confronting Americans, and the design of contemporary American policy is to a great extent grounded on certain assumptions about Soviet behavior.

All adult Americans recall that the USSR was, along with Britain, one of the major allies of the United States in the successful war against the Axis, and that the same three powers took the lead in preparing the world for the reestablishment of peace. At what point did the mainspring of great-power cooperation go wrong? When, where, and how did the Soviet threat manifest itself? This chapter is designed to suggest some answers to these questions.

The rise of Soviet revisionism

The pivot of our discussion of Soviet policy is the assumption that the USSR is a revisionist power. For whatever reasons, Russian leadership emerged from the war committed to a policy of seeking further advantage, and apparently willing to capitalize upon postwar disorganization

253

and distress by any expedient means. Since the United States accepted the contrary status of being and behaving like a status-quo power, the cold war was from the beginning a massive struggle between attackers and defenders of the general shape of the postwar settlement.

The Wartime Policy of the USSR. Many Americans were unnecessarily shocked at the Soviet Union's determination to follow an active and opportunistic policy after the war. Moscow had given adequate warning of its intentions all through the era of active combat; her postwar policy should not have occasioned such surprise. Beginning in 1939 with the annexation of a large part of Poland, and culminating with the mass looting of Manchuria in 1945, Soviet military operations were always at the immediate service of a set of political objectives. Russian goals may be generally categorized as an attempt to establish the physical security of the state, and involved three major concerns: (1) the rectification of Soviet frontiers, particularly with regard to territories that Russia had lost after 1917 (Poland, the Baltic States, Bessarabia); (2) the elimination or abasement of hostile regimes on Soviet frontiers (Finland, Turkey); (3) the reestablishment of traditional spheres of Russian influence (northern Iran, the Balkans). Although Soviet policy was to go far beyond these goals in the postwar era, they remain today as apparently fundamental to Soviet policy.[1]

The Breakup of the Wartime Alliance. American attitudes during the war, public and official alike, tended frequently to magnify unduly the actual area of agreement between the United States and the Soviet Union. Basic harmony of ends between Moscow and the West was confined to a common interest in the military defeat of the Axis, and included only the most general and vague reassurances about the final shape to be taken by the peace settlement. Even on such purely procedural matters as the timing of a cross-Channel invasion of Europe or the terms of Soviet entry into the war against Japan, there was great confusion of purpose and considerable open disagreement. But the military effort progressed withal in an atmosphere of general cooperation.

It was in the latter days of the fighting, when in 1944 and early 1945 the dimensions of the ultimate victory were becoming apparent, that the developing divergence of interest between Moscow and the West came into the open. As the allies turned to the task of postwar planning, serious cleavages developed. Soviet policy remained consistent with its fundamental revisionism; Britain and the United States assumed the posture demanded by their status-quo orientation.

---

[1] See, for example, Anatole G. Mazour, *Russia Past and Present* (New York: D. Van Nostrand Company, Inc., 1951), Chapters 26, 27.

This mutual opposition manifested itself on almost all the specific issues that came under discussion, of which three were most important for the future: (1) the disposition to be made of the Axis states, particularly Germany and the reparations she was to pay; (2) the post-liberation status of eastern Europe, epitomized by the problem of Poland; (3) the nature of the United Nations and the place of the great powers in its structure. On each of these points a distinct Soviet position developed, marked by a single-minded pursuit of its own advantage, an apparent unconcern for peace, order, and stability in the abstract, and an unwillingness to accept substantial compromise. So clear had it become that allied unity had dissolved that peace-making became from the outset an admitted conflict between the Soviet and the West. The grand alliance did not survive the crisis that had given it birth.[2]

The Soviet's Search for Advantage. At this point we may generally characterize the evolving Soviet policy at the close of the war as a search for advantage. Stalin began with a revisionist assumption that the USSR was to seek to improve its position in the future. It is relatively unimportant to us here whether this decision to take the policy offensive was a wartime development or a long-standing (though often ignored) ideological commitment; in 1945 it was clear that Moscow was determined to win whatever rewards were available for the taking.

It is axiomatic that revisionist policies succeed best in periods of stress, insecurity, and disorganization. Such, as we saw in Chapter 9, was the condition of the world in the wake of World War II. Conditions were everywhere tailored to Soviet purposes: Europe was prostrate, Asia in ferment, and the fabric of international relationships badly disrupted by twelve years of Hitler, the last six having been years of war. Moscow had ample opportunity to use its newly rationalized position of power to force rearrangements to its advantage. Russian hegemony broke out of its traditional limits and flowed in all directions as the Kremlin sought to profit by the badly roiled waters of international affairs.

SOVIET POSTWAR POLICY

Before examining the specific moves made by the Soviet Union during 1945, 1946, and early 1947—the pre-cold war period during which Moscow was able to move with relative freedom and without particular fear of effective opposition—we should first make some general observations about the nature of its policy.

---

[2] For general discussions of deteriorating relations with the Soviet, see Cordell Hull, *Memoirs* (New York: The Macmillan Co., 1948), Chapters 105, 106; and James F. Byrnes, *Speaking Frankly* (New York: Harper & Bros., Inc., 1947), Chapters 2, 3, 4.

General characteristics

We have already noted that Soviet policy was fundamentally revisionist. This means that in practice it was dynamic, expansive, and alert to seize such initiatives as offered themselves. The USSR was impatient with long-standing commitments and traditional patterns; Russian leadership conceived of the international order as being infinitely fluid. According to their apparent hypothesis, almost any situation was susceptible of manipulation and exploitation by a sufficiently determined and ingenious Soviet policy. Moscow's approach to the world was therefore posited on its ability to transform relations and to direct the course of events to its liking.

The Exploitation of Great-power Status. From the very outset the Soviet insisted on the maximum exploitation of its status as a great power. Stalin seemed to relish his unusual position as an equal among the mighty and his government was diligent in capitalizing upon it. Three trends of Soviet action stemmed from this principle.

(1) The Soviet stressed and magnified the role of great-power consultation in making and maintaining the peace. Outstanding examples of this tendency were the denial of jurisdiction to the United Nations over all problems of settlement with the Axis, and the Soviet demand for the veto in the Security Council; another was Moscow's preference for the Foreign Minister's Conference as a tool of diplomacy.

(2) The USSR began to assert the traditional prerogative of a great power of having an interest in and being consulted on any international question into which it chose to intervene. It is a common characteristic of great powers that their concerns are total; no issue is too remote for them to claim the right to help determine its outcome. Indication of this tendency was provided by Soviet interest in such issues as the fate of the Italian colonies and the partition of Palestine.

(3) The Soviet began to demonstrate the all-too-familiar lack of regard for the opinions of small states that has in the past been a normal accompaniment of great-power status. Small nations were regarded as annoyances when they claimed rights as against Moscow; the rest of the time they were ignored except as targets of Soviet expansionism. This principle reached its full flower in the development of satellitism.

The Assumption of Disharmony of Interest. A second basis characteristic of Soviet policy was its assumption that no community of interest existed between the USSR and any state not under its control. The Soviet leaders entered the postwar world officially committed to the doctrine that Moscow would have to look only to itself for its salvation,

256

and that the motives of other states ranged from the highly questionable to the openly hostile. As a result, the USSR seemed to place no trust in pledges of good faith or in collective guarantees; its working hypothesis stressed rather the impermanence of such arrangements and concentrated instead on the creation of situations absolutely under Moscow's control.[3]

This outlook made Moscow a most troublesome negotiator. Assuming that noncommunist states were incapable of any interest not unalterably opposed to the continued existence of the USSR left little room for maneuver and none for compromise. Every discussion with the West became a no-quarter battle in which the Soviet set minimum objectives for itself and would accept nothing less; offers of partial settlement by the other states were deemed to be admissions of defeat and were met by demands for further concession. So long as Moscow postulated the failure of any community of agreement Soviet policy was destined to remain beyond stabilization.

Soviet relations with the United States

Naturally enough, the Russian decision to break the pattern of wartime cooperation and to initiate a policy of unilateral revisionism required that it reorient its relations with the United States. During the war Moscow had been officially friendly with Washington, although this was a friendship with definite reservations; by mid-1945, however, this attitude had become an encumbrance on the Soviet's postwar plans. Relationships with America were thereupon deliberately transformed from amicability to hostility.

The Change in Attitude. The new Soviet position became apparent before the end of the war. Even before the death of President Roosevelt the Soviet propaganda line had begun to minimize American contributions to the war, to discredit American motives before and during the fighting, and to discover ideological justification for the assumption that the United States was bound to plot the destruction of the Soviet system.[4]

After victory, Moscow's "hate America" approach solidified. Official Russian policy pretended to discover the reason for American hostility in the distortion of President Roosevelt's intentions by his successors;

---

[3] For the doctrinal roots of this assumption, see Nathan Leites, *The Operational Code of the Politburo* (New York: The McGraw-Hill Book Co., Inc., 1951), Chapters 9, 10, 11, 14, 20.

[4] Robert Sherwood, *Roosevelt and Hopkins* (New York: Bantam Books, 1950), Chapter XXXII, "Beginnings of Dissension."

unofficially the condemnation of everything American became much more general. By the end of 1945 Russian-American relations had become tense; by mid-1946 the conflict was open.

The new Soviet attitude was demonstrated in more than propaganda; at every operating level Russian harrassment of the United States was obviously an established principle. By 1946, Foreign Minister Molotov was perfecting what came to be known as "the diplomacy of vituperation" in his dealings with Secretary of State Byrnes as the foreign ministers sought vainly to make peace with Germany; various Soviet representatives at the United Nations, notably Andrei Vishinsky, were using that sounding board to ridicule, indict, and condemn the United States to the world; wherever Soviet and American representatives came into direct contact, as in the occupations of Germany and Korea, Soviet behavior had become deliberately uncooperative, provocative, and contemptuous.

Open Competition. The policy of hostility to the United States was amplified by the adoption of an action principle: open competition with America. In every area of the world and on every functional issue, a Soviet policy was swiftly developed as a counterpart to each move of the United States. On occupation and reparations policy, on the development of the United Nations, on colonial and imperial questions, and on atomic energy control—to cite only a few of the more important issues—Moscow took stands that were admittedly relevant to its original revisionist orientation but the detailed implementation of which was to some extent inspired by its determination to demonstrate disagreement with the United States. Analyzing this period from the perspective granted by time, a good case can be made that the Soviet was often more concerned with differing with the United States than it was with the specifics of the program it was following.

The Escape from Inferiority. This last point suggests another aspect of Moscow's American policy, difficult to measure exactly but possibly of great significance. The USSR seems to have been determined to force the United States to accept it as an equal in every way: in status, in power, in prestige. What perplexed a great many Americans was the fact that, under the glow of good fellowship arising from the end of the war, the United States was apparently willing to grant such equality. The inability of the two states to communicate successfully, however, added a massive misunderstanding to the developing policy clash. The Soviet tended to insist upon exactly those symbols of equality most likely to annoy American prejudices, and often attempted to win their acceptance by violent and direct propaganda attack on the United States. The

258

almost predictable result was a total American refusal to give any ground at all to Soviet prestige, a position that was to become almost a fixed element of American policy and a basic principle of the cold war policy of the United States.

The Soviet Union and the United Nations

Soviet attitudes toward the United Nations during the early history of the organization provided further clues to Russian policy. With the popular American conception of the United Nations as an instrument for interstate cooperation directed at the institutionalization of peace, the USSR had no sympathy. Moscow instead brought to the organization its own great-power preoccupation and its assumption of the absence of any genuine community of interest.

The United Nations as a Tool. Underlying the Soviet approach to the United Nations was the basic judgment that the United Nations' sole justification was as a tool of Moscow's foreign policy. Certain Russian objectives were most efficiently pursued through the United Nations; some foreign-policy techniques were more effective when employed there. For these purposes the USSR was willing—almost eager—to employ the institutions and mechanisms provided. Other United Nations functions were thought to be politically dangerous; some procedures violated the Soviet's conception of the organization's appropriate role. These "undesirable" aspects of the United Nations system Moscow set itself to arrest or at least to minimize. Finally, the Soviet felt that a large area of United Nations activity was simply irrelevant to itself; this portion was simply ignored. There was clearly no intention on the Soviet's part to make the organization the substantive or the procedural center of its policy; rather the United Nations was to remain as one of its available techniques of foreign policy, to be used when and to the extent to which it was appropriate.[5]

The Soviet Union and the Security Council. The Soviet idea of the United Nations was clearly indicated by its conduct on the Security Council. The great-power veto became the USSR's method of guaranteeing that its status would be inviolate. Any measure that carried a threat —however remote—to any Russian interest, the Soviet was prepared ruthlessly to void by means of a negative vote; at the same time Moscow shrewdly expected to capitalize on the reluctance of the other permanent

---

[5] See Rupert Emerson and Inis L. Claude, "The Soviet Union and the United Nations," *International Organization* (February, 1952), pp. 1 ff.

members to veto in their turns. Thus the Security Council was put substantially at Russia's mercy; it could deal only with those questions that the Soviet permitted and its solutions had to meet Soviet specifications in order to gain the requisite great-power unanimity. Moscow went so far as to argue that its veto extended to whether or not a question was placed on the agenda; this would have completed the Russian victory. This final power, however, was denied.

The Propaganda Weapon. The principal value Russia seemed to find in the General Assembly was as a platform for propaganda. Soviet theorists had only contempt for the idealistic conception of the General Assembly as the "parliament of man" or the "collective conscience of mankind"; ideologically, only the proletariat had a conscience and most of the members of the United Nations were noncommunist states. But the great forum of the General Assembly provided a built-in global audience for Soviet arguments, and from its very first session Russian spokesmen took full advantage of it. Out of General Assembly sessions emerged the outlines of Soviet anti-Americanism, of its emergent anti-colonialism, and of its series of sensational disarmament proposals. Here the Soviet could claim and receive equal time with its western opponents to appeal to the uncommitted states and to the discontented masses everywhere in the world. Some of what turned out to be the most lasting and significant Soviet propaganda victories (on such issues as disarmament) were won in the arena of the General Assembly.

The Rejection of ECOSOC. In marked contrast to its vigorous exploitation of the opportunities it found in the Security Council and the General Assembly, the Soviet largely ignored the economic and social activities of the United Nations. It participated in the work of the Economic and Social Council (ECOSOC) itself and of its commissions, but with obvious lack of interest and energy; one interesting exception was its feverish attachment to the work of the commission drafting a world declaration of human rights. Except for the Universal Postal Union, the World Health Organization, the International Telecommunications Union, and the World Meteorological Organization, the Soviet Union boycotted the specialized agencies; even its membership in WHO was terminated in 1949 for the alleged reason of exorbitant cost. It was not until the cold war changed character in 1954 and 1955 that the Soviet indicated any interest in the other specialized agencies,[6] and even went so far as to join the United Nations Educational, Scientific, and Cultural Organization.

---

[6] See Daniel S. Cheever and H. Field Haviland, *Organizing for Peace* (Boston: Houghton-Mifflin Co., 1954), pp. 193-4.

Both ideology and realistic politics help explain the USSR's abstention from the economic and social work of the United Nations. Ideologically, there was no reason for a socialist state to cooperate with capitalist societies in attempting to improve the economic and social lot of men; according to Marxist dogma, such reform could come about only after a proletarian revolution that would rebuild society on a more substantial base. Communists could argue, therefore, that Moscow was lending more real assistance to workers everywhere by intriguing to destroy capitalism than it would by cooperating with bourgeois democracies. Politically, it was apparent that Russia's policy would thrive best in a distraught world; to stabilize economic and social conditions might well interfere with the satisfaction of Soviet desires. There was no reason for the USSR to take any pains to speed the return of orderly existence; on the contrary, there were many reasons to interfere with it.

The development of satellitism

What the Soviet conception of its great-power status and its assumption of disharmony of interest meant in practice was shown in its relationships with its smaller European neighbors of Eastern Europe. Permanently friendly relations between Moscow and a smaller state were possible on only one basis: the status relationship the world came to call "satellitism."

The Meaning of Satellitism. What was satellitism? As the relationship developed, it became clear that the price of Russian friendship for a small state was the complete subordination of its foreign policy to Soviet control. The international mission of a satellite became reduced to contributing its share to the accomplishment of Russian designs. In theory, it was not absolutely necessary for a satellite to become a communist state on the Soviet model; the minimum requirements of satellitism were satisfied with an appropriate international orientation.[7] The complex of historic, ethnic, religious, and economic forces in Slavic Europe, Hungary, and East Germany, however, left Moscow no convenient stopping place short of the complete reconstruction of the states in that region; in no other way could the Kremlin exercise sufficiently close control over their foreign policies.

Once a satellite's status was formalized, it lost its freedom of international action. Its position was that of a member of the Soviet team and

---

[7] This condition is perhaps represented by Finland's relationship with the Soviet. Although internally a free democracy, and not overtly a satellite of the Soviet, nevertheless it is noteworthy that Finland's foreign relations are carefully conducted so as not to antagonize the USSR.

of the instrument of a foreign policy that remained peculiarly Russian. Moscow's enemies were its enemies; Moscow's friends were its friends. Its traditional objectives were measured against Soviet policy; to the extent that the USSR was gratified by any satellite's success, such goals were permitted. When any conflict arose, Soviet objectives naturally took precedence.

The Application of Satellitism. The principle of satellitism was put into practice in those areas of Europe that were liberated from the Nazis by the Red Army. In the wake of Soviet military forces came teams of civilian political specialists, composed both of Russians and of natives of the particular state who had been indoctrinated during periods of exile in the USSR. These groups rapidly made contact with local resistance forces and hastily put together provisional governments under the sponsorship of the Red Army. The new regimes were called "democratic"— a word whose effective synonym was "anti-Nazi"—and were ostensibly broadly-based coalitions of all acceptable political factions. As time went on, it became clear that the coalition structure was a mere facade; the dominant element was the local communist element that drew its strength from its liaison with the Russian army and the Russian party commissars.[8]

The single exception to this pattern was Yugoslavia, where the indigenous strength of Marshal Tito's partisans and the aid they received from the West made it possible for a communist-style people's government to be established without the appearance of Russian troops. This single difference was to have a profound effect on the later development of Russo-Yugoslav relations.[9]

In all the east and southeast European states entered by Soviet forces except Czechoslovakia and Hungary, the principles of satellitism were applied during 1945 and 1946. Bulgaria, Yugoslavia, Albania, Romania, Poland, and the Soviet zone of Germany were swiftly brought under effective communist control; the process of purging all unsympathetic elements of the coalition was begun almost as soon as the regimes were established. In Czechoslovakia and Hungary Soviet plans did not succeed so swiftly; genuine coalitions with anti-communist elements were voted into office in reasonably free elections, not to be disbanded until the coups of 1947 and 1948. Even with these two exceptions, however, the Soviet created within less than two years a tightly-knit bloc of supporters whose foreign relations were completely under Moscow's control

---

[8] For a deft summary of this technique, see Lennox Mills and Charles M. McLaughlin, *World Politics in Transition* (New York: Henry Holt and Co., 1956), pp. 576-581: "The Technique of the Inside Job."

[9] Hamilton Fish Armstrong, *Tito and Goliath* (New York: The Macmillan Co., 1951); see also Fitzroy Maclean, *The Heretic* (New York: Harper & Bros., 1957).

and that formed a buffer belt from the Baltic to the Adriatic, insulating Russia from the West.

The Rationale of Satellitism. The rationale of satellitism had several components that help explain why the Soviet was compelled to move so strongly in dealing with its immediate neighbors. (1) The Soviet conception of great power-small power relations demanded such a pattern, since large and powerful states were supposed to dictate to smaller and weaker ones. (2) The Russian assumption of a lack of any community of interest with noncommunist states indicated a need for complete control. (3) Russia was reversing the *cordon sanitaire* of the 1920's, throwing up a buffer zone between itself and the West. The flat plain of Poland had served as a highway for two invasions from the West within a single generation. (4) Ideology urged the expansion of the proletarian revolution by capitalizing on such favorable opportunities. (5) The historic Russian role as "protector of the Slavs" coincided with these other factors in persuading Moscow to make Slavic Europe a Russian province. All together, the combination of considerations of prestige, of security, of ideology, and of nationalism made a sufficient case for the Soviet doing something it would have had difficulty in avoiding doing anyway.[10]

EARLY SOVIET MOVES

For roughly the first two years following the surrender of Germany, the Soviet gained major advantages from the disorganization of the West and the slowness of the United States to grasp the implications of Russian policy. During this brief period the USSR was able to score a number of significant victories and to establish a position relatively well suited to receive the western counterattack. To trace each of the complex and varied maneuvers of Soviet policy during this period would be tedious and to a large extent unnecessary for our purposes. We shall confine ourselves to a rapid survey of the major trends.

Europe

Europe was the major theater of the cold war from the beginning. Soviet expansionism began in Europe, and Russian efforts there have

---

10 On satellitism, see Owen Lattimore, "Satellite Politics: the Mongolian Prototype," *Western Political Quarterly* (March, 1956), p. 37 ff; Czeslav Milosz, "Poland: Voices of Illusion," *Problems of Communism* (May-June, 1956), pp. 26 ff; E. D. Stillman and R. H. Bass, "Bulgaria: A Study in Satellite Non-conformity," *Problems of Communism* (November-December, 1955).

been continuous. The development of concerted Russian strategies for the Far East and the Middle East was not to come until later and then only in response to drastic changes in conditions; the Soviet program in Europe was full-grown the moment peace arrived.

Germany. Early Soviet policy toward the problem of Germany may be divided profitably into three subsections. In each of them the Soviet acted vigorously, apparently unconcerned that its actual policies often tended toward self-contradiction.

(1) The first matter was that of occupation policy. The USSR's version of the quadripartite occupation required that its own zone be treated as a captured province. Soviet-occupied Germany was almost sealed off from the other three zones and the Russians argued that four-power coordination was to be implemented only at the topmost level of the ACA. Here the Soviet veto was effective in blocking policies of which it disapproved. Within its own zone, the "democratization" and "denazification" directives formulated at Potsdam gave Moscow ample justification to proceed swiftly to the creation of a satellite regime for east Germany.

(2) The second issue was reparations. The Soviet stripped its own zone of Germany of almost everything that was both portable and valuable in the guise of reparations, and then presented an enormous bill that it claimed was due from west Germany. It made no impression on Moscow to point out that the United States, Britain, and France were occupying Germany at a loss, and that there was a net input of western currency (almost entirely dollars) that almost exactly matched what the Soviet was taking out. To the other three powers it seemed as if the Soviet demand for reparations was insatiable.

(3) The final broad concern was the negotiation of a peace settlement. Although all four powers were pledged to the principle of German unity, the Soviet refused to consider any reunification formula that did not put Germany virtually at the mercy of Russia. The most it appeared willing to accept was a permanently impotent Germany always under the guns of Russian troops across the Polish border; the Soviet obviously preferred a political structure for Germany that would facilitate its eventual capture by a communist coup. Western policy rapidly hardened in the face of Soviet insistence on hegemony over Germany; negotiations on a peace treaty finally broke down early in 1948.[11]

Western Europe. Soviet policy in Western Europe was executed pri-

---

[11] A convenient summary of the interallied negotiations over Germany is given in James P. Warburg, *Germany: Key to Peace* (Cambridge, Mass.: Harvard University Press, 1953).

marily through its control over the indigenous communist parties there. Although capable of exerting considerable pressure in Scandinavia and the Low Countries, Russian policy concentrated on the key states of France and Italy. With communists included in the cabinets of both states, a concerted program of alternating pressure and persuasion was exerted on their tottering democratic governments. Parliamentary maneuvering was combined with "direct action"—strikes, riots, boycotts, and similar tactics. The object of this policy was to bring about either the collapse of democracy and its replacement by communist regimes or the modification of French and Italian foreign policy in the direction of a pro-Soviet orientation. Outside France and Italy, communist pressure was a complicating annoyance rather than an open threat, although conditions existed that made possible future communist moves.[12]

Eastern Europe. Our discussion of satellitism has already outlined the general content of Soviet policy in eastern Europe. We need at this point only to stress the continuing Russian effort to weld its bloc into a monolithic entity. The Soviet attempted to force all the satellites to orient their policies entirely toward Moscow, to cut their relations with the West to the bare minimum, and to recast their economies, social structures, and governments on the Russian model. Under Soviet direction economic, political, and military agreements were made with each of the small states that validated Russian control.

The Middle East

The early phase of Soviet policy in the Middle East is explicable more with reference to Russian history and tradition than to either rational policy judgment or the imperatives of ideology. During this period Moscow was involved in three sectors of the Middle East, all of time-honored significance to pre-Leninist Russia. Two—the Balkans and Turkey—centered about the question of the Straits; the third—Iran— was a memento of nineteenth-century Russian imperialism.

The Greek Civil War. Soviet intervention into the Greek civil war that flared immediately after that country's liberation was something of a violation of pledges it had made at Yalta. At that conference Stalin had agreed that Greece fell into the British sphere of influence. When civil war broke out between the British-sponsored monarchist government and communist-led guerrillas, however, the Soviet could not restrain itself. Operating through the convenient device of its satellites that bor-

---

[12] See Mario Einaudi, Jean-Marie Domenach, and Aldo Garosci, *Communism in Western Europe* (Ithaca, N.Y.: Cornell University Press, 1951).

dered on Greece—Albania, Bulgaria, and Yugoslavia—large amounts of aid were given to the rebels. Moscow's Greek policy was the first unmistakable demonstration to the West that the Soviet was willing to break its word, and played a large part in influencing the broader counter strategy that the United States devised. We will recall that it was this same Greek crisis that precipitated America into active opposition to the Soviet and touched off the cold war.

Turkey and the Straits. Soviet pressure on Turkey had two objects. More important was Moscow's insistence on some revision of the Montreux Convention (1936) that controlled the straits (the Bosporous and the Dardanelles, connecting the Black Sea and the Mediterranean). The Soviet sought modifications in the agreement giving Russia a privileged position in these strategic waters. Of lesser significance, probably important primarily as a bargaining counter, the Soviet also demanded frontier rectifications along its common frontier with Turkey, mainly in Armenia. The Turks, although their long period of neutrality during the war had prevented their establishing firm contacts with the West up to this time, resisted all Soviet advances and were ultimately rewarded with American aid in 1947.

Iran. Soviet forces had moved into Northern Iran in 1941 to protect a major supply route for United States lend-lease materials that ran from the head of the Persian Gulf to Soviet Azerbaijan. At the end of the war, the Soviet presented the Iranian government with a series of demands that centered on oil concessions in northern Iran. The presence of Soviet forces served as an eloquent threat; not content, Moscow created a communist-led movement that demanded an "independent" state of Azerbaijan, to be carved out of Iranian territory. Iran made some token concessions but otherwise stood fast, and in early 1946 the first serious crisis of the postwar era seemed to be developing. Iran took a complaint to the United Nations and, although no formal enforcement action was decided upon, Moscow withdrew its troops in return for some (later repudiated) concessions by the Iranian government.[13]

The Far East

Early Soviet policy in the Far East, as in the Middle East, centered on problems and areas that had a long history in Russian policy: Manchuria, China proper, and Japan.[14]

---

[13] See the account of this episode in George Lenczowski, *Russia and the West in Iran, 1918-1948* (Ithaca, N.Y.: Cornell University Press, 1949).

[14] On this region generally, see Max Beloff, *Soviet Policy in the Far East* (New York: Oxford University Press, 1953), and David Dallin, *The Rise of Russia in Asia* (New Haven, Conn.: Yale University Press, 1949).

The Rape of Manchuria. The Soviet Union entered the war against Japan just a few days before V-J Day, but nevertheless moved rapidly to garner massive rewards for its brief military effort. Its major prize was the capture of the rich Chinese province of Manchuria that had been ripped away by Japan in 1931 and set up as the puppet kingdom of Manchukuo. Moscow rapidly stripped this territory of a great deal of its industrial equipment and liquid wealth. After seizing this great prize and occupying the key Manchurian ports of Port Arthur and Dairen, the Soviet loomed as the dominant land power in the Northern Far East.

The Chinese Civil War. Once established in Manchuria, Moscow began to play a part in the rapidly developing Chinese civil war. It refused to turn over the Japanese outposts it captured to Kuomintang forces, but surrendered them instead to the communists; it transferred great quantities of captured Japanese equipment to its ideological brethren; it refused to permit the use of Manchurian ports by the Kuomintang naval forces and military transports. In every way possible, short of actual participation in the fighting, Soviet policy gave aid and comfort to the forces of Mao Tse-tung.

What made the Russian attitude so disruptive was that it was another indication of the Soviet's willingness to violate its own promises. In early 1945 a Sino-Soviet treaty of friendship had been concluded, by the terms of which Stalin had accepted the Chiang Kai-shek government as the legitimate ruler of all China. Only a few months later the Soviet was obviously supporting the opposite faction in a new struggle for total control over China. It is true that Soviet support for the Chinese communists was never open and overt in the more acute phases of the conflict; nevertheless, its conduct in the immediate postwar period contributed significantly to the eventual communist victory.[15]

Revenge on Japan. The Soviet took what revenge it could on Japan for the long record of humiliation that began in 1905. It presented Japan with a reparations bill that, if taken seriously, would have by itself destroyed the Japanese industrial potential. By the terms of the Yalta agreement Moscow had been promised the Kurile Islands and southern Sakhalin, and Stalin moved quickly to occupy these strategic territories. The final and, as events turned out, the most important of Moscow's anti-Japanese moves was the occupation of that part of Korea that lay north of the 38th parallel. Soviet armies poured across the Manchurian

---

[15] Among the many recent studies of Sino-Soviet relations, three of the most reliable and useful are Henry Wei, *China and Soviet Russia* (New York: Van Nostrand, 1956); Robert C. North, *Moscow and Chinese Communists* (Stanford: Stanford University Press, 1953); and Howard L. Boorman, Alexander Eckstein, Philip E. Mosely, and Benjamin Schwartz, *Moscow-Peking Axis: Strengths and Strains* (New York: Harper & Bros., Inc., 1957).

frontier in the wake of Japan's surrender, and threatened for a time to overrun the entire peninsula; they were arrested only by an emergency movement of American forces that took control of the south.

The net impact of the Soviet's series of moves in the Far East was to make Russian power dominant in the entire area except for Japan. Western governments, remote from the scene and unprepared for the speed of Russian exploitation of Japan's sudden collapse, were caught off guard; Moscow's central position in Far Eastern affairs was not fully realized until the communist victory in the Chinese civil war in 1949.

SOVIET FOREIGN-POLICY TECHNIQUES

What made Soviet policy particularly baffling for western statesmen, and especially annoying for Americans, was the radically different technique developed by Stalin and his associates. The postwar USSR brought a unique methodology to the problem of advancing its national interest, and its opponents found themselves confronted by a phenomenon with which they had no experience. A major but immeasurable proportion of Soviet success in the immediate postwar period was due to the inability of American policy-makers to cope with the unexpected combination of techniques used by Moscow.

We may consider Soviet techniques under two heads. The first is the transformation of diplomacy at Russian hands; the second includes the non-negotiatory devices the Soviet adopted to supplement its unusual concept of diplomacy.

The transformation of diplomacy

As the Soviets began to use diplomacy on a large scale as an affirmative_ instrument for the achievement of national objectives, they made substantial modifications in it. In theory, in scope, and in method the historic idea of the diplomatic instrument was discarded and something much broader and more powerful was substituted. Western negotiators were first amazed, then frustrated, and finally angered by what the Russians did, but none denied the effectiveness of the new technique.[16]

The Diplomacy of Attack. The classic conception of diplomacy

---

16 Philip E. Mosely, "Some Soviet Techniques of Negotiation," Chapter 10 in Raymond Dennett and Joseph E. Johnson, eds., *Negotiating with the Russians* (Boston: World Peace Foundation, 1951). The entire volume is very instructive on the manner in which the Soviet conducted diplomatic encounters.

viewed negotiation as a means of adjusting differences between states, as a harmonizing and accomodating instrument, and as a substitute for armed conflict. According to this notion, a "successful" negotiation was one that culminated in the resolution of a dispute and that furnished each party a proportionate share of the object in controversy. To this idea the Soviet gave no service.

The Russians conceived of diplomacy as a technique of attack. Whether or not agreement was reached was secondary to the really important consideration: whether or not the negotiation had, in any strategic or tactical sense, improved the Soviet position. Diplomacy was at the very least a quasi-military instrument; it was most appropriately used to strike the enemy where he was weakest. There was no inherent virtue in agreement as an end in itself; accepting a settlement incorporating less than what the position promised was equivalent to total defeat. Thus in certain situations the Soviet interest was served by accepting a settlement, and in such cases Russian diplomats proved easy to deal with. In other instances, however, Soviet policy demanded that the question be kept unsettled, and diplomacy was thus turned to the unfamiliar task of keeping a dispute alive rather than of resolving it.[17]

This procedure was most effective before the West, particularly the United States, began to understand its rationale. During this early period, American negotiators were bent on ending the East-West controversy on almost any terms and were eager to dispose of issues by some form of honorable compromise. The Soviet shrewdly played on this typically American desire and kept attempting to extract concessions in return for always-illusory promises of eventual agreement. As soon as the United States perceived the real motivation behind Soviet dilatory tactics in bargaining, the diplomacy of attack began to lose its power.

Vituperation as a Technique. The philosophy of attack implicit in Soviet diplomacy was emphasized and materially implemented by the astonishing tone in which relations were conducted. Soviet diplomats raised vituperation to the level of an art—or perhaps it would be more accurate to call it a science, for it was done with deliberate purpose and for calculated effect. Negotiations with the Russians were conducted amid a barrage of violent language, open threats, accusations of bad faith, and uninhibited mockery. Western representatives came to expect but never grew accustomed to having their most sincere and innocuous proposals greeted by a chorus of invective and abuse. In more ordinary days such tactics would have led to major crisis and possible war, but

---

[17] Ideological justification of this position was easy to discover; examples can be found in Leites, *Operational Code*, Chapters 15-20.

to the Soviet it was all in the day's work; this was the way diplomacy was to be conducted.

The unrestrained violence of Soviet language had at least two distinct purposes. In the first place, it might anger the opposition and provoke replies in kind. Soviet theory held that this would give the Russian diplomats an advantage, since they themselves were perfectly cool-headed in their tirades while their opponents were likely to lose judgment in their rage. The deliberate provocation of anger was the first objective of the vituperative technique. Second, extreme language frequently served a valuable propaganda purpose and also was an excellent delaying tactic. Negotiations that degenerated into futile name-calling sessions could not arrive at any concrete results. It was soon discovered that Moscow's signal that it was ready to begin serious bargaining often took the form of a significant relaxation in the tone of its language. When real understandings were to be reached, vituperation had no place.

This last point merits some further consideration. Diplomacy by insult was not diplomacy at all, but really a means of escaping its necessity. The chief target of intemperate language was usually not the diplomats on the other side of the table, but the vast outside audience. Violent accusations did not often persuade Moscow's adversaries to change their position, but they scored many propaganda successes. When the Soviets were ready to come down to cases and to reach decisions, it was usual for them to request private sessions free of publicity. Here old-fashioned give-and-take was possible.

The Refusal to Compromise. Soviet diplomacy never contemplated reaching a solution by significant compromise. The classic technique of the alternation of proposal with counter-proposal, gradually narrowing the area of disagreement between the parties, was unthinkable to the Kremlin. Instead, Russians negotiated by stating a position upon which they absolutely insisted, and monotonously repeating their proposals over and over in increasingly violent language until either the opposition gave in or negotiations were broken off.

Starting as they did from an assumption of absolute conflict of interest with all noncommunist states, there was no ideological justification for genuine compromise with the West. It was preferable to yield nothing, to continue struggling for the inevitable victory. Settlements were reached by diplomatic means only when the Soviets had achieved complete victory or when the Kremlin was satisfied that all the possible advantage had been wrung from the situation. Under the latter circumstances accepting a settlement, even if only a temporary one, might often be expedient. The Soviet never settled unless it was absolutely necessary; a stalemated situation was often better left unresolved if there were any possibility of its ultimate reopening. In such a case a completed negotiation might embarrass later Russian decisions.

The Bombshell Technique. Another device chosen more for its psychological effect than for its contribution to effective negotiations was the "bombshell." Soviet diplomats made most effective use of surprise. By suddenly introducing a new agenda item, by announcing a complete reversal of position, by repudiating an implicit (sometimes explicit) understanding, or by any of a dozen other methods, Russian negotiators sought to create an atmosphere of consternation and mystery. Carefully calculating their effect, series of surprises were sometimes brought forth in the hope that the opposition would become either demoralized or depressed. Usually the Soviet was uninterested in seriously pursuing the new lines it opened up by the bombshell device; its purpose was served when it had had its effect on the other negotiators (and perhaps on public opinion abroad as well.)[18]

The Manipulation of Procedure. One final diplomatic technique, closely allied to the bombshell, remains to be mentioned. This was the Soviet skill at manipulating matters of procedure to Moscow's eventual substantive advantage. No discussion with the USSR could begin without a seemingly interminable wrangle about procedure. Questions that Americans were likely to dismiss as mere mechanics, such as seating arrangements, the order of presiding, and so on, were seized on by the Russians as pretexts for long (and often angry) argument.

Western diplomats were often caught in a dilemma by this device. If they fought the issue out, tempers were exacerbated and valuable time lost that could more profitably be spent on the substantive items of the agenda. On the other hand, if they accepted Soviet proposals on procedure, they found themselves in a double danger. Apparently innocent procedural details (such as the preparation of the agenda) often turned into formidable substantive questions in the hands of the Soviet; in addition the USSR vigorously exploited the minor prestige victories it won on procedural matters by alleging them to be symptoms of western weakness. In the end, the democracies elected to accept the challenge to a procedural dispute and battled most such quarrels through to the end, demanding a concession from the Soviet for each one they made themselves. So extreme became the procedural quarrel that agreement on an agenda finally came to be popularly thought of as an augury of success

---

[18] Secretary of State Byrnes had extensive experience with the bombshell. See his *Speaking Frankly*, especially Chapter 7: "London Again and Paris Twice."

in a negotiation, for at least it demonstrated that the Soviet was willing to talk seriously.

Soviet non-negotiating techniques

Soviet diplomacy was closely articulated with a variety of direct methods of foreign policy. This is not in itself remarkable; all statesmen seek to mesh diplomatic pressures with economic, psychological, and military methods. But the Soviet contribution was distinctive in the new dimensions that were added to the whole idea of direct action. We may say generally that Moscow's transformed diplomacy was matched by an equally unusual methodology in other techniques.

Subversion. Perhaps the most distinctively Soviet direct technique was that of subversion. Under the direction of the Kremlin, the systematic undermining of foreign governments was elevated to the level of a standardized procedure of foreign policy. The worldwide apparatus of communist parties provided the vehicle for this device; its application was closely coordinated with other policy techniques, diplomatic and direct.

In this connection, by "subversion" we mean the deliberate attack on a government and the loyalty pattern of its people by a group of its own nationals acting on behalf of and under the direction of the Soviet Union. It was only rarely that the subversive method was employed with the intention of going the whole way and bringing the government down in ruins; indeed, only in the Czech and Hungarian coups can clear instances be found of this extreme. Normally, subversion had more limited objectives.

Initially its purpose was to weaken the government against which it was aimed by the creation of internal cleavages, the intensification of domestic crisis, the diversion of official and public attention, or the creation of distrust between people and rulers. Such weakening as these tactics were able to produce was of some value for its own sake, but was sought primarily for its effect in reducing the ability of such a government to resist Soviet pressure applied through other—and often more orthodox—channels. This called for careful control of the subversive elements lest they move too suddenly and too far. Instances of both premature revolutionary activity and excess zeal can be found during 1945 and 1946. All in all, in selected cases the method of subversion proved extremely efficacious in extending the effectiveness of Soviet policy.[19]

---

[19] Philip E. Mosely, "Soviet Exploitation of National Conflicts in Eastern Europe," and Stephen Kertesz, "Methods of Soviet Penetration in Eastern Europe," in Waldemar Gurian, ed., *The Soviet Union: Background, Ideology, Reality* (Notre Dame, Ind.: University of Notre Dame Press, 1951).

Propaganda. Soviet propaganda was another non-negotiatory technique that Moscow was able to employ in a new way. Firm believers on ideological grounds in agitation and propaganda, the Russian leaders fitted large-scale propaganda campaigns into their foreign-policy effort. Soviet propaganda was remarkable on three counts: its violence, its volume, and its flexibility. The vituperative language of Soviet diplomacy paled into near-insignificance alongside the vocabulary of invective that formed the vehicle of Moscow's propaganda line. Epithets not normally used in civilized society, let alone in the more dignified circles of international intercourse, became the stock in trade of Soviet propagandists. Both for domestic consumption and for export, Moscow's message was couched in highly inflammatory language.

The Soviet expended great effort and considerable money in devising perhaps the most elaborate propaganda network the world had ever seen. Local communist parties were transmission belts, and party newspapers and other periodicals were filled with the orthodox Moscow doctrine; operating deficits of these publications were made up by the Soviet government. Every Soviet diplomatic mission was a disseminating and coordinating center for propaganda. Major efforts were made to enlist fellow travelers in all states who, although not identified formally with the party, would serve Moscow's purpose as apologists.

Finally, Soviet propaganda proved remarkably flexible, considering the rigid ideology it was ostensibly expounding. Despite the Marxist imperatives, Russian appeals proved capable of reaching widely different groups of people, of a great variety of social, cultural, and economic backgrounds. The routine Soviet propaganda approach seized upon the principal grievance of a foreign people and then polarized its problem. It told the discontented that all their troubles were the fault of the American-dominated capitalist world, and offered Soviet policy as the panacea for whatever troubled them. By shrewd manipulation of all forms of social maladjustment, communist propaganda was able to move such dissimilar groups as French peasants, Italian factory workers, Chinese coolies, Indian intellectuals, and Guatamalan stevedores.[20]

The Fait Accompli. Soviet policy also made effective use of the *fait accompli.* This, the operational counterpart of the diplomatic bombshell, involved a sudden and usually dramatic move taken without warning. Its rationale stressed that such a step would present other states with a radically altered situation with the aftermath of which they could do

---

[20] See Ernst B. Haas and Allen S. Whiting, *Dynamics of International Relations* (New York: The McGraw-Hill Book Co., Inc., 1956), Chapter 9, "Propaganda and Subversion," for a discussion of these topics in behavioral-science terms, with some reference to the USSR. See also I. Ducachek, "The Strategy of Communist Infiltration," *World Politics* (April, 1950).

nothing. The stripping of Manchuria, the purges of noncommunist elements in eastern Europe, and the abandonment of the policy of denazification in east Germany were early examples of this device in operation.

The essence of the *fait accompli*, at least as used by the USSR, lay in confining its use to situations in which other states were unable to take retaliatory action without serious inconvenience. Sudden action the result of which is to produce a riposte more often than not produces an undesirable outcome; the Soviet Union was to learn this from the western reaction to the Berlin blockade.

The Military in Soviet Policy. The postwar policy of the USSR demonstrated that its policy-makers had a clear understanding of the strengths and weaknesses of the military as a technique of foreign affairs. Generally speaking, the Soviet armed forces served two foreign-policy purposes.

Initially, they won and held most of the eastern European satellites; during the early coalition period in several of the Slav states, the position of the communists would have become untenable had it not been for the presence and the active intervention of the Red Army. The army also played its central part in the administration of Soviet-occupied Germany, assisting both in the establishment of the pro-Soviet regime there and in the mass transfer of wealth undertaken in the guise of reparations.

The second function of the military in Soviet strategy was as a threat, sometimes overt and sometimes implicit. The sudden demobilization of the American forces in Europe and the Far East after the war left Russian forces as the only significant power-in-being. The Soviet's military posture in Europe was particularly impressive. With its troops present in force as far West as central Germany and Austria, Russia was able to hold the remainder of Europe in a constant state of uneasiness. No opposition worthy of the name existed short of the Atlantic coast; in 1947 estimates of how long it would take Soviet armies to overrun Europe ranged from five days to three weeks. With this much of an immediate and obvious military preponderance on the spot, and faced with only the putative threat of American nuclear weapons, the Soviet Union was in an admirable position to press its own more extreme demands. Small states in the Middle East were likewise forcibly made aware of the proximity of Soviet military power.

Summary. The presence of the Red Army in central Germany, the admitted subversive tactics of communists in western Europe, the unceasing barrage of confusing and divisive propaganda, and the reliance upon a revolutionary and violent diplomacy combined to give Soviet policy in 1945 and 1946 an extremely powerful impact. The boldness of the design of Russian action seemed to be matched by ample skill in its execution. It is no wonder that the western world, led by the United States, seemed bemused and ineffectual in its attempts to cope with this new threat that followed so swiftly on the heels of the Nazis.

THE AMERICAN PERCEPTION OF THE THREAT

The United States was not caught completely off guard by the rapidly developing Soviet menace, despite the many attempts to "prove" this point that have been made by both special pleaders and serious scholars. There was enough of a heritage of misunderstanding and tension left over from the war to make American policy-makers cautious and quizzical, if not openly suspicious, as they faced the Soviet after the surrender of Germany and Japan. It is well known, for example, that President Roosevelt's last state paper before his death was a message to Prime Minister Churchill expressing concern about Stalin's latest moves.

The difficulty faced by the United States, rather than being one brought on by naivete and self-deception, grew essentially out of a well-intentioned belief that Soviet obduracy, despite its frustrating quality, could eventually be dissolved by patience and the development of mutual understanding. It was not until some practical experience with the radical implications of Russian plans had been gained by President Truman and his aides that a consistent American policy could develop.

The end of "appeasement"

A number of politicians, journalists, and historians of an iconoclastic turn of mind have characterized American policy toward the USSR during 1945 and 1946 as one of "appeasement." This highly elastic term, of imprecise content but clear import, carries the implication that American policy-makers and negotiators during these critical two years were concerned only with "handing over central Europe and China to the communists." In point of fact, of course, these two years were for the United States a period of evolving purpose and growing understanding. The Soviet began with certain advantages; until American policy could develop effective countermeasures it was only to be expected that Moscow would continue largely to have its way.

275

The First Year: American Concessions. There is ample ground for contending that the period from mid-1945 to mid-1946 was one in which the United States made substantial concessions and the USSR made off with most of the booty.[21] During this year the great powers were primarily engaged in attempting to work out a peace settlement, and negotiations, covering many subjects, went on almost continuously. We have remarked on the general area of disagreement that developed between the Soviet and the United States; it extended to almost every point of detail that fell within the general problem of peacemaking. On at least three major issues Moscow was able to win important victories.

First, the Soviet was permitted to develop a distinct occupation policy of its own in its areas of Germany and Austria. Not only were the Russians enabled to make over east Germany and to strip their area of Austria, but the operation of the veto on the ACA made it possible for them to obstruct the creation of any coherent policy by the West. Second, and connected with the first, the United States made a long series of concessions on the troublesome issue of reparations, making large deliveries of both capital equipment and finished goods from the western zone of Germany. Each time the reparations question was discussed it seemed as if the Soviet bill grew larger. Finally, in the negotiations that led to the peace treaties with the Axis satellites in 1947, Moscow was able to make good its claim for sizeable indemnities from Italy and a variety of territorial concessions from the minor states.

Why did the United States acquiesce in all these—and many other—Soviet demands? We have already hinted at part of the reason. Probably the most important factor explaining American lack of resistance was a practical one: the United States had very little with which to resist. Neither military power nor economic power nor psychological power nor—be it admitted—a strong diplomacy was available to American policy-makers as they sought to stem the wave of Soviet aggrandizement.

Second, and almost as important, there was an element of almost philosophical detachment in the American view of the postwar settlement. The aftermath of the war was thought of as a part of the war era, and not as an integral part of the postwar period. Peacemaking was attacked as the last phase of the war itself, to be disposed of as quickly as possible so as to free the American people for the important long-range

---

[21] The most valuable sources for ascertaining the thinking of high-level American personnel during this period are their various memoirs, particularly James F. Byrnes, *Speaking Frankly,* and former President Harry S. Truman's two volumes, *Year of Decisions* and *Years of Trial and Hope* (Garden City: Doubleday, 1956).

tasks of the future. The American attitude therefore stressed making peace on almost any terms that would ensure Soviet cooperation in building the permanent world order. The preservation of a satisfactory working relationship with Moscow was conceived of as an objective that was worth a very high price.[22]

American Doubts. The United States was willing to coexist with Soviet intransigence in peacemaking. Amid growing concern over the real outline of Soviet designs, Secretary of State Byrnes struggled for a year to bring the Soviet to some acceptable terms on the peace settlement. The true cause of the final American break with the USSR was not the interminable squabble over the peace treaties, but the growing American realization that Soviet ambitions went far beyond merely appropriating whatever was available in the wake of a general war. It became clear that Moscow was not prepared to agree on any base for permanent co-operation with the West; instead of attempting to bring stability the Soviet was interested in perpetuating instability.

In Chaper 12 we shall analyze the motives for American policy in the cold war. We may anticipate somewhat, however, by stressing that the American decision to oppose the Soviet on a broad front was not due entirely, or even principally, to Moscow's provocative behavior during 1945 and 1946, nor was it prompted by any desire to deprive the Soviet of the fruits of its victory over the Nazis. The American rupture with the Soviet grew out of the American policy judgment that, in at least the foreseeable future, the USSR was going to persist in seeking to upset the existing distribution of rewards in international society. This was the doubt that ended the period of concessions.

The beginnings of a policy

"Get Tough with Russia." When American mass opinion and the calculations of American officials agreed that a major modification was needed in the attitude of the United States toward Soviet dynamism, the first move was actually a negative one. The new American approach was summed up in the popular phrase "get tough with Russia." In every possible way the United States sought to demonstrate new resistance to Soviet demands, a new willingness to brave and endure Molotov's ire,

---

[22] A very articulate statement of this position was made by Sumner Welles in 1946. See his *Where Are We Heading?* (New York: Harper & Bros., Inc., 1946), pp. 369-383.

a new determination to present positive counter proposals to match those emanating from Moscow. In the early stages, of course, there was little the United States could do except in a negative way; most American action amounted to being as unyielding and obstinate as the Soviets were themselves.

What concessions could be repudiated were ended. Reparations deliveries from Germany to the Soviet were halted; in September 1946 Secretary Byrnes made a speech at Stuttgart, Germany, that marked a landmark in American policy. He declared that henceforth the United States was going to develop its own policy for Germany without regard to the now-shattered working principles of four-power unamimity. Four-power negotiations over a German peace treaty took on a new sharpness as the United States began to repay the Soviet in some of its own coin.

"Patience and Firmness." But at its best getting "tough with Russia" was an almost spontaneous reaction without a solid policy base. As 1946 drew to a close, a new phrase replaced the earlier one: "patience and firmness" was the watchword of the more solidly conceived approach that the United States was developing.

The implications of the new tag were more than verbal. "Getting tough with Russia" was a last echo of the traditional American penchant for basing policy decisions on emotional attractions or repulsions. Its effectiveness was confined to the ultimately irrelevant demonstration that Americans were capable of being as "tough" as Russians and that they were no longer subject to being manipulated freely by the Soviet leadership. This point was worth making in itself, but its utility for the long-range purpose of the United States was sharply limited. Something of longer purview was necessary if American efforts were not to be dissipated in a futile effort to defeat the Soviet in a game of muscle-flexing.

"Patience and firmness" carried definite connotations that helped prepare the American public for the broad-gauge policy that was being devised. Patience was necessary because the developing contest with the Soviet was obviously destined to endure for a long time; it was not the sort of crisis that could be settled and forgotten within a few months or years. Americans needed to gird themselves for an indefinite, but certainly protracted, period of tension and recurrent crisis. Firmness also foreshadowed the design that was in the making. For a long to come American-Soviet relations, at least as the United States viewed them, were to be based on a continuing assumption of mutual conflict and hostility. The United States was bent on carrying on foreign policy in a novel climate—novel at least for what purported to be a period of

278

peace. Pressure was going to be applied upon the Soviet, and defenses were to be built to resist Soviet power. The American people were to learn during the next decade more of the implications of "patience and firmness" as the cold war developed and matured.

American policy, as it developed into a pattern of action, rested on a judgment about Soviet intentions, purposes, and motivations. We shall examine the analysis to which the United States subjected Soviet policy, together with the responses selected, in Chapter 12.

11 : American capabilities

In Chapter 1 we noted that the concept of state capability refers to the tools and techniques that a state has available to use in accomplishing its objectives and advancing its interests. Now that we have laid some of the groundwork for our consideration of American foreign policy and have examined both the operating concept of interest and the major external factors affecting American policy since 1945, the next step in our analysis is a somewhat more detailed study of the capabilities of the United States.

FORMULATING THE PROBLEM

The techniques of capability analysis, as we pointed out earlier, do not yield results of mathematical precision. We can discuss American capability intelligibly only after carefully recognizing the limits on what we are attempting and stating the assumptions upon which we are proceeding. We cannot manipulate the concept in a vacuum; on the other hand, an elaborate catalogue of "factors" would be of only minor usefulness to us. We shall attempt to formulate our problem in terms that will permit us enough leeway to reach helpful (if only tentative) conclusions and at the same time will prevent us from attempting overmuch.

The limits of capability analysis

Relativity, Dynamism, and Time. At the outset we should restate the three most important qualitative factors in the notion of capability that affect its applicability. (1) State capability is highly relative, as to other states, as to objectives, and as to time; no state is "capable" in a vacuum. (2) Capability is a dynamic condition whose contributory elements are always changing. A state's capability to accomplish an objective is always either rising or falling; it cannot remain static. (3) Finally, time has a

280

major impact on capability. Comparative analyses may be made either on the basis of existing information (and by that token are always obsolete) or on the basis of the projection of trends, and thus must involve a large element of guesswork.

The Concrete Context. One other limit on capability analysis seems to be even more fundamental. No study of a state's capability can be made without some reference to what it is that the state is capable of doing. In other words, a concrete context is a prerequisite to an intelligible capability study; the more detailed the context, the more valid the analysis.[1] It is also true that capability analysis is always undertaken with reference to a set of (implicit or explicit) assumptions regarding objectives and strategy, both of the state itself and of the other states involved. Comparative capabilities, therefore, are most usefully analyzed with regard to a particular problem situation, because under these circumstances it is possible to determine both the various state objectives and the commitments to be made in considerable and specific detail.

This problem will be with us throughout this chapter. The context of our analysis must be total, and the objectives of the United States must be postulated in the broadest possible terms. We shall, therefore, remain at a high level of generalization; there will be all too obvious limits on the precision with which we can draw conclusions from the raw data we discover. What this chapter incorporates is really something of a preliminary study; our later estimates of American capability in narrower situations will build upon the less specific conclusions we shall reach here.

Assumptions of this analysis

In this chapter we shall be assuming the analytical role of the "nonparticipating observer"; that is, we shall make our judgments independently of the strategic requirements of contemporary and continuing American policy. This will give us great breadth in analysis, but at the

---

[1] Harold Sprout, a pioneer in the development and refinement of the concept of state capability, emphasizes the contextual element in his treatment of the term, particularly with reference to the role of the estimator: "... capability analysis, by which the military, diplomatic, industrial, or other capacities [sic] of states are described, evaluated, and compared, consists mainly of estimating the opportunities and limitations which the estimator judges to be significant with reference to various hypothetical contingencies." Harold and Margaret Sprout, *Man-Milieu Relationship Hypotheses in the Context of International Politics* (Princeton, N. J.: Center of International Studies, 1956), p. 47; reprinted by permission. The present author is indebted to Professor Sprout for much of the theoretical structure upon which the analysis in this chapter rests.

same time will deprive us of the special point of view of the official decision-maker. We have suggested earlier some of the substantive assumptions of our approach; we may list them here serially:

1. American capability will be considered in relation to the over-all foreign-policy problem of the United States rather than to any particular issues within it.

2. The objectives of American policy to the attainment of which the capability of the United States is put are those stemming naturally from the concept of American national interest discussed in Chapter 8.

3. The situational context in which American capability will be analyzed is the broadest possible one: the world as it emerged from World War II and as it has evolved since that time.

4. The major operational problem of American policy calling the nation's capability into question has been the Soviet threat; the most frequent comparison with another state has been with the Soviet Union.

Operating under this set of assumptions, our study of the capabilities of the United States, although largely independent of specific issues, is nevertheless geared intimately to the course of American foreign policy since 1945. From a catalogue of sources of strength and evidences of weakness, we shall be able to reach certain conclusions about the pattern of American policy and its possible future modifications.

TANGIBLE ELEMENTS IN AMERICAN CAPABILITY

We listed the tangible elements of state capability in Chapter 1; there we found them to include geography, population and manpower, natural resources, industrial and agricultural production, and military organization and power-in-being. On each of these we may comment briefly as they appertain to the United States.

Geographic factors in the American position

We shall assume that the fundamentals of American geography are common knowledge and do not require reiteration. What we shall consider here are some of the specific ways in which American geography confers strength or weakness (actual or potential) on the United States.[2]

---

[2] Among the more useful summaries of the American geographic position are Gordon S. Darkenwald, "Geographic Foundations of Continental United States," in G. Etzel Pearcy, Russell Fifield, and associates, *World Political Geography* (New York: Crowell, 1948), and Harold and Margaret Sprout, eds., *Foundations of National Power*, second ed., Chapter VIII, "The American Realm in World Politics."

Geographic Advantages of the United States. In the light of the conditions of world politics in the twentieth century, we may conclude that the United States has been fortunate in the geographic material with which it has been obliged to work. In the light of the more common criteria by which states are measured geographically, the United States ranks consistently high.

In area, the continental United States incorporates just over three million square miles, the fifth largest state in the world. Its topography, although varied, is nevertheless generally favorable, permitting (under modern conditions of transport) easy movement into and across its area. The climate is generally temperate, although great variations are found; with certain exceptions rainfall is adequate and in some areas abundant. The soil is generally fertile.

No strong neighbors menace American security. The eastern, the western, and a large part of the southern frontiers of the United States are formed by the open sea; its common boundaries with Canada and Mexico do not constitute security problems. The coastlines furnish many excellent ports; the United States has easy access to the high seas and to the rest of the world. In general we may say that, except for a few points noted below, the effect of geography is to make a near-maximum contribution to American capability.

Shortcomings of American Geography. The major geographic handicaps of the United States are functions of distance. In the first place, for Americans both internal and external distances are usually great. The longest east-west dimension in the United States is 2,807 miles; from north to south it is 1,598 miles. Airline distances to points abroad are similarly great: New York-Paris is 3,630 miles; Seattle-Tokyo, 4,700; New York-Rio de Janiero, 4,840.

We should emphasize, however, that sheer distance is not automatically a shortcoming, but might well actually be a source of advantage. To the extent that American policy emphasizes defense, distance from hostile centers is still an advantage, even under conditions of modern aircraft and missiles. But if—as is the case—the major preoccupation of the United States is to extend its influence outward from its own shores, the greater the distance to be traversed the greater the difficulties of doing so.[3] This should, however, be calculated against the corresponding difficulties faced by other states who may also be operating at great distances from their own bases. Internally, distance also has a complicating effect, stemming primarily from the pattern of population distribution. The

---

[3] This idea is developed by Kenneth Boulding, in "Economic Issues in International Conflict," *Kyklos*, VI (1952), 97ff.

283

clusters of people along east and west coasts are separated by the vast underpopulated area of the Great Plains, the Rockies, and the inter-mountain basin.

Internal distance becomes even more significant when another geographic handicap is considered: the concentration of population and industry in a relatively few areas. One of the often-alleged advantages of size to a state is the facility of dispersal. The fact remains, however, that important portions of American activity cluster within certain confined geographical areas, particularly in Southern California and in the so-called "Boston-Chicago-Washington" triangle. Such uneven human and economic spacing raises questions both of vulnerability to modern weapons and of the efficient distribution of goods through the entire area of the United States.

Population and manpower

The human base of American capability is a population estimated in 1957 to surpass 170,000,000. The more sophisticated analysis of population figures requires us to consider additional factors to sheer numbers; these demographic ponderables throw more light on the present and future importance of American manpower.

Demographic Pattern of the American People. There are approximately one million more females in the United States than there are males. In recent years the median age has risen to its highest point in history: 30.1 years. This rise in the median age occurred as the result of a great increase in the number of people over 65 years of age; late estimates put the total as over 15 millions. These were balanced, however, by the nearly 40 millions under 18 years of age. Between 18 and 65, in the age brackets of maximum effectiveness, clustered the bulk of the American people. The total manpower pool (male and female) for military and industrial service was nearly 90 millions.

Population density varies widely in the United States. In 1950 the national average was 50.7 persons per square mile; the three states that most closely approximated this figure were Florida (51.1), Iowa (46.8), and Georgia (58.9). In contrast to these averages, however, were such concentrations as were found in Rhode Island (748.5), New Jersey (642.8), and Massachusetts (596.2), as well as such underpopulated states as Nevada (1.5), Wyoming (3.0), and New Mexico (5.6).

Two additional distributional factors are of some significance. In 1950, 64 per cent of the American people lived in urban areas. The northeast, with 79.5 per cent, was the most urbanized region; the west and north-central regions ranked next with urban percentages of 69.8 and 64.1 respectively; the south trailed with only 48.6 of its people urbanized. The other important datum is that of racial distribution. In 1950 there were 134.9 million white persons in the United States and 17.4 million non-whites; of the latter, just over 15 million were Negroes.

Population Trends. The basic population trend in the United States is one of numerical growth, at a higher rate than was the case earlier in the century. Between 1940 and 1950 there occurred a 14 per cent increase compared with only a 7 per cent increase during the previous decade; an estimated 9 per cent increase took place during the first six years of the 1950's. If this rate were to continue through 1960, a total gain in excess of 16 per cent can be forecast.

Vital statistics bear out this conclusion. The birth rate has stabilized at something over 24 per thousand per year; the death rate has steadily declined to its present rate of slightly over 9.6 per thousand. As long as these trends continue, the American population will grow steadily at a slowly increasing rate. One result of the decline in the death rate is the slow rise in the median age, now for the first time over 30 years.

Demographic Conclusions. From the point of view of sheer statistics, the American manpower situation is absolutely favorable except in comparison with China, India, and the Soviet Union. Americans constitute a numerous people whose steady increase to the neighborhood of 200 millions is—barring unexpected catastrophe—probable.[4] There is no reason for us to assume that any likely American policy would fail because of a shortage of raw manpower.

In addition, the United States has certain intangible manpower advantages that do not show up in a mere population tally. We shall consider them at greater length in a later section of this chapter, but we may say at this point that they rise generally from the demographic "quality" of the American people. The high levels of literacy, tool skill, technological orientation, formal education, and cultural homogeneity require that the verdict of pure numbers be revised upward. In productive efficiency, in aptitude for modern warfare, and in other categories of manpower utilization, 50 million Americans (for example) have more impact than do two or three hundred million other people without this relative head start. Except for certain situations involving sheer weight of numbers

---

[4] Some demographers of repute, however, are not convinced that the birth-death rate patterns of the last fifteen or twenty years are anything more than a statistical aberration. They do not share the opinion expressed in this paragraph, and we should note that such a dissent exists.

(such as a large-scale ground war), the manpower of the United States is thought to be adequate.

Natural resources

The American Resource Endowment. The United States is among the more fortunate states of the world in its natural resource endowment. Many of the materials most critical to the capacity to execute foreign policy are present within the United States or immediately available outside its borders. Crucial shortages exist, and are increasing in number; other reserves are nearing depletion. The general picture is not so serious, however, as to require deep anxiety. Most of the resource problems that exist promise to be soluble by the normal devices of foreign policy and do not present major dilemmas.[5]

The most basic category of materials includes coal and iron—the foundation of modern industry. American known coal reserves are conservatively estimated to be adequate—at present rates of consumption—for a thousand years. Domestic iron ore reserves of high quality are dropping rapidly—production from Minnesota's Mesabi Range fell 65 per cent between 1953 and 1954—but recent discoveries of rich deposits in Labrador and Venezuela open the prospect of ample supplies for certainly the next forty or fifty years, and perhaps for a century.

Energy sources—in addition to coal—are also substantial. The United States leads the world in the production of hydroelectric power and has vast untapped resources for further exploitation. Exact American petroleum reserves cannot be formulated because the rate at which new reserves are "proved" exceeds that of actual production by approximately one billion barrels a year; proved reserves in 1956 surpassed 30 billion barrels. Other rich petroleum pools exist in Venezuela and Canada, while American industry has made extensive investments in the incredibly rich oil fields of the Middle East.

The United States is in a less favorable position with regard to other industrial raw materials. The common ferroalloy metals—manganese, chromium, nickel, vanadium, cobalt, and so on—must be largely imported and stockpiled. So must large percentages of the critical nonferrous metals, including tungsten, copper, tin, and lead. Food, fiber, and timber

---

[5] Extensive data on resources may be found in the Report of the President's Materials Policy Commission, *Resources for Freedom* (Washington, D. C.: U. S. Government Printing Office, 1952).

resources, on the other hand, are generally adequate, although certain commodities within this class—such as coffee, hemp, and wool—must be procured abroad.

The Dependence on Foreign Supplies. Thus we can see that the United States, for all its enviable position with reference to the basic raw materials, is nevertheless dependent on foreign sources for what are yet small —though critical—amounts of those resources vital to the maximum realization of its potential. What does this mean for American policy?

Nature distributed the important resources very unequally throughout the world. Whereas the early industrial centers grew up where coal and iron appeared in reasonably close proximity, today the major deposits of the newly important minerals are frequently in Africa, Central and South America, and Asia. American policy has concerned itself with the problem of guaranteeing adequate supplies of these items.

However much the United States might wish to preserve its freedom of maneuver in a region—Central Africa, for example—steps to gain access to such critical raw materials as there may be there must take precedence. The protection of sources of supply is a fixed dimension of American policy, and it is fortunate that at the present time enough of each material needed can be found within the portions of the world outside the Soviet sphere to which the United States can gain access. Any increase in the territory controlled by Moscow might have serious repercussions for America's resource position.

Another common aim of United States resource policy, growing out of the necessity of maintaining American strength vis-a-vis the Soviet, is to deny Moscow access to foreign resources that—if added to the Soviet potential—would lessen the gap between the two states. The petroleum of the Middle East—vitally important to the Soviet but at present only of secondary significance to the United States—is a prime example.

Industrial and agricultural production

Of the tangible elements of capability, the one most directly pertinent to the contemporary role of the United States is that of industrial and agricultural production. The three we have so far discussed are relatively fixed; there is little a state can do about its geography, its population, or its resource endowment—at least in the short run. But what a people does on its own land to transform raw materials (which are, after all, only a potential source of power) depends to a great extent upon human

287

will. Industrial and agricultural production is an index of the results derived from purposive activity by individuals and by government.

The Measure of American Industrial Strength. Industrial production is at the same time the predominant economic activity in the United States and the major contributor to American power in international affairs.[6] Americans are generally sensitive to the major role played in their own lives by industry, and many have some appreciation of its place in foreign policy, but the exact configuration of American industrial strength is difficult to visualize.

The United States includes less than 6 per cent of the land area of the world and slightly more than 8 per cent of its people, yet since 1945 the United States has consistently outproduced all the other states of the world combined, at least as far as strategic commodities are concerned. Americans produce three-fifths of the world's telephones, four-fifths of the automobiles, 70 per cent of the crude petroleum, three-fifths of the pig iron, and over half the cotton and lumber. The American industrial machine has a nice balance between capital and consumer production; war and postwar experience have indicated that it is technically a relatively simple matter to shift emphasis from one to the other. The flexibility and versatility of American industry is an important element in national strength.[7]

Few economists today would venture to predict a production ceiling for American industry. During World War II industrial production expanded to two and a half times its 1935-9 level in the face of the loss of a substantial portion of the labor force to the armed forces.[8] Since 1950 industry has proved capable of handling $30-40 billion annually of government orders for military goods while at the same time increasing its output of consumer items. The expansion of industry in peacetime is aided by extensive applied research conducted both by industry itself and by private and government agencies.

Not the least significant aspect of American industrial strength is the fantastically elaborate network of transportation and communication facilities that tie the United States together and connect it intimately with the rest of the world. The steady expansion of air transportation

[6] A semi-popular but graphic treatment of the trends in American production was provided by the series of twelve monthly articles in *Fortune* (January-December 1955) under the general title of "The New Economy."

[7] Klaus Knorr, in his recent *The War Potential of Nations* (Princeton, N. J.: Princeton University Press, 1956), qualifies this judgment sharply but concludes that it retains a good deal of its validity, even under conditions of nuclear weapons.

[8] See Geoffrey H. Moore, *Production of Industrial Materials in World Wars I and II* (New York: National Bureau of Economic Research, 1944).

288

facilities and, beginning in 1956, the development of an entirely new Federal superhighway system have gone far to improve an already efficient transportation pattern; communications networks have likewise been extended.

Weaknesses and Vulnerabilities. The over-all picture of American industry is one that makes it a central element in American strength. This optimistic generalization must be tempered by the recognition of certain shortcomings that may be classified as inherent weaknesses or as vulnerabilities to external pressures.

By "weaknesses" we mean only those built-in difficulties that bear on industry's contribution to American strength; no judgment is intended here on the social, economic, political, or psychic values that may attach to any of the conditions we shall mention. All we are concerned with is the simple issues of capability to accomplish foreign policy objectives.

In these terms we may briefly stipulate five such weaknesses in the American industrial machine. (1) Being a private enterprise system posited on competition, maximum efficiency through unified and coordinated effort is often difficult to achieve. (2) The industrial plant is so closely knit that maladjustment in one small segment may be rapidly transmitted to all parts of the economy. (3) There is a growing shortage of certain categories of key personnel, particularly middle- and high-level executives. (4) Long-range prospects are clouded by a relative overemphasis on applied research at the expense of more fundamental—although less obviously profitable—basic research. Dramatic demonstration of the inadequacy of American basic research was afforded by the entire nation's embarrassment at Moscow's "Sputniks" in the autumn of 1957. (5) Certain key sectors of the economy, such as the machine-tool industry, are inadequately developed; strains and delays follow any unusual demand on these sensitive areas.

The vulnerabilities of the American industrial plant are somewhat better known; we shall list what are perhaps the three most significant. (1) The heavy concentration in the northeastern quarter of the nation and along the New York-Chicago axis; this has been only partly alleviated by planned and unplanned dispersal.[9] (2) The critical role played by labor relations; the growing sense of responsibility of organized labor has not yet obviated the danger inherent in work stoppages of various sorts. (3) The dependence of so much of American industry on stockpiles of key raw materials that must be imported. Any interruption in the flow

---

[9] "Planned dispersal" is a problem complicated by the reluctance of interests adversely affected to cooperate. An apt example is provided by real estate and labor groups in such areas as New England.

of ferroalloys, other critical metals or certain chemicals would disrupt great areas of American industrial production.[10]

The Agricultural Balance. Agricultural production in the United States is remarkable for the enormous output derived from the efforts of only a small portion of the national labor force. In 1954 there were less than eight and a half million persons employed on the nation's 5.4 million farms; of the 1.1 billion acres in farms, only 337 million acres were planted to crops. The remainder was largely pasture or grazing land, with a smaller portion in timber. Farm income in 1954 was just under 30 billion dollars. The total number of American farms has been slowly decreasing since 1920, while the mean acreage has shown a corresponding slow increase. Farm tenancy is also on a slight rise.

From American farms pours a steadily increasing flow of agricultural products that far surpasses American capacity to consume, making possible both the export of farm goods and the accumulation of embarrassingly large surpluses. The United States leads the world, usually by a large margin, in the production of corn, raw cotton, wheat, and oats. The beef cattle, dairy cattle, and hog population of the United States is the largest in the world; America leads in the production of meat, milk, and dairy products.[11] The only agricultural products that Americans cannot grow themselves are those requiring tropical or other special weather conditions. The United States is unquestionably the leading agricultural nation in the world today. We must also point out, however, that some agricultural economists question the future ability of the United States in this regard, citing increasing population and declining soil fertility as possible handicaps.

The only food products imported into the United States in significant quantities are coffee, sugar, and cocoa; imported fibers include sisal and wool. Although there is considerable importation of other goods, such supplies are either unessential luxuries or are in direct competition with

---

[10] See Jules Backman, *War and Defense Economics* (New York: Rinehart & Co., 1952); George A. Lincoln and associates, *The Economics of National Security* (New York: The Macmillan Co., 1954); Seymour E. Harris, *The Economics of Mobilization and Inflation* (New York: W. W. Norton and Co., Inc., 1951); Albert G. Hart, *Defense Without Inflation* (New York: Twentieth Century Fund, 1951). All these works deal with the impact of defense, war, mobilization, and foreign policy on the American industrial plant. See also Knorr, *War Potential of Nations* (Princeton, N. J.: Princeton University Press, 1956).

[11] It was notable that Soviet leaders boasted frequently during 1957 that Russia would catch up with the United States in meat and milk production in the "near future." Apparently this was part of the new emphasis on the production and distribution in consumer goods in the USSR. Some speculation suggested that this had considerable significance for the future of Soviet-American relations.

domestic sources. The enviable agricultural situation of the United States not only gives it the capacity to resist pressure on its food supplies to which other states might be vulnerable, but also—in an era of widespread food shortage—gives it a weapon of great versatility and sometimes controlling effect. The availability of food has several times been of real value to American policy-makers.

Military power

Military power is at the same time the most obvious element in a state's capability and the most difficult to assess accurately except in the most short-run of situations. Power-in-being is never more than a (possibly large) fraction of a state's potential; the men and materials available to a state in any context are susceptible of being employed according to different strategic and tactical theories. The mission to which armed force is put influences the techniques of its employment; the new technology of warfare has increased the relative importance of power-in-being. The most that we can do is to sketch the outlines of the problem and to suggest one or two of the operational decisions that must be made before serious calculation of American military capability can be undertaken.

American Military Power. Unless the United States should be put to the ultimate test of survival, it is impossible to set a maximum figure for American military power. In mid-1945, during the mobilization peak of World War II, there were 12,300,000 Americans in the armed forces; during 1945 the armed services spent 78.7 billion dollars. At the same time, there yet remained a surplus—both of manpower and of resources—that had been untapped during the war.

The armed force maintained by the United States in a readiness condition during the cold-war period represented the best guess of what was necessary, but nevertheless the subject of military policy provoked recurrent dispute. During the mid-1950's, military manpower averaged about 3 million with the trend slowly downward; the Army and the Air Force each included roughly one million; the Navy and the Marine Corps divided the remainder on a rough 3-to-1 basis. Military expenditures averaged about 38 billion dollars, with the trend slowly upward. The disarmament negotiations with the USSR that reached the point of "seriousness" in mid-1957, included proposals for cuts in troop totals to 2.5 million men, and this raised prospects of a reduction in the power-in-being of the United States. The suspension of these negotiations during the summer, the growing domestic clamor for the adoption of a strategy of

291

"limited war" by the United States, and the recalculations forced by the revelation of Soviet technological prowess in its space satellite program, all threw new doubt on the prospects of such a reduction as 1957 drew to a close.

Weapons-wise, any figures must be largely guesswork, since the exact amounts of available equipment are kept secret. In 1955, for example, the Air Force had approximately 9,000 first-line aircraft and 2,500 less efficient ones, divided roughly 60-40 between tactical and strategic types. The Navy had in service or in ready reserve some 800 vessels, of which 35 to 40 were capital ships (battleships or heavy carriers). The naval air wing had approximately 1,700 operational aircraft. The Army's weapons, due to their almost infinite variety, do not permit a summarization; one suggestive estimate is that the United States now has some 1,600 modern tanks in operation.

The Importance of Strategic and Tactical Theory. We shall discuss current American military policy and the controversy surrounding it in Chapter 15. We may suggest here, however, that the present military posture of the United States emphasizes the so-called "new look" dating from 1953 and 1954.[12] Under this concept the major American effort is to be made in strategic air power with a concentration on nuclear weapons; the military mission of the Air Force is both that of a deterrent and of a decision-forcing instrument in the event of actual combat. The Army and the Navy have roles in support of the Air Force in case of all-out war; in a limited war context they are expected to hold their own with the corresponding forces of any possible enemy.

Although the tactical doctrine of the armed services has been worked out in great detail in terms peculiar to each branch, we may nevertheless suggest some principles common to all three. We might call these the "American tactical theory." Stripped to their essentials, they can be stated as follows: (1) American armed forces stress mobility, speed, and flexibility in performing their missions. (2) Aggressiveness is emphasized as being most parsimonious of both manpower and material. (3) Machine power—in the broadest sense—is both more efficient and more expendable than manpower; in tactical situations emphasis is placed on weapons and machines rather than on the commitment of large bodies of men. (4) The tactical goal of all branches is firepower, whether from the ground, from the sea, or from the air; the object of maneuver is to subject the enemy to overwhelming fire.

[12] See W. W. Kaufmann, ed., *Military Policy and National Security* (Princeton, N. J.: Princeton University, 1956); for a semi-official "retreat" from this position, see John Foster Dulles, "Challenge and Response in United States Policy," *Foreign Affairs* (October, 1957).

How Much Mobilization? One of the ubiquitous problems facing any responsible statesman, and one that endlessly complicates judgments on absolute or relative state capability, is the sliding relationship between actual military power-in-being and theoretical potential. For the United States it has proved difficult in the postwar era to decide on a mobilization level that satisfies all the categories of requirements.

American military theory, relying on citizen-armies and heavy industrial production as the preferred ways of winning wars, has always insisted that the peacetime military establishment had only one real mission: to buy time against the enemy until war-level mobilization was attained. This system served the United States well throughout the nineteenth century and brought victory in World Wars I and II. The technology of modern war, however, has reduced the value of mobilization and production planned to occur after the outbreak of hostilities. The advantages of surprise are so great that a three-week war (or, for that matter, a three-hour war) is a real possibility. Thus it follows that the United States might well have to fight and win a total war with only the personnel and equipment it had available at the moment the first bomb fell.[13]

But to remain constantly prepared to retaliate overwhelmingly to any possible attack is beyond American capacity—or that of any people. Americans, for reasons at the same time economic, political, ideological, and psychic, refuse to live forever on a total-war footing. Some bearable compromise between all-out readiness and underpreparedness has had to be devised. Any solution must take account of the changing nature of the threat confronting the United States, of its relative imminence, of the tolerance of Americans toward taxation and conscription, and of the general climate of world politics.[14] The result has been that since 1945 a persistent struggle, no less fierce because confined within a reasonably

[13] In this connection, Adlai Stevenson's presidential campaign of 1956 stressed the inefficiency of selective service as a method for manning a modern military establishment. On one occasion he called for a professionalized and highly paid armed force. See *New York Times* (October 19, 1956). Early in 1957 the "Cordiner Committee" recommended substantial incentive pay increases for members of the armed forces so as to retain them in service—a move toward the concept of professionalism. *New York Times* (April 27, 1957). Although the Budget Bureau rejected most of the proposals, in May the Defense Department made a move toward putting such a plan in effect insofar as 350,000 specialists were concerned. *New York Times* (May 9, 1957).

[14] In this connection, the announcement in mid-June 1957 that American troops were beginning their planned withdrawal from Japan, coming at the same time that disarmament negotiations were nearing what seemed to be a climax, seemed to indicate that major modifications in American military dispositions were in the making. See article by James Reston in *New York Times* (June 23, 1957).

narrow range of alternatives, has raged over the amount and the kinds of the American mobilization potential that should be kept in readiness.[15]

The solution accepted to date, as we have briefly considered it above, is only the latest in what has become a long series. It is probable that newer ones may be taking their turn in precedence as part of the unending process of attempting to adjust American military power-in-being to the requirements of American policy.

INTANGIBLE ELEMENTS OF CAPABILITY

We now turn to the intangible factors that affect the way in which the tangibles are employed and often set outer limits to their usefulness. We must first, however, make one final remark about the catalogue in the preceding section: even the most concrete element of capability has intangible implications that modify its significance in practice. Geography, population, and resources seem to be fixed entities that can be manipulated objectively, yet each of them gains its final relevance and value only in terms of human assumptions about them. Production and military power are even more obviously functions of human perception and will, and no automatic answers about state capability can be derived from any generalizations about these two. Even the tangible elements of capability, therefore, have indefinite dimensions of choice; at the level of all-out effort, this is often thought of as the "will to fight."[16]

This is even more the case, of course, when we take up the group of considerations that we are calling the intangibles. Here there are by definition very few concrete data on which to found generalizations; here we must recognize from the beginning that each element is measured on a sliding scale and that any conclusion we reach is subject to immediate revision. The most that we can attempt in this section is to raise the kind of questions that offer some relevance to our general inquiry, and to suggest certain broad conclusions that arise from measuring the United States with our set of yardsticks.

Political, economic, and social structure

This broad heading refers to the way in which the American people are organized for the accomplishment of political, economic, and social

---

[15] See, as major contributions to this debate, Henry A. Kissinger, *Nuclear Weapons and Foreign Policy* (New York: Harper & Bros., Inc., 1957); see also Robert E. Osgood, *Limited War: Challenge to American Strategy* (Chicago: University of Chicago Press, 1957), and Secretary Dulles's article (footnote 12).

[16] See Knorr, *War Potential of Nations*, Part II: "The Will to Fight."

purposes. Each area deserves extended treatment; our effort here is the poorer because we cannot give them the attention they merit. Our consideration of the American social order will be confined to the most direct implications of the political, economic, and social system of the United States for the accomplishment of American foreign policy.

The Nature of American Society. The American political, economic, and social system remains, despite the massive strains to which it has been subjected during the past half century, one of the most impressive monuments to human freedom the world has ever known. Founded and operated on the principle of encouraging the maximum of meaningful individual choice commensurate with the accomplishment of common goals, the United States has preserved its essential doctrine in the face of pressures both internal and external.[17]

Politically, the United States is organized into a federal democracy that institutionalizes private rights, limited government, and the determination of policy by the mass will. Economically, the partially free enterprise system retains its vigor although subject to extensive and increasing public control. The American social system is one of the least stratified in the world, permitting broad mobility both upward and downward as well as laterally.

The energizing principle of freedom in the major areas of life, however, has become subject to broad limitations largely stemming from the rising concept of bigness. Big government menaces much of the democratic myth as people stand outside the political process rather than participate in it; the major function of the mass is often conceived as that of serving as audience for the deliberations of the ruling elite. Big business and big labor together control much of economic life and their struggles work great inconvenience and frequent hardship on the unorganized public.[18] Socially, the cult of conformity and the rise of "middle-class America" have given much of American life undertones of drabness, uniformity, and rigidity that do violence to the dream of a free society.[19] These trends,

---

[17] Many scholarly and statistical analyses of American society provide extensive raw data for this generalization. Very suggestive, however, are three recent books by non-social scientists that are remarkable for their insights: Louis Kronenburger, *Company Manners* (Indianapolis: The Bobbs-Merrill Co., 1954), Jacques Barzun, *God's Country and Mine* (New York: Harper & Bros., Inc., 1954), and Russell Lynes, *A Surfeit of Honey* (New York: Harper & Bros., Inc., 1957).

[18] This theme is elaborately developed in John K. Galbraith, *American Capitalism: the Concept of Countervailing Power* (Boston: Houghton-Mifflin Co., 1952).

[19] David Riesman, Nathan Glazer, and Reuel Denney, *The Lonely Crowd* (New Haven, Conn.: Yale University Press, 1950); Russell Lynes, *The Tastemakers* (New York: Harper & Bros., Inc., 1954); William A. Whyte, *The Organization Man* (New York: Simon and Schuster, 1956).

rather than proving the total collapse of the American system, are instead a measure of the extent to which American professions fall short of actuality. Their influence on the vigor of the foreign-policy effort of the United States is not yet great, although some observers are confident that it will increase.

Strains in the Body Politic. In addition to the generalized threat of bigness in American life, there are specific maladjustments within the political, the economic, and the social sphere that create internal stresses. Each of them has direct influence on the broad questions of foreign policy and on the way in which it is executed. We shall mention only a few of the most important of them.

In government, two issues defy final solution today and both are engaging the attention both of scholars and of practitioners. The first is the problem of discovering the working basis of federalism in the twentieth century. These are extremists on both sides; the states rights advocates who insist on the denigration of national authority and the transfer of broad grants of power to state and local governments, and the supernationalists who argue for increased federal power and the abasement of the states to the status of administrative districts. Somewhere between these two positions a more satisfactory balance must ultimately be found.[20] The second problem concerns the accurate determination of the majority will. When apathy limits voting in presidential elections to 60 per cent of the eligibles, and if "engineers of consent" can mobilize public opinion on call by the use of techniques of advertising and mass communication, there is obviously something out of tune in American democratic processes.

In economic life, problems abound. Perhaps the two most important are the trend toward larger and larger units of production, symbolized by the rash of corporate mergers that broke out during 1954, 1955, and 1956. How to continue to enjoy the advantages of large-scale production while avoiding monopolistic trends is a many-sided problem. The other issue, as much social as economic, has to do with the future of agriculture. The family farm, as a way of life as well as an economic unit, seems to be heading toward extinction. The consequences of any such outcome would be of deeper significance than to the limited number of persons directly involved.

In social relations, the two leading issues (or at any rate, two leading issues from among several) are the troublesome questions of inter-racial

---

[20] See Arthur Macmahon, ed., *Federalism: Mature and Emergent* (New York: Columbia University Press, 1955), and K. C. Wheare, *Federal Government* (New York: Oxford University Press, 1947).

adjustment and the changing nature of the family in American society. Both racial conflict and family disorganization have results that extend into many other areas of social life, and both have a stubbornness that defies simple solutions. Some observers fear that either or both of them threaten to work basic changes in America that would radically alter the fundamentals of the entire American system. Whether or not their eventual importance will be this great, there is no doubt of their constantly eroding effect and the need for their resolution.[21]

Is Major Change Necessary? We frequently hear arguments to the effect that American society, American government, and the American economy are unsuited to the problems of foreign policy, and that great change in the American social order will be necessary before the United States can cope successfully with the world. It is often said, for example, that the American government should remake itself on the British model, that public opinion should leave foreign-policy decision-making to experts, that the economy should be overhauled in the direction of government planning and control, and that egalitarian social doctrine has no place in the essentially aristocratic business of international affairs.

Even if these propositions have some theoretical validity, they have only slight practical relevance. For better or worse, the United States will be obliged to live with the social order it has inherited from the past; rapid and thorough remodeling is simply out of the question. The most that planning and direction can do is to exert a moderate directing influence on the course of evolution, and to shape—within limits—the America of the future. Radical reconstruction of American society, to be accomplished within a relatively short time span, is beyond the capacity of anyone.

Educational and technical level

Modern political power is inseparably wedded to modern technology, and the capacity of a state to exert pressure to accomplish its objectives depends in large measure on the extent to which its people have mastered contemporary techniques. An examination of the educational level and technical competence of Americans throws some light on American capability in this respect.

---

[21] On race relations, see Gunnar Myrdal, *An American Dilemma* (New York: Harper & Bros., Inc., 1944); on family problems, see Earnest Burgess and Harvey Locke, *The Family: from Institution to Companionship* (New York: American Book Co., 1953) and Ruth S. Cavan, *The American Family* (New York: Crowell, 1953).

American Education and "Know-how." The American people are the beneficiaries of the most elaborate program of mass education in the world. Free public education is available to everyone through high school, and low-cost higher education at public expense is almost universal. Just what results has the United States had from its extensive educational effort?

In 1952, 97.2 per cent of the population over 14 years of age was at least minimally literate, and the figure has since inched higher. The school population, fed by the increased birthrates since 1945, passed 40 million in 1956 and promised to soar over 50 million by 1963. In 1950 the median level of educational accomplishment was 9.3 years of schooling; the leading state was Utah, with 12 years, and the lowest-ranking was Georgia, with 7.1. In 1954, nearly 293,000 bachelor's degrees were granted by American colleges and universities, 57,000 received some form of master's degree, and 8,996 doctorates were awarded. On the score of formal education, Americans are making extensive use of the opportunities open to them.

We should also recognize a factor more difficult to measure. Americans live in a technological culture and they have shown remarkable aptitude for coping with it. American familiarity with the machines and the gadgets of modern civilization enables the United States to absorb the new products of industrial ingenuity and to use them effectively. The facility with which Americans employ the tools and techniques of technology—what is often called "know-how"—has become a byword in much of the world. Americans think of themselves as well-educated, and to a considerable extent the assumption is justified—at least on the scores of literacy and tool skill.

Potential Shortages: Engineers and Scientists. The American educational and scientific picture is not so attractive when certain categories of highly trained specialists are examined. In 1954, 22,329 engineers were graduated from American colleges, and 4,204 master's degrees and 594 doctorates were awarded in engineering. These totals fell far short of actual and anticipated needs for these specialists; the estimates of what could be profitably absorbed per year ranged from 35 to 50 thousand engineers per year, and 15 to 20 thousand scientists, including three times as many Ph.D.'s and Sc.D.'s as are now being produced. Especially critical in the "scientific" category are physicians and research scholars in medicine.

These current shortages promise to become even more acute in the future as trends in higher education reveal a growing disinclination among students to submit to the rigorous discipline necessary for scientific education. Some commentators laid the blame for this condition on the prevailing philosophy among public-school educational leaders that emphasizes "adjustment to life" as a "democratic" base for education and dismisses intellectual training as "sterile" and "aristocratic." In 1956, government recommendations looked toward a program of encouraging and subsidizing promising scientific and technical students to build up this manpower pool to a satisfactory level. This proposal received a very much more favorable reaction from the public as well as from educators following the American debacle in the missile race with the Soviet in 1957.

Potential Shortages: Educated Persons in General. There is a more general and pervasive problem in American education. In 1954 the National Manpower Council's report revealed a chronic shortage of trained "brainpower."[22] Although the elementary schools are crowded and college enrollments are booming, there is an inadequate supply of thoroughly trained personnel in almost every area of scholarship, pure and applied.

As American foreign policy involves more and more areas of American life, the need for genuine experts becomes more pressing. Economic pressures, the declining standards in public secondary education, the urge to conform and to avoid distinction (what David Riesman calls "other-directedness"), and a hyperconcentration on economic security have been suggested as explanations for the lack of interest among Americans for thorough intellectual training. Whatever the explanation, it is obvious that the inadequacy in the supply of educated men and women represents a substantial limitation on the capacity of the United States to accomplish the goals of its foreign policy.

National morale

Morale is defined by Webster as "condition as affected by, or dependent on, such moral or mental factors as zeal, spirit, hope, confidence, etc." The importance of such a concept to any consideration of state capability can scarcely be overestimated. From the point of view of the operating statesman, morale is a measure of the extent to which his people are united behind their government and its mission and of the extent to which they will actively cooperate in accomplishing the ends of national policy.

American Morale: Characteristics and Problems. Without attempting at this point the thankless task of estimating the state of popular morale in the United States, we may nevertheless advance some tentative sugges-

---

[22] National Manpower Council, *A Policy for Skilled Manpower* (New York: Columbia University Press, 1954).

tions about the character of the morale of the American people. There is a constant "morale problem" in the United States, and policy-makers must be always alert to its requirements.

The state of American morale at any given time is materially affected by three factors. (1) There is a tendency for wide, relatively sudden, and frequently rapid shifts in the prevailing mood of the public. (2) American morale is notoriously sensitive to short-run or temporary influences, such as a sudden crisis or unexpected good news. (3) It is easier to maintain high morale on negative issues than on positive ones; that is, Americans traditionally are more at home when they are opposing some state than when they are pursuing an objective of their own.

Government morale policy, dealing with a public opinion and mass attitudes that are subject to extensive and frequent modifications, cannot be rigid. The constant concern of American statesmen is to keep morale relatively constant in its acceptance of the objectives and procedures of the government. This requires effort to anticipate the swings of popular sentiment and to meet them with appeals designed to restrain both excessive optimism and extreme depression.

Not only is there a question about how much information to make public, but related issues of how to treat the information that is released are also pertinent. If relations with the public are wrapped in crisis, sudden and extensive popular reaction is to be expected; a more relaxed or unconcerned presentation will calm down some of whatever popular tensions exist. Both dictatorial and popular governments must be aware of the state of national morale, but a democracy like the United States must develop more elaborate strategies for dealing with it.[23]

Morale and Discipline. From the point of capability analysis, of course, national morale is an index of the degree to which a people will follow its leaders through the vicissitudes of foreign policy and, while doing so, exert maximum effort in the accomplishment of public tasks. We might say that by "morale" we really mean "endurability": the capacity to perform efficiently under prolonged stress. If this is what we mean by morale, then obviously another factor enters into its makeup besides "zeal, spirit, and hope"; this is the matter of mass discipline. It seems probable that some societies (Germany and Japan during World War II, for example) have been able to maintain a satisfactory level of performance by the sheer force of discipline even after hope and spirit had fled. There is

---

[23] For some further discussion of morale strategies, see the present author's *Principles of International Politics* (New York: Oxford University Press, Inc., 1956), pp. 87-9.

a good deal of doubt, however, whether such would be the case in the United States; American behavior does not place so high a premium on discipline as does that of some of the other national groups.

Morale: the Central Issue? A very good case can be made that the morale of the American people—their "zeal, spirit, hope, confidence, etc." —is the central problem of American capability. Whether the American effort in world affairs is well planned and energetically executed, whether American policy will "succeed" or "fail," will in the last analysis depend on whether or not the mass of Americans play their various parts effectively. Statesmen may plan and negotiate forever, but their efforts will be sheer futility without the active cooperation and allegiance of the people. It is not over-optimistic to conclude that the broad-gauge pattern of American policy is one that does not overtax the maximum capability of the United States; the major unanswered question is whether or not the American people will become sufficiently convinced of the worth and the desirability of their policy to make the necessary effort. On these grounds national morale becomes a matter of highest importance for American foreign policy.

International strategic position

Perhaps the most relative of the elements of state capability is the factor of strength or weakness that arises from the general strategic position of the state in the world. The situation of a state wih regard to strategic advantage or disadvantage depends on the mission that the state sets for itself. If its goals are limited to what it can gain by its own resources, it is thereby in a better position than if it needs help from other states to accomplish its objectives. If it must devote a large portion of its resources to the defense of its homeland against powerful and aggressive neighbors, it is deprived of part of its ability to prosecute its own purposes at greater distances. Here is the case of a state's ability to achieve its objectives being at least partially determined by the very objectives it selects.

America's Need for Allies. It is beyond doubt that the United States for the indefinite future is going to be required to work in close harmony and cooperation with other states. The objectives of American foreign policy—summed up in an earlier chapter as the achievement of a world of peace, order, and stability—by their very nature require that the United States forge a series of close and long-lasting agreements with all like-minded states. The prosecution of the cold war also has necessitated that

Americans ally themselves with over forty states and fit their policy into a common framework.[24]

To the considerable extent to which the United States is closely tied to its many allies, American freedom of action (and, consequently, American capabilities) are reduced. The kind of alliance the United States prefers to enter into (because of its greater usefulness and flexibility) is one that is genuinely voluntary and that springs from a sensed identity of interest. In dealing with its allies, Washington must therefore preserve the free and voluntary character of the alliance by minimizing the force component of capability and by seeking the maximum return from the exploitation of consent. Intra-alliance relationships are therefore sharply conditioned by America's need for allies.

The same is generally true with regard to all free-world programs undertaken collectively, whether against the USSR in the cold war or—less frequently—in situations not directly stemming from the East-West conflict. The United States must temper the intensity of its policy moves and confine its actions to measures that are acceptable to the other states with which it is acting in concert.

An apt illustration of the inhibiting effect of alliances upon American freedom of action was provided by the Suez crisis of 1956 that grew out of Egypt's seizure and nationalization of the Suez Canal Company. Throughout the entire complex negotiations, including special international conferences, direct diplomatic negotiations, discussion before the Security Council of the United Nations, and extensive propaganda campaigns, American policy was at least partially governed by the necessity of maintaining a common front with France and Britain.[25] In the process, the United States was obliged to take a much less forthright stand than might have been the case had it been free to act completely according to its own desires. It was no longer under such compulsion after Britain and France took military action on their own initiative, and American policy then developed with unwonted speed.

Allies: Strength or Weakness? The vexations inherent in intimate and long-lasting cooperation among sovereign states have caused periodic resentments among segments of the American people. The whole idea of alliances is recurrently called into question; each crisis in the free world produces renewed pleas for the United States to "go it alone."

[24] For a succinct official statement of the United States' need for allies, see President Truman's *First Report to Congress on the Mutual Security Program* (Washington, D. C.: U. S. Government Printing Office, 1952), pp. 2-7.

[25] On several occasions, when Secretary of State Dulles intimated that the United States was following an "independent" course on some issues, strong British and French protests were immediately voiced. See *New York Times* (October 3, and October 10, 1956).

This position, however rationally it may occasionally be argued, is ineluctably based on a frankly emotional premise. It seems to grow out of two disparate sources: an evocation of a happier past and an urge to vent the inevitable frustrations attendant upon a multi-dimensional foreign policy. For the United States seriously to seek to dismantle the alliances it has so painfully put together would involve far more than merely abandoning one foreign-policy technique and substituting another in its place.

To take on a purely lone hand would require—if collapse were not to be swift and ignominious—a drastic truncation of the objectives of American policy and the abandonment of most of the world to its own fate (or to the clutches of the Soviet camp). It would further the transformation of American society into the true "garrison state," heavily mobilized, constantly on the alert, and eroding all remaining private rights in the name of national security. Put in terms of practical alternatives, the opponents of alliance find themselves defending a position whose costs would far outweigh the advantages alleged to accrue from a more extensive area of American "freedom."

A less extreme view of the pros and cons of the alliance structure of the United States would argue, even after admitting the embarrassments that have appeared and will continue to appear, that the United States cannot afford to do without them. So long as the current concept of national interest retains its applicability, the American government must fit its policy within the framework of an alliance system. That valuable freedom of maneuver is sometimes sacrificed thereby no one will deny; that frequently the United States is forced to do things it really does not want to do seems obvious; that many of the alliances seem to be more advantageous to the other parties than to the United States is a suspicion that will not down.

Even after admitting all these—and many other—unpleasant side effects of the free-world pattern, it seems demonstrable that, save for two or three possible exceptions, the United States gains more than it loses from its arrangements with other states. For each diminution in capability vis-a-vis an ally, a greater gain is won in some other policy area. Under the policy pattern America is now following, some such calculation must lie behind each commitment undertaken.

SOME TENTATIVE CONCLUSIONS

After our rapid survey of the various factors, tangible and intangible, that bear on the question of whether the United States has the wherewithal to accomplish its objectives, we have now arrived at the point at which we must put our investigations together. The only purpose of capability analysis, regardless of the level of specificity at which it is pursued, is to answer concrete questions about actual situations, and our discussion in this chapter is aimed at this goal. Does the United States "have what it takes" to accomplish the ends it has set for itself?

The needs of American policy

Before we can answer the question as we have just asked it, we must first clarify what the needs of American policy will be in the foreseeable future. Here again we must generalize broadly, recognizing that situational changes might present entirely new problems of which we have no inkling at the present time. But our exegesis of the fundamentals of American national interest has laid down a series of objectives, both automatic and derived, whose pertinence promises to be long-lasting and within the definition of which almost any conceivable pattern of events can be fitted. Basing our judgment on this set of "givens," we may stipulate three kinds of long-range needs of future American policy.

Long and Extensive Effort. Of one thing we may be sure at the outset: the United States is involved in a long-term operation and the demands of foreign policy will be enduring, extensive, and varied. If our summation of the goals toward which Americans are moving is correct, and if we have accurately delineated the situational backgrounds and the nature of the primary motivation represented by the Soviet threat, long-range capability calculation thereby gains an importance unexpectedly great. Short-term judgments retain much usefulness, but if American efforts are to be carefully distributed over a relatively lengthy time span, the most important consideration is the goal that lies at the end of the greater period. The experience of the years since 1945 has also made certain that foreign policy is to continue to absorb a large share of American energies, interests, and wealth. Multiformed action in the military, economic, diplomatic, and propaganda areas is a certainty for an indefinite period.

Cooperation with Other States. A second apparent need of American policy in the future is that of the continued development of bases of cooperation with all other states that accept the basic ingredients of the American blueprint for the future. We have concluded that the cold war makes it necessary for the United States to have allies; the same is obviously true of whatever pattern world affairs take when the intensity of the Soviet-American conflict is reduced. The present and future content of American policy must be shaped within the limits imposed by a close-knit cooperative system and executed—if not always jointly with all states concerned—at least only after gaining intra-alliance approval and authority.

And, of course, cooperation has an organizational dimension of another form: the United Nations system. The UN has become such a normal arena of American foreign-policy activity that often it is not thought of as a "cooperative" venture at all. But its entire reason for being is joint action, and its machinery is for the purpose of making such action more effective. It would be difficult to conceive of how any major portion of American interest can be satisfied without extensive (but not necessarily total) reliance on the United Nations.

Understanding and Commitment at Home. A third need—and, as we suggested in discussing morale, perhaps the most critical—is that of popular understanding and acceptance of, and commitment to, the objectives of American policy. The American people have been called on since 1945 to play a role for which neither their traditions nor their inclinations had fitted them; to participate intimately and unceasingly in international affairs, conducted at a continuously high level of tension but with only a few climaxes to provide fulfillment and release. Even for a people accustomed to the perplexities of international politics the experiences of the first decade of the cold war would have been difficult to bear; for Americans the new world of the postwar era has been a constant trial. The remarkable point is not that some groups of the population have become disillusioned and have either lapsed into apathy or espoused extremist proposals, but rather that the bulk of Americans have retained most of their perspective and their conviction that the road their government is taking will eventually lead them to the goal they seek.

If, as seems increasingly likely, the nature of the cold war is changing and American policy is entering a new phase, the United States will have great need of this continuing commitment on the part of its people. If international politics is moving away from the twilight of war into some less supercharged atmosphere, the strains on Americans will become even more acute. It will be easier to argue in favor of less effort and less attention when the menace of atomic war has receded. It is at this point that serious understanding of the broader outlines of American policy can come to the rescue of the emotional fixation that has kept many citizens going since 1945. Without the concrete symbol of a potential enemy upon

305

which to vent their hostilities, Americans must call on their faculties or reason to suggest justifications for the inconveniences and strains that will accompany American foreign policy in the future as in the past.

American objectives and American capabilities

Finally we now come to answer the question implicit in this entire chapter: do American capabilities square with American objectives? Is the United States going to be able to meet the requirements of its own policy, at least under such conditions as we can foresee? At the end of our discussion, we may no more advance a categorical answer than we could at its beginning. The best we can do is to divide it into two parts, about one of which we have some certainty, but about the other of which we can do no more than conjecture.

First, there is little ground to quarrel with the general proposition that the pattern of American objectives is within the theoretical capacity of the United States, at least within any probable set of circumstances. Were Americans to mobilize all their potential and commit it to the accomplishment of their present foreign-policy goals, there would be adequate means at hand to achieve the end. To put it briefly, we may say that the United States *can* eventually reach its objectives, at least as they are phrased today.

The other, equally blunt, question comes at the matter from another direction: *will* the United States have available, at the appropriate place and at the right time, enough of its capability to surmount each of the obstacles it will be called on to meet? The potential is there, at least as far as rational calculation can suggest, but whether the skill of American policy makers and the understanding of the American people will prove equal to the operational mission of mobilizing, committing, and employing it is a question to which no one yet knows the answer.

The Adequacy in Tangibles. Taking into account the mission, the situation, the nature of the threat, and the operating principles of the United States, the tangible raw materials of capability would seem to be adequate for the purpose as presently formulated. The American geographic situation is advantageous; the manpower balance—when modified by qualitative considerations—is satisfactory and promises to improve relatively and absolutely; the resource endowment is sufficient if prudently managed. Industrial and agricultural production have no inherent imbalances sufficient to threaten the continuation of their present and possible high levels; American military capacity, backed by technology and an elastic industrial plant, can be raised to almost any point that seems today to be possibly necessary. In each of the five tangible classifications are certain shortcomings; we have attempted to indicate at least some of the more important of them. None, however, seems beyond control or to be of such importance as to inhibit seriously future American efforts. On the score of the visible and tangible factors of capability the United States receives a satisfactory rating.

The Area of Uncertainty. It is, of course, the intangibles that provide the grounds for such doubts as may exist about the future. Questions bristle at every point. Will the American social order survive the strains of the coming decades, or is a quasi-totalitarian garrison state the only way to organize Americans for long-term coordinated effort? Will Americans match the Russian educational effort in training enough scientists, engineers, and technicians to meet national needs; alternatively, if American education should become science-oriented, will it mean the end of the humanistic, liberal education that has contributed so largely to the American version of the "open society"? Will American morale be equal to the task it faces; can rational calculation replace emotional fervor as the guide to mass attitudes toward foreign policy? Can the United States live indefinitely in close relationship with 40 or 50 other nations, each bent on its own purposes and most of them aggravatingly different in culture, tradition, and social structure?

These questions, and the hundreds more like them that could be raised, constitute the area of uncertainty about American capabilities. No one has any capsule solution to the problem they raise, but their relevance to our concern seems unquestionable. It is not the part of a textbook to exhort its readers, but it does not seem inappropriate at this juncture to suggest that in the ability of the American people to cope with the intangible factors determining the success or failure of the United States in its international mission will be found one of the most important tests of the applicability of the democratic idea to the conditions of the twentieth century.

part 6:

AMERICAN POLICY IN ACTION

12 : The pattern
of American policy

In Chapter 8 we developed an outline of a concept of national interest that the United States seems to be using as its guide in the middle of the twentieth century. In Chapters 9, 10, and 11 we then elaborated the major situational factors affecting American action in the period beginning with the close of the war of 1941-5. Chapter 9 summarized the state of the world in 1945; Chapter 10 considered the Soviet threat; Chapter 11 examined American capabilities.

These two sets of considerations—a dominant idea of interest and a set of situational elements confronting the United States—provide the raw material out of which American foreign policy is fashioned. In this chapter we shall describe the outcome of the interaction of the American concept of interest and the prevailing situational factors since 1945. Our approach will be one of attempting to delineate the "pattern" of American policy: the set of assumptions upon which decisions have been based and the action formulas that have grown from these decisions.

WHY THE COLD WAR?

The end of World War II found the United States in a uniquely favorable position. All its visible enemies had been defeated and were under occupation; all its powerful associates were bound together in an international mechanism for postwar cooperation: the United Nations. As Americans seemed to see it, the future policy of their government was to be largely one of binding up the wounds of the war and of initiating programs to eliminate the maladjustments and tensions that yet re-

311

mained in the world. The era of peace, order, and stability seemed within grasp, if not actually at hand. Americans, it must be admitted, grasped only a few of the complexities and difficulties of the task they faced, but even so their lack of dismay and their bouyant hope seem remarkable to us today.

It was into this apparently idyllic picture that the Soviet intruded itself. Americans were generally quite slow to grasp the Soviet threat for what it was; as late as 1948 they had only begun to comprehend the implications of the status to which the United States had fallen heir. When, as we have already seen, the United States realized that peace had yet to be won, the action principles of its national interest asserted themselves. The cold war was on.

The American response to the Soviet threat was at first purely emotional. Washington, backed by popular approval, decided to "get tough with Russia," and the first phase of American cold war policy consisted largely of replying to each Russian *"nyet"* with a thunderous "no." However satisfying it might have momentarily been to bruised egos, in the long run this approach was merely to compound futility. Gradually, as American policy took form and the people grew more accustomed to coping with permanent crisis, a more coherent picture of why the United States was involved in the cold war took shape. The nature of the controversy became more clear; Americans began to learn what they wanted from Russia.

Non-reasons for the cold war

To keep our own analytical decks clear, we ought first to examine briefly some of the explanations for American cold-war policy that have (or have had in the past) considerable vogue, despite the fact that all of them represent at least partial misemphases. So much mass emotion has been involved in the development of American strategy that an entire mythology has been created to "explain" and "justify" a phenomenon whose rationale is not especially complex.

Communism. Americans are not mainly concerned with fighting communism, nor with fighting the USSR because it is officially a communist state. Communism as an ideology and the Soviet Union as a communist state both existed long before 1945, yet Americans did not feel themselves particularly menaced prior to the end of the war in that year. No principle of the American political tradition and foreign policy is more firmly grounded than that of noninterference in the internal affairs of

312

other states—particularly large and powerful ones. It would violate both democratic ideology and American national interest to base a long-range policy on popular hostility to any belief system in the abstract, however repugnant it might be on moral grounds.[1]

Dictatorship. Neither does the United States oppose the Soviet simply because of the existence of the dictatorial form of Russian government. Americans have no necessary political quarrel with any form of government, no matter how reprehensible it may be in theory. The United States has often proved (and, indeed, is proving today) that it can do business with a dictatorship that is—from the American point of view—well-behaved. The concern of the United States is not with the existence of a dictatorship, but rather with policy that that dictatorship might pursue.

Power. Some "super-realists" attempt to explain American antipathy to the Kremlin in terms of a simple power rivalry.[2] Moscow is the only capital in the world in a position to challenge Washington, they say; only the Soviet stands between the United States and world dominion. From this premise they conclude that Americans must therefore destroy Russia and then assume their rightful place as rulers of the world.

This frightening idea never had very many adherents in the United States (and virtually none at all outside American frontiers). It reached its peak of popularity during the early days of the cold war, and has declined steadily ever since. Whatever validity it possesses depends on whether or not the United States is actually bent on hegemony. It would be difficult to reconcile such an objective with America's basic interest in peace, order, and stability; it would conflict as well with almost all the ingredients of the national tradition. The United States has no absolute objection in principle to a strong Russia; on the contrary, if Soviet friendliness were guaranteed, American interest would demand the maximization of Russian strength.

Expansionism. Finally, the United States is not involved in the cold war simply because of Moscow's interest in expansion. To the extent that Russian interests can be classified as "legitimate" (admittedly a difficult distinction to pinpoint in practice), there is no reason for the United States always to oppose increases in Soviet power, prestige, or well-being. We may grant that there are inherent limits on what America would conceive of as permissible Soviet aggrandizement, and perhaps these bound-

---

[1] A position directly opposed to that taken in this paragraph has been often advanced with great sincerity; one of the most able advocates of the doctrine that communism is the real enemy of the United States is Anthony Bouscaren, in *America Faces World Communism* (New York: Vantage, 1953).

[2] An influential exposition of this doctrine is James Burnham, *The Struggle for the World* (New York: John Day, 1947).

aries might prove in fact to be unacceptable to the Kremlin; with reference to the basic principle, however, we may safely say that the United States has no eternal interest in keeping the Soviet forever inferior to America.

What the United States wants from the communists

The Procedural Base of American Policy. The reason why the United States fights the cold war is much simpler than any explanation based on ideology, or governmental forms, or power, or expansionism. American opposition to the Soviet, as we suggested in Chapter 8, is based on procedural grounds. The postwar policy of the Kremlin has been based primarily upon the perpetuation of crisis and the use of disorder, violence, and revolution as operating techniques. This alone would be sufficient to keep the United States hostile to the Soviet as long as Moscow plays the foreign-policy game by such rules. Americans went into opposition as soon as they realized fully that Stalin did not share their concept of a world of peace, order, and stability marked by a general acceptance of the status quo and the cooperative solution of problems. They will remain there until his successors change their minds and their tactics. At that moment, when the Soviet accepts procedural rules as well as their substantive implications, the cold war will end. It will not, of course, be replaced by total agreement and friendliness; Soviet-American controversy in a non-cold war era, however, would be much easier of adjustment and less likely to break out of control.

The Limits of American Demands. What, then, do Americans want from the communists? The United States does not demand the obliteration of communism, but only that it no longer be used as a technique of international disorder. It does not demand that the Kremlin dictatorship be dissolved, but only that such form of government not be forcibly exported to smaller states. It does not demand that Russian power be destroyed, or even drastically reduced, but only that it be put to serve a socially useful purpose. It does not demand that the Soviet abandon its traditional concern for Russian security, prosperity, and prestige, but only that its leaders interpret these objectives more realistically and pursue them in an orderly fashion. In short, the United States does not demand that Moscow surrender; an American victory in the cold war could be brought about by a mere procedural change by the communist leadership. The United States will be satisfied when the Soviet agrees to

314

conduct its foreign policy on the same basis as do most civilized states.[3]

This is the major objective of the United States vis-a-vis the Soviet. We must distinguish it carefully from what Americans often say their objectives are; the United States often overstates its case for reasons of diplomatic bargaining, international propaganda, or domestic politics. In times of crisis, official and unofficial spokesmen (particularly U.S. Senators) are prone to say a great deal more than they mean; radio, television, and newspaper comment frequently goes even further.

But anything more than the limited goal we have stipulated would do a good deal of violence to the basic requirements of the American situation. To demand the destruction or the abasement of the USSR would be extremely dangerous. It would either produce total war with its attendant horrors, or prove unattainable and doom the United States to deep frustration. What is more, what sort of world might follow the utter elimination of Soviet power? Some analysts, as we have seen, would be quick to point out that this would mean unchallenged American mastery of the world. We may inquire, however, how many Americans really hunger for that lofty but shaky eminence? And who could guarantee that the United States would actually be in a position to dominate the globe after a destructive total war with the Soviet?

The Goals of American Policy. We may put American goals in simple and homely language by saying that the United States wants to "housebreak" the Soviet. The entire pattern of American policy is aimed at convincing the Kremlin of two points, one positive and one negative. Negatively, the United States is attempting to persuade the Soviet dictators that the way they have chosen, the way of disorder, violence, and crisis, will not produce victory; frustration and failure will instead be their reward. Positively, the United States is prepared to prove that the Kremlin's reasonable interests and objectives—or at least those that are compatible with world political stability—can be successfully and satisfactorily attained only by cooperative effort in a climate of peace and order. This, stripped to its essentials, is the basic American view of the cold war.

---

[3] See for example the formulation of the issues made by then Secretary of State Dean Acheson in 1950, in a speech, "Tensions Between the United States and the Soviet Union" (Department of State Publication 3810): "The United States is ready ...to cooperate.... But it takes more than one to cooperate. If the Soviet Union could join in...we could all face the future with greater security. We could look forward to more than the eventual reduction of some of the present tensions. We could anticipate a return to a more normal and relaxed diplomatic atmosphere and to progress in the transaction of some of the international business which needs so urgently to be done."

The Pattern of American Policy

The free world and the cold war

Where does the noncommunist world fit into this picture? American policy toward the free states flows naturally from American interests and assumptions. In practice the United States tends to deal with the free world at two different levels.

Long-term Harmony of Interest. There is a fairly large group of states, including especially most of those within the orbit of western culture, whose circumstances and level of development lead them to share largely in the basic American interest in peace and order. It was only natural for such states, including (among others) the Commonwealth of Nations, France, and the Low Countries, to find a good deal of common ground with the United States. They have as great a concern as has the United States with finding effective programs that might lead to the creation of a more stable world society. Although the United States is also allied with most of this group against Soviet expansionism, the close cooperation that exists is to a large extent independent of the cold war. The United States would be virtually as intimate with them even if there were no Soviet threat.[4]

Arrangements of Convenience. Another group of noncommunist states, however (and also at least one communist one), for a variety of reasons each peculiar to the state involved, is not as interested as is the United States in institutionalizing stability, but have instead revisionist ambitions of their own. Some of them, nevertheless, feel themselves menaced by Soviet policy. With such governments, including such otherwise dissimilar cases as Yugoslavia and Spain, the United States has made alliances of convenience against a common danger. In these agreements no commitments are exchanged or expected concerning the day that Russian policy no longer furnishes a possible cement of alliance. In the meantime these sometime associates serve a necessary purpose from the American point of view and gain concrete advantages for themselves. Many Americans find themselves uncomfortable in alliance with such questionable associates, but each party to any such arrangement gains something by it and American policy would be less effective without them.

Ambiguities in American Free-world Policy. The bifurcated nature of America's attitude toward the free world is perhaps the most subtle and certainly one of the most frequently misunderstood aspects of American

---

[4] This idea permeated the original conception of American economic assistance to Europe. See the text of Secretary of State Marshall's speech at Harvard University on June 5, 1947, in which he outlined the proposed program. *New York Times* (June 6, 1947).

policy. It is easy for Americans to think of the "free world" as a unit, as a weapon to be used against communist power. They find it difficult to recognize valid grounds for disagreement among its members. They classify noncommunist states that do not actively join the western alliance as "neutralist" and drift into thinking of them as at least quasi-communist. They cannot understand how India, although outspoken in criticism of many anti-communist moves by the West, nevertheless receives favors and deference from the United States, while Spain, "the most anti-communist state in Europe," has only a tenuous connection with the free world and is dealt with gingerly and at arm's length.

The Cold War and the Long View. This, and most analogous paradoxes, can be largely resolved in terms of American long-run interest. The cold war, despite its contemporary significance, is actually only a phase in a larger program. The United States cannot afford to concentrate entirely upon the Soviet; it must be prepared for the day when the cold war has been liquidated and the way is again open for positive action in behalf of the kind of world Americans want. The United States must, even in the present circumstances, make such moves in this direction as it can. The problem of world order will outlive the Soviet threat.

At the same time, the frustration of the Kremlin's immediate plan is the first order of business. In order to resist the Soviet, the United States must mobilize as powerful a force as possible, and aid from any source is welcome. It would be too much to expect that the entire group of 40-odd states with which the United States is allied would agree in their long-range plans. Americans realize that they are putting aside many future quarrels in return for promises of immediate support against Moscow. The end of the cold war would probably be the signal for an outburst of new disputes between the United States and many of its allies; indeed, even the relaxations in Soviet-American tensions in 1955 and 1956 produced exactly such intra-alliance disputes.

The American experience is not unique. Many governments have wrestled with the problems stemming from an inconsistency between their long-range interests and their immediate objectives. Americans can only hope that the pattern of their foreign policy will prove to have sufficient flexibility and breadth to point a way through the inevitable difficulties of the future.

CONTAINMENT: ASSUMPTIONS AND PROGRAM

American policy since 1945 has not been merely a haphazard business of putting out "brush fires" as they have flared up. Brush fires there have been in plenty; underlying all of Washington's calculated moves, however, and giving point to many emergency measures as well, has been a reasonably well-rationalized plan. Its execution has been uneven and provocative of controversy, yet in its essentials it has furnished what we might call a blueprint for American action for the past decade or more. The American strategy and tactics have been grounded upon a detailed analysis of the nature of the Soviet threat and the selection of a general line to meet the varying forms in which Russian expansionism developed. Known by several names, none has proved as durable as the policy's original informal title. In this chapter we shall call the American plan and policy by its popular name of "containment."[5]

The present era is almost the first time in American history that the United States government has acted upon a theory of foreign policy; never before have Americans attempted to apply a consistent body of doctrine to an evolving international situation. Despite the persistence with which certain generalizations were invoked as guides to action during the nineteenth century, the United States since 1945 has surpassed the record of any earlier period in the degree to which it has set its course in harmony with a set of basic premises.

Soviet motivations

The fundamental assumption upon which the American government has proceeded is easily stated: Soviet policy is inherently expansionist. Let alone, the Kremlin would continue indefinitely to bring more and more of the world under its domination. Why did Americans conclude that Russia would always expand? What, in George F. Kennan's words, did the government believe were "the sources of Soviet conduct"?

The Mixture of Motives. Attempts to demonstrate conclusively that Russian behavior since 1945 has been the result of a single overriding

---

[5] Any discussion of "containment" must rely heavily on the writings of George F. Kennan who, as chief of the Policy Planning Staff of the State Department in 1947, made a major contribution to its conception and also helped make it public property by means of a justly famous magazine article ("X," "The Sources of Soviet Conduct," *Foreign Affairs* [July, 1947]; reprinted in H. F. Armstrong, ed., *The Foreign Affairs Reader* [New York: Harper & Bros., Inc., 1948], and in George F. Kennan, *American Diplomacy 1900-1950* [Chicago: University of Chicago Press, 1951]). Although what we shall be discussing here is more the actual practice of American policy rather than its theoretical formulation by Mr. Kennan, any systematic analysis of the past decade of American policy must be greatly in his debt. The catalogue of Soviet motivations that follows here is drawn largely from his writings.

motivation have not been particularly successful. The safest judgment emerging from more than fifteen years of analysis seems to be that Soviet policy arises from a mixture of motives. Several individual factors may be isolated, but their interaction, the extent to which each modifies the others in practice, and which one is primarily responsible for any single policy move all are yet impossible to show accurately.

This much, however, we may accept confidently: any single-factor theory of Soviet behavior explains either too much or too little for the purposes of American foreign policy; none adequately incorporates all the relevant facts. The United States, as a matter of sheer self-defense, has been obliged to adopt the thesis of multiple motivation of Soviet action.

The Roots of Soviet Action. Soviet leadership, in making policy decisions, seems to be subject to three different pressures. The first arises from communist ideology, the second from Russian history and tradition, and the third from the peculiar dynamics of dictatorship in a police state.[6]

Thus Marxism-Leninism and its later variants impels them toward conflict with the capitalist world, assures them of inevitable victory, and teaches them that time is forever on their side. Russian historical tradition gives them a grip on their people and sets them in pursuit of objectives sanctified by time; the Kremlin has driven toward the Straits, has demanded Balkan hegemony, and has established spheres of influence in central Asia and the Far East.

The compulsions of dictatorship create certain imperatives for the ruling clique in Russia. The continued survival of the regime requires—as was the case in Imperial Rome—"bread or circuses." The expectations of a higher standard of living for the masses have not materialized in any significant way; the brave new world has remained largely a dream. There is a constant danger that the Russian people might become impatient with the pie that remains forever in the sky. The apparatus of the police state therefore becomes essential as the only way to guarantee the security of the regime if the better life for all remains out of reach. If no bread be forthcoming, circuses become vital; if the circuses fail, then the bread must be made available.

Soviet policy therefore has attempted to provide a scapegoat for the unsatisfactory conditions at home; it is all the fault of the imperialist West

---

[6] In contrast to these three as listed by Kennan, see Waldemar Gurian, "Permanent Features of Soviet Foreign Policy," *Yearbook of World Affairs, 1947* (London: Stevens, 1947); reprinted in Hans J. Morgenthau and Kenneth Thompson, *Principles and Problems of International Politics* (New York: Alfred A. Knopf, 1951). Professor Gurian finds the "two mainsprings" of Soviet policy to be "utopianism" and "cynical realism."

that is encircling the worker's Paradise and is ever plotting a war of destruction. And so the myth of self-defense is polished up and made to serve as a rationalization of domestic oppression. Its outcome is what has been called "defensive aggression" or "aggressive self-defense"; according to this doctrine, the Soviet expands only to forestall the West.

The Nature of Soviet Action. Thus ideology, history, and the greed for power all affect the minds of the top layer of the Soviet hierarchy. Which is the fundamental level of being? Which would be, in the final analysis, the controlling factor if the teachings of the three were to contradict each other?

During the early postwar period, this was a purely academic question; as long as Stalin lived all three made the same point: expansion. Not in rigid conformity to any blueprint or detailed plot, of course; if any plot existed it was certainly one of the weirdest and least consistent in history. Russian policy called for a constant outward pressure in all directions, probing along the perimeter until a weak spot was discovered through which Soviet power could flow. Indeed, this has sometimes been called the "strategy of the amoeba." Its result was a steady expansion of the Soviet sphere between 1945 and 1950 that gratified all three Soviet motivations.

The Need for a Choice. In order to fashion a policy, however, the United States had to determine for itself the most deeply rooted of the three influences. It made a great deal of difference to America's future policy what it felt to be basic to Soviet behavior. If ideology were fundamental, the United States would have to prepare to deal with fanatics who were immune to reason and who might well stop at nothing to achieve their goal of world communism. If "Russianism" were the inspiration for Moscow's policy, there were ample historical guides provided for the United States by the two centuries of British struggle with Czarist imperialism. If the Soviet leaders were first of all political adventurers who were most concerned with retaining their power, American statesmen again would be able to draw upon the rich store of experience that Western man had accumulated in coping with this type of political force. The direction of American policy depended on this initial decision.

The American decision

After a good deal of painful study, complicated by lack of experience with the Soviet and the shortage of Americans equipped with the necessary knowledge and insights, American policy-makers finally reached a decision.

The Rejection of Ideology. It was apparent that Marxist-Leninist ideology was important to the Soviet as a tool of policy, as a guide in new and unfamiliar situations, and as an orienting and idea-shaping influence. The framers of American policy could not, however, bring themselves to believe that it was the ultimate answer to Moscow's behavior. The doctrine itself was simply too flexible.

Communist dogma had been interpreted and reinterpreted so many times by Soviet leaders that it could be used to provide a theoretical justification for any policy at all, or even for several mutually contradictory ones. Even hardened communists grew dizzy from keeping up with all the twists in the party line. It was undeniable that ideological versatility aided Russian policy; it could be applied to support and justify anything the high command decided to do. This very strength, however, made it unreliable as a guide to Moscow's future conduct.[7]

The Limits of Historicism. In the same way, the influence of Russian history and tradition, although great, was finally not thought to be basic. Much of Moscow's policy was in the historic Russian pattern, but more of it was not. Lithuania, for example, was traditionally a Russian sphere, but East Prussia never was. Tradition might serve a purpose in winning mass support for the regime, and undoubtedly played its part in suggesting possible channels for expansion.[8] It failed, however, to explain enough of Soviet policy for the United States to safely accept it as controlling.

The Compulsions of Dictatorship. The conclusion seemed, if not obvious, at least probable that the Soviet leadership, when finally judged, was composed of men who were first of all dictators with all the strengths and weaknesses of the breed. They were dictators with a difference, of course; Russian and Marxist influences endowed them with peculiar characteristics. But beneath the veneer of ideology and patriotism, the men in the Kremlin were driven by the same compulsions that have obsessed political adventurers in many other places: a lust for power and an urge to preserve and expand it.

The Significance of the Choice. This judgment, if accurate, had profound importance for the United States. It meant that, if driven into a tight corner, the leaders of Russia would probably react primarily from a desire to save their own power and to preserve their regime. It meant that the Soviet system was subject to the stresses and strains of any dictatorship, most conspicuously a conspiratorial psychology permeating the

---

[7] See, however, Barrington Moore, Jr., *Soviet Politics: The Dilemma of Power* (Cambridge, Mass.: Harvard University Press, 1950). Moore argues the opposite position, especially on pp. 404-12.

[8] See Julian Towster, "Russia: Persistent Strategic Demands," *Current History* (July, 1951).

bureaucratic structure and an incessant competition for power. It meant that Soviet policy was, rather than a carefully worked-out timetable and battle plan, a highly experimental and pragmatic program subject to frequent revision in the light of changing circumstances. It meant that the dictators would be likely to stake their survival on a policy only after carefully calculating its probable effect on their own security. It meant, finally, that the leaders, although vicious and unprincipled men, were basically rational and could be dealt with by a rationally conceived policy.[9]

Containment: basic elements

Upon this assumption—that the USSR's policy was that of a dictatorship modified but not controlled by ideological and traditional influences —the United States has built its anti-Soviet policy. The program was designed to take advantage of the enemy's weaknesses and to minimize his strengths. It called for action upon an unprecedentedly broad front, and of a variety of forms at first undreamed of and now—after more than ten years—still bewildering to many Americans. It put the United States at the center of a web of complicated relationships extending from Norway to Japan, from Labrador to Cape Horn.

The First Phase. Containment visualized several phases of American action against the Soviet, although only the first ever became a matter of general comprehension by the public. This initial line required the United States to take a position all along the perimeter of the Soviet world and to resist any further advance by Moscow. Wherever Soviet outward pressure increased, there also would American resistance become stronger. America committed itself to meet each threat as it presented itself, by such action as was appropriate to the particular time, place, and conditions. The United States adopted no single pattern of resistance, but instead reserved its freedom to choose techniques demanded by the form of Russian expansionism it was meeting, whether political, psychological, or military.

This decision pledged the United States to hold an enormous arc extending from the North Cape in Norway down through central Europe, the Middle East, and South Asia, and then turning northeastward and

---

[9] Thus Kennan says: "...it will be clearly seen that the Soviet pressure against the free institutions of the western world is something that can be contained by the adroit and vigilant application of counter-force at a series of constantly shifting geographical and political points, corresponding to the shifts and manœuvres [sic] of Soviet policy, but which cannot be charmed or talked out of existence." "Sources of Soviet Conduct," by X. *Foreign Affairs* (July, 1947). Copyright by Council on Foreign Relations, Inc. Reprinted by permission.

running up through Southeast Asia, China, Korea, and Japan. This was the geopolitical "shatter zone" abutting on the Soviet Heartland. This was the crucial area; if Moscow was to be stopped short of total domination of Eurasia, America must draw a line and hold it before Russian power broke out to the open sea. In 1947, when the United States launched this program, the American people were almost totally unprepared for the demands it was to make; despite the loss of China and half of Indochina to communist control since that year, however, the United States has held the line tolerably well.

The Second Phase. For many Americans this is all there ever was to it; the United States was to "stop communism," and that was what containment was all about. Unfortunately, the problem of American policy was never this simple. Stopping the Soviet threat would not eliminate it, and for the United States to sit forever on the cold war would be a poor way to fulfill American goals of a better world, a strange version of the peace, order, and stability that is the announced American objective. The theorists of containment had anticipated stalemate as the most probable outcome of the first phase of American action, and had devised a strategy to follow up any success the United States might enjoy in holding the line.

Their formula was based on the pattern of American policy and its assumptions about the kind of people the Russians were. In its essentials the second phase of American policy called for the United States to exploit its own advantages, to capitalize on the difficulties inherent in the Soviet position, and ultimately to confront the Kremlin with such an unfavorable situation that peaceful accommodation with the free world would be the only convenient way for the leadership to escape with the regime intact. Put thus baldly, the doctrine might sound over-simple. It had, however, sound reasoning and considerable historical evidence to lend it credence.

The Rationale of the Second Phase. Soviet policy was expansionist, Americans reasoned, but it was also opportunistic. This meant that it would continue to expand only as long as it met weakness. Confronted by equal strength, Moscow would stop; met by superior power, it would recoil. This has been the key to the entire American approach.

The first objective of the United States was the stabilization of the line of containment by plugging up the soft spots through which the Soviet threatened to move. The American government planned then to create "situations of strength": particular areas at various places along the line of containment where the United States enjoyed superiority over Soviet power and could apply controlling pressure on its own part. The advan-

323

tages that could produce such local preponderance, we should note, were not necessarily military; any relationship could suffice if its net effect was to give the United States a policy leverage. If the Soviet found itself in a clearly inferior position, the reasoning ran, it would withdraw rather than risk open defeat.

Why did the United States feel it necessary to win local victories at all? The answer to this question lies in the controlling American theory of Soviet motivations. The Russian leaders, unable or unwilling to fulfill their promises of domestic plenty made to their people, needed a dynamic foreign policy as an outlet for the powerful energies they had liberated in their people. If, by containment, the United States could deny them release, enormous frustrations would result. Internal pressures, pent up, would multiply their effect; the ubiquitous stresses within the Soviet structure would worsen.

This, we should remember, might result from a mere negative program of containment. The United States, the argument ran further, could heighten the effect and speed up the process of reversing Soviet dynamics by scoring significant if limited victories within the compass of its own situations of strength.

Since power and its distribution (and enjoyment) are generally thought to be the primary concerns of any dictatorship, the intramural struggle within the Soviet hierarchy would probably intensify if foreign policy were not to produce a constant flow of victories. The luckless bureaucrats officially tagged with responsibility for failure would be ousted and humiliated;[10] new plans, put forward by other members of the high command, would replace those that had failed. The demoted leaders would seek to obstruct and inhibit their successors as they pursued their own vindication; competition for rank and status, never far submerged in the Soviet system, would come out into the open. This, added to the embarrassing necessity of explaining away defeats to the mass of the Russian people, would compound an already difficult situation.[11]

The Need for Restraint. So the second phase of American policy—the attempt to roll back Soviet power at points where the United States enjoyed local superiority—had as its object the intensification of stress within the Soviet government. Such a development, it was contended, would hasten the moment at which the leadership would cry quits and undertake to prosecute Russian policy by a different and—from the

---

[10] The ouster of Dimitri Shepilov, Soviet foreign minister during the Suez and Hungarian crises in late 1956, was widely interpreted in the United States as being a punishment for his lack of success. See, for example, *Newsweek* (March 11, 1957).

[11] See, for an official statement of this thesis, Charles E. Bohlen, "Creating Situations of Strength," *Department of State Bulletin* (August 4, 1952).

American point of view—more satisfactory method. This was a more delicate matter, however, than might appear at first glance.

The United States had always to plan its victories carefully, allowing the Kremlin the opportunity to withdraw gracefully with its prestige intact. If America were over-militant, if it forced the Soviet so tightly into a corner that the stability of its regime were directly menaced, the Russians in their desperation might choose war rather than accommodation. This would be fatal; total war with Moscow was just what the United States was seeking to avoid.[12]

American local victories had to be just convincing enough that the Soviet would retreat, yet not so obvious that the leaders could not rationalize them to their people. It has proved difficult for Americans generally to grasp this point. Why not, if the United States has the communists in a real vise, put the pressure on and force either Moscow's surrender or its destruction? This way the United States might eliminate the cold war in one blow and solve all its problems. Like virtually all short-cut solutions to foreign policy, this argument raises more issues than it resolves.

In the first place, there is very little reason to believe that anything short of military defeat would force the USSR to capitulate. Second, trying to force surrender runs a grave risk of provoking total war. Third, if American pressure were to prove unexpectedly successful, and if it should undermine the Soviet regime without causing war, the most probable consequence would be a new—and certainly a bloodier—Russian revolution.

This last might sound like an ideal solution on first hearing, but it would defy good sense to argue that a new upheaval in Russia, complete with probable international intervention and certain widespread unrest, would serve the American interest in peace, order, and stability. Revolution may indeed again come to Russia, but to provoke it deliberately is no part of the American plan.

We must also remember that the hoped-for change in Soviet tactics is within the power of decision of the Soviet policy-makers themselves. They alone began the cold war, and only they can end it short of bloodshed. The most the United States can safely attempt to do is to speed up the process by increasing the pressures on the leadership and by being always ready to act promptly when (and if) signs of change should appear. What is the United States prepared to do if and when the contra-

---

12 Kennan says: "...it is a *sine qua non* of successful dealing with the Soviet that the foreign government in question should remain at all times cool and collected and that its demands on Russian policy should be put forward in such a manner as to leave the way open for a compliance not too detrimental to Russian prestige." "Sources of Soviet Conduct." Reprinted by permission.

dictions in the Kremlin's position force Russia into an "agonizing reappraisal" of its own policy?

The framework of accommodation

Up to the present time Americans have been mainly concerned with the theory and practice of containment, whose objective it is to convince Moscow that its policy of unilateral revision of the status quo by tactics of subversion, intrigue, and violence simply does not pay. We have seen, however, that the American approach has a further objective, positive where the first is negative. The United States hopes to persuade the Soviet to accept its offers of peaceful cooperation and the orderly satisfaction of justifiable Russian desires. It is the carrot and the stick of the fable; containment is the stick, driving Moscow away from its goal; accommodation is the carrot, tempting the Soviet into abandoning its unattainable objectives by means of satisfactory compromises.

The Failure of the Second Phase. The cold war, as it progressed between 1946 and 1954, eroded American political consciousness to the point where many Americans lost sight of this long-run goal. Washington tended to take the easy way; faced with the necessity of obtaining popular agreement to sudden and far-reaching action, high officialdom all too frequently floated programs on a wave of crisis. The crisis was often real, and there was little desire deliberately to deceive the public; one result of the "crisis approach," however, was to fix in the public mind the image of the Soviet as an inscrutable and implacable enemy, whose intentions were transparently evil and whose persistence was inhuman.[13]

The public—guided by some less responsible elements of the press—adopted a set of clichés by means of which the problem of Soviet expansionism was fitted into a simple stereotype. "You can't trust the Russians," "the only thing they understand is force," "no appeasement," "their tactics may change but never their objectives": the list is sizeable. As Americans became accustomed to constant Soviet hostility, most of them forgot—if they ever realized—that American policy had actually looked to the day when the Kremlin (although not necesesarily anymore friendly) was willing to act cooperatively.[14] When and if this moment arrived, cold-war techniques—and the cold-war psychology—would be largely obsolete.

---

[13] In this connection, Winston Churchill's characterization of Russia as "a riddle wrapped in a mystery inside an enigma" became almost a cliché. See a criticism of this attitude by George Fisher, in his review of John L. Stipp, *Soviet Russia Today* (New York: Harper & Bros., Inc., 1956), *Saturday Review* (March 16, 1957, p. 16).

[14] See S. Grover Rich, "Negotiation from Strength: the Psychological Problem," *Antioch Review* (September, 1952). Professor Rich stresses this point.

The Need for Realism. It will not be enough for the United States merely to hold out its blueprint for a better world. Any proposal it advances must be attractive enough to the Soviet leaders that they will want to accept it. Americans, if they wish a peace of accommodation, must take the USSR as it is; its attainment remains impossible as long as so many segments of the public claim to oppose peace with Moscow until the Kremlin sincerely repents and apologizes for obstructing American policy.

If repentance and apology are what the United States is working for, then truly the cold war will go on forever. On the other hand, a rational image of American national interest can be constructed that does not require that the USSR should love the United States or that it should agree on everything. All America really insists upon is that Russia behave itself.[15]

This formulation makes the problem of reaching agreement a practical one. Formulas must be devised that include what the United States must have and at the same time promise enough advantages to the Kremlin so that its leadership can accept these terms without fear of drastic domestic repercussions or a fatal loss of international prestige.

Minimum Basis of Accomodation. There has been relatively little inclination in the United States to consider the minimum bases of a practical settlement with the Soviet Union. Many Americans insist that peace will come only when the Soviet abandons eastern Europe, retreats to its 1939 boundaries, dismantles its worldwide apparatus of Communist parties, disarms drastically, and ends its "interference" in the Middle East, south and southeast Asia, and the Far East.

If these are actually the minimum American requirements, peace is far off. They would require the Soviet to liquidate its policy, renounce its objectives, and leave itself virtually defenseless and at the mercy of the United States. We may find it difficult to imagine a situation in which the Soviet leadership would accept such a proposal as an alternative to war; military defeat itself could scarcely exact a higher price. No dictatorship (nor any other government, for that matter) would dare lightly to risk accepting a settlement so obviously humiliating.

But it is not at all clear that these requirements are actually the least the United States can safely insist upon. Must America deny Moscow any protection against such a threat as a resurgent Germany? Can anyone categorically deny that the Russians have no reason to fear another invasion from the West, the fourth since 1815? Does the Soviet indeed have to be militarily impotent for the United States to feel secure? Would

---

[15] See George Kennan's article, "America and the Russian Future," *Foreign Affairs* (April, 1951), for his estimate of what changes in the Soviet system the United States may reasonably expect to come about.

peace be worth conceding the USSR a clear right of continued existence as a great power? Granting an American concern with permanent world order, these questions and others like them would seem to be obviously rhetorical. Peace—real peace, the goal of American policy—would be worth its price.

Principles of Accommodation. It would be frivolous for us to suggest any detailed terms on which Soviet-American accommodation could be based; they would have to depend on the particular conditions prevailing at the moment any such agreement was reached. We can, however, lay down what might be the guiding principle of any American negotiator working out such details: the United States is willing to make any grants to Soviet interest that would ensure Russian cooperation in a peaceful world but that would not compromise the fundamental American position.

The United States cannot ever "trust" the USSR the way individuals trust each other. This generalization, however, does not invalidate the prospect for lasting accommodation; nations cannot ever safely "trust" each other in that way. Trust and good faith, however, have never proved to be a solid base for viable international agreement, however much they may serve as frosting on a cake of accommodation.

The real stuff of lasting agreement between states is a harmony of interest. We may assume that the Soviet leadership—never abandoning for a moment their conspiratorial outlook—will keep only those agreements that individual and mutual interest demands be kept. It is immaterial to the United States whether the Kremlin abides by its promises because of the positive advantage accruing therefrom or because of its fear of the consequences of breaking faith.[16] Both motivations have a place in American thinking; it is the carrot and the stick. The American

---

[16] In this connection, Walter Lippmann, in criticizing the Kennan hypothesis in *The Cold War* (New York: Harper & Bros., Inc., 1947), p. 60, made this point about accommodation: "At the root of Mr. X's philosophy about Russian-American relations and underlying all the ideas of the Truman Doctrine there is a disbelief in the possibility of a settlement of the issues raised by this war. Having observed, I believe quite correctly, that we cannot expect 'to enjoy political intimacy with the Soviet regime,' and that we must 'regard the Soviet Union as a rival, not a partner in the political arena,' and that 'there can be no appeal to common purposes,' Mr. X has reached the conclusion that all we can do is to 'contain' Russia until Russia changes, ceases to be our rival, and becomes our partner.

"The conclusion is, it seems to me, quite unwarranted. The history of diplomacy is the history of relations among rival powers, which did not enjoy political intimacy, and did not respond to appeals to common purposes. Nevertheless, there have been settlements. Some of them did not last very long. Some of them did. For a diplomat to think that rival and unfriendly powers cannot be brought to a settlement is to forget what diplomacy is all about." (Reprinted by permission)

problem, therefore, is one of devising a settlement that will make the joint effect of the carrot and the stick sufficient to commit Moscow firmly and—perhaps—irrevocably to cooperation.

THE PATTERN APPLIED

Most Americans can recall the major events of the first decade of the cold war. This story is retold chronologically in the next chapter, so at this point we need only make a summary estimate of the pattern of American policy as it demonstrated itself in practice and some analyses of certain special problems it presented.

Successes and failures of the pattern

Europe: Holding the West. As the United States looked over the long line it had pledged itself to defend in 1946-7, several weak spots seemed to demand immediate attention. The gravest danger of a Soviet break-through was in western Europe. The democracies of the West needed protection against the twin dangers of communist subversion and Russian military aggression. The United States moved quickly, broadly, and—to some extent—over-enthusiastically to meet the threat. Economic aid was poured in via ECA and its successors; military agreements and political commitments were reached in a series of steps culminating in an expanded NATO; a steady—if not devastatingly effective—drumfire of propaganda was launched.

Europe was doubly important to the United States.[17] Not only was it the richest prize within the Soviet's grasp, but the democracies figured largely in American plans. It was not enough for the United States to prop up western Europe so the region would not fall victim to the Kremlin; Europe was to become a "situation of strength" and was to play its cooperative part in future struggle with the USSR. By 1957, balancing unquestioned progress against some equally obvious failures, it was clear that at least a significant beginning had been made on this task.

First Defeat: China. If Europe represented the first relative American success, Asia was the scene of the first, and so far the greatest, defeat for the United States. By 1947 the situation in China had deteriorated so badly that the Kuomintang government was doomed; the only way for

---

[17] See Edward Mead Earle, "A Half-Century of American Foreign Policy: Our State in Europe, 1898-1948," *Political Science Quarterly* (June, 1949).

the United States to "save" China was by major war and—rightly or wrongly—Americans were unwilling to go so far.[18] The communist victory upset the line of containment even before it was clearly drawn; communist power had reached the open sea. A rapid recalculation of the situation, however, pointed out a way to escape the worst effects of this setback.

A New Position in the Far East. Communist sea power was too weak to capitalize fully on the new advantage it had gained by the capture of China. The United States accordingly drew a new line of containment along the chain of island groups that fringe the Asiatic mainland. The Philippines, Formosa, Okinawa, and Japan became fixed points upon which was based a mobile screen of sea and air power to contain Communism at the water's edge. This was admittedly a makeshift, but it served the purpose surprisingly well. American reorientation in the Pacific was emphasized by a favorable peace treaty with Japan in 1951 and a series of later agreements that were aimed at making that country into an anti-communist outpost, an offshore anchor (like Great Britain) of the ring of containment.

The Pattern and the Korean War. From the point of view of this global pattern, North Korea's aggression in 1950 was another communist attempt to break through the ring, this time by the technique of military force. To remain consistent with its announced policy, the United States was required to resist this move as it had all earlier ones. South Korea itself was not actually indispensible to the American perimeter—as Secretary of State Acheson had intimated in an often-quoted but as often deliberately misunderstood statement early in 1950. Blocked from further expansion by revolution, by propaganda, or by diplomacy, the communists attempted open war in Korea. The American purpose was to halt communism militarily as was already being attempted economically and politically.

The Southern Arc. Along the southern segment of the Eurasian arc, neither spectacular success nor crushing defeat took place during the first ten years of the pattern's application. The United States made a little progress in the Middle East; it kept the Arab-Israeli quarrel from flaming into open war until late 1956, and made the "northern tier" of the Middle East—Turkey, Iran, and Pakistan—relatively secure by the Baghdad Pact. It had no luck with India, whose refusal to commit itself kept Russia at bay but also frustrated American policy. The effort in southeast

---

[18] See Secretary of State Acheson's letter of transmittal of the "China White Paper" in 1949: "The unfortunate but inescapable fact was that the ominous result of the civil war in China was beyond the control of the government of the United States." *United States Relations with China* (Washington, D. C.: U. S. Government Printing Office, 1949), p. xvi.

Asia was, on balance, more unsuccessful than otherwise. Thailand and the Philippines were at least partially won for the West, but Burma and Indonesia followed India's neutralist lead, while Indochina and Malaya flamed with open communist rebellion.

A Ten-Year Trial Balance. How had the United States fared in ten years? The original line had undergone some modification, both unfavorably and favorably; American losses in Asia were to some extent offset by Yugoslavia's at least partial defection from the communist camp and by the appearance of obvious cracks in the Soviet's belt of satellites. Europe was comparatively stable, although not yet completely organized. The Far East, although uneasy and potentially explosive, was at least temporarily tenable. South and southeast Asia were worrisome; political and economic instability, communist-led civil war, and Indian-style "neutralism" all seemed to make this region a likely target of Muscovite pressure. The Middle East seethed with internal pressures and Soviet probing. All in all, however, we can say that the policy had paid off; Soviet expansionism had been largely stopped. By mid-1955, it seemed as if world politics approached balance—or stalemate.

The pattern and the public

Any foreign policy must be grounded in consensus, regardless of how this mass approval is brought into being. This is especially true in a democracy. How did containment fare with the American public during these ten years, and to what extent did popular attitudes influence its execution?

The Popularity of Containment. There is no doubt that containment, at least during its heyday, was genuinely popular with the American people. It served the controlling version of the national interest, and at the same time provided a necessary outlet for some of the powerful emotions engendered by the stresses of the postwar period. The world after 1945 was a confusing and frustrating arena for a relatively uninformed and unsophisticated people. Coping with indigestible problems, truculent enemies, fractious allies, and the inscrutable processes of history made many Americans irritable, hostile, and impatient. Containment gave Americans the opportunity to say "no" as often as they pleased and yet glow in the certainty that such behavior was actually serving a real purpose. It took a number of years for this attitude to begin to wear off.

American Negativism. The most conspicuous characteristic of American attitudes during the cold war has been their essential negativism.

331

The United States accepted a policy line whose ultimate goal is international agreement, but the mass of the American people have often acted as if they feared agreeing with anybody. The practice of containment has made much of the nation behave as if America had a vested interest in the cold war, as if it were afraid of peace.

This negativism has concentrated on the largely hypothetical danger of appeasing Russia. "Appeasement," in this context, has meant making any concessions at all to Russian interest. So obsessed have Americans been with the possibility of being seduced into an unfortunate capitulation that they have lost much of their sense of purpose and their confidence in their ability to hold their own. The mass response to problems has too often been an attempt to exorcise a demon by incantation while refusing to face concrete issues. This attitude created, and in turn has been fed by, the "crisis policy" of the American government; many moves have been presented to the people as something they ought to approve of simply because they were certain to irritate the Kremlin.

The Over-emphasis on the Soviet. Perhaps the greatest failure of American public opinion has been its fixation on the problem of Russia. Although theoretically the cold war is only an interruption in the orderly development of a rational American policy, in practice the menace of the USSR has largely dominated the public mind. Analytically Americans see Moscow at the root of most of their difficulties—even though, as sometimes has happened, other factors are responsible. Operationally the United States tends to make the Soviet the immediate target of each policy move, even though the issue may be uninvolved in the cold war.

This had led to two different embarrassments. First, it has proved to be difficult to keep Soviet policy in any kind of perspective; Americans have often overestimated Soviet power as grossly as they once underestimated it. The second unfortunate result of American Russophobia has been a tendency to misjudge specific problems. Since Russia was the only concern, Americans have felt little need to familiarize themselves with the situational details of problems. Local forces and local issues have often been either ignored as insignificant or arbitrarily distorted to fit a cold-war mold. America's policy toward its allies has had only one object, and a short-range one at that: to force the states along the Soviet frontier to become vocally anti-communist and to join actively in a political and military alliance against Moscow. By 1955 considerable evidence had accumulated that this had been one of the least successful enterprises of the United States.

The Confusion of Ends and Means. Another shortcoming of American policy brought about by public attitudes has been a frequent confusion of ends and means. The entire containment policy is a means to an end, the attainment of a working basis of understanding with the Soviet. Each step presumably has been aimed at the intermediate goal of bringing Moscow to the point of settlement on some mutually acceptable basis.

As the cold war has hardened into something resembling a way of life, however, its place in over-all American policy has become blurred. The long view has been almost forgotten, and victory over the Kremlin and its allies has been substituted for the ideal of mutual accommodation. Americans demand unconditional surrender from their enemies, and who cares what lies beyond that happy day?

Each particular problem—German rearmament, the Suez Canal, the revolt against imperialism, and many others—has come to gain a unique significance divorced from any general strategic plan. Their relevance to larger concerns has been forgotten; the application of "containment" to defeat Moscow on the battleground of the issue has become the single purpose of American action.

American Inflexibility. What the confusion of ends and means has meant in practice has been great inflexibility in approach. The wooden and mechanical quality of much of American policy has been a far cry from its original intention.[19] The pattern demanded steadfastness and tenacity in purpose, it is true; in operation, however, it demanded great flexibility. The United States was supposed to meet the Soviet threat in the form in which it presented itself, allowing always for great variety in Russian techniques. Rather than to pursue a single line, America was supposed to employ methods varying according to time, place, and circumstances.

Instead, the United States staked out fixed positions and held to them grimly; it developed a limited battery of techniques and insisted that each problem in the endless series could be dealt with by dollars, guns, or "information." The more pressure Moscow applied, the more insistent the United States became upon clinging to methods tried and true. There seems to have been little desire to overhaul the American approach or to frame possible bases for realistic compromise.

Something like a Maginot-line complex came to be grafted onto what had been originally a concept of flexible defense. For several years after 1947 Soviet policy-makers kept battering themselves in frontal attacks on the line of containment, while ignoring tempting opportunities to hit the United States where its ideological flanks or its political rear were

---

[19] See the suggested ways of recapturing flexibility contained in the reports of the American Friends Service Committee, *The United States and the Soviet Union* (New Haven: Yale University Press, 1950), and *Steps to Peace* (1951).

exposed. It was not until the Kremlin initiated (what we call later in this chapter) the "new" cold war that the fuller implications of American rigidity became apparent.

The Imitation of the Soviet. The longer the negative and inflexible aspect of containment remained dominant, the more the United States (at least superficially) came to resemble the Soviet. Unconsciously, as Washington searched for new techniques of resistance, the United States came to adopt many of the very practices it was opposing. Many Americans learned to think of foreign policy in terms verging upon the totalitarian; they developed an emotional preference for military methods, subversion, and other avenues of "direct action"; the American government fell into the trap of attempting to dictate to its allies, just as Moscow was doing to the satellites. The distinction between Moscow's policy and Washington's dwindled; to some uncommitted peoples, the apparent goal of the United States was to be just like the Russians but to be better at it than the Russians were.

"Liberation"

The presidential election of 1952 provided the occasion for a fairly systematic attempt to reshape the pattern of American policy as it had developed up to that time. This reappraisal grew out of widespread popular dissatisfaction with the frustrations of containment, and was fed by the partisan fires of a heated electoral campaign. It never emerged as a full-fledged action program; its major utility was as an electioneering device. Its brief heyday is important to us because of the new light it threw on the fundamentals of the pattern of American policy.

The Indictment of Containment. By the time of the 1952 campaign, the cold war had stabilized into a more or less equal stalemate. Both sides had made their basic commitments and neither proved to be able to break the impasse into which they drifted by any expedient means. The American people, grown familiar with the requirements of the role they were playing, began to find fault with it.

The first charge in the popular indictment of containment boiled down to the claim that it never seemed to get anywhere. It did not spell out any clear objectives. It called for constant effort, directed to no visible purpose except an adamant anti-Soviet line and the neutralization of each of an interminable series of crises.

Containment also failed, Americans said, because it produced no victories. It furnished neither a sense of accomplishment nor any standards by which to measure progress. Its greatest successes were "silent": American action had prevented many unfortunate things from happening. But these were negative, and a steady diet of stalemate had not proved nourish-ing. Americans were hungry for real, positive success over which they could feel proud and from which they could draw courage for future struggles.

It seemed also as if the United States was always on the defensive and that containment robbed it of any initiative. Despite the evidence that this was the way it had to be—given the original terms of reference of American policy—there is no doubt that their defensive posture was irksome to many Americans. The United States was obliged to stand fast under an infuriating barrage of communist insult and provocation. Even when a crisis permitted psychic release in national action, mass frustra-tions were never fully satisfied. American moves were scrupulously limited to exactly what would neutralize communist pressure or, at best, to what would restabilize the situation on the basis of the status quo ante.

A final objection to American policy in 1952 was a traditional one: it cost too much. The military budget and the international commitments made under its terms seemed to many Americans to be out of all propor-tion to what the United States was receiving in return. Some political leaders detected a demand by the public either for more results from the foreign-policy investment or else a reduction in its cost.[20]

The "Liberation" Formula. The formula of "liberation," advertised as a substitute for and an improvement upon containment, was originally the creation of the "radical right" wing of the Republican party. As the electoral campaign of 1952 developed, the doctrine was adopted as party policy by the Republican leadership, and the Eisenhower victory was thought by many to be a mandate to put it into practice.

"Liberation" was tailored to meet each of the major objections to con-tainment.[21] It had a concrete and realizable objective: the rollback of communist power from the places into which it had expanded, and the liberation of the captive and satellite areas of eastern Europe and Asia. It promised clear-cut victories over the Soviet: short-run triumphs ac-companying each phase of the rollback, and finally Moscow's surrender as communism became caught in a steadily worsening position. It pro-claimed the end of the defensive in American policy: the United States was finally to assume the initiative, mount offensives against the Soviet, and gain the satisfaction that containment had denied it. And—for many the best of all—it was to cost a great deal less in money, manpower, and

---

[20] A serious attempt to invalidate containment and to substitute a much more limited policy was made by Senator Robert A. Taft in his *A Foreign Policy for Americans.*

[21] The most ambitious attempt to provide a theoretical rationale for liberation was made by James Burnham, in his polemic, *Containment or Liberation?* (New York: John Day, 1953).

335

anxiety. Victory, said the Republicans, could be won without economic strain or the danger of war.

What was ironical, considering the heated language of the campaign, was that "liberation" was not the complete break with the past that both its friends and its enemies proclaimed it to be. Its roots lay in the very doctrine of containment that many were busy repudiating. We may recall that arresting Soviet expansion was planned as only the first step in the design of American policy; once the line of containment was stabilized, the United States had intended from the beginning to go forward and to create "situations of strength" as a prelude to final settlement. This is exactly what the "liberators" were promising; to accomplish it, they would build on what the "containers" had already accomplished.

The Rationale of "Liberation." At any rate, "liberation" purported to call for a new grand strategy. The United States was to abandon the defensive and to seek out the Soviet where Moscow was weak and America was strong. The frontier of communist expansion would be driven back; Americans would no longer wait for Russian moves before taking action themselves.

Preventive war—or any form of military aggression—was of course ruled out, but every form of nonviolent attack was to be pressed to the maximum. The United States was to apply economic pressures ruthlessly, subvert communist regimes, encourage and subsidize resistance movements behind the Iron Curtain, step up the propaganda offensive, and give no ground before communist counterattacks.

Eastern Europe was an obvious first target. Satellite resistance to Soviet domination was apparent; why else did Moscow feel compelled to purge, to reprimand, and constantly to re-indoctrinate the "friendly" regimes there? If the United States could step up its pressure sufficiently, it might well touch off a chain reaction that would drive the Kremlin to cover. Breaking open satellite resistance would either destroy Russian control in eastern Europe or would make Moscow tighten its grip so as to hold on—thus weakening Russia vis-a-vis the rest of the world. Either outcome would be a net gain for the United States.

What worked in Eastern Europe might work in Russia itself. A policy of liberating the Ukrainians, the White Russians, the Baltic peoples, and the several submerged populations of Soviet Asia had unlimited prospects. There was no logical stopping place to the rollback short of the Kremlin walls themselves; at the very least, if the Soviets were kept busy trying to put down rebellions in their own domains they would have neither time, interest, nor capability to undertake further expansion.

Military policy was also to be different. The United States would fight no more little wars, no more Koreas. American armed might was not to be dissipated in stopping aggressions chosen by Moscow for their nuisance value or for their debilitating effect on the United States. America was no longer to foil aggression in one place only to let the communists escape to plot more moves in other parts of the world.

American military power was to have a role primarily political. It was initially to serve as a deterrent, threatening total war on the Kremlin in "massive retaliation"[22] for any outbreak, even a minor one. Ultimately, American superiority—especially in nuclear weapons and in air power— would be a major element in forcing a final peace. This general notion was elaborated into the famous "new look" in defense, discussed in detail in Chapter 15 below.

The Failure of "Liberation." If the doctrine of "liberation" had any final value, it lay in the debate it provoked. The underlying assumptions of American policy were brought again into public awareness during the recurrent controversies over foreign policy that filled the Eisenhower administration. The action program called for by "liberation" was questionable at best, and it was rapidly rendered obsolescent by the rapid development of the cold war between 1953 and 1958. Today most of the debate has primarily historical value, and only a significant modification in American defense policy remains as a monument to the hypothesis of the rollback.[23]

The new cold war

What invalidated the premises and the conclusions alike of the doctrine of "liberation" was the major change in Soviet tactics in the cold war that became apparent during 1954 and 1955. The new line had been in the making ever since Stalin's death, but came out into the open after the "summit" conference of 1955. The Soviet offensive changed character and American replies, although still conceived within the original pattern, had to be framed in new terms. A new cold war was being fought.

The Shift in Soviet Tactics. The Soviet line in the new cold war was different in many ways from the Stalin formula; perhaps the simplest way to characterize it is to call its approach to the West "soft," in contrast to the "hard" line identified with Stalin. It apparently called for the

---

[22] The phrase was apparently first used by Secretary of State John Foster Dulles in January, 1954, in an address before the Council on Foreign Relations (*New York Times,* January 13, 1954), but the principle itself is an integral part of the broader theory of liberation.

[23] Even James Burnham radically revised his ideas. See his "Liberation: What Next?" *National Review* (January 19, 1957), and the debate touched off by this article in later issues of the magazine.

abandonment of military aggression or its threat; even the vituperation that the world had grown to accept as a normal concomitant of Moscow's policy was minimized from time to time. Ideological weapons were downgraded as well. Primary trust was placed in economic techniques such as trade agreements, technical cooperation, purchase credits, and so on. Russia was seeking to win consent to its policy rather than coercing acquiescence; Soviet moves were undertaken in harmony with protestations of sweet reasonableness and mutual good will.

Soviet policy also acquired a new set of targets. The Kremlin ceased trying to break through the ring of containment; the network of alliances had proved adequate to hold back direct Russian pressure. Instead Moscow concentrated on the "neutrals": the uncommitted peoples of Asia and Africa. It wooed these states with soft and nonideological words and with tempting offers of economic and political assistance. By emphasizing nonpolitical action, by employing a "strategic" (what one author defines as an "indirect"[24]) approach, the Kremlin was able to breach the line of containment by simply leaping over it. Early maneuvers in the new cold war won the Russians significant victories in Burma, in Egypt and Syria, and in North Africa. A major reorientation in Soviet policy was also suggested by Moscow's initial conciliatory tactics toward the satellite rebellions in Poland and Hungary late in 1956, although the Hungarian episode culminated in a policy of bloody suppression.

The Modification in the American Pattern. American understanding of and reaction to the new Soviet approach was slow—perhaps unnecessarily so—in developing. It seemed to many Americans as if something dazzlingly new had been unveiled by Soviet strategists, and for many months the United States found itself unable either to grasp the significance of the new attack or to devise effective countermeasures.

This did not have to be such a problem. If Americans had recalled the original foundations of their policy and had sloughed off the Russophobe and militarist deviants of the containment hypothesis, the general line of American policy would have been clearer. The purely military phase of American policy had largely achieved its purpose by 1955; the Soviet leaders gave evidence of being convinced of the folly of armed adventure outside the Iron Curtain. Now that Moscow had developed new measures of expansion, these same fundamentals could be called on to point the way to new American counterstrokes appropriate to the nature of the threat. How well the United States has met this challenge is partially suggested in later chapters, but its final success or failure will be told by history yet to be written.

[24] B. H. Liddell Hart, *Strategy* (New York: Praeger, 1954).

13 : A decade of cold war, 1947-1957

T he major ingredient in the history of American foreign policy since 1947 has been the ebb and flow of the cold war. Despite the pressing dilemmas confronting the United States in every part of the world and the difficult decisions they have forced, the attempt to meet the continuing menace of Soviet expansion has provided the continuing thread of American action and decision.

This chapter is an attempt at an overview of the cold war. Many items of detail are mentioned whose discussion will be deferred until later chapters. Its purpose is to furnish a generalized historical perspective of the phases into which the first cold-war decade can be divided that might provide a background for our later evaluation of current problems.

We shall give conceptual unity and sequence to this period by using the analytical notion of "bipolarity." By this term we mean a fundamental assumption implicit in the cold war, embodying two basic characteristics: (1) the principal antagonists, the United States and the USSR, oppose and repel each other at all points, just as do opposite poles on a magnet; (2) all the other states in the world are drawn—again by analogy with a magnet—toward one pole or the other. Thus, a bipolar world is one neatly divided into two totally opposing camps, with no states remaining permanently aloof from such arrangement.

Bipolarity as the governing assumption of the cold war has passed through three different stages, each occupying a roughly equal time period. The first phase, from early 1947 to the onset of the Korean war in 1950, was a period during which the idea of bipolarity was evolving and winning acceptance as the dominant rule of world affairs. The second, the era of total stalemate in great-power relations, extended from

1950 to the end of the 1954 Geneva Conference; this was the era of bi-polarity dominant. Beginning in 1954 and continuing at least for three years more was what we call the "new cold war," marked by the gradual dissolution of the bipolar construct. As the rigid two-power system began to break up into a closer approximation of the multi-state system, many of the operating assumptions of the early cold-war era began to lose some of their validity.

CONTAINMENT: THE EVOLUTION OF BIPOLARITY, 1947-1950

The American assumptions about Soviet behavior and the policy neces-sary to cope with it found the United States largely unprepared for the mission it had assumed. The first period of American action was therefore devoted to two related if dissimilar tasks: coping with short-run crisis and developing capabilities and procedures for the long-range program that lay ahead. By 1950 the methods of American bipolar policy had largely stabilized; this precision in technique, however, was not matched by an equally clear understanding of the specific goals and objectives the United States was pursuing.

First steps in containment

The Problem. The problem of the United States in 1947 can be simply stated. Soviet influence, operating from a secure base inside Russia, was pressing outward in all directions. Eastern Europe had already fallen to Moscow; the Middle East lay almost defenseless; in the Far East the new power situation left the Soviet as the major factor in China and a con-trolling participant in East Asian politics. Of the areas immediately con-tiguous to the Soviet heartland, only south Asia—protected by the Hima-layan barrier—seemed relatively safe, at least for the moment.

The line the United States had drawn to defend varied in its suitability. In some areas it was natural and more or less defensible (the northern frontiers of Turkey, Iran, and Afghanistan); in others it was artificial, difficult, and complex (such as the interzonal boundary in Germany, the 38th parallel in Korea, and the northern frontier of Greece). A natural first step was the selection of techniques to hold this line against what-ever pressure Moscow might exert.

Crucial Area: Europe. It was obvious that the United States could not defend the entire ring simultaneously; some system of priorities was needed. The situation, however, permitted of little discussion. Western Europe—especially France and Italy—was, if not the weakest link in the chain, at least the most endangered. The Middle East, torn by the Greek "civil war," represented at the moment a more localized threat; Asia seemed sufficiently quiet that action—although probably ultimately necessary—might safely be postponed.

Europe's central role in the cold war was not alone due to its vulnerability. It was an immensely valuable prize, either to the USSR or the United States. It contained over 200 million people, highly industrialized and technically proficient, and was of major military and political significance. Americans had deep cultural affinities for Europe as well; its defense seemed to many to be a matter of coming to the assistance of close relatives. Wartime experience had also left its mark. The common defense against Nazi authoritarianism underscored the determination of the United States to make Europe the scene of its first organized stand against Soviet expansion.[1]

Retooling at Home. But the decision to act against the Soviet and to defend Europe meant little in itself. Between 1945 and 1947 the United States had tried its best to leave behind both the war and wartime ways of thought. Military demobilization was a fact; economic readjustment to full peacetime production was under way; government organization for foreign affairs was imperfect and bore the marks of the extensive extemporization of the war years. Even more inhibiting was what we might call American "psychic demobilization." Although the utter unconcern of the immediate postwar period had given way by 1947 to a deep disquiet over the burgeoning Soviet threat, there was relatively little public awareness of the future requirements of American policy.

The government, therefore, was obliged to move slowly. With the Greek crisis as a pretext, Selective Service was enacted early in 1947, but was not put to immediate use in the rebuilding of American military power. Beginnings were made at preparing for economic mobilization. New organizational measures, such as the unification of the armed services and the reorganization of the Department of State, were put into effect; new agencies (the National Security Council, the Central Intelligence Agency) were established. But this retooling was more preparatory than operational. Almost by default, the "brush fire" technique of moving breathlessly from crisis to crisis became the accustomed way of doing business.

---

[1] For a sympathetic study of Europe on the eve of the cold war, see Barbara Ward, *The West at Bay* (New York: W. W. Norton & Co., Inc., 1948).

Economic and military aid

With Europe the area of primary concern, and with the immediate danger being that of economic and political collapse preceding a series of communist revolutions, emergency moves were obviously called for. The tottering economic-political structures of western Europe needed propping up to retain their viability until a more comprehensive political and military policy could be devised. American cold-war policy began as a result with programs of economic and military aid.

The Truman Doctrine. The first overt step is known to history as the "Truman doctrine," formulated and expressed in March, 1947. The inability of Britain to sustain its commitments to the pro-western government in Greece transferred the burden of holding back communist expansion to the United States.[2] President Truman, on March 12, proposed to Congress that extensive military and economic aid be extended to Greece (and Turkey) so as to hold back the Soviet: ". . . it must be the foreign policy of the United States to support free peoples who are resisting attempted subjugation by armed minorities or by outside pressure. . . ." The United States, Mr. Truman insisted, should be willing "to help free peoples to maintain their free institutions and their national integrity against aggressive movements that seek to impose on them totalitarian regimes."[3] After over two months of heated debate in Congress and among the general public, the Greek-Turkish Aid Bill of 1947 was approved, but only after specific assurances had been given that the broader doctrinal implications of the measure (suggested in the quotations above) did not represent any fixed commitment. The direct impact of the Truman Doctrine was restricted to Greece and Turkey, but no one doubted that a precedent had been set.

The Marshall Plan. The Truman Doctrine had been an avowedly emergency measure aimed at a particular crisis point. Unless the United States was prepared to dissipate its substance in an endless series of such moves, a broader program was needed. Emergency relief would not solve Europe's problem; basic and permanent rehabilitation might well do so. This realization prompted the more ambitious "Marshall Plan" and the later ECA.

---

2 See Joseph M. Jones, *The Fifteen Weeks* (New York: The Viking Press, 1955), for a thorough account of this period.

3 John C. Campbell and staff, *The United States in World Affairs, 1947-48* (New York: Harper & Bros., Inc., 1948), p. 33. Data in this chapter through 1954 have largely been drawn from this valuable series of annual volumes written by the staff of the Council on Foreign Relations. The Truman message is in the *Department of State Bulletin* (March 23, 1947), p. 536.

The popular name of the American aid program came from its first specific expression in a speech by Secretary of State Marshall at Harvard University in June 1947.[4] He offered the prospect of large-scale American aid to the battered European economy. This was, however, no invitation for a mass raid on the American treasury; he attached certain important qualifications to the suggestion.

The initiative, he declared, must come first from the European states themselves. Furthermore, European participation in any program must be based on the maximum of self-help and mutual aid by the participating states, thus demanding extensive intra-European cooperation as a prior condition to grants from the United States. Mr. Marshall made clear that the United States would extend aid only within a regional framework and not in a mutually contradictory and competitive system of single-nation programs.

The European states moved quickly. After first forcing Moscow to oppose the plan openly (and thereby to admit to the distressed Europeans that the Soviet was more concerned with its own expansion than with their welfare) and then to apply great pressure on its satellites to stay out, sixteen western European states met in Paris in July. Out of this conference grew the Organization for European Economic Cooperation (OEEC) that was to do yeoman service in coordinating the American aid program in Europe. The conference estimated a need of eight billion dollars to cover the "dollar gap" for 1948 and a four-year program of $22.4 billion.

At home the Marshall program was translated into law. Once the measure came before Congress, one subtle but important change occurred that was to become increasingly important in the future. Originally ERP was conceived as a positive program aimed at moving the United States closer to its own long-term goal by helping to create an area of peace, order, and stability; under the pressure of political controversy, it developed into an admitted anti-Soviet move. This changed its context to a considerable extent and, with it, the direction of a good deal of later American policy.

Eventually, after long and heated debate, Congress passed the bill as the Foreign Assistance Act of 1948 and authorized $5.3 billion for the European program. Smaller amounts were added for Greece, Turkey, and China. With this move the United States took the first great step in the direction of bipolarity.[5]

---

[4] Text of speech in *New York Times* (June 6, 1947).

[5] See Henry Bayard Price, *The Marshall Plan and Its Meaning* (Ithaca, N. Y.: Cornell University Press, 1955).

Military Aid: MDAP. The Marshall Plan was limited to economic aid; the United States, however, had already broadened its program to include military assistance. The Greek-Turkish aid bill had involved the supply of military items, particularly to Turkey. It was not until the ratification of the North Atlantic Treaty (1949), however, that systematic military aid became an integral part of American policy. In July 1949 the Military Defense Assistance Bill was presented to Congress; in October it was passed and the Military Defense Assistance Program (MDAP) was inaugurated. In the original bill, one billion dollars was authorized for military assistance to the signatories of the North Atlantic Treaty, and over 300 million for specified nonsignatories (Greece, Turkey, Korea, the Philippines, and Kuomintang China).

The beginnings of alliance

Aid programs, however meritorious in themselves, could not accomplish everything the United States had in mind. If containment were to hold Moscow in check, the free world had great need of unity. So long as the noncommunist states remained isolated, each dependent only upon itself for its continued existence, Moscow would enjoy a great advantage over most of the states it confronted. No American aid, regardless of its content or amount, could equalize such small states as Norway, Iraq, or Korea vis-a-vis the Soviet.

The next great need of the free world, therefore, was for coordination of policy and defense. Only by joint effort could the Kremlin be brought to a halt. The United States, on its part, also felt the need of a more elaborate organization. The magnitude of the American mission was so great that only by careful coordination could the task be kept within manageable proportions.

These considerations indicated strongly that Washington should attempt to create a network of alliances with friendly states. If the United States was to expect that the small states should agree to stand fast against Soviet pressure, an equivalent pledge would have to be made by Americans. The old bugaboos of "fixed commitments" and "entangling alliances" had to be set aside; the twentieth century had convinced even the most unregenerate isolationists that Washington's Farewell Address no longer provided a complete blueprint for future American action. The structure of the free world was to rest on a foundation of exchanged pledges of joint action incorporated in hard-and-fast alliances.

The Rio Pact (1947). The history of American alliances since 1947 demonstrates one of the truisms of international affairs: an alliance can be built only upon a predetermined area of shared interest. Each of the major pacts made by the United States has been born only after the prior discovery of this harmony of interest among the participants. As might have been expected the first mutual-security pact the United States consummated was in an area in which this harmony was already elaborately developed: Latin America.

Building on the improved tone of inter-American relations dating from the liquidation of dollar diplomacy and its replacement by the Good Neighbor during the 1930's, and capitalizing on the record of hemisphere cooperation during the war, the United States nailed down Latin American agreement as its first move. During the summer of 1947 an Inter-American Conference for the maintenance of continental peace and security, meeting at Brazil's summer capital of Petropolis, drafted the Rio Pact, known officially as the Inter-American Treaty of Reciprocal Assistance. This instrument made mutual defense the rule within the Americas.[6]

All the signatories pledged joint action in case of an act of aggression against any of them, whether arising within or without the hemisphere. Action could also be taken on "any fact or situation" which might endanger the peace, even if not distinguishable as an "aggression." Joint action was to follow consultation; a decision to act taken by two-thirds of the signatories bound all of them. No state, however, was pledged to use armed force without its consent.[7]

The Rio Treaty was followed up by American military aid to Latin America; it was not until 1951, however, with the creation of the Organization of American States, that formal institutional machinery was made available to execute the guarantee.

The North Atlantic Treaty (1949). By 1949 it had become clear that another American step was due in Europe. The economic aid program, by revitalizing Europe's economy, had intensified Moscow's opposition. Just as the likelihood of communist revolt faded due to domestic stability, the prospect of Russian military attack in Europe increased. American action against this danger was necessary.

The North Atlantic Treaty, finally negotiated in April, 1949, was the instrument by which this step was taken. By this document the 12 signatories (the United States, Canada, Britain, France, Italy, Belgium, the Netherlands, Luxembourg, Portugal, Iceland, Denmark, and Norway)

---

[6] See Edgar S. Furniss, "The U. S., the U. N., and the Inter-American System," *Political Science Quarterly* (September, 1950).

[7] For specific provisions, see pp. 419-20 below.

entered into an engagement to keep the peace among themselves and to resist aggression jointly. An attack on one would be an attack on all; consultation and collective action were to take place according to automatic procedures.

Always with an eye on the United States Senate, American negotiators pointedly refrained from including any promise of the automatic commitment of armed force without a declaration of war, but this was virtually a technicality. Both the MDAP and the strategic planning that followed the ratification of the treaty put the United States in a position that left little room for American equivocation if the guarantee were ever to be put into effect.[8]

Thus by 1950 the United States had succeeded in tying two highly sensitive areas, Latin America and western Europe, into a mutual security system that seemed destined to grow. There remained great segments of the ring of containment whose stabilization had not yet been attacked systematically, especially the Middle East, south Asia, and southeast Asia. But during the first phase of the cold war—what we might call the European period—American alliances bulked large in the developing bipolar structure.

Issues outside the anti-Soviet context

We have already suggested that the American fixation on the Soviet gave rise to some distortion in American policy. Even more serious than the misinterpretation of specific relationships and problems was the tendency in the United States to overlook or to minimize events that did not fit a narrow cold-war pattern. Prior to 1950 at least three crises occurred whose eventual significance was largely missed in Washington and that were destined to return later to plague the United States. Among these were the Palestine problem, the birth of India, and the Indonesian revolution.

Palestine. American policy toward the creation and development of the Republic of Israel is an issue of great complexity. Here we are interested primarily in the impact of cold-war thinking on the United States

---

[8] A useful survey of the rationale of the treaty and of the circumstances surrounding its ratification is Halford L. Hoskins, *The Atlantic Pact* (Washington, D. C.: Public Affairs Press, 1949); see also Blair Bolles, *The Armed Road to Peace* (New York: Foreign Policy Association, 1952)....For more recent appraisals, see Massimo Salvadori, *NATO: A Twentieth-Century Community of Nations* (Princeton, N. J.: D. Van Nostrand Company, Inc., 1957), and Gardner Patterson and Edgar S. Furniss, Jr., *NATO: A Critical Appraisal* (Princeton, N. J., Princeton University Conference on NATO, 1957).

during the crisis arising from the partition of Palestine and the Arab-Israeli war.

During these events, the cold war impinged on American policy in two ways. First, the United States was keenly aware of the actual and potential significance of Middle East petroleum. "Oil politics" involved a two-pronged effort to keep the petroleum reserves of Iraq, Iran, Saudi Arabia, and the minor shiekhdoms from falling into Soviet hands and, as part of the same policy, to guarantee their permanent exploitation by the West. American action therefore sought the retention of the practical maximum of Arab good will.[9]

The second influence of cold-war thinking was more broadly oriented. Stability in each region was an objective of containment; crisis in any area along the Soviet periphery might offer tempting opportunities for Muscovite exploitation. America therefore sought a swift and peaceful end to the dispute on almost any mutually tolerable ground, arguing that even an imperfect solution would be in American interest if only it were reached peacefully. It was in support of this doctrine that Washington so strongly supported the armistice negotiations and subsequently opposed any recourse to violence by either party.

There were, of course, other factors influencing American opinion during this period. Disinterested humanitarianism, partisan politics, British pressure, and several others may be distinguished. But it would be difficult to prove that cold-war psychology played a lesser part than any of these; certainly the tenseness of Soviet-American relations precluded the possibility of many otherwise valid alternatives. The United States was to reap some of the harvest of this error during the later Middle East crisis of 1956-7.

The Partition of India. The 1947 crisis over the partition of India was likewise seriously misinterpreted by American statesmen. With the actual course of events the United States had of course little to do; the major American miscalculation was in assaying the results.

As Washington saw it, India and Pakistan—once freed from British rule—would automatically side with the West, and especially with the United States. It seemed axiomatic that democratically-inclined peoples, newly independent, would find common cause with Americans, who so long ago set the pattern of liberation. The Indian and Pakistani ruling classes were western-trained and anti-communist; Britain's withdrawal from India was generally regarded as guaranteeing two recruits for the free world.

---

[9] See Benjamin Schwadran, *The Middle East, Oil, and the Great Powers* (New York: Praeger, 1956).

The easy assumption that India and Pakistan would follow the broad path to the western alliance proved false; totally for India, partially for Pakistan. Two unsuspected factors help explain American misjudgment: the fiery quality of Indian nationalism and its near-frantic insistence on the substance as well as on the forms of independence, and the depths of Indian resentment against anything that smacked of colonialism. Indian "neutralism," so puzzling to Americans in later years, could have been more easily foreseen in 1948 had not Americans been so prone to equate noncommunism with anti-communism. It was not for nearly a decade that the United States was to learn how vast the gap actually is between these two ideas.[10]

The Indonesian Revolution. Cold-war thinking nearly led the United States seriously astray during the Indonesian revolution. Americans did not become really aware of the revolt in the former Netherlands Indies until 1948, and by that late date certain habits of thought had already developed. Two points stood out in the American view of the crisis: an American ally was being weakened by a native revolt, and the Indonesian movement was frankly revolutionary. Revolution against an ally of the United States was perilously easy to classify as a communist enterprise, and Washington was reluctant to take a firm stand in favor of independence. Not until the Dutch had forfeited much American good will by repeated violations of their word did the United States exert any considerable pressure for a peaceful settlement and to support United Nations moves toward Indonesian independence.

This hesitancy sowed an unhappy harvest. Indonesians found it difficult to forgive what seemed to them to be a weak American attitude and saw in the United States a potential defender of an outworn colonialism. This was an unjust stricture; American confusion during the revolution grew out of the methods of analysis imposed by the anti-Soviet campaign rather than from any animus toward colonial independence. But, for good or ill, the damage was done and the United States later had ample cause to regret it.

The dynamics of bipolarity

As the American reaction to the Soviet threat crystallized, a dynamic of bipolarity was developed. Certain operational assumptions came to

---

[10] See F. S. C. Northrop, "Asian Mentality and United States Foreign Policy," in *Lessons from Asia*, ed. E. M. Patterson, *The Annals* (July, 1951); also Eleanor Roosevelt, *India and the Awakening East* (New York: Harper & Bros., Inc., 1953), p. 115.

underlie the planned moves of both sides; within very broad limits the cold-war cycle become fairly well stabilized.

The Focus of American Policy. By 1947, the United States had abandoned hopes for positive results from any direct negotiation with the Soviet, at least until Moscow had been persuaded of the futility of its policy of force. Once the cold war was well launched, relations with the Soviet were reduced to the minimum and American policy concentrated instead on the organization of the free world.

America had only one goal: the creation of a defensible line of containment. No serious discussion with the Soviet needed to be undertaken until the power balance had been stabilized in the world; better still, until the West had its own "situations of strength" in existence. The United States thus largely ignored the Soviet except insofar as Moscow interfered with American efforts to organize the free world.

The Agreement to Disagree. To the extent to which contact with the Soviet was impossible to avoid—and this was a considerable extent indeed, considering the many meetings in the United Nations, in the occupations of Germany and Japan, at international conferences, and so on—the policy of the United States was based on an implicit "agreement to disagree" with the USSR. Regardless of the question, it became axiomatic that the American and Soviet positions would be diametrically opposed. Such opposition did not incorporate any real hope by either party that it might persuade the other or win any victories; the agreement to disagree was rather the most obvious indication of the totality of the cold war. Both sides counted on the other's objections as a fixed situational element. When, by quirk of history, the United States and the USSR found themselves on the same side of a question (as on the Palestine issue), their mutual embarrassment was obvious.

The Elimination of Power Vacuums. Direct controversy between the two giants was relatively rare; more frequent were battles by proxy. Both the United States and the Soviet, once the cold war had been "declared," sought to perfect the bipolar idea. This required the progressive elimination of the so-called "power vacuums": those states and regions that were as yet undeclared in the cold war.

When the cold war began in 1947, the leading power vacuum was China, where the Communist-Kuomintang civil war was about to reach full fury. In Europe the best-known example was, of course, Germany. Less important uncommitted areas included almost all of the Middle East, much of southeast Asia, Japan, and Korea. Indian independence added the Indian subcontinent to the list of future battlegrounds of the cold war.

The struggle for the power vacuums required both direct pressure on the uncommitted governments and the use of a variety of indirect methods. Both Moscow and Washington enlisted partisans in each of the battleground states and fought the battle through them. In Germany, east and west Germany were pitted against each other; in China, the Kuomintang opposed the communists; in Korea, the north faced the south. Some of these areas were won by the communists, most notably China; others, like Greece and Iran, were saved for the West. The only overt loss of an ally suffered by either side during this period was Yugoslavia's defection from the communist camp; China's status as an ally of the West never became sufficiently formalized after 1945 to count the communist victory as a real minus for the United States in spite of its plus value to Moscow.

Direct Clash: Berlin. The most open confrontation between East and West before 1950 was the Berlin crisis of 1948 and 1949. Its details are too complex to fit in our space;[11] certain of its aspects, however, are relevant to the broader trends of the cold war.

Berlin was the first open test the Soviet made of American determination and American strength. It was important for Moscow to know that the United States was both willing and able to meet coercion with counterpressure. Berlin also stiffened the United States; the Soviet's stubborn and uncompromising attitude hardened American determination to carry containment through to completion. It was also during the Berlin affair that Washington first succeeded in mobilizing public opinion as a weapon against the Soviet.

Most significant of the implications of Berlin was that the issue was finally brought to the point of an acceptable compromise. Moscow, faced with a stabilized power situation and a worsening public opinion, was willing to call a halt to its dynamism. This development (consummated in May, 1949) was a dramatic vindication of the Kennan theory, and convinced American policy-makers of the fundamental accuracy of their assumptions. Moscow, faced by equal pressure, had shown it would stop; it seemed reasonably safe to conclude that the Kremlin would recoil if faced by superior power.

STALEMATE: BIPOLARITY DOMINANT, 1950-1954

We cannot specify the precise date at which the United States and the

---

[11] See Lucius Clay, *Decision in Germany* (Garden City: Doubleday, 1950) and Walter B. Smith, *My Three Years in Moscow* (Philadelphia: J. B. Lippincott Co., 1949). The diplomatic sequence is related in John C. Campbell, *The United States in World Affairs, 1948-49* (New York: Harper & Bros., Inc., 1949).

USSR lost their freedom of maneuver and became caught by the inexorabilities of the logic of the two-power system. The closest we come is to place it somewhere in the period beginning with the final victory of the communists in China and ending with the outbreak of the Korean war, although the atomic explosion in the USSR in September, 1949, was undoubtedly the major single event signalling the culmination of bipolarity. By the beginning of 1954, at the earliest, other forces had asserted themselves to the point that the successful maintenance of bipolarity became impossible. The outcome of the 1954 Geneva Conference revealed that other principles were at work undermining the two-power world; both great states then set about readjusting their approaches.

The Korean conflict

The Korean conflict was at once the most important single element of the rigid cold-war era and its most meaningful symbol. The bloody and inconclusive battle that lasted from 1950 to 1953 was the high point both in the Soviet expansionist policy and in the containment effort of the United States. In its prosecution the bipolar principle received its most severe tests and eventually developed cracks under the pressure. In its indecisive resolution, the Korean struggle epitomized the impact of the cold war on the issues of world affairs.

Cold War in the Far East. Between 1947 and 1950 the policy of the United States had concentrated on Europe. China and Korea, it is true, had been included in the American aid program, but this move was dictated more by domestic politics than by serious policy decisions. By 1950, however, a series of events in Asia had alerted the United States to the portentous fact that new arenas were being found for the East-West struggle.

First, and most importantly, the fall of Chiang Kai-shek and the triumph of Mao Tse-tung in China sounded a warning to Washington, even though no clear American policy was developed in response. Other indices of the broadening of the cold war were the Hukbalahap crisis in the Philippines, the worsening situation in Indochina, and the constant rumblings out of divided Korea. When open war came to the latter country in 1950, it was a strident indication that Communism—at least temporarily balked in Europe—was seeking compensation in Asia.[12]

---

[12] See Robert Payne, *Red Storm over Asia* (New York: The Macmillan Co., 1951), and O. O. Trullinger, *Red Banners over Asia* (Boston: Beacon, 1951).

The Cold-war Significance of Korea. American leadership thought of the Korean war as a part of a larger policy whole. Korea was an example of a different technique—military force—put to serve the standard communist goal of expansion. Whether the Soviet deliberately planned the aggression to test American determination—a claim very popular during the war—is immaterial (although a good deal of evidence points to the contrary). Moscow seized on the war and sought energetically to capitalize on it. The United States reasoned that its real enemy in Korea was neither Korea nor China, but rather the Soviet itself. American policy was therefore derived from an application of the basic principle of containment to the peculiar conditions prevailing in Korea, and added up to the restraint of Communism by equal military force. General MacArthur's more extreme views confused the issue but did not alter the outcome.[13]

One consequence of Korea was the identification of Red China with the Soviet. The active entry of Chinese troops in the Korean fighting and the participation of China in the truce negotiations removed whatever doubt remained about the direction the new regime would take. Henceforth Peking was assumed to be Moscow's most faithful ally.

The United States and Collective Security. The Korean war offered the United States the opportunity to test the strength of the lines of alliance it had been forging. Although military action in Korea was undertaken in the name of the United Nations, the 15 states that joined the United States and the Republic of Korea in resisting the communist attack formed a roughly accurate list of those states that were most in agreement with American policy.

The United States fought in Korea not primarily in defense of any abstraction called "collective security," but in response to the dictates of national interest. The other active members of the United Nations Command joined on the same basis; only those whose concern about Soviet expansionism approximated that of the United States or whose operating version of national interest demanded the closest possible relations with the United States made a decision to fight. Others, less directly concerned, supported the principle and the name of the United Nations in a variety of less extensive ways; some, as a matter of fact, ignored it completely.

And yet, despite the mixture of motivations, Korea offered some proof

---

[13] General MacArthur's views were dramatically presented in his address to a joint session of Congress after his recall from the Far East. See *New York Times* (April 20, 1951).

of the validity of the notion of collective security. A sizeable number of states not deeply involved in the fate of Korea itself nevertheless were moved to commit military force to the principle of peaceful process. If it be true—as seems obvious—that the American objective of a world of peace, order, and stability must be widely shared before any state can attain it, the Korean experience revealed that considerable agreement on it existed and proved that joint action in its behalf is feasible, if admittedly difficult.

The Korean Crisis and the Free World. On the other hand, the polarizing effect of the cold war created stresses within the ranks of the noncommunist states. Americans had fallen into the habit of using the term "free world" to include loosely all states outside the Soviet orbit and to assume that all of them agreed generally with United States policy. This generalization, always an oversimplification, broke down badly as a result of the intensity of the Korean struggle and the growing militancy of the United States. Serious rifts were caused in what had seemed in 1950 to be an unbroken front against the USSR.

India was the principal defector. Mr. Nehru had approved the 1950 finding of aggression against North Korea; as the war wore on, however, his disenchantment grew. General MacArthur's decision to proceed northward past the 38th parallel smacked of aggression to India; the 1951 General Assembly resolution condemning China as an aggressor seemed needlessly provocative. By 1953 India had carved out a self-styled position of noncommitment in the cold war and had brought along with itself a number of Asian states that came to be known as the "Arab-Asian" bloc.[14]

Even the closest allies of the United States, Britain and France, found much to complain of during the war. Britain protested the rigidly anti-Chinese tone of American policy; France felt that American concentration on victory in Korea obscured any understanding of the serious issue in Indochina. The lesser associates of the United Nations forces had similar objections whose general import was that the United States was imposing purely American aims on a collective enterprise.

This complaint was the more serious because of the widespread suspicion that the United States had—at least temporarily—lost sight of its calculated objectives and was committed to total victory over China at whatever cost. It cannot be said that the Korean war materially im-

---

[14] For a summary of the circumstances surrounding India's decision for neutrality, see *Major Problems of U. S. Foreign Policy, 1952-3* (Washington, D. C.: Brookings, 1953), pp. 251-55, "The Problem of India."

proved American relationships with the free world, while some uncommitted states were lost by American attitudes. By the time of the truce in 1953, bipolarity (at least at the American pole) was losing much of its appeal for the smaller states.

The Korean Truce. The end of the Korean war brought no settlement. The military truce, itself a patchwork of stalemate, did not lead to any political resolution of the issues that had precipitated the war. The major point had been made by the West that communist expansion by force would be resisted as vigorously as would any other form. This, after all, was really all that could be proved by containment, and in these terms the Korean effort was successful.

But in a larger sense the issue of Korea epitomized the dilemma of the cold war. The USSR was seeking to extend the frontier of the communist world; the United Staes was dedicated to the frustration of this goal. Neither policy could produce lasting settlements; victory was possible by either party only if complete surprise were achieved. Once both sides had committed their power, an inconclusive quarrel broken off by mutual consent was inevitable, at least if neither side was interested in precipitating total war. Neither dared go further without risking undesirable consequences; by the same token, neither could conveniently retreat. Diplomacy could discover a point of rough equilibrium at which to stop, but could not dispose of the issues.[15]

United States Security Pacts in the Pacific. The shift in American attention to the Pacific produced between 1950 and 1953 a spate of new alliance agreements covering various sectors of the Far East. Washington negotiated a peace treaty with Japan in 1951 and supplemented it with a mutual security pact in 1953. In 1952 a similar defense agreement was concluded with the Philippines. The same year the ANZUS (Australia, New Zealand, United States) treaty was consummated. A security treaty was negotiated with the Republic of Korea after the 1953 truce. During this period also the Nationalist Chinese government on Formosa began to receive large amounts of American aid and Formosa's relationship with the United States was formalized late in 1954 when still another mutual security agreement was made with Chiang. The Korean war thus forced the United States to extend its alliance network throughout the Far East.[16]

---

[15] For a thorough discussion of American policy on the Korean episode, see Leland M. Goodrich, *Korea: A Study of United States Policy in the United Nations* (New York: Council on Foreign Relations, 1956).

[16] For details of these commitments, see below, pp. 421-2.

The "mutual security" context

The powerful mass emotions created by the Korean war and the evolution of American policy brought about a significant new trend in American thinking during this period. Between 1947 and 1950 the United States worked at shoring up the weak spots in the line of containment and made only a beginning at organizing a working system. During the next phase the United States built its policy toward the free world largely on the concept of "mutual security."

American policy from this point onward contemplated the formation of hard-and-fast agreements with its associates; firm military and political commitments were thought to be preferable to constant adjustment of policy to bring about harmony in the face of a dynamic Soviet policy. Promises from its allies to take specific action under certain circumstances enabled the United States to calculate in advance the extent and the amount of the support it could command in a given situation. As a result of this orientation technical assistance, foreign aid, informational programs, and diplomatic policies were modified to fit the requirements of the concept of mutual security.

The Shift to Military Planning. The mutual-security phase of American policy was really initiated by the North Atlantic Treaty in 1949, but the public was sufficiently resistant to military foreign-policy moves that little progress was made until after the onset of the Korean war. The commitment of American forces to that struggle was the signal for a change in the content of American policy.

Many Americans believed that the reasons for the major military build-up, the conceptualization of the cold war as a quasi-military operation, the emphasis on military foreign aid, and the extension of the American security frontier to the Far East, the Middle East, and North Africa were part of the program to win the Korean war. Actually, the United States never really intended to "win" the war in the MacArthurian sense, and the larger significance of the conflict was its role in making military planning and action palatable to the American people. Korea coincided in time with the reshaping of American policy, but was only in a remote sense its cause.

New Dimensions of American Aid. "Mutual security" was most apparent in the new version of American aid. "Economic aid" on the model of ECA was submerged and made only a minor part of the program as "defense support"; military aid of the MDAP type became the core. The Mutual Security Act of 1951 made it a prerequisite of American assistance that the recipient country unequivocally place itself in support of the United States in the cold war and subscribe to the general foreign policy of the free world. The "technical assistance" program, originally nonpolitical, nonmilitary, and noncoercive, was absorbed into the mutual security concept and put to serve the same paramilitary purpose. The entire foreign-assistance program was geared to the necessity of creating a modernized, coordinated, and efficient military force in the free world capable of resisting any new communist military adventure.[17]

The Development of NATO. Mutual security was most elaborately developed in Europe, where the North Atlantic Treaty had been the first successful application of the principle in an area directly menaced by the Soviet. In 1952 Greece and Turkey adhered to the pact (despite their relatively great distance from any part of the North Atlantic) and the permanent organization of NATO was set up.

The crux of the NATO concept was the establishment of a single unified defense force for western Europe under the general direction of a civilian body representing all the treaty members. The fourteen signatories pooled their resources for the joint defense of their area; goals for rearmament were set and supplemented with American aid.[18]

In 1948, at Bogotá, there had been created the Organization of American States, growing out of the Rio Treaty of 1947 and dedicated to implementing that instrument in much the same general way as NATO was to execute the North Atlantic Treaty. The OAS was much more loosely organized and conspicuously omitted the elaborate defense planning that characterized NATO.

The Impact on the Free World. The mutual-security orientation of the new American policy served further to polarize American policies. As aid from the United States came to require the acceptance of American leadership (often called domination) and an overtly anti-Soviet orientation, a number of states (particularly in Asia) found the price too high. They argued that Washington was giving them no real choice; to accept American aid was to forswear their independence and to make them more anti-Soviet than they cared to be, while to reject assistance from the United States was to leave themselves helpless before any overt Soviet pressure.

The smaller states in Asia divided sharply over this issue. India,

---

[17] See *Major Problems of U. S. Foreign Policy, 1952-3*, pp. 123-6, "Recovery and Rearmament."

[18] The structure of NATO as of 1952 is conveniently summarized in Blair Bolles, *The Armed Road to Peace: An Analysis of NATO.*

Indonesia, and Burma led in the formation of the "neutral" bloc; Pakistan, Thailand, the Philippines, Korea, and nationalist China accepted American terms. Despite the advantages accruing from the adherence of the latter group, the policy of forcing the smaller Asian nations to "stand up and be counted" resulted in the opening of serious gaps in the wall the United States was attempting to build against communist expansion. In later years Moscow was to prove adept at exploiting some of these weaknesses.

Even in Europe, where American leadership was strongest, "mutual security" produced both resentment and resistance. Many Europeans felt that the United States was pushing them too rapidly and too far in hostility to Moscow. Americans often overlooked the impact of rearmament and militarization on the shaky economies and governments of Europe. Another common plaint was that the United States—so firmly committed to military resistance to the Soviet—was neglecting both the dangers of nonmilitary expansion and the opportunities for constructive negotiation with the Soviet.

Major European trends

While the more spectacular events of the cold war were taking place in Asia between 1950 and 1953, the struggle continued in Europe as well. Here, with less room for maneuver, the period was marked generally by a continuation and intensification of trends set in motion as early as 1947.

Toward European Integration. The ECA had been posited on the principle of European cooperation, and its administration brought the participating states a perceptible distance down the road toward integration. The North Atlantic Treaty likewise implicitly contemplated a single "defense community" to include all western Europe. Also supporting the trend were the powerful mass movements in Europe that insisted that regional consolidation was a positive good rather than merely an unpleasant necessity brought on by Europe's exposed position between the giants.

Between 1950 and 1953 the United States did what it could to speed up the movement toward European union. The European Coal and Steel Community (the "Schuman Plan" for the consolidation of the steel industry in the six states of "little Europe") received both encouragement and concrete support. The abortive European Defense Community (for a common European army) received extensive support as well in Washington. Even the Council of Europe, more broadly based but less powerful than the other two, was encouraged as a wholesome trend. By 1954 it had become apparent that complete European integration was yet a long time off, but it was also evident that intra-European cooperation had reached a new peak and would probably continue to evolve.[19] This development was generally gratifying to the United States.

West Germany and the Cold War. By 1950, the United States had already included west Germany within the aid program and had sponsored the creation of the Bonn government; in 1949 Washington had accepted the principle of rearmament for free Germany. The next phase of the cold war saw new elaboration of American policy toward Germany.

The official end of the war with Germany came in 1952 by a treaty with Bonn. The problem of American policy was thus reduced to the discovery of a formula that would bring Germany into the western defense system on a basis acceptable to both the French and the Germans and at the same time that would not precipitate a total crisis with Moscow. The European Defense Community (originally a French proposal) seemed to be the most attractive of the many schemes. When this failed late in 1954, the United States settled for Germany's membership in NATO and in the intra-European alliance known as Western European Union (WEU).

During this period—as both earlier and later—American policy was constantly bedeviled by the problem of German reunification. Although Washington was willing to endure a divided Germany indefinitely, Bonn was not; the Soviet possessed a trump card in its occupation of east Germany. The United States was recurrently uneasy that the Germans might let their concern with unification obscure their alliance with the West. Chancellor Konrad Adenauer labored mightily to keep his government in line with American policy, and earned a major debt of American gratitude for his effort.[20]

The Consolidation of Bipolarity: Yugoslavia and Spain. As the cold war matured in Europe, the United States extended its ranks to include all states whose anti-Soviet orientation was strong enough to lead them into open opposition to Moscow. As a result there were added to the "free world" such oddly assorted (and "free" in only a highly technical sense) states as Yugoslavia and Spain. Yugoslavia's status as an outcast

[19] For a compelling argument by a leading European, see Paul Raymond, *Unite or Perish* (New York: Simon and Schuster, 1951); see also F. S. C. Northrop, *European Union and United States Foreign Policy* (New York: The Macmillan Co., 1954).

[20] See James F. Warburg, *Germany: Key to Peace* (Cambridge: Harvard University Press, 1953).

by Moscow made it willing to accept American aid and to fit itself—albeit reluctantly and with many backward looks—into the defense system of the West. Spain accepted a 1953 agreement with the United States whereby Madrid provided facilities for American bases in return for American aid. These moves left Switzerland, Sweden, and Finland the only European states outside the direct Soviet orbit that were not linked with the American security system.

Soviet policy, 1950-1954

What was the Soviet doing during the period that American policy was at its most rigid? Granted the bipolar assumption, it was natural that Moscow's attitude should be the reciprocal of Washington's. The Soviet sought steadily to implement bipolarity on its side of the Iron Curtain. Not until the death of Stalin were there any hints that the Soviet attitude might mellow, and even eighteen months later it was doubtful whether anything really new had been added to the Soviet outlook.

Total Hostility. Direct Soviet-American relationships continued as arid and unproductive as they had been ever since 1947. Moscow loudly protested an utter lack of confidence in American intentions. All possible differences with American policy were discovered and vigorously exploited. Even such innocuous enterprises as the 1952 and 1956 Olympic games became the occasion for ill-tempered and ferocious competition with the United States. Not until Yacob Malik opened the door for truce negotiations in Korea in 1951 was it possible to discover any major subject on which the United States could negotiate constructively or coherently with the Soviet.

The Korean Conflict. The Soviet gave extensive aid to the communists in Korea; economic, military, and technical assistance were extended to Moscow's ideological brethren. The 1954 Geneva Conference saw the Soviet participate as spokesman and defender of the communist cause in opposition to the United Nations.

The Consolidation of the Soviet Sphere. The Kremlin moved speedily to unify its own sphere. Eastern Europe was knit together in a complex of economic, political, and military pacts that perfected the pattern of satellitism. "Nationalist deviationism" in any form was ruthlessly suppressed. Satellite military forces were modernized with Soviet equipment; joint defense plans were worked out that reduced the armies of eastern Europe to the status of shock troops for the defense of the Soviet itself.

Communist China, with western doubts about its orientation removed after 1950, was brought squarely into Moscow's camp. The Soviet engaged itself in a long-term program of aid for China in return for Peking's allegiance to the Soviet system.[21] The adherence of China was a great gain for the Soviet, even though in the future—particularly after Stalin's death—Peking was to prove to be a troublesome and fractious ally, unwilling to accept the permanently subordinate place demanded of all close associates of the Soviet.

The Attempt to Split the West. As the power vacuums disappeared one by one and as the two camps sought to consolidate themselves, the major ingredient of Moscow's policy came to be a continuous attempt to split the free world. The American-led coalition was strong enough to hold Soviet ambitions in check; any new Russian successes had as a prerequisite the disruption of the western team.

The favorite hunting ground of the Soviet was, of course, Germany. By dextrous manipulation of the German urge for unity Moscow could raise one extraneous issue after another to delay the accomplishment of the goals of the West. Germany was useful also in another way: the issue of its rearmament provided a lever by which Moscow could excite France and further complicate inter-allied relations. Another device useful to the Soviet was the frequent suggestion that, in return for scrapping NATO or German rearmament or some other western project, Moscow might be willing to consider an over-all settlement of outstanding problems. This played on the natural eagerness of Europe to be freed from the more onerous burden of the cold war. Despite the USSR's inability finally to detach any of the allies, the cumulative effect of the Soviet splitting technique was a constant annoyance to the United States.

Climax: Indochina

The frustrating inconclusiveness of the Korean settlement presaged the end of the naked bipolar principle in international relations, but it was not until late 1954 that its final consequences were openly recognized. The Indochina crisis of that year and its stalemated settlement were the climax and the finale of the attempt to create the pure two-power world.

The Indochina Struggle. The Indochina affair is relevant to the broader cold-war picture in two different ways. First, it was almost entirely a battle by proxies. Communism was represented on the firing line by the Viet Minh; Chinese and Russian participation was limited to various forms

---

[21] Henry Wei, *China and Soviet Russia* (Princeton, N. J.: Van Nostrand, 1956).

360

of aid. French and pro-western Vietnamese forces fought on the anti-communist side, using materiel largely provided (after 1950) by the United States. Indochina was thus the cold war in microcosm: Moscow and Washington fought for Indochina by supporting partisan groups native to the country rather than by participating themselves. The second important fact about the Indochina crisis was that both sides, when faced with the likelihood of direct involvement in the war, drew back and accepted a time-buying compromise rather than to risk a repetition of Korea. Cold-war issues in an era of stalemate were as insoluble by hot war as they were by diplomacy.[22]

The Consequences of Stalemate. The Geneva Conference of 1954 ended hostilities in Indochina without disposing of any of its problems. This was the familiar pattern of stalemate to which the world had grown accustomed—if not inured—since 1947. But the Geneva Conference brought some hard reflection in its wake that contributed largely to the change in the character of the cold war.[23]

Geneva proved beyond doubt that nothing was ever settled finally under the conditions of bipolarity. Communists knew (and, after the death of Stalin, could admit at least to themselves) that the 1947-style techniques of expansion had outlived their usefulness. Western techniques of resistance had proved capable of holding back Soviet expansion. The development of nuclear weapons had progressed to the point that any policy that even in theory might require total war had become obsolete. Some new dimensions of policy had to be discovered or the whole Soviet effort would grind to a standstill.

For the United States, Geneva provided the final vindication of containment but also proved its inherent limitations. "Meeting force with force" would hold the communists back, but it was not especially useful in advancing toward the world of peace, order, and stability. New tactics seemed also to be called for by the West.

THE NEW COLD WAR: BIPOLARITY IN DECLINE, 1954–1957

The third and most recent phase of the cold war began immediately after the 1954 Geneva Conference. Bipolarity lost its grip and a more flexible international order began to appear. Why was the two-power world breaking up?

[22] For background material on Indochina, see Ellen Hammer, *The Struggle for Indochina* (Stanford, Calif.: Stanford University Press, 1954).

[23] The work of the Conference is summarized in Claude Buss, *The Far East* (New York: The Macmillan Co., 1955), pp. 647-50.

In the first place, many governments not directly involved in the great-power struggle found perpetual stalemate intolerable. Unable to accomplish any of their own major objectives because of the pervasiveness of the cold war, and facing the inability of the major antagonists to settle their own quarrel, more and more states overtly or covertly began to ignore the great powers in the prosecution of their own foreign policies.[24]

The two super-powers themselves realized the futility of uncomplicated total opposition. The Soviet had won everything it could by the old methodology of force; the United States was prepared to move into the second stage of its long-range policy as we have formulated it. Since Moscow never abandoned its basic revisionist premise and the United States its status-quo orientation, the new cold war that was being born would demand no new basic relationships. Moscow was destined to remain on the offensive, Washington to defend, counter-attack, and attempt to stabilize.

As of the moment this is written, no one can say where the new cold war will lead. There are those who feel that the USSR has entered a one-way street and that its adoption of a noncoercive policy is a preview of its eventual membership in an orderly society of nations. On the other hand, many hold a more pessimistic view: the Soviet's new tactics, they say, were dictated by international expediency or internal stress. This argument continues by alleging that—whenever an opportune moment presents itself—the Kremlin is prepared to resume the belligerency it temporarily laid aside. Soviet extremism in crushing the Hungarian revolt in November, 1956, and in dealing with Anglo-French-Israeli action in Egypt at the same time seemed to lend credence to this explanation. It was in this connection that the Kremlin's internal crises of July and October 1957, were so carefully analyzed in Washington. Both schools of thought agree, however, that the abandonment of bipolarity offers new opportunities to the United States.

The summit and after

The most spectacular event in the new phase of Russo-American relations was the unmistakable signal of its beginning: the sensational

---

[24] The Anglo-French military action against Egypt in October and November 1956 was—at least up to that time—the most dramatic instance of major states abandoning the cold-war framework for the direct advancement of their own interests. It was not surprising, therefore, that both states met opposition not only from the small states but also from both the United States and the Soviet.

"summit" conference of July, 1955, at Geneva, where President Eisenhower, Premier Bulganin, Prime Minister Eden, and French Premier Faure met face to face and cast about for some new way to attack the problems of the cold war. Surrounded as it was by world-wide publicity and deeply involving the emotions of much of mankind, the summit conference stands out as one of the most significant moves of the cold-war era.

Background for the Summit. For several years before 1955 there had been a widespread, if rather wistful, hope that, if the opposing leaders could deal directly and informally with each other, the worst aspects of the cold war could be liquidated. World War II, we recall, had set a pattern for such conferences. During 1954 and early 1955, the Soviet (under the new leadership of Premier Bulganin and party leader Khrushchev) repeatedly urged some form of top-level conference to make a frontal assault on over-burdensome problems.

The American government had been reluctant to begin direct and extensive negotiations with the Soviet again unless some assurances could be forthcoming that real progress would be made. Negotiation for its own sake Washington had long since abandoned, and arousing groundless hopes would be injurious to American morale. But early in 1955 the United States—prodded by its allies—began to reconsider. Moscow was much more insistent than heretofore, and external evidence hinted that a major readjustment in Soviet policy might be brewing. If such indeed were the case, a new try at direct conversations might prove helpful. Even if agreement could not be reached on specifics, there was some advantage in gaining an early insight into the new pattern of Soviet thinking. In May the United States agreed to the conference, and a new phase in Soviet-American relations was initiated.

The Meeting. The conference had a four-item agenda: (1) the future of Germany; (2) European security arrangements; (3) East-West trade; (4) interpersonal contacts across the Iron Curtain. The meetings went forward in an unusual atmosphere of good fellowship and amicability. The leading figures were obviously President Eisenhower and Premier Bulganin and their exchanges provided the highlights of the sessions.

The world watched Geneva closely between July 18 and 25. The conference represented new hope for a more orderly world; any decision reached there would hold enormous consequences for everyone. For the first time in a decade peace seemed almost within grasp.

The Summit Decisions. The conference failed to reach any concrete agreements on the first three items of its agenda and only a limited understanding on the fourth. Although on specifics some pessimists have labeled Geneva 1955 as a failure, there was one vastly important agreement reached (although never formalized officially) and several others outlined by implication.[25]

The most basic agreement at the summit was the frank exchange of pledges between President Eisenhower and Premier Bulganin that—at least as long as either of them was in charge of his government—neither state would go to war against the other. This simple admission changed the entire character of the cold war. After the summit, no cold-war policy was entertainable that would necessitate consummation by total war; neither side could any longer construct a program on the assumption that aggressive war was the ultimate intention of its adversary. The Geneva pledge has governed the interaction of both states ever since despite recurrent crisis.

Less explicit was another understanding that questions of organizing peace and reducing tension were to be of much higher priority in the future than in the past. The Geneva conferees took official notice that much of the world was weary of a diet of constant crisis; they determined to explore much more seriously any prospects for its alleviation. New importance was therefore given to issues of security systems and arms limitations; President Eisenhower's sensational "open sky" inspection proposal, made on the last day of the conference, came to epitomize the search for new dimensions of peace. A final consensus, equally unspecific, was reached on an attempt by both sides to discover means to reduce the harassing quality of East-West relations by the development of new avenues of friendly contact.

Aftermath of the Summit. Geneva, for all its breathless atmosphere of hope, was discouragingly unproductive of detailed solutions to concrete problems. The follow-up conference of foreign ministers in October, 1955, broke up in complete failure and the American isolationist fringe shrieked that the summit had been at best a delusion, at worst a snare. Some of the worst fears of the pessimists seemed realized during the Suez crisis of November, 1956, when Moscow threatened open war on Britain and France unless they withdrew their expeditionary forces in the Canal Zone.[26]

And yet as the months wore on, even this apparent new militancy did not conceal that the summit had ratified a new basis for Soviet-American competition. Direct intergovernmental relations became more cordial;

[25] See Pitman B. Potter, "The End of the Cold War," *American Journal of International Law* (October, 1955).

[26] See text of the Soviet notes to Britain and France on November 3, 1956, *New York Times* (November 4, 1956).

discussion of concrete issues became possible; compromises were actually worked out on minor points; even the 1956 threats by the Soviet were preceded by an invitation to Washington to join in a joint Russo-American policing action in Suez. More noticeable, if perhaps less immediately significant to political issues, was the improvement in interpersonal contacts. Apparently genuine friendliness frequently replaced hostility between individuals of the two nations; the Soviet even opened its doors to that ubiquitous spokesman for democracy and free enterprise, the American tourist. In this kind of atmosphere the old cold-war slogans began to lose much of their appropriateness; the development of new operating hypotheses was undertaken by American policy-makers.[27]

The new face of Soviet policy

As the summit faded into history, Americans realized that Moscow had been perfectly candid in professing its wish to end the total-hostility phase of the cold war. Soviet policy (irrespective of its ultimate objectives) acquired a new face. The old "hard" line of vituperation, force, propaganda, and subversion was subordinated; the Kremlin tried to show the outside world, and especially the United States, a facade of good fellowship, reasonableness, and a sincere dedication to peace. Soviet influence, forwarded by these new techniques, began to spread to new areas. The new face of Russian policy in 1955 gave rise to some troublesome problems for the United States.

The Soft Approach to America. The new Soviet line stressed cooperativeness and friendliness toward the United States. Issues such as disarmament, European security, free movement of persons, and other problems either untouchable or useful only for propaganda became the subjects of serious and open discussion. Even more important than the agenda of Soviet-American parley was the climate in which they went forward. Bulganin and Khrushchev, notably the latter, attempted to create an aura of bluff good-natured candor to replace the humorless and desperate milieu of former exchanges. In dozens of minor ways the Kremlin

---

[27] A sharp example of the new Soviet line was Premier Bulganin's congratulatory message on President Eisenhower's reelection in 1956. Coming immediately after a week of great international tension highlighted by Moscow's war threat, Bulganin's note described Mr. Eisenhower as a "great statesman . . . whose aspirations are the relaxation of world tension and establishment of peaceful relations between all states. . . ." Quoted in *The Atlanta Constitution* (November 9, 1956); reprinted by permission.

attempted to erase the memory of its vituperative past and to put its relations with the West on some new footing.

The Hungarian and Middle Eastern crises of late 1956 seriously conditioned the effect of the soft approach. The savagery with which Moscow suppressed Hungary's abortive revolt and the chill menace of Russia's near ultimatums to France and Britain seemed to be an unhappy Soviet regression to the Stalinist era.[28] But through this entire episode, particularly as it affected the Middle East, Russia took pains to maintain cordial contact with the United States and the United Nations and seemed eager not to disrupt the improved climate of Soviet-American relations.

Even at its most *gemütlich*, Soviet policy never concealed its dedication to the same general objectives as formerly. Competition was as absolute as ever; the Russian leaders never pretended that they contemplated an era of total reconciliation with the United States. But "softness" to the Soviet possibly meant that, while disagreement with the United States was inevitable, such disputes could be prosecuted at a much lower level of tension and with techniques less than total. It became popular to call this the theory of "competitive coexistence," and both words were important in the American judgment of Soviet intentions. Moscow was apparently planning to compete, but it was also planning to coexist indefinitely.

New Soviet Techniques. The Russians took the lesson of Geneva to heart; after 1955 some drastically new techniques were grafted onto the old methodology. These generally emphasized persuasion rather than coercion, and stressed winning voluntary support rather than forcing obedience. This new methodology had four specific channels of implementation: (1) a constant advocacy of the cause of peace and an avoidance of extreme positions except in its defense; (2) a vigorous championing of the cause of small states, particularly that of colonial and ex-

---

[28] During the height of these two issues, there was a good deal of speculation that the new Soviet policy was an indication of a return to power of Mr. Molotov, the ex-Soviet foreign minister whose head was the price Marshal Tito demanded for his reconciliation with Moscow. Molotov was represented as heading a "Stalinist" faction unalterably opposed to the soft approach of the Khruschchev-Bulganin clique who had degraded Stalin's memory. This impression (as well as Khrushchev's victory over the Stalinist faction) was confirmed by the sensational purge of July, 1957, as the result of which Molotov, Georgi Malenkov, and Lazar Kaganovich (the core of the Stalinist group) were summarily removed both from their membership on the party Presidium and their official positions. At the very moment of his victory, Khrushchev published in *Pravda* a "platform" in which he pledged continued coexistence between different economic and political systems, and asserted that the Stalinists had been attempting to question his stand on that point. See *New York Times* (July 4, 1957). This stand was reaffirmed in October, when Marshal Zhukov was demoted.

colonial peoples in dispute with their erstwhile masters; (3) an extensive program of foreign aid, both military and economic, with emphasis on the latter;[29] (4) an all-out "cultural offensive" that went far to melt the Iron Curtain at least for certain neutral states. What baffled the United States was that this program largely consisted of techniques identified with America and in the execution of which the United States had felt it enjoyed a natural advantage. By the middle of 1956 Moscow's new design had created a large if indefinite pool of free consensus that raised the prospect of the eventual near-isolation of the United States.

New Areas of Penetration. The Soviet's new line did not make it willing to disgorge any of the gains it had won by its hard policy. Satellite unrest in 1956 was greeted by a reluctant acquiescence in a new "national communist" orientation for Poland, but Hungary's attempt to break away entirely was met by the full weight of Soviet military power. Its new techniques, however, won Moscow victories in areas formerly barred to it by American containment.

The major targets of the new policy were the uncommitted states that had refused bipolarity or who had escaped from it. The Arab world—especially Egypt and Syria—were among the first to respond to the "milk and honey" approach; significant progress was also made in India, Burma, and Indonesia. Equally important, Russia's unusual moderation won it support in many places in Europe after the de-Stalinization campaign of 1956 got underway. This last harvest of good will, however, largely went by the board as the result of the Hungarian massacres. Even in the neutral world, American championing of peaceful process at the time of the Anglo-French-Israeli invasion of Egypt (coming at the same time as the Soviet attack on Hungary) undid much of Moscow's appeal except among some of the Arabs.

The rise of neutralism

Even at its peak, bipolarity was never absolute; there were always a few states outside the cold war. The Korean crisis made it possible for several others to divest themselves of their attachment; during 1954 and 1955 still others took advantage of the general relaxation of great-power relations. By 1956 "neutralism" had become a powerful force in world affairs, rivalling either of the two power blocs.

---

[29] On the famous trips to Asia and to Great Britain made by Bulganin and Khrushchev in prosecution of the Soviet's economic offensive, see "The Happy Hypocrites," *The Economist* (December 17, 1955).

A Decade of Cold War, 1947–1957

Neutrals and the Cold War. Before 1954 the lot of a cold-war neutral was an unhappy and dangerous one. Both sides were committed to the obliteration of power vacuums and great pressures were exerted on holdouts. As soon as the violent phase of the cold war ended, however, and especially after the summit conference, what had formerly been a perilous status became a preferred one.

When intimidation and force were replaced by persuasion, the neutrals —subject to bidding by both sides—gained the most. As long as a neutral could guarantee its freedom of choice, it could permit itself to be wooed first by one camp and then the other, reaping benefits from each transaction.[30] Skilled neutrals such as Burma's U Nu, Indonesia's Ali Sastromidjojo, and Yugoslavia's Tito kept the ball of competitive coexistence bouncing indefinitely and cashed concrete dividends of grants, loans, trade agreements, and political concessions, as well as intangible but equally important ones of prestige.

Under such conditions, to a number of states neutralism seemed a doctrine and nonidentification seemed a position far preferable to joining either side. So seductive was its appeal that the tragic outcome of the apparently successful Hungarian revolution in 1956 was at least a partial result of that nation's attempt to become a neutral itself by breaking free of Soviet domination.

The Spread of Neutralism. Neutralism gained converts both among governments and among peoples. In addition to the original Indian-inspired Arab-Asian group that dated from 1951, other states in 1955 and later staked out a neutral position and announced their willingness to deal equally with both sides (or, as cynics pointed out, to be equally bribed). Leading members of this latter group of noncommitted states were Yugoslavia after its 1956 reconciliation with Moscow, Egypt (although President Nasser virtually broke all ties with the West over Israel and Suez), Ceylon, and Laos. Even in states in which no formal policy modification was undertaken, the desire to withdraw from direct involvement and to concentrate on their own affairs exerted a perceptible influence on the thinking of many people on both sides of the Iron Curtain.

Neutralism and World Politics. The resurgence of neutralism was due to the relaxation of the grip of the two major powers; the more neutralism grew, the less Russia and the United States were able to control it. By the end of 1957 it was having an impact on world affairs in several directions.

---

[30] See Hamilton F. Armstrong, "Neutrality: Varying Forms," *Foreign Affairs* (October, 1956), and Vera M. Dean, "What Is the United States Policy on Neutralism?" *Foreign Policy Bulletin* (August 15, 1956).

First, the appearance of a distinct "third force" in the world restored some closer approximation of the classic mechanism of the multi-state system. The neutrals were not content only to be courted by East and West; instead they acted increasingly on their own to serve their own interests and to intervene directly into the Soviet-Western dispute. This was clearly demonstrated by the 1956 General Assembly resolutions on both the Hungarian massacre and the invasion of Egypt; in both cases the neutrals took the lead in condemning great-power action. Bipolarity seemed to be giving away to a more complex and delicately balanced system.

Second, the increasing flexibility of world affairs gave a new relevance to the United Nations. The neutral bloc in the General Assembly, counting both its regular members and its sometime adherents, could frequently muster a majority. Thus the United States and the Soviet each faced the prospect of being on the losing side of a world opinion mobilized by the smaller neutrals. Both major powers sought to reassure them, but at least up to the crises of 1956 the Soviet enjoyed greater success. On these latter occasions, the United States suddenly seized the leadership of the entire neutral world, and there was a good deal of speculation both within and without the United States as to whether this move foreshadowed an entirely new American approach to the uncommitted states.

Third, the neutral bloc also represented a real although qualified victory for the small states. During the height of bipolarity it seemed as if small states were obsolete and faced the early loss of their identities in one of the two monolithic groupings. By 1956, however, the neutrals had largely rationalized their position. Small and weak states no longer feared extinction by the giants; indeed, there were those who claimed that minor powers would ultimately decide the cold war. The new role of the small power was dramatically demonstrated by the multi-nation, small-power United Nations Emergency Force rapidly mobilized in 1956 to enforce the cease-fire resolutions in the Middle East. Its members symbolized world public opinion insisting on a peaceful solution of a vexatious crisis.

New components of American policy

The new cold war placed strains on the United States. Containment, even with its faults, had developed a powerful myth in its support, and the American people and their leaders were reluctant to jettison techniques developed at such great cost. This hesitation left the Soviet free to exploit the advantages of its new techniques while most Americans were at a loss to explain how Moscow could win such formidable victories.

The desired new components of American policy were not impossible to discover. They were to be found for the taking within the general framework of American action since 1947. What was needed was a general overhaul of programs in the light of new conditions, the most important of which was that world affairs (despite Soviet threats) had largely left the quasi-military phase behind. By mid-1956 this realization was coming home to Americans and, despite the digression of the 1956 presidential campaign, the rethinking of American policy had been begun.

Finishing Touches on Mutual Security. Before abandoning the mutual security context, however, the United States added three more agreements to its series of collective-defense pacts. In 1954 a Southeast Asia Security Treaty was concluded that united the United States, Britain, France, Australia, and New Zealand with the Philippines, Thailand, and Pakistan in the defense of the southeast Asian area against aggression (not, be it noted, against only communist aggression).[31] In the same year formal status was lent to American defense of Formosa by a Nationalist China-United States agreement. In 1955 the Baghdad Pact (in which the United States was a silent partner rather than an actual member) brought together Britain, Turkey, Pakistan, Iraq, and Iran in what Washington hoped would be the nucleus of a defense system for the entire Middle East. This last maneuver split the Arab world and provoked strenuous responses by Egypt, Syria, and Saudi Arabia, as well as by Israel.[32]

Changing Relations with the Free World. The new temper of world affairs forced the United States to modify its relations with the free world. The problem was to discover an affirmative cement to hold the free world together rather than merely relying on the negative fear of the Soviet.

As long as the great danger from Moscow was military attack, American leadership was unchallenged if for no other reason than that on the United States rested final responsibility for keeping the free world free. Such a position was not calculated to produce popularity, nor was American behavior toward the allies especially suited to winning friendship and respect. This was of little moment, however; the common danger was so great as to submerge most differences.

---

[31] In this connection, the present author's "The United States, Great Britain, and SEATO: A Case Study in the *Fait Accompli*," *Journal of Politics* (August, 1956), discusses the Anglo-American dispute surrounding the negotiation of the pact. Details of this American commitment can be found below, p. 418.

[32] The diplomacy of the formation of the Baghdad Pact is summarized in George Lenczowski, *The Middle East in World Affairs*, second ed. (Ithaca: Cornell University Press, 1956), pp. 260-65.

The lessening of the military threat eased this situation. No longer did the free world have the same cohesiveness in the face of a common enemy; the bonds of alliance began to fray and, in a few minor cases such as Iceland, to weaken perceptibly. In 1956 the whole issue grew acute when Britain and France deliberately deceived the United States about their intentions to invade the Suez Canal Zone. The free world, as long as it rested only on an opportunistic, anti-communist foundation, had no guarantee of permanence.

The United States, after having built the coalition, thereby acquired the responsibility of holding it together. This called for new measures to draw the anti-communist states together on an affiirmative basis of joint interest. Among early examples of such moves were the attempt in 1956 to transform NATO into a politico-economic union, the new American efforts at disarmament negotiations, and the aggressive promotion of the 1953 "atoms-for-peace" proposal into the International Atomic Energy Agency.[33] Much more spectacular was the new intimacy demonstrated by all the NATO powers after Moscow's technological coups in missiles and the investigation of outer space in October 1957. Proposals for a NATO pool of scientific information and personnel received favorable hearings both in the United States and among its allies.

Coping with the Neutrals. American policy-makers were officially upset by the rise of neutralism (although there was some doubt about whether they were as displeased as they sometimes seemed). In any case, after 1955 the United States faced the problem and soon came to two conclusions. First, any attempt to use coercion on the neutrals would be useless and possibly dangerous. They had made good their escape from the bipolar structure and American pressure might well only drive them closer to the Soviet. Second, the necessary minimum objective of American policy should be the maintenance of their neutral status. The neutrals were not aligned with the United States, it is true, but neither were they pro-Soviet. If the most the United States could accomplish was to guarantee their noncommitment to Moscow, then at least that much should be done. Within the boundaries formed by these two propositions, American policy took its shape.

New Approaches to the Soviet. By 1957 the pattern of American relations with the Soviet had not yet become clear. America had in some degree met Russia's request for a more relaxed tone in their mutual con-

---

[33] The Statute of this body was submitted for Senate approval of United States adherence on March 21, 1957; Senate approval was given in June. *Department of State Bulletin* (April 15, 1957), p. 615. A summary of the Statute can be found on pp. 618-624 of the same issue of the *Bulletin*.

tacts, and the climate of world affairs had thereby improved—save for a few crises. But substantive agreement had not emerged from happier procedural situations. The issues that first divided the Soviet from the United States remained unresolved and the cold war continued.

It seemed likely, however, that Washington would eventually accept the Soviet challenge to competitive coexistence, if for no other reason than that no attractive alternative seemed available. Stepping up the intensity of the conflict would be disastrous, and calling it off by mutual consent seemed impossible. The new Soviet threat had to be met by measures appropriate to its dimensions.

The new cold war did give the United States an opportunity to pick up particular points of controversy and—aided by the new climate—to bring them to successful solution. Through 1956 and 1957 they continued to be minor, having to do with the movement of persons, international trade, or minor political concerns, and a new optimism over disarmament. But optimists pointed out that it is out of this sort of thing that areas of major agreement are built, and that this augured well for the future; even pessimists admitted that cultural exchange with the USSR could hardly be dismissed as merely a breathing space before a total war. Both groups could also admit that a more civilized basis of relationships was necessary before there could be any broad settlement of disputes. The Soviet breakthrough in rocketry and the blow to American pride caused by "Sputnik" in late 1957 precipitated a reassessment of the course of the cold war. No responsible official, however, seriously contended that the altered Soviet-American relationship presaged any major reversal of the ongoing trends, at least as long as the United States could compete on a roughly equal basis with Moscow.

part 7:

CONTINUING ISSUES IN
AMERICAN POLICY

14 : Continuing political issues in American policy

Within American foreign policy as we have outlined it in the preceding chapters we have found a number of "continuing issues." These are problems stemming from the general policy line the United States has been pursuing that are peculiar in that they do not permit of any final resolution. Each has been met within the context of a given set of circumstances, but each change in the situational milieu has required that new answers be given to the old questions. Because they promise to be of long duration, we would profit by discussing at least the most important of these continuing issues.

As we take them up in this section of our study, we will break them down into four functional areas, corresponding roughly to the four channels by way of which states usually execute their policies: the political (or diplomatic) area, the military area, the economic area, and the psychological area. This chapter deals exclusively with issues of a political import; there follows one devoted to each of the other three. It seems scarcely necessary to point out again—we have made this point several times earlier—that these classifications are valid primarily as convenient foci of discussion. In practice the political, military, economic, and psychological dimensions of foreign policy blend into one another and form component parts of a single operational entity.

In this chapter we shall examine four diplomatic-political areas of continuing and fundamental concern to the over-all structure of American policy. Each represents a significant complex of issues; each has great relevance to American action in other areas, both geographic and functional; each has had a variety of answers recommended and, in some cases, attempted. The four we have selected are the issues (1) of American relations with the great powers, (2) of American relations with the free-world alliance, (3) of American relations with international organization, and (4) of American policy toward the smaller states generally and toward the issue of anti-colonialism specifically.

THE UNITED STATES AND THE GREAT POWERS

By the "great powers" in the contemporary world we mean (in addition to the United States) the USSR, Great Britain, China, and India. This listing reflects the new dynamics of world politics and differs markedly from any made at any earlier period of history. With this group of states collectively and with each of them individually American relations are destined to continue to be important, perhaps central. With regard to each of them certain complicating factors exist that make the establishment of a firm orientation difficult.

At least as of the moment this is written, we cannot lay down any generalizations about American policy toward the entire group. The course of world affairs since 1945 has been characterized by deep and bitter divisions among the major states and we have no reason to believe that this condition will soon be changed. Our discussion, therefore, will deal individually with the Soviet and with Britain, and (because of certain fundamental similarities) jointly with India and China.

The future of American-Soviet relations

No one can envisage any possible situation—barring the total eclipse of civilization in the wake of a general war—in which the United States and the Soviet Union would not be the two most powerful states in the world. If this be so, it follows that Soviet American relations will continue to be the bedrock of American policy, as they have been since 1945. There has been surprisingly little inclination in the United States to consider the long-term future of Soviet-American relations; as American experience accumulates, however, a greater sensitivity toward the necessity of such speculation seems to be dawning.[1]

The Alternatives. We may approach the question initially by cataloguing the possible alternatives. We may safely stipulate that American-Soviet relations in the future can follow only one of three broad paths: their general tone will either improve, remain generally the same, or deteriorate.

---

[1] An outstanding recent example is Henry L. Roberts, *Russia and America: Dangers and Prospects* (New York: Harper & Bros., Inc., 1956).

Deterioration in the presently tense cold-war atmosphere is possible only if relations break down into open war; it strains the imagination to conceive of any non-war relationship that could be more hostile than the cold war has been since 1947. The middle alternative, the continuation of the present cold war on approximately its current level of intensity, would leave room for considerable maneuver by both sides (such as the hard-soft continuum in Soviet policy) but would not open any route of escape from the present stalemate.

From the American point of view improvement in Russo-American relations could come about in any of three ways. First, Moscow might undergo a change of heart and surrender totally, adjusting Russian policy to American requirements on all issues. Second, the cold war might be called off by mutual consent and be replaced by an (implicit or explicit) agreement by both sides to ignore each other as much as possible. Third, a set of compromises on outstanding issues adding up to a *modus vivendi* could be worked out, thus providing a firm if limited basis for coexistence. Each of these, from the American point of view, would constitute an improvement in the tenor of Soviet-American relations.

The Probabilities. Taking into account both the trends of world politics and the predilections of the American people toward the prevailing concept of national interest, we may arrange these alternatives in a rough scale of probabilities. None of the outcomes is automatic; which of them actually occurs will depend in large measure upon deliberate decisions made by both American and Soviet policy-makers. But we may nevertheless project contemporary factors into a series of estimates of greater or lesser likelihood.

It seems safest to assert initially that the middle alternative, the indefinite prolongation of the cold war, is the least likely as the dominant note in long-range Soviet-American relations. We have seen that at least three factors are working to change the present character of the great-power struggle: the impatience of the other states of the world with a conflict that denies them solutions to their own problems; the growing demand among Americans for some new policy that will provide the sense of movement, purpose, and accomplishment that the cold war denies them; and the inability of the Soviet system to endure for long a policy whose main result is frustration. Together these three provide a great impetus to the trend toward changing the cold war into something else.

Ever since the 1955 Geneva Conference, the third alternative has also declined in probability. It is too much to say that total war between the United States and the USSR has been ruled out; only wilful blindness or utter fatuity would permit us to claim that there is no prospect of a worsening of Russo-American relations. But the latter years of the cold war have shown that statesmen on both sides of the Iron Curtain are taking pains to avoid the necessity of having to support policies with total war; each side has warned the other of certain interests that are vital and would be supported by war,[2] and each side has been studiously avoiding the application of extreme pressure on the other. Nor is it likely that either would seek to step up the pressure beyond its present level; both have reduced their margins of error to the point that any reckless step might trigger off the conflict both wish to avoid.

The various ways in which American relations with Moscow might improve are of differing degrees of probability. The possibility that the Soviet might be willing to ignore the United States, and that America would reciprocate, is perhaps the least likely of all the alternatives we are considering. The requirements of national existence in an interdependent world are such that, even if both states were willing to avoid each other in international contacts, such a development would be practically impossible. The necessities of world affairs make continued Soviet-American relations inevitable.

Almost as remote a possibility is the prospect of a Soviet surrender. We may safely disregard it as long as the present Russian regime retains its identity and its mission. Only a major upheaval inside Russia, one of a size sufficient to force a reconstitution of the government, could bring to power a group of rulers willing to accept the renunciation of what the Soviet had been attempting since 1945. Such an outcome, as we have suggested earlier, is unlikely but not impossible; it is of a low enough order of probability, however, that the United States dare not base its policy on its coming about spontaneously.

For the United States deliberately to seek to bring about such revolution would be a policy of some hope for success but with considerable attendant danger. The communist dictators, faced with the erosion of their power, might risk everything in an all-out attempt to destroy the United States; alternatively, even an anti-communist regime in Moscow might not be willing to abandon enough of the foreign policy of its predecessor to please the United States. The latter outcome would leave the United States virtually where it started.[3]

---

[2] For example, the Soviet made unmistakably clear in 1956 that it would regard direct American intervention in eastern Europe as a cause for war, while the "Eisenhower doctrine" made the same point about overt Soviet aggression in the Middle East.

[3] The writings of James Burnham, however, urge such a policy on the United States, especially his *The Coming Defeat of Communism* (New York: John Day, 1950).

The final possibility of improvement in Soviet-American relations is that of a gradual relaxation brought about by a progressive mutual accommodation of policy. This, as we have indicated in earlier chapters, is the outcome implicit in the over-all design of American policy. We have indicated the reasons for American confidence that the eventual outcome of the cold war will be the stabilization of Russo-American relations on a mutually tolerable level. It is this conviction that a climate of cold war can and will be changed to one of toleration and a modicum of cooperative action that has inspired the architects of American policy to proceed in the direction the United States has gone since 1947. Some other judgments of probability would have resulted in an entirely different approach.

Yet we must conclude this rapid survey of alternatives and probabilities with an obvious but necessary reminder. Accommodation is the most probable outcome of Soviet-American tensions, but it is by no means the inevitable or the only one. Its consummation requires good will and effort on both sides, and we need not be pessimists to point out that these preprequisites are not yet visible in Soviet behavior nor—to be candid—in any great measure in American conduct. Much remains to be done before such a happier day arrives.

Possible Areas of Agreement. We cannot predict the final form of Soviet-American accommodation nor when such an agreement could be reached. We can discover, however, certain issues in the general cold-war context that seem more susceptible to relatively early successful attack than do most of the others. In no particular order of priority, we may suggest four bones of contention between East and West the later history of which gives some grounds for optimism about their final resolution: (1) the reunification of Germany; (2) a security agreement and system for Europe; (3) reduction in armaments (discussed in Chapter 15); (4) the expansion of East-West trade and economic life generally.

Each of these questions seems to have received considerable reanalysis by both states since the summit conference of 1955 (on the agenda of which they all appeared). There is some reason to believe that both sets of leaders are more willing today to accept a viable compromise on them than at any point previously, and that negotiations on each of them are destined to increase in seriousness. Success in any (or all) of them would not, of course, end the cold war, but it would contribute largely to what might become an evolving pattern of accommodation.

The Policy Implications. Some of the implications for American policy of such an estimate of the future have been suggested in earlier chapters. At this point we need only to stress one or two general considerations. Probably the most important point is that the United States should seek to maintain a larger consistency in the face of circumstances that are often mutually contradictory; we have seen evidence of failure in this regard in Chapter 13. There is real need for a general policy line that concentrates on moving the United States as steadily as possible toward its long-term goal and also provides a rationale for short-range policies. Its continued lack would tend to make American action a series of limited undertakings, consistent neither with each other, with past commitments, nor with future plans.

An apt illustration of the dangers to which American policy is subject was provided in the late months of 1957. Under the shocks of "Sputnik" and the resultant Soviet intransigence, sectors of American opinion reacted violently. The dominant note in the comment was an insistence that the United States resume its bipolar posture and rebuild its policy on a primarily military base. So great became the clamor for sudden and drastic action to "catch up" with the Soviet that President Eisenhower felt compelled to make a series of addresses to the nation in which he attempted to fit the recent events into a larger framework and to reassure Americans that the new dimensions of Soviet strength did not in themselves require any major overhauling of American policy.

It would seem logical for us also to suggest that the general frame of American policy should be more directly oriented toward its expected outcomes. At the present time, any particular American action seems to be posited on some one of four mutually contradictory assumptions about Soviet-American relations. Segments of policy assume the inevitability of total war; others presuppose eventual Soviet surrender, the indefinite continuation of the cold war, or the achievement of accommodation. While admitting that a sound policy seeks to take account of all possibilities, it would seem justified for us to argue that greater emphasis could profitably be placed on the alternative that America feels most likely and that the others be given appropriately subordinate places. Greater economy of effort and clarity of purpose might well result from such a reordering of objectives.

Britain and the United States

Anglo-American relations have been the core of affirmative American policy since the end of World War II. Despite some inescapable controversy and considerable misunderstanding, the problems of American policy toward Britain have been matters more of detail than of fundamental orientation. Agreement on basic premises is as great as can ever be the case between two major states, and prospects for any different basis of relationships are remote.[4]

Britain: the Key Ally. From the moment that the United States began to implement its postwar policy decisions, Britain has been its key ally. A high degree of coincidence of interest, both in general terms and on a remarkably large number of specifics, has resulted in a long series of joint policy moves and a group of more elaborate collaborative enterprises. In the network of American alliances, Britain has bulked large; London participates in NATO, SEATO, and the Baghdad Pact for the Middle East. The United States has resisted all Soviet invitations to negotiate directly with Moscow on most questions of interest to Britain. In the United Nations close Anglo-American cooperation has been the normal practice, whether in the Security Council, the General Assembly, or any other organs. In the fields of technical assistance, of military and economic aid, and of propaganda, British cooperation has given American policy an extra impact. Even more significant that the specific projects on which British and American policies have been harmonized has been the constant and usually close consultation between the two capitals. Recent diplomatic history provides few such impressive examples of close and mutually satisfactory relations between allies in time of peace.

Anglo-American Disputes. The closeness of Anglo-American relations has been affected to some significant—although minor—extent by a series of annoying disagreements. These have been most apparent when open breaks between the allies have taken place (the most serious was American opposition to Britain's invasion of the Suez Canal Zone in 1956) but there has been a constant undercurrent of tension that has colored relations when it has not directly controlled them.

These conflicts between Britain and the United States grow out of causes both general and specific. Perhaps most fundamental is the inevitable stress caused by the great disparity in power between the two states. For Britons, long accustomed to considering themselves as citizens of the world's leading power, to take second place to a young and inexperienced America has been difficult. Anti-Americanism has complicated the partnership from its very outset. We must also admit that American attitudes have often not been calculated to soothe outraged British sensibilities, and frequently Anglo-American controversy has been a matter of embattled nationalisms nagging at each other.

---

[4] From among the many studies of Anglo-American relations, we may suggest Henry L. Roberts and Paul Wilson, *Britain and the United States* (New York: Harper & Bros., Inc., 1953) and Leon Epstein, *Britain: Uneasy Ally* (Chicago: University of Chicago Press, 1954).

But Anglo-American antagonism has had a more solid policy root as well. Despite the real harmony of interest on fundamentals, in many areas of the world British and American objectives have conflicted. On these points real disputes have arisen. Mention of a few of the more important of them will suggest both the scope and severity of the disagreements.

In Europe, London has been generally unenthusiastic about European integration and has slowed its pace markedly by abstaining from the Coal and Steel Community and the Defense Community, while successfully resisting attempts to make the Council of Europe a viable instrument of European action. It was not until after the Suez debacle in 1956 that the British government, under the leadership of Harold Macmillan, turned openly to Europe via the proposed common market plan and the atomic pool known as EURATOM. In the Far East, Britain opposed American policy toward communist China to the point of itself extending recognition to the regime of Mao Tse-tung. In southeast Asia the British resisted the American plan to enlist the southeast Asian states in their own defense and, in SEATO, obliged Washington to settle for less than it had originally hoped for. And, of course, the Middle East crisis of 1956 saw Anglo-American disagreement go to the point that the United States used open coercion on Britain following London's decision to act independently and in defiance of the United States.

Maintaining the Tie. Anglo-American controversy is always fuel for headlines on both sides of the Atlantic; the question is deeply involved in domestic politics in both nations, and each frequently finds in the other a convenient scapegoat for its own frustrations. Yet there is little possibility that the working agreement or the harmony of interest between the two states might dissolve. Both are status-quo powers; both recognize the need for substantive change in many world relationships if stability is ever to be attained; both insist that the necessary change be peaceful. Real disagreement arises only from the differing specifications each has for what would be an optimum solution to its own problems. The identity of purpose, however, is sufficiently great that each has ample room in which to adjust its differences in behalf of maintaining the tie that is so profitable and so necessary for both. Anglo-American relations will never be idyllic, but they will probably continue to be largely harmonious and cooperative.

The new powers: India and China

India and China are the two new great powers in the arena of world politics. The United States, itself a relative newcomer to this small circle, has had difficulty in orienting itself to deal with them. Its perplexity has been shared by the other major states and, be it noted, India and China as well have found it troublesome to devise effective policies vis-a-vis each other. The world has not yet become accustomed to having so much of its power located in these inexperienced hands.

Asian Centers of Power. Not the least of the difficulty is a byproduct of history. The present era is the first time since the birth of the state system that as many as two of the great powers have been Asian. A further complication is the fact that Japan, the first major Asian state, acted generally like a western nation in its foreign policy; Tokyo's behavior, although extreme and provocative, was nevertheless comprehensible to westerners. India and China, on the other hand, although they have the external trappings of western-style statehood, nevertheless have brought something new and distinctively Asian to great-power politics. The West cannot easily cope with Asian power, particularly when it is applied to the pursuit of objectives framed with an unfamiliar and distinctively Asian turn.

The United States has a special problem in confronting these two states, both in their own right and as representatives and spokesmen for a newly-militant Asia. Americans, as we have seen, have escaped most of the effects of what we might call the "post-imperialist psychosis" that complicates so much of European policy toward Asia. The United States, never a major imperialist power in Asia, has had little direct concern with the decay of empire there. Its problem has grown instead out of the heavily missionary background of American attitudes toward the Orient. Public opinion in America, although generally favorable toward the aspirations of Asians, nevertheless cannot seem to escape a patronizing attitude toward them. Asians frequently are thought of primarily as subjects for industrialization, westernization, or—in some cases—civilization. Americans want to save Asia from itself; that many Asians do not particularly want to be saved from themselves by Americans is either ignored or brushed off as irrelevant.

This unconsciously invidious approach has produced a reaction often puzzling to Americans: it has frequently infuriated Asians more than does the openly imperialist policy of European states. It irritates Americans to see that Britain has had generally greater success with both India and China than has the United States, despite the British record of imperialist conquest and exploitation. American "do-goodism" has had only limited effect, possibly because its psychic motivation has been apparent to its subjects.[5]

---

[5] This point is made generally by William O. Douglas, in *Strange Lands and Friendly People* (New York: Harper & Bros., Inc., 1951), and Chester Bowles, in *Ambassador's Report* (New York: Harper & Bros., Inc., 1954) and *The New Dimensions of Peace* (New York: Harper & Bros., Inc., 1955).

Continuing Political Issues in American Policy

The Problem of India. It is difficult to characterize American relations with India within any brief compass. They are many-sided, confused, and rapidly changing. In some areas reasonably good understanding prevails, while in others disagreement is nearly total. The basic tenor of the relationship is made complex by the fact that both states must largely improvise in dealing with each other; neither has any long history or controlling tradition to give shape to the relationship. Indian affairs remain one of the more unclear aspects of American policy.

As we indicated in Chapter 13, the United States originally assumed that an independent India would be pro-western and would find ample ground on which to agree with the United States. Washington's failure to communicate meaningfully with New Delhi and India's conception of its international role as not calling for immediate commitment in the cold war brought about a speedy worsening of Indian-American relations. The policy estrangement that endured from 1950 to 1957 had its roots in massive misunderstandings on both sides. Both American mass opinion and most politically articulate Indians insisted on judging one another in terms of stereotypes with only tangential relevance to actual policy problems. Both governments—particularly the American—struggled to break through the fog of emotion that complicated the development of a base for a stable relationship.

As the United States saw Nehru's India, the major problem was India's apparent attempt to be all things to all people. American analyses frequently found five mutually contradictory lines of Indian policy. (1) India considered itself a great power and insisted on being dealt with as such. (2) India also wished to lead and to speak for the small states and newly-independent regimes everywhere. (3) India had ambitions of Asian leadership. (4) India was determined on a literal version of neutralism: to remain entirely outside the scope of the cold war. (5) India was deeply determined to mediate the cold war and to bring peace to the world. Mr. Nehru's inability to reconcile these divergent objectives made India's policy subject to misinterpretation by all shades of American opinion.[6]

Especially annoying to the United States was India's approach to Soviet-American relations. Mr. Nehru and his advisers apparently felt that the mediator's role required that India maintain good relations with the communist world; there was some evidence also that India was greatly impressed by the Soviet's material achievements.[7] The upshot of this

[6] See Werner Levi, *Free India in Asia* (Minneapolis: University of Minnesota Press, 1952), for an analysis of Nehru's Asian policy.

[7] This point is made by William O. Douglas, in *A Russian Journey* (New York: Harper & Bros., Inc., 1956).

concern was that India felt itself compelled to show sympathy and cordiality toward the USSR and communist China, while feeling free to indulge its official disagreements toward the United States by chilly formality and anti-American propaganda. Americans reasoned that Nehru felt that it was safer to insult the United States than the Soviet; annoying as this attitude might be, Washington was forced to admit that it had some basis in fact.

The Hungarian crisis of 1956 and American policy during the contemporaneous Middle East imbroglio provided a possible ground for some reorientation of Indian-American relations. Mr. Nehru was both repelled by Soviet brutality and impressed by Washington's willingness to support Asians against America's European allies. His visit to Washington in December of that year raised some hopes that relations between the United States and India might be entering a new phase. Though concrete results of this conference were slow in coming, some observers felt that the most troublesome stage was over and that a beginning at real understanding had been made. More difficulties arose, however, from India's later incorporation of part of Kashmir into its own boundaries, and the future of Indian-American relations clouded again.

The Problem of China. Chinese affairs, long a concern of the United States, acquired a new dimension after 1949. The problem was no longer the familiar one of helping to build a China whose territorial integrity and political independence would be secure, but rather that of coming to terms with a China whose strength was unquestionable but whose intentions were open to serious question.

The new problem of China has three ingredients. First, China is now free from (at least Western) tutelage and, partly under Soviet sponsorship, is aggressively prosecuting its own foreign policy. Second, China is a communist state and constitutes the most populous unit in the camp hostile to the United States. Third, China is openly revisionist, seeking in a variety of ways to improve its international position. American policy has been slow to devise a strategy adequate to cope with this new manifestation of Chinese political dynamism.[8]

The base of a good deal of American policy toward China after 1949 was an apparent determination not to accept the fact of communist domination of the mainland. The United States withheld recognition

---

[8] For one set of recommendations about American policy, see W. W. Rostow, with Richard W. Hatch, *An American Policy in Asia* (New York: John Wiley, 1955). This volume is an outgrowth of W. W. Rostow and others, *The Prospects for Communist China* (New York: John Wiley, 1954). Another attempt at the same goal was made by Edwin O. Rieschauer, in *Wanted: An Asian Policy* (New York: Alfred A. Knopf, 1955).

of the Peiping regime, blocked communist representation of China in the United Nations, and openly supported Chiang Kai-shek's regime on Formosa. In general American action toward the Peiping government seemed built on the premise that Mao's victory was only a temporary interruption in the rightful occupation of power by the Kuomintang. Open American combat against Chinese "volunteers" in Korea and Peiping's provocative and belligerent behavior subsequently hardened American determination not to yield an inch to the communists either in principle or in practice.

By 1955 there was a widespread suspicion in official circles that this no-quarter policy was not yielding dividends proportionate to its cost; its ultimate implementation would logically call for affirmative American steps looking toward Mao's downfall, either by open war or by subversion. Failing a "power policy" to topple the regime, the rewards of militancy were not impressive. American rigidity on China had brought about a rift in the western alliance, while many Asian states were repelled by a policy that could be interpreted as fundamentally anti-Asian. Chinese affairs, for example, were not the least cause of Nehru's anti-Americanism. There seemed to be some ground for arguing that greater American flexibility might open new doors for American efforts to contain communism in Asia.

The heart of the matter, as Washington saw it, was the exact nature of Sino-Soviet relationships. Throughout 1955 and 1956, the impression grew that the two communist giants were not in total harmony despite the frequent parades of ideological solidarity. The disagreement, although still veiled, grew apparent in the aftermath of Soviet behavior in Hungary in 1956 as Chou En-lai made no secret of his distaste for Soviet brutality in Budapest and openly praised the "national communism" of the new Gomulka regime in Poland. Hopes grew in the United States that there was a real possibility of a break in the communist front in Asia.

The United States, in the autumn of 1955, began direct discussions with the Chinese. In relative privacy, American and Chinese representatives in Geneva discussed an agenda officially confined to the subject of the nationals of each state held captive in the other, but actually covering a much broader range of questions. Chou En-lai's new line on great-power relationships stressing the need for international cooperation (made public late in 1956) also opened a vista of a possible future rapport. The new China bulked large enough in the future of world affairs for the regularization of Sino-American relations to be a major question to the United States.

386

AMERICAN-ALLIED RELATIONS

Having to maintain relationships with more than 40 allies in time of peace is a completely novel experience for the United States. "Allies" traditionally are a by-product of war; when the United States has been at peace American tradition has insisted on the working minimum of fixed commitments. The cold war, however, forced the United States to accept the leadership of a massive coalition for the prosecution of free world policy. This new posture has required that Americans accustom themselves to the peculiar requirements of policies framed and executed within a multi-state context. Problems both of theory and of practice have grown out of this situation, and the subject of American-allied relations is one which the United States has yet to resolve satisfactorily.

American theories of alliance

The Myth of the "Free World." The basic bipolar assumption of American policy after 1947 contributed to the development of what we might call the "myth of the free world." Americans tended to assume that the world consisted of two groups of states, the communist and the noncommunist blocs, the one led by Moscow and the other by Washington. American policy has had certain objectives; the United States has been supported by a number of allies. If every state in the world were on one side or the other, and if the dividing line between them was the choice between freedom and communism, it was then only a short step to reason that all anti-communist states shared the same value system and the same general foreign-policy pattern.

This is the notion of the "free world." Americans seem to feel that the alliance of which their government is the leader is (or ought to be) a monolithic entity that opposes Moscow's pretensions with a single purpose and a single effort. United States policy often purports to speak for all its allies on a great variety of questions, and the revelation of intra-alliance disagreement often throws much of American public opinion and leadership into a strange catalepsy. Americans are fond of the shibboleth of "the unity of the free world," a notion often more pervasive than relevant. The "free world" is a concept of great importance, but in practice it has demonstrated significant limitations as an analytical focus for policy.

Students of international affairs know that the western alliance, like all alliances, is founded on coincidence of interest among its members, and that it cannot be interpreted as covering any substantive or procedural points by sheer implication. Cooperation among the allies is ensured only in those areas of action covering which ironclad agreements, embodying predetermined degrees of harmony, have been worked out. To assume that agreement on any single point implies agreement on any other point is not only to prepare the way for later disillusionment and disappointment, but frequently also to weaken the working effectiveness of such alliances as exist.[9]

The United States: Leader or Partner? Equally important to the issue of American-allied relationships is the question of the role of the United States within the alliance pattern it has worked out. There is considerable disagreement among Americans and foreigners alike about the nature of American responsibility to its associates and the degree of authority the United States is to be permitted in committing other members to courses of action they may not wish to follow.

This has often been put as a "leader-partner" dichotomy. In the most general analytical terms, the United States has only two alternatives open to it in dealing with its allies. It may, on the one hand, assume a position of absolute leadership, to which its power, its wealth, and its prestige seemingly entitle it. Alternatively, it may adopt a position of a partner and participate in (but not control or dominate) the formulation of joint policy. Although many gradations are possible on one side or the other of this proposition, and the dichotomy itself may be a questionable one, the two choices seem to represent a not unjust statement of the practical alternatives.

Between 1947 and 1954, the controlling theory in the United States was that of leadership.[10] The United States, paying much of the bill for the construction of the free world alliance, insisted on attempting to call the tune. Both in the development of intra-alliance relationships and in the common front presented to the Soviet world, American wishes were paramount. The weakened condition of many noncommunist states made it difficult and often impossible for them to resist American pressure, and a number of European, Asian, and Latin American countries were (as they saw it) coerced into accepting a purely American formula for the solution of a joint problem. This tendency reached its height during the Korean war, when American militancy caused serious rifts

---

[9] This point is elaborately developed by George F. Kennan, in *Realities of American Foreign Policy,* in Chapter II: "The Non-Soviet World."

[10] Reitzel, Kaplan, and Coblentz, *United States Foreign Policy, 1945-1955,* p. 429.

in the western alliance and forced India and its associates to break with the free world and to adopt a self-styled neutrality.

What caused considerable disquiet, even among the states most in agreement with the United States, was what American "leadership" of the alliance often meant in practice. Western Europe particularly harbored serious doubts of the wisdom and the skill of American policy-makers and its leaders questioned the implicit (and sometimes explicit) claim that only the United States knew the right answers to the questions facing the free world.[11] The inclination among many Americans to regard any deviation from the American line as evidence either of a lack of moral fiber or of a half-concealed admiration for Communism often irritated Europeans who considered themselves guilty of no more reprehensible offence than of differing with Washington over how to accomplish a particular objective. American leadership also showed a disconcerting tendency to interpret "western" objectives in purely American terms, and to assume (in a paraphrase of a statement attributed to then Secretary of Defense Charles E. Wilson) that "what is good for the United States is good for the free world." Some plaintive voices were even heard to inquire what in practice was the difference between Soviet satellitism and American leadership of its allies.

The potentially and actually disruptive effect of such a theory of leadership brought about an attempt at a change of policy and some modification in American practice. In mid-1954, President Eisenhower asserted that the United States was henceforth to adopt the partnership theory in dealing with its allies, and that the era of attempted dictation was over.[12] This decision had been brought about by the unfortunate consequences of the strong line and the accumulating evidence that coercion of the allies was becoming increasingly difficult. Secretary Dulles, abandoning the hard line vis-a-vis the free world as abruptly as he had the theory of "liberation" in dealing with the Soviet empire, spent the bulk of his effort during the first Eisenhower administration in a series of long negotiations designed to make the partnership concept a workable one. Persuasion instead of dictation, the adjustment of policy to a mutually satisfactory base instead of the imposition of an American formula, and a greater fund of patience in coping with allied disagreements came to be the marks of the new approach.

---

[11] Raymond Aron, *The Century of Total War* (Boston: Beacon Press, 1954), pp. 322-24. Mr. Aron, a distinguished French publicist, argues that the real cause of Europe's resentment at American leadership is Europe's realization of its own weakness.

[12] *New York Times* (August 5, 1954).

Partnership, of course, had its own pattern of difficulties. Its implementation required that the United States accept often extensive modifications of its own demands on the alliance, and also to accept open disagreement and occasional defiance from its associates. Both of these results had unfortunate repercussions among the American people. Partnership to a critical observer often looked perilously like a lack of decision, a failure of will, or an unworthy search after popularity abroad. Allied criticism of American action was met by equally hostile popular reactions in the United States. The American government, once it relaxed its efforts to enforce conformity from the other states of the free-world complex, was attacked by its own constituents for being too weak and by its allies for being yet too dominating.

The growth of neutralism, a predictable outcome of the partnership concept, brought down new torrents of criticism among Americans. As long as the United States was committed to avoid coercion in its relations with the noncommunist states, it was obliged to accept the possibility that some of them would use their newly guaranteed freedom of action to develop independent courses. When this actually happened, objections were heard both from those who condemned the government for weakness in permitting the neutrals to stray and from those who argued that a more sympathetic American policy would have prevented any such deviation.

It was also obvious that partnership, as an action principle, was not especially easy of application. However much the President and his advisers may have wished to transform the western alliance into a community of free peoples in which the United States was but the first among equals, such Elysium could be only imperfectly attained. Americans would not permit their own interests to be disregarded in the formulation of joint policy, and even a limited truncation of American objectives proved to be unpalatable to articulate elements of American opinion. In response to considerable public pressure the American official attitude stiffened considerably, and by mid-1956 several of the western allies were again convinced that at least some of the more unfortunate (from their point of view) manifestations of "leadership" were again controlling in Washington. The old warnings about the quality of American policy and the inept manner of its execution began to circulate again, especially in the capitals of western Europe. This attitude contributed to the Anglo-French decision to develop an independent policy in the Middle East late in 1956.

Partnership was revived in late 1957, when the Soviet satellite program brought all the NATO countries to a new realization of their mutual weakness. Higher levels of cooperative enterprise were immediately projected at the Decmber, 1957 meeting of the NATO Council, clouded as it was by President Eisenhower's illness.

The "Senior Partner." It has proved difficult to resolve the leader-partner controversy in any absolute terms. Very few Americans really want the western alliance to be reduced to a featureless collection of satrapies applauding every American move; even fewer, however, feel that American interests would be adequately cared for if free world policy were made by some agency in which United States influence was in a clear minority. There are some valid grounds, furthermore, for arguing that America's power preponderance carries with it not only the privilege of playing the leading role in formulating common policy, but also the responsibility for doing so. The United States may not be the only state in the free world with interests that must be considered, but certainly both its concerns and its capacity to fulfill them far surpass those of any of its allies. Free-world policy must be in some large measure American policy. One way out of the dilemma would seem to lie in some such notion as that of the "senior partner." If the United States were to devise its policy in the light of an enlightened awareness of the real needs and wants of its associates, if it were able to enlarge its concerns to take account of at least the most important of the common interests of the alliance, and if it were to concentrate its major effort on those projects that genuinely reflect such community of interest as exists, there would seem to be some ground for hoping that intra-alliance tension could be held to a minimum without adopting either extreme position. No conceivable formulation, of course, could guarantee that American-allied relations would be always harmonious and that joint policy would reflect unanimity. The problem, however, is not that of institutionalizing perfection, but the less lofty one of constructing some American theory of alliance that would enable the free world to maximize its efforts on the points of agreement and to hold its controversies to a level sufficiently low as not to impair the achievement of common goals.

Problems of alliance

The issue of leadership or partnership is important in the American theory of alliance because of certain problems that have arisen within the structure of the free world. There are several fundamental grounds for tension whose consequences must be expected and to which adjustment must be made by all participants. Some of these problems grow out of the nature of alliances in general and are in no sense peculiar to the free world in the cold war, while others are functions of the special circumstances and times that confront the noncommunist states in coping with the Soviet menace.

Disparities of Strength. Perhaps most relevant to the crises of the free world is the fact that there is such a great disparity of strength between the United States and all of its allies. America's 40-odd associates include states of all sizes and degrees of strength, from such miniscule entities as El Salvador, Luxembourg, and Haiti to such extensive, populous, and relatively powerful states as Britain, Pakistan, and Brazil. None of them, however, is capable of matching American strength except in an occasional category. Much as the United States may wish to rationalize the partnership theory of alliance, the stubborn fact remains that American power towers over that of any of America's allies.

It is not so clear, however, whether American strength is greater than that of all its allies combined; it might be possible to balance the capabilities involved so as to create a situation in which American power was overshadowed by the combined weight of the allies. Such a calculation, however—in addition to its problematical nature—would suffer from an irrelevance to any easily conceivable situation. The American alliance pattern is not a single entity, but rather a group of multi- and bi-lateral pacts. United States membership is the only point common to all of them. Mobilizing all these otherwise largely competitive states in support of the single objective of overbalancing American power would involve an almost total revolution in world political relationships. Whether or not the United States outweighs all its allies is a consideration of only remote significance to the actual workings of the free-world system.

It is undeniable, however, that the disparity of strength among the allies creates problems, of which the central one is that of the role of the United States. The major goal of the free world's political effort is the development of a unified policy not dominated by the United States but to which America will lend adequate support. This would be difficult to work out even if all the partners were of approximately equal stature; in a situation in which one member is overwhelmingly powerful it becomes extremely complex.

Intra-alliance Conflicts of Interest. One troublesome dilemma of the free world is how to dispose of the conflicts of interest among its members. These, as we know, are inescapable as long as the American bloc is not structured into a simple spokesman-satellite pattern. To what extent are allied interests to be subordinated to American concerns; how far will the United States go in adjusting its wishes to those of its allies; how much independence of action should allies be permitted in following their own purposes; what, in practice, is to constitute a "rupture" of the alliance; how should conflict between two or more of its allies be dealt with by the United States: these are only a few of the recurrent questions stemming from the central fact that membership in the free world does not entail the abandonment of national objectives.

Certain rough principles have been developed by the United States to guide it in some of these problems. Under the partnership principle after 1954, American leadership made a real attempt to work for the development of a joint policy on major issues. On the central problem of Russo-western relations, Washington steadfastly refused to deal with the Soviet except in company with its major allies (we should note, however, that in principle some American freedom of action was expressly reserved on certain questions, although never exercised). Even on the tangled Middle Eastern situation, the United States labored (energetically if not especially effectively) for a common front on the Suez issue until Britain and France chose to act on their own and invaded the Canal Zone.

This latter crisis demonstrated what at least the Eisenhower administration felt to be the permissible limits of independent action by its allies. No free world state could count on either American support or American approval if it pursued its own interest to the point of violating the basic American interest in peaceful process and the procedural status quo. American opposition to Britain and France in that dispute was a natural application of the action principles of American policy.

By 1955 and 1956, the United States had also initiated a policy of attempting to develop new common interests among the members of its alliance to minimize the prospect of a rupture of the free world. A negative interest holds a grouping together only as long as the common threat endures; a more positive purpose would provide for a longer-lasting bond. The new emphasis in American policy given to such issues as peaceful atomic development, an economic and social dimension to NATO, and issues of international trade are all aimed at minimizing the prospect that internal disharmonies of interest would fray the alliance as the direct Soviet military threat lessens.

Nationalist Resentments. Emphasis on the common purposes of the western alliance should not obscure the fact that many of the states with which the United States is associated harbor fundamental nationalist resentments toward America. Latin America was prepared to revive the bogey of Yankee imperialism; Europe tended to remember American isolationism of the 1920's, distrusted American inexperience, impetuosity, and naivete, and rebelled against its own overtly subordinate status; Japan remembered its half-century of hostility; Asia and the Middle East objected to America's missionary orientation and feared American political and cultural hegemony. Each of these forces, never completely subdued and occasionally dominant in particular states, served to vitiate many otherwise constructive enterprises.[13]

Americans proved slow to grasp these nationalist biases and to adequately allow for them. Either they were overlooked entirely in the bland confidence that American generosity, strength, and good intentions were obvious to all, or else they were put down to the machinations of pro-communist propaganda and hence put down as unworthy. It was not until Americans realized they were in danger of becoming "unpopular"—a fate regarded by many Americans in their personal lives as being worse than death—that many of the implications of nationalist hostility became apparent. Then its effect was largely to awaken equivalent hostilities within the general American public, and a surly distrust to some extent replaced the enthusiastic reformism of another day.

The new attitude was as unrealistic and as destructive of intelligent planning as had been the old. It would seem that the full efficiency of the western alliance must wait upon the willingness both of Americans and of the other peoples of the free world to modify or suspend the worst of their nationalist hostilities in the interest of a common purpose they all agree is of primary importance.

THE UNITED STATES AND INTERNATIONAL ORGANIZATION

American attitudes and behavior toward international organization provide one of the most impressive and instructive contrasts with the period of the 1920's and 1930's. The rebirth of isolationism that followed World War I took its characteristic form from the spontaneous and consistent effort to avoid "entanglement" in the League of Nations system; for millions of Americans the League epitomized the devious world of diplomacy they were seeking to shut out. We have already noted how this frame of mind was outmoded by the pressure of events during the war years and how the United States was one of the founders and principal architects of the United Nations system. Throughout the entire period since 1945, American commitment to the principle of interna-

---

[13] Reitzel, Kaplan, and Coblentz, *United States Foreign Policy*, pp. 355-56.

tional organization, though not total, remained consistently high, and the maintenance, strengthening, and employment of the United Nations endures as a cardinal procedural principle of American policy.

The United States and the United Nations

The United Nations Idea in American Policy. It seems scarcely necessary to elaborate upon the meaning of the "United Nations idea." The framers of the Charter knew better than any one else that they were not drafting a constitution for a world government, and that the United Nations could never be any more than a mechanism for the more efficient implementation of such will to cooperate as existed among the membership. The "United Nations idea" that made the organization such a hopeful portent in its early days and that revitalized it again during the latter months of 1956 was the hope that states generally would accept the principle that United Nations procedure was the type of action most conducive to permanent improvement of world relations; the goal was to funnel the great majority of all national policy moves through United Nations channels. The organs of the Charter were thought of as instruments for the harmonization of national interests rather than for the creation of entirely new policies.[14]

How has the United States reacted to the challenge of the "United Nations idea"? On balance, we may say that America has made a reasonably good record in acting through United Nations channels, but by no means an exceptional one. The major elements of postwar American policy have been executed both within the United Nations and outside it; the most important cold-war moves, such as the alliance system, Point 4, economic assistance, and so on, have generally been independently executed. Washington took care, however, to make all its actions square more or less directly with its obligations and privileges under the Charter.[15]

The most spectacular example of American reliance on United Nations procedures was, of course, the series of General Assembly resolutions in 1956 condemning Soviet behavior in Hungary and the Anglo-French-

---

14 See Daniel S. Cheever and H. Field Haviland, *Organizing for Peace* (Boston: Houghton-Mifflin Co., 1954), ch. 28: "The New Diplomacy and World Order."

15 The mutual-security pacts of the United States, for example, make specific reference to the obligations of the parties under the Charter. See *Disarmament and Security: A Collection of Documents, 1919-1955* (Washington, D. C.: U. S. Government Printing Office, 1956 pp. 531 (NATO), 599 (Philippines treaty), 600-601 (ANZUS), 607 (Japanese treaty), 608-9 (Formosa treaty), 612-13 (SEATO), 650 (Rio Pact).

Israeli invasion of Egypt. Here, at a crucial moment in American policy, President Eisenhower placed American trust almost entirely in the mechanisms of international organization and—to the surprise of considerable segments of American public opinion—discovered that in at least this case the essentials of American policy were adequately achieved. Much of the world wondered if this dramatic move foreshadowed a much greater emphasis on the United Nations in future American action. American popular reaction to this move reflected a major upsurge in public support of the United Nations.[16]

The United Nations as a Tool. In general the attitude of the United States toward the United Nations has been the same as that shared by the other great powers. To a major state with global interests, extensive commitments, and a sensitive nationalism, the notion that all policy is to be executed in the chambers of the United Nations cannot help but be considered somewhat naive. The characteristics of United Nations action —publicity, majority vote, the preponderance of small-state opinion, leisureliness, and the disavowal of other than collective force—often are felt to be overly constraining to great powers.

The normal view among the permanent members of the Security Council (who, with India, constitute the group of "major powers" in the organization) is to consider the United Nations as a tool of national policy. Like any policy technique, on appropriate occasions its use is mandatory, at other times either expedient, immaterial, undesirable, or inimical. The decision by such a government whether or not to "go to the United Nations" is not based on any preference for such action in the abstract, but rather upon the circumstances of the case and the nature of the objective sought.

These generalizations roughly characterize the American approach to the United Nations. As a status-quo state interested in stabilizing world relationships, it has been appropriate for the United States to find work-

---

[16] A Gallup Poll published in the Atlanta *Journal-Constitution* on December 9, 1956, made this clear. On the question "How important do you think it is that the United States try to make the United Nations a success—very important, fairly important, or not so important?" the comparative percentages for 1952 and late 1956 were as follows:

	1952	*1956*
Very important	77	85
Fairly important	10	8
Not so important	6	3
No opinion	7	4

The same poll pointed out that the percentage of people who felt that the United Nations was doing a "poor job" had steadily declined from 36 per cent in 1951 to 11 per cent in late 1956. Reprinted by permission.

ing through the United Nations expedient a larger share of the time than would such revisionist states as the Soviet Union or Yugoslavia. But despite the relatively favorable record America has made compared to the USSR, many of the smaller states complain that American policy has often bypassed international action in behalf of unilateral procedures.

In defense of American policy, it might be pointed out that the first dozen years of the world's experience with the United Nations had demonstrated that the organization had definite limits beyond which it had no usefulness. Constructed on the principle of great-power cooperation for peace, it proved itself powerless to cope with the cold war in any but the most indirect ways. The United States was obliged to take direct action in prosecuting the anti-communist struggle simply because no effective means existed to act through the United Nations.

A good case could be made to the effect that significant portions of longer-range American planning (looking beyond the cold war) did take the United Nations into account, and that the "tool" view of the organization in no way embodied a negative judgment about its usefulness in appropriate situations. According to this argument, direct American cold-war policy was in preparation for the day that the United Nations would be able to function effectively in affirmative action for a more stable world.

The United States, the United Nations, and World Public Opinion. The Middle-East crisis of 1956 provided a dramatic demonstration of this thesis. World public opinion (particularly in the uncommitted states) turned sharply against Britain, France, and Israel following their invasion of Egypt. Acting through the United Nations, the United States was able to mobilize this opinion into an overwhelming majority demand that the three states evacuate their conquered territory at once. The weight of American and United Nations disapproval was too heavy for the three capitals to bear and all eventually submitted to the decisions of the General Assembly. Washington attempted also to create the same force of opinion on the issue of Soviet interference in Hungary and, although the results were slower and less spectacular, evidence accumulated that even the Soviet was to some extent amenable to the pressure. Not even a communist dictatorship can long withstand a near-unanimous condemnation by a world opinion mobilized and speaking with a single voice through the United Nations.

The broader lesson contained in this event was not lost in Washington. In escaping from the illusions of the interwar period, Americans had lost much of their former faith in international public opinion as a tool of policy. Although moral force was admittedly not the only ponderable in international affairs, American policy-makers had fallen into the error

397

of thinking that it had no effect whatsoever. The unexpected power demonstrated by the United Nations had implications for the future of American policy. If the United States could keep its policy generally in harmony with the demands of mass opinion throughout the noncommunist world, a powerful new weapon would have been added to the American armory. The problem of the United Nations in American foreign policy thus acquired a new dimension; how to keep the formidable majorities amassed during these two crises together in support of American aims. The so-called "Eisenhower Doctrine" for the Middle East, approved by Congress in March, 1957, was the first step in this effort; the strong American support given King Hussein of Jordan during the disturbances of April 1957 and later in the year was also regarded as a move toward consolidating this position.

The United States and supranational organization

The drastic redistribution of power brought about by the war caused a renewed interest in the question of supranational political organization. The concentration of strength in the two new giants made most of the states of the world acutely aware of their own insecurity and set them thinking about ways to escape this unhappy situation. One of the frequently discussed techniques of doing so—particularly in the early postwar period—was the creation of political entities on a basis greater than the national state.

The extensive discussion and the tentative beginnings at the implementation of the idea raised an issue of some pertinence to the United States. It did not become a central question during the first dozen years after the war, but no one dares say unequivocally that the problem will never become critical to Americans. In its details it had relevance at two levels, that of regional federation and of world government.

The United States and Regionalism. As far as the noncommunist world was concerned, American policy toward regionalism was favorable.[17] The more tightly organized the free world became, the better for the United States. We must point out, however, that this sympathy with regional supranational groupings did not go so far as to suggest that the United States itself might join in such an undertaking. The creation of new vehicles of government was up to smaller and weaker states; the United States was determined to preserve its own freedom of action.

---

[17] An interesting analysis of the problem in a context of "sociological jurisprudence" was made by F. S. C. Northrop, in *European Union and United States Foreign Policy*.

Thus Washington spurred the creation of the European Coal and Steel Community, the European Defense Community, the projected European common market, and the Europe-wide atomic pool known as "Euratom," but turned a deaf ear to the proposals from private sources on both sides of the Atlantic suggesting the creation of some federal superstructure incorporating the "Atlantic Community." Americans had come far in their new comprehension of world affairs, but at no time after 1945 were they willing to submerge American sovereignty in any "superstate." Even such a natural grouping as the states of the North Atlantic region was kept at the intergovernmental level of NATO rather than carried forward in any more elaborate framework. Other suggested regional groupings outside Europe received less attention in Washington and never went far toward fruition by means of American support.

The United States and World Government. The same general theme ran through the less-than-cursory attention paid to the question of world government after 1945. Official policy, backed by the bulk of public opinion, usually dismissed the entire idea as the crackpot scheme of a group of visionary idealists; some patriotic organizations hinted darkly that the movement was at least quasi-communist.[18] It is true that under the cold-war conditions between 1947 and 1957 there was little immediate relevance to a discussion of whether or not the United States should forthwith merge its sovereignty with that of the Soviet, its western allies, and all the neutrals in a single mechanism of world government. The problem of the United States was phrased more in terms of a formula for survival rather than for the transformation of all political relationships.

And yet, as we suggested in an early discussion, the ultimate implications of American national interest in the postwar era could not be dismissed indefinitely. If peace, order, and stability on a worldwide basis were actually the interests that the United States was pursuing and was determined to pursue in the future, at some point the question of supranational organization would have to be faced. The history of societies everywhere demonstrates that social stability is feasible only within an elaborate pattern of institutions; the more complex the working institutional structure, the greater is the stability and predictability of human behavior. If peace, order, and stability were to mean anything in terms of final purposes, the issue of whether or not the United States would be willing to carry its interests to the point of promoting world government would have to be resolved some day.

---

[18] As a representative sample of this latter attitude, see Joseph P. Kamp, *We Must Abolish the United States: the Hidden Facts Behind the Crusade for World Government* (New York: Constitutional Education League, 1950). The Appendix, entitled "Communist Frontiers and Subversive Socialists," is particularly interesting.

SMALL STATES AND ANTI-COLONIALISM

An issue that was relatively late in making its appearance in American policy and that could only with difficulty be fitted into an exclusively cold-war mold is the bifurcated question of American policy toward the small states of the world generally and toward the related burning problem of anti-colonialism. After 1954 some analysts insisted that this question, rather than the more widely-discussed one of direct Soviet-American relations, would hold the key to the success or failure of American policy over the long term.[19]

The two issues are distinct but so closely connected that they can conveniently be discussed together. Not all small states are anti-colonial, nor are all ex-colonial states small. Enough states fit both categories, however, and the questions grow from such similar roots that their combined impact on American policy is exerted in the same general direction.

The small states and the cold war

The "small states" of the world include the fifty or so smallest members of the international society, although drawing a definite line between small, medium, and medium-large states is difficult.[20] Their general approach to the cold war has been governed essentially by the fact of their absolute and relative weakness and their groping attempts to find some common cause in restraining the super-powers.

Small-state Groupings. The small states have fallen into a number of subgroups of varying degrees of formalization. Each is distinct enough, however, to have something of a character and at least the elements of a common policy of its own.

As of early 1957, there were five such groupings active in world politics and it appeared as if one of them were undergoing further fission into two separate blocs. These were: (1) the Latin American bloc; (2) the Commonwealth states other than Britain; (3) the small states of western Europe led by Scandinavia and the Low Countries; (4) the Soviet satellites; and (5) the "Afro-Asian" bloc. This latter group, under the pressures of the Middle-East and Hungarian crises of 1956, gave some indica-

---

[19] See, for example, Chester Bowles, *Africa's Challenge to Americans* (Berkeley: University of California Press, 1956).

[20] One interesting attempt to establish criteria of size (both in area and in population) is made in Samuel Van Valkenburg and Carl L. Stotz, *Elements of Political Geography*, second ed. (Englewood Cliffs, N.J.: Prentice-Hall, Inc., 1955), pp. 54-55.

tion of splitting into an exclusively Arab bloc and a South-Southeast Asian grouping. The effect of these groups was most obvious in the United Nations, where the requirements of public voting and overt alignments made them apparent; in the patterns of diplomatic maneuvering, increasing intra-group solidarity was shown by all of them after 1954, even including (at least during the relaxation of Soviet militancy during 1955 and 1956) the Eastern European satellites of the USSR.

The Rise of Neutralism. Beginning in 1954, each of these groups, acting in the ways open to it in its special circumstances, began increasingly to show inclinations toward neutralism in the cold war. The Afro-Asians, under India's leadership, led the way, followed at irregular intervals and with varying degrees of freedom by the others. The extent to which each group was consistent within itself in its commitment to neutralism and the nature and importance of the moves it took depended in practice upon each state's location with respect to the great powers. Nehru's group was least involved, and could make the first and—as yet—the greatest move out of the cold-war orbit. Latin America on the western side and the Soviet satellites on their part had the least freedom of movement and were able to change their positions only slightly. The European small powers, with their tradition of neutrality, discussed the prospect openly but made no overt break; the Commonwealth members (other than those in south Asia) stayed with the West but only after considerable analysis of their positions. '

Why the small states chose neutralism is no great mystery, and is a question we considered in Chapter 13. It seems fair to summarize their position as one that found the cold war to be a great-power struggle, and one in which their interests as small powers were involved only peripherally. They were perfectly willing (within limits) for the United States and the Soviet to settle their differences if only they would leave the rest of the world alone.

American Policy. American attitudes and policy toward the small states between 1947 and 1957 passed through three perceptible stages, corresponding roughly to the three phases into which we divided the cold war in Chapter 13.

Up to about 1950, the bipolar assumptions of the United States considered all small states as actual or potential allies of one of the two great leaders, and a neutral small state was unthinkable. American policy was therefore aimed at winning as many as possible of these states to the camp of the United States.

Between 1950 and 1954, the United States became officially aware of the distinct groups into which the small states were dividing themselves, with the first obvious ones being Latin America, the Commonwealth, and the Afro-Asians. The strength of the new group orientation of these states was first shown in the General Assembly and later in various regional conferences (such as Commonwealth Conferences, the Bandung Afro-Asian Conference in April, 1954, and various inter-American meetings).

The third stage of American comprehension of the small-state problem came with the recognition of the basic identity of interest of all minor powers when they have a free opportunity to express it, demonstrated most dramatically in the United Nations votes on the Middle-East crisis of 1956. In the most important vote, every member of the five groups listed (except Australia and New Zealand) agreed to demanding a cease-fire and the withdrawal of the forces invading Egypt.[21]

If the latter development of small-state consciousness were to continue, and if the bipolar structure of the world were to continue to dissolve, American policy was increasingly destined to take account of the combined force of the minor powers. With United Nations membership rising to 82 (after the admission of Japan in 1956 and Ghana and Malaya in 1957), and with the vast majority being small nations, the extent to which these states could mobilize a united public opinion would be the measure of their effect on world politics. Very few observers could be found who were certain that this impact would be a minor one. One index of their growing power was their success at the 1957 General Assembly in forcing the United States to agree in principle to a broadening of the membership of the Disarmament Subcommission to include small-power membership.

The United States and anti-colonialism

"Anti-colonialism," a word symbolizing a potent force in world affairs today, is a product of the contemporary era. Since 1945 the great colonial empires of the nineteenth century have been rapidly melting away; coincident with this development (and to some extent its cause), there has appeared a vast current of opinion that condemns as immoral and illegal the very principle of imperial rule. The source of this attitude is found in the nationalist aftermath of the successful colonial revolutions in Asia and Africa after 1945, but it is by no means confined to ex-colonial peoples. There has always been something of a guilty conscience in the

---

[21] For a summary of American policy toward the uncommitted states up to early 1956, see Reitzel, Kaplan, and Coblentz, *United States Foreign Policy*, pp. 314-18, 453-7.

western world about the subjugation of alien peoples, and this has come to the surface since the end of the war. The ex-colonial states and the mass support they command in the West (to say nothing of the encouragement they receive from the USSR) have combined to make the word a rallying point for some of the most potentially explosive forces in the modern world.[22]

The Meaning of Anti-colonialism. Anti-colonialism has meaning in a variety of contexts. At its simplest, it stands for the rapid and total dismantling of all forms of imperialism. To borrow the language of the Charter (Article 73), anti-colonialism insists that the category of "non-self-governing peoples" be eliminated from the world's political vocabulary. It is the right of one people to rule over another—regardless of any extenuating circumstances—that the missionaries of anti-colonialism are busy denying.

But anti-colonialism in practice goes much further. It does not stop with attacking the legal relationships of ruler-colony, but challenges what some of its practitioners call the "colonial mentality." This means that the task of anti-colonialism is not ended by a declaration of independence, but that it does further to a variety of social, economic, and (especially) psychic goals. Anti-colonialism will not be content until ex-colonial states are accepted as full and equal partners in the world political process, until equality of deference is accorded them, and until their purposes and objectives are judged to be as important and as inherently worthy as those of older nations. This has meant inevitably that anti-colonialism has come to carry unmistakable overtones of racial equality, of the relative merits of different civilizations and culture, and of a demand for industrial and technological parity.

The Impact on the United States. The United States was, in its inexperience with imperialism as practiced by Europe, totally unprepared for the violent effect of anti-colonialism on the pattern of international politics. At a time when Washington was laboring to construct a framework of unity for the free world, and when some of its major partners were the world's leading colonial powers, it seemed a regrettable and almost irrelevant digression when the new states of Asia began to raise the issue of anti-colonialism.

The slowness of American response to the new force led many Asian leaders to conclude that the United States had proved false to its own

---

[22] See Kenneth Robinson, "World Opinion and Colonial Status," *International Organization* (November, 1954); for a critical appraisal of the impact of anti-colonialism on the United Nations, see Vernon Aspaturian, "The Metamorphosis of the United Nations," *The Yale Review* (Summer, 1957).

revolutionary and anti-imperialist tradition. They feared that Americans had been seduced by Britain and France into becoming apologists for an "outworn" imperialist outlook, and that American policy had acquired a racist character that classified the new states as "lesser breeds without the law." With some reluctance and regret, many anti-colonialists turned to the Soviet as being more sympathetic toward the aspirations of freedom and equality that they harbored.

This development again caught the United States off guard. The new turn in the anti-colonial attitude caused sharply divided opinions among Americans. Some argued that this proved the essentially communist nature of the revolt against imperialist authority, and urged that the United States join vigorously in suppressing independence movements aimed at destroying the bonds of empire. Others contended that the liquidation of empire and the appearance of new states was inevitable and that several hundred millions of newly independent people were soon to be added to the world political community. These new states and peoples would constitute a powerful factor, one that the United States would ignore only at its own peril.

A New American Policy? From 1947 to 1956, American policy on this issue was never clarified. Washington, reluctant to weaken its European allies, did little overtly and very little more covertly to speed the withdrawal of imperial authority, but neither did it ever unequivocally oppose the forces of independence. Put in the opposite way, it can be said that the United States mildly encouraged the colonial states to continue imperial rule, but on a more enlightened and humanitarian basis, while at the same time giving studiously nonspecific indications that it retained its traditional adherence to the principle of self-determination. The upshot was that neither the European states nor the anti-colonial peoples were satisfied.

American policy, however, took what appeared to be a dramatic turn in 1956. The split with Britain and France over the invasion of Egypt won Washington expressions of support and loyalty from the entire ex-colonial world. President Eisenhower's explanation of American action as being in defense of the rights of small nations and of the principles of legal equality and justice for everyone seemed to most Asians to be what they had been hoping the United States would say. When American policy remained consistent throughout the crisis, and as Vice-President Nixon went off on a widely-publicized tour of the new nations of Africa, it seemed to many as if a radically new departure in American policy was undertaken. The world watched anxiously to see what precise forms the American attempt to come to terms with anti-colonialism would take.

404

15:   Continuing military issues in American policy

A t various points in the preceding chapters we have alluded to the military ingredient in American foreign policy. We have noted that one of the characteristics of the post-1945 era is the closer interrelation of military, political, and economic factors in the foreign relations of the United States. Americans, to whom military affairs were a matter to be traditionally dealt with in a crisis atmosphere of war or near-war, have been obliged to devise a consistent military policy for times that, if not truly peaceful, were at least not marked by all-out warfare. With little of consistent tradition to guide the United States, and with the stakes in national and international power and prestige so high, it is no wonder that the first decade and more of the postwar era witnessed no entirely satisfactory resolution of the military issues in American policy.

In this chapter we shall examine three of the broader and more persistent questions that have arisen since 1945. We shall first deal with American military policy in general, considering the military mission of the United States and examining the controversy between the advocates of a "balanced force" and those of the "new look." Next we shall take up American overseas defense obligations, both in extent and in nature. Finally we shall summarize the problem of arms limitation, reduction, and control, often stereotyped in the popular term "disarmament."

UNITED STATES MILITARY POLICY

The American military mission

The military establishment of any state is an instrument of the state, to be used for the implementation of appropriate policies. As such, it is a

405

part of the arsenal of techniques any goverment has at its disposal. The military mission of the United States, therefore, is inseparable from the totality of American policy objectives and is comprehensible finally in terms of the contribution it makes to their accomplishment.[1]

Granted the nature of American foreign policy and the concept of national interest which it serves, we may say generally that the American military mission is to put the armed might of the United States at the service of international peace, order, and stability. We have stipulated that this is most expeditiously accomplished by preserving the procedural status quo and working desirable substantive change. In this way, American armed forces exist for the purpose of deterring a potential revisionist state (an "aggressor") from seeking to advance its policy by armed attack on the United States security sphere and of warding off such an attack by active combat if one should occur.[2]

The Deterrent Mission. The story is told that General Curtis LeMay, Commander of the Strategic Air Command of the United States Air Force, once said: "If war comes, SAC will have failed in its primary mission." Whether or not this is an accurate quotation, the idea it expresses is central to much American military thinking. American military power has the primary mission of preventing wars from happening; for a status-quo nation such as the United States, the most successful wars are the ones that never have to be fought.

Under conditions of modern technology, deterring a potential aggressor is only partially a matter of defensive ability. Although the race to develop effective neutralizing techniques to nuclear bombs, supersonic aircraft, guided missiles, rockets, and so on is neverending, the offense in warfare yet enjoys the advantage over the defense that it gained at the beginning of World War II. Today, the most elaborate and expensive defenses can afford only partial protection against modern weapons. Military security, therefore, tends to be largely a function of a nation's ability to retaliate to attack. No sane leader will attack another state if he is certain he will be overwhelmed in return; only a foolhardy one will launch a modern total war if he is convinced that his enemy can and will reply with an equal amount of force. Modern warfare, to be a good bargain, requires an enormous margin of superiority. Deterrence, therefore, in theory does not require absolute superiority over any possible enemy or even

---

[1] See W. D. Puleston, *The Influence of Force in Foreign Relations* (New York: Van Nostrand, 1955), especially chapters 2, "Land, Sea, and Air Forces as Factors of Peace," and 7, "Averting War by Means of Force."

[2] See Edgar W. Furniss, Jr., *American Military Policy* (New York: Rinehart & Co., 1957).

equality with him; adequate reprisal power to discourage attack is sufficient to accomplish the mission, even if the total available is less than that of the enemy.

The Combat Mission. But the American military machine must be prepared to deal with the situation arising from an overt resort to arms by an enemy; it must be prepared to fight and win any probable war. This is a more familiar problem to Americans; it has seemed to many as if this is the true and natural mission of the United States Army, Navy, and Air Force.

But here again the impact of modern weapons has complicated what was once a reasonably clear and simple problem. Modern war, in practice, can assume either of two forms: total war for total objectives, or limited war for limited goals (what is sometimes called today the "brush-fire" war). Each presents its own technical problems, and each—and this has been the source of much difficulty—requires its own planning and level of "preparedness."

Total war, as we have seen, will probably be won by the side that achieves absolute surprise and buries its enemy in a rain of nuclear bombs. It is conceived of as a quick and sudden assault of a size sufficient to destroy or to impair fatally the enemy's capacity to strike back. Limited war, however, refers to a struggle prosecuted without recourse to total weapons and for objectives that are by that fact themselves limited.

The major question surrounding limited war since 1945 has been one of utility. It is possible, even under modern conditions, to prevent a limited war from growing into an all-out struggle; Korea, Indochina, and Palestine all proved this point. But since the era of total weapons was born, no limited war directly involving major states has been able to produce a final solution to the political problems that were responsible for the conflict in the first place. This is a limitation that affects the United States perhaps less than it does the revisionist states, for a stalemated war for America can never be anything less than a qualified victory; for all states, however, it throws much doubt on the efficacy of any form of war other than the total.[3]

American combat missions, therefore, must take two forms. The United States must be prepared to accept the challenge of total war if any aggressor presents it. Americans must also face the necessity of coping with limited wars of all types; "brush fires" may break out at any moment and the United States must have the ability to extinguish them if it be

---

[3] See, in this connection, Robert E. Osgood, *Limited War: the Challenge to American Strategy* (Chicago: University of Chicago Press, 1957), and Henry A. Kissinger, *Nuclear Weapons and Foreign Policy* (New York: Harper & Bros., 1957).

thought desirable. America must recognize, however, that the probability of winning any meaningful affirmative victory by limited war is at best a very low one, and that stalemate will often be the most that can be achieved by any such effort. Short of winning a war of survival, it can be argued that the most important American military mission is preventing big wars rather than winning small ones. This is true not because the small conflicts are unimportant in themselves, but because of the difficulty of "winning" them while keeping them small.

Balanced force vs. new look

This formulation of the American military mission is the one presently controlling within American government circles, but it is by no means the only one that has been advanced. We alluded earlier to the controversy over the optimum form of the American military establishment. Although fought out before the public largely in terms of the conflicting responsibilities of the three armed services, it actually was (and is) an outgrowth of a fundamental disagreement over the nature of the military problem facing the United States and the theory to be adopted in solving it. As we discuss it in this section, we shall view it in the form of a dispute between the concept of a "balanced force" and that of the so-called "new look" in American defense.

Little Wars or Big Wars? We will recall that the original containment hypothesis of American foreign policy called for the United States to resist further communist expansion at whatever time and in whatever form it appeared. In military terms, this meant that American armed force would repel any Soviet-inspired attempt to break through the ring by war, and that adequate American military power would be committed to hold the line. The Korean war provided the first clear test of this principle.

Korea proved to be an extremely frustrating experience for Americans; it would be impossible for us to suggest any enterprise more calculated to fray American nerves and to destroy American perspectives than a war fought under such conditions. There were technical military reasons for questioning American policy in Korea; it defied the historic American theory of war to fight a holding action indefinitely and to refuse to force a battlefield decision.[4] There was also some doubt about the worth of a

---

[4] This was the major point in General MacArthur's attack on administration and United Nations policy in Korea. See Charles A. Willoughby and John Chamberlain, *MacArthur, 1941-1951* (New York: The McGraw-Hill Book Co., Inc., 1954), pp. 421-2.

policy that left it up to the enemy to decide when, where, with what weapons, and for what objectives to fight. It became popular to warn of the "bleeding" effect of such a policy: Moscow, according to this argument, could use its initiative to force a series of profitless little wars on the United States and thus to bleed America to death.

In discussing the theory of "liberation" in Chapter 12, we pointed out that this dogma called for a new military policy, one that came to be known popularly as "massive retaliation." According to this doctrine, the United States—although not totally abandoning the "little war" field to the communists—came to concentrate instead on the big-war problem. Instead of meeting each "brush fire" directly, the United States emphasized the true source of the difficulty, the Soviet itself. Any new war (of whatever size), Washington said, might be met not by equivalent resistance at the point of outbreak but instead by "massive retaliation" at "places and times" of America's own choosing. Thus deterrence became the preferred method of dealing with the danger of limited war as well as that of total war.

The New Look in Defense. Beginning in 1953, the Eisenhower administration began reshaping the structure of the American military establishment in conformity with the new doctrine. The "new look" [5] had two major components: (1) a reduction both in expenditure and in manpower—headlined on occasion as "more bang for a buck"; (2) a new strategic theory based frankly on American industrial and technological superiority.

Defense budgets were scaled down to approximately $33 billion in fiscal 1955. After that year the total moved slowly upward again as the cost of new weapons programs continued to mount, reaching $38 billion in fiscal 1957. Manpower was likewise reduced, dropping nearly to the 2 million mark during 1957.

These new directions were possible, according to official doctrine, because of the new strategic theory. Essentially this new dogma involved a concentration upon air power as the central vehicle of applying force and upon nuclear weapons as being most appropriate to the mission the United States was adopting. Underlying both of these foci of concentration was the basic assumption that the American military problem was one "no longer calling for rearmament by a specific date of peak

---

[5] The term apparently was first used by Defense Secretary Charles E. Wilson in June, 1953, while testifying before the Senate Committee on Appropriations on the 1954 defense budget. Wilson promised "a new look at the entire defense picture." *Hearings on the Department of Defense Appropriations for 1954,* Senate Committee on Appropriations, 83rd Congress, 1st Session (Washington, D.C.: U.S. Government Printing Office, 1953), p. 6.

danger, but as requiring a gradual build up and steady maintenance over an indeterminate period." [6] For the long pull America was to put its trust in science and technology as a means of offsetting Soviet preponderance in manpower and in conventional weapons. Despite the strenuous objections of some military personnel who felt themselves slighted in the redefinition of missions and of other observers who found partisan politics at least partially at the root of the new principles, the United States government moved steadily to make the "new look" a reality.

The Assumptions of "Massive Retaliation." The doctrine of "massive retaliation," if it were to be taken seriously as the operating principle of American defense policy, rested on a number of assumptions that were independent of the technical issues of budgets and the conduct of warfare. Five of them were of primary importance. (1) All three services would agree on the principle of the "new look." (2) American superiority (qualitative and quantitative) in nuclear weapons would be maintained. (3) The only threats to United States military security would come from the communist world. (4) The decision to employ the weapons of totality would be a unilateral one by the United States. (5) Public opinion, inside the United States and the free world, and among the uncommitted nations, could be safely ignored.

One need not be a partisan in the triangular Army-Navy-Air Force dispute to be convinced that these assumptions have never been simultaneously realized in practice. None of them has been constantly operative, and it has been rare since 1953 to find as many as three of them applying at one time. Each is open to serious question.

The argument against the first simply denies that interservice agreement and consensus, let alone unanimity, has ever existed. The second is challenged on the ground of the history of the development of Soviet nuclear weapons; in the spring of 1956 General LeMay could assert the possibility of early Russian leadership both in aircraft and weapons.[7] The General's point was dramatically confirmed in 1957, when in rapid succession the Soviet fired a hydrogen bomb, announced a successful inter-continental missile, and launched several space satellites. In the welter of confusion in the United States that ensued, President Eisenhower admitted that Moscow had indeed gained weapons superiority in some fields. The third is the least open to question, although many security threats to the United States can be suggested that might arise from other than Soviet sources.

---

[6] Reitzel, Kaplan, and Coblentz, *United States Foreign Policy, 1945-1955*, p. 347. Reprinted by permission.

[7] See General LeMay's testimony before the Symington subcommittee of the Senate on April 27 and 30, 1956. *New York Times* (April 28 and May 1, 1956).

The fourth runs counter to the entire alliance system of the United States and caused immediate resistance among America's European associates. The fifth was rapidly invalidated by the growth of neutralism and the success of Moscow's "peace and disarmament" campaign during 1955 and 1956.

The "new look" was not inseparable from the doctrine of "massive retaliation." It was possible to justify a smaller and more efficient armed force geared into a retaliatory strategy on some basis other than that of meeting every danger with the threat of nuclear assault. The increasing inexpediency of the doctrine stimulated a series of bitter arguments among service personnel, the public, policy-making officials, and within the free-world alliance. By the end of the first Eisenhower administration there were indications that the rigor of the massive retaliation thesis had been somewhat relaxed; [8] the "Eisenhower Doctrine" of 1957 clearly assumed the likelihood of American participation in any new Middle-East brush fire.

Inter-service Disputes. Complicating the objective evaluation of the "new look" in defense and of "massive retaliation" as the theory for its implementation was the continuing squabble among the three uniformed services. Basic strategic development was obscured by well-publicized barrages of claims and counter-claims by the Army, Navy, and Air Force for privileged positions in the new military machine. In the course of the running battle by the three, however, the various alternatives were thoroughly aired.

Underlying the controversy, and dating back to its initial flareup at the time the armed services were "unified" by the National Security Act in 1947, was the widespread notion among professional military men of all branches that the future belonged to air power. The older services hoped to redefine their own missions so as to give them authority over such air weapons as were appropriate to themselves; the Air Force, itself newly independent of Army control, sought to acquire and to perpetuate a monopoly.

A large, if undiscoverable, share of the devoted care with which each service prosecuted its own case was due to the sincere conviction each held that its own strategic principles, tactical doctrine, and dedicated personnel was best fitted to provide for the security of the United States. We must also recognize, however, that all three services were not unaware of the career implications of the new nature of defense. The service that was granted central responsibility would receive the lion's share of prestige, high rank, and appropriations. Each service felt impelled, therefore,

[8] Reitzel, Kaplan, and Coblentz, *United States Foreign Policy,* pp. 444-5.

not only to press its own claims but also to deprecate and often to deride the assertions of the other two.

The "Revolt of the Admirals." The first open split among the services in response to the new developments in defense occurred in 1949 and is known as the "revolt of the admirals." The Navy, reacting sharply to Secretary of Defense Johnson's termination of construction on a "super-carrier" (the Navy's bid for air-atomic power), erupted in charges against the Air Force. The Secretary of the Navy resigned, correspondence highly critical both of unification and of Air Force policy was circulated, and Congressional investigations aired the whole matter. Although no overt surrender was involved, the Navy won concessions in public opinion and super-carrier construction was resumed a few months later.[9]

General Ridgeway's Protest. The Korean war submerged interservice disputes for several years. The next open flareup came in 1955, on the occasion of the retirement of General Matthew B. Ridgeway from the office of Army Chief of Staff. General Ridgeway, in a letter to Secretary of Defense Wilson, criticized the dismantling of Army strength in favor of the questionable doctrine of "massive retaliation," and made his points public property in his autobiography.[10] Although a small storm was produced by the dissent of such a widely respected and admired Army figure, no noticeable change in policy was undertaken.

The 1956 Disputes. The Army, disturbed by the growing trend in official thinking to place more and more reliance on air power as the central weapon, was not content. Reacting to the 1956 hearings on air power held by Senator Stuart Symington's subcommittee (Senator Symington himself had formerly been Secretary of the Air Force), and jolted by the clear assumption of the Air Force that the other services had missions purely auxiliary to its own, the Army launched its own offensive. Late in May a series of news "leaks" occurred that added up to a frontal attack on the entire airpower concept.[11] The Air Force retaliated in kind, and the whole controversy broke out all over again.

Secretary of Defense Wilson, himself under considerable fire from his political opponents, the supporters of the Army's position, and most news columnists and commentators quieted the disturbance by an unprecedented news conference at the height of the dispute. He appeared with

---

[9] Timothy W. Stanley, *American Defense and National Security* (Washington, D.C.: Public Affairs Press, 1956), pp. 94-5.

[10] General Ridgeway's letter was printed in full in the *United States News and World Report* (July 29, 1955); his autobiography, Matthew B. Ridgeway, *Soldier* (New York: Harper & Bros., Inc., 1956).

[11] See the *New York Times* (May 19-22, 1956), especially the dispatches of Anthony Liviero.

the three chiefs of staff and the three service secretaries, and each of the uniformed commanders solemnly pledged support to official policy and denounced what their subordinates had been saying.[12]

A few months later Mr. Wilson attempted to settle the specific issues that had precipitated the most recent quarrel: the allocation of responsibility for the development and employment of guided missiles, and the extent of the Army's control over aviation. We shall consider these points below, but here we may point out that on both counts the Air Force was again the victor; even a reduction in the projected strength of the Air Force because of the increasing power of Army anti-aircraft missiles and rockets failed to lift the gloom into which the Army leadership fell. The dispute broke out all over again late in 1957 as the Army won back some missile competence in the race to have an American space satellite.

The "Balanced Force" Argument. We must not infer from the Air Force victory of 1956 that the "new look" doctrine reigned unchallenged; its opponents had a substantial case of their own. Even without the "massive retaliation" appendage to the theory of atomic-air power, a very solid argument could be made (and was made) in favor of the concept of a balanced force.

Its central thesis was, of course, that atomic strategy was feasible only as long as the United States enjoyed great superiority in that category of weapons. Once atomic stalemate was achieved, the utility of total war *for either side* was reduced to the vanishing point. From that moment, the only sort of warfare at all likely to occur was limited war in peripheral areas.[13] Total weapons of whatever type were held to be useless in any such local struggle; the United States would be forced to rely on conventional weapons and tactical nuclear ones, used in conformity with time-tested strategic concepts. The basic problem was the familiar one of applying force appropriate to the objective sought. If total weapons were all that were available, a small objective would either have to be abandoned or achieved by methods out of all proportion to the goal.

The Army and the Navy both espoused this position; the Army was perhaps more deeply interested in its adoption because of its greater stake in the issue (the Navy, we must remember, had been granted a real if limited atomic competence of its own and was willing to adapt itself to the "new look"). Considerable intellectual effort was expended in

---

[12] *New York Times* (May 22, 1956).

[13] This point was strongly made by Henry A. Kissinger in his articles in *Foreign Affairs:* "Military Power and the Defense of the 'Grey Areas'" (April, 1955), "Force and Diplomacy in the Nuclear Age" (April, 1956), and "Strategy and Organization" (April, 1957).

hammering out a doctrinal position justifying the "balanced force." [14]

No one can say that the inter-service controversy and the "new look"-"balanced force" dispute is ended. The United States must continue to make its own decisions about the optimum method of securing its own defense in terms of the nature of the security threat it faces and the human and technological resources it has available. No answer can be absolute; any significant change in any of the variables might provoke another round in what has proved to be a long-lived argument.

The allocation of responsibility

The inter-service controversy has been, among other characteristics, a disagreement about respective roles and missions. Not the least cause of the conflict is the difference in the way each service presents its claim. From this fundamental divergence in point of view has grown much of the subsequent confusion of purpose.

The Navy adopts a "task force" theory of organization and contends that there should be within the Navy itself everything necessary for the accomplishment of its mission. The Army, on the other hand, is more concerned with command; under Army command (for the Army, committed to the conquest and occupation of the enemy's territory, considers itself the only possible winner of real victory) there should be everything —regardless of service identification—necessary for victory. The Air Force has a simpler theory: anything that flies belongs to the Air Force. These three theories of mission were obviously destined to clash.

The Key West Agreement. The basic understanding reached on the roles of the services is the so-called Key West Agreement of 1948, revised and expanded slightly by subsequent directives. Under this agreement, the services are given missions based on their respective "primary functions" in land, sea, and air operations. Each has collateral functions that blend into the primary function of one or both of the other two branches. The Army was given primary responsibility for Army anti-aircraft artillery units, thus giving it access to the guided missile field; the Air Force was, among other points, given authority over "strategic air warfare" and for providing "close combat and logistical air support to the Army."

---

[14] See W. W. Kaufmann, ed., *Military Policy and National Security* (Princeton, N. J.: Princeton University Press, 1956). Lieutenant General James M. Gavin is quoted as saying about this volume: "This is the Army's story," *Army* (May, 1956).

Naval air power (including, presumably, naval employment of atomic bombs) was guaranteed.[15]

The original agreement and its later amendments resolved some points but left others unsettled:

> Primary interest in the development of *amphibious* techniques was granted to the Marines, while primary concern with *airborne* operations was given to the Army. *Anti-submarine warfare* was made a primary function of the Navy and a collateral function of the Air Force. *Air transport* was assigned to the Air Force. But there were many areas of ambiguity. *Air Defense* was made a primary function of all three services. *Army aviation* was not discussed at all. Nor was any mention made of *guided missiles*. Strategic bombing was made a primary function of the Air Force....[16]

Direct inter-service agreements and directives from the Secretary of Defense served to eliminate or to minimize some of the failures of understanding left after the Key West Agreement and its amendments of 1949 and 1953. By 1956 the principal points of controversy remaining involved authority over guided missiles and rockets on the one hand and the Army's possession and employment of its own aviation on the other.

The Missiles Decision. During the 1956 dispute all three services had brought up the issue of missiles, praising their own and deriding the others. For all three it was a central problem. If the warfare of the future was to become increasingly robotinized and if ground-to-ground, air-to-ground, ground-to-air, and air-to-air missiles, carrying nuclear warheads, were to become the decision-forcing weapons, the share of authority of each service over the general missile field was a vital concern. The public became familiar with the names of "Nike," "Talos," "Redstone," and other missiles, and the initials "ICBM" (the intercontinental ballistic missile with a projected range of 3,000-5,000 miles) also acquired the status of a household word.

The November 1956 directive of Secretary Wilson attempted to cut the Gordian Knot.[17] The Army was limited to missiles with a *200-mile range* for use against *tactical targets* with its *zone of operations* (defined as 100 miles beyond the front line and 100 miles to the rear). The Air Force was given jurisdiction over all *land-based missiles* with a range of over 200 miles. Thus existing missiles were divided (the Air Force won control over the Army's "Jupiter," an intermediate-range ballistic missile)

---

[15] The Key West agreement is reproduced in Stanley, *Defense and Security*, pp. 176-88.

[16] Stanley, *Defense and Security*, p. 89. Italics in original. Reprinted by permission.

[17] The directive is summarized in *New York Times* (December 2, 1956), iv: 1.

and the development of the long-range ICBM was granted exclusively to the Air Force. This was a major defeat for the Army and, according to its more pessimistic supporters, cast a cloud over its future. This quarrel broke out again a few months later in the controversy over the court-martial of an army missile expert who had reduced his objections to the Wilson directive to writing. The officer was convicted and reprimanded, but meanwhile the Army had received a valuable opportunity to air its disagreement with the Wilson decision. Army supporters were quick to point to the Soviet successes in rocketry as proof of their case and, late in 1957, rewon at least some of the ground they had lost the previous year.

Army Aviation. The Air Force's victory was as complete on the issue of Army aviation. For some time the Army, envious of the Navy's integral air arm and the fact that each Marine division has its own tactical air wing, had been agitating in favor of some such arrangement for itself. It had stressed the difficulties of dealing with Air Force commanders who were not under Army control, and of the danger and inefficiency of having to negotiate tactical air support, troop transport, and airlift operation under combat conditions.

Secretary Wilson nipped this campaign in the bud. In the same directive as that incorporating the missile decision, the Army was forbidden to provide its own close-combat air support. Its aircraft, furthermore, were limited to those required for battle-zone operations (as defined above) and their functions were confined to essentially Army purposes, such as observation, reconnaissance, and the airlift of Army personnel and materiel. This decision seemingly certified the position of the Air Force as the key service in the American defense scheme.

AMERICAN OVERSEAS DEFENSE COMMITMENTS

A major feature of American policy during the cold war has been the development and elaboration of a series of overseas defense commitments. For the first time in its history, the United States had found it necessary both to enter into firm alliances with foreign states and to deploy its military forces on the territory of its allies. A logical consequence of this development has been the adoption of the policy of supplying the associates of the United States with materiel for their own defense and for the security of the alliance.[18]

---

[18] An elaboration of this point is undertaken by Herbert Agar in *The Price of Power: America since 1945* (Chicago: University of Chicago Press, 1957).

As of 1957 the United States was allied with 43 different states. These ties included four multilateral treaties and a number of bilateral arrangements. The obligations covered the major areas of the world: western Europe via NATO, southeast Asia via SEATO, the southwest Pacific by means of ANZUS, the western hemisphere through OAS, and the Far East by a series of bilateral agreements with the Philippines, Nationalist China, the Republic of Korea, and Japan. The Middle East alone did not involve any direct American commitments up to early 1957, but the Middle East crisis of 1956 and the passage of the Eisenhower Doctrine in 1957 resulted in a much more intimate American relation with the "Baghdad Pact" powers.

The patterns of alliance

Although all the 43 states with which the United States had military agreements were, in one sense or another, "allies," the nature of the obligation incurred by the American government differed from one pact to another. Each merits mention in order to clarify just what Americans have obligated themselves to do.

The NATO Commitment. Both the most binding commitment accepted by the United States and the most elaborate institutional implementation are found in American action under the terms of the North Atlantic Treaty of 1949. NATO is, as American leadership delights in pointing out, the keystone of all contemporary American policy, and our consideration of American alliances should begin with it.

The principal obligation under the Treaty is contained in Article 5. Its language is important enough to merit quotation:

> The Parties agree that an armed attack against one or more of them in Europe or North America shall be considered an attack against them all; and consequently they agree that, if such an armed attack occurs, each of them, in exercise of the right of individual or collective self-defense recognized by Article 51 of the Charter of the United Nations, will assist the Party or Parties so attacked by taking forthwith, individually and in concert with the other Parties, such action as it deems necessary, including the use of armed force, to restore and maintain the security of the North Atlantic Area.[19]

Later provisions define the geographic area included by the pact and the

[19] *Disarmament and Security: A Collection of Documents, 1919-1955,* Committee Print, Subcommittee on Disarmament, Committee on Foreign Relations, United States Senate, 84th Congress, 2d Session (Washington, D.C.: U.S. Government Printing Office, 1956), pp. 530-31.

relationships of the treaty to the Charter of the United Nations, and provide for the creation of a North Atlantic Council for implementing the execution of the treaty. It was thrown open to adherence by any other European state "in a position to further the principles of this Treaty" upon unanimous invitation of the members. Under these terms, the original 12 signatories (Belgium, Canada, Denmark, France, Iceland, Italy, Luxembourg, Netherlands, Norway, Portugal, United Kingdom, and the United States) have accepted the later membership of Greece, Turkey, and West Germany.

The SEATO Obligation. The Southeast Asia Collective Defense Treaty of 1954, the negotiation of which was preceded by a sharp dispute between the United States and the United Kingdom, is not as precise as the North Atlantic Treaty in specifying either the action to be taken by the parties or the danger which the treaty is designed to meet. Article 4 contains the general pledge:

> 1. Each Party recognizes that aggression by means of armed attack in the treaty area against any of the Parties or against any State or territory which the Parties by unanimous agreement may hereafter designate, would endanger its own peace and safety, and agrees that it will in that event act to meet the common danger in accordance with its constitutional processes.[20]

Section 2 of the same Article dealt with a slightly different contingency. If the "inviolability or the integrity" of any party or of any protected territory "is threatened in any way other than by armed attack or is affected or threatened by any fact or situation which might endanger the peace of the area," the parties will consult together immediately to agree on measures to be taken for the common defense. We will note that Section 1 does not provide for consultation in the case of armed attack, but that Section 2, covering other dangers, requires consultation and the formulation of common measures.[21] Later provisions of the treaty, in much the same way as had the North Atlantic treaty, define the area covered, establish a Council, and relate the treaty to the Charter.

The ANZUS Obligation. The Australia-New Zealand-United States security treaty, negotiated in 1951 and put into effect in 1952, involves a commitment less comprehensive than the North Atlantic Treaty and

---

[20] *Disarmament and Security*, p. 612. The "State or territory which the Parties may hereafter designate" referred to the Associated States of Indochina (Laos, Cambodia, and Vietnam), barred from entry into any such pact.

[21] This distinction is generally thought to be a gesture in the direction of the Asian neutrals, who—led by Nehru—distrusted the narrowly anti-communist orientation of NATO and were interested in provisions offering protection against any renewed Asian colonialism.

more akin to the SEATO obligations. Articles III and IV are the pertinent provisions:

> ARTICLE III. The Parties will consult together whenever in the opinion of any of them the territorial integrity, political independence or security of any of the Parties is threatened in the Pacific.
>
> ARTICLE IV. Each Party recognizes that an armed attack in the Pacific Area on any of the Parties would be dangerous to its own peace and safety and declares that it would act to meet the common danger in accordance with its constitutional processes.[22]

It is noteworthy that nowhere in the treaty is the term "Pacific Area" defined, although what would constitute an armed attack on a Party is declared to include "an armed attack on the metropolitan territory, ... on the island territories under its jurisdiction in the Pacific, or on its armed forces, public vessels, or aircraft in the Pacific." [23] Other provisions are not exceptional, except that Article VIII authorizes the ANZUS Council to maintain a consultative relationship with "States, Regional Organizations, Associations of States, or other authorities" in the Pacific area in a position to contribute to the security of the region.

The OAS Obligation. American commitments with regard to the western hemisphere were accepted in the Inter-American Treaty of Reciprocal Assistance of 1947. This document, the first of the mutual-security pacts brought about by the United States and to some extent the model for all subsequent ones, is both more detailed in its provisions and more complex in its structure than are the others we have considered.

Article 3 contains the general guarantee and authorizes individual action on behalf of the group:

> ARTICLE 3. 1. The High Contracting Parties agree that an armed attack by any State against an American State shall be considered as an attack against all the American States and, consequently, each one of the said Contracting Parties undertakes to assist in meeting the attack in the exercise of the inherent right of individual and collective self-defense....
>
> 2. On the request of the State or States directly attacked and until the decision of the Organ of Consultation of the Inter-American System has been reached, each one of the Contracting Parties may determine the immediate measures which it may individually take in fulfillment of the obligation contained in the preceding paragraph and in accordance with the principle of continental solidarity.[24]

Article 6 defined the situations that would make the treaty applicable:

> ARTICLE 6. If the inviolability or the integrity of the territory or

---

[22] *Disarmament and Security*, p. 600.

[23] *Disarmament and Security*, p. 601.

[24] *Disarmament and Security*, p. 650.

the sovereign or political independence of any American State should be affected by an aggression which is not an armed attack or by an extra-continental or intra-continental conflict, or by any other fact or situation that might endanger the peace of America, the Organ of Consultation shall meet immediately in order to agree on the measures which must be taken in case of aggression to assist the victim of the aggression or, in any case, the measures which should be taken for the common defense and for the maintenance of the peace and security of the Continent.[25]

Article 7 authorized the parties to terminate a conflict between two or more American states on the basis of the "*status quo ante bellum*," and to take action to maintain inter-American peace. Article 9, without attempting a definition of "aggression," listed as examples "unprovoked armed attack by a State against . . . another State" and "invasion, by the armed forces of a State, of the territory of another State" by trespassing "boundaries demarcated in accordance with a treaty, judicial decision, or arbitral award" or "territory under the effective jurisdiction of another State." Article 17 provided that the Organ of Consultation should take its decisions by a two-thirds vote of the signatories. Thus the treaty made a major attempt to minimize inter-American conflict.

The United States and the Baghdad Pact. The last of the multilateral regional agreements in which the United States has an interest is the so-called Baghdad Pact of 1955. This treaty, originally an agreement between Iraq and Turkey and expanded by the adherence of Iran, Pakistan, and Great Britain, is more of a declaration of common purpose than an exchange of specific engagements. Article 1 points out merely that

> Consistent with article 51 of the United Nations Charter the High Contracting Parties will co-operate for their security and defence. Such measures as they agree to take to give effect to this co-operation may form the subject of special agreements with each other.[26]

The American attitude toward the pact was summarized in the joint communique issued at the end of the Eisenhower-Eden conference of January, 1956:

> We discussed the work of the Baghdad Pact and agreed upon its importance for the security of the Middle East. . . . We believe that it serves the interests of the area as a whole and provides no reason for impairing the good relations we wish to maintain with nonmember countries.
>
> The United States government will continue to give solid support to the purposes and aims of the pact and its observers will play a constructive part in the work of its committees.[27]

---

[25] *Disarmament and Security*, p. 651.

[26] *Disarmament and Security*, p. 643.

[27] Communique of February 1, 1956, *Department of State Bulletin* (February 13, 1956), p. 233.

In accordance with this attitude, American cooperation and aid was undertaken with regard to the pact members. The Middle East crisis of 1956 impaired the relationship of Britain with the other members, and considerable speculation developed in the United States that Washington might find it desirable itself to enter the Baghdad Pact. This conjecture reached fruition at the Eisenhower-Macmillan conference at Bermuda in March, 1957. In the communique issued at the close of the discussion, the two chief executives announced the "willingness of the United States, under authority of the recent Middle East joint resolution, to participate actively in the work of the Military Committee of the Baghdad Pact." [28]

Bilateral Obligations. The United States has entered into bilateral security arrangements with five states: the Philippines, Japan, Korea, and China in the Far East, and Spain in Europe. Each of these has its own peculiarities.

The earliest was with the Philippines, negotiated virtually simultaneously with the ANZUS agreement in 1951. Its language is in some parts exactly the same. Article IV, for example, makes the identical pledge as Article IV of the ANZUS treaty, and Article III, providing for consultation, differs from the ANZUS provision only in specifying that the vehicle of consultation shall be the Foreign Ministers (or their deputies) of the two states.[29]

The treaty with Japan, also negotiated in 1951, is unique among the American security pacts because of the one-sidedness of its commitments. This imbalance grew out of the provisions of the 1946 Japanese constitution that prohibited that nation from maintaining any armed forces. Obviously, under such an arrangement Japan could not make any contribution to mutual defense that would involve military power. Article I of the treaty was its heart:

> Japan grants, and the United States of America accepts, the right, upon the coming into force of the Treaty of Peace and of this Treaty, to dispose United States land, air, and sea forces in and about Japan. Such forces may be utilized to contribute to the maintenance of international peace and security in the Far East and to the security of Japan against armed attack from without, ... [30]

In return for this guarantee, Japan agreed in Article II not to grant, without American consent, "any bases or any rights, powers or authority whatsoever" to the armed forces of any third power. The treaty was to

---

[28] Text of communique in *Department of State Bulletin* (April 8, 1957).

[29] *Disarmament and Security*, pp. 598-99.

[30] *Disarmament and Security*, p. 606.

expire, according to Article IV, when there should have come into force United Nations arrangements of "such alternative individual or collective security dispositions" as would satisfactorily provide for peace and security in the "Japan Area."

The pact with the Republic of Korea, negotiated after the truce in the Korean war in 1953, included most of the concepts that this brief catalogue has made familiar. Article II provides for consultation if either party is "threatened by external armed attack." Article III states that an armed attack on the territory of either party would be dangerous to the peace and safety of the other; both agree to act "in accordance with ... constitutional processes." Article IV, in the same way as had the Japanese treaty, conferred the right "to dispose United States land, air, and sea forces in and about the territory of the Republic of Korea." [31]

The 1954 treaty with Nationalist China followed what was by this time the standard pattern for Far Eastern pacts; it provided for consultation, action according to constitutional processes to meet danger of armed attack, and the disposition of American forces on Formosa and the Pescadores. Because of the somewhat anomalous status of the Chinese government, the territorial limits of the treaty were restricted for China to "Taiwan and the Pescadores" and for the United States to "the island territories in the West Pacific under its jurisdiction." [32] This provision was widely interpreted as constituting official American recognition of the Taipei regime's claim to de jure sovereignty over Formosa.

The agreement with Spain, entered into late in 1953, was much less specific and much more restricted in scope than any other of the bilateral pacts. It represented the consummation of a hard bargain between Madrid and Washington. The United States agreed to extend military aid to Spain "during a period of several years to contribute to the effective air defense of Spain and to improve the equipment of its military and naval forces. ..." Spain, on its part, agreed to permit the United States to construct bases in Spain and engaged itself to acquire the land necessary for that purpose; such areas, however, were to remain "under Spanish flag and command," and Spain was to "retain the ownership of the ground and of the permanent structures which may be constructed thereon." Despite the limited nature of the obligation assumed by both sides, the agreement was generally regarded as bringing Spain within the alliance framework of the United States.[33]

---

[31] *Disarmament and Security*, pp. 607-8.

[32] *Disarmament and Security*, pp. 608-610.

[33] *Disarmament and Security*, pp. 537-39.

Military aid programs

Beginning with the first Mutual Defense Assistance Act in 1949, the United States has consistently supported its political and military commitments to its allies with programs of military aid. The various major phases of the effort to equip the military establishments of friendly nations we have considered in earlier chapters. At this point we need only consider the policy in its present more or less stabilized form.

What Is "Military Aid"? We ought first to clarify what we (and the United States government) mean when we say "military aid." The term has figured in political and journalistic discussion to such an extent and with such a variety of meanings that a great deal of confusion has resulted. In our discussion we shall be using the term as officially defined by the United States government.

The President's "Tenth Semiannual Report on the Mutual Security Program" classified mutual-security assistance as follows:

> Direct military assistance under the mutual security program is extended by providing weapons and other military supply items, by carrying out training programs, and by sharing in the financing of joint military facilities.
>
> Nonmilitary assistance is extended in one of three ways, depending on how the needs and circumstances of the participating country relate to the policy objectives of the United States: (1) defense support and technical cooperation; (2) development assistance and technical cooperation; or (3) technical cooperation alone.[34]

"Defense support" is defined in the same document as being

> designed to help certain countries which are receiving military assistance to support appropriate levels of military strength while also maintaining and promoting political and economic stability. Such support involves furnishing economic resources to enable the recipient country to undertake defense activities that otherwise would not be possible or to increase the recipient's capacity to do so in the future.[35]

"Military aid," therefore, includes direct military assistance and defense support. Although it is possible (and the International Cooperation Administration finds it convenient to do so) to subsume development assistance and technical cooperation under the general notion of aid with a mutual-security purpose, their relationship to military concerns is

---

[34] *Report to Congress on the Mutual Security Program,* September 20, 1956 (Washington, D.C.: U. S. Government Printing Office, 1956), p. 14. The data in this section are drawn from this *Report.*

[35] *Report to Congress on the Mutual Security Program,* p. 14.

admittedly peripheral. The figures that follow are confined to the first two categories, direct military aid and defense support.

How Much Military Aid? Fiscal 1956 is a convenient year to use as an example in discussing military aid. By that year the "new look" military concept had become standardized and the American government had rationalized its military plans, both domestic and international, on something resembling a long-term basis. The 1956 totals, therefore, represent what Washington assumed was a "normal" year in military assistance.

During fiscal 1956, the obligations incurred by the Department of Defense (for direct aid) and the International Cooperation Administration (for defense support) totalled $1,975,000,000. Of this amount $843 million was in direct aid, while the remainder was for defense support.

During the first six months of 1956, $1.9 billion worth of military equipment and supplies was shipped abroad. Over half (by value) of the items consisted of aircraft and related items; 40 per cent was ground-force equipment. The remainder went for naval items. These deliveries brought to $14.2 billion the cumulative total of military equipment and supplies furnished since the program began in 1949. Ammunition, tanks, and aircraft accounted for over two-thirds of all the materiel; 61 per cent of all supplies were for ground forces.

Who Receives Military Aid? Direct military aid during fiscal 1956 was heavily focused on Europe. Almost two-thirds of the $1.9 billion went to America's western allies, largely to the NATO nations. The Asia-Pacific area was next, with about one-quarter of the total. Although the exact distribution was classified, it was admitted that the major Asian recipients of direct military aid were Taiwan, Korea, the Philippines, and Vietnam.

Defense support, however, presented a contrasting picture. Almost half of the $1.5 billion total, almost $727 million, went to Asia; Korea alone received nearly $320 million. The other major Asian recipients were Taiwan and Vietnam, although all the Far Eastern nations except Indonesia and Japan had allocations; the smallest (for the Philippines) was $23 million. In South Asia only Pakistan was included; in the Near East and Africa only Greece, Iran, and Turkey. In Europe, the only defense-support programs were in Germany, Spain, and Yugoslavia, with a small allocation for regional activities. No defense support was given in Latin America.[36]

---

[36] In fiscal 1957, the patterns changed only slightly. Military aid programs totalled $1.5 billion, with 40 per cent going to Europe during the first six months and 33 per cent to the Far East. In defense support, more than two-thirds of the amount programmed between July 1 and December 31, 1956, went to Korea, Taiwan, and Vietnam. *Report to Congress on the Mutual Security Program* April 27, 1957 (Washington, D.C.: U.S. Government Printing Office, 1957).

Thus in Europe the emphasis in military aid was on direct end-item supply and cooperative defense, while in Asia it tended heavily toward defense support. This promised to be a continuing pattern for an indefinite period unless a sudden overturn in the course of international relations should demand some radical revision of the entire philosophy of military aid. An indication of one such possible reversal was the American aid program focussed on the Middle East early in 1957. Major commitments of economic and military aid for selected Arab states were authorized by this program, and many experts expected some major change in the general pattern of American policy as a result.

ARMS LIMITATION IN UNITED STATES POLICY

Our final military issue—which is only partly military in nature, since it conveys heavy overtones of political, economic, and psychological relevance—is the troublesome question of the international regulation and limitation of armaments. In Chapter 6 we considered the high points in the "disarmament" effort of the 1920's and early 1930's; in some respects the history of the attempt to devise a workable scheme of armament control since 1945 is a continuation of the story of the interwar period. Certain factors peculiar to the contemporary era, however, have made the issue of arms limitation both more frustrating and more important than ever before in American history.

At the beginning of this brief examination of the issues and problems involved in the international limitation of armaments, we should again point out that what we are discussing here is not the emotion-packed concept of "disarmament." No one in responsible office has ever seriously proposed that all nations should lay down their arms and, in the words of the spiritual, "study war no more." The more cumbersome but more exact phrase "arms limitation" describes what we are to consider here: the attempt to discover some basis for a multilateral reduction in the level of national armaments and for guaranteeing that interstate contacts will remain confined within the limits prescribed by these more modest military establishments.

The arms race with the Soviet Union

What has changed the issue of arms limitation from a nonspecific concern for a better world to a matter of practical urgency for the United States is the ominous dimensions assumed by the massive arms race with the Soviet Union. History teaches that in international affairs (as in other areas of social life) there operates a concept known as the "expectation of violence." When social conditions habituate individuals to the probability of a recourse to violence, the prospect of its employment in settling disputes increases. In the relations of rival states, there seems to be a positive correlation between the respective levels of armament and the expectation of war. This suggests, but by no means proves, that an arms race between the USSR and the United States tends to make war between them more likely.

In any case, by 1957 the intensity of the arms competition between the two giants had become a cause of much concern, both within the United States and among America's allies. Public pressure multiplied on both governments to make some new efforts to break through the obstacles and to release the world both from the economic burden of armaments and from the menace of nuclear holocaust. It seemed probable that both major powers would take advantage of any period of relaxation in tension to make some new explorations. The issues of arms limitation had acquired a new siginficance.

The Arms Race and the Cold War. How the arms race had begun was well known. As soon as the cold war began in earnest, the United States began to rearm. Never planning to match the Soviet preponderance in manpower generally and in ground armies in particular, America's effort centered on the development of mobile and highly effective air and naval defense units; the principal weapons in which the United States placed its trust were atomic. Moscow's reaction to the failure of atomic-control discussions was to intensify its own "crash" program for the development of nuclear weapons; its success in 1949 prompted the United States in turn to strengthen its own ground defenses and to construct the extensive alliance system to contain Soviet expansionism. By 1950 the arms race was on in earnest.

Since that date the cold war has had a clear arms-competition dimension. Each policy step by both sides has been taken with due regard to the new military situation created thereby; each side has attempted to score points at the expense of the other by making the best possible propaganda out of each new armament development. It is because this process seems to be self-perpetuating and has no visible end that so much support has been lent to the attempt to call a halt.

Categories of Competition. Any discussion of armaments since 1945 must take account of the fact that the military equipment of both major states falls today into two categories: "conventional" and nuclear. One of the most vital—but yet unsettled—questions is the relationship of these two to each other. In totting up a nation's armed power, how many infantry divisions equal one hydrogen bomb? No easy formula has yet been devised to answer this obviously pertinent question, and without one it is extremely difficult to make intelligent estimates of military parity.[37]

The United States has recognized that it would be politically inexpedient for the free world to attempt to match Soviet ground power. The United States has sought to keep its own and its allied armies superior to the Soviet on a man-for-man basis, and to maintain a sufficiently large ground force to serve as a deterrent in time of peace and as a delaying factor in the event of combat. The major American effort has been in maintaining a controlling lead over Russia in strategic air power, in nuclear bombs, and in missiles of all types. The obvious American strategy has been to use its lead in the newer weapons to offset Soviet superiority in the conventional ones. This was why the revelation of Soviet progress in missiles caused such a strong reaction in the United States in the autumn of 1957.

The Kremlin's position, however, has been exactly the converse. Although Soviet atomic-nuclear progress has been well-advertised, there seems to be no controlling necessity for Moscow to aim to surpass the United States in the newer weapon fields. Russia's leaders have seemingly conceded the United States much of its technological head start. Soviet policy has worked to build up Russian atomic-air-missile power to the point where it would virtually neutralize American capability in this respect (not necessarily, be it noted, equalizing it), and then to count on Russian ground superiority to confer a controlling preponderance. We have seen that it is this prospect that motivates the advocates of the "balanced force" theory of American defense.

In the tense climate of East-West relations, however, clear policies were difficult to discover. The unprejudiced observer might feel justified in feeling that the arms race was nearing totality as both sides made every effort to gain some sort of leverage over the other.

The United Nations and disarmament

The United Nations has been the focus of all postwar attempts to limit and control armaments. The history of the negotiations in that body over this question is a complex, confusing, and only intermittently

---

[37] This problem is discussed in Knorr, *The War Potential of Nations*, Chapter 14: "The Present State of War Potential."

427

interesting one. From it, however, certain important lessons have been learned about the future possibilities of armaments control.

The Charter and Arms Limitation. It is worth noting at the outset that the Charter does not call either for "disarmament" or the "reduction of armaments"; it speaks instead of the "regulation of armaments." [38] It was expected at San Francisco that armed force would exist in a United-Nations dominated world, but that it would be put only to the purpose of guaranteeing international peace and security. Charter provisions calling for the creation of a United Nations armed force and for the temporary earmarking of certain national contingents for United Nations use further underscored the point. Military power and armaments were to have a place—limited, controlled, and subordinate, but a place nonetheless—in the world of the United Nations.

"The Diplomacy of Embarrassment." The long and tortuous course of negotiations in the various organs of the United Nations looking toward the creation of a system of regulated armaments is of little interest to us here. As soon as the issue got caught up in the cold war, any real prospect of arms control was dissipated. The inability of the United Nations mechanisms to check the course of the great-power conflict was nowhere more dramatically demonstrated than in the failure of disarmament.[39]

What was remarkable about these unproductive discussions, however, was the tack taken by both the USSR and the United States. Each was interested in and advocated an arms-control formula that would give it a policy advantage; Washington advanced proposals that would have forever denied Moscow nuclear parity while the Soviet plainly wished to pull America's atomic teeth while maintaining its own primacy in conventional weapons. Each saw the impossibility of achieving its major goal and settled down instead to what we might call the "diplomacy of embarrassment."

Both sides propagandized their proposals in the name of "peace." Each devised specific formulas that sounded attractive to the smaller states but were so worded as to be unacceptable to the other. Rejection of any scheme was followed by accusations of bad faith and "warmongering." Each side was hoping to extract the maximum policy and public-relations value from an obviously foredoomed negotiation. By early 1948 disarmament discussions were hopelessly deadlocked; no more serious attempts were made until 1955.

---

[38] Article 26.

[39] This point is made clear in Leland M. Goodrich and Anne P. Simons, *The United Nations and the Maintenance of International Peace and Security* (Washington, D.C.: Brookings, 1955), chapters 21, 22.

428

The summit and disarmament

Disarmament acquired a new significance as one result of the general relaxation of cold-war tensions following the 1955 summit conference. Through all the ups-and-downs of Soviet-American relations since that meeting, the issue has remained steadily alive to the point that some observers feel that an agreement on arms control and inspection would be the signal for a fundamentally new turn in the cold war and is the most likely area within which the first steps in agreement and accommodation might be taken.

The "Open Sky" Proposal at the Summit. On the last day of the summit conference, President Eisenhower broke open the whole subject of arms control by a sensational proposal on the issue that had been the stumbling block of most early negotiations, that of adequate safeguards and inspection. After stressing the importance of the subject and the obstacles met earlier, he addressed himself directly to the Soviet Union:

> I propose, therefore, that we take a practical step, that we begin an arrangement, very quickly, as between ourselves—immediately. These steps would include:
>
> To give to each other a complete blueprint of our military establishments, from beginning to end, from one end of our countries to the other, lay out the establishments and provide the blueprints to each other.
>
> Next, to provide within our countries facilities for aerial photography to the other country—we to provide you the facilities within our country, ample facilities for aerial reconnaissance, where you can make all the pictures you choose and take them to your country to study, you to provide exactly the same facilities for us and we to make these examinations, and by this step to convince the world that we are providing as between ourselves against the possibility of great surprise attack, thus lessening danger and relaxing tension.[40]

Mr. Eisenhower went on to propose that the Subcommittee on Disarmament of the United Nations "give priority effort to the study of inspection and reporting."

The Eisenhower-Bulganin Correspondence. The "open-sky" proposal electrified the world, rapidly coming to symbolize an entirely new approach to ending the arms race. More importantly, it touched off a new round of discussions and negotiations that, although slow to produce concrete results, nevertheless narrowed the ground of disagreement between the two states and kept the hopes of 1955 alive through the crises of 1956 and into 1957.

---

[40] *Disarmament and Security*, p. 340.

Most expressive of the changed mental state of the leadership was the Eisenhower-Bulganin correspondence on arms control, a phenomenon unusual both in its dimensions and in the obvious determination of both governments to keep open this channel of direct contact. It was initiated in September, 1955, with Premier Bulganin's formal reply to the Geneva proposal; the next 18 months saw five additional letters from Moscow alternating with replies by Washington. In all of the letters a determinedly friendly tone prevailed, except for Mr. Eisenhower's reply to the Bulganin letter of October 17, 1956, that urged the abandonment of the further testing of hydrogen bombs.[41] In November 1956, Bulganin's letter finally accepted the principle of aerial inspection, but within such a geographically delimited area (a few hundred miles on either side of the Iron Curtain) that the American reaction was one of further disappointment.[42] But the American government continued to press on, seeking the final concession from the Soviet that would open the door to constructive negotiation.

The Eisenhower-Bulganin correspondence was generally conceded to be a hopeful portent because it epitomized the seriousness with which the states principally concerned were viewing the issue of arms limitation. The maintenance of frequent communication between the very top levels of the two governments made it possible for them immediately to exploit any agreement that might be reached. There was some feeling that the direct discussions were moving the United States and the USSR closer together; at least it seemed safe to conclude that they were at least not drifting further apart.[43]

The New Round of Negotiations. The enthusiasm of the summit era was translated into an outburst of activity in the Disarmament Subcommittee of the United Nations. A series of hopeful negotiations were undertaken in the two years following the Geneva proposal, with the United States, Britain, and France submitting working papers of various sorts designed to give effect to the new desire for action.[44] Until the heads of the major states could arrive at some agreement in principle, however, the negotiations could not have a sound basis. No significant

---

[41] Mr. Eisenhower objected strenuously to raising the point in the midst of a presidential campaign that had been featured by Adlai Stevenson's attempt to make the same point a campaign issue. See *Department of State Bulletin* (October 29, 1956), p. 662.

[42] See President Eisenhower's reply to this proposal, in *Department of State Bulletin*, (January 21, 1957), p. 89.

[43] Reitzel, Kaplan, and Coblentz, *United States Foreign Policy*, pp. 449-450.

[44] See *Disarmament and Security*, pp. 347-351 (United States), pp. 354-355 (Great Britain), pp. 355-366 (France), pp. 366-367 (3-power proposal, November, 1955).

progress was made although it was discovered that the differences between the two camps had lessened. The entire ten-year history of the effort at arms control made clear that no agreement could be reached as long as the United States and the USSR continued to prosecute the cold war and to make the arms race an indispensable part of their policies.

The new round of negotiations that opened in the spring of 1957 in the United Nations Subcommittee on Disarmament, however, provided new fuel for hopes that had begun to flag. Focusing much more clearly on limited agreement rather than on the all-at-once disarmament-inspection-control formula of earlier years, both the United States (represented by Mr. Harold Stassen) and the Soviet gave evidence that they were closer to an agreement than ever before. Not only were the negotiations carried on in an atmosphere unwontedly "businesslike," [45] but the proposals themselves represented major concessions by both sides. The central problem at this series of talks was to make a beginning, however small, on the task; suggestions of a place to start included "open-sky" inspection of the Arctic, control posts throughout Europe, partial "open-sky" inspection of the USSR and the United States, and a temporary ban on weapons testing. Though it was impossible to predict what would finally emerge from the negotiations, prospects for some agreement seemed brighter in mid-1957 than they had for a decade.

The discussions eventually bogged down, to be transferred to the 1957 General Assembly. Here both great powers discovered that the smaller states were insistent that negotiations be continued and, furthermore, that the Subcommission be expanded to include some of their number. Coming at a moment when the missile race was reaching a new intensity, at least some optimists hoped that small-state participation might break the great-power deadlock.

The prospects for arms limitation

Where did the arms-limitation issue stand after more than a decade of more or less serious attempts to solve it? What can we say about the prospects for regulation and control of national armaments?

The Implications of "Disarmament." Among the American people, even the searing experiences of the cold-war era had not entirely eliminated their historic antipathy to things military and warlike. "Dis-

---

[45] President Eisenhower used this word in his press conference of May 8, 1957. *New York Times* (May 9, 1957).

armament"—stigmatizing the tools of war as illegal and immoral and adopting some "higher" standard for international politics—retained much of its original grip on the emotions of broad sectors of the American body politic. Although the obviously sinister intentions and behavior of the Soviet served consistently to inhibit the mass urge to divest the nation of the burden and the threat of a high level of military expenditures and of mobilized power, there seemed to be a general feeling that the perils of national existence would be eliminated or drastically reduced if only weapons could be put away.

Of course, the American government had no such uncomplicated objective in mind as it dealt with the Soviet. Washington, consistent with the Charter's injunction to "regulate" rather than to eliminate armaments, never aimed at anything approximating the popular image of disarmament. The realistic objectives of the United States were two: (1) the development of a system of control over national military establishments sufficient to make impossible the achievement of strategic surprise by an aggressor; (2) the reduction of armament levels to a point sufficient to relax tension and allow relations to go forward on a more nearly normal basis.

A serious hiatus in communication developed between the public and the government; neither a common policy ground nor mutual understanding existed between policy-makers and most of their constituents. The mass public was and remained largely unaware of what was involved in the complicated series of disarmament negotiations, while American leadership failed to realize the extent to which the fear of nuclear war paralyzed the judgment of the public. The development of a coherent American policy could not progress until a greater cohesion developed on the implication of disarmament.

Disarmament and Security. The postwar arms-reduction issue teaches much the same lesson as that taught by the experience of the interwar years. Disarmament, by itself, is not a cause of peace, but rather a reflection of it. Since 1945 it has proved impossible, just as it was between 1922 and 1932, to separate the issues of disarmament and security. As long as armed force remains the only ultimately efficacious method of guaranteeing national security, states are going to retain their military machines. They will agree to a reduction in arms levels only to the extent that they become convinced that their security problems will be solved by other methods.

Within the circles of academic speculation there is a real cleavage on the point of the relative importance of disarmament and security. There is a sizeable body of opinion that finds certain "positive" values in disarmament. This argument contends that even—or especially—at a moment of crisis, measures to reduce arms levels and to call off an arms race result in affirmative gains in security for everyone involved. On this basis, the time to disarm is just at the moment when affairs seem at their most tense; the beneficent effects of a reduction in armaments will extend to other policy areas, and the creation of an atmosphere of mutual confidence will be expedited.

On the other hand, an equally strong argument is frequently made that disarmament cannot ever precede the establishment of binding security agreements. This was the theory behind Premier Bulganin's suggestion in the summer of 1956 that the first step in arms reduction be the negotiation of a nonaggression pact between the United States and the Soviet Union. It has also been the apparent basis of American action; implicit in United States policy has been the assumption that disarmament could be implemented only if and when Moscow fundamentally changed its foreign policy and minimized its threats to the peace and security of the world. In the round of discussions beginning in March, 1957, however, the United States gave the impression that it no longer insisted on political agreements as an integral part of any arms reduction program; Mr. Harold Stassen, the American representative, expressed his willingness to consider arms proposals on their own merits. Soviet reaction to this changed American stand produced for a time, as we have suggested, a different climate and new hope for agreements.

It seems unnecessary for us to attempt a solution to this "chicken-or-egg" dilemma as to which condition leads to the other. We can be just as informative and on much safer ground if we merely stipulate that disarmament and security are inextricably intertwined and that no formula for one can permanently exclude the consideration of the other. As long as a reduction in arms cannot be imposed by fiat on a major state, if it is to come at all it must come voluntarily. No state will consent to a reduction in its military capacity unless it is convinced that the arms it is giving up are genuinely surplus and not needed. The problem of arms control must be attacked within a total context if it is to yield a solution.

Arms Reduction and Accommodation. What is this total context? Of what larger whole is the issue of arms limitation a part? In attempting to answer this question we come back very nearly to our original starting place.

The arms race is not the cause of the cold war, but is rather one of its symptoms. The original root of the disarmament issue lies in the fundamental divergence in national interest between the United States and the

Soviet. So long as this conflict continues, and so long as there remains the remotest possibility that the disagreements might be prosecuted to the point of open warfare, each side will insist on retaining the practical maximum of armed strength. The arms race is thus one facet of the total policy controversy between the two contemporary giants, and can be dealt with only in connection with the other points at issue.

Thus we may opine that the road to large-scale arms limitation and reduction will really open only at some time in the future of Soviet-American relations when the trend toward mutual accommodation has accumulated sufficient impetus. Only when the resolution of outstanding issues on a basis of substantial compromise is a dominant concern, and when "coexistence" is not a propaganda phrase but rather a formula for problem-solving, can large-scale plans for arms control be discussed realistically.

This might be thought a pessimistic view. Yet, if our analysis in the earlier part of this book has any validity, it would seem to be the most probable one. Weapons are tools of policy; when new policies no longer call for execution by military means, the weapons can be discarded. Any proposal for disarmament advanced before substantial political agreement has been reached (or at least before some sort of "agreement to agree" has been ratified by both parties) is at best irrelevant and at worst possibly dangerous. It may be that the first fruit of any such joint decision to reduce the level of conflict might be an understanding on arms control. There is, however, no way for this to happen before an appropriate broader decision is made at the highest policy level.

16 : Continuing economic
issues in American policy

"Economic issues in American policy" is a phrase with two possible meanings; which of them we select will affect the nature of our discussion in this chapter. On the one hand, it may refer to the general range of concerns that are included in the notions of "economic foreign policy" or "international economic relations," primarily involving the pattern formed by the economic objectives and interests of the American people and the techniques used to serve them. The phrase may equally accurately connote, however, the purely economic dimension of total American policy, including both the economic components of American national interest and the economic techniques the United States government employs to advance it.

What makes this dual meaning important to us is that there is a considerable degree of contradiction in the implications of the two meanings. An "economic foreign policy," with objectives drawn from the free-enterprise doctrine accepted at least in principle by most Americans, cannot be thoroughly reconciled with the course of American foreign policy since 1945. The larger questions of national security and the prosecution of the cold war have imposed a number of policies on the United States that cannot be squared with any traditional or rational image of "economic foreign policy" that would call for the maximization of private profit and the free flow of goods, services, credit, and persons.[1]

---

[1] "In short, although economic and military developments tend to be shaped by the same forces, a considerable gap separates our strategic and economic interests. How to bridge this strategic gap—rather than any dollar gap—is the central problem our foreign economic policy must overcome." Samuel Lubell, *The Revolution in World Trade and American Economic Policy* (New York: Harper & Bros., Inc., 1955), p. 40. Reprinted by permission.

In one sense this dualism reflects a dilemma on which we have re-marked previously: the tendency in the actual conduct of foreign policy for short-run programs, stemming from contemporary situational im-peratives, to run counter to long-term objectives. Statesmanship must be constantly alert to keep such conflicts to the irreducible minimum; its function is to labor to create a total policy design broad and flexible enough to encompass all such contradictions and to keep the nation's efforts moving along a path that, although broad, nevertheless leads in the desired direction.

Our discussion will, as it must, select one of the two meanings upon which to concentrate and will consider the other only to the extent that it is relevant to the first. We shall deal in this analysis, as we have attempted to do throughout this study, with the broader aspects of American foreign policy: the "economic issues" we shall consider are those that bear upon the over-all mission that the United States has set itself and problems that it encounters. We shall discuss initially the basic issue of the impact of American foreign policy upon the national economy. We shall then take up two of the more significant problems of American policy with a uniquely economic pertinence: American economic assistance to foreign states and American trade policy.

FOREIGN POLICY AND THE AMERICAN ECONOMY

It is obvious that the major weapon upon which the United States has relied in its struggle against the Soviet Union has been its economic power. Unable to match Russia in manpower, military mobilization, "political warfare," or subversion, America has counted on balancing the scales by its unique ability to produce and distribute goods and its posses-sion of a highly organized and effective economic machine.[2] The key role of economic capability has given rise to certain fundamental questions about the relationship of foreign policy to the American economy.

The costs of foreign policy

Foreign policy, involving as it does such a large share of the ex-penditures of the government, is admitted to cost a great deal of money.

---

[2] James P. Warburg, in *The United States in a Changing World* (New York: Put-nam, 1954), pp. 425-31, gives a dramatic account of how this decision was originally reached in 1947-8.

So much, indeed, that sectors of the general public, egged on by ideological, political, or opportunistic opponents of the trend of American policy, have come to entertain a genuine fear that the expenditure forced by international affairs will "bankrupt" the United States. Generally speaking, this attitude tends to go hand in hand with a relative unawareness of the exact costs of foreign policy and their relation to the national wealth or the gross national product. It would be salutary, therefore, to begin our discussion with some consideration of just how much foreign policy costs.

The Dollar Cost of Foreign Policy: 1957. Expenditures for foreign policy fall into three budget catogories: national security, mutual security, and international affairs and finance. The dollar cost for a given year is instructive: we have selected fiscal 1957, covering the period from July 1, 1956, to June 30, 1957, as an illustration. Expenditures in this period were typical of recent trends.

ESTIMATED FOREIGN-POLICY EXPENDITURES, FISCAL 1957[3]
(In millions)

National security:

Department of Defense:

Army	8,581	
Navy	9,732	
Air Force	16,890	
Other	801	
TOTAL DEFENSE		36,005
Atomic energy control and development	1,940	
Stockpiling and defense production expansion	759	
TOTAL NATIONAL SECURITY		38,704

Mutual Security:

Military	2,600	
Economic, technical, and other	1,500	
TOTAL MUTUAL SECURITY		4,100

International Affairs and Finance:

Economic and technical development	[1,500]*	
Other (Export – Import bank, etc.)	962	
Foreign information and exchange activities	133	
Conduct of foreign affairs	155	
TOTAL INTERNATIONAL AFFAIRS AND FINANCE		1,250
TOTAL FOREIGN-POLICY EXPENDITURES		44,054
Less receipts		723
TOTAL NET COST		43,331

* This figure appears twice in the budget, but is counted only once in the total.

Thus, out of a total estimated government expenditure for fiscal 1957 of

---

[3] Data extracted from *The Budget of the United States Government for the Fiscal Year Ending June 30, 1958* (Washington, D.C.: U.S. Government Printing Office, 1957), pp. M27, M34 (Budget Message of the President).

$68.9 billions, over $43 billions were expended for purposes directly connected with foreign affairs. Within the remaining $24 billions, another large amount—perhaps as much as $5 billions—was used to finance programs, the impact of which on foreign policy was almost as direct. The costs of foreign policy are not only large in themselves, but constitute the most important single charge on the government's budget.

Foreign Policy and the Gross National Product. But billions of dollars printed in a table are difficult to visualize; the sheer size of the amounts involved serves to obscure both the meaning and the relationships of the totals. More relevant for our purposes is the relationship between the gross national product (GNP) and that portion of it that is devoted to foreign-policy purposes. In a table prepared by Walter S. Salant of the Brookings Institution, this relationship is demonstrated graphically.[4] We are extracting from the table here to clarify the point. Data are in billions of dollars.

GROSS NATIONAL PRODUCT AND ITS DISTRIBUTION AMONG NATIONAL DEFENSE, FOREIGN AID, AND ALL OTHER USES, IN 1947 PRICES, 1946-1955

Year	GNP	National Defense (less military grants abroad)	Foreign Aid and Military Grants Abroad	All Other Uses	
				Total	Per Capita (in dollars)
1946	233.8	21.2	6.0	206.6	1461
1950	264.7	12.7	4.3	247.7	1633
1952	293.3	36.8	4.4	252.1	1606
1953	306.5	38.9	5.5	262.1	1642
1954	300.5	32.4	4.0	264.1	1626
1955	318.8	29.8	3.7	285.3	1726

Thus, to quote Mr. Salant:

It [the table] indicates that the increase in total production was great enough to permit expansion of the combined total of defense and foreign aid between 1950 and 1953 without reducing the volume of goods and services used for other purposes in any year. It also shows that the total volume of goods and services available for these other purposes decreased in only one year of the postwar period, that it increased 38 per cent over the whole period, and that this increase was sufficiently rapid to permit an increase of 18 per cent per capita, despite the increase in population.[5]

[4] Reitzel, Kaplan, and Coblentz, *United States Foreign Policy*, p. 379n. See also Appendix D out of this volume, entitled "Defense, Foreign Aid, and Other Uses of Output, 1946-1955," pp. 480-84, in which Mr. Salant gives a number of comparative tables covering this ten year period. Reprinted by permission.

[5] Reitzel, Kaplan, and Coblentz, *United States Foreign Policy*, p. 378n. Reprinted by permission.

The data contained in this table would suggest that the costs of foreign policy have not represented any great strain on the American economy. Americans have been able to bear the burden of maintaining a sizeable military establishment and of conducting a foreign policy heavily loaded with economic programs without impoverishing themselves. On the contrary, with the share of the GNP available for maintenance of the standard of living increasing both relatively and absolutely, large foreign-policy expenditures have had no measurable inhibiting effect on the much-lauded American standard of living.

Trends in Foreign Policy Costs. The costs of foreign policy, viewed historically, demonstrate certain clear trends. Once again we may most profitably present the information in tabular form.[6] Data are in billions.

YEARLY TOTALS FOR MAJOR FOREIGN POLICY EXPENDITURES

Expenditure	1948	1949	1950	1951	1952	1953	1954	1955	1956	1957*	1958*
† Major nat'l security	11.8	12.9	13.0	22.4	43.9	50.3	46.9	40.6	40.6	40.9	43.3
‡ Int'l affairs and finance	4.5	6.0	4.6	3.7	2.8	2.2	1.7	2.1	1.8	2.3	2.4

* Estimated.
† Includes military assistance and direct forces support.
‡ Includes economic and technical development.

On the basis of these figures, it appears that, dollar-wise, American foreign-policy spending has reached something of a plateau at upwards of $40 billion for "major national security" or military spending, and something over $2 billion for nonmilitary programs. Since the end of the Korean war the figures have remained relatively constant, varying only slightly to reflect the fluctuation of the price level and the changing pattern of international affairs. This judgment, however, is conditioned by the possible inaccuracy of the Eisenhower administration's judgment that the long-pull objectives of American policy are at last coming into view and that the best course for the United States is to stabilize its programs in a continuing steady effort to reach these goals. Any sudden shift in world relationships, either favorable or unfavorable to the United States, would throw these trends out of line and would create entirely new requirements for foreign-policy spending.

Can the United States afford its foreign policy?

In one sense, the question at the head of this section is unnecessary; there is no doubt that the United States can afford the foreign policy

---

[6] *U.S. Budget for 1958*, p. 1149.

it is presently carrying on. It has been doing so for a decade and—despite some danger signals in the economy—there seems to be no real danger that the demands of foreign policy will place any insuperable burden on the economic capacity of the United States.

But, as we shall indicate in a moment, there is another sense in which the question has great relevance. We may refer momentarily back to our discussion of American capabilities in Chapter 11. We concluded there that American capacities are in general adequate to the mission the United States has set for itself. The United States *can*, we suggested, meet all the foreseeable tests; what was much less certain, however, is whether the United States *will* do so. So long as there remains an area of relatively free choice, no one dare state unequivocally that Americans will decide that they can afford their foreign policy.

The "Layer of Fat" in the Economy. Economists point out that despite the great expenditures the United States has been making in the foreign policy field and the constantly rising GNP and standard of living, the national economy has not been operating at peak efficiency. There remain segments of plant, manpower, and finance capital that are not being used at full effectiveness; there is, in other words, a residue of productivity that has not yet been fully called on. Speaking theoretically, therefore, it seems reasonable to assume that the United States could if it wished increase its foreign-policy expenditure by an indefinite but certainly considerable amount without having any significant effect at all on the standard of living. A simple expansion of productivity to take up the slack would make available great amounts of goods and services for public purposes without reducing the total available for other purposes.[7]

This "layer of fat" in the national economy—the unused (or inefficiently used) productive capacity—may well be the secret economic weapon of the United States. As long as it exists it provides something

---

[7] In his provocative study, *The Revolution in World Trade*, Samuel Lubell has a typically suggestive statement on this point (p. 40):

"Currently the tendency is to think of our surplusses as costly liabilities. But two world wars and the whole course of the postwar period have shown that the free world's strongest *single* asset is the ability of the American economy to generate sizable surpluses of every kind, from food and machinery, to medicine and clothing. . . .

"Although the heads of many foreign governments do not seem to realize it, our productive reserves are the cushion which permits them to sleep in political stability and freedom. For some time ahead most of the world is likely to continue to be living on the thin edge strategically and, in many cases, economically as well. By far the greatest contribution the United States can make to the well-being and security of the rest of the world is to remain economically strong, a reservoir of productive resources capable of meeting any emergency." (Italics in original; reprinted by permission.)

of an answer to the question we asked above: the United States can afford its foreign policy as long as it retains in uncommitted reserve considerable increments of economic power. Until international requirements force the United States to go beyond this point—that is, until the demands of foreign policy grow to the stage where they require that serious inroads be made in the supply of goods and services available for civilian use— the United States is living within its means.

The Impact of Popular Preferences. Webster defines "afford" in the sense in which we are using it as "to incur, stand, or bear without serious detriment (as to financial condition ... etc.)." Whether or not the United States can afford its foreign policy, therefore, depends in the final analysis on whether the American people, acting through their political channels, decide that the cost of international relations is causing "serious detriment" to their standard of living. A popular decision at any time that foreign affairs are costing too much would be immediately reflected in a cut in government outlays to a level felt to be tolerable.

There is no doubt that Americans are willing to support great deprivations in private economic life if they are convinced that the external peril is real enough to justify them. This fact is at least a partial explanation for the "crisis technique" that surrounded so much of American programming between 1947 and 1953. The policy of the Eisenhower administration, however, has made much of eschewing this approach and of concentrating instead on commitments of a long-term nature and planning for coordinated policies extending over a period of several years. This method, although minimizing the risks of going "too far, too fast," involves dangers of its own.

In view of the mercurial swings of American public sentiment in response to stimuli frequently slight or even irrelevant, a long-range plateau-type policy may at times be thought too expensive and at others too niggardly. Particularly in moments of relative relaxation may the public pressure for a lower rate of expenditure become politically impossible to resist. At these times the danger of unwise retrenchment is the greatest.

In at least three areas this pressure is constant and on occasion dominant. First, of course, we must mention taxation. Foreign policy must be financed with tax revenue, and paying high taxes when the international scene seems quiet is abhorrent to many Americans. Second, government policy interferes with "normal" economic relations, particularly international trade. Pressure groups constantly agitate for policy modifications in their favor; some wool growers in the United States, for example, feel that they cannot afford a policy calling for any reductions on the duty on Australian wool. Finally, foreign policy obliges the government to compete with private interests for certain key resources, of which atomic fuels, electric power, and water supplies are examples. In special cases, individuals affected in this way often feel that they can no longer afford a foreign policy that represents such a direct cost to them. When such special resistances gain mass support, the likelihood of cutbacks in policy implementation grows.[8]

Can the United States afford peace?

A question of a significance only remote in contemporary affairs but of potentially major importance is whether or not the United States can afford peace. We have seen that the cold war, at least at its present level, is bearable; we know also that the United States has fought a major war and avoided a postwar depression. But what if the economic stimulus provided by foreign-policy spending of all sorts (consuming, as we have seen, roughly 10 per cent of the GNP), should suddenly come to an end? Would there be, as some political figures contend, an immediate depression? Does the United States need the cold war to maintain its prosperity?

The Economic Effect of Peace. These are questions which no one can answer in vacuo; the proof of the American economic pudding must be the eating. Certain points, however, permit some generalization.

We must initially distinguish between two different ways in which peace could "break out." If the whole pattern of American postwar policy were to be made suddenly obsolete by a dramatic collapse of the Soviet regime, the economic questions that would then be posed would indeed be formidable and would call for rapid—perhaps emergency—action. On the other hand, if the cold war were to relax gradually, the American government would have time to shift its policy emphases little by little from a quasi-war basis to some other areas of expenditure.

To be more specific: major savings in the cost of foreign policy, of a size sufficient to present a problem to the adjustment capacity of the

---

[8] The great furor touched off by Secretary of the Treasury Humphrey's assertion that expenditures called for in the 1958 budget were too great for fiscal safety and that the trend was toward a depression "that would curl your hair" led to much agitation for budget cuts. The most frequently suggested reductions were in foreign aid programs. See *New York Times* (January 21, 1957) for Humphrey's statement. The pressure for budget cuts grew so great that President Eisenhower went directly to the people in a series of television and news-conference appeals in the spring of 1957, hoping to use his great personal popularity to swing popular sentiment behind what he called a "necessary" program.

American economy, can be achieved in only one major category: armaments spending. Other areas of government outlay for foreign policy represent only relatively negligible totals. The economic problem of peace would most probably be presented in the form of a great reduction of government appropriations for military purposes, and it is in this area that the clearest difference between a rapid shutoff and a gradual slowdown is demonstrated.

Were there to take place wholesale demobilization, speedy contract cancellation, renegotiation of purchases, and the other apparatus of rapid transition with which Americans became familiar during 1945 and 1946, this would mean that roughly 10 per cent of the GNP would suddenly become surplus. If no corrective action were taken, massive unemployment, price drops, and deflation would bring on an economic crisis potentially rivalling the depression of 1929. On the other hand, if the cutback in military expenditures were more gradual, its impact could be spread out over a longer period and—even in the absence of palliative government action— the pressure at any one time would not be so great.

Government Policy. If the situation we have suggested comes about (and, although no one flatly predicts this eventuality, very few will deny its possibility), there are several different lines the national government might follow in meeting the danger. We must remember that such a condition of peace is included in the formulation of American interest that we are employing in this study, and that it would defy good sense to view the accomplishment of one phase of basic national interest as a catastrophe to be avoided. The problem might be phrased as that of constructing economic order and stability in a world to which political peace had suddenly come.

In the event that the cold war relaxes gradually, the United States stands committed to maintain a high level of international spending for an indefinite time. As long ago as 1953, President Eisenhower pledged that the United States would devote substantial portions of any savings brought about by disarmament to a fund for "world development and reconstruction." [9] From the domestic point of view, maintaining prosperity while readjustment takes place is primary; it is a happy coincidence that one technique for accomplishing this purpose also directly advances the foreign policy of the United States. If world stability and order are to follow peace, American financial assistance will be needed. The fact that such a policy will also play a part in maintaining domestic economic health only makes more probable the fulfillment of the pledge.

---

[9] In his speech to the American Society of Newspaper Editors, April 16, 1953. See *New York Times* (April 17, 1953).

In the event of a sudden shutoff in the cold war, however, the major problem will be that of emergency action. The American economy contains a number of built-in stabilizers and anti-depression mechanisms that would cushion the shock,[10] including the Social Security System, the Full Employment Act, and the Federal Deposit Insurance Corporation. But emergency action to "prime the pump" (in the phrase of depression days) would be needed to get the economic wheels turning again at full speed. One author lists the following emergency devices to infuse a sudden new supply of money into the economy so as to buy time until longer-purview policies became effective:

> Reduce excise taxes for one year only, with notice that at the end of the year they are to be restored.
> Cut lower bracket income taxes and make the cut show at once in the rate of withholding....
> Reduce letter postage to one cent for one year and other rates enough to please the business men....
> Offer generous grants-in-aid to states and municipalities if they will act within a month to make a corresponding reduction in sales and real estate taxes for the current year.
> Pay a 100 per cent bonus on social security benefits.
> Give away large quantities of government-held agricultural surpluses to countries where goods are scarce.
> Stockpile steel, rubber, and other storable materials, with special consideration for foreign suppliers who may be especially fearful of a slump.
> Announce that military aid promised to allies will not be cut, but will be available to help with their relief costs, stiffen their foreign exchange position, and generally bolster their strength and confidence.[11]

Once these emergency measures (or any of the dozens of others that might be mentioned) had been taken, more gradual policies aimed at a smoother readjustment could be initiated. Without the breathing spell gained by quick stopgap devices, however, a serious slide would be a real danger.

FOREIGN ECONOMIC ASSISTANCE

We have discussed some of the aspects of military aid and defense support extended by the United States to friendly nations in another chapter. In the present connection we are primarily interested in the over-all economic implications of foreign aid, not only that portion oriented toward defense, but also including development assistance, technical assistance, and private overseas investment.

---

[10] See David Cushman Coyle, "Leaning on the Kremlin," *Virginia Quarterly Review* (Spring, 1954), p. 192ff.

[11] Coyle, "Leaning on the Kremlin," pp. 202-203. Reprinted by permission.

Foreign aid: amount and impact

The Economic Dimensions of "Foreign Aid." How large have American aid programs been, and of what size are they today? The summary figures indicate both amounts and trends: [12]

FOREIGN AID EXPENDITURES, FISCAL 1949—FISCAL 1958
(In millions)

Category	1949	1950	1951	1952	1953	1954	1955	1956	1957*	1958*
Military Assistance	415	130	991	2,442	3,954	3,629	2,292	2,611	2,600	2,600
Economic and Tech. Dvpt.	5,880	4,442	3,506	2,584	1,960	1,511	1,960	1,616	2,096	2,075
Total, Foreign Aid	6,295	4,572	4,497	5,026	5,914	5,140	4,252	4,227	4,696	4,675
Total Expenditure of U.S.		39,507	39,606	44,058	65,408	74,274	67,772	64,570	66,540	68,900	71,807

* Estimated.

Thus we see that the total foreign-aid bill was highest during fiscal 1949, and that it has been reduced significantly since that year in the face of a steady rise in the national income, the GNP, and the standard of living; the percentage of the total government expenditure represented by aid programs has not changed significantly since the onset of the Korean war.

When price adjustments are made to reflect all figures in 1947 prices, a somewhat different picture emerges. Including only the fiscal years 1948–1955, 1949 was the peak year in foregin-aid expenditures, with a total of $5,913 million in all forms of aid; the 1955 total was $3,706 million, the lowest annual figure for the entire period (this contrasts with the 1955 dollar total of $4,252 million in current prices shown by the budget figures).[13]

Our earlier discussions of the over-all impact of foreign policy on the American economy made the point that to the extent that international obligations constitute a net drain on the available goods and services, the primary stress occurs at the point of military expenditures rather than in foreign-assistance programs. This generalization appears to be borne out by the statistics we have quoted. At particular pressure points in the economy, however, there could be some cause for complaint that foreign assistance might actually work a hardship on Americans. This contention

---

[12] U.S. Budget for 1958, p. 1169.

[13] These figures from table, "Conversion of Foreign Aid from Current to 1947 Price Basis," by Walter S. Salant, in Reitzel, Kaplan, and Coblentz, United States Foreign Policy, p. 483. Abstracted by permission.

is offset, however, by the considerable, if immeasurable, extent to which foreign assistance programs have stimulated other, more normal trade activities and thus brought about a net economic gain to the United States.

The Global Scope of American Aid. Despite its relatively small dollar volume as compared to the total expenditures of the United States government, the American aid program has brought the United States into direct contact with the economies of virtually all the countries of the free world. Whether American economic assistance is by means of direct supply of military end-items, defense support, development aid, or technical cooperation, the United States and its policy exert a significant effect on economic affairs in the entire noncommunist world.[14]

As of the end of fiscal 1956, direct military support was being extended to at least 19 states. Of these, 12 were in Europe: the 11 European members of NATO and Yugoslavia. Four were in the Middle East: Greece, Turkey (both of which were members of NATO), Iran, and Pakistan. In "free Asia," Korea, Taiwan, and free Vietnam were included. The difficulty of drawing a clear line between "direct military assistance" and "defense support" makes it impossible to prepare any more exhaustive list. The new Middle East program of 1957 promised to add other states to this group.

ICA assistance, being "other than military," was easier to pinpoint. In fiscal 1956, 48 nations received ICA assistance: nine in the Far East, five in South Asia, eleven in the Near East and Africa, three in Europe, and twenty in Latin America.

The breakdown by type within each region is interesting. ICA assistance, as we have seen, falls into three categories: defense support, development assistance, and technical cooperation. The following table indicates the different programs in each region.[15]

ICA OBLIGATIONS IN FISCAL 1956, BY REGION
(In millions)

Region	Total $	Defense Support	Development Assistance	Technical Cooperation
Far East	760.5	726.7	—	33.8
South Asia	192.2	97.3	70.7	23.1
Near East and Africa	259.1	188.7	—	32.0
Europe	110.1	110.1	—	—
Latin America	71.3	—	44.1	27.1

[14] A very valuable and complete economic analysis of American aid programs up to 1953 is William A. Brown and Redvers Opie, *American Foreign Assistance* (Washington, D.C.: Brookings, 1953).

[15] Extracted from table, "ICA Obligations in Fiscal Year 1956," in *Report to Congress on the Mutual Security Program* (September 20, 1956), p. 18.

Within each region the further breakdown among countries provides further clues to the political ends the aid program is designed to serve. We shall cite only a few examples.

In south Asia, the entire defense-support appropriation went to Pakistan, while almost 70 per cent of the development assistance and nearly half the technical cooperation funds went to India. In the Near East-Africa group, defense support was confined to Greece, Iran, and Turkey, while development assistance was given only to Israel, Jordan, Lebanon, and Libya. All the states in the three Asian regions had some form of technical cooperation budget in operation. In Latin America, only Bolivia, Guatemala, and Haiti were included in development assistance, but 19 states (excluding only Argentina) were covered by technical cooperation. None of the latter programs, however, were very large; the Brazilian, involving some $3.6 million, involved the largest total.

The Future of American Aid. No issue has caused more bitter debate among Americans than the question of foreign aid and its future. To some it is simply a "giveaway," inspired by quasi-socialists who want to dissipate the American substance in a mad burst of vapid philanthropy; to others it is a foredoomed attempt to "buy friends" who cannot be bought; to still others it is stupid to arm, modernize, and develop potential rivals, adversaries, and competitors. On the other hand, its defenders claim it is—in one form or another—not only the most efficient weapon of American policy, but indeed an absolutely essential method of holding back communism without war. The ups and downs of the aid budgets over the years not only reflect the changes in the international scene but also roughly indicate the currents of public opinion and legislative interest in the question.

Despite the constant verbal resistance to the very idea, however, there has never been any all-out attempt made to cut off the flow of aid entirely; controversy has centered rather about how best to extract political advantage from such aid as is given. Nor has there been any agreement about the future of American aid programs. The President's *Report on the Mutual Security Program* of September, 1956, alluded to the necessity of adapting the program to meet new conditions, and pointed out that "intensive studies" of the entire program were being undertaken to devise a policy adequate to the existing situations.[16]

---

[16] The first of these "intensive studies" was released on December 22, 1956, by Chairman J. P. Richards of the House Foreign Affairs Committee. It was the product of the deliberations of the committee's staff, and proposed a general re-thinking of the entire aid program. Among its most important recommendations were: (1) a relaxation of the American restrictions on free-world trade with the Soviet bloc; (2) a legislative and administrative separation of military assistance from

Following the Middle East crisis of late 1956, there was a great deal of discussion, both of the "inside story" variety and at the level of sheer gossip, that the administration was planning a massive increase in and reorientation of aid. Seeking to capitalize on the new entree into the neutralist world gained by the American action on Suez, American planners set about calculating how best to accomplish long-standing objectives in this new situation. The President's special message on Middle East policy of January 5, 1957, calling for an extensive and string-free aid program for the region, was the first result of this reappraisal.[17] Expectation was general that other proposals would amplify this beginning at a new theory of foreign aid. Complicating the future, however, was the contemporaneous public and congressional objections to the size of the Federal budget and the demand for a lower level of expenditure.

Technical assistance

Technical assistance, the "bold new program" first broached in President Truman's inaugural address in 1949, has never reached the dimensions once hoped for it. Although, as we have seen, there were 45 country programs and three regional programs in operation at the end of fiscal 1956, the total expenditure of slightly over $150 million by no means represented the maximum exploitation of the possibilities of the program. The future of technical assistance remained one of the unresolved issues in American policy.[18]

---

economic aid; (3) a deemphasis of free world resistance to the Soviet and an emphasis on "common interests and cooperative relationships which are not connected with the Soviet Union at all"; (4) a realization that the Soviet's economic offensive be recognized as a substantial threat; (5) a shift to loans rather than grants as the vehicles of American aid, but on an objective basis and without attempts to force others to agree politically with the United States; (6) a stress on the maintenance of the European alliance and on traditional, rather than "exotic" weapons. *Foreign Policy and Mutual Security,* Committee Print, House Committee on Foreign Affairs, 84th Congress, 2d session, (December 24, 1956). The later reports were issued in March, 1957. One, by a Presidential Commission of Citizen Advisers, headed by Benjamin Fairless, urged retention of foreign aid for "a very long time," but stressed that priority should be given to countries with which the United States is militarily allied and that greater emphasis be placed on loans repayable in dollars rather than on grants. The other group, the International Development Advisory Board, headed by Eric Johnston, called for a substantial increase in capital investment and technical assistance to underdeveloped areas, even at the expense of military aid. The two reports split sharply on American aid policy toward the neutrals. See *New York Times* (March 10, 1957), iv, 2.

17 See President's message in *New York Times* (January 6, 1957).

18 See Chapter 2, "The Viewpoint of the United States," in Eugene Staley, *The Future of Undeveloped Countries* (New York: Harper & Bros., Inc., 1954), for a convenient summary of the background and objectives of Point IV and the entire technical assistance concept.

The Failure of Technical Assistance. Perhaps the most controlling consideration affecting the development of technical cooperation has been its inclusion, ever since 1951, within the mutual-security concept. Such technical assistance as has been extended since that date has been geared to generally the same political-military purposes as the other forms of American aid. There has been little official inclination to rely on technical assistance, by definition slow-acting and of long-range scope, for the accomplishment of relatively speedy political purposes. Direct military assistance, defense support, and—in special cases—development assistance can all be counted on to do the visible task much more speedily. Congress has been particularly prone to view Point IV as a policy of only limited relevance to the cold war, and to be reluctant to move very energetically in its implementation.[19]

But technical cooperation, considered on its own merits, has proved vulnerable to criticism on other grounds. Many of its advocates are easy to portray as zealots with little practical sense; the "quart of milk for every Hottentot" charge is often used to refute the more extreme proponents of the virtues of the exportation of American "know-how." "Boondoggling" is bad enough; even more directly in point is the charge made that the development of industrial capacity in the underdeveloped areas of the world would merely create new competitors for American industry and thus would be—to use another hackneyed phrase—a case of the American "cuckoo fouling its own nest." [20]

Financing Technical Assistance. But the policy objections to the program have not been the major reasons why Point IV has never really gotten off the ground. The major failure of the enterprise has been its inability to attract enough finance capital to make possible the many projects suggested. In the beginning it was expected that American government participation in technical cooperation would be confined to making available technically competent personnel; financing would come either from the indigenous sources in the host country (rarely) or (more commonly) from American private investors. This goal has never been reached; American private capital has been reluctant to go into the under-

---

19 We will recall that mutual-security assistance, as officially defined, sets technical cooperation as an appendage either to defense support or to development assistance before admitting it to be a technique of aid in its own right. See page 183. As a summary of the question in the Spring of 1957, see E. W. Kenworthy, "Washington Takes a New Look at Foreign Aid," *New York Times* (March 27, 1957), iv, 9.

20 For example, Congressmen from cotton-producing states generally opposed the original American offer to help finance Egypt's Aswan Dam, made in early 1956. Their reasoning was simple; any increase in available water would increase Egypt's cotton production, thus strengthening a potential competitor for world cotton markets. See remarks of Senator George of Georgia, *New York Times* (April 28, 1956).

developed areas and Congress has been unwilling to provide any significant amount of government funds for development purposes.[21] The fiscal policy of the World Bank (the International Bank for Reconstruction and Development) has also been extremely cautious, restricting loans primarily to self-liquidating projects. Very few development programs can qualify on these grounds.

The United States government has attempted in several ways to stimulate the flow of private capital overseas. It has made intensive studies of the impediments to foreign investment,[22] and has made what improvements it could in the "investment climate." In this connection it has used the extensive consultative facilities provided by the General Agreement on Tariffs and Trade (GATT; 1947) frequently to urge other states to remove at least the more irksome of these impediments.

The International Finance Corporation. Another recent step was taken in July, 1956, by the creation of the International Finance Corporation, the purpose of which was stated to be as follows in a White House press release:

> The objective of the new organization is to encourage the growth of private enterprise by providing, in association with local and foreign investors, risk capital for financing the establishment, improvement, and expansion of productive private enterprises in member countries when other sources of funds are not available on reasonable terms.[23]

The IFC began its existence with 31 members and capital subscriptions of over $78 million. Reports indicated that 20 other nations intended to join IFC as of the early part of 1957 and that its total capital would reach $100 million. Its function, at least from the American point of view, was described as follows:

> We regard this new institution as more than a financing institution. Its importance rather lies in the fact that it will work to bring together potential investors and investment opportunities.
>
> To insure that the IFC does not become merely another financing institution, governments have wisely avoided putting large sums of money at its disposal. This should result in its keeping its original purpose and make it extremely unlikely that in the great majority of cases its participation in an individual enterprise will be a small minority one.[24]

---

[21] The figure for fiscal 1957 was $152 millions. Studies in 1957 indicated that the United States could easily afford $1 billion annually for these purposes. See the Kenworthy article above.

[22] See, as an elaborate example, *Factors Limiting U.S. Investment Abroad*, a report prepared by the Office of International Trade, Bureau of Foreign and Domestic Commerce, U. S. Department of Commerce (Washington, D.C.: U.S. Government Printing Office, 1954). Part I was subtitled: "Survey of Factors in Foreign Countries"; Part II, "Business Views on the U.S. Government's Role."

[23] *Department of State Bulletin* (October 22, 1956), p. 634.

[24] John C. Baker, "Financing of Economic Development," *Department of State Bulletin* (September 3, 1956), p. 396; this entire speech, made before the 22d session

The safest conclusion we can reach about the problem of financing that the development of the technical assistance program raises is to echo the words of John C. Baker that "confidence plays an important part in creating an atmosphere favorable to the movement of capital." [25] Technical cooperation and its objectives have proved to be extremely difficult to rationalize in the midst of a paramilitary cold war; confidence of a sort adequate to lure timorous investors out of hiding cannot very easily be engendered by an incessant iteration of the twin threats of Soviet military aggression and of domestic communist revolution. Whether the conclusion the United States would draw from this lesson of seven years would be to abandon technical assistance entirely or to separate it from its uncomfortable resting place in the mutual security program was unpredictable as of early 1957.[26] The major unsettling of American policy brought about by the Middle East crisis and the contemporaneous stresses within the Soviet bloc gave some hope that new decisions contemplating a major expansion of technical assistance might be in the making. The re-emphasis on armaments triggered off by the events of the last months of 1957, however, once again threw a cloud over the future of Point 4.

UNITED STATES TRADE POLICY

An economic issue of immediate pertinence to the total of American foreign policy is the question of the status of international trade. Perhaps in no area has it proved more difficult to bring together the competing requirements of a cold-war orientation to immediate issues and a long-term interest in the economic implications of peace, order, and stability.

America's strategic economic position has made it possible for the United States to use international trade as a weapon against the Soviet. Denying exports to hostile nations or extending trade and exchange concessions to friendly ones, and the employment of promises or threats to do either while bargaining, have proved generally useful to American negotiators. What the use of trade control as a tool of policy has meant, however, has been a systematic denial of the pledges of "normal" trade

of ECOSOC on August 4, 1956, is authoritative regarding current official thinking on the subject. Of interest was Mr. Baker's clear identification of disarmament with American support of SUNFED (Special United Nations Fund for Economic Development). No major American contribution to SUNFED could be expected, Mr. Baker indicated, until arms control resulted in substantial reductions in the American military budget.

25 *Department of State Bulletin* (September 3, 1956), p. 396.

26 The Richards report of December, 1956, and the Johnson report of 1957, however, seemed to foreshadow some attempt to revitalize the original Point IV concept. See footnote 16 above.

relations made by the United States on other occasions. Freely-operating "multilateralism" in international economic relations has been a casualty of the cold war. The United States has been unable thoroughly to rationalize this confusion of purpose.

Domestic developments have also complicated the problem. The free-enterprise economy of the United States has resisted both forms of government pressure, either toward greater control of trade in the national interest or toward a genuine attempt at the liberalization of international trade. Instead the American economy has been greatly affected by the world-wide urge toward economic nationalism, and considerable pressure-group agitation toward protectionism, boycotts, government-subsidized trading, and other manifestations of "unilateralism" have been a constant factor in government decisions. All of these matters enter into United States trade policy and affect the broader pattern of American policy.[27]

The problems of trade

International trade, for the United States, has presented a series of problems since 1945 that have made the development of a coherent trade policy very difficult. As we shall discuss them here, they break down into three broad categories: the announced pledge of multilateralism and what has happened to it, the existence of the "dollar gap" vis-a-vis the free world, and the political significance of trade, both with the communist bloc and the noncommunist states.

The Pledge of Multilateralism. The United States entered the postwar era committed in principle to multilateralism in international economic relations, the increase of international trade, and the maximum possible freedom for all forms of interstate economic contacts.[28] The American position in 1945 was flatfootedly in favor of immediate and extensive action to reduce the barriers to trade and to stimulate the flow of goods and services in all directions across national frontiers. The concrete meas-

[27] Samuel Lubell, in *The Revolution in World Trade*, says (p. 26): "To attempt to reassert the doctrine of free trade or free competition in its old laissez-faire sense is unworkable in view of the prevailing pressures for government intervention from both domestic and foreign sources. Yet expanded government intervention, in itself, offers no solution either, if only because the pressures for government action that arise from domestic sources, are so often in such violent conflict with the needs of international stability." Reprinted by permission.

[28] See, as the most forthright statement of this position, *Proposals for Expansion of World Trade and Employment*, Department of State publication 2411 (Washington, D.C.: U.S. Government Printing Office, 1945).

ures the United States (in association with Britain) proposed included tariff reduction and cooperative action by all trading states to create a climate more favorable to trade; particularly important in American (and British) thinking was the early negotiation of the General Agreements on Tariffs and Trade (GATT) and the creation of the International Trade Organization (ITO).

Unfortunately, neither economics nor politics permitted the pledge of multilateralism to be effectively translated from the realm of principle to the area of practice. The cold war grew in importance until it relegated the "normal" economic relations of nations to the indefinite future; even if the Soviet threat had not materialized, in any case the economic dislocation left in the wake of the fighting would have required extensive and long-lasting corrective action. The first postwar decade saw the United States government clinging to its pledge of ultimately freer trade, but unable to make any major progress toward that goal in the face of constant political crisis provoked by the Soviet and recurrent economic trouble at various points in the free world.

The Dollar Gap. From the point of view of pure economics (assuming for the moment that in this context "economics" can be separated from "politics") official American policy asserted that the reopening of trade channels after 1945 was obstructed by four factors: (1) restrictions imposed by governments; (2) restrictions imposed by private combines and cartels; (3) fear of disorder in the markets for certain primary commodities; (4) irregularity, and the fear of irregularity, in production and employment.[29] In practice, however, all of these proved less important than one that American economists and policy-makers foresaw only dimly in 1945: the dollar gap.

The dollar gap—or, more technically, the balance-of-payments problem—is a question of great complexity and a long history. To do it justice in economic terms would require a longer discussion than we can afford.[30] We may perhaps be able to put it simply and nonscientifically without distorting the concept out of recognition.

In essence the dollar gap after 1945 meant that the free-world nations wanted and needed American goods, but lacked the means to pay for them. In international trade, payment for American goods in the first instance may be made in dollar credits, but ultimately the payments must balance; if Europe (for example) were to continue purchasing American commodities over any protracted period, it would be obliged to sell an

---

[29] *Proposals for Expansion of World Trade and Employment*, pp. 12-18.

[30] See, for a theoretical discussion, J. E. Meade, *The Balance of Payments* (London: Oxford University Press, 1951).

equivalent amount of goods in dollar markets. In 1945 the free world could neither produce saleable goods nor gain access to dollar markets. This was the dollar gap: the margin between a nation's import requirements from the dollar area and its available dollars or dollar-earning capacity.

So great was the dollar gap for all except a very few states that to talk about "normal trade" was preposterous. The United States was forced (both for economic and for political reasons) to undertake large-scale programs of aid to the free world ("unilateral transfers," to use the delicate phrase) so as to keep some trade flowing and to accomplish the minimum objectives of foreign policy. This program was concentrated in Europe, where (in an industrialized society) the problem was more acute; the elimination of the dollar gap in unindustrialized nations (primarily raw-material producers) was to be accomplished by longer-range programs, primarily Point IV development assistance.

The intensification of the cold war after 1950 brought about, as we have seen, a shift in American aid policy that emphasized rearmament rather than economic recovery. This put a new strain on the economies of the European nations, and threatened to reopen the dollar gap that had begun to narrow.[31] The end of the first decade of the cold war saw a long-term, self-regulating system of free international trade still being subordinated to requirements of mutual security and the cold war. No one in mid-1957 was able to predict when the balance-of-payments problem would be brought back to manageable size and the principles of multilateralism would be again controlling in trade.

The Political Implications of Trade. But there were additional reasons why multilateralism was ignored. When the nature of the Soviet threat was made clear and the outlines of an American policy were inked in, America's strategic economic position dictated the use of trade as a political weapon. Since 1945, the use of trade as a tool of foreign policy has taken two forms: (1) the Soviet bloc has been generally excluded from the American trading area; (2) trade concessions have been used to weld the free world into a more cohesive entity. Bipolarity as a policy demanded that the Soviet sphere be boycotted by the entire free world, and American policy has worked to this end. The Battle Act, passed by Congress in 1951, was designed to deny American economic aid to any nation that traded with communists, and much effort was expended by American negotiators to persuade allies and neutrals alike that they should have no dealings with Moscow.

---

[31] See W. Diebold, *Trade and Payments in Western Europe* (New York: Crowell, 1952).

The policy, however bravely it might be stated, was never fully implemented. Too many noncommunist states were faced with economic problems that the United States could not (or would not) solve, and the communist bloc offered too many tempting bargains. American tariff policy left, from the point of view of allied nations, a great deal to be desired. There was always a certain amount of trading across the Iron Curtain, even at the height of bipolarity; the rise of neutralism after 1954 and the coincident decline of the two-power concept made it out of the question to restrict free-world trade with the communist empire. By 1957, although the United States was careful not to undertake any full-fledged reconsideration of its policy, the volume of East-West trade was at a postwar high and promised to increase steadily.

Just as the effectiveness of bipolar control of East-West trade diminished, so did the utility of using intra-free world trade as a means of unifying the American bloc. This is not to say that the economic interdependence of the western world diminished; what declined was the ability of the United States to hold its allies in line by economic means. As long as the other western states were free to deal economically with the Soviet Union, they were less amenable to control by Washington. The aftermath of the Suez intervention of 1956, however, was to precipitate economic and financial crisis in Britain and to cause serious dislocation on the Continent. The revelation of Europe's weakness evoked new suggestions that the United States uses its economic power to force total compliance from its allies. There was little indication, however, that America was particularly interested in any such move; American policy was more concerned with the progressive dismantling of bipolarity than with its rebirth.

ITO and GATT

In the postwar world multilateral international trade has been subordinated to the twin pressures of domestic planning and economic nationalism on the one hand and of the demands of foreign policy on the other. A clear demonstration of this generalization is the history of the attempts to formalize multilateralism into international institutions. The International Trade Organization, the Charter of which was hailed as a great forward step, has never come into existence; the General Agreement on Tariffs and Trade, although provocative of much negotiation and some reduction in tariffs, has had only a negligible effect on trade patterns.

The Failure of ITO. The ITO Charter was drawn up at the United Nations Conference on Trade and Employment, held at Havana in 1947–8.[32] It was the culmination of the 1945 American *Proposals* and, in general, provided for an organization charged with the duty of bringing about an increase in the flow of international trade. Even though the Charter contained many exceptions to the general principles of free trade (made on behalf of nations that were in difficulties and that demanded the right to take unilateral remedial action), the theory of the document was clearly in the tradition of multilateralism.

The ITO was stillborn; the Charter remains as a monument to the hopes of the early postwar era, but the organization never came into existence. Failure of the United States to ratify the instrument doomed the entire undertaking, and after 1950 the executive branch ceased even to attempt to win congressional approval. In 1955 President Eisenhower attempted to gain consent for American entry into the Organization for Trade Cooperation, a less elaborate offshoot of ITO. This too proved too much for newly-protectionist Senators to accept, and there was little hope after that date that the United States would—at least in the contemporary climate of domestic and foreign policies—take this step in implementation of its promise of freer trade.

Negotiations under GATT. The General Agreement on Tariffs and Trade was entered into in 1947.[33] It is actually an understanding providing for multilateral tariff bargaining among the signatories. Under its terms periodic meetings of the Contracting Parties are held (11 through 1956) at which bilateral and multilateral discussions go on, either for reciprocal tariff reductions or for ironing out particular trade difficulties.

Although the first decade of GATT failed to bring about any wholesale reductions in tariffs, there was no doubt that it filled a real need. Twenty-three nations originally adhered to the agreement; by 1956 the number had risen to thirty-five, including most of the major trading states of the free world. The membership included eight states of the Commonwealth, fourteen in Europe, eight in Latin America, four from the Afro-Asian region, and the United States.

The GATT negotiations, in addition to bilateral and multilateral tariff discussions, have concentrated upon certain semipermanent problems obstructing free trade. Among these have been the issue of import

---

[32] United Nations, *Charter for an International Trade Organization*, United Nations Conference on Trade and Employment, Havana, Cuba, 1947-8 (New York: United Nations, 1948).

[33] U.S. Department of State, *The General Agreement on Tariffs and Trade and Texts of Related Documents* (Washington, D.C.: U.S. Government Printing Office, 1950).

quotas [34] (imposed usually by nations in serious balance-of-payments difficulties), currency convertibility, and price stabilization on primary commodities (usually agricultural). Despite the fairly general good-will with which these problems were attacked, most of the participating states felt sincerely that their own problems were important and unique enough that exceptions to general rules should be made in their case. Understandable as this was, and justifiable as many of the claims were, this emphasis on discovering loopholes in GATT rather than attempting to make forward progress could not but be a disappointment to those who hoped for an increase in trade as a contribution to stability in the world.

New Trade Problems. As the postwar era moved well into its second decade, most of the old trade problems continued to complicate international economic relations. In addition, growing out of evolving conditions were some new trade issues that were to require either that new American policies be developed or that old decisions be rethought. Of these, the two most significant were the new dimensions of the question of East-West trade and the development of new free-trading areas.

We have already considered East-West trade in the context of bipolarity. As the cold war continued to change its form after 1954, questions of trade became, if not more important, at least more widely discussed. A good case could be made that one of the best ways to guarantee Moscow's acceptance of the procedural status quo was to tie the Soviet down by economic and trade commitments. On this basis, some arguments were heard after the summit in 1955 that Washington should take the lead in proposing expansion of trade with the Soviet sphere. On the other hand, both American economic nationalism and a certain school of cold-war thinking found any trade concessions to Moscow to be totally abhorrent, and this group contended that opening American markets to communist penetration would be surrender comparable to the worst appeasement of Hitler. This division in American public opinion took place in the face of growing demands from the western allies for a liberalization of American policy on East-West trade and a steady increase in commercial agree-

---

[34] The State Department press release discussing the 11th session of the Contracting Parties made the following comment about American action on import restrictions at this 1956 meeting: "...the U.S. delegation held bilateral consultations with the delegations of 13 countries.... These discussions covered import restrictions maintained by these countries on specific commodities which created a hardship to U.S. producers or were unduly discriminatory toward U.S. goods. In each case the U.S. delegation suggested that the other country consider whether a relaxation of the restriction could be made without disrupting that country's balance of payments position. Industrial products were discussed with eight countries, agricultural products with five, and fisheries products with four." Quoted in *Department of State Bulletin* (December 3, 1956), p. 895.

ments between Moscow and the Afro-Asian nations. During 1957, the United States moved at least partially to satisfy the urge for trade between the communist bloc and the free world states, particularly in Europe.

Potentially of even greater importance to the future of world economic relations was the movement toward the creation of new free-trade areas in various parts of the world. A number of smaller states—primarily in Europe—after 1945 began to find advantage in consolidating themselves either into free-trade areas or into customs unions.[35] Atlhough the United States, along with the other signatories of GATT, approved of such measures as steps toward an increased and liberalized trade, there is no question that their establishment, particularly as among major trading nations, would have a significant impact on the course of trade.

The postwar pattern was set by Belgium, the Netherlands, and Luxembourg, who partially consolidated their economies in a customs union known colloquially as "Benelux." Although the projected goals of this program were not reached, by 1956 several other projects had gone into the planning stage. One involved negotiation among the six states of "little Europe,"—the Schuman Plan states of France, west Germany, Italy, and Benelux—of a full-fledged customs union; the document was signed in early 1957, and the crucial ratification—by France—took place in July of that year. Another went beyond this and looked to the day when the OEEC states (the 16 Marshall Plan nations) should be united in a free-trade area with the six-state customs union as its core. The most interesting aspect of this latter proposal was the announced willingness of Great Britain at least to negotiate the matter. Up to 1956 British policy had contended that London's commitments to the Empire and Commonwealth would prevent British participation in any such project. There was a good deal of speculation that a major revolution in British policy was in the making, growing out of London's apparent decision to merge —at least partially—its economy with that of western Europe.

Another interesting free-trade area was in the making in Latin America. Under the leadership of Nicaragua, a treaty was developed (to go into effect by 1960) which within ten years would have the effect of eliminating all tariffs on trade among Nicaragua, El Salvador, Costa Rica, Guatamala, and Honduras.

Free-trade areas and customs unions had some implications for the United States and other exporting nations that were at least potentially

---

[35] Both a free-trade area and a customs union involve the elimination of tariff barriers among the countries comprising the area. A customs union, however, establishes a common tariff applicable to all imports from outside the area, while in a free-trade area each nation retains its own tariff schedules except vis-a-vis each other.

disturbing. If several nations enacted multilateralism as among themselves, but then used their mutually improved position to deal as a unit with the rest of the world on a bilateral basis, the over-all trade situation of the world would not have been particularly improved. GATT, in authorizing such measures, required that any free-trade or customs-union agreement should not result in tariffs or other protections higher under the new arrangement than they were before, and that tariff preferences for particular outside countries should not be increased. GATT also required that any trading-area agreement should be submitted to the contracting parties for review.[36]

The rebirth of American protectionism

The title given this section may actually be unintentionally misleading. It is at best debatable whether or not American protectionism ever reached such desuetude that we may speak of its present importance as a "rebirth." In any case, the sense of our discussion here is clear; the bulk of American opinion and policy, despite powerful economic evidence to the contrary, is still wedded to the principle of the protective tariff. Arguments based on history, economic doctrine, the requirements of foreign policy, or simple humanity all fail to move the high-tariff advocates. They deny the necessity to compete with foreign production in the American market and apply the historically familiar techniques of pressure politics to keep the United States a high-tariff country.

American Tariff Policy. The basic American tariff law is still the Smoot-Hawley Tariff of 1930, the highest tariff in American history and a major contributing factor to the depression of the early 1930's. The Roosevelt New Deal never repealed this law; such reduction in its prohibitive rates as was accomplished prior to 1941 was by means of the Reciprocal Trade Agreements program (1934). By this device the President negotiated executive agreements for tariff reduction with one nation at a time. He was authorized to lower existing rates by up to 50 per cent in exchange for corresponding concessions. Under the widely used most-favored-nation clause, such reductions in American duties were extended to most other countries as well.

The Trade Agreements program is often thought of as a landmark of

---

36 The Contracting Parties, at their 11th session, "regretted that there had not been an examination of the customs union" between France and Tunisia (effective January 1, 1956) before its establishment. *Department of State Bulletin* (December 3, 1956), p. 897.

New Deal foreign policy, and yet in retrospect we can see that it failed to bring about really important reductions in American tariffs. Congressional pressure has been constant ever since the enactment of the original law in 1934 against any such thorough-going overhaul of American imposts, and each legislative renewal of the Act has brought more limitations on the freedom of executive action. Most revelatory was the so-called "peril point" legislation, originally added to the Act in 1947. Under its terms, the Federal Tariff Commission must fix the point at which foreign goods can compete with any American industry. If tariffs are below this point, Congress must be informed. This carries the implicit threat of legislative increase of rates if the President were to persist in cutting tariffs beyond what Congress felt to be tolerable.

The Pressures of the Tariff. Actually, of course, the American people are not (and never have been) of a single mind on tariff policy. Significant sections of the economy have vested interests in a high protective tariff wall, while others—either less numerous or less well-organized and vociferous—are concerned with increased trade and lower tariffs. Into which group a particular industry falls, of course, depends largely upon its competitive status vis-a-vis foreign goods.

An industry in an inferior competitive position—cotton textiles or precision watches, for example—is insistent on high tariffs to protect its domestic market. An industry concentrating on domestic sales and without significant foreign competition is largely indifferent to tariff considerations. An industry whose export sales are large and important and whose leaders realize the balance-of-payments implications of international economic relations tends to demand reductions in duties. The first and last groups participate most heavily in tariff pressure politics.

Historically (up to 1914), American industry was generally protectionist and American agriculture (producing raw materials for export and purchasing industrial products) argued for freer trade. The nineteenth-century Republican party, dominated by industrial leaders, was the high-tariff party; the Democrats, led by Southern agriculture, was identified with low rates. The tariff long was considered one of the issues on which party positions were genuinely distinguishable.

Under contemporary conditions, however, the party positions have become strangely confused as the international trade requirements of industry and agriculture have become nearly reversed. Much of American industry depends on exports for its profit margin, while agriculture—many of its overseas markets gone—today demands insulation from the price-depressing mechanisms of the world market. So far has this gone that the 1956 Democratic platform contained a somewhat equivocal pledge to restudy the reciprocal trade agreements program so as to offer a more adequate protection to American producers.

Examples of Protectionism. It would be impossible for us to catalogue the specific victories won by advocates of protection for particular commodities. Mention of a few of the more recent ones, however, will illustrate the variety of the pressures. In recent years the American watch industry won a major tariff concession against the importation of Swiss watches, and the Midwest dairy farmers won a temporary restriction against the import of cheese and other dairy products. Bicycle manufacturers have agitated against the rapidly developing preference for European bicycles among American consumers, and cotton textile producers during 1955, 1956, and 1957 engaged in a well-coordinated and well-financed effort to impose quotas on Japanese imports of textiles.

The most thorough-going victory for protection, of course, is that won by the "farm bloc." The entire pattern of government farm policy is an attempt to give American agriculture a preferred domestic economic position, immune from the influence of either the home or the foreign market. In this enterprise support prices and government purchase of commodities are as much a part as are tariffs and quotas on imports. Various agricultural industries, such as the production of sugar beets and of wool, enjoy privileged positions with the American consumer; others, such as the "basic crops" covered by support prices, need not fear foreign competition as long as their prices are guaranteed by government purchase at a level safely above the world price.

The Advocacy of Economic Internationalism. The anti-protection position has been officially adopted by the executive branch ever since 1945. Presidents Truman and Eisenhower have both accepted the commitment that the cause of economic multilateralism was so much in the American interest that it required wholesale revision of American trade policies. From the Gray Report [37] in 1950 to the Randall Commission's report [38] in 1954, administration leaders have opposed the protectionist trend. Their failure to head it off, however, reveals the extent to which economic internationalism has failed to take hold among the American people.

Although certain leading industrialists, such as Mr. Clarence Randall himself and Mr. Henry Ford II, have advocated an entirely new approach to tariff policy, and despite the fact that they have been to some extent

---

[37] Gordon Gray and others, *Report to the President on Foreign Economic Policies* (Washington, D.C.: U.S. Government Printing Office, 1950).

[38] Commission on Foreign Economic Policy, *Report to the President and the Congress* (Washington, D. C.: U. S. Government Printing Office, 1954).

supported by trade associations (notably the United States Chamber of Commerce), a low-tariff position is still relatively uncommon among the general public. Interest in tariff revision is frequently thought of as vague "do-goodism" and simple-minded internationalism, and the most earnest arguments of such groups as the League of Women Voters are shrugged off by "practical" politicians.

Protectionism and American Foreign Policy. There seems to be considerable reluctance among leaders of the public to face squarely the economic implications of the long-range policy of the United States. If and how peace, order, and stability can be ensured without gearing the American economy into an international system is a question never thoroughly debated by the public.[39] It may well be that such a thorough airing of the problem will have to precede the development of an American policy adequate to the demands of the controlling concept of American interest.[40]

---

[39] See Gunnar Myrdal, *An International Economy* (New York: Harper & Bros., Inc., 1956), for an argument on this point.

[40] See H. Piquet, *Aid, Trade, and the Tariff* (New York: Crowell, 1953).

17 : Continuing psychological issues in American policy

I t has become banal to observe that "the cold war is a struggle for the minds of men," and that the only permanent victories that the United States can hope to win in its search for a world of peace, order, and stability are to be found in the realm of human preferences and desires. Despite the platitudinous nature of such statements, however, we cannot deny the central relevance of mass states of mind on both sides of the Iron Curtain and elsewhere to the accomplishment of American objectives and the advancement of American national interest. No catalogue of the continuing issues in American policy would be even approximately complete without an examination of some of those pertinent concerns whose major impact is in the area of attitudes, beliefs, and other psychological manifestations.

We indicated earlier that there is no closed category that we can dub the "psychological." Every move made by the United States, regardless of its primary focus, has its psychological overtones; Washington has largely abandoned the concept of psychological warfare as a distinct dimension of action. We shall not, therefore, discuss narrowly psychological concepts in this chapter. Instead, we shall take again the general position that we adopted in the two previous chapters, and shall consider a number of issues of broader import that have a specific psychological implication.

We shall first comment on the question of whether or not the cold war is a "battle of ideas"; that is, we shall attempt to discover the extent to which the Russian-American controversy is an "ideological conflict" and what place ideological considerations have within in. We shall next attempt to analyze American propaganda, as to content and as to purpose. A final section, on the maintenance of American morale, will include a discussion of American popular reaction to the propaganda of foreign states and the various "morale policies" used by the government to achieve and maintain the desired level of public morale.

THE COLD WAR AS A BATTLE OF IDEAS

Among the more hotly disputed points stemming from the general line of American policy since 1947 has been a basic disagreement among analysts and the general public about whether or not (and if so, the extent to which) the cold war is actually a struggle between ideologies. That there has been an ideological quarrel between East and West seems beyond question; the controversy, at least among Americans, grows out of the conclusions that can safely be drawn from this admitted divergence in ideological outlook.

Many questions of great policy importance are answerable only by a determination of the ideological content of the cold war; a few of them might profitably be mentioned. We should note, however, that the discussion in this section of the chapter will not attempt to answer these questions in detail; its purpose will be rather to suggest a few factors that might influence the responses that any citizen would make to them.

Some of the more frequently argued points are the following: (1) Is America's real enemy communist ideology or Soviet expansionism? (2) Is ideological conflict inevitable between communism and democracy? (3) Must ideological disagreement result in overt policy clashes? (4) Is ideological war inevitable? (5) Can the cold war ever be amicably adjusted? (6) Must the cold war go to the point at which one ideology exterminates the other? (7) Can the behavior of the USSR (or, for that matter, the behavior of the United States) be predicted on the basis of ideological imperatives?

The ideological front

What has been the ideological front of the cold war? In what forms have ideological differences been prosecuted?

Ideological Disagreements. There is no need for us to examine the many detailed points of disagreement and differences between the Soviet and the American belief systems. To do so would require an elaborate analysis of both societies and the roots of their beliefs[1]. We may perhaps make the central point, however, that both ideologies are "total" in the sense that from either may be derived an ideological position on almost any foreign-policy issue. Taking opposing positions on a number of basic philosophic dichotomies—such as free will (democracy)-determinism (communism), or individualism (democracy)-collectivism (communism) —the ideological confrontation of the two systems is as nearly absolute as we can imagine.

We should also note here that it is important to keep clear which level of ideological disagreement we are discussing. Although each belief system exists in a "pure" form to which people and government alike render homage (Marxism for communists; the "natural-rights" dogma of the Declaration of Independence for Americans), the officially-sanctioned credo of each government today represents a significant departure from such original formulation. Nor are we speaking here of such difference as may exist between announced ideology and actual policy, but rather of the distinction between official working doctrine and its older—and presumably purer if not always simpler—form. The ideological controversy most pertinent to our analysis is that between the presently controlling belief systems within the respective societies and governments, and not between the relatively rigid philosophical formulations of Karl Marx and Thomas Jefferson.

Ideological Conflict. The ideological issues between American-style democracy and Russian-style communism are infinite, but we may conveniently group them under three main headings: [2] (1) the world role to be played by the two states and their relations vis-a-vis each other; (2) the preferred political system for all states—western parliamentary democracy vs. communist "people's democracy"; (3) the preferred economic system on which ultimately to organize the entire world—capitalism vs. socialism. In each of these three broad areas, absolute disagreements exist; in each, ideological controversy is prosecuted vigorously.

Ideology as objective

Any ideology has as one of its essentials a vision of the world as it ought to be and as it will be when truth finally triumphs. This means

---

[1] See, among many studies on this point, William Ebenstein, *Today's Isms* (Englewood Cliffs, N. J.: Prentice-Hall, Inc., 1954), and H. B. Mayo, *Democracy and Marxism* (New York: Oxford University Press, 1955).

[2] This formulation is found, in somewhat more detail, in the present author's *Principles of International Politics* (New York: Oxford University Press, 1956), pp. 379-80.

that an ideology incorporates a set of ideological objectives: goals derived from the summary absolutes of the dogma. If the ideology is accepted by the bulk of the people of a state, the attainment of those objectives in the real world becomes the putative responsibility of that state's government.

It is clear that both the Soviet and the American ideologies as officially enunciated today lay down such policy objectives. Such ideological concerns can be classified as positive and negative; that is, some call for the destruction of conditions inimical to the doctrine, while others demand the affirmative accomplishment of states of affairs deemed desirable.

Soviet Ideological Objectives. Soviet ideological objectives can be grouped in three categories, called for convenience economic, social, and political.

(1) Economic objectives. Negatively, Soviet ideology calls for the destruction of private property as an institution and capitalism as a system of production. Positively, capitalism is to be followed by "socialism" that will provide a cure for each of the evils for which private property is responsible.

(2) Social objectives. Negatively, the social classes whose existence depends on private property—the aristocracy, the capitalists, and the bourgeoisie—are to be liquidated, either by conversion and "re-education" or by violence. Positively, the class structure is to be replaced by a reconstituted classless community of "workers, peasants, and intellectuals."

(3) Political objectives. Negatively, all regimes dominated by socio-economic groups hostile to Soviet beliefs (the capitalists and the bourgeoisie) are to be either destroyed or transformed, and all foreign policies opposing Soviet aims are to be defeated. Positively, anti-communist democracies and autocracies alike are to be remade into "people's democracies" on the Soviet model and an era of total ideological peace is to be ushered in.[3]

These objectives as we have stated them are drawn fairly directly from orthodox Marxist-Leninist-Stalinist sources. Since Stalin's death in 1953, however (and to some extent previously), successive official reinterpretations of communist doctrine have blurred the sharper edges of the ideological blueprint. It is no longer necessary, at least according to some formulations of the official line, for the Soviet to act incessantly to destroy the capitalist democracies; coexistence may now be ideologically respect-

---

[3] Many detailed analyses of Soviet ideological goals have been made. We shall cite only two: R. N. Carew Hunt, *Theory and Practice of Bolshevism* (London: Bles, 1950): and Hans Kelsen, *The Political Theory of Bolshevism* (Berkeley and Los Angeles: University of California Press, 1948), especially pp. 26-39.

466

able.[4] "Socialism" itself, as defined today, permits private property, savings banks, and some free-market economic activity. The newer exegeses of Soviet holy writ so inhibit the impact of the older ones that it is extremely difficult for us to be precise about just what contemporary Soviet ideology demands as objectives. We may be reasonably safe in assuming, however, that at bottom Soviet ideology demands the same goals as heretofore, and that what is different is largely detail regarding time, procedure, and priority.[5]

American Ideological Objectives. The United States—fortunately or unfortunately—has no such rigid belief system that purports to impose a set of controlling foreign-policy objectives. Americans, proud of being a nonideological people—and so ill-equipped historically for foreign policy—have no detailed and consistent set of traditional ideological objectives.[6] We may, however, extrapolate certain foreign-policy concerns out of the general pattern of American beliefs.

Generally speaking, America's ideological objectives in foreign policy tend to be more negative than positive, to concentrate more on enemies to be defeated and obstacles to be overcome than on concrete aspirations. Ideologically the United States opposes any form of authoritarian regime, although the extent to which this opposition becomes active depends largely on the extent to which the particular autocracy impinges directly on the American consciousness. Violations of individual freedom contradict American predispositions, whether in the economic or political realms. Once involved, American ideological hostilities tend to become extreme and to harden in stereotyped—almost absolute—terms.

Positively, American mass beliefs hold that all people everywhere will eventually accept the essentials of the American system.[7] The victory of American ways over all competitors is foreordained; ultimately the world will consist entirely of democatic political systems, fluid societies, and capitalist economies. This ideological objective is deemed certain of even-

---

[4] This was the position taken by Nikita Khrushchev when he submitted to an unprecedented television interview by a panel of American newspaper correspondents, presented over the Columbia Broadcasting System on June 9, 1957. See *New York Times* (June 10, 1957).

[5] See W. W. Rostow and others, *The Dynamics of Soviet Society* (New York: W. W. Norton and Co., Inc., 1953), pp. 92-97, for an analysis of the evolving role of ideology in contemporary Soviet society.

[6] We will recall that in our earlier discussion of the "American tradition" in foreign policy, we pointed out that long-standing American *objectives* grew out of history and experience, while such ideological tradition as Americans had was concentrated on *methods* of foreign policy rather than on substantive objectives.

[7] For a recent expression of this position, see Robert Strausz-Hupé, "The Balance of Tomorrow," *Orbis* (April, 1957).

tual achievement; many people seem to think that ideological vindication will come to Americans as the result of no more taxing effort than that of setting a good example and remaining faithful to their own beliefs. The direct foreign-policy implications of this outlook we have had occasion to remark upon in earlier chapters.

With the destruction of ideological enemies bulking so much larger than the accomplishment of positive ideological ends, it is natural that official and semi-official analyses of the American ideological position should stress the inherent conflict between the Soviet and the United States. There is a minor tendency to emphasize the positive solidarity of the United States with the free world, but such efforts are usually aimed at the practical end of buttressing the working alliance against the USSR. So little ideological concern has been given to the shape of any past-cold war world that a cynical observer might be pardoned for wondering if American ideology today teaches that the destruction of the Soviet empire and the elimination of the Russian threat would usher in Utopia.

Ideological Objectives vs. Operating Policy. How important have the rival ideologies proved to be as controlling elements in the foreign policies of the two adversaries? In hazarding an answer to this important question, we must again seek to generalize as the only way to avoid a long and detailed comparison of preachments with practices.

The history of the cold war reveals that both states have used ideology as the dominant guide to policy only when no more trustworthy criteria have been available. When either Moscow or Washington was faced with a decision for which history, experience, logic, or a clearly understood concept of interest failed to prepare it, ideological considerations were most likely to be called upon.[8] In other situations, in which the demands of time and place and the compulsions of history and interest were more clearly grasped, policy was at least to some extent liberated from ideology.

This generalization, although applicable to both states, is perhaps more directly relevant to Soviet policy. This is generally due to the greater formalism and rigidity in communist dogma. American doctrine, confined more to abstractions with a predominantly moral orientation, does not pretend to be universally applicable or to furnish precise answers to questions of detail; American policy-makers have never been able to rely on the teachings of an absolutist belief system. Even so, in the early days of the cold war, Washington often drew inspiration to act from generalized principles about human nature that stemmed from the controlling belief pattern in the United States.

---

[8] Early American policy toward the Indochina war and early Soviet attempts to penetrate the Middle East (in both cases prior to 1954) are examples of policies grounded more on ideology than on more concrete bases.

Most of the policy decisions originally rooted in ideology have been eventually modified by both sides. Some, proving to be good and workable programs in their particular contexts, were retained; the Soviet approach to the Asian revolution, for example, was thoroughly feasible as a working policy (at least up to the Hungarian massacres of 1956) although it grew initially out of an ideological base.

We may conclude, however, that the actual conduct of both the United States and the Soviet Union—as apart from what both sets of leaders have said—indicates that ideological considerations are not primary in their respective foreign policies. Objectives, the motivations of which are purely belief-centered, have been accepted only in default of better ones. To the extent that any may be clearly identified in operative policy decision, we may safely conclude that they remain distinctly subordinate to other, more immediate concerns.[9]

Ideology as technique

If we accept the generalization that ideological objectives are of relatively little importance to the participants in the cold war, how then can we explain the great extent to which ideological issues figure in its conduct? It seems probable that ideology, although of limited value as a goal-setting mechanism for either the Soviet or the United States, is of great service as an instrument for executing policy and for achieving ends determined by other criteria. Ideology's major pertinence to the cold war would then seem to be its use as a technique of policy implementation.

"Psychological instruments of policy" or the "psychological channel of power" are concepts long familiar to students of international affairs.[10] The nature of the cold war and the perhaps controlling importance of winning the allegiance of uncommitted millions of men has raised this

---

[9] A number of well-qualified analysts, however, differ sharply with this conclusion. Some argue that the Soviet's orientation is totally ideological and that communist theory is the enemy the United States must defeat; others see the cold war simply as a titanic struggle between truth and falsehood and call for unremitting effort by the United States, not only to vanquish communism but to make good the final victory of American beliefs. The best-known advocate of the latter position is James Burnham, whose various writings develop this theme. See especially Chapter III, "The End of Traditional Diplomacy," in his *The Coming Defeat of Communism* (New York: John Day, 1950).

[10] See, as an early example, the sophisticated discussion in Frank L. Simonds and Brooks Enemy, *The Great Powers in World Politics*, new ed. (New York: American Book Co., 1939), pp. 149-52.

vehicle of policy to an unprecedented strategic significance. Just as military force has become less useful in normal interstate relations by the evolution of technology, psychological techniques using ideological concepts have become increasingly important. If, as we suggested at the beginning of this chapter, the only permanent victories are those won in the minds of men, it would seem to make good sense to argue that the most significant weapons of foreign policy are those that have their effect on the human psyche.

Soviet Ideological Techniques. We have previously alluded to many specific examples of Soviet ideological technique. We may summarize it here as a continuing attempt to identify communism everywhere with the dissatisfactions, aspirations, animosities, and fears of whatever group in any state Moscow feels is most useful for its purposes.[11] In some states this may be the submerged mass just beginning to stir, as in much of southeast Asia; on the other hand, the Kremlin has no aversion to sustaining or supporting an oligarchy of power even against the wishes of the bulk of the local population, as it has done in many of its satellites and in such ostensibly noncommunist states as Syria. Whatever element in the society is most likely to support Soviet ambitions or to accomplish Soviet purposes can be the recipient and perhaps the beneficiary of Russian communist ideological support.

Moscow's negative ideological emphasis is on portraying the United States as the enemy of the downtrodden everywhere. America is identified with monopoly, capitalist exploitation, imperialism, and war.[12] By discrediting the United States in ideological terms, the Soviet hopes to accomplish two purposes: first, to weaken American influence and the effectiveness of American policy; second, to procure a more favorable hearing for its own claims. The Soviet's primary goal is to alienate people from the United States and then, on the old principle (made much of by Moscow's propaganda) that "the enemy of my enemy is my friend," to win them to the acceptance of its own position.

Moscow's major victory on the ideological front, of course, has been its success in establishing a communist party in virtually every noncommunist state. These parties, serving under the Kremlin's orders, provide a ready-made pipeline into the social structure of every host state, and the

---

[11] A provocative analysis of Soviet ideological methods, interpreted in the light of the doctrines of modern psychology, is "Ferreus," "The Menace of Communist Psychological Warfare," *Orbis* (April, 1957).

[12] Perhaps the most successful example in recent years was the germ-warfare charge leveled at United States forces in Korea. Its receipt in Asia was unexpectedly favorable for the Soviet.

ideological message is the more effective for being propagated by natives. Soviet diplomatic and other official emissaries maintain close contact with local communists and coordinate their activities.

American Ideological Techniques. American ideological techniques are generally the reciprocal of the Soviet's. Like the Russians, Americans insist that they are interested in the welfare of all men everywhere and that American beliefs promise the most for the future. American ideology stresses human freedom, national self-determination, and individual economic well-being.

This last point has been hotly debated; some observers argue that emphasizing economic betterment under American-style capitalism is a total refutation of the materialistic philosophy of communism, while others insist that the incessant reiteration of the material comforts resulting from adherence to American ideas makes the United States an advocate of a "bathtub and television" culture that entirely neglects the spiritual side of man.[13] Whatever its impact on foreigners, however, there is no doubt that most Americans feel that their high standard of living is in some way an outgrowth of their belief system, and it is only natural for an export ideology to make much of what so many Americans feel is important.

American ideology, as we suggested above, in practice is heavily oriented toward opposition. The major use to which ideological weapons have been put has been in the forging of the free-world complex. In this endeavor the ideological concept of the "free world" has been put to extensive use in developing a common ground on which all noncommunist nations could stand. The operative ideology seems to presuppose a simple dichotomy between communism and freedom, and to count as ideological brethren all nations on the non-Soviet side of the dividing line.

Some difficulty has arisen because of the natural but unfortunate popular tendency to make "freedom" (in the sense of opposition to communist expansionism) a working synonym for "democracy," peaceful intent, or a shared interest in the American version of the status quo. Despite the apparent ambiguities in the ideological position of the United States, however, the actual identity of interest among the major noncommunist states has made the ideological approach to the construction of the anti-Soviet alliance a frequently useful tool.

The major complaint we can level at the use of ideological techniques

---

[13] See Chester Bowles, *The New Dimensions of Peace* (New York: Harper & Bros., Inc., 1955), pp. 368-372, for a discussion on this last point. See also, for a theoretical analysis of the issue in a cultural framework, F. S. C. Northrop, *The Meeting of East and West* (New York: The Macmillan Co., 1947), pp. 454-8. Barbara Ward, in *The Interplay of East and West* (New York: W. W. Norton and Co., Inc., 1957), directs herself to this point as well.

by the United States has been the significant disparity between American professions and the actual policy of the United States. If self-determination, individual freedom, and economic well-being are the cornerstones of America's ideological position, the extent to which American action fails to exemplify these abstractions is one measure of the inadequacy of American policy. A considerable body of opinion holds that either because ideology has been neglected in shaping decisions or because the American ideological position has been inadequately presented to the world, a considerable gap exists between principles and practice and that this opening in American defenses has been exploited by the Soviet.[14]

Verdict on a decade

To the extent that the cold war is actually a battle of ideas, how has the tide run during the first decade? Can we reach any general conclusions about the relative success of the United States and the USSR in the struggle for the minds of men? Although recognizing that these are treacherous waters indeed, we may suggest some general conclusions.

Russian Balance Sheet. Before venturing any estimate of Soviet success in winning converts, we should establish some rough criteria of measurement. The Kremlin has had several operational goals in mind, and has made different degrees of progress toward each of them.

The Soviet's announced primary goal—its major "ideological objective" —has been to win converts to the total official ideology of the USSR, the entire communist apparatus of dialectical materialism, the dictatorship of the proletariat, the classless society, and so on. In this area its success has been minimal and, considering the entire period from 1947 to 1957, perhaps negative. The internal dissensions that rocked the Soviet orbit during 1956, capped by the Hungarian atrocities, caused widespread defections from communist ranks in many parts of the world. Even before these episodes, however, it had become obvious that throughout the world communists were tending to organize into tiny, almost clandestine revolutionary groups instead of becoming major political forces in their own nations. In only a few states—France, Italy, and China, for example —did communism ever become anything like a mass movement organized under a rigid ideological roof.

In their second ideological purpose—winning foreign support for the foreign-policy objectives of the USSR—the Soviet leadership had some greater success. Once the overtly "hard" line generally identified with

---

[14] A restrained argument of this position was made by T. V. Smith, "The Ideological Strength and Weakness of the American Position," *Annals* (November, 1951).

Stalin was suppressed in favor of an advocacy of peace, disarmament, and reconciliation, the Soviet discovered large segments of opinion, both in the neutral world and within the ranks of the West itself, that were becoming more disposed to listen to Moscow. Soviet espousal of the cause of underdeveloped and colonial peoples also gained considerable popular approval and some overt diplomatic cooperation from the Asian bloc. This attack, however, lost a good deal of momentum after mid-1956.

Moscow's greatest ideological success, however, came in its effort to discredit the United States. Here both American failures and the inability of the United States to present its position convincingly made it possible for the Soviet to claim that events were corroborating its denunciation of everything American. Much of the noncommunist world, distressed by its own weakness, by the heavy-handed manner in which much of American policy was executed, and by its dependence on American largesse, found comfort in accepting Soviet attempts to explain United States action in the most sinister terms. This approach, although it led to only limited pro-Sovietism, served Russian purposes nevertheless by impeding American efforts and can be counted as a major ideological victory.

The American Record. The American record on the ideological front is (for Americans) one of the less encouraging aspects of the first decade of the cold war. If we apply the same general criteria as we used on the Soviet record, we find little evidence to justify American self-congratulation.

On the count of winning converts to the total American ideology, there is no indication of any but miniscule success. A lack of agreement at home about what the American ideology actually is and a general preference for emphasizing those aspects of American belief most likely to offend exotic cultures (material comfort, mechanization, and armed might) have resulted in only a relatively short list of converts. Americans today realize that they are much less "popular" throughout the world than they were a decade ago, and their perplexity at this development is matched by their resentment.[15]

The record of winning ideological support for American foreign

---

[15] Edward W. Barrett, in the concluding paragraph of his study of the American information program, *Truth Is Our Weapon* (New York: Funk & Wagnalls, 1953), makes this comment: "When we Americans consistently put our case before the people of the world in a way which shows we respect their intelligence, we will be well on our way. In the world of today there is an enormous stock of good will toward us.... America can mobilize this force of good will effectively when it determines to pursue vigorously and *consistently* the aim reflected in the Declaration of Independence—to behave and to speak out of a decent respect to the opinions of mankind." (P. 300; italics in original. Reprinted by permission)

policy is an uneven one; broad swings can be detected from acceptance to rejection of the American ideological defense of particular policy moves. The enactment of ECA was one high point at which American arguments were listened to sympathetically; United States opposition to Britain and France at the time of the Suez invasion of 1956 was another, although before a different audience. Other moves, such as America's insistence upon European rearmament after 1950 even though such a policy endangered economic stability, have caused widespread cynicism about American sincerity.[16] The equivocal American position on anti-colonialism and imperialism also created considerable disaffection from United States leadership, on the part both of the imperial nations and the ex-colonial states themselves.

American ideological obstruction of communist designs was more successful. The constant exposure of the contradictions between Soviet beliefs and Soviet practice impeded Russian policy in many areas. American success was greatest in those regions, such as western Europe, where considerable ideological harmony already existed with the United States; in Asia, the American anti-communist message was so confused with other purposes that its edges were often blunted. Just as unfortunate American actions and statements helped the Soviet discredit the United States, occasional senseless Russian moves played into America's hand. The most impressive of these gaffes was of course Russia's unabashed brutality in dealing with the Hungarian rebellion in 1956.

The State of the Ideological Battle. Ideological conflict within the cold-war context has been, on the basis of the record of a decade, inconclusive. Neither side has scored any great or convincing victory by winning major increments of loyalty from uncommitted peoples nor by gaining converts from its opponent. The major effect of the ideological battle has been negative; each side has had some profit from its attempt to demolish the other's position. One conclusion, however, emerged from the ten-year record of ideological disputation that had great relevance for the future: the effectiveness of ideological argument as a technique of foreign policy seemed to depend, in the long run, upon the extent to which actual policy could be reconciled with purported beliefs. The mere advocacy of absolute principles of social, economic, or political organization had only a limited effectiveness by itself; when coupled with demonstrable implementing action, however, ideology not only heightened the effect of other tactics of policy implementation but acquired a significant impact in its own right.

---

[16] This point is developed by Salvador de Madariaga, "Why the United States Is Universally Disliked," *The New Leader* (May 6, 1957).

UNITED STATES PROPAGANDA: PURPOSE AND CONTENT

The United States is deeply involved in a propaganda war, most obviously with the USSR but also to some extent with the great majority of the states with which it has relations. This situation is one facet of America's commitment to a total foreign policy. It is a relatively new, and for most Americans a somewhat distasteful, outgrowth of the new stature of their nation; Americans do not yet feel thoroughly at home in a systematic attempt to influence other peoples by overtly persuasive techniques. But to forego propaganda would be to concede the psychological battleground to the enemy and, despite the fundamentally non-ideological character of the cold war and most of American policy, to allow such a possibly fruitful area to go by default to the Soviet would be to place American policy under a major handicap. The American situation is by no means so advantageous that the United States can allow other states to enjoy a field day in propaganda unimpeded by American countermeasures.

The purposes of American propaganda

What are the purposes of American propaganda? What does the United States hope to accomplish by its efforts? In judging the propaganda program of the American government we must keep in mind the objectives it is designed to attain.

What Can Propaganda Accomplish? The many definitions of "propaganda" agree that it is generally a technique of persuasion, and that its general objective is action taken by the recipient(s) of the sort desired by the propagandist. Any propaganda campaign, private or official, must accept the practical limits laid down by the concept itself.

Psychological studies agree, furthermore, that appropriate action will not follow a propagandist's appeal unless the recipient's own attitudes were favorable to the receipt of the message. Attempting to persuade tribal groups of native Africans to purchase electric refrigerators would be pointless unless the Africans themselves were aware of what they were missing by not having these appliances. In the jargon of American advertising, this is known as "creating a demand." In the same way, urging a foreign population to rise against its oppressors is of no use unless the people themselves realize that they are oppressed, nor is there any value in begging such a people to support American policy unless they feel that the United States is actually trying to help them.[17]

We may thus subdivide the propagandist's purpose into two different tasks, one precedent to the other. Government propaganda may in the first place concentrate on the creation of a climate in which the propagandist's appeals are favorably received. Advertising men are familiar with this process as "building good will" or "institutional advertising." After the image of the propagandizing nation as a friendly, likeable, and well-wishing people has been constructed on a lasting basis, the second phase of propaganda can be undertaken. At this point open appeals for action may be made, drawing their effectiveness from the base of good-will created by earlier programs.

This two-phase operation, as we describe it, is obviously schematic. In the case of the United States, there already exists a "reservoir of good-will" in many parts of the world on which Washington can draw to float its appeals for direct action. This predisposition to listen to American propaganda grows out of popular impressions of the United States that have come from dozens of sources in addition to the official informational facilities. In such cases the United States need devote only a small amount of time and effort to the creation of a "set to action," and can move directly to its specific programmatic message. But in dealing with peoples whose attitude toward the United States is either indifferent or hostile, an indispensable first step is the discovery of some channel into the foreign society that will procure a favorable hearing for whatever America has to say. Only such a route, properly exploited, can serve to transmit propaganda with a political purpose.

The Targets of American Propaganda. We must also distinguish the various groups that form the targets of American government propaganda. Each of them presents a separate problem; for each of them a separate program has been devised.

The first target of propaganda is, of course, the American people. Public support of the policies undertaken by the leadership is vital; full attention must be paid to the maintenance of public confidence. The second target group consists of America's allies; the object here is to maintain the solidarity of the alliance and to win continuing diplomatic agreement with American moves. The third consists of the states of the

---

[17] See D. Lincoln Harter and John Sullivan, *Propaganda Handbook* (Philadelphia: 20th Century Publishing Co., 1953), Chapter 7, "The Aims of the Propagandist"; and Daniel Lerner, "Effective Propaganda: Conditions and Evaluation," in Daniel Lerner, ed., *Propaganda in War and Crisis* (New York: George Stewart, 1951), pp. 344ff:

"neutral" world; the United States attempts to gain their friendship and support and, if that prove impossible, at least to strengthen their anti-Soviet orientation. Finally, and most obviously, the fourth propaganda target is the communist empire in the Soviet orbit. In this area the United States seeks fundamentally to impair or destroy the loyalty patterns of the peoples of the Soviet world and to set them against their governments.[18]

The vehicles of American propaganda

The United States uses every available method to disseminate its message and operates in virtually every region of the world. The direction of the American propaganda effort is, as we noted in an earlier chapter, under the administrative control of the United States Information Agency (USIA), operating both in Washington and in the field under the policy direction of the Department of State.

The Propaganda Media. A rapid summary of the extent to which the various media were employed during a recent six-months period (January-June, 1956) illustrates the broad variety of techniques available. (1) Television: 460 USIA programs were telecast by 150 stations in the free world. (2) Radio: the Voice of America broadcasted in 43 languages, with an average of 23 hours and 15 minutes daily in Russian alone. (3) Motion pictures: 65 documentary and feature films, and over 100 newsreel releases, were distributed during the half-year. (4) Press: the International Press Service distributed 27 million leaflets, pamphlets, and posters, published a daily news bulletin of 8000 words, and began publication of the Russian-language *America Illustrated* for distribution in the USSR. (5) Books: the Information Center Service set up a number of new centers and expanded book holdings of older ones. In addition the USIA maintained an Office of Private Cooperation, enlisting the help of private American citizens in the President's "People-to-People" program. Americans abroad were encouraged to supplement the official propaganda by personal and informal efforts.[19]

Field Organization. The USIA is organized for field operations into four regional groups: American Republics, Far East, Europe, and Near

---

[18] This listing is similar to the one suggested by Barrett, in *Truth Is Our Weapon*, p. 290n.

[19] These categories and data from U. S. Information Agency, *Sixth Review of Operations, January 1-June 30, 1956* (Washington, D. C.: U. S. Government Printing Office, 1956), pp. 6-16.

East-South Asia-Africa. Twenty-three countries are included in the American Republic posts, employing 128 Americans and 595 "locals"; the largest missions were in Brazil and Mexico. In Europe there were 17 countries covered with 365 Americans and 2,649 locals in 1956; these figures were reduced by the budget-cutting 85th Congress in 1957. Fourteen Far Eastern nations were hosts to USIA missions, employing 266 Americans and 1,663 locals; the largest mission was in Japan. In the vast Near East-South Asia-Africa region, 26 different countries figured, with a staff smaller than for the Far East (236 Americans and 1,404 locals); the mission in India was the largest in the region, followed closely by that in Pakistan.

The message of the United States

What is the content of American propaganda? What message does the United States distribute abroad through the elaborate mechanisms that we have outlined? On what stimuli does the American government count to provide the action abroad that it hopes for?

"*Truth Is Our Weapon.*" In his authoritative study of the early stages of the American propaganda effort, former Assistant Secretary of State Edward W. Barrett laid down what is still the controlling principle of American information policy:

> In the contest for men's minds, truth can be peculiarly the American weapon. It cannot be an isolated weapon, because the propaganda of truth is powerful only when linked with concrete actions and policies.... Yet, because truth is generally on our side, it can be our decisive weapon if we will only profit from past lessons and employ it with wisdom, consistency, and responsibility.[20]

Truth can indeed be the decisive American propaganda weapon, if only it remains accurate to say that "truth is generally on our side." Less committed to the "big lie" as a policy technique than is the Soviet, and free by its own decisions to implement its commitment to tell the truth, the United States enjoys a massive advantage in the battle of persuasion.

The development of modern methods of communication and the mass media by means of which simultaneous and instantaneous communication is possible with hundreds of thousands of people has placed a premium on the propaganda of truth. Maintaining the efficiency of lying propaganda is fantastically difficult when only a modicum of effort will enable

---

[20] Barrett, *Truth Is Our Weapon*, p. ix. Reprinted by permission.

almost any target people to check one nation's claims against another's. Any propagandist caught in a barefaced untruth thereby creates a barrier against all his subsequent efforts to penetrate; each exposed lie makes the lot of the persuader that much more difficult. Theodore C. Streibert, then Director of USIA, put the point this way in 1956:

> If the "world's people" are to understand the issue in this contest, we must effectively counter the hostile propaganda of world communism and, at the same time, vigorously project abroad the truth of what we stand for.[21]

We must not suppose, however, that the "truth" that is the American weapon is (or even should be) always the whole truth. What goes into propaganda should be truthful—for reasons both of conviction and of expediency—but this does not imply that American messages must tell everything there is to be told. Propaganda, after all, is persuasive; it would call its very purpose into question to include—out of a single-minded devotion to the ideal of truth—information that might vitiate the persuasive message.

Understanding the United States. A most important aspect of the American message is that devoted to broadening foreign understanding of the United States and the American people. We must never forget that American ignorance of foreign cultures, particularly of the exotic ones of Asia and Africa, is matched by an almost equal lack of comprehension of the United States abroad. Such impressions of Americans as those had by most foreigners—even many sophisticated Europeans—is largely garnered from the output of Hollywood. Very few Americans would care to be judged everywhere by the picture of American life depicted in the films. The cultivation of a real listening and reading audience for American propaganda has required initially the creation of a more sophisticated understanding of the United States in most foreign countries.

A good deal of USIA activity, therefore, has been concentrated on the presentation of various nonpolitical insights into American life, in an attempt to portray Americans in terms that even relatively untutored foreigners can understand and approve of. A partial catalogue of recent USIA offerings reveals the variety of ways in which this mission has been discharged. Films have been produced on American labor, on the life of Thomas A. Edison, and on the working of American capitalism. The Voice of America has long been broadcasting programs of jazz music. The International Press Service produced a factual collection on *Elections in the U.S.—1956.* A monthly TV sketch of everyday life in the United

---

[21] USIA, *Sixth Review of Operations*, p. 1.

States, *Report from America,* received much favorable comment in Britain. The general effort has been made to break through the political barriers to interpersonal communication and to make American propaganda something more closely resembling an instance of "peoples speaking to peoples." [22]

Specific Propaganda Lines Relevant to Policy. American propaganda, however, does not confine itself to background material and audience conditioning. The USIA also stresses particular lines that have immediate relevance to American policy, either by offsetting Soviet propaganda or by advancing an ongoing project of the United States. Great care is taken to keep the number of such emphases being made at any one time as small as possible so as to minimize the danger that each message might be obscured by the others. During the first half of 1956, for example, USIA stressed four main themes, making them a large part of its program in all media and in all parts of the world. As described in its report, they were: (1) "The USSR versus Josef Stalin," a detailed analysis of the anti-Stalin campaign in the Soviet; (2) the story of *People's Capitalism* (the meaning of American capitalism for the individual), told in photo exhibits, pamphlets, a film, news articles, and a Voice of America series; (3) the American disarmament program, featuring the "open sky" proposal; (4) the "shining vision" of atoms-for-peace. Each of these four was immediately pertinent to the current policy of the United States.[23]

The shortcomings of American propaganda

We suggested earlier in this chapter that the first decade of the cold war was marked either by a stalemate or by a relative Soviet victory in the ideological struggle. Unless we are willing to admit that there is an inherent superiority in communist dogma, it would seem that America's lack of success can be attributed to a failure in communicating American ideas to the world—in other words, in propaganda techniques. We cannot, however, explain away this difficulty on the ground of a lack of knowledge of the technical problems of persuasion since, after all, it is in America that advertising (the "engineering of consensus") has become both an art and a science. The shortcomings of the American propaganda

---

[22] Llewellyn White and Robert D. Leigh, *Peoples Speaking to Peoples* (Chicago: University of Chicago Press, 1946). This volume is the Report on International Mass Communication by the wartime Commission on Freedom of the Press. The report is very pertinent to our discussion in this chapter.

[23] USIA, *Sixth Review of Operations,* pp.1-5.

effort must lie somewhere else than in the inadequacy of the message itself or in a lack of technical skill in its transmission.

The deepest-rooted cause of the ineffectiveness of American propaganda would seem to be found in the rather common lack of understanding, both in government and among the general public, of the nature, limitations, and effectiveness of the propaganda instrument. Far too often, the implications of propaganda have been either overestimated or underestimated, and the execution of the persuasive task has been either overenthusiastic or half-hearted. With such a record, the remarkable point is not that American propaganda has not been as effective as that of the Soviet, but rather that the disparity between the two is not greater than it is. For this we may thank impartially the essentially solid ideological position of the United States and the frequently astonishing ineptitude of Soviet ideologues.

We may list the major shortcomings of American propaganda under four heads, each varying in degree of importance but all of major pertinence to the future program of the United States.

The Expectations About Propaganda. Americans have swung between extremes in their expectations of what could be accomplished by propaganda. One extreme may be represented by the abortive "political warfare" movement in 1953, when official Washington seemed to think that a magic formula of persuasion could be discovered that would demolish the Soviet threat quickly and cheaply.[24] At the other end we may put the niggardly attitude of Congress toward the entire propaganda effort in the backwash of Senator McCarthy's investigation of the Voice of America; during 1953 responsible lawmakers were arguing that the entire propaganda machine should be dismantled and the money put into bigger and better bombs and aircraft. A similar drive was undertaken by Congress in 1957 under the compulsions of the "economy" war cry of that year.

Even as of the moment of this writing, we cannot say that the United States has a clear understanding of what its propaganda can do, what it is expected to do, and what will follow the achievement of any of its objectives.[25] There was something almost shocking, for example, in the insistence of the State Department that its "liberation" propaganda of 1952 and 1953 had had nothing to do with precipitating the Hungarian rebellion in 1956.

The Relationship Between Propaganda and Policy. Edward L. Barrett's

---

[24] A strategy for this method was suggested by John Scott, in *Political Warfare* (New York: John Day, 1955).

[25] Compare Barrett, *Truth Is Our Weapon, Chapter* 15: "Home-front Foes."

warning that "truth is powerful only when linked with concrete actions and policies" is particularly apposite to the issue of American responsibility for the Hungarian revolt. That the United States never officially pledged overt support to nationalist rebellions in the Soviet orbit may be true, but unofficially the impression (aided to some extent by the private voice of "Radio Free Europe") was general that the United States would lend concrete assistance to any people that arose against Soviet domination.[26] When no such assistance was coming, disillusionment was widespread and many accusations of bad faith were heard.

The American record of promises—both explicit and implicit—not fulfilled by action is too long for any partisan of the United States to feel comfortable. Americans are often perturbed when foreigners do not take the unsupported word of the United States, either about its good intentions or about its willingness to act under certain circumstances. It goes against the American grain to admit it, but history (at least as viewed by foreigners) teaches that many American commitments have been repudiated, often in response to changing domestic political currents. To the extent to which American propaganda is not consonant with or implemented by policy, the propaganda itself becomes almost valueless and may on occasion actually prove harmful.

Unintentional Propaganda. Americans are also largely unaware of the broader dimensions of propaganda. Not all the persuasive messages from the United States are disseminated by USIA; Americans do not realize the extent to which every facet of their lives is under constant scrutiny throughout the world. The bitter language of politics, including accusations of treason; the isolated cases of racial violence and the much more common patterns of racial discrimination; the towering corporate structure of mergers, combines, and cartels; the vulgarity and ostentation of much of American life; these too are part of the American propaganda message. Their effect often is to vitiate much of the overt informational activity of the government. How, USIA representatives abroad are often asked, can the United States be sincere about individual liberty, human dignity, and economic well-being when at home racial, religious, economic, and cultural discrimination is common, political rights are denied, monopoly capitalism is rampant, and cultural life is being reduced to a dead mediocrity? Such questions, of course, reveal inaccurate information and distorted inferences: the fact remains, however, that to the extent to which these propaganda devices are operative (and others we might men-

---

[26] Perhaps the most important single element in creating this impression was the Republican party's adoption of the "liberation" hypothesis during the 1952 presidential campaign.

tion, such as the ubiquitous Hollywood film), the task of the official propagandist becomes more complicated and difficult of achievement.[27]

Translating Abstractions into Specifics. At the operating level, the major inadequacy in American propaganda shows up in translating the abstractions of American ideological predispositions into specific appeals. Making American propaganda intelligible to its targets has not been simple, nor has the record of performance improved notably during the latter period of the cold war.

What we are saying is that American propaganda, in making such concepts as individual liberty or economic well-being the bases of specific appeals, has failed to clothe these notions with referents intelligible to the actual wants or needs of the target people. The American criterion has instead tended often to be what the "average" American means by these terms, and the net impact of the American message has been to exhort the Greek, the Indonesian, the Sudanese, or the Bolivian to become just like the middle-class citizen of Peoria, Illinois.[28]

Painting rosy pictures of life in America, complete with skyscrapers, television, and indoor plumbing makes few converts among peasants whose major concerns are with shaking free of the local moneylender and learning to read. Instead of inspiring a desire to emulate the United States, such appeals usually leave the observer unmoved; frequently, indeed, they stir up actual resentment and soften up resistance to Soviet persuasion. American self-praise, particularly when American policy can be interpreted as contradicting ideological professions, often helps no one except the Soviet.

To the extent to which American propaganda is pitched at a level to which its audience is responsive—whatever the audience and whatever that appropriate audience level might be—there is a greater likelihood that a sympathetic hearing can be obtained. As long as the specifics of propaganda fail to reach mass audiences because of their unintelligibility, mass responses are impossible. How to increase the audience for the American message is a problem of growing significance.

THE MAINTENANCE OF AMERICAN MORALE

Perhaps the most crucial psychological issue in American foreign policy has nothing at all to do with United States propaganda abroad. It is, of

---

27 See C. D. Jackson, "Private Media and Public Policy," in Lerner, *Propaganda in War and Crisis*, pp. 328ff.

28 Barrett makes this point in a number of places, especially in Chapter 21: "The Quest for a Formula."

course, the question of the mental state of the American people; can it be maintained at a level adequate to provide the necessary support for American policy?

We discussed American morale as a capability factor in Chapter 11. There is no need for us again to go over the ground we covered there, particularly with regard to the relevance of popular morale to the long-range mission of the United States. At this point we shall discuss only one problem bearing on the state of national morale, that of American reaction to foreign propaganda, and then we shall canvass briefly the various approaches to public opinion that we call the "morale policies" of the United States government.

American reaction to foreign propaganda

"Propaganda" and the American People. Americans, we have pointed out, are a suspicious people in international relationships, and they have also a deep-rooted cultural antipathy to being taken in by any sort of over-smooth and glib sales-talk. From these two sources has grown a prevailing popular attitude: "propaganda" in international politics (and in many other areas as well) is a dirty word. In the mass mind, propaganda is put to an ulterior purpose, and almost always that purpose is against the better interests of whoever is being propagandized. Furthermore, propaganda carries distinct overtones of deceit: it is almost by definition thought to be compounded of untruths, half-truths, suppressed facts, and deliberate misinterpretations.

This attitude toward anything overtly labeled "propaganda" has made the lot of the foreign specialist in persuading Americans a particularly unhappy one. He must disguise his message so that it does not seem like propaganda at all; he must, in the jargon of the television commercials, do a "soft sell" rather than a "hard" one. Even so, the remarkable aspect of the total foreign propaganda effort in the United States is the relatively minor impact it has had—with certain important exceptions.

Foreign Propagandists in the United States. With perhaps one or two exceptions, each foreign diplomatic mission in the United States maintains some organization for the dissemination of propaganda and information. The name most commonly given them is that of "information service," and their clientele is divided between the American press (and other mass media) and the general public. Each foreign propaganda agency or individual is required to register with the United States Department of Justice, and their activities are subject to some government control. Perhaps most typically American is the requirement that each piece of literature must bear a notice that its source is a registered foreign propaganda agency and that "registration does not imply" that the information contained is vouched for by the United States government. The Justice Department thus seems to be interested in giving the consumer fair warning that the document he is perusing is admittedly "foreign propaganda." [29]

Registration and labeling serve to inhibit the effectiveness of many "information services," although all of them have a large area of action, producing press releases, answering questions and requests for information, and in general attempting to gain as large an audience as possible for their material. Some of them, however, are further handicapped by small staffs and inadequate and inefficient facilities; in contrast we may point to the model propaganda service in the United States, the British Information Services. The B.I.S. has a network of regional offices throughout the United States and offers an almost bewildering variety of materials.

Often much more valuable to a foreign state than its own information service, however, are the voluntary groups of Americans that, each for its own reasons, spring up to advance the "friendship" between the United States and the nation it is interested in supporting. There is at least one such organization for most of the states with which the United States has any but the most peripheral relations, and Britain, France, Italy, and other states have several. Among the most important are the English-Speaking Union (Great Britain) and the Zionist Organization of America, which is affiliated with the World Zionist Organization and works in a variety of ways to advance the interests of Israel. These private organizations, led by prominent Americans and usually elaborately organized down to the local community level, can prosecute the cause of the foreign state in an effective way totally barred to official propagandists.

The Rejection of Soviet Propaganda. The USSR has failed almost completely to gain any sympathetic audience among Americans. Its propaganda seems crude and banal, and its ability to affect American attitudes turns out often to be the exact reverse of its intent. For this the Soviets can blame both their own ineptitude—their appeals aimed at Americans

---

[29] The statement used on British material reads: "This material is filed with the Department of Justice, where the required registration statement under 56 Stat. 248-258 as an agency of the British Government is available for inspection. Registration does not imply approval or disapproval of this material by the United States government."

betray an appalling ignorance of what Americans are like and of what mass wants, fears, and concerns actually are—and the vigorous counter-propaganda carried on by the American government. Washington at-temps to bar Soviet propaganda from American distribution except on a strict *quid pro quo* basis and exerts considerable effort to warn the American people of the deceitfulness and evil intent of Soviet appeals.

Americans generally are aware that the Soviet is attempting to prop-agandize them—perhaps overly so.[30] Although the militancy of American resistance has relaxed perceptibly since 1952 and 1953, there is no doubt that most people today are highly sensitized to the danger of being trapped by the wiles of communist arguments. Such a normal and ordinarily commendable concern was distorted out of all reason during the red scare of the early 1950's in which the late Senator Joseph Mc-Carthy of Wisconsin figured so largely. During this period anyone who deviated from the Senator's version of orthodox Americanism ran the risk of being accused of "following the communist line"—an offense that, though never made specific, was made to seem subtly treasonable. Since the 1955 summit conference and the evidence of Soviet weakness that accumulated during 1956 and 1957, the controlling American at-titude seemed to be one that no longer fears communist propaganda as a virus against which there is no defense but a closed mind, although it retained a near-total skeptcism about the content to Russian arguments.

"Sputnik," however, seemed to reverse this trend. The realization that Americans were not automatically the world's greatest scientific and technological geniuses caused a serious (although temporary) loss in popular perspective. During the last months of 1957 the old warnings about Soviet propaganda again filled the airwaves and the editorial pages of the nation, and the public was urged to be on its guard against tempta-tion to surrender to Khrushchev's "sputnik diplomacy."

Successful Foreign Propaganda. A few states have been able to make their propaganda widely effective in the United States, both through direct contact with the public and via domestic informational media. Each of this small group of states has certain advantages—ethnic, cul-tural, or historic—that create affinities with a mass American audience and guarantee a sympathetic hearing. Each of them also—for perhaps the same reasons—has had the assistance of extensive private organizations

---

[30] Nikita Khrushchev's appearance on an American television network in June, 1957, threw the nation's editorialists into a frenzy of concern lest innocent Americans be seduced by the Russian's appeal. For an acid comment on this outburst, see Gilbert Seldes, "America and the Face of N. Khrushchev," *Saturday Review* (June 29, 1957).

in the United States that have worked in close cooperation with official representatives.

Certainly the most successful has been Great Britain. Based upon the superlatively efficient B.I.S., and aided by virtually every Briton temporarily or permanently resident in the United States, Britain has had an extensive network of transmission centers. Amicable relations with news media, friendships with national and local leadership elites, a delicate restraint in capitalizing on the fact of linguistic, cultural, and economic ties, and a uniformly helpful and courteous attitude have made British propagandists the envy of American informational personnel. The British have been able to condition American attitudes into receptiveness of London's position on many issues.

During the confused days of the Suez crisis of November, 1956, for example, the British position received extensive and friendly discussion in all media, to the point where serious doubts were raised among Americans of the wisdom and effectiveness of the policy their government had adopted. The crisis receded, however, before anyone could tell whether the British wedge had driven home to the point where American public opinion might force the United States government to modify its policy. The success of the British campaign, however, eloquently testified to the efficiency of British propaganda, and the later evolution on American policy on the Middle East suggested that many of London's shafts had struck home.

Another state with a good record of influencing American attitudes is Israel. Here again something of a ready-made consensus has aided Israel's propagandists, and here also a voluntary apparatus has done yeoman service. But the Israeli government has also shown much imagination in its campaign (particularly in emphasizing the social-service aspect of Israeli domestic policy and in stressing the "western"—pro-American —nature of its experiment in government) and the number and variety of pro-Israeli groups in American society are one indication of its success.

Vivid proof of the effectiveness of Israeli efforts to influence American attitudes was provided during February and early March of 1957. During the crisis caused by Israel's refusal to evacuate the Gaza strip and the Gulf of Aqaba, the American government seemed inclined to accept the possibility of a General Assembly resolution to impose sanctions on Israel. Israeli propagandists, professional and volunteer, succeeded in creating a mass opposition to this move to the point that for Washington to have gone ahead with the project would have touched off a major internal dispute. Fortunately, the crisis was compromised and the full strength of the pro-Israel sentiment was never put to the test.

487

Nationalist China has also shown great ability to gain a hearing for its cause. Chiang Kai-shek's official governmental mechanisms for propaganda in the United States is only a skeleton, but he has been aided by many volunteers. Whether or not there is a "China Lobby" of Nationalist officials and influential Americans—as has been charged [31]—it is a a fact that Taiwan's propaganda has won a large and highly sympathetic audience, both within government circles and in the public at large. Not the least effective weapon in this campaign has been the winsome personality of Madame Chiang. Its major purpose has been to keep the United States committed to the defense of Taiwan and to oppose American recognition of communist China; in both it has had a great degree of success.

The Lack of a Mass Audience. Except for the states mentioned and perhaps one or two other, however, the story of foreign propaganda in the United States is briefly told: it has had no great and continuing effect because of its failure to achieve a steady mass audience. Americans, buffeted by news, background information, and interpretations of international issues virtually around the clock, have no great urge to seek out information from foreign sources to supplement their heavy domestic diet. The information services of such states as Spain, Laos, Paraguay, or Iceland—to cite a few more extreme examples—never reach large segments of the American public except in very special circumstances. If they penetrate news media, they have a somewhat greater impact, but in this effort there is such fierce competition that many states receive little other than routine coverage.

American government "morale policies"

We know that government action in foreign policy must be backed by active mass support by the public. On any but the most minor, short-run matters, mere passive acceptance of what is decreed in Washington is insufficient; what is needed over the long term is an informed, alert, and insightful public opinion that understands the reasons why the government acts the way it does, that has confidence in official leadership, and that cooperates with officialdom in executing the decisions out of which foreign policy is made.

One need not be a pessimist to point out that—if this be an accurate

---

[31] See the series of articles by Charles Wertenbaker and Philip Horton, "The China Lobby," in *The Reporter* (April 15 and 29, 1952).

representation of what high "national morale" involves—American mass attitudes leave much to be desired. We know both from our earlier discussion and from our own experience that mass apathy toward the details of international issues is a problem of growing dimensions, that mass emotional clichés all too often are substituted for rational attempts to perceive the national interest, that interest groups and political parties are ever at work to impair public confidence in the leadership of opposition groups, and that the level of public understanding and discussion of international questions is often discouragingly low.

Without attempting to pass any kind of judgment here on the prospect for the improvement of public attitudes, we may safely stipulate that the present state of national morale constitutes a continuing operating problem for the American government. Judicious care must be taken that the level of active committed support be retained sufficiently high to guarantee a workable consensus, and that opposition forces be restrained at a safe pitch. A variety of different techniques have been developed for this purpose; which one is used in any particular circumstance depends upon the situational factors and the objective in view.

The "Crisis" Approach. The "crisis" approach was most useful during the earlier stages of the cold war, when public comprehension of the nature and requirements of American policy was rudimentary. With its general outline all adult Americans are familiar; a particular policy move was identified with an international crisis calling for immediate American action, and speedy and unquestioning acceptance of the government's proposal was asserted to be the only way to stave off the danger. Disagreement, delay, or alternative proposals were alike dismissed as perilous; the official cry for "unity" attempted to drown out dissent.[32]

The methodology of crisis, as long as the crisis is real and the measure under consideration is suited to the problem, has a real utility. Granting popular lack of information and reluctance to act, undoubtedly it has frequently made steps possible that would never have been taken otherwise. Perhaps the most significant example is the fairly rapid passage of the ECA; this complex enterprise might very well have been sunk in a morass of partisan debate and the quarrels of competing interest groups had it not been wrapped in a cloak of anti-Soviet crisis.

But the "crisis approach," as it matured, began to reveal certain inherent shortcomings; perhaps the gravest was the danger of constantly crying "wolf" when the wolf never came. As popular sophistication grew

---

[32] As an illustration, see the story of the unveiling of the Truman Doctrine and its public reception in J. C. Campbell, *The United States in World Affairs, 1947-48* (New York: Harper & Bros., Inc., 1948), pp. 34-38.

and as the domestic opponents of the trend of American policy found leadership and slogans, it became more and more difficult to convince mass opinion that the crisis was real or that such a crisis as existed was not due to the bungling of American policy-makers. To secure consensus on a crisis basis in those circumstances required that the level of tension be driven higher and higher to the point where a real possibility arose that the public might be oversold on the danger and that public opinion might force unwanted extremes of action. As American policy progressed, less and less reliance was placed after 1950 on crisis as a means of maintaining morale.

Crisis techniques were revived, however, late in 1957. Faced with what was generally thought to be an overpowering necessity to launch a "crash" program to overtake the Soviet both in the exploration of space and in the development of long-range missiles, much of American officialdom dusted off the well-worn mechanism of crisis. Military leaders, Congressmen and Senators, and bureaucrats vied with each other in portraying the desperate peril into which the United States had drifted and in demanding far-reaching action and major "sacrifice" to regain' "security."

The "Calm-and-Firm" Approach. Largely replacing crisis psychology was what we might call the "calm-and-firm" approach. Here governmental leaders sought to maintain an atmosphere of calmness, of circumspection, and of rationality as they faced problems, and to communicate these characteristics to the public. As long as the leadership refused to get excited, the argument ran, the public would not; if the President coolly suggested that American interest demanded that some particular policy be followed, his detachment might well prove contagious.

This method proved to be especially well suited to President Eisenhower, comporting as it did with his own personality and with his theory of the Presidency. His popularity with the people and the confidence in his judgment and good intentions shared throughout the population made his approach to morale building quite successful.[33] Opinions among students differed as to whether the administration's addiction to the "calm and firm" technique tended toward popular complacency and apathy, but there was no doubt that the national temper was calmer after 1953 than it had been previously.

---

[33] An apt example of the Eisenhower technique was the President's radio-TV address to the nation on the evening of October 31, 1956, as the Middle East crisis was developing. In this speech he announced his intention to put the problem before a special session of the General Assembly of the United Nations. His manner, as well as his words, emphasized calmness and the avoidance of extremes. Text of speech in *New York Times* (November 1, 1956).

Perhaps the basic question, although an empirically unanswerable one, about the worth of this method was whether or not it was being practiced on a population whose level of information, insight, and understanding had been significantly raised by its experience since 1945. If such were the case, there was no need for a more frenzied program to maintain morale; if not, the "calm and firm" technique was actually concealing serious gaps in the working relationship between government and people. Administration critics pointed to the public's total befuddlement in the face of Sputnik as proof of the failure of the President's policy. In the resultant furor, the Chief Executive provided almost the only calm voice.

The Encouragement of Public Debate. Among Americans, the admitted necessity of effective leadership does not go so far as to permit the mass public to be excluded from the policy-making process. We have seen how major departures in policy must often be submitted to public debate before a dependable consensus can be obtained. Permitting and encouraging such debate of issues before any official decision is made is a morale technique of relatively infrequent application, but of great importance under appropriate circumstances.

The usual signal for a public "great debate" is the launching of a trial balloon by some (usually nonresponsible) government spokesman.[34] It is seldom that it is labeled as such, but news comment and the ubiquitous interest groups can be counted on to identify it. If the issue is important and controversial enough, the debate begins. In its course a consensus is either reached or identified, and at its end the policy-makers are equipped to act—although not possibly in the way they had originally hoped.

From our point of view here, the significant aspect of such great debates is their effect on morale. Once everyone interested has had the opportunity to express himself and to pay his respects to his opponents, and once a more or less firm verdict has been rendered on the subject of the debate itself, a great clearing of the air can usually be discerned. The issue itself tends to pass from the area of the controversial and—except for a usually small minority of recalcitrants—the mass attitude is generally one of satisfaction with the action. It is very rare for any such debate to be reopened, and rarer still for a decision to be reversed.

The principal danger in the technique is the fact that, as long as the debate is on, there is no firm policy on the issue under discussion and

---

[34] Such a trial balloon was sent up on April 16, 1954, by an "anonymous high administration source" (Vice President Nixon). His speech implied that the administration was preparing to commit ground forces to the Indochina war. The resulting public debate convinced the administration that public sentiment was opposed and the project was abandoned. Speech reported in *New York Times* (April 17, 1954).

it might transpire that unexpected events would work to the significant disadvantage of the United States during such a hiatus. It is to guard against this possibility that government officials permit such debates to gain momentum only when a reasonably protracted delay in reaching a decision will not work any undue hardship on American interest—or else when it is simply impossible to head off the debate.

The Education of the Public. Perhaps the ideal type of morale policy, but one that we must admit has been of limited application, is the education of the public. We discussed the major dimensions of the problem in our analysis of a democratic foreign policy in Chapter 7, and there is little that we need add here to that statement. To the extent that national morale is based on fundamental agreement on what the public wants, on how generally to obtain it, and on the major obstacles standing in the way, other morale policies are made unnecessary. Everyone involved in making foreign policy would agree on the importance of this type of morale.

The rapid pace of foreign-policy decisions since 1945, the interminable succession of crises, the inescapably political implication of foreign affairs, and the limiting effect of the bureaucratic psyche all have combined to reduce formal public education by government to the status of a pious hope rather than that of a serious objective. This is not to say that government officials do not do a major job of education in obtaining a working consensus, but merely that such an outcome is a by-product rather than an end in itself. In the course of developing a crisis formula, of spelling out "calmness and firmness," or of touching off a trial balloon debate, educational outcomes are inevitable. But there has been little attention paid to the enrichment of public understanding in situations independent of specific policy proposals.

We must admit that such a proposal smacks—at least to Congress and to broad segments of mass opinion—rather much of the "public enlightenment" technique identified with totalitarian propaganda. Overtly propagandizing the American people—although admittedly in their own interest—is a policy difficult to defend before a public notoriously suspicious of all propagandists. It will require more maturity on the part of both the bureaucrats and the legislators before a workable system of public education can be devised. In the meantime popular sophistication on international issues must grow primarily from the efforts of interested private agencies and from the outcomes of other morale policies of the American government.

part 8:

LOOKING AHEAD

18 : *The next phase*

The United States has come far in the last 30 years. Even the most casual look at the history of the international adventures of the American people will reveal an enormous difference between contemporary popular attitudes toward foreign policy and those of a generation ago. For most Americans in the 1920's, the politics of nations was a subject in which they had little interest and less involvement. The Great Depression, the rise of the dictators, World War II, and the tensions of the cold war have fundamentally changed the American outlook. Most adult Americans have undergone a rapid—if sometimes painful—education in the basic principles of international politics, particularly as they apply to the United States.

We are both humbled and gratified if we contemplate in retrospect the road the American people have traveled in gaining their understanding of the nature of foreign policy. Although it is a record indisputably marked by many failures, we cannot escape some feeling of satisfaction that the United States has done as well as it has. By many objective standards America's conduct of its external relations justifies serious crticism for faults of insight, determination, technique, and vigor. We have attempted to make such a critique throughout this study. Yet, without denying any of the details of such an indictment, we may also find in that same record considerable evidence of the mass good sense and mass goodwill that are indispensable both to democratic theory and to a workable system of popular government. The history of American foreign policy, particularly of that portion of it that begins in 1945, is—like most histories—a tale in which good and bad are almost indiscriminately mixed.

But our major purpose in this book is not to pass judgment on the past. Foreign policy is a continuous process; it has no end, at least as long as the

United States retains its identity in a world of sovereign states. In studying American foreign affairs, what happened yesterday is always less important than what will happen tomorrow; the significance of the past is to be found in the future. Unless our study in some way is relevant to the problems with which the American government and the American people will have to cope in the years ahead, its value will be purely antiquarian. We must, if we are to give our analysis here a broader function, conclude it with some attempt to look ahead.

The road to the future

The goal of all social science is prediction, but very few social scientists would argue seriously that their techniques have discovered laws of universal applicability that can serve as predictive criteria. We may look into the future; in doing so, however, we realize that our vision is weak. The most we can grasp is the immediate foreground, where the very near future is fitfully illuminated by both the present and the past; beyond that point is shadow in which we can do no more than to detect certain broad outlines whose details usually defy analysis, frequently even description. The rest of the future remains impenetrable, at least with the tools we have available.

The difficulty and the danger of predicting, however, in no way excuses us from making the attempt to do so. Realizing the certainty of error in details and the possibility of serious misjudgment of major factors, we must nevertheless use such knowledge and understanding as we have in an effort to pierce the unknown. In justification for our temerity, we may hope that our successes will outweight our failures and that, by reducing the number of the otherwise countless variables, we may make rational judgment easier when the future has become the present. If our analysis in this book has any vindication at all, it would seem to be found in such guides as it provides to making general predictions of relative probabilities.

The Past and the Future. Our study in this volume has been largely historical. This has been, at least in one sense, inevitable; by the time that they have come to our attention, the data with which we have been concerned have already escaped from the present into history. Almost all social study is therefore historically oriented. But our historical perspective has had a broader purpose. We have attempted to consider the past, both recent and remote, in the light of its relevance to the future.

We are by no means suggesting that the key to the riddle of what is

496

yet to come can be found in the record of what has already occurred. Whether or not history "repeats itself" is an argument vigorously prosecuted by various philosophers of history, but it is not one especially appropriate to our purposes. This book has championed a thoroughly non-deterministic interpretation of human motivation, and it would be the most glaring of inconsistencies at this late stage to argue that the problems of American foreign policy could be solved by riding the crest of some metaphysical "wave of the future." History is important to us not because it provides detailed answers to particular problems, but because of the object lessons it teaches and the sense of continuity it provides.

The Impossibility of Prediction. What we are saying, of course, is that we cannot predict the future on the basis of the past. The foreign-policy process as we have analyzed it involves, more than anything else, an adjustment of action to a constantly-changing milieu. Policy is consistent when the interest it serves and the long-range objectives it is seeking remain relatively constant; particular courses of action may (and often do) differ from and contradict one another in great degree. The only way that a unique historical event could serve as a predictive tool would be for all the relevant circumstances to repeat themselves in exactly the same sequence and relationship, and for the passage of time itself to be of no importance. Such a repetition of events, although logically conceivable, is so improbable as to be of no practical use as a guide to conduct. Prediction in detail of future events is not the province of the historical method, at least as applied to American foreign policy.

The Future Road. We may, however, suggest a positive value of our historical point of view. The past is considered here as the "road to the future." History is a continuous stream; from the perspective gained by historical study and from the discovery of trends in the past whose effects promise to extend beyond the present, we may gain some light on what lies ahead.

The figure of the road is appropriate in several metaphorical senses. Like most roads, on this one we can see that part that lies immediately ahead, but not our ultimate destination. We know, however, where we want to go and we have some reason to believe that this road will take us there. A road has boundaries, warning signs, and frequently carries traffic other than our own vehicle. It has forks and crossroads, each of which calls for the consultation of maps and guidebooks and a decision as to which alternative to follow. And, finally, most roads require conscious effort if we are to travel them; only a few are consistently downhill and permit uninterrupted coasting.

And so we may generalize that our concern with the past is with the light—admittedly dim—that it may throw as we move into the future. We must be prepared for the possibility of suddenly being required to revise our calculations as new conditions invalidate our assumptions, and our willingness to predict must be conditioned by many cautions. Normally we will not dare go beyond a fairly high level of generalization. But unless we are willing to resign ourselves to incessant surprise, we must use our techniques to suggest some guides to purposive behavior.

Focus: the Next Phase. Our major interest, therefore, must be carefully delimited. We must concentrate upon that segment of the future that we can see the most clearly and in which the forces rooted in the past will have their most foreseeable impact. This means, of course, that we shall concern ourselves primarily with the near future. By restricting our essays at forecasting to the immediate next phase of history, we will be better able to minimize the impact of the unpredictable fortuities that will throw off our calculations and to clarify the alternatives of action on the basis of which decisions must be made relatively soon. Ours is essentially a modest predictive effort; in making it we shall constantly be impressed by how much remains to be done before the "science of international politics" will have justified its name.

The renaissance of flexibility

Our reflection on the recent past as it impinges on the immediate future brings us quickly to one general conclusion. The pattern of international relationships, badly distorted by the strains of the era of World War II and rigidly formalized by the operative dynamic of bipolarity, is again moving toward its more typical state of flexibility. Many of the classical theories of international relations were suspended by new factors dating from the rise of the dictators in the 1930's and the revolution in world affairs brought on by that catastrophic series of events. New doctrines were advanced to take the place of those that were seemingly outmoded, drawing their inspiration from the modified conditions under which the state system was operating. Much of American policy since 1945 has been built on this new group of principles. As the international scene has again changed character in an apparent swing back to its former condition, many of the postulates of contemporary American action are being drastically revised.

The Increasing Scope of Maneuver. The new flexibility of international politics is most dramatically evidenced by the increasing room for maneuver that many states are discovering. For a decade after the end of the war, almost all states except the Soviet Union and the United States found themselves caught in a system which either permitted no alternatives at all or provided such a limited number of open choices that the freedom of action was more illusory than real. Only the giants had any maneuverability; we have also seen, however, how the acceptance of the bipolar concept reduced their flexibility almost to the vanishing point.

During recent years, however, this drift toward a constantly narrowing range of choice has been largely reversed. The bipolar system seems to be dissolving and, at any rate, is much less controlling; old alignments are breaking up, some new ones are being formed, and governments everywhere are exploiting new areas of meaningful choice. Each of the successive relaxations in the control over world affairs exercised by the dispute between the major powers has presented the majority of all the other states with a new and much broader pattern of practical alternatives. Though not especially pleased by this development, even the United States and the Soviet Union themselves have been forced to choose from among alternatives that only a short while previously did not exist. Maneuver is now possible in international politics on a scale undreamed of only a few years ago.

Without attempting to suggest the eventual outcome of this new trend, we may postulate that the maximization of maneuver will continue at least into the immediate future. The forces that have brought flexibility back into world affairs are to a great extent beyond the control of individual governments; they grow out of the dynamism of the international process itself. The restoration of any version of bipolar rigidity does not seem within the capacity of any state today (or even of any likely grouping of states). It may be that eventually this contemporary flexibility will prove temporary, and that it will again be replaced by some more confining principle. We cannot, at least at the present time, isolate the factors that might have this effect, however, and all we may safely say is that great room for maneuver will continue to be characteristic of international affairs in at least its next phase.

New Alignments. It would seem to be nearly inevitable that the rediscovery of areas of maneuver among states would lead to the disruption of the hard-and-fast alignments of the cold-war era and the creation of new ones appropriate to contemporary conditions. As a matter of fact, this process is already well advanced. States of all sizes and of varying interest patterns are exploring new policy lines, taking advantage of their recently-acquired freedom. In doing so, they discover new harmonies and new conflicts, new friends and new enemies. Each such new relationship gives rise to new possible understandings, agreements, and alignments.

Not only do the new partnerships involve strange participants, but the terms of the arrangements themselves are similarly departing from the cold-war pattern. The cooperative undertakings that are emerging from the new conditions are all more circumstantial, more tentative, and more limited in scope and duration than were their predecessors of the bipolar era.

States are no longer driven, often against their will, into one or another of the great camps whose interplay dominated the world for so long. Today (and probably tomorrow as well) many states are free to pick and choose their allegiances, and the number is steadily increasing. Once an understanding with an ally has been reached, it by no means implies the total commitment that was implicit in most of the earlier groups of agreements. States choose associates today with an eye to particular objectives, and an ally well suited to one project may be totally inappropriate to another. As a rule, also, the current type of alliance would seem by its very nature to be short-lived; limited-purpose understandings negotiated in a changing context tend not to outlast either the achievement of the common goal or its abandonment as beyond reach.

We have no reason to assume that the process of choosing new partners for virtually each dance will not continue. Like many trends in world affairs, it seems at least to some extent to be self-accelerating; the prospects are that it will become even more pronounced before any limiting reaction sets in. In this instance also we see the possibility that the world may eventually return to something very much like the nineteenth-century system of international relations, where combinations—at least among the major nations—were assumed to be infinitely fluid and in which diplomacy consisted mainly of picking one's way through a system incorporating very few fixed points.

New Demands on Diplomacy. If the world continues to move in the direction of greater flexibility, the classical adjustment mechanism of diplomacy will regain much of its lost importance. Diplomatic maneuver has been seriously handicapped in a cold-war atmosphere, and the techniques of compromise and *quid pro quo* have almost atrophied with disuse. But if international relationships again become marked by great unpredictability and fluidity, the role of bargaining via emissary will again become central to the process of maintaining a satisfactory relationship.

However, although much of the old diplomacy can be and will be transferred to the new era, it can never aspire to the dominant position it held in the days of Metternich and Canning. Under conditions of modern technology, the consequences of diplomatic failure are so great that any negotiator must feel some degree of inhibition as he seeks to adjust differences and to reach viable compromises on important issues. The permanently magnified roles of public opinion on the one hand and of warfare on the other will continue to limit indefinitely the scope of effectiveness of even the most skillful and best-intentioned diplomats.

Despite the admitted handicaps under which future diplomacy will labor, its mission will be uniquely important. With a newly flexible system providing room for extensive maneuver and with the likelihood that working partnerships will continue to change rapidly, the system of states will require a new set of effective controls if it is to avoid the twin dangers of breakdown and explosion. These controls can be successfully applied only by high-level (and high-type as well) diplomacy, especially in a world in which the recourse to war becomes an ever more suicidal gamble.

The Consequences of Flexibility. The renaissance of flexibility is having increasingly important consequences for the United States. Americans generally do not fully appreciate that the era in which they grew to international maturity was an abnormal one. The cold-war era, featuring total hostility and rigid alignments, provided the international environment in which the United States accepted the consequences of great-power status and world leadership. Bipolarity, total objectives, total techniques, and the flight from compromise have become popularly accepted in the United States as the normal way in which international affairs are conducted.

The new flexibility of the international order has come as an unwelcome shock to many Americans. The United States had serious difficulty in coming to terms with the cold war, but the principal psychic problems were largely overcome between 1947 and 1954. The narrow scope of American action within the two-power world became familiar; the incantation of the mystic words of "containment" and "no appeasement" served to minimize frustration. The United States during the early part of the cold war seemed to derive some more or less melancholy satisfaction from "facing the facts" and fulfilling its limited responsibilities.

Now, with the dissolution of bipolarity a growing probability and with the necessity at hand of prosecuting American interest in an atmosphere grown more complex, less stable, and less amenable to American control, something very much like popular resentment has developed at the loss of the sense of certainty provided by the closed system of the cold war. There is an interesting note of half-concealed regret in many of the comments on the new trends in American policy. The United States, although aware that the lessons so painfully learned must be at least partially discarded as unreliable guides to the future, is not particularly pleased about it.

Americans must keep in mind, however, that the bipolar system was never a "normal" way of doing international business. The state system was founded on flexibility and freedom of sovereign choice, and the narrow range of alternatives presented to most nations during the height of the cold war was an aberration from the classic pattern of international affairs. The United States has no choice; it must adjust both its own policy and its way of doing business to a more nearly typical situation as the world moves farther away from the narrow Russian-American struggle into a more varied set of concerns.

We might enumerate a long list of the demands that a new climate of international affairs will make on the United States. We can, however, summarize them conveniently here into three more or less basic needs: (1) a clarification of the notion of national interest and its full acceptance by the public, so as to provide greater consistency to policy in a context grown much more changeable; (2) a much more realistic, and therefore more relativist, attitude toward the whole scope of foreign policy, including a popular willingness to accept partial solutions to problems as the best available substitute for interminable controversy or war; (3) a new set of governmental mechanisms (or the improvement of existing ones) for reaching and implementing decisions, that will enable the United States swiftly and effectively to meet sudden changes in the milieu. These, applied in detail to the concerns of foreign policy, would provide at least a beginning at the adaptation of American policy to the requirements of a system in which flexibility and fluidity are the norms rather than the occasional exception.

The possibility of explosion

We must not permit ourselves, in our appreciation of the opportunities presented by it, to overlook the fact that the trend toward flexibility carries within itself its own dangers. During the era of its dominance, bipolarity had one great advantage: it dammed up the explosive forces of world affairs and fairly well obviated the probability of an outbreak of uncontrolled international violence. By denying the viability of all alternatives except one—or at best a few—the two-power world minimized the prospect of explosion. It extracted a high price for its success by largely preventing the compromise resolution of conflicts of interest, but this does not obscure the value of what it did accomplish. A flexible world order, in which the number of alternatives open at any one time is much greater, removes this safeguard. The next phase in international affairs will probably be one that—at least in this regard—will be much more dangerous.

Dangers of a Transitional Era. The world is well into a transitional era, and is already suffering the frustrations and indecisions that are inevitable when a generation is caught "between two worlds, one dead and the other unable to be born." The familiar landmarks by which statesmen have guided their course since 1945 are melting away, and the new ones destined to replace them have not yet been discovered. Such a period has its peculiar dangers, and especially so for Americans.

Perhaps the most compelling peril is that of impatience. Americans are by tradition doers; when a situation is moving rapidly, there is a powerful mass urge to jump into the middle of things and to attempt to cope with the active forces. The tendency in the American public to demand a "showdown" is strongest at times of actual or potential change, and the temptation to act boldly might well become impossible to resist. And yet, it is just at the moment of transition that bold, forthright action might prove the most destructive of long-range objectives; taking strong moves without understanding and isolation of the relevant factors might be much worse than taking no action at all. If we base our judgment on the recent record of the American people, we have some reason to fear the possibility of thoughtless action stemming from the need to discover some release from compounded frustration.

Almost as great a danger is that of miscalculation. Americans have accumulated considerable experience in dealing with a situation of great peril, the cold war. We must recall, however, that most of the effort of the United States was confined to dealing with a single force. No such mass familiarity exists with a highly dynamic context in which many forces are operative simultaneously. In such an environment there is a greater possibility that misjudgment of a single crisis situation might bring in its train unsuspected consequences. This situation makes the need for patience all the more pressing; when failure awaits him who miscalculates, the danger of doing "too little, too late" may well be less than that of attempting too much, too soon. No action should be taken without a maximum effort to verify the judgements on which it is based.

This raises the question of timing. Time is always a factor of importance in statecraft, but a fluid situation increases its relevance. When change occurs relatively frequently as the result of the combination, coincidence, or conflict of forces running loose in the world, time factors will bulk larger than they have in the relatively stabilized cold-war era. Among the considerations with a distinct time dimension we may mention the optimum moment for making a particular move, the speed with which action can be taken in response to unexpected demands, and the anticipation of moves taken by other states.

503

Frustrated Dynamisms. A transitional era increases the possibility of explosion in another sense. We have suggested that the cold war served to canalize most of the powerful forces of world politics into the relatively narrow channel of Russian-American conflict. Anti-colonialism, economic and social tension, nationalism, and technological advance were among the dynamisms that were put to the service of the cold war between 1945 and 1954. As long as the United States and the USSR were able to control the major trends of world politics, these forces were kept under fairly close control and the danger of their causing an outbreak of extreme action was minimized. The transitional era of flexibility, marked by the reduction in great-power control, makes it more likely that the contemporary dynamisms of world affairs will break loose and provoke an entirely new set of crises.

The last weeks of 1956 provided the world with dramatic proof of this tendency. Even at this early date in the age of flexibility, nationalism in Hungary and a combination of nationalism and anti-colonialism in the Middle East brought about the most serious crises in several years. In both cases the problems arose from the new inability of both Moscow and Washington to exercise the total control over their respective spheres that they had formerly done.

The United States must prepare itself to cope increasingly with the impact of these freshly liberated forces. Part of the explanation for the apparent dissolution of bipolarity can be found in the growing strength of these dynamisms to the point that they could no longer be held in check. Now they are virtually free of control; discovering mechanisms to restrain their excesses while preserving and capitalizing upon the opportunities they offer for constructive action will constitute one of the major problems of American foreign policy.

What About World War III? Considering the possibilities of explosion brings us naturally to the prospect of World War III. Throughout this entire book we have deliberately avoided any extended discussion of the probability of and the possible results of a third total war. This has been due to other reasons than the mere wish to avoid a subject both unpleasant in itself and not susceptible to rational analysis; from the analytical point of view, ours has been a "probabilist" study stressing the more likely outcomes, and the deliberate selection of total war as a technique of policy is a relatively remote one.

We can say this in terms of our assumptions. We have posited a relatively high level of rationality among American policy-makers and in the leadership groups of other states as well. As long as we can safely assume that the world's decision-makers will apply the normal criteria of pru-

504

dence and prevision to their actions, we can be safe in relegating total war to the category of the logically unthinkable and the empirically improbable. Our analysis of American policy has attempted to demonstrate how the objectives of American interest can be achieved without recourse to all-out military action.

But the rationality of statesmen is only an analytical assumption. We cannot safely predict that all decisions will be reached as the result of a relatively detached weighing of all the probable outcomes of each of several alternatives; indeed, we cannot even predict that any particular decision will be made in that fashion. Too many irrational factors enter into human choice for the assumption of rational decision to receive more than partial statistical verification. As long as the possibility exists that any political leader possesses the power to decide for total war, we must allow for conflict.

The peculiar and poignant feature of the next phase of international politics, if it turns out as we expect to be one in which maneuver is maximized and alternatives are more numerous, is that the danger of all-out war is materially increased. As long as the explosive forces could blow in only one direction, the problem of their containment was capable of being simply stated, even if fantastically difficult of solution. The American theory has been that restraining Moscow would mean restraining all the potentially disruptive factors in the world. But today World War III may be begun in any of dozens of places, by any of at least 60 states, and for any of thousands of possible reasons. The problem of maintaining peace in the future will have many more facets; the difficulties involved in the effort may be individually less taxing, but their increased number will add new complexities and strains to the burden Americans are now carrying.

A popular foreign policy

Throughout our study one theme has been implicit; we have stated it on several occasions. Here, at the very end, it is most appropriate for us to formulate it once more. American foreign policy is, as the title of this book states, really the foreign policy of the American people. On this assumption the whole of the effort of the national government is based; on its validity will depend the eventual success or failure of the entirety of American policy.

America's national interest is drawn in the first instance from the wants and needs of the mass public and the individuals that make it up; objec-

tives are selected and pursued with constant reference to popular acceptance and approval; operating techniques must remain within the limits
laid down by popular preferences. Important decisions must receive
popular ratification. American capability to reach goals depends in large
measure upon popular morale. In almost every realm of analysis we have
entered, we have met the fact that in the United States a deliberate and
extensive attempt is made to include the public in the policy process, and
that the policy is largely a reflection of what the public wants.

This intimate relationship between the leaders and the people is generally taken as a matter of course; it is axiomatic to Americans that foreign
policy, like any other area of government action, is subject to mass control. Like so many of the other rights of democratic government, however, it carries with it a corresponding duty, and there is good reason to
believe that this aspect of popular foreign policy is not sufficiently understood by the spokesmen for the public.

Whether or not the American people can fulfill the duties of participation in foreign policy in the next phase of history is the central question
we must leave unanswered. We cannot foretell whether or not American
popular understanding will prove equal to the new tests; we do not know
whether or not American emotions will stand the new strains to which
they will be put. The issues may well hold the key to how successful the
United States will be in reaching its objectives in the years ahead.

We have already noted the increase in comprehension, insight, and
commitment that took place within the United States during the decade
of bipolarity. We can be gratified that so much has been accomplished.
But we cannot forget that this problem, though serious, was essentially
narrow—almost one-dimensional: the containment of the Soviet. Our
discussion has indicated to what extent American attitudes tended to make
the cold war almost a way of life and how single-answer formulas to
attack complex problems contributed to the partial ossification of what
was originally a highly flexible and subtle policy. With the change in
the climate of international politics that we are forecasting, new and
vastly more complicated lessons will need to be learned.

The pace of events will undoubtedly increase; the variety in the answers
demanded will grow; the probability of immediately visible returns for
efforts expended will further diminish. All these are conditions for which
the sophistication gained during the cold war will not provide adequate
answers. The preservation of the democratic process in policy-making
will require that the public play its part in revising the American methodology to make it consonant with the new conditions the United States
will be facing.

506

If popular intelligence, good will, patience, tolerance, and good humor prove adequate to the task, the problem will not be beyond solution. Unless we are willing to admit an inherent inferiority in American policy-makers as compared with those of other states, we may assume that the technical requirements of the new foreign policy will be adequately met. The real problem will lie in the kind and degree of support and cooperation that official personnel will receive from their constituents.

If the American people cannot adapt their habits of thought and action to the new conditions of foreign affairs, one of two alternatives will undoubtedly be adopted by American leadership. On the one hand, the officials may follow public attitudes into the catastrophe that awaits all nations that cannot adequately cope with their environment; on the other, officialdom may deliberately break the tie with public sentiment, deal with foreign policy assues as they think best, and manipulate the public on some frankly elitist hypothesis. Either of these would be fatal to the American ideology and destructive of cherished American values.

The future will provide new tests for the concept of a popular foreign policy. The first great problem, the acceptance of responsibility for continuous planned action, was solved in the crisis era of the cold war. The second, the development of criteria by which to steer in executing an affirmative policy in a changing, insecure, and relativistic milieu, lies ahead. We can hope that this equally important test will be met, at least as successfully as was the first, and perhaps well enough that the next phase will see significant progress toward the long-range goals of American policy.

Recommended readings

Note: This reading list is highly selective. To include all the books of interest and relevance to a student of American foreign policy would require a list covering approximately as many pages as are in this book. What follows here is a selection of titles whose inclusion is based on at least one of the following three criteria: (1) unique relevance to the thesis of this study; (2) major significance and lasting impact on the study and practice of American foreign policy; (3) recent publication and promise of future importance. All the books in this list deal more or less directly with the theory and practice of American foreign policy; studies of the policies of other nations or the detailed analyses of problem areas are, with a few exceptions, not included.

Almond, Gabriel A., *The American People and Foreign Policy.* New York: Harcourt, Brace and Co., 1950. A leading book on the subject with a pronounced social-psychological orientation. It stresses the role of elites in forming mass opinion and raises serious questions about the validity of the democratic myth as applied to foreign-policy issues.

American Friends Service Committee, *The United States and the Soviet Union.* New Haven: Yale University Press, 1949. Subtitled "Some Quaker Proposals for Peace." The first clear voice in the cold-war era that called for great-power reconciliation and the mutual relaxation of tension. Of continuing relevance today as the cold war evolves.

American Friends Service Committee, *Steps to Peace.* No publisher, 1951. An elaboration of the general theme outlined in *The United States and the Soviet Union:* relaxation, reconciliation, accomodation. Makes a number of concrete suggestions.

Armstrong, H. F., ed., *The Foreign Affairs Reader.* New York: Harper & Bros., Inc., 1947. A collection of leading articles from *Foreign Affairs,* including Eugene Staley, "The Myth of the Continents," Sir Halford Mackinder, "The Round World and the Winning of the Peace," and "X," The Sources of Soviet Conduct."

RECOMMENDED READINGS

Bailey, Thomas A., *America Faces Russia*. Ithaca: Cornell University Press, 1950. A history of Russian-American relations, written in a sprightly style. The final chapters stress the need for mutual understanding and the development of realistic policies by both states.

Bailey, Thomas A., *A Diplomatic History of the American People*. 5th ed. New York: Appleton-Century-Crofts, Inc., 1955. A textbook with an emphasis on public opinion and mass attitudes. Written with a generous dash of humor and a keen eye for the ridiculous, it makes surprisingly easy reading. Unimportant details tend to be omitted in the interest of preserving dramatic sweep.

Baldwin, Hanson W., *The Price of Power*. New York: Harper & Bros., Inc., 1948. An early postwar study of the military and diplomatic requirements of America's position. It argues that heavy military demands need not create a "garrison state"; the author calls for a "feet-in-the-mud, eyes-on-the-stars" combination of realism and idealism.

Barnes, Harry Elmer, ed., *Perpetual War for Perpetual Peace*. Caldwell, Idaho: Caxton, 1953. The most comprehensive "revisionist" attack on the Roosevelt foreign policy during and after World War II. The authors include some of the best-known and most literate revisionist publicists, whose sincerity in rejecting FDR's work matches their dedication in opposition to him during his lifetime. Interesting and authentic presentation of this point of view.

Barnett, Vincent, ed., *The Representation of the United States Abroad*. New York: the American Assembly of Columbia University, 1956. Papers presented at the ninth American Assembly in 1956. Problems of diplomatic, military, economic, and informational representation are discussed by experts, many of them practitioners themselves. The recommendations generally tend toward professionalism in representation and less interference from political leadership in Washington. The key role of the resident American ambassadors is stressed.

Barrett, Edward W., *Truth Is our Weapon*. New York: Funk & Wagnalls, 1953. A pioneering study of American informational policy in the battle of ideas. The author, a former Assistant Secretary of State, analyzes the assumptions of American propaganda, makes a critical evaluation of them, and prescribes the outlines of a future policy based on the principle that "truth is our weapon."

Beloff, Max, *Foreign Policy and the Democratic Process*. Baltimore: Johns Hopkins University Press, 1955. Professor Beloff, a noted British historian, finds much to criticize in the way democracies grapple with foreign policy, and he documents his charges. He offers little comfort to doctrinaire elitists, however; he argues that the problem is not insoluble and makes some suggestions for its resolution.

Bemis, Samuel F., *A Diplomatic History of the United States*, 4th ed. New York: Henry Holt and Co., 1955. One of the standard histories. It stresses the more formal side, including the details of negotiation and of treaties. Sober, balanced, factual, and impressive. An indispensible reference work.

Bingham, Jonathan B., *Shirt-sleeve Diplomacy: Point 4 in Action*. New York: John Day, 1954. An informal defense of Point 4 by the former acting administrator of the Technical Cooperation Administration. It stresses the personal impact of technical assistance on its recipients and argues that only in this way can an unequivocal refutation of communist dogma be presented.

Bowles, Chester, *Africa's Challenge to America.* Berkeley: University of California Press, 1956. Mr. Bowles argues for an affirmative American policy toward Africa, claiming that the NATO fixation of the United States has left Washington without a policy, while the Soviet has moved aggressively in Africa.

Bowles, Chester, *The New Dimensions of Peace.* New York: Harper & Bros., Inc., 1955. The author's prescription for a more affirmative and flexible American foreign policy. Most interesting are his demands for a new approach to Asian dynamism and for an identification of the United States with anticolonialism.

Brookings Institution, *The Administration of Foreign Affairs and Overseas Operations.* Washington, D.C.: Brookings, 1951. A detailed study of the administration of overseas programs by the American government. Stresses administrative reorganization and clearly spells out the alternatives. Very influential on subsequent official policy.

Brookings Institution, *The Changing Environment of International Relations.* Washington, D.C.: Brookings, 1956. The Brookings Lectures, 1956. Six lectures by experts on the new milieu of international politics and its significance to the United States. It covers the roles of technology, new political forms, economic factors, and the rise of new states in Asia. Consistently provocative.

Brookings Institution, *Major Problems of United States Foreign Policy.* Washington, D.C.: Brookings, 6 vols. 1947-54. An annual series, ending in 1954. Contains convenient summaries of events and a detailed analysis of major problems for each year. Each volume also contains a "problem paper" dealing with a large issue. Embodies the "policy paper" method borrowed from government practice.

Brown, William A., *The United States and the Restoration of World Trade.* Washington, D.C.: Brookings, 1950. An attempt to place GATT and ITO in a historical and policy setting and to show the importance of revived trade to American foreign policy.

Brown, William A., and Redvers Opie, *American Foreign Assistance.* Washington, D.C.: Brookings, 1953. A study of American foreign assistance programs between 1940 and 1952, with emphasis on the postwar period. It pulls together the various types of aid and the forms of their administration.

Burnham, James, *The Struggle for the World.* New York: John Day, 1947. An influential exposition of the total theory of the cold war, arguing that the prize is the world and that American objectives must include the destruction of the Soviet and the utter obliteration of communism. This book and the author's later ones provide a good deal of the intellectual ammunition for the advocates of this position.

Byrnes, James F., *Speaking Frankly.* New York: Harper & Bros., Inc., 1947. The highly personal account of Secretary of State Byrnes as he sought

511

(vainly) to bring the Soviet to agreement on a peace settlement. In conjunction with President Truman's *Memoirs,* an invaluable aid in recapturing the American mood as the cold war was beginning.

Cheever, Daniel, and H. Field Haviland, *American Foreign Policy and the Separation of Powers.* Cambridge: Harvard University Press, 1952. An analysis of legislative-executive conflict in the making and executing of American foreign policy. Although the authors suggest several administrative reforms, their major appeal is for greater harmony and trust.

Cheever, Daniel, and H. Field Haviland, *Organizing for Peace.* Boston: Houghton-Mifflin Co., 1954. An important textbook that transcends the limits of the form. It is a mine of information, historical and structural, and also makes a persuasive argument for more intelligent use of the new opportunities provided by international organization.

Cohen, Bernard C., *The Political Process and Foreign Policy.* Princeton: Princeton University Press, 1957. An analytical study of the "political process" as it operates in foreign-policy making in the United States. It is a case study of the making of the Japanese peace settlement and generally is unsympathetic to rigid elitist hypotheses.

Cook, Thomas I., and Malcolm Moos, *Power Through Purpose.* Baltimore: Johns Hopkins University Press, 1955. A restrained and diligently "realistic" defense of the moral basis of American foreign policy. Idealism, the authors say, is a powerful reality in the world today; by seizing and exploiting moral leadership the United States can win ample international support to deal with its problems. "Morality," to the authors, means generally democracy and freedom.

Council on Foreign Relations, *The United States in World Affairs,* 9 vols. New York: Harper & Bros., Inc. 1947-57. An annual series, entirely narrative and historical. Most useful for running down information too recent to be in standard reference works or too scattered to permit ready discovery in other histories. Each volume in the postwar series (an earlier series was published during the 1930's) maintains a nice balance between factual detail and narrative sweep.

Cressey, George B., *How Strong Is Russia?* Syracuse: Syracuse University Press, 1954. A brief survey of the geographic, human, resource, and economic factors in the capability of the USSR, by a distinguished geographer. Some of his conclusions have been challenged, both by geographers and by experts on the Soviet.

Dahl, Robert, *Congress and Foreign Policy.* New York: Harcourt, Brace and Co., 1950. The author elaborates the reasons for the limited role that Congress (and Congressmen) play in American foreign policy, and suggests some remedies. Can profitably be read in conjunction with Cheever and Haviland's *Separation of Powers.*

Dennett, Raymond, and Joseph E. Johnson, eds., *Negotiating With the Russians.* Boston: World Peace Foundation, 1951. A series of studies by various Americans who have had the experience of direct negotiations with Soviet diplomats. Invaluable for insights into the Russian theory of diplomacy.

Dulles, John Foster, *War or Peace*. New York: The Macmillan Co., 1957. Reissued with new foreword. The Secretary of State's personal analysis of the cold war, written three years before he took office. Readers of the book will gain many clues to Mr. Dulles's personality and method of doing business. Although generally consistent with the grand design of his personal philosophy as outlined here, Mr. Dulles's record in office reveals many contradictions in detail with his principles.

Elliott, William Y., *et al.*, *The Political Economy of American Foreign Policy*. New York: Henry Holt and Co., 1955. An overview of the economic aspects of American foreign policy, by a study group of experts. Rather technical, but valuable because of its success at demonstrating the interrelatedness of political and economic concepts in foreign policy.

Elliott, William Y., *et al.*, *United States Foreign Policy: Its Organization and Control*. New York: Columbia University Press, 1952. A study-group report on governmental organization for foreign policy, contemporaneous with the Brookings study and a number of other works.

Ellis, Howard, *The Economics of Freedom*. New York: Harper & Bros., Inc., 1950. An early analysis and rationalization of economic aid to Europe, phrased primarily in economic terms. The findings must, of course, be interpreted today in the light of later events.

Feis, Herbert, *The Road to Pearl Harbor*. Princeton: Princeton University Press, 1950. The most balanced of the postwar attempts to "explain" Pearl Harbor. Mr. Feis avoids the "devil" theories of other writers and distributes praise and blame more or less impartially. President Roosevelt is largely exonerated from the more extreme charges made in other studies.

Finletter, Thomas K., *Power and Policy: U.S. Foreign Policy and Military Power in the Hydrogen Age*. New York: Harcourt, Brace and Co., 1954. A former Secretary of the Air Force blueprints a military-political strategy for the U.S., marked by an increased emphasis on air-nuclear preponderance and a more determined effort at disarmament. The author sees little probability that the cold war can be compromised; it must, he says, either become total or be liquidated by disarmament. A provocative and important book.

Fosdick, Dorothy, *Common Sense and World Affairs*. New York: Harcourt, Brace and Co., 1955. The purpose of this book is stated in the title. The author, a former member of the Policy Planning Staff of the State Department, appeals for the application of twelve "principles of common sense" to questions of foreign policy. She hopes in this way to break public apathy and to narrow the gap between citizen and statesman.

Fox, William T. R., *The Super-Powers*. New York: Harcourt, Brace and Co., 1944. Mr. Fox, writing toward the close of World War II, saw the United States, the Soviet, and Great Britain as the super-powers of the postwar world, and called on them jointly to police the world to maintain peace. His prescription was not followed, but the book's title added a new descriptive epithet to the vocabulary of international affairs.

RECOMMENDED READINGS

Furniss, Edgar S., Jr., ed., *American Military Policy*. New York: Rinehart and Co., 1957. An over-all view of the military component of American foreign policy. The author finds the military to have five missions: (1) defense of the American continent; (2) refereeing interallied disputes; (3) regional security; (4) defense of weak neutrals; (5) reduction of armaments. In each of these, armed force cooperates with other tools of policy.

Gibson, Hugh, *The Road to Foreign Policy*. Garden City: Doubleday, Doran and Co., 1944. An older book by a pioneer career diplomat. He justifies the professional and makes a number of telling points against the backseat driving of the Washington bureaucracy. Many of his arguments sound as if they were based on yesterday's headlines rather than on events of 15 or 20 years ago. Things do not, he seems to say, change very much in the State Department or among the American people.

Goldman, Eric F., *The Crucial Decade: America 1945-1955*. New York: Alfred A. Knopf, 1956. A vivid account of the first postwar decade in the United States, valuable for the light it throws on public attitudes while American foreign policy was being formed. Professor Goldman has a facile style that recreates this crucial decade effectively for those who remember it, and makes it live for those too young to recall it.

Goodrich, Leland M., *Korea: A Study of U.S. Policy in the United Nations*. New York: Council on Foreign Relations, 1956. The author finds much to defend and much to criticize in American behavior in the United Nations during the Korean crisis.

Graebner, Norman A., *The New Isolationism*. New York: The Ronald Press, Inc., 1956. According to this thesis, "nationalism" and "isolationism" have captured control of American policy since 1952. The book does not include any consideration of American policy in the Middle East crisis of 1956.

Gross, Feliks, *Foreign Policy Analysis*. New York: Philosophical Library, 1954. An attempt at the development of a methodology for analyzing foreign policy as part of a "social process," with emphasis on factors of power and ideological considerations.

Haines, C. Grove, ed., *The Threat of Soviet Imperialism*. Baltimore: Johns Hopkins University Press, 1954. A symposium of experts deal with the question of Soviet expansionism. Various opinions are offered, but in general the authors see little likelihood of an early shift in Soviet strategy, although greater tactical flexibility is expected.

Halle, Louis J., *Civilization and Foreign Policy*. New York: Harper & Bros., Inc., 1955. Another book by an ex-member of the Policy Planning Staff. The author puts foreign policy in the context of the social aspirations of the American people. Noteworthy is his development of the concepts of "force" and "consent" in the achievement of foreign-policy ends.

Hilsman, Roger, *Strategic Intelligence and National Decisions*. Glencoe, Ill.: The Free Press, 1956. An astute and detailed study of the role of strategic intelligence in reaching policy decisions.

Hull, Cordell, *The Memoirs of Cordell Hull*, 2 volumes. New York: The Macmillan Co., 1948. Valuable for its evocation of the New Deal foreign policy and the events leading up to American entry in World War II.

Huntington, Samuel P., *The Soldier and the State*. Cambridge: Harvard University Press, 1957. A new approach to a theory of civil-military relations, designed to be applicable to contemporary conditions in the United States. Propounds some novel hypotheses.

Huszar, G. B. de, ed., *Persistent International Issues*. New York: Harper & Bros., Inc., 1947. An early postwar symposium discussing a series of non-political issues of world affairs, mainly economic. The proportion of correct guesses about what would prove pertinent is remarkably good. The book is a necessary reminder that international politics has dimensions of personal and private import.

Jones, Joseph M., *The Fifteen Weeks*. New York: The Viking Press, 1955. An introspective study of the period between February 21 and June 5, 1947 (from the beginnings of the Truman Doctrine to Secretary Marshall's Harvard speech), during which time the outlines of current American policy were being laid down.

Kaplan, Morton A., *System and Process in International Relations*. New York: John Wiley, 1957. A major attempt to bring all of the international political process within the bounds of a conceptual system. Very provocative of insights into American policy.

Kaufmann, W. W., ed., *Military Power and National Security*. Princeton, N. J.: Princeton University Press, 1956. A symposium on national military and security policies. Consistently opposed to the air-nuclear theory of warfare and of American security policy; inclined to accept the theory of limited war in peripheral areas as the major problem of military planning. Generally favorable to the Army's position in the interservice controversy.

Kennan, George F., *American Diplomacy, 1900-1950*. Chicago: University of Chicago Press, 1951. One of the really important recent books. Mr. Kennan's historical knowledge may be, as experts have pointed out, shaky; no one can challenge, however, the impact of his ideas on American policy. See chapter 6, "Diplomacy in the Modern World," and his two *Foreign Affairs* articles, reprinted here. Also available in a paperback edition.

Kennan, George F., *Realities of American Foreign Policy*. Princeton, N. J.: Princeton University Press, 1955. A further development of the ideas expounded in his earlier book, more directly applicable to the cold war. Originally a series of lectures, the book retains the simplicity associated with oral delivery.

Kissinger, Henry A., *Nuclear Weapons and Foreign Policy*. New York: Harper & Bros., Inc., 1957. An ambitious attempt to reconcile the new dimensions of warfare with the requirements of American foreign policy. Essentially a defense of "limited nuclear war" as a viable alternative to either total war or policy frustration. Most provocative, though its real relevance has yet to be demonstrated.

RECOMMENDED READINGS

Knorr, Klaus, *The War Potential of Nations*. Princeton, N. J.: Princeton University Press, 1956. A re-evaluation of the concept of "war potential" in an era of nuclear weapons. The author concludes that the notion retains validity, and carefully analyzes the kinds of data that are employed in its application. Data used are drawn primarily from the period of World War II.

Langer, William L., and Everett Gleason, *The Challenge to Isolation; The Undeclared War*. New York: Harper & Bros., Inc., 1952, 1953. A detailed two-volume study of American diplomacy from 1937 to Pearl Harbor. The authors generally approve Roosevelt's policy and have harsh words for its opponents.

Lerner, Daniel, ed., *Propaganda in War and Crisis*. New York: George Stewart, 1951. A collection of readings covering the general background of contemporary propaganda, its role in foreign policy, organization for propaganda, and an evaluation of its effects. With so many authors, the effect is somewhat uneven, although the editor's introduction provides a valuable conceptual framework.

Lippmann, Walter, *The Cold War*. New York: Harper & Bros., Inc., 1947. A riposte to George Kennan's article on the "Source of Soviet Conduct." Mr. Lippmann challenges the containment thesis as destructive of intelligent diplomacy and urges a less rigid policy.

Lippmann, Walter, *The Public Philosophy*. Boston: Little, Brown and Co., 1955. A polemic, arguing that most of the troubles of contemporary political life (including the international) stem from the runaway effect of popular wishes and emotions. Mr. Lippmann pleads for a return to a sense of "decency" and a due regard for the superior claims of experts in the formation of public policy. Available also as a paperback.

Lubell, Samuel, *The Revolution in World Trade*. New York: Harper & Bros., Inc., 1955. A sparkling little book taking a refreshingly different point of view on American trade policy. It denies the validity of the old low-tariff argument, and calls for a rethinking of trade policy in terms of America's total foreign-policy concerns. Mr. Lubell is not an economist; perhaps his book is the more interesting for that reason.

McCloy, John J., *The Challenge to American Foreign Policy*. Cambridge: Harvard University Press, 1953. By the former U.S. High Commissioner to Occupied Germany. The "challenge" to American policy is to develop some alternative policies for the exclusively military ones the United States has relied on in dealing with the Soviet threat. An influential book.

Macmahon, Arthur W., *Administration in Foreign Affairs*. University, Alabama: University of Alabama Press, 1953. A series of lectures. Far more inclusive than the title suggests; the author's reflections on the impact of administrative considerations on foreign affairs throw considerable light on the substantive problems of American foreign policy.

Markel, Lester, *et al.*, *Public Opinion and Foreign Policy*. New York: Harper & Bros., Inc., 1949. A symposium, directed mainly at evaluating the "public information" policy of the American government on foreign-policy matters. The consensus is that the government, and particularly the State

Department, is falling down on the job of "mobilizing" public sentiment in support of government policy. Most of the conclusions are as valid today as they were in 1949. Less consideration is given to the problem of making the government more responsive to public opinion.

Marshall, Charles B., *The Limits of Foreign Policy*. New York: Henry Holt and Co., 1954. The author, a former State Department official, stresses the limits inherent in foreign policy, and pleads for greater public awareness of the actual dimensions of the task facing the United States and the practical alternatives open to the government.

Mayo, H. B., *Democracy and Marxism*. New York: Oxford University Press, 1955. A literate and deft analysis of Marxist thought in its many ramifications. The last two chapters set Marxism in opposition to democratic thought.

Mikesell, Raymond F., *United States Economic Policy and International Relations*. New York: McGraw-Hill Book Co., Inc., 1952. A scholarly study of the foreign economic policy of the United States, stressing both historical development and the impact of recent situational changes. The new concept of American interest, the author feels, will eventually find expression in new economic policies.

Mills, C. Wright, *The Power Elite*. New York: Oxford University Press, 1956. An angry book, asserting that America is actually ruled by an interlocking "power elite" drawn from corporate, military, and political leadership. The democratic myth has never received more abrupt nor total decapitation. The thesis of the book, if it can be substantiated, would seem to have obvious implications for American foreign policy.

Morgenthau, Hans J., *In Defense of the National Interest*. New York: Alfred A. Knopf, 1951. An earnest defense of the national interest as the preferred basis for American foreign policy. The author is especially impatient with morality and legality, and calls for a clear-sighted concentration on fundamentals. He is less explicit, however, in explaining how the national interest is arrived at in a particular context.

Northrop, F. S. C., *European Union and United States Foreign Policy*. New York: The Macmillan Co., 1954. A study in "sociological jurisprudence," to quote the subtitle. Professor Northrop argues that the "living law" of much of Europe already argues for union and urges the United States to act energetically to transform this moral consensus into positive union.

Ogburn, William F., ed., *Technology and International Relations*. Chicago: University of Chicago Press, 1949. A series of papers stressing the cumulative impact of the new technology on the course of international relations. By and large, the papers have stood the test of time very well.

Osgood, Robert, *Ideals and Self-interest in America's Foreign Relations*. Chicago: University of Chicago Press, 1953. A critical analysis of American motivations in foreign policy since 1900. By and large, the author claims, American actions have grown out of self-interest, whether enlightened or otherwise; morality and idealism, he says, have often been self-deceiving subterfuges.

517

Recommended Readings

Perkins, Dexter, *The American Approach to Foreign Policy*. Cambridge: Harvard University Press, 1952. A series of lectures that together paint a picture of American foreign policy as springing from indigenous American culture. A major purpose of the book is to refute the charge that the United States is drifting into an imperial policy of its own.

Plischke, Elmer, *Conduct of American Diplomacy*. New York: Van Nostrand, 1950. A textbook study of the mechanisms by which American diplomatic representation takes place, including the processes of treaty-making, international conference, and international organization.

Pratt, Julius A., *A History of United States Foreign Policy*. Englewood Cliffs, N.J.: Prentice-Hall, Inc., 1955. The newest full-dress history of American foreign policy. By and large it concentrates upon the history of policy rather than on the details of negotiation. Well-written and thorough.

Price, Harry Bayard, *The Marshall Plan and Its Meaning*. Ithaca: Cornell University Press, 1955. An able analysis of the Marshall Plan, written from the perspective of several years. The ECA is judged both in the light of its specific accomplishments and of its relationship to subsequent American policy.

Randall, Clarence B., *A Foreign Economic Policy for the United States*. Chicago: University of Chicago Press, 1954. The author was chairman of the "Randall Commission" on foreign economic policy. This is his personal plea for a more liberal international trade and finance program.

Reinhardt, George C., *American Strategy in the Atomic Age*. Norman: University of Oklahoma Press, 1955. An army officer's version of American strategy. He hopes to "stabilize" the two-power world by forcing victory through the preponderance of the West. His announced aim is to avoid a war rather than to win one.

Rieschauer, Edwin O., *Wanted: An Asian Policy*. New York: Alfred A. Knopf, 1955. The author, an expert on the Far East, here presents the fundamentals of Asian policy for Americans. He discusses the background of American interests in the light of historical development and suggests, on the basis of this overview, some of the principles that might underlie a coherent American policy.

Riesman, David, Nathan Glazer, and Reuel Denny, *The Lonely Crowd*. New Haven: Yale University Press, 1950. A pioneering study into the changing American character. Valuable in foreign-policy study because of its image of the "other-directed" man whose major goal in life is to "adjust" and to "belong to the group." The implications of this social type for the notion of a democratic foreign policy are fundamental and disturbing. Published also in a paperback edition.

Reitzel, William A., Morton A. Kaplan, and Constance G. Coblentz, *United States Foreign Policy 1945-1955*. Washington, D.C.: Brookings, 1956. A historical-topical study of American policy, concluding with a number of open-ended questions about specific issues. The tone is generally judicious and balanced; such preferences as the authors may have are usually well-hidden.

Roberts, Henry L., *Russia and America: Dangers and Prospects*. New York: Harper & Bros., Inc., 1956. An attempt to analyze American-Soviet relations in the context of the "new" cold war. The emphasis throughout is on the necessity of developing a more flexible American policy to meet the new forms in which the Soviet threat will present itself. A most thoughtful book.

Rostow, W. W., with Richard W. Hatch, *An American Policy in Asia*. New York: John Wiley, 1955. A brief attempt to do much the same thing that E. O. Rieschauer does in *Wanted: An Asian Policy*. Certain important issues are analyzed in terms of American interest; the authors feel American policy should concern itself increasingly with the dangers of political and economic erosion and less with those of a military attack.

Sapin, Burtin M., and Richard C. Snyder, *The Role of the Military in American Foreign Policy*. Garden City: Doubleday, 1954. An examination of the present and possible future part played by military personnel, military concepts, and military objectives in American foreign policy, with some attention given to the execution of policy by military means.

"competitive coexistence," which to the author requires that the United

Scott, John, *Political Warfare*. New York: John Day, 1955. A manual for States engage in "psychological warfare, economic pressures, political wedges, cultural campaigns, and assorted skulduggery." Very stimulating reading, even though some of his proposals might strike the timorous as somewhat risky.

Slessor, Sir John, *Strategy for the West*. New York: William Morrow & Co., 1954. A Britisher's defense of the air-nuclear strategy for driving communism "back within its borders." Interesting as a European development of the American "massive retaliation" doctrine. The author was a Marshal in the Royal Air Force.

Smith, Louis, *American Democracy and Military Power*. Chicago: University of Chicago Press, 1951. A historical study of the principle of civilian control over the military in the United States. The author has some fears that the traditional relationship might be altered by the requirements of modern foreign policy.

Snyder, Richard C., H. W. Bruck, and Burton M. Sapin, *Decision-making as an Approach to the Study of International Relations*, Foreign Policy Analysis Series #3. Princeton, N.J.: Princeton University, 1954. A trailblazing methodological study, emphasizing the way in which foreign-policy decisions (mainly American ones) are made. Provocative of much discussion and not a little controversy, this little monograph promises to bulk increasingly large in the literature of international relations.

Sprout, Harold, and Margaret Sprout, eds., *Foundations of National Power*, 2nd ed. New York: Van Nostrand, 1951. A standard collection of international relations readings that has had a major influence on recent thinking. The chapter on the United States is of major significance.

Sprout, Harold, and Margaret Sprout, *Man-milieu Relationship Hypotheses in the Context of International Politics*. Princeton, N.J.: Center of International Studies, 1956. A monograph containing an overview of the various

519

ways in which environmental factors may be considered in analyzing international politics. The authors feel no single hypothesis is universally valid, and that several are useful for particular purposes.

Spykman, Nicholas J., *America's Strategy in World Politics*. New York: Harcourt, Brace and Co., 1942. An early attempt to formulate a geopolitical strategy for the United States. Often thought of as one of the first steps in "realistic" thinking about American foreign policy. Basically oriented to geography, but of a much broader scope. A fundamentally important book.

Staley, Eugene, *The Future of Underdeveloped Countries*. New York: Harper & Bros., Inc., 1954. Primarily concerned with the political implications of economic development, particularly for the United States. Communist techniques of penetration of the underdeveloped areas are contrasted with democratic proposals; the author is by no means certain that economic development automatically brings political democracy in its train.

Stanley, Timothy W., *American Defense and National Security*. Washington, D.C.: Public Affairs Press, 1956. A historical sketch and evaluation of the 1947-56 decade in national security policy, written by an official of the Department of Defense while on leave at the Harvard Defense Studies Program. An unusually valuable synthesis of the complex story of the evolution of the defense establishment of the United States.

Strausz-Hupé, Robert, Alvin J. Cottrell, and James E. Dougherty, eds., *American-Asian Tensions*. New York: Praeger, 1956. Case studies of tensions in American relations with two neutral Asian states (India and Indonesia), two Asian allies of the United States (Japan and the Philippines), and one noncooperative Asian state (Egypt).

Stuart, Graham, *American Diplomatic and Consular Practice*, 2nd ed. New York: Appleton-Century-Crofts, Inc., 1952. The standard manual on the subject.

Sulzburger, C. L., *The Big Thaw*. New York: Harper & Bros., Inc., 1956. A *New York Times* correspondent analyzes the cold-war policy of the USSR after the death of Stalin. He argues that more recent Soviet policy, because more flexible, represents a graver danger than did the old hard line; he also feels that Titoism may prove to be Moscow's eventual stumbling block.

Tannenbaum, Frank, *The American Tradition in Foreign Policy*. Norman: University of Oklahoma Press, 1955. An evocation of the theory of the "co-ordinate state" as the basis of American foreign policy: equal rights for each political unit. The author rejects *Realpolitik;* he was one of the antagonists of Hans J. Morgenthau in a "great debate" on American national interest. This volume might be read as an answer to Morgenthau's *In Defense of the National Interest*.

Toynbee, Arnold, *The World and the West*. New York: Oxford University Press, 1953. The noted historian's speculations on the impact of the West on the remainder of the world. His major point is that the other peoples are borrowing western techniques and using them against their inventors, thus creating a problem that all western nations must face jointly. Particularly pertinent to Americans is Chapter 5, "The Psychology of Encounters."

Truman, Harry S., *Memoirs* (vol. I: *Year of Decisions;* Vol. II: *Years of Trial and Hope*). Garden City: Doubleday, 1955, 1956. The former President's own recollections, full of detail and personal insights. Fascinating reading.

Vandenburg, A. W., Jr., ed., *The Private Papers of Senator Vandenburg.* Boston: Houghton-Mifflin Co., 1952. The role of the leading Republican advocate of bipartisanship during the early phases of the cold war. Particularly interesting is the story of the Senator's part in the passage of ECA.

Vinacke, Harold M., *The United States and the Far East, 1945-1951.* Stanford: Stanford University Press, 1952. A historical survey of American policy, subtitled "A Record of Aims, Achievements, and Frustrations." It is notable for its balance and the author's refusal to select heroes or villains from among its characters.

Warburg, James C., *The United States in a Changing World.* New York: Putnam, 1954. A colorful interpretation of American foreign policy by by a well-known publicist. The later chapters provide a convenient summary of the author's views of American cold-war policy up to 1953.

Ward, Barbara, *The Interplay of East and West.* New York: W. W. Norton & Co., Inc., 1957. The plea for intercultural accomodation between East and West, made by the famous British commentator on world affairs.

Ward, Barbara, *Policy for the West.* New York: W. W. Norton & Co., Inc., 1951. An appeal for Western cooperation before the Soviet threat. A sequel to the same author's *The West at Bay.* Miss Ward is willing to face the prospect of "practical federalism" as a possible outcome of Western cooperation.

Ward, Barbara, *The West at Bay.* New York: W. W. Norton & Co., Inc., 1948. A skillful summarization of the dilemma of the West in 1948, calling for western association under American financial sponsorship.

Welles, Sumner and Donald McKay, eds., *The American Foreign Policy Library.* Cambridge: Harvard University Press. A valuable series for the "general reader," each volume prepared by an expert. Even the older titles are valuable for their points of view and their insights. The series includes the following:

> Brinton, Crane, *The United States and Britain,* rev. ed. 1948.
> Brown, W. Norman, *The United States and India and Pakistan,* 1953.
> Cline, Howard F., *The United States and Mexico,* 1953.
> Dean, Vera M., *The United States and Russia,* 1947.
> Fairbank, John K., *The United States and China,* 1948.
> Hughes, J. J., *The United States and Italy,* 1953.
> McKay, Donald, *The United States and France,* 1951.
> Perkins, Dexter, *The United States and the Caribbean,* 1947.
> Rieschauer, Edwin O., *The United States and Japan,* 1950
> Scott, F. D., *The United States and Scandinavia,* 1950.

Recommended Readings

Speiser, E. A., *The United States and the Near East*, rev. ed., 1949.

Thomas, L. V., and R. N. Frye, *The United States and Turkey and Iran*, 1951.

Whitaker, Arthur P., *The United States and Argentina*, 1955.

Whitaker, Arthur P., *The United States and South America: the Northern Republics*, 1948.

Westerfield, Bradford W., *Foreign Policy and Party Politics*. New Haven: Yale University Press, 1955. A statistical and interpretative study of bipartisanship in American foreign policy, particularly as expressed in Congressional votes on key issues. Conclusions tend toward the advocacy of the concept of "extrapartisanship" rather than pure "bipartisanship." Valuable both for its data and for its provocative insights.

Index

C